COLLECTANEA HELLENISTICA

IV

Collectanea Hellenistica

IV

THE BILINGUAL FAMILY ARCHIVE OF DRYTON, HIS WIFE APOLLONIA AND THEIR DAUGHTER SENMOUTHIS

(P. Dryton)

BY

Katelijn VANDORPE

Postdoctoral Fellow of the Fund for Scientific Research - Flanders (Belgium)
K.U.Leuven and UFSIA

with a contribution on the 'Alexandrian Erotic Fragment' or 'Maedchens Klage'
by ***Peter Bing****, Associate Professor of Classics, Emory University*

PUBLIKATIE VAN HET COMITÉ KLASSIEKE STUDIES, SUBCOMITÉ HELLENISME
KONINKLIJKE VLAAMSE ACADEMIE VAN BELGIË
VOOR WETENSCHAPPEN EN KUNSTEN

BRUSSEL
2002

KONINKLIJKE VLAAMSE ACADEMIE VAN BELGIË
VOOR WETENSCHAPPEN EN KUNSTEN

Paleis der Academiën
Hertogsstraat 1
1000 Brussel, Belgium
http: //www.kvab.be

D/2002/0455/15
ISBN 90 6569 901-5

Printed by Universa Press - 9230 Wetteren - Belgium

Contents

NOTES FOR THE READER

In the transcriptions of Greek texts the Leiden system is used. The transliteration of demotic follows the standard system as described in *Enchoria* 10 (1980), p. 11-13.

The edition caused some practical problems, such as the references to Greek and demotic documents. I have preferred a uniform system for both Greek and demotic texts, and thus chosen to cite the documents by publication number as is common in Greek papyrology and in some demotic editions. I distinguish systematically between Greek and demotic publications by adding "dem." (P. dem. or O. dem.) to the demotic editions (see p. 421). I have also opted for a uniform system for the text edition. Greek papyrus editions usually have an apparatus criticus in which, among other things, wrong readings by previous editors are recorded. I found it convenient to introduce a similar apparatus criticus for the demotic text editions so that the reader has an overview of the corrected readings without having to consult the commentary. Most of the demotic texts are accompanied by facsimiles, as tradition requires, but I also made facsimiles of some difficult Greek texts, in particular accounts and lists (Texts 39, 40, 41, 42, 43, 44).

This volume numbers 24 plates, but not all of the photographs have been reproduced. The choice is not arbitrary: these are plates of 1) texts of which no photographs or facsimiles are otherwise available, or 2) texts to which new fragments have been added; in the latter case, a collage often had to be made which led to an inferior quality of the plate, since the fragments had to be copied on a larger or a reduced scale. In the future I hope to provide the majority of the photographs on the World Wide Web.

Preface

At the end of 1988 I started to work on a PhD dissertation, which I finished three and a half years later. Surprisingly, it has taken almost ten years to translate it from Dutch into English.

The family archive which is presented in this volume has become well-known among papyrologists and historians as the Dryton-archive. My research, however, has shown that women played a central role in the archive and the temptation has been strong to name it after a woman, that is after Dryton's wife Apollonia and their daughter Senmouthis. But in the end the typically Belgian tendency to compromise prevailed over feminism, for I chose as title "The Bilingual Family Archive of Dryton, his Wife Apollonia and their Daughter Senmouthis", which retains the old name of the archive but at the same time stresses the role women played (see also p. 12). Unfortunately, the women introduced in the title are lost in the abbreviation P. Dryton, which I have preferred for practical reasons.

The archive was discovered at the end of the 19th century and via the antiques market ended up in collections all over the world. The editions of the texts are scattered over several publications. Although the family archive was quite famous for almost a century, it was never edited as a whole. One of the reasons was undoubtedly the bilingual character of the archive: there are 29 Greek, 25 demotic and 5 Greco-demotic or demotic-Greek texts. These are all documentary texts, except for the Greek poem (Text 50) copied on the back of an old loan. P. Bing, who I met during a stay in Cambridge, accepted my offer to deal with this literary text.

The present volume is more than a re-edition of texts. New fragments and new texts are included and a new approach is proposed for the reconstruction of the archive, an approach I call "museum archaeology". The results are summarized on p. 9-11. This already substantial volume contains the text edition proper and is preceded by a brief introduction. The reconstruction of the archive and of other archives from the same town of Pathyris will be discussed in a second volume, which also contains an elaborate introduction to the family of Dryton, Apollonia and Senmouthis: The Archives from Pathyris Reconstructed. With an Introduction to the Bilingual Family Archive of Dryton, his Wife Apollonia and their Daughter Senmouthis (Collectanea Hellenistica).

It is appropriate to thank several people. Most of all I am grateful to my mentor W. Clarysse, who suggested the subject. He supported me with his never ceasing enthusiasm and offered numerous valuable comments. I am also deeply indebted to D.J. Thompson for her sound insight in historical problems. She also undertook the heavy task of correcting and polishing my "Dutch" English. P. Van Dessel helped me checking last minute changes. Any shortcoming remains my responsibility alone.

I profited much from the advice of the readers of my dissertation, who were so kind as to make their notes available: the late J. Quaegebeur (KULeuven) who introduced me to Egyptology and especially to demotic; the late E. Van 't Dack (KULeuven) who suggested the publication of this volume in the series Collectanea Hellenistica of the Koninklijke Academie; L. Mooren (KULeuven) who supported me through the years in my academic career, and P.W. Pestman whom I must thank in a special way. I was most welcome in the Papyrological Institute of Leiden, which he led at the time I studied there. He shared my interest in Pathyris and stimulated to continue my research on Pathyris' archives. He was also so generous as to inform me about a new fragment of Text 17.

I also profited from the advice and help of several other people. I owe a special debt of gratitude to U. Kaplony-Heckel who knows the demotic (published and unpublished) material of Pathyris very well and who generously shared her knowledge on several occasions (see especially Texts 12 and 15). In addition, U. Kaplony-Heckel and V. Massa kindly informed me about a text from Moscow which was discovered by D. Devauchelle (Text 7 descr.).

I should like to thank S.P. Vleeming for his generosity as well. Over the years he has given me helpful comments on several demotic documents from Pathyris.

Furthermore, I am most grateful to A.M. Donadoni and V. Massa for permission to disclose information on ostraka from the Egyptian Museum of Turin (Texts 54 descr. and App. C descr.). I also had interesting discussions with V. Massa on the temple oaths from Pathyris in general.

C.A.R. Andrews is much thanked for her permission to consult and to include information on papyri which will be published in a volume prepared by the late A.F. Shore (Texts 9, 10 and 26 descr.).

I would also like to express my gratitude to R. Pintaudi and G. Messeri who were so kind as to send me copies of small fragments from Pathyris which are kept in the Bibliotheca Medicea Laurenziana (Florence).

J. K. Winnicki kindly agreed to publish his facsimile of graffito App. B, a.

Finally, I should like to thank B. Van Beek who solved my computer problems.

I should like to express my gratitude to several collections and to their staff for their help and hospitality when I studied the original texts: the British Library, the British Museum, the Egyptian Museum of Cairo, the Egyptian Museum of Turin, the Louvre Museum and the Papyrussammlung Universität Heidelberg.

Several collections kindly provided photographs. Permission to reproduce the papyri and ostraka in the present volume has been granted by: the Archäologisches Institut der Universität Zürich, the Bibliotheca Medicea Laurenziana (Florence), the British Library, the British Museum, the John Rylands Library, the Louvre Museum, the Papyrussammlung Universität Heidelberg, the Pierpont Morgan Library in New York, the Sorbonne Bouriant collection, and the Staatliche Museen zu Berlin.

My thanks are further due to the Fund for Scientific Research-Flanders (FWO) for the grants of Aspirant and of Postdoctoraal Onderzoeker which enabled me to pursue my research. I wish to express my gratitude to the Academie for accepting this work for publication in the series Collectanea Hellenistica.

Finally, I wish to thank my parents and Jan for their help and moral support over all these years.

Katelijn Vandorpe, 4 oktober 2001, Heverlee

OWNERS OF THE ARCHIVE AND FAMILY TREE

An exhaustive study of the archives from Pathyris, especially the family archive of Dryton, is to be found in Vandorpe, *Archives from Pathyris* (2001).

Papyri and ostraka from Pathyris

The southern Egyptian town of Pathyris (modern Gebelein) received a military base after the fierce revolt in Upper Egypt under the reign of Ptolemy V (205-186 B.C.). As a consequence, several soldiers of the Ptolemaic army were settled in the area. The town was gradually hellenized and has yielded hundreds of Greek and demotic papyri from that flourishing period. But in the beginning of the first century B.C. Upper Egypt was again gripped by a new rebellion. Though Pathyris remained loyal to the Ptolemaic house, it was finally besieged by the rebels and went down when the revolt was suppressed by Ptolemy IX Soter II in 88 B.C. Documentation, so abundant from c. 186 B.C. onwards, ended abruptly: no Pathyris papyri or ostraka are found after 88 B.C.

The major part of the papyri and ostraka from Pathyris originate from clandestine excavations. They turned up via the antiques market in several collections. It was and still is the task of papyrologists to reconstruct the archives from which these texts derive. One of these archives has become well known as the archive of Dryton, son of Pamphilos: his papyri (often fragmentary) are found in collections all over the world (see the Concordances, p. 433-440).

The reconstruction of the family archive of Dryton and museum archaeology

See especially Vandorpe, *Archives from Pathyris* (2001), §22-27 (Museum archaeology put to work: the reconstruction of the Dryton archive).

Compare the survey of the texts of the archive, p. 18-20.

A Dryton's archive, as it has hitherto been pieced together, was reconstructed on purely prosopographical grounds (Vandorpe, *Archives from Pathyris* (2001), §23).

B I was able to extend the archive, first in the traditional way, either by finding new fragments of published texts

C or by discovering new texts with the name of a member of Dryton's family (see Vandorpe, *Archives from Pathyris* (2001), §24).

D The extension of the archive through what I call museum archaeology (tracing the dates of acquisition by museums and other collections) is, however, much more significant. It gives, among other things, an answer to the question as to who preserved the archive of Dryton after his death. I confine myself here to the most important results (see in more detail Vandorpe, *Archives from Pathyris* (2001), §14-27).

- A number of published and unpublished papyri may be attributed to the archive thanks to museum archaeology (Texts **9-10**, **20**, **37-38**, **42-44**). Additional arguments for the attribution are prosopographical data (such as the name of Myrsine, a slave girl of Dryton's family) and the identification of the handwriting as that of Dryton or his son Esthladas (see §64-66 and Vandorpe, *Archives from Pathyris* (2001), §25, 2).
- *Kaies, son of Pates.* — Some Pathyris loans share a common name: the soldier Kaies, son of Pates. Dryton's oldest daughter Apollonia alias Senmouthis was married to a Kaies, but unfortunately the name of Kaies' father is never recorded. In Pathyris only two people are known who bore that name, both of them soldiers: Kaies, son of Pamenos[1], of whom no archive is preserved, and Kaies, son of Pates, who has his own humble archive of loans. Kaies' archive has never been linked to that of Dryton.

  Museum archaeology has now established that the papyrus archive of Kaies, son of Pates, originally stems from the same, early, illegal excavation as that of Dryton. This makes it probable that the Dryton and Kaies papers were in fact parts of a single archive (see Vandorpe, *Archives from Pathyris* (2001), §25, 3). In addition, museum archaeology of the ostraka confirms that there are strong ties between Kaies, son of Pates, and Dryton's oldest daughter Apollonia alias Senmouthis (see §57-58 and Vandorpe, *Archives from Pathyris* (2001), §26).

  A study of the Dryton archive must incorporate the Kaies texts (Texts **23-28**, **51-53**), for it would be illogical to consider, on the one hand, the divorce contracts of Dryton's daughters (= Kaies' sisters-in-law) and Dryton's granddaughters (= Kaies' daughters) as a part of the archive, and to exclude, on the other hand, the loan contracts of Kaies. For the divorces and marriages took place after Dryton's death and the contracts were preserved by Kaies and his wife. By separating these groups of texts, one would create an archive that ignores the family-by-marriage, and even worse, the later owner of the archive (see below).
- *Phagonis, son of Panebchounis.* — A certain Phagonis, brother of the famous Peteharsemtheus[2], caused some problems during my museum research. For it could be proved that the family archives of Dryton and Peteharsemtheus were completely separate, except for two papyri, the only two papyri in which Peteharsemtheus' brother Phagonis acts alone: a Greek loan of salt (Text **29**) and a demotic deed of partnership (Text **49**). In the other texts belonging to the Peteharsemtheus archive, Phagonis always acts together with his brothers. The solution was provided by an unpublished marriage contract in the British Museum (Text 9). It records the information that in 95 B.C. Phagonis married a girl called Tbokanoupis, the granddaughter of Dryton and the daughter of the above-mentioned Kaies and Apollonia alias Senmouthis. What looked like a problem for my museum archaeology in fact proved that after his marriage Phagonis added his own papers to the archive of his parents-in-law (see Vandorpe, *Archives from Pathyris* (2001), §25, 4).
- *Ostraka.* —Archives of ostraka are usually considered archives *sui generis*. Museum archaeology of the ostraka relating to Dryton's family suggests, however, that in this case they were found together with the papyrus archive and that the last (or second last) owners were Dryton's daughter Apollonia alias Senmouthis, and her husband Kaies, son of Pates

---

1 Pestman, 'Pathyris II' (1963), p. 15-53, no. 28.
2 Pestman, 'Pétéharsemtheus' (1965), no. 55.

(Texts **51-58**; see §57 and Vandorpe, *Archives from Pathyris* (2001), §26). There are no ostraka preserved of the previous generation of owners of the archive, Dryton and his wife Apollonia.

- *The Erbstreit dossier.* — The so-called Erbstreit dossier relates to disputes within the family of Dryton's wife Apollonia. The contents suggests that it was preserved by cousins of Apollonia who finally won the "Erbstreit". Apollonia and her sisters are only involved in the initial phase of the "Erbstreit". Museum archaeology affirms that the Erbstreit dossier does not form part of the family archive of Dryton and his wife, with the exception of the petition Text **33** and **33bis**. This petition is generally considered part of the "Erbstreit", but concerns a dispute between Apollonia, her sisters and their uncle Kallimedes and has nothing to do with the "Erbstreit" (see Vandorpe, *Archives from Pathyris* (2001), §25, 1 and §37).

The story of the archive

The family archive has always been called the archive of Dryton. But the new archive, as proposed in this volume, gives a more nuanced picture. It gives an answer to the question: what happened to the family archive after Dryton's death? It was already known that some papyri, such as the divorce contracts Texts 5, 6 and 8, dated from after the death of Dryton, but it was not clear who preserved them.

Owners of the archive (see family tree, p. 17)

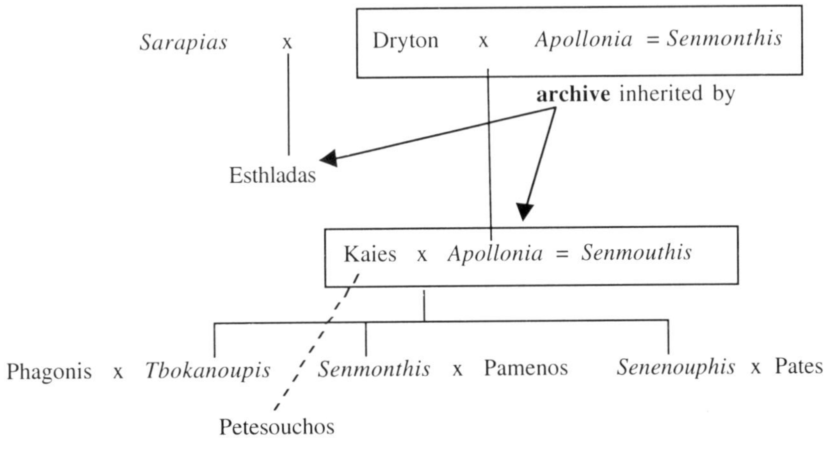

After Dryton's death, in or shortly after 126 B.C., in my view the family archive was transferred to one or more heirs. One would expect Esthladas, Dryton's oldest son, to inherit the archive. There are, however, few documents preserved which belonged to Esthladas and none of these dates from the period after Dryton's death. I assume that the family archive was split up, as was the remainder of Dryton's inheritance (see §14 and §21-22):

(1) some of the papers went to **Esthladas**, Dryton's oldest son of his first marriage, and are now lost; among these were undoubtedly the more important papers of Dryton which are missing (such as title deeds).

(2) The preserved part of the archive

(a) contains some old papers of Dryton and Esthladas, most of them being relatively unimportant: old loan contracts (Texts 11, 12, 21, 22), Dryton's first marriage contract (Text 1), petitions (copy: Text 31 and perhaps the original petition Text 32), private accounts and lists (Texts 37-40, 42-44);

(b) contains also several relatively important papers from Dryton's wife Apollonia: loan contracts (more recent than those of Dryton: Texts 13-20), original petition (Text 33);

(c) has been enlarged after Dryton's death with three divorce contracts (Texts 5, 6, 8), two marriage contracts (Texts 7, 9) and with one petition (Text 34), all related particularly to Dryton's oldest daughter and her three children.

Apparently, this part of the archive (2a-b-c) was inherited by Apollonia alias Senmouthis, Dryton's oldest daughter from his second marriage (there were no sons). It became the family archive of **Apollonia alias Senmouthis and her husband Kaies**. This Kaies, son of Pates (see above), added his own papers to the archive. It is not surprising that the couple also kept the divorce contracts of two of the sisters(-in-law), the divorce or marriage contracts of their three daughters and two papers of their son-in-law Phagonis.

My proposal is confirmed by the ostraka, which I consider part of the family archive (see §57 and Vandorpe, *Archives from Pathyris* (2001), §26). Ostraka are usually related to the last (or last two) generation(s) of owners of an archive. This is also the case with the ostraka from Dryton's family: these are all connected with Dryton's oldest daughter, Apollonia alias Senmouthis, and her husband Kaies, son of Pates, the last (or second last) owners of the archive (see below, Overview, periods 3-4).

A women's archive?

Dryton always played a dominant role in the story of his family. But the new archive, as proposed in this volume, provides another picture. The new reconstruction shows the prominent role of women for two reasons: (1) the important papers not of Dryton, but of his wife Apollonia alias Senmonthis are preserved making up a substantial part of the archive, (2) the archive as it was inherited by their oldest daughter Apollonia alias Senmouthis has come to us and not the part inherited by Dryton's oldest son Esthladas. This is not yet exclusively a women's archive (there are still papers of Dryton, his son and his son-in-law Kaies), but the role women play here is much more prominent than has ever been realized. The temptation has been strong to call it, for instance, the archive of mother and daughter Apollonia, as these two women rather than Dryton are the central persons, but the archive has since so long been known as the archive of Dryton that is better to retain his name in the title of this edition. Furthermore, I prefer to use the Greek name of the mother (Apollonia) and the Egyptian name of the daughter (Senmouthis) in the title: the mother saw in her marriage to the Cretan Dryton an opportunity to present herself as a Greek woman, whereas the daughter married an Egyptian soldier and returned to Egyptian tradition[3].

---

3 Vandorpe, 'Apollonia, a Businesswoman' (2001).

Overview

Period 1 *The archive of Dryton, son of Pamphilos: his early years and his first marriage*

c. 174-150 B.C., Thebes and Diospolis Mikra

Dryton's father Pamphilos probably emigrated from Crete to Egypt under the reign of Ptolemy III or IV. Dryton was born c. 192 B.C. He calls himself a Cretan and was a citizen of the Greek polis Ptolemais in Upper Egypt. He served as a cavalry man in several places. Before his first marriage, he lived for a while in Thebes, where he visited various royal tombs and left graffiti (App. B). Afterwards he served in Diospolis Mikra, where, in 164 B.C., he married Sarapias, citizen of Ptolemais. She bore him a son, Esthladas. It is not clear how the marriage came to an end. They either divorced or Sarapias died. In any case, Sarapias is never heard from again and Esthladas was raised by his father.

Papers of Dryton

11 Gr.	Greek loan of wheat to Dryton	174	Diospolis Megale
12 Dem.	Demotic loan of money by Dryton	171	Diospolis Megale
1 Gr.-Dem.	The first Greek will of Dryton	164	Diospolis Mikra

Compare

App. B Gr.	Greek graffiti of Dryton	s.d.	Western Thebes

Period 2 *The archive of Dryton and Apollonia alias Senmonthis: Dryton's second marriage and his death*

150 - c. 126 B.C., Pathyris

Dryton served at the latest by 150 B.C. in the troops of the eponymous officer Diodotos. One of his colleagues, Ptolemaios alias Pamenos, was infantry man of the same unit. Dryton, who was at that time c. 42 years old, married Ptolemaios' oldest daughter, Apollonia alias Senmonthis, on 4 March 150 B.C. Apollonia was still a young girl and descended from a Cyrenaean family. The family had already lived in Egypt for three or four generations and was Egyptianized for the most part. Dryton and his son went to live with Apollonia in Pathyris. She bore him five daughters, the oldest being Apollonia alias Senmouthis; the youngest two girls were born when Dryton was c. 60 years old.

At some time after his second marriage (and before 137/130 B.C.) Dryton was promoted to cavalry officer: he became a hipparch of the epitagma-unit, that is the highest unit of the cavalry in the Ptolemaic army. In or shortly after 126 B.C. Dryton died.

Papers of Dryton

31 Gr.	Greek diagraphe and petition (copy perhaps by Dryton)	140-131/130
32 Gr.	Greek petition from Dryton	137-130

35 Dem.	Demotic letter to Dryton	150-126/115
39 Gr.	Greek account written by ?Dryton	c. 137/136
40 Gr.	Greek account written by Dryton	135
43 Gr.	Greek account written by ?Dryton	after 154/153-143/142
44 Gr.	Greek account written by ?Dryton	after 150-143/142

Papers of Esthladas, Dryton's oldest son of his first marriage

4 Gr.	The third Greek will of Dryton (copy by Esthladas)	126
21 Gr.-Dem.	Greek receipt for Patous on behalf of Esthladas	after 140
22 Gr.	Greek acknowledgement of debt by Esthladas	after 140
37 Gr.	Greek list of temple goods and account written by ?Esthladas	B.C. 139
38 Gr.	Greek list of traveller's items written by ?Esthladas	after 153/152 or 142/141
42 Gr.	Greek list of traveller's items written by ?Esthladas	134
48 Gr.-Dem.	Greek fragment with a king's oath by Esthladas	145-116

Papers of Dryton and his wife Apollonia alias Senmonthis

36 Gr.	Greek letter from Esthladas to Dryton and Apollonia	130

Papers of Apollonia alias Senmonthis

2 Gr.	The second Greek will of Dryton	150
3 Gr.	The third Greek will of Dryton (agoranomic copy)	126
10 Dem.descr.	Demotic loan of wheat and barley to Panas, grandfather of Apollonia	164
13 Dem.	Demotic loan of spelt by Apollonia	179-133
14 Dem.	Demotic loan of corn by Apollonia	179-133
15 Dem.	Demotic acknowledgement of debt (wheat) to Apollonia	139
16 Gr.	Greek loan of wheat by Apollonia	131
17 Gr.	Greek loan of money by Apollonia	129
18 Dem.	Demotic loan by Apollonia	128
19 Gr.	Greek loan of money by Apollonia	127
20 Dem.-Gr.	Demotic acknowledgement of debt (barley) to Apollonia	after 150
33 Gr.	Greek petition from Apollonia and her sisters	136
33bis Gr.	Greek petition from Apollonia and her sisters (draft or copy)	136
41 Gr.	Greek account written by ?Dryton on behalf of Apollonia	135
45 Dem.	Demotic account of Apollonia	after 141/140

Period 3 *The archive of Dryton's oldest daughter Apollonia alias Senmouthis and her husband Kaies, son of Pates*

c. 126 – 91 B.C., Pathyris

Papers of Kaies, husband of Dryton's oldest daughter

Papyri

23 Dem.	Demotic loan of money by Kaies	124-116
24 Dem.	Demotic acknowledgement of debt (barley) to Kaies	118
25 Gr.	Greek loan of wheat by Kaies	117
26 Dem.descr.	Demotic loan of wheat by Kaies	116
27 Dem.	Demotic loan of wheat by Kaies	112
28 Dem.	Demotic acknowledgement of debt (barley) to Kaies	after 135

Ostraka

51 Dem.	Demotic receipt of measurement for Kaies	B.C. 108
52 Dem.	Demotic harvest tax receipt for Kaies	108
53 Dem.	Demotic harvest tax receipt for Kaies	107

Papers of Apollonia alias Senmouthis, Dryton's oldest daughter, and her younger sisters

Papyri

5 Dem.	Demotic divorce agreement for Aphrodisia alias Tachratis, sister of Apollonia alias Senmouthis	123
6 Dem.	Demotic divorce agreement for a daughter of Dryton	123-100
34 Gr.	Greek petition from Apollonia alias Senmouthis and her sisters	115-110

Ostraka

54 Dem.	Demotic tax receipt for pigeon house for Senmouthis, her sisters and Senminis daughter of Stotoetis	108
55 Dem.	Demotic tax receipt for pigeon house for Senmouthis	101
56 Gr.	Greek tax receipt for pigeon house for Senmouthis	100
57 Gr.	Greek tax receipt for pigeon house for three daughters of Dryton	100
58 Dem.	Demotic account recording Senmouthis and her cousin	s.d.

Papers of Kaies' and Apollonia's children and son-in-law

7 Dem. descr.	Demotic marriage contract of Senenouphis, daughter of Kaies and Apollonia	107-101
8 Dem.	Demotic divorce agreement for Senmonthis, daughter of Kaies and Apollonia	100
9 Dem. descr.	Demotic marriage contract of Tbokanoupis, daughter of Kaies and Apollonia	95
29 Gr.-Dem.	Greek loan of salt with demotic receipt for Phagonis, son-in-law of Kaies and Apollonia	105
49 Dem.	Demotic deed of partnership of Phagonis, son-in-law of Kaies and Apollonia	94

Period 4 *The archive after Kaies' death*

91-88 B.C., Pathyris

Kaies died in 91 B.C. As mentioned above, the documentation from Pathyris ended abruptly in 88 B.C. Who preserved the archive in the period 91-88 B.C. is not clear, since no texts have reached us from that short period: his wife Senmouthis or their oldest daughter Senmonthis? The latter married and then divorced her husband Pamenos in 100 B.C.; there is no evidence of a new marriage. Or was the archive inherited by Kaies' son Petesouchos or by another, married daughter, such as Tbokanoupis, wife of the above-mentioned Phagonis? In the latter case, it would be strange that the marriage contract Phagonis made for Tbokanoupis was kept in their archive, rather than that of a family member, as is usual.

I have tried to reconstruct the archive for the period 174-91 B.C. New evidence relating to the last three years of the archive (90-88 B.C.) may still surface. In 88 B.C., when the town of Pathyris went down after the suppression of the revolt in Upper Egypt by the king, this archive was buried for almost two thousand years, as were the other papyri from Pathyris.

Doubtful cases

There are two texs which were maybe part of the family archive of Dryton, but which are not published here: P. Grenf. I 42 and P. dem. Fs. Berl., p. 287 (= P. dem. Heid. inv. no. 781b), see Vandorpe, *Archives from Pathyris* (2001), §25, 5.

Family Tree

Pros. = a prosopographical study of the family members of Dryton and his wives Sarapias and Apollonia is to be found in Vandorpe, *Archives from Pathyris* (2001), chapter V.

Legend

I, I, III, ...	generations
~	double name
italic	woman's name
x	married
/x/	married and divorced
(°)	additions to the family tree found in Ritner, 'Property Transfer' (1984)
▭	owners of the archive

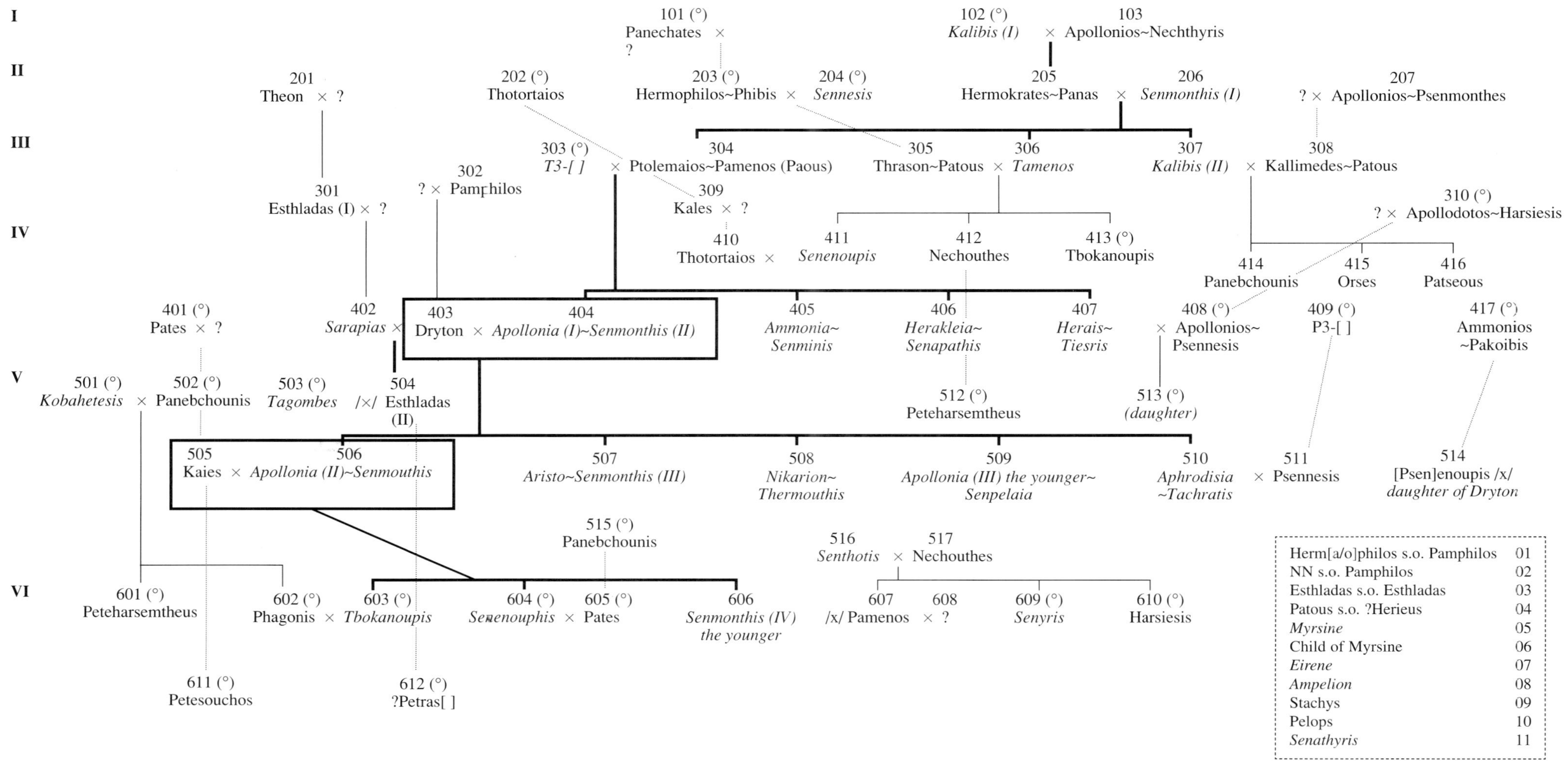
I
II
III
IV
V
VI
101 (°) Panechates × ?
102 (°) Kalibis (I) × 103 Apollonios~Nechthyris
201 Theon × ?
202 (°) Thotortaios
203 (°) Hermophilos~Phibis × 204 (°) Sennesis
205 Hermokrates~Panas × 206 Senmonthis (I)
207 ? × Apollonios~Psenmonthes
301 Esthladas (I) × ?
302 ? × Pamphilos
303 (°) T3-[ ] × 304 Ptolemaios~Pamenos (Paous)
305 Thrason~Patous × 306 Tamenos
307 Kalibis (II) × 308 Kallimedes~Patous
309 Kales × ?
310 (°) ? × Apollodotos~Harsiesis
401 (°) Pates × ?
402 Sarapias × 403 Dryton × 404 Apollonia (I)~Senmonthis (II)
405 Ammonia~Senminis
406 Herakleia~Senapathis
407 Herais~Tiesris
408 (°) × Apollonios~Psennesis
409 (°) P3-[ ]
410 Thotortaios ×
411 Senenoupis
412 Nechouthes
413 (°) Tbokanoupis
414 Panebchounis
415 Orses
416 Patseous
417 (°) Ammonios ~Pakoibis
501 (°) Kobahetesis × 502 (°) Panebchounis
503 (°) Tagombes /×/ 504 Esthladas (II)
505 Kaies × 506 Apollonia (II)~Senmouthis
507 Aristo~Senmonthis (III)
508 Nikarion~Thermouthis
509 Apollonia (III) the younger~Senpelaia
510 Aphrodisia ~Tachratis × 511 Psennesis
512 (°) Peteharsemtheus
513 (°) (daughter)
514 [Psen]enoupis /x/ daughter of Dryton
515 (°) Panebchounis
516 Senthotis × 517 Nechouthes
601 (°) Peteharsemtheus
602 (°) Phagonis × 603 (°) Tbokanoupis
604 (°) Senenouphis × 605 (°) Pates
606 Senmonthis (IV) the younger
607 /x/ Pamenos × 608 ?
609 (°) Senyris
610 (°) Harsiesis
611 (°) Petesouchos
612 (°) ?Petras[ ]
Herm[a/o]philos s.o. Pamphilos 01
NN s.o. Pamphilos 02
Esthladas s.o. Esthladas 03
Patous s.o. ?Herieus 04
Myrsine 05
Child of Myrsine 06
Eirene 07
Ampelion 08
Stachys 09
Pelops 10
Senathyris 11

SURVEY OF THE TEXTS

I. WILLS, MARRIAGE AND DIVORCE

Introduction §1-§32

1 Gr.-Dem.	The first Greek will of Dryton	B.C. 164	A
2 Gr.	The second Greek will of Dryton	150	A
3 Gr.	The third Greek will of Dryton (agoranomic copy)	126	B
4 Gr.	The third Greek will of Dryton (copy by Esthladas)	126	A
5 Dem.	Demotic divorce agreement for Aphrodisia alias Tachratis, daughter of Dryton	123	A
6 Dem.	Demotic divorce agreement for a daughter of Dryton	123-100	A
7 Dem. descr.	Demotic marriage contract of Senenouphis, granddaughter of Dryton	107-101	C
8 Dem.	Demotic divorce agreement for Senmonthis, granddaughter of Dryton	100	B
9 Dem. descr.	Demotic marriage contract of Tbokanoupis, granddaughter of Dryton	95	D

II. LOANS AND RECEIPTS

Introduction §33-39

10 Dem.descr.	Demotic loan of wheat and barley to Panas, grandfather of Apollonia	164	D
11 Gr.	Greek loan of wheat to Dryton	174	A
12 Dem.	Demotic loan of money by Dryton	171	C
13 Dem.	Demotic loan of spelt by Apollonia	179-133	C
14 Dem.	Demotic loan of corn by Apollonia	179-133	A
15 Dem.	Demotic acknowledgement of debt (wheat) to Apollonia	139	C
16 Gr.	Greek loan of wheat by Apollonia	131	A
17 Gr.	Greek loan of money by Apollonia	129	B
18 Dem.	Demotic loan by Apollonia	128	C
19 Gr.	Greek loan of money by Apollonia	127	A
20 Dem.-Gr.	Demotic acknowledgement of debt (barley) to Apollonia	after 150	D
21 Gr.-Dem.	Greek receipt for Patous on behalf of Esthladas	after 140	A
22 Gr.	Greek acknowledgement of debt by Esthladas	after 140	A

A = Text of the old Dryton archive — **B** = Text of the old Dryton archive + new fragments — **C** = New text attributed to the Dryton archive on prosopographical grounds — **D** = New text attributed to the Dryton archive on the basis of museum archaeology, see p. 9-11.

23 Dem.	Demotic loan of money by Kaies	124-116	D
24 Dem.	Demotic acknowledgement of debt (barley) to Kaies	118	D
25 Gr.	Greek loan of wheat by Kaies	117	D
26 Dem.descr.	Demotic loan of wheat by Kaies	116	D
27 Dem.	Demotic loan of wheat by Kaies	112	D
28 Dem.	Demotic acknowledgement of debt (barley) to Kaies	after 135	D
29 Gr.-Dem.	Greek loan of salt with demotic receipt for Phagonis	105	D
30 Gr.	Greek loan of wheat by a descendant of Dryton?	131-113	A

III. Petitions

Introduction §40-43

31 Gr.	Greek diagraphe and petition (copy perhaps by Dryton)	140-131/130	B
32 Gr.	Greek petition from Dryton	137-130	A
33 Gr.	Greek petition from Apollonia and her sisters	136	A
33bis Gr.	Greek petition from Apollonia and her sisters (draft or copy)	136	A
34 Gr.	Greek petition from Dryton's daughters	115-110	A

IV. Letters

Introduction §44-46

35 Dem.	Demotic letter to Dryton	150-126/115	A
36 Gr.	Greek letter from Esthladas to Dryton and Apollonia	130	A

V. Lists and accounts

Introduction §47-55

37 Gr.	Greek list of temple goods and account written by ?Esthladas	139	D
38 Gr.	Greek list of traveller's items written by ?Esthladas	after 153/152 or 142/141	D
39 Gr.	Greek account written by ?Dryton	c. 137/136	C
40 Gr.	Greek account written by Dryton	135	A
41 Gr.	Greek account written by ?Dryton on behalf of Apollonia	135	A
42 Gr.	Greek list of traveller's items written by ?Esthladas	134	D
43 Gr.	Greek account written by ?Dryton	after 154/153 -143/142	D

A = Text of the old Dryton archive — **B** = Text of the old Dryton archive + new fragments — **C** = New text attributed to the Dryton archive on prosopographical grounds — **D** = New text attributed to the Dryton archive on the basis of museum archaeology, see p. 9-11.

43 App. dem.	Demotic loan of corn	154/153 -143/142	D
44 Gr.	Greek account written by ?Dryton	after 150 -143/142	D
45 Dem.	Demotic account of Apollonia	after 141/140	A

VI. VARIA

Introduction §56

46 Gr.	Greek fragment of a division or an agreement	after 150	A
47 Gr.	Greek fragment of an agreement made by Dryton	s.d.	C
48 Gr.-Dem.	Greek fragment with a royal oath made by Esthladas	145-116	C
49 Dem.	Demotic deed of partnership of Phagonis	94	D
50 Gr.	The 'Alexandrian Erotic Fragment' or 'Maedchens Klage'	after Oct. 174	A

VII. OSTRAKA

Introduction §57-62

51 Dem.	Demotic receipt of measurement for Kaies	108	D
52 Dem.	Demotic harvest tax receipt for Kaies	108	D
53 Dem.	Demotic harvest tax receipt for Kaies	107	D
54 Dem.descr.	Demotic tax receipt for pigeon house for Senmouthis, daughter of Dryton, her sisters and Senminis, daughter of Stotoetis	108	C
55 Dem.	Demotic tax receipt for pigeon house for Senmouthis, daughter of Dryton	101	A
56 Gr.	Greek tax receipt for pigeon house for Senmouthis, daughter of Dryton	100	A
57 Gr.	Greek tax receipt for pigeon house for three daughters of Dryton	100	A
58 Dem.	Demotic account recording Senmouthis, daughter of Dryton, and her cousin	s.d.	A

VIII. APPENDICES

Introduction §63

Appendix

A Gr. descr.	Greek cheirographon of the Peteharsemtheus archive written by Dryton	136
B Gr.	Greek graffiti by Dryton	s.d.
C Dem. descr.	Demotic temple oath for Esthladas	124

A = Text of the old Dryton archive — **B** = Text of the old Dryton archive + new fragments — **C** = New text attributed to the Dryton archive on prosopographical grounds — **D** = New text attributed to the Dryton archive on the basis of museum archaeology, see p. 9-11.

CHRONOLOGICAL LIST OF THE TEXTS

DATED TEXTS

11 Gr.	Greek loan of wheat to Dryton	174
12 Dem.	Demotic loan of money by Dryton	171
1 Gr.-Dem.	The first Greek will of Dryton	164
10 Dem.descr.	Demotic loan of wheat and barley to Panas, grandfather of Apollonia	164
2 Gr.	The second Greek will of Dryton	150
15 Dem.	Demotic acknowledgement of debt (wheat) to Apollonia	139
37 Gr.	Greek list of temple goods and account written by ?Esthladas	139
App. A Gr.	Greek cheirographon of the Peteharsemtheus archive written by Dryton	136
33 Gr.	Greek petition from Apollonia and her sisters	136
33bis Gr.	Greek petition from Apollonia and her sisters (draft or copy)	136
40 Gr.	Greek account written by Dryton	135
41 Gr.	Greek account written by ?Dryton on behalf of Apollonia	135
42 Gr.	Greek list of traveller's items written by ?Esthladas	134
16 Gr.	Greek loan of wheat by Apollonia	131
36 Gr.	Greek letter from Esthladas to Dryton and Apollonia	130
17 Gr.	Greek loan of money by Apollonia	129
18 Dem.	Demotic loan by Apollonia	128
19 Gr.	Greek loan of money by Apollonia	127
3 Gr.	The third Greek will of Dryton (agoranomic copy)	126
4 Gr.	The third Greek will of Dryton (copy by Esthladas)	126
App. C Dem.	Demotic temple oath for Esthladas	124
5 Dem.	Demotic divorce agreement for Aphrodisia alias Tachratis, daughter of Dryton	123
24 Dem.	Demotic acknowledgement of debt (barley) to Kaies	118
25 Gr.	Greek loan of wheat by Kaies	117
26 Dem.descr.	Demotic loan of wheat by Kaies	116
27 Dem.	Demotic loan of wheat by Kaies	112
51 Dem.	Demotic receipt of measurement for Kaies	108
52 Dem.	Demotic harvest tax receipt for Kaies	108
54 Dem.descr.	Demotic tax receipt for pigeon house for Senmouthis, daughter of Dryton, her sisters and Senminis, daughter of Stotoetis	108
53 Dem.	Demotic harvest tax receipt for Kaies	107
29 Gr.-Dem.	Greek loan of salt with demotic receipt for Phagonis	105
55 Dem.	Demotic tax receipt for pigeon house for Senmouthis, daughter of Dryton	101

8 Dem.	Demotic divorce agreement for Senmonthis, granddaughter of Dryton	100
56 Gr.	Greek tax receipt for pigeon house for Senmouthis, daughter of Dryton	100
57 Gr.	Greek tax receipt for pigeon house for three daughters of Dryton	100
9 Dem. descr.	Demotic marriage contract of Tbokanoupis, granddaughter of Dryton	95
49 Dem.	Demotic deed of partnership of Phagonis	94

TEXTS DATED APPROXIMATELY

13 Dem.	Demotic loan of spelt by Apollonia	179-133
14 Dem.	Demotic loan of corn by Apollonia	179-133
50 Gr.	The 'Alexandrian Erotic Fragment' or 'Maedchens Klage'	after Oct. 174
43 App. dem.	Demotic loan of corn	154/153 -143/142
43 Gr.	Greek account written by ?Dryton	after 154/153 -143/142
44 Gr.	Greek account written by ?Dryton	after 154/153 -143/142
38 Gr.	Greek list of traveller's items written by ?Esthladas	after 153/152 or 142/141
35 Dem.	Demotic letter to Dryton	150-126/115
20 Dem.-Gr.	Demotic acknowledgement of debt (barley) to Apollonia	after 150
46 Gr.	Greek fragment of a division or an agreement	after 150
48 Gr.-Dem.	Greek fragment with a royal oath made by Esthladas	145-116
45 Dem.	Demotic account of Apollonia	after 141/140
31 Gr.	Greek diagraphe and petition (copy perhaps by Dryton)	140-131/130
21 Gr.-Dem.	Greek receipt for Patous on behalf of Esthladas	after 140
22 Gr.	Greek acknowledgement of debt by Esthladas	after 140
39 Gr.	Greek account written by ?Dryton	c. 137/136
32 Gr.	Greek petition from Dryton	137-130
28 Dem.	Demotic acknowledgement of debt (barley) to Kaies	after 135
30 Gr.	Greek loan of wheat by a descendant of Dryton?	131-113
23 Dem.	Demotic loan of money by Kaies	124-116
6 Dem.	Demotic divorce agreement for a daughter of Dryton	123-100
34 Gr.	Greek petition from Dryton's daughters	115-110
7 Dem. descr.	Demotic marriage contract of Senenouphis, granddaughter of Dryton	107-101
47 Gr.	Greek fragment of an agreement made by Dryton	s.d.
58 Dem.	Demotic account recording Senmouthis, daughter of Dryton, and her cousin	s.d.
App. B Gr.	Greek graffiti by Dryton	s.d.

Greek and Demotic Texts

I

WILLS, MARRIAGE AND DIVORCE

Dryton and his three wills (164-126 B.C.) : §1. Introduction

Dryton's first will (May-June 164 B.C.) : §2. Survey. — §3. Dryton's will and his first marriage. — §4. 'Dryton's wives: two or three?'. A problem solved. — §5. Division of the inheritance. — §6. Epitropos formula. The appointment of a "testamentary executor" or "guardian"? — §7. Identity of the epitropos. — §8. The other clauses. — §9. Witnesses. — §10. Verso.

Dryton's second will (4 March 150 B.C.) : §11. Survey. — §12. Problem of date and place solved. — §13. Dryton's will and his second marriage. — §14. Division of the inheritance. — §15. Appointment of the epitropos. — §16. Witnesses. — §17. Verso.

Dryton's third will (29 June 126 B.C.) : §18. Survey. — §19. Dryton's will and his impending death. — §20. Dryton's last and final testament. — §21. Division of Dryton's real estate. — §22. Division of Dryton's moveable property. — §23. Non-recurrent obligations for the children. — §24. Recurring obligations for the children. — §25. Maintenance of the wife and two youngest daughters. — §26. Some conclusions. — §27 Witnesses.

Marriage and divorce among Dryton's offspring (c. 126-95 B.C.) : §28. Dryton's son Esthladas. — §29. Dryton's daughters. — §30. Dryton's granddaughters. — §31. The marriage contracts. — §32. The divorce agreements.

Dryton and his three wills (164-126 B.C.)

§1. *Introduction.* — Dryton owes his fame in the papyrological world in part to his Greek wills. He has left us at least *three* of these. It is not clear whether the fragmentary Text 46 is part of a will or another kind of contract. *If* it is part of a will, it is certainly not a copy of Dryton's second will, as generally assumed, but of a *fourth*, otherwise unknown will, drawn up between 150 and 126 B.C. (see Text 46, Introduction).

Dryton's wills become all the more important if one considers that — apart from the Greek Petrie wills copied in the notary's office of Krokodilopolis in the Fayum (238-225 B.C.)[1] — only eleven Ptolemaic wills have come to light[2]. Five out of them were discovered in Pathyris: P. Grenf. I 24 (139-132 B.C.), *AfP* 1 (1901), p. 63-65 (123 B.C.), and the three wills of Dryton.

These Greek διαθῆκαι[3] are wills in the true sense of the word: the heirs succeed to the inheritance after the decease of the testator. The original deed of the Greek wills of the second and first centuries was kept at the office of the agoranomos. The testator and his heirs each preserved a copy[4].

Alongside the Greek will, there is the Egyptian "division", a form of *donatio inter vivos*: the testator divides his belongings between his children, who become joint owners of their part while the testator lives and owners on his or her death. Such a document is called *sẖ dny.t pš* *(deed of division)*. It was initially drawn up in demotic, but two Greek counterparts occur, which are clearly influenced by Egyptian law. These are therefore called Graeco-Egyptian wills: in a παραχώρησις or cession the testator "concedes" to a heir part of his inheritance; in a δόσις or donation he "donates" possessions to his heir(s). All these types of "wills" are found in Pathyris[5].

---

1 For a survey, see P. Petr.2.I.The Wills, p. 15.
2 P. Petr.2.I.The Wills, p. 12-13; Clarysse, 'Ptolemaic Wills' (1995), p. 88-89.
3 For the general structure of the *diathekai*, see Clarysse, 'Ptolemaic Wills' (1995), p. 89-93.
4 See Pestman, 'Agoranomoi' (1985), in Pap. Lugd. Bat. XXIII, p. 28.
5 See Clarysse, 'Ptolemaic Wills' (1995), p. 93-98; Depauw, *Companion* (1997), p. 144-145; for a demotic deed of division from Pathyris, see, *e.g.*, Ritner, 'Property Transfer' (1984); for the *parachoresis* and *dosis* in Pathyris, see Pestman, 'Agoranomoi' (1985), in Pap. Lugd. Bat. XXIII, p. 28-30.

Dryton's first will (May-June 164 B.C.) **(Text 1)**

§2. *Survey*

Basic information
- drawn up in Diospolis Mikra by the agoranomos Dionysios.
- in the month Pachon of year 6 of Ptolemy VI, Ptolemy VIII and Kleopatra II = between 31 May and 29 June 164 B.C.
- at the occasion of his first marriage to Sarapias.

Sources
- copy by the agoranomos, for Dryton and his family (= Text 1).
- mention of the first will is made in Dryton's third will of 126 B.C. (= Text 4, l. 4-6).

Dryton's family situation

Dryton is about 28 years old when for the first time he enters a legal marriage (σύνειμι κατὰ νόμους, Text 4, l. 4). His wife Sarapias is — like Dryton — a citizen (ἀστή) of the southern Egyptian polis Ptolemais (pros. 402). They have a son, Esthladas, born circa 158 B.C., who will also become a citizen of Ptolemais (pros. 504). As the will is drawn up in Diospolis Mikra, despite the fact that there was a notary's office in Diospolis Megale (see Text 11 of 174 B.C.), we may assume that Dryton either lived or was quartered there.

---

§3. *Dryton's will and his first marriage.* — Dryton's first will was undoubtedly drawn up on the actual occasion of his first marriage to Sarapias, as has often been suggested[1]; thus N. Lewis: «and indeed it is hard to imagine why else a young man of eighteen or so[2] should draft such an instrument»[3]. This assumption is confirmed by Dryton's second will, on the verso of which it is explicitly stated that Dryton's (second) marriage took place on the same day as the composition of the will (see §13).

§4. *'Dryton's wives: two or three?'. A problem solved.* — Quite recently, G. Messeri Savorelli has discovered in the Bibliotheca Medicea Laurenziana some fragments of Dryton's first will; these were published in 1990 (= Text 1). Before this discovery, we knew of this will only through Dryton's third will (Text 4, l. 4-6) of 126 B.C.: the first testament was drawn up δ̣ιὰ του ἐν Διὸς πό(λει) τῆι μι(κρᾶι) ἀρχείου ἐπὶ Διονυσίου ἀγορανόμου ἐν τῶι ϛ (ἔτους) ἐπὶ τοῦ Φιλομήτορος, *in the archeion in Diospolis Mikra, before the agoranomos Dionysios, in the 6th year of the reign of Philometor.* The date has provoked discussion: is it the 6th year of Ptolemy VI's reign (176/175 B.C.) or the 6th year of the joint reign of Ptolemy VI, Ptolemy VIII and Kleopatra II (165/164 B.C.)?[4] The first editor of Text 4 opted for the latter date[5]; few shared his view[1].

---

1 Bouché-Leclercq, *Histoire des Lagides* IV (1907), p. 112; Winnicki, 'Ein ptolemäischer Offizier' (1972), in *Eos* 60, p. 348.

2 N. Lewis supposed at that time that Dryton's first will was redacted in 176/175 instead of 165/165 B.C.; in 176/175 B.C. Dryton was c. 18 years old.

3 Lewis, 'Dryton's wives' (1982), in *Chron. d'Ég.* 57, p. 317.

4 See, *e.g.*, L. Mooren, in *Ancient Society* 5 (1974), p. 144 n. 43.

5 P. Grenf. I 12, l. 14 and note; I 21, l. 5 and note.

Most scholars preferred the date 176/175 B.C.[2] This preference had, however, consequences. In his article 'Dryton's Wives: Two or Three?' N. Lewis assumed that Dryton drew up his first will (of 176/175) on the occasion of his first marriage; he doubted if Dryton then married Sarapias, since they had a son Esthladas only 18 years later (circa 158 B.C.). Lewis continued: «All of which invites us to consider, as another possibility, that Dryton married in 176/5 a woman whose name we do not know, who produced no living issue, and who died or was divorced some time prior to circa 160 B.C., when Dryton married Sarapias, who then bore him a son a year or two later. In sum, there is sufficient reason, I think, to keep open the possibility that Dryton married X in 176/5, took Sarapias as his second wife circa 160, and Apollonia alias Senmonthis as third wife circa 150 B.C.» Hence his question: 'Dryton's Wives: Two or Three?'[3].

A passage from Dryton's third will (Text 4, l. 4-5) strongly suggests that the will of year 6 was made for Sarapias, and not for an unknown woman:

"I bequeath (...) to Esthladas, my son by" Σαραπιάδος ... ἧι συνήμην γυναικὶ κατὰ νόμους καὶ κατὰ διαθήκην [τὴν κεχρηματισμένην] διὰ τοῦ ἐν Διὸς πό(λει) τῆι μι(κρᾶι) ἀρχείου ἐπὶ Διονυσίου ἀγορανόμου ἐν τῶι ς (ἔτους) ἐπὶ τοῦ Φιλομήτορος, "Sarapias (...) the woman with whom I have lived legally and in accordance with a will which was drawn up in the archeion of Diospolis Mikra, before the agoranomos Dionysios, in the 6th year of the reign of Philometor".

Some scholars have taken κατὰ νόμους with Σαραπιάδος . . . ἧι συνήμην γυναικί and considered καὶ κατὰ διαθήκην as belonging to *I bequeath (...) to Esthladas.* In this case, the sentence does not stand up, with an inexplicable καί between κατὰ νόμους and κατὰ διαθήκην. J. Mélèze-Modrzejewski attributes the unfortunate phrasing to «une maladresse du rédacteur de ce texte»[4].

The problem of the date and of the two or three wives has been solved by the discovery of Dryton's first will, published by G. Messeri Savorelli in 1990 (Text 1). The fragmentary papyrus offers the necessary information to establish the date:

- (ἔτους) ς Παχώ[ν], *year 6, Pachon* (l. 3)
- [μην]ὸς Παχὼν [ ], *month Pachon* (l. 11)
- remains of the protocol with names of the eponymous priests (l. 3-10).

The will dates to the 6th year [known data], the month of Pachon [new data; the day is lost]. The preserved names of the eponymous priests allowed the editor to attribute the 6th year to the joint year of Ptolemy VI, Ptolemy VIII and Kleopatra II, that is 165/164 B.C., as once

1 G.A. Gerhard, in *Philologus* 63 (1904), p. 508, n. 3 and p. 557, n. 168; Bouché-Leclercq, *Histoire des Lagides* IV (1907), p. 112, n. 1; Mooren, *Prosopography* (1975), no. 0192.

2 Plaumann, *Ptolemais* (1910), p. 32, n. 1 and p. 65; Pestman, 'Pétéharsemtheus' (1965), in Pap. Lugd. Bat. XIV, p. 49; Winnicki, 'Ein ptolemäischer Offizier' (1972), in *Eos* 60, p. 348; Mélèze-Modrzejewski, 'Dryton le crétois' (1984), p. 375, n. 4; Pros. Ptol. III 7662.

3 Lewis, 'Dryton's wives' (1982), in *Chron. d'Ég.* 57, p. 317-321 and Id., *Greeks in Ptolemaic Egypt* (1986), p. 89-91.

4 *E.g.*, Mélèze-Modrzejewski, 'Dryton le crétois' (1984), p. 375, n. 3.

suggested by the first editor of Text 4. Dryton can be credited with three wills, but with only two wives[1].

§5. *Division of the inheritance.* — We know little about Dryton's first will, due to the fragmentary condition of the papyrus. Text 4, which mentions this will casually, is, unfortunately, also sparing with its information.

The first will (Text 1, l. 13-17) has only left:

ἐὰν δέ τι ἀνθρώπ[ινον πάθω, καταλείπω καὶ δίδωμι - c. 40 -] Σαραπιά[δ . . Ἐσθλάδου τοῦ Θέωνος ἀστῆ . . ἧι σύνειμι γυναικὶ κατὰ νόμους - c. 4 - διὰ - c. 9 -] .ου καὶ δι' ἐμοῦ [- c. 22-]ωι ạὐτ.[- c. 16 - Ἄλλωι δὲ οὐθ]ενὶ οὐθὲν καταλ[είπω οὐδὲ δίδωμι],

"But if I suffer mortal fate, I bequeath and give - - - Sarapias, daughter of Esthladas son of Theon, a citizen, the woman with whom I live according to the laws - - - and through me - - -. I neither leave nor give anything to anybody else."

The "disinheritance clause" [ἄλλωι δὲ οὐθ]ενὶ οὐθὲν καταλ[είπω οὐδὲ δίδωμι] is usually found in general legacies: the formula stresses that the testator is bequeathing his whole estate[2]. As there are no children, Dryton apparently leaves behind all his belongings to his wife Sarapias, presumably on the condition that she stays in the house and does not live together with another man (Text 1, fragment 9); a similar condition is stipulated in Dryton's third will (see §25-26). This legacy to his wife Sarapias is confirmed by the demotic summary on the verso of the will (see §10). A legacy to the wife is often attested in the Greek Petrie Wills (238-225 B.C.)[3] and, for instance, in *AfP* 1 (1901), p. 63-65, from Pathyris[4]. It is not clear whether the wife has real ownership or solely usufruct[5]. Dryton appointed maybe also a future son as heir. Such a clause is found in, for instance, P. Petr.[2].I.The Wills no.17, l. 25: the testator bequeaths his estate to his wife and ἐάν τί μοι ἐπιγένηται ἐξ αὐτῆς παιδίον, "to the child(ren) she may bear me". In his second will Dryton equally leaves part of his possessions to the children who may yet be born (see §14).

§6. *Epitropos formula. The appointment of a "testamentary executor" or "guardian"?* — According to H. Kreller the epitropos is «der Vertrauensmann, dem man etwas anvertraut (ἐπιτρέπειν)»[6]. He distinguishes between (1) an individual entrusted by the testator with the execution of the will, and (2) a individual entrusted with his still minor children, that is a guardian. The testators in the Petrie wills usually appoint the ruling royal family as epitropoi (ἐπιτρόπους δὲ αἱροῦμαι). They are doubtless testamentary executors. A private person is

---

1 Nonetheless, N. Lewis leaves open the possibility that Dryton had three wives: if Dryton was born c. 192 B.C., as is generally acknowledged, «this would have made him about thirty years old when he contracted the marriage and executed the will of 164. (...) One is to suppose that when he married Sarapias in 164 she was his second wife, not his first»; N. Lewis doubts, however, whether Dryton was born c. 192 B.C.; in his view Dryton was born later and «was a young man of normal marriageable age when he married his first wife, Sarapias (...) this would have been his first marriage», see Lewis, 'Drytoniana' (1993), p. 111-112. For Dryton's birth date (c. 192 B.C.), see pros. 403.

2 Kreller, *Erbrechtliche Untersuchungen* (1919), p. 348-349; P. Petr.[2].I.The Wills, p. 40-41.

3 P. Petr.[2].I.The Wills, p. 34.

4 *AfP* 1 (1901), p. 63-65.

5 See the discussion in P. Petr.[2].I.The Wills, p. 34.

6 Kreller, *Erbrechtliche Untersuchungen* (1919), p. 374-375.

rarely chosen as epitropos in the Petrie wills; if so, he is appointed epitropos either alone or together with the royal family. In these cases the epitropos formula is introduced by ἐπίτροπον δὲ καταλείπω, "as epitropos I leave". There are five examples of such a clause[1]. In four of them there is (possibly)[2] mention made[3] of a son or child; only in the case of no. 16, l. 28 is no child mentioned by the testator, who is 85 years old. W. Clarysse considers the epitropos in these examples of the third century B.C. as testamentary executors[4].

In the petition Text 33 of the Dryton archive, the context of the formula οὔτε κατὰ διαθήκην ἀπολελειμμένοι ἐπίτροποι (l. 7-8) evidently points to the appointment of "guardians" for the minor daughters (135 B.C.). In wills of the Roman period, in the *divisiones parentis inter liberos* and in particular types of marriage contracts an epitropos or guardian is often appointed for the minor children (καθιστάναι ἐπίτροπον).

What about the epitropoi in Dryton's first and second will: are they testamentary executors or guardians? Thus far scholars have assumed them to be guardians, even for children who were not yet born, as would be the case in Text 1[5]. This is, however, far from a simple matter.

- In his first and second will, (the notary of) Dryton('s will) applies the expression ἐπίτροπον δὲ καταλείπω, as in the Petrie Wills, where epitropos has the meaning of testamentary executor. The passages in Dryton's will are, however, fragmentary: the addition of αὐτῶν (*viz.* the children) after ἐπίτροπον is possible, pointing then to the sense of guardian; the genitive in [ὁμ]οίως δὲ κ[αὶ Ἐ]σθλάδου τοῦ Ἐσθλάδ[ου] in the second will might again suggest the latter meaning ("I leave as epitropos Herm[a/o]philos (...), a relative of Dryton, equally of Esthladas, son of Esthladas", see §15).
- Text 4, l. 5-6 refers to the first will, which διασαφεῖ τά τε ἄλλα [καὶ ἐπίτροπον Ἑρμ .φιλο]ν ὄντα συγγενῆι κατέστησεν, "records among its dispositions the appointment of Herm[a/o]philos as epitropos, being a relative", there is no space left after ἐπίτροπον for supplementing αὐτοῦ (*viz.* Esthladas). This rather points to the meaning of testamentary executor.
- When making his first will, Dryton did not yet have children. To consider the epitropos mentioned in this will as a guardian for future children is possible, but it would then be a unique example.

Epitropos in Dryton's wills, "Testamentary executor" or "guardian"? A new question, hard to answer. I prefer the former meaning of executor of his will.

---

1 Kreller records only one example; see, furthermore, P. Petr.².I.The Wills, p. 41, n. 72 and 73; Clarysse, 'Ptolemaic Wills' (1995), p. 91-92.

2 P. Petr.².I.The Wills no. 1, l. 71-73; no. 8, l. 4.

3 P. Petr.².I.The Wills no. 15, l. 8; 18, l. 12.

4 P. Petr.².I.The Wills, p. 41.; see also Kreller, *Erbrechtliche Untersuchungen* (1919), p. 376 («Testamentsvollstrecker»); in a will of 218 B.C. a son is appointed epitropos of his mother; here, epitropos is considered as a mistake for kyrios, see Taubenschlag, *Law* (1955²), p. 173 and n. 13.

5 Kreller, *Erbrechtliche Untersuchungen* (1919), p. 377-378, who is misled, however, by a wrong addition in the lacuna Text 2, l. 21: ἐπιτρο[πευομένοις - - -], instead of ἐπίτρο[πον δὲ καταλείπ]ω; Sel. Pap. I 83; Mélèze-Modrzejewski, 'Dryton le crétois' (1984), p. 375 («tuteur (?)»); Pomeroy, *Women in Hellenistic Egypt* (1990), p. 105; Messeri Savorelli, 'Frammenti del primo testamento' (1990), p. 435, n. Fr. 6 («tutore»).

§7. *Identity of the epitropos.* — Text 4 informs us that Dryton's first will διασαφεῖ τά τε ἄλλα [καὶ ἐπίτροπον - - -[1]]ν ὄντα συγγενῆι κατέστησεν, "records among its dispositions the appointment of an epitropos - - -, being a relative" (Text 4, l. 5-6). Dryton's first will Text 1 is somewhat fragmentary where it records the epitropos: he is a son of Pamphilos (Text 1, l. 18), a kinsman [of Dryton] (l. 17? and fragment 6) and belongs to the misthophoroi of the cavalry (l. 18).

In his second will of 150 B.C. Dryton similarly appoints an epitropos (Text 2, l. 21-22): Herm[a/o]philos son of Pamphilos, a relative of Dryton and belonging to the same deme as Dryton, Philoteris.

The details for the person of the epitropos of the first and the second will correspond on major points. It is plausible that Herm[a/o]philos also served as epitropos of the first will; therefore, I have added Herm[a/o]philos as name of the epitropos (see Text 4, l. 5-6). He is probably a brother or half-brother of Dryton (pros. 01).

§8. *The other clauses.* — The remaining clauses of the first will are quite fragmentary. Probably it was forbidden under the will to pledge (part of) the estate, as long as the future heir was not an adult, and a penalty was determined should the terms of the will not be observed.

§9. *Witnesses.* — Of the total of (probably) six witnesses, traces of four of them remain. One bore the name Antiochos or the ethnic Antiocheus (fragment 10), a second one the ethnic [- - -]αντινος (l. 26) and at least two were cavalrymen ([ἱππ]εῖς l. 28). The witnesses apparently were, as was Dryton, Greek soldiers or cavalrymen.

§10. *Verso.* — The back of the will has a demotic summary: "- - - which Dryton, son of Pamphilo[s, has drawn up] for the woman [Sarapias, daughter of Esthladas]". It is curious to find a demotic summary in the archive of a Greek. The note was made either by an Egyptian who looked after the will temporarily, or by Kaies, the later owner of the Dryton archive, who knew Egyptian better than Greek (pros. 505).

---

[1] I have added Herm[a/o]philos as name of the epitropos in the text edition, see below.

Dryton's second will (4 March 150 B.C.) **(Text 2, not Text 46)**

§11. *Survey*

Basic information

- drawn up in Latopolis before the agoranomos Ptolemaios.
- on 4 March 150 B.C.
- on the occasion of his second marriage to Apollonia alias Senmonthis, of Cyrenaean origin, who lives in Pathyris.

Sources

- copy by the agoranomos, for Dryton and his family (= Text 2).
- the fragmentary Text 46 is, in our opinion, *not* a copy of this will, see §1 and Text 46, Introduction).

Dryton's family situation in 150 B.C.

Dryton's first wife Sarapias has died or divorced Dryton. He has a son by her, Esthladas, who is about eight years old. Dryton marries for the second time, again in accordance with the laws (cf. σύνειμι κατὰ νόμους, Text 4, l. 13). His second wife is a young woman, Apollonia alias Senmonthis (pros. 404), whose ancestors were Cyrenaean immigrants: she carries the ethnic Κυρηναία, although her family is now fully egyptianized. Dryton probably met her through her father Ptolemaios (pros. 304), since both belong to the same military detachment of Diodotos.

Apollonia lived with her family in Pathyris. Since in 150 B.C. there was no Greek notary's office in Pathyris or in neighbouring Krokodilopolis (see §34), the couple goes south to Latopolis, where the agoranomos Ptolemaios draws up Dryton's second will.

---

§12. *Problem of date and place solved.* — For a long-time there has been speculation as to the precise date of Dryton's second will[1]. According to the eponymous priests of Ptolemais named in the protocol, the deed was drawn up between 152/151 and 145 B.C. N. Lewis assumed that the marriage could not have taken place later than 152/151, since Apollonia is recorded in the petition Text 33 (l. 11-12) as having become an adult in year 30 (according to N. Lewis 152/151)[2].

On the place of redaction the will contained until recently only fragmentary data: [- - -]ν πόλει (l. 13). Grenfell suggested that the will was drawn up in Krokodilopolis, Pathyris' sister-town (see Vandorpe, *Archives from Pathyris* (2001), §4). The will would then be the first witness to the existence of a Greek notary's office in Krokodilopolis, the next testimony dating

---

[1] See, *e.g.*, Bouché-Leclercq, *Histoire des Lagides* IV (1907), p. 112 (149/148 B.C.); Winnicki, 'Ein ptolemäischer Offizier' (1972), in *Eos* 60, p. 344 (c. 148 B.C.); P.W. Pestman, in Pap. Lugd. Bat. XIX (1978), p. 33 (151-145 B.C.); Lewis, 'Dryton's wives' (1982), in *Chron. d'Ég.* 57, p. 319-320 (152-151 B.C.).

[2] Lewis, 'Dryton's wives' (1982), in *Chron. d'Ég.* 57, p. 320: «When did a girl in Ptolemaic Egypt cease to be minor? When she married, . . . As the marriage made her ἐνήλικος, enabling her to file the petition of 152/1, the marriage cannot have taken place later than that year».

ten years later (141/140: P. Amh. II 45). G. Messeri Savorelli and P.W. Pestman adopted this proposal in their studies of the agoranomoi[1].

The discovery of a new fragment by W. Clarysse in 1986[2] clarifies the ambiguities. The tiny fragment contains interesting details; the verso has a summary with the exact date (6 Mecheir year 31 or 4 March 150 B.C.) as well as the place of redaction: Latopolis (Text 2, verso). Place of redaction and date of the second will are now firmly established and generally accepted[3].

§13. *Dryton's will and his second marriage.* — It is assumed that Dryton's first will was made on the occasion of his marriage (see §3). For the second will one can be sure, since the note on the verso records "the marriage (γάμος) of Apollonia with Dryton took place in Latopolis, before the agoranomos Ptolemaios, in year 31, 6 Mecheir". As the will written on the recto was also drawn up in the month of Mecheir (l. 13) before the agoranomos Ptolemaios (l. 14), it is obvious that the redaction of the will and the actual marriage coincided.

The will was, apparently, the only type of marriage contract that was made. Dryton's first marriage is said to be established "legally and in accordance with a will (which ...)" (σύνειμι κατὰ νόμους καὶ κατὰ διαθήκην, Text 4, l. 4). Dryton's second marriage also has a legal base (σύνειμι κατὰ νόμους, Text 4, l. 13) and a legal testament was also drawn up on the occasion of this marriage, as shown by the note on the verso.

A marriage contract is nowhere mentioned, as it is, for instance, in the testament BGU VI 1285 (1st cent. B.C.): the testator is married according to a cohabitation contract (σύνειμι κατὰ συγγραφὴν συνοικεσίου, l. 6-7)[4]. E. Seidl notes: «Die etwas weniger zahlreichen griechischen Eheurkunden sind in der Literatur heftig umstritten. Auch bei ihnen herrschte der Grundgedanke, daβ die Ausstellung einer Urkunde notwendig sei»[5]. For Dryton's marriages, the wills apparently took over the function of marriage contracts.

§14. *Division of the inheritance.* — Dryton divides his whole estate: τὰ ὑπάρχοντά μοι πάντα ἔγγαια καὶ ἔπιπλα (l. 18), "all my immovable and movable property" and he neither leaves nor gives anything to anybody else: ["Ἄλλωι δὲ οὐθενὶ οὐ]θ̣ὲν [καταλ]είπω οὐδὲ δί[δωμι] (l. 24). This general legacy is accompanied by one specific legacy to his son Esthladas[6].

• *Apollonia, wife of Dryton.* In his second will Dryton bequeaths nothing to his second wife; this is different to the case in his first will, in which Sarapias is named heir (see §5). H. Kreller[7] argues it was the normal procedure not to bequeath the estate to the spouse; she would only receive usufruct. According to the Petrie Wills, however, the surviving wife often inherits the whole estate either alone or jointly with her children.[8] In the Pathyris will *AfP* 1 (1901), p.

---

1 Messeri Savorelli, 'Lista degli agoranomi' (1980), p. 206-207, n. 35; Pestman, 'Agoranomoi' (1985), in Pap. Lugd. Bat. XXIII, p. 16, no. 1.

2 Clarysse, 'Le mariage et le testament' (1986), in *Chron. d' Eg.* 61, p. 99-103 = SB XVIII 13330.

3 See, *e.g.*, Lewis, 'Drytoniana' (1993), p. 110.

4 For this type of marriage contract, see Taubenschlag, *Law* (1955²), p. 113.

5 Seidl, *Ptolemäische Rechtsgeschichte* (1962), p. 181.

6 Kreller, *Erbrechtliche Untersuchungen* (1919), p. 348-349; P. Petr.².I.The Wills, p. 37-40.

7 Kreller, *Erbrechtliche Untersuchungen* (1919), p. 176-178; 194-195.

8 P. Petr.².I.The Wills, p. 34-35; Clarysse, 'Ptolemaic Wills' (1995), p. 90.

63-65, the legal wife (σύνειμι κατὰ νόμους) is bequeathed the major part of the testator's belongings; his sons by another, apparently illegal wife, only inherit one bed and one mattress.

Apollonia is not mentioned at all in Dryton's second will, nor is the usufruct of his estate, to which she was no doubt entitled, recorded. In his third and last will, Dryton will explicitly provide for Apollonia, though only for four years and on the condition she lives blamelessly in the house, where she has to take care of her two youngest daughters (see §25).

• *Esthladas, son of Dryton by his first wife.* Esthladas comes into half of Dryton's estate (τὸ ἥ[μισυ], l. 20), as well as Dryton's military equipment: his weapons and his service horse (τὰ ὅπλα καὶ τ[ὸν ἵππ]ον ἐφ' οὗ στ[ρατεύομαι], l. 20). Greek soldiers often left their military equipment as a specific legacy to one of their sons, since it could not be divided. Soldiers of the Petrie Wills, for instance, bequeath their horse, armour, stathmos and/or kleros to one of their sons[1].

• *The children who may be born during their marriage.* Any children who may be born in the future, regardless of their number or gender, inherit the remaining part of the estate, that is the other half of Dryton's belongings ([τὰ δὲ λοιπά], l. 21). Thus Esthladas, being the oldest son and child of a former marriage, is privileged. In Dryton's last will, the same division of the inheritance will be maintained, but will be specified in more detail (see §22-23).

§15. *Appointment of the epitropos.* — Dryton presumably appoints the same epitropos as in his first will: Herm[a/o]philos, son of Pamphilos, a relative, probably a (half-)brother of Dryton (see §7; pros. 01). Even more problematic is the mention of Esthladas, son of Esthladas: "As epitropos I leave behind Herm[a/o]philos, son of Pamphilos, of the deme Philoteris, a relative of Dryton, son of Pamphilos, equally of Esthladas, son of Esthladas" (ἐπίτρο[πον δὲ - c. 2 - καταλείπ]ω Ἑρμ[.]φιλο[ν] Παμφίλου Φιλωτέρε[ιον Δρ]ύτωνι Πα[μφίλου ὄντα συγγενῆ, ὁμ]οίως δὲ κ[αὶ Ἐ]σθλάδου τοῦ Ἐσθλάδ[ου], l. 21-23). The use of the genitive for the name Esthladas suggests Herm[a/o]philos is also epitropos of this Esthladas, apparently a family member of Dryton's first wife Sarapias (pros. 03). This would point to the meaning of epitropos as "guardian" and not of "testamentary executor" as I suggested above (see §6). This Esthladas would then be a minor, Dryton being his guardian.

It is, in my opinion, more likely that the wrong case has been used (genitive instead of accusative): Esthladas, son of Esthladas, is probably an adult, maybe brother of Sarapias, who would be appointed co-epitropos.

§16. *Witnesses.* — The passage with the names of the six witnesses is fragmentary. They are apparently Greeks (l. 27: Apollonios, son of Asklepiades, from Aspendos; l. 28: Herakleides; l. 31: Herodos — a Persian name? —, bearing a Persian father's name Arsakes). At least one of them belongs to military circles: he is a cavalryman of the detachment of Ptolemaios, son of Ptolemaios (l. 30). Finally, at least one witness is a Persian of the epigone (l. 29).

§17. *Verso.* — The verso of the will has a Greek note, probably written by the agoranomos (see §12).

---

[1]   P. Petr.[2].I.The Wills, p. 35, 37-39; Clarysse, 'Ptolemaic Wills' (1995), p. 91.

Dryton's third will (29 June 126 B.C.) (Texts 3 and 4)

§18. *Survey*

Basic information
- drawn up in Pathyris before the agoranomos Asklepiades.
- on 29 June 126 B.C.
- apparently shortly before Dryton's death.

Sources
- Text 3 is a copy by Areios, scribe of the agoranomos Asklepiades, intended for Dryton and his family; the text contains a copy, with abbreviations, of the will proper (col. I, l. 1-34), the name of the testator (col. I, l. 35) and of the witnesses (col. II).
- Text 4 is a copy, probably by Esthladas, Dryton's oldest son. The text contains a copy, with abbreviations, of the whole will; the name of the testator and the witnesses' list are not copied. The will proper is quite well-preserved in Text 4, unlike that of Text 3; indeed Text 4 helps to fill the lacunas of this latter text .

Dryton's family situation in 126 B.C.

Dryton is about 66 years old and several years before was promoted to cavalry officer. His son Esthladas is circa 32 years.

Dryton has five daughters by his second wife Apollonia. Three of them are grown-up, two still minors. One of his older daughters, Tachratis (pros. 510), will be married soon; the two other mature girls are probably already married.

---

§19. *Dryton's will and his impending death.* — Several details of Dryton's final will show that it had to be drawn up hurriedly, shortly before his death.

The six witnesses of a Greek will are usually Greeks, often Greek soldiers, who sign the will in Greek. In Dryton's will four out of the five or six witnesses are, however, Egyptians who cannot write Greek and have, consequently, signed in demotic. The scribe who copied the will notes that there were at the time no people available who were able to write Greek (Text 3, col. II, l. 25-28). In Pathyris there were indeed few people who mastered the Greek language. If necessary and if there was time, it was nonetheless possible to bring together enough individuals who could write Greek, as is shown by the Greek Pathyris will of the Egyptian testator Pachnoubis, who in 123 B.C. found five Greek-writing witnesses (*AfP* 1 (1901), p. 63-65). The redaction of Dryton's final will was apparently unexpected and could not be postponed until sufficient Greek-writing witnesses were available.

In addition, the will contains several terms which presuppose that Dryton expects to die in the very near future: (1) In Text 4, l. 9 Dryton mentions a half-finished dovecote; he clearly does not expect it will be finished while he is living. — (2) In Text 4, l. 11, Dryton bequeaths an open lot intended for a dovecote; in l. l. 16-17 he charges Esthladas and his daughters to bear the cost of the dovecote jointly until it is completed. — (3) According to Text 4, l. 14, Esthladas is to cede about one square metre of his open lot for the construction of a baking oven. — (4) The two youngest daughters are to be maintained until they are eleven years old, or for a period of eleven years (Text 4, l. 19). — (5) Dryton's daughter Tachratis is to be given a dowry of twelve copper talents (Text 4, l. 19-20). Tachratis will indeed marry soon after the redaction of the will, since she divorces three years later (in 123 B.C., see Text 5). For the two youngest daughters, still minors, no provision is made for a dowry.

The introductory clause seems to contain a counter- argument: "I bequeath and give all my immovable and movable property, cattle and *everything I may acquire besides*" (καταλείπω καὶ [δίδωμι τὰ ὑπάρχοντά μοι ἔγγαι]ά τε καὶ ἔπιπλα καὶ κτήνη καὶ ὅσα ἄν προσεπικτήσωμαι, Text 4, l. 3). This is, however, a standard clause for Pathyris testaments: the same clause is found in a will of 123 B.C., drawn up by the same scribe Areios (see Text 4, introduction). Moreover, the sentence in Dryton's will containing this phrase, is misconstrued, since Areios wished to maintain the standard clause.

§20. *Dryton's last and final testament.* — Dryton's third and last will does not consist of a general legacy, as were his preceding two wills. He does bequeath his whole estate (l. 2-3: καταλείπω καὶ [δίδωμι τὰ ὑπάρχοντά μοι ἔγγαι]ά τε καὶ ἔπιπλα καὶ κτήνη καὶ ὅσα ἄν προσεπικτήσωμαι), but he subdivides it in several specific legacies. In the end, the division turns out to be consistent with the terms of the second will (see §14): half of the estate as well as the military equipment are left to Esthladas, the remaining half to his five daughters.

The reason why Dryton describes in detail what is bequeathed to whom, is probably due to the fact that he has children from two marriages. Through specific legacies he can prevent rows after his death. A similar case is found in the Petrie wills, some hundred years before: Peisias, equally a Greek officer, had a son of a first marriage and married a second time. His last will clearly specifies what is left to his son and what is bequeathed to his second wife[1]. W. Clarysse observes: «No doubt the second marriage of the testator caused some friction between the child(ren) of the first marriage and their stepmother»[2].

In his last will Dryton also imposes various obligations on his children (see §23-24). An epitropos or testamentary executor is not appointed, as in his former wills, probably because Esthladas is grown-up and can make the necessary arrangements himself.

§21. *Division of Dryton's real estate.* — Dryton's immovable property (ἔγγαια) is also mentioned in several other papyri of the archive. Only a short survey of the division is given here (for a full survey, see Vandorpe, *Archives from Pathyris* (2001), chapter VI).

• *The vineyard with appurtenances in the Pathyrite nome.* Dryton's vineyard is located on the east bank of the Pathyrite nome, in a barely fertile region called the Kochlax (ἐπὶ τοῦ Κόχλακος τῆς Ἀραβίας τοῦ Παθυρίτου, Text 4, l. 8). This vineyard is left to Esthladas. According to a petition from Dryton's daughters ten years later (Text 34), half of the vineyard seems, however, to belong to the girls. What exactly happened, remains unclear[3]. One must,

1 P. Petr.2.I.The Wills 13; Clarysse, 'Ptolemaic Wills' (1995), p. 91.

2 P. Petr.2.I.The Wills, p. 158, comm. on l. 6-7.

3 Compare Lewis (*Greeks in Ptolemaic Egypt* (1986), p.101): «Feeling that his father's will was less than fair to his half-sisters, that collectively they ought to share equally with him in everything (...), Esthladas deeded them half-ownership of the land after he inherited it. Whether his stepmother had a hand in leading him to that decision we shall never know.»

however, keep in mind that according to Dryton's (earlier) second will, all immovable property was to be divided between Esthladas and children who might be born in the future.

• *The house in Pathyris.* It is not made clear where Dryton's house, listed among his real estate in his last will, is located. It seems certain that his house in Pathyris is meant. As the will is made in the latter town, it was not necessary to name the town where the house is located. Some parts of the house are assigned to Esthladas, others to Dryton's daughters. Dryton's house consists of:

- a vaulted room (οἶκος κεκαμαρωμένος or καμάρα) and other rooms with appurtenances (οἶκοι καὶ χρηστῆρες).
- at least one courtyard or αὐλή.
- open lots (ψιλοὶ τόποι) and dovecotes (περιστερῶνες) located around the house.

An earlier "division"
Some details in the will point to an earlier division of parts of the house: to the youngest daughter Apollonia the younger, only a few years old, has been assigned the vaulted room (Text 4, l. 9); Petras- - , son of Esthladas (pros. 612) has a τόπο̣[ς - c. 6 -]ς (Text 4, l. 10), and Esthladas already owns an open lot near the house (Text 4, l. 9-10).

Division according to Dryton's last will
(1) "To Esthladas I bequeath (...) the dovecote, the other, half-finished dovecote, a courtyard of which the boundaries are, south: open lots of the said Esthladas, north: a vaulted room of Apollonia the younger, east: a lot - - of Petras- - son of Esthladas, west: an open lot of Esthladas, as far as the door opening to the west." (τὸν περιστ]ερῶνα κ[α]ὶ τὸν ἄλλον ἡ̣μιτέλεστον καὶ αὐλὴν ὧν γείτονες νό(του) ψιλοὶ <τόποι> τοῦ αὐ(τοῦ) Ἐσθλάδου βο(ρρᾶ) οἶκος κεκαμαρωμένος Ἀπολλω(νίας) τῆς νεω(τέρας) ἀπη]λι(ώτου) τόπο̣[ς - ca 6-]ς Πετρασ[. .]υ̣ τοῦ Ἐσθλάδ̣[ο]υ̣ λι(βὸς) ψιλὸς τόπος Ἐσθλάδου ἕως τῆς ἀνεῳ̣γμένης θύ(ρας) ἐπὶ λίβα, Text 4, l. 9-10)

The courtyard, dovecote and half-finished dovecote are assigned to Esthladas. That the courtyard is bequeathed to Esthladas is readily understood, since it is bounded by open lots belonging to Esthladas.
(2) "The remaining rooms with appurtenances, on old - -, an open lot intended for a dovecote down from the door of Esthladas and to the west of the vaulted room, I give to Apollonia, Aristo, Aphrodisia, Nikarion and Apollonia the younger, my five daughters." (τοὺς δὲ λο(ιποὺς) οἴκους καὶ χρηστῆρας [καὶ π]α̣λ̣α̣ιὰν [- c. 5 -] καὶ ψιλὸν τόπον εἰς [π]εριστερῶνα ἀποδεδειγμένον ὑποκάτω τῆς Ἐσθλά(δου) θύ(ρας) καὶ ἀπὸ λι(βὸς) τῆς καμάρας δίδωμι [Ἀπολ]λωνίαι καὶ Ἀριστοῖ καὶ Ἀφροδισίαι καὶ Νι[κα]ρίωι καὶ Ἀπολλωνίαι νεωτέραι οὖσι $\overline{\epsilon}$, Text 4, l. 10-11)

The remaining part of the house with appurtenances, as well as an open lot to the west of the house designated for a dovecote (see also l. 16-17), are assigned to the five daughters.

• *Real estate in Perithebas.* The will informs us that "Of the remaining building(-site)s and open lots in the Ammonieion(-quarter) in Diospolis Megale and in the Kerameia, Esthladas is to have half, Apollonia and her sisters half." (τὰ δὲ λο(ιπὰ) οἰκόπεδα καὶ ψι]λ̣οὶ τόποι ἐν Δι(ὸς) πό(λει) τῆι μεγά(λῃι) ἐν τῶι Ἀμμω(νιείωι) [κ]α̣ὶ ἐν τοῖς Κεραμείοις ἐχέτω Ἐσθλάδας κατὰ τὸ (ἥμισυ), Ἀπολλω(νία) δὲ καὶ ἀδελφαὶ κατὰ τὸ (ἥμισυ), Text 4, l. 14-15).

Dryton owns building(-site)s and open lots in the nome of Perithebas[1]: some are located in the Ammonieion[2], a quarter of the metropolis Diospolis Megale, other plots in the Kerameia[3], modern Medamud to the north of Diospolis. Dryton distinguishes between building(-site)s and open lots, both in cities or towns, not on the fields. Open lots (ψι]λ̣οὶ τόποι) are free from buildings, but structures may be built on it in the future, whereas building(-site)s (οἰκόπεδα) may already contain constructions or buildings («un bien immobilier qui prend souvent la forme d'un bâtiment»[4]).

Esthladas inherits half of the real estate in Perithebas, whereas his sisters the other half.

§22. *Division of Dryton's moveable property.* —

• *Military equipment.* As already stated in his second will (see §14), Dryton leaves his military equipment to his son Esthladas: his weaponry and the horse on which he campaigned (Text 4, l. 3-4).

• *Four domestic slaves.* In his former wills, Dryton never explicitly mentioned domestic slaves. One cannot conclude that he did not have slaves at that time, as the former wills were general legacies, without mention of specific legacies, except for the military equipment. In his last will Dryton states that "to Esthladas I bequeath (...); of the four domestic slaves (I give to Esthladas) those named Myrsine and her (child - -); the remaining two female slaves called Eirene and Ampelion, (I leave) to Apollonia and her sisters." (Ἐσθλάδαι . . . ἀπὸ τῶν οἰκετικῶν σωμάτων δ̅ ὧν ὀνόματα Μυρσίνην καὶ ταύτης [- c. 12 - · τὰ δὲ] λοιπὰ θη̣[λ]υκὰ β αἷς ὄνομα Εἰρήνην καὶ Ἀμπέλιον Ἀπολλωνίαι καὶ ταῖς ἀδ(ελφαῖς), Text 4, l. 4-7).

The sentence is not clearly phrased, with the result that A.S. Hunt and C.C. Edgar thought Esthladas was to inherit four household slaves: «of the household slaves I gave him 4, whose names are Myrsine and ταύτης [τὰ γ̅ παιδία, "her three children ?]»[5] — with the strange position of ταύτης in front of the article. The girls would then be left the two remaining female slaves. Dryton would, consequently, have had six slaves in total. As R. Scholl has already observed, in the lacuna after Μυρσίνην καὶ ταύτης [- c. 12 -] one expects the name(s) of the child(ren)[6]. The lacuna is, however, too small to contain three names of children. Furthermore, a petition of Dryton's five daughters some ten years later records that the girls inherited half of the domestic slaves: μέρ[ους] ἡμίσους . . . τῶν οἰκετικῶν σωμάτ[ων] (Text 34, l. 8-10).

---

1 For the nome of Perithebas, see Vandorpe, 'Outline of Greco-Roman Thebes' (1995), in Pap. Lugd. Bat. XXVII, p. 230.
2 See Vandorpe, 'Outline of Greco-Roman Thebes' (1995), in Pap. Lugd. Bat. XXVII, p. 213.
3 See Vandorpe, 'Outline of Greco-Roman Thebes' (1995), in Pap. Lugd. Bat. XXVII, p. 221-222.
4 Husson, *Oikia* (1983), p. 209-211.
5 Sel. Pap. I 83.
6 C. Ptol. Sklav., p. 232.

It is more obvious to assume — with B.P. Grenfell, the first editor of the will[1] — that the number "four" is not used independently, but belongs to the preceding noun (ἀπὸ τῶν οἰκετικῶν σωμάτων δ̅) and thus points to the total of Dryton's slaves: of the four slaves, Esthladas inherits two: Myrsine and her child (pros. 05 and 06), whose name is lost in the lacuna; a nice parallel is found in P. Petr.2.I.The Wills, 13, l. 9: παιδίσκην Ἀβίσιλαν [κ]αὶ ταύτης θυγατέρα Εἰρήνην. One of Dryton's accounts, which I recently discovered, records that Myrsine gave birth to a child; the *terminus post quem* of the account is 154-142 B.C. (Text 43, see pros. 05). When Myrsine bore her child somewhere between 154-142 and 126 B.C. (date of the will), Esthladas was between 12 and 30 years old. So it is possible, as R. Scholl already suggested[2], that Esthladas is the father of Myrsine's child and therefore inherits them both. This tempting proposal remains, however, a hypothesis.

The two remaining female slaves Eirene (pros. 07) and Ampelion (pros. 08) are assigned to the five daughters. Furthermore, the will records that "They (the five daughters) are to possess the two female slaves (...) in equal shares for their households according to the division I have made." (τὰ θη[λ]υκὰ β̅ σώμα[τ]α . . . ἐξ ἴσου κυριευέτωσαν ταῖς οἰκίαις καθ' ὃν πεποίημαι μερισμόν, l. 13). Other papyri inform us that a heir can possess, for instance, "the third part" of a slave and can even sell that part[3].

• *The wagon with its equipment.* The ἅμαξα σὺν τῆι ἐπισκευῆι or wagon with equipment (Text 3, col. I, l. 12 and Text 4, l. 8-9) is left to Esthladas. Ἐπισκευή (equipment) usually comes in the plural, but here in the singular; the harness is undoubtedly meant with the benefit of which a horse or cow could pull the wagon. Dryton's wagon is also mentioned in one of his accounts, in which he rents the wagon (Text 44, verso l. 1-2).

• *The cow.* Dryton's five daughters inherit the cow (ἡ βοῦς, Text 4, l. 13), which "they are to possess (together with the two female slaves) in equal shares for their households according to the division I have made" (ἐξ ἴσου κυριευέτωσαν ταῖς οἰκίαις καθ' ὃν πεποίημαι μερισμόν). The latter formula "according to the division I have made" is only relevant for the two female slaves mentioned in the will in an earlier passage. The cow has not been recorded before. Dryton must have owned more cattle, as is shown by his accounts (κτήνη, see Text 43, recto l. 1). Except for the cow, cattle is, however, only mentioned in the stereotypical introductory clause: "I bequeath and give all my immovable and movable property, cattle and everything I may acquire besides" (καταλείπω καὶ [δίδωμι τὰ ὑπάρχοντά μοι ἔγγαι]ά τε καὶ ἔπιπλα καὶ κτήνη καὶ ὅσα ἂν προσεπικτήσωμαι).

• *The symbola of grain and money, and the furniture.* All Dryton's remaining belongings, his symbola for grain and cash, as well as his furniture, will be divided in half shares ([τἆλλα ὑ]πάρχοντά μοι πάντα σύμβο(λά) τε σιτικὰ [κ]αὶ ἀργυ(ρικὰ) καὶ ἔπιπλα πάντα

---

1 P. Grenf. I 21, introduction; see also Pomeroy, *Women in Hellenistic Egypt* (1990), p. 105.
2 C. Ptol. Sklav., p. 232.
3 Biezuńska - Małowist, *L' esclavage dans l' Egypte gréco-romaine.* II (1977), p. 124-127.

κατὰ τὸ (ἥμισυ), Text 4, l. 16). The σύμβο(λά) τε σιτικὰ [κ]αὶ ἀργυ(ρικὰ)[1] could theoretically be loans in cash and kind, since the term symbolon can have the meaning of a notarial loan contract (see §34), especially in demotic documents where the term symbolon is used as a loan word[2]. In Greek texts the expression συγγραφαὶ δανείου is preferred. Moreover, not a single loan contract is preserved for Dryton himself since he lived in Pathyris (from 150 B.C. onwards).

It is more plausible to interpret those symbola as did M. Launey[3]. Soldiers were paid in kind or in money. They received an acknowledgement that entitled the owner to a certain amount of grain or money. Such an acknowledgement was called a symbolon. Concerning the fact Dryton leaves his symbola to his children, M. Launey observes: «Cela signifie visiblement que les σύμβολα n' étaient pas mensuels, mais valables au moins pour une année et que, comme le *stathmos* et le *kléros*, on pouvait les léguer»[4]. Those symbola as well as the furniture were divided in half shares: half for Esthladas and half for his five sisters.

§23. *Non-recurrent obligations for the children.*

• Two obligations are concerned with Dryton's house with appurtenances. (1) Esthladas has to construct a baking oven on one of his open lots ("Esthladas shall give, from the open lot granted to him facing his door to the west, 4 square cubits for the site of an oven" [δότ]ω δὲ Ἐσθλάδας ἀπὸ τοῦ δεδομένου αὐ(τῶι) ψιλο[ῦ τ]όπου ἀπέναντι τῆς θύ(ρας) αὐ(τοῦ) ἐπὶ λίβ[α] πή(χεις) ἐμβαδοὺς δ̅ εἰς κλιβάνου τόπον, Text 4, l. 14). (2) Esthladas and his sisters have to pay jointly the expenses of a new dovecote ("Esthladas, Apollonia and her sisters shall pay in common the expenses of building the dovecote, (that is) the intended dovecote until they have finished it", δότω δὲ Ἐσθλά(δας) καὶ αἱ περὶ Ἀπολλωνίαν κατὰ κοινὸν [εἰς οἰκ]οδομὴν περιστερῶνος ἀνηλώματα ε[ἰς] τὸν ἀποδεδειγμένον περιστερῶνα ἕως ἂν ἐπιτελέσωσι, Text 4, l.16-17).

• Dryton's daughter Tachratis is about to marry in the near future (compare her divorce agreement of 123 B.C., Text 5). Dryton provides a dowry: "They (Esthladas and his sisters) shall give to Tachratis for a dowry 12 copper talents out of the common funds" (δότωσαν δὲ Ταχράτει εἰς φερνὴν [χαλκο]ῦ (τάλαντα) ιβ ἐκ τῶν κοινῶν, Text 4, l. 19-20). A dowry of 12 copper talents or 72,000 drachmes is a very generous gift. The dowries mentioned in demotic marriage contracts from Pathyris have an average value of 16,000 drachmas. The highest dowry amounts to circa 42,000 drachmas[5]. We have to go to Djeme (Memnoneia) to find a dowry of the same level: a demotic agreement of 125 B.C. records a dowry of 12 talents (72,000 drachmas) for an Egyptian girl called Senamounis, daughter of Pechytes (see also §26)[6].

---

[1] A.S. Hunt and C.C. Edgar, in Sel. Pap. I 83: «corn and money contracts»; Lewis, *Greeks in Ptolemaic Egypt* (1986), p. 100: «loans in kind and money»; Pomeroy, *Women in Hellenistic Egypt* (1990), p. 106 does not translate symbola; R. Scholl, in C. Ptol. Sklav., p. 230: «Korn- und Geldverträgen».

[2] Clarysse, 'Greek Loan-Words' (1987), p. 30, no. 78.

[3] Launey, *Les armées hellénistiques* (1949-50), p. 770-775.

[4] Ibid., p. 773.

[5] P. dem. Ryl. 20 (= P. dem. Eheverträge 39) from 116 B.C.

[6] P. Choach. Survey 29.

§24. *Recurring obligations for the children.* — The recurring obligations concern the maintenance of Dryton's wife and his two youngest daughters. Dryton wants his son and older daughters to maintain their mother and younger sisters jointly (κατὰ κοινὸν) or out of common funds (ἐκ κοινοῦ): "Esthladas, Apollonia and her sisters shall jointly give (...) to Apollonia alias Senmonthis, my wife, *for 4 years*, if she stays at home irreproachably, for the maintenance of herself and her two daughters, every month 9.5 artabas of wheat, 1/12 (artaba) of kroton and 200 copper (drachmas). *After 4 years* they shall make the same provisions from common funds to the two younger daughters for 11 years." (δότω δὲ Ἐσθλά(δας) καὶ αἱ περὶ Ἀπολλωνίαν κατὰ κοινὸν . . . Ἀπολλωνίαι τῆι καὶ Σεμμώνθει [τῆι ἐ]μῆι γυ(ναικὶ) ἐτῶν δ̄ ἐὰν παραμείνηι ἐ[ν τῶι] οἴκωι ἀνέγκλητος οὖσα εἰς τροφὴν αὐ(τῆς) καὶ ταῖς β̄ θυγατράσιν ἑκάσ(του) μη(νὸς) (πυροῦ) θ (ἥμισυ) κρότω(νος) ιβ χα(λκοῦ) Σ [καὶ] μετὰ δ ἔτη τὰ αὐτὰ μετρήματα [δότ]ωσαν ταῖς β̄ νεωτέραι<ς> ἐκ κοινοῦ ἕως ἐτῶν ια, Text 4, l. 16-19).

This passages poses two major problems:
(1) Are the "two daughters" (ταῖς β̄ θυγατράσιν) who are to be maintained during the first four years, the two oldest or the two youngest of Dryton's five daughters, being

Apollonia — Aristo — Tachratis — Nikarion — Apollonia the younger.

If the two oldest (Apollonia and Aristo) or next daughters down (Aristo and Tachratis) are meant, as assumed by most scholars[1], then they are not yet married. In that case maintenance is not provided for the two youngest daughters (Nikarion and Apollonia the younger) for the first four years.

I prefer, however, to interpret the "two daughters" as being the two youngest girls (Nikarion and Apollonia the younger), who are still minor and whose maintenance Dryton provides explicitly for after the first four years. In this case, the two oldest daughters (Apollonia and Aristo) are married and are maintained by their husbands; Tachratis is about to be married (see §23).
(2) Does ἕως ἐτῶν ια point to the duration of the maintenance ("for 11 years")[2] or to the age of the two youngest daughters ("until they are 11 years old")[3]? For the indication of the duration a genitive is used in the preceding passage (ἐτῶν δ̄), which would rather point to the meaning "until they are 11 years old" of ἕως ἐτῶν ια. It is, though, unlikely that the two youngest girls were no longer to be maintained by the family after the age of eleven.

In conclusion, I assume that the two youngest girls were to be maintained by the family for four years together with their mother and afterwards for a further eleven years without their mother.

§25. *Maintenance of the wife and two youngest daughters.* — Dryton does not leave any of his belongings to his second wife Apollonia. She is, however, to be maintained for four years

---

1 A.S. Hunt and C.C. Edgar, in Sel. Pap. I 83, note (perhaps the second and third daughters, but the meaning is rather obscure); Lewis, *Greeks in Ptolemaic Egypt* (1986), p. 101 (two next oldest daughters).
2 Thus A.S. Hunt and C.C. Edgar, in Sel. Pap. I 83; Mélèze-Modrzejewski, 'Dryton le crétois' (1984), p. 376; Lewis, *Greeks in Ptolemaic Egypt* (1986), p. 101; Pomeroy, *Women in Hellenistic Egypt* (1990), p. 106.
3 Thus R. Scholl, in C. Ptol. Sklav., p. 230.

from the common funds administered by the children, on the condition that she stays at home free from reproach. She is thus allowed to live in Dryton's house. If she cohabits with another man, who can provide for her, the maintenance by Dryton's children is to be ended. Parallels for this disposition are not found. Only a Ptolemaic will from the third century B.C. contains a clause that reminds us of Dryton's disposition: the Greek testator gives to his wife the right to live in one of his houses[1].

Apollonia receives for herself and for her two youngest daughters every month 9.5 artabas of wheat, 1/12 (artaba) of kroton (castor beans) and 200 copper drachmas. The same items return in the Egyptian marriage contracts, which can contain a clause on the maintenance of the wife during marriage: corn, oil — usually two varieties — and a fixed amount of money (money for clothes and food, and pocket money)[2]. The exact amounts are then given for one year, but the wife, of course, receives the items monthly.

9.5 artabas (circa 285 litres) of wheat monthly for Apollonia and her two daughters is a large amount (see Text 4, l. 18 comm.), as 1 artaba is sufficient for one person a month — for comparison: the Egyptian woman gets on average 480 litres barley a year, that is 40 litres a month. The castor seed (κροτών)[3] can be used for the lighting: the oil from 1/12 artaba castor seed suffices for two to three hours lighting. Castor oil is, however, rather used by women for their personal hygiene: castor oil is used (with natron) as a soap. When the slave Myrsine gives birth to her child, she receives from Dryton 2.5 artabas of castor seed, presumably also for hygienic reasons (Text 44, verso l. 4). As the amount of 200 copper drachmas is somewhat low — one artaba of wheat costs 1200 drachmas in that period[4] —, it is probably meant as pocket money.

After four years the two youngest daughters receive the same amounts for a further eleven years (or until they are 11 years old, see §24). Their mother Apollonia is no longer maintained through the common funds. Other texts inform us that she has inherited from her father and that she was an active business woman (see Vandorpe, *Archives from Pathyris* (2001), chapter V); hence Dryton's very last wish: "Whatever properties Semmonthis appears to have acquired as belonging to herself, while living with Dryton, she shall be the owner" ("Οσα δ' ἂν φαίνη[ται ἐ]π̣ίκτη(τα) ἔχουσα ἡ Σεμμῶνθις ὄντα αὐτῆι συνοῦσα Δρύτωνι κυριευέτω αὐτῶν, Text 3, col. I l. 32-33; Text 4, l. 20-21).

§26. *Some conclusions.* — Esthladas, Dryton's oldest child and his only son, inherits half of Dryton's property. In addition, Dryton leaves him his military equipment, as is often the case with Greek soldiers (see §14 and §22). The privileged position of the eldest son in wills seems to be a Greek as well as an Egyptian custom[5].

---

1 P. Petr.[2].I.The Wills 3, l. 76; comm. p. 40.

2 Pestman, *Marriage* (1961), p. 145-150; E. Lüddeckens, in P. dem. Eheverträge, p. 260-262.

3 D.B. Sandy, 'Egyptian terms for Castor', in *Chron. d' Eg.* 62 (1987), p. 49-52; Id., *Vegetable Oils* (1989), p. 35-54.

4 Reekmans, 'Ptolemaic Copper Inflation' (1951), p. 111.

5 See Kreller, *Erbrechtliche Untersuchungen* (1919), p. 149-154; E. Seidl, 'La preminente posizione successoria del figlio maggiore nel diritto dei papiri', in *Rendiconti del' Istituto Lombardo, classe di lettere e scienze morali e storiche* 99 (1965), p. 185-192; P. dem. Mattha, col. VIII, l. 30 - col. IX, l. 22 (see also K. Donker Van Heel, *The Legal Manual of Hermopolis. Text and Translation* (Uitgaven vanwege de Stichting "Het Leids Papyrologisch Instituut" 11), Leiden 1990, p. 93-103; Pestman, ' "Inheriting" in the Archive of the

The five daughters of Dryton inherit the remaining half of Dryton's estate. Thus each of them is left 1/10 of the whole property. Not included in this 1/10 part, however, are the dowries. According to his third will of 126 B.C., Dryton's daughter Tachratis receives the generous dowry of 12 copper talents (see §23); the two oldest daughters are at that time probably already married and thus have received their *pherne*; for the two youngest daughters no provision is made for a dowry in Dryton's last will; their maintenance is, however, provided for for several years (see §25). In demotic documentation there are some examples where dowry and/ or maintenance are given to a daughter instead of a share of the inheritance[1]. Dryton's daughters received both: a dowry or maintenance and part of the inheritance.

Dryton's second wife Apollonia does not inherit from her husband. He only provides for her maintenance for four years, under the condition she does not live with another man during that time. This disposition is probably influenced by two facts: (1) Apollonia is somewhat younger than Dryton (pros. 404): she can build up a new life with another man; (2) Apollonia has her own property and thus her own means of making a living; already in the past she has proved to be a successful business woman[2].

§27. *Witnesses.* — At least five witnesses have signed the will (Text 3, col. II). Six is the usual number of witnesses in Greek wills[3]. In the lacuna above col. II of Text 3 there is certainly place for the signature of a sixth witness. *AfP* 1 (1901), p. 63-65, drawn up three years later in the same notary's office in Pathyris by the same clerk, has only five signatures; this witness list is, however, followed by οἱ ἓξ τακτόμι(σθοι), "the six taktomisthoi", which shows that six witnesses were expected; as suggested by H. Kreller, the copyist probably skipped one witness[4].

There are not enough witnesses available who have mastered the Greek language when Dryton's will is drawn up (for the reason, see §19). As a consequence four of them sign in demotic. In the copy of the will that contains the witness list (Text 3, not Text 4), the scribe translates the demotic signatures into Greek and adds apologetically that there were at the time insufficient people available who knew the Greek language. The last witness Ammonios (pros. 417) signs in Greek. He is the son of Areios, the scribe who draws up Dryton's last will in the notary's office of Pathyris. Also for the Greek will *AfP* 1 (1901), p. 63-65, equally written by his father Areios, he turns up as a witness. This Ammonios will succeed to his father as scribe; his son Psenenoupis (pros. 514) will marry one of Dryton's daughters.

The four other witnesses sign in demotic. They are important personalities in the town. One of them, Patous son of Horos, is the hypepistates of Pathyris. The three others hold prominent priestly offices. Patous son of Herieus is, in my view, the priest with whom Dryton's family often has contacts (pros. 04). Nechouthes is the son of Thotortaios and brother of Nechthminis, both monographoi of the Hathor temple in Pathyris (see Text 3, comm. on l. 48).

Theban Choachytes' (1987), p. 61-62; W. Clarysse, in P. Petr.2.I.The Wills, p. 25-26; Clarysse, 'Ptolemaic Wills' (1995), p. 95-96.

1 See Pestman, ' "Inheriting" in the Archive of the Theban Choachytes' (1987), p. 59; P. Choach. Survey 29.

2 See Vandorpe, *Archives from Pathyris* (2001), chapter V; Ead., 'Apollonia, a Businesswoman' (2001).

3 Kreller, *Erbrechtliche Untersuchungen* (1919), p. 315-316; P. Petr.2.I.The Wills, p. 42.

4 Kreller, *Erbrechtliche Untersuchungen* (1919), p. 315, n. 5, who cites still another example.

Finally, the priest Schotes is well-known to us, since a small archive of his son Harsiesis has been found (see Vandorpe, *Archives from Pathyris* (2001), §38).

It seems conspicuous that the names of the witnesses are preceded by ἔγραψεν ("Has written"), otherwise unattested in Greek wills. «Daß diese Form für eine Zeugenunterschrift singulär wäre, hat schon Naber l.c. betont», notes H. Kreller[1]. The reason is, however, simple. The signatures of witnesses on several types of demotic contracts is always preceded by *sẖ* ("Has written", see, for instance, Text 23). When translating the four demotic signatures into Greek, the scribe has translated *sẖ* as ἔγραψεν and has erroneously added ἔγραψεν also before the name of the last witness, who signed in Greek.

There remains one problem, as has already been pointed out by P.W. Pestman. Two of the priests are called Persian: «ce qualificatif indiquerait, à l' époque de notre texte, que l' homme en question appartient à l' armée (...) tant Nechoutês que Patous sont des prêtres, descendants de bonnes familles sacerdotales égyptiennes, et n' entretiennent (...) aucun rapport avec l' armée»[2]. In my view, the scribe has added the status designation himself — the first time he has added it later, above the line (Text 3, l. 48). The reason could be that witnesses of Greek wills are usually Greeks or belong to the category of the Persians. The scribe would have added the latter status designation to the priests in order to normalize the witness list.

---

1 Kreller, *Erbrechtliche Untersuchungen* (1919), p. 324.

2 Pap. Lugd. Bat. XIX, p. 35, comm. on l. 6.

Marriage and divorce among Dryton's offspring **(c. 126-95 B.C.)**

§28. *Dryton's son Esthladas* (pros. 504). — Compare App. C.

Married and divorced from Tagombes, before 29 August 124 B.C.

Marriage and divorce agreement were probably kept in the archive of a family member of Tagombes and are now lost.

The only, coincidental, information on Esthladas' marriage life is found in a demotic temple oath of 29 August 124 B.C., concerned with problems resulting from the divorce (App. C). The text informs us that Esthladas was married to and divorced from a woman called Tagombes. Their marriage contract appears to have been a *sẖ n ḥm.t*, a "deed concerning the wife", a frequently attested type of marriage contract in Pathyris (see §31).

§29. *Dryton's daughters.* — Compare Texts 5 and 6.

• *Dryton's oldest daughter Apollonia alias Senmouthis* (pros. 506)

Married to Kaies, son of Pates (pros. 505).

Her marriage contract was in all probability kept in the archive of a family member and not in the archive kept by herself and her husband Kaies, which has survived; the contract is now lost.

• *Aphrodisia alias Tachratis* (pros. 510)

Married to Psennesis, son of P- - - after 29 June 126 B.C. (pros. 511).

Divorced on 25 March 123 B.C.

The divorce agreement Text **5** was kept in the archive of Aphrodisia's family (*viz.* the archive of Dryton and his offspring), whereas the marriage contract had probably to be returned to her ex-husband and is now lost.

Aphrodisia married soon after the redaction of her father's last will on 29 June 126 B.C. This will stipulated that she should be given a dowry of 12 copper talents (see §23). The man she married was a soldier, registered in the camp of Krokodilopolis and called Psennesis; his father's name is for the most part lost in the lacuna, but could have been Pmois. The couple were divorced soon afterwards: the divorce agreement dates from 25 March 123 B.C.

• *A third daughter of Dryton* (pros. 507, 508 or 509)

One of Dryton's three other daughters married and was divorced from [Psen]enoupis, doubtless the son of the agoranomos Ammonios (pros. 514).

Divorced between 123-100 B.C.

The divorce agreement, Text **6**, has been kept in the archive of the family of the daughter (*viz.* the archive of Dryton and his offspring); the marriage contract had probably to be returned to her ex-husband and is lost.

The date of the divorce agreement is lost but can, on palaeographical grounds, be dated to the period 123 - 100 B.C. Taking account of the age of Psenenoupis (pros. 514), I assume that he married one of the two youngest daughters of Dryton, Nikarion or Apollonia the younger, somewhere between 115 and 100 B.C

§30. *Dryton's granddaughters.* — Compare Texts 7, 8 and 9. The only grandchildren of Dryton we have information on are Senmonthis, Senenouphis and Tbokanoupis. They are children of his oldest daughter Apollonia alias Senmouthis and her husband Kaies, who took over the part of Dryton's archive that has survived and added their own papers, among them the divorce and marriage contracts of their daughters, see p. 12.

• *Senmonthis the younger* (pros. 606)
Married to Pamenos, son of Nechouthes (pros. 607).
Divorced on 21 September 100 B.C.
The divorce agreement Text **8** has been kept in the archive of her parents (*viz.* the archive of Dryton and his offspring), whereas the marriage contract had probably to be returned to her ex-husband and is lost.

• *Senenouphis* (pros. 604)
Married in the period 107-101 B.C. to Pates, son of Panebchounis (pros. 605).
The marriage contract Text **7** has been kept in the archive of her parents (*viz.* the archive of Dryton and his offspring) and is of the type *sẖ n ḥm.t*, "deed concerning the wife" (see §31)

•*Tbokanoupis* (pros. 603)
Married on 16 March 95 B.C. to Phagonis, son of Panebchounis and brother of the well-known Peteharsemtheus (pros. 602).
The marriage contract Text **9** is kept in the archive of Tbokanoupis' parents (*viz.* the archive of Dryton and his offspring) and is of the type *sẖ n ḥm.t*, "deed concerning the wife" (see §31).

§31. *The marriage contracts* (Texts 7 and 9 and compare App. C). — The only marriage contracts found among the papers of Dryton's family belong to the granddaughters Senenouphis (Text **7**) and Tbokanoupis (Text **9**). The contract made by Esthladas is occasionally mentioned in a temple oath (App. **C**). In all cases the contract is a *sẖ n ḥm.t*, a "deed concerning the wife"[1].

The *sẖ n ḥm.t* is an agreement settling the financial side of a marriage. It need not be drawn up on the actual occasion of the marriage (it might be drawn up later) nor was it a necessary condition for a valid marriage. It is in fact not a real contract, but a unilateral deed, since it only contains a statement made by the husband. The deed becomes legally valid when the woman receives it. If she accepts the deed, she agrees with the stipulations recorded in it[2]. These stipulations are described in the following paragraphs[3]:

• The deed fixes the amount of the *šp*, the "gift" by the bridegroom. This gift consists of an amount of money, to which sometimes a quantity of corn is added. The gift is usually not of a high value. In the case of early marriage contracts the gift is handed over to the father of the

1 Compare Depauw, *Companion* (1997), p. 139-140.
2 See Pestman, *Marriage* (1961), p. 21-32.
3 See Pestman, *Marriage* (1961), passim.

bride, later to the bride herself, but from c. 230 B.C. onwards the *šp* became fictitious and was only paid to the woman in case of a divorce.

The gift to Tbokanoupis consists of 100 deben + 10 artabas of wheat. The same amounts are found for Pathyris in P. dem. Ryl. 20 and 27, P. dem. Strasb. 43 and P. dem. Adler 14. In other marriage contracts from Pathyris lower amounts are recorded: 100 deben + 5 artabas of wheat and even 10 deben + 5 artabas wheat.

• The husband can promise to pay a fine if he repudiates his wife. This stipulation is optional and is not found in the marriage contract of Tbokanoupis.

• The husband promises to accept the eldest son who may be born to his wife during their marriage, as his eldest son, and to bequeath his property either to this eldest son — as is the case in the marriage contract of Tbokanoupis — or to all their children.

• Finally a detailed list is made of the so-called *nkt.w n sḥm.t*, "goods of a woman". These are private goods the woman brings along with her to her husband's house, such as jewels, mirrors, jars, copper money and clothes, of which the most important is doubtless the *in-šn*, a kind of veil (maybe the bridal veil)[1]. The woman remains the owner of these goods, but the husband can dispose of them. In case of dissolution of the marriage, the husband has either to return these goods to the woman or to pay their counter value; the goods and their counter value are often listed in detail in the marriage contract.

Among the goods which Esthladas' wife brought along with her, were two *in-šn*-veils[2] having together a value of three talents or 900 deben, a large amount, as well as some copper money (the precise amount is lost). Among Tbokanoupis' goods were: probably an *in-šn*-veil of which the value is lost in the lacuna, a basin, a sieve and a jar. The latter three items have together a value of 190 deben. In Senenouphis' marriage contract several goods are listed which she brought along with her, among them an *in-šn*-veil worth 600 deben and a *swḥ3* (egg, see Text 45, l. 10) worth 50 deben. The total value of these goods adds up to 2140 deben or 42,800 drachmas plus a small amount of silver and gold, which is a large amount: 15 other demotic marriage contracts from the period 118-88 B.C. record values between 500 and 2170 deben; two undated contracts have amounts of 3070 and 3000 deben, respectively (the major part originates from Pathyris)[3].

§32. *The divorce agreements* (Texts 5, 6 and 8). — Three divorce agreements have been preserved in the archive of Dryton and his family; they date from the period 123-100 B.C. They are juridically of great importance, since only one other divorce agreement from the 2nd century B.C. has been preserved (P. dem. Tor. Botti 16[4], Thebes, 29 December 114 B.C.). The three divorce agreements from Pathyris are of the "short" type (compare §34 (Notarial deeds)) and their clauses find their parallels especially in the Theban deed just mentioned of 114 B.C. A survey of the barely ten Egyptian divorce agreements, which cover the period 542 -

1 See E. Lüddeckens, in P. dem. Eheverträge, p. 289-291; Pestman, *Marriage* (1961), p. 94-95.

2 See E. Lüddeckens, in P. dem. Eheverträge, p. 289; Pestman, *Marriage* (1961), p. 95.

3 See Pestman, *Marriage* (1961), Diagram A: no. 38-52; not dated: P. dem. Cairo II 30681 and P. dem. Ryl. 42. See now also the seven 'Frauensachen-Listen' on ostraka from Pathyris, published by Kaplony-Heckel, 'Pathyris II' (1994), no. 46-52 and see p. 28.

4 Corrections by K.-Th. Zauzich, in *Enchoria* 2 (1972), p. 88.

100 B.C., and more details on the dissolution of marriage in general, are provided by P.W. Pestman[1].

Contrary to marriage contracts, divorce agreements do not mention a single detail as to the financial consequences of divorce. They only treat the status of the woman: with this deed she is able to prove that she is again free and is allowed to take herself another husband.

In Text 8 the papyrus is broken off at the bottom, after the names of two witnesses. The witnesses' names are written in other hands than the body of the contract; the text is thus the original deed. Of the two remaining texts (Texts 5 and 6) the lower part with the names of the witnesses is lost. Most divorce agreements, among them P. dem. Tor. Botti 16, are signed by four witnesses. One can assume the same number of witnesses for the three divorce agreements Texts 5, 6 and 8.

---

1 Pestman, *Marriage* (1961), p. 58-79 and diagram Z; see also Depauw, *Companion* (1997), p. 140.

1

THE FIRST GREEK WILL OF DRYTON
Agoranomic copy

Plate I (recto); see facsimile of verso below

[New collage]

Diospolis Mikra[1] | 14 fragments [see the description] | 31 May - 29 June 164 B.C.

Bibliotheca Medicea Laurenziana, P.L. III/155 [bought by Vitelli in Egypt in Jan. 1901 for the Bibliotheca Medicea Laurenziana, where the fragments arrived in 1906].

The *recto* has been published by **G. MESSERI SAVORELLI**, 'Frammenti del primo testamento di Dryton?, in *Miscellanea Papyrologica in occasione del bicentenario dell' edizione della charta borgiana* (Pap. Flor. XIX), Florence 1990, p. 429-436 (= **SB XX 14579**). The demotic résumé on the *verso* of fragment 3 has remained **unpublished**.

Photograph. — Plate I (recto); see my facsimile of the verso below; ed. pr., plate 41 (recto and verso).

Description. — Only fourteen tiny fragments of Dryton's first will are preserved. The dimensions of the three largest fragments are (H. x W.): fragment 3 = 2.8 x 3 cm, fragment 5 = 3.2 x 2.8 cm and fragments 7 and 13 together (see Figure) = 6.6 x 3.8 cm. The bottom margin (see fragment 14) measures 1.2 cm, the right-hand margin (see fragments 12 and 13) 0.4 to 1.3 cm and the left-hand margin (see fragment 4) at least 0.3 cm.

The text on the front is written along the fibres in a small, well-cared-for agoranomic handwriting. The pen ran 'uphill' towards the right of the text. The verso is called "bianco" by the editor, who adds in a footnote that there is one line of demotic on the back, running across the fibres (see fragment 3).[2] It is a so-called résumé. As the résumé has been written on the upper part of the verso, the papyrus was rolled from bottom to top.

Introduction

Positioning of the fragments (see Figure below)[3]. — G. Messeri Savorelli transformed fourteen tiny fragments into the first will of Dryton. This was a brilliant discovery.[4] She was able to position six out of the fourteen fragments: fragments no. 1 to 4, 13 and 14. Fragment 13 with the lines 22-28 can be moved up to the lines 18 to 21, or moved down below lines 22 to 28; hence my line indication 22 +/-x in the edition. Fragment 14 with the date, making up the end of the will, can be moved more to the right or to the left. I was able to position one more piece with certainty: *fragment 7* fits fragment 13; the fibre structure, which does not run parallel in that passage, is identical and the text runs on as follows (see l. 25-26):

25] ̣ν διομολο|γουμένου (ed.: ̣νδιομολ ̣ *and* ̣ουμένου)
26]αντι|νος (ed.: αντιν̣ *and* νος)

---

[1] Not Diospolis Megale, as proposed as a possibility in SB XX 14579, note on l. 9. See §4 and Text 4, l. 5 where the first will of Dryton is said to be redacted in Diospolis Mikra.

[2] Messeri Savorelli, 'Frammenti del primo testamento' (1990), p. 429, n. 3.

[3] The numbering of the fragments is based on the edition of G. Messeri Savorelli.

[4] Lewis, 'Drytoniana' (1993), p. 111.

It has been possible to place two further fragments with high probability; the two lines on *fragment 12* (see l. 15-16) undoubtedly continue on fragment 4 (see l. 16-17):

fragm. 12 (l. 15): ̣ου καὶ fragm. 4 (l. 16): δι' ἐμοῦ
fragm. 12 (l. 16): ἄλλωι δὲ οὐθ]ενὶ οὐθὲν fragm. 4 (l. 17): καταλ[είπω

G. Messeri Savorelli already suggested to supplement the lacunas of fragment 12 as ἄλλωι δὲ οὐθ]ενὶ οὐθὲν [καταλείπω, though without linking it with fragment 4.

L. 2-3 of fragment 5 are undoubtedly part of the epitropos-formula and can thus be positioned as well (see l. 17-18).

Of the fourteen fragments five cannot be positioned precisely. Fragment 6 is probably part of the epitropos-formula (l. 17-18), fragment 10 of the witness list (l. 26-29). Fragment 9 mentions in l. 3 a fiscal fine and thus has to be connected with the penalty clause of l. 20. Finally, the text of fragments 8 and 11 cannot be identified at all.

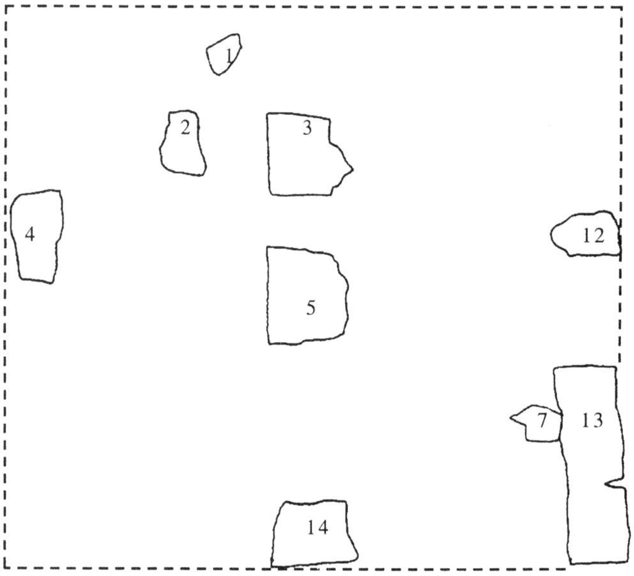

The position of nine of the fourteen fragments of Dryton's first will

Supplementing the lacunas. — Some scanty data made it possible for G. Messeri Savorelli to reconstruct the dating formula with the names of the eponymous priests. This reconstruction shows that one line numbered 72 to 83 letters.

l. 1-2: the editio princeps does not mention how many lines are lost in the beginning of the will. As the name of the kings as well as the title and name of the eponymous priest of Alexander and the deified Ptolemies are known,[1] the opening of the will can be reconstructed

1 See Pap. Lugd. Bat. XXIV, no. 126.

on the example of P. Tebt. III 811: this papyrus dates from 166/165 B.C. and is one year earlier than our text. My supplement numbers 159 characters, in other words two lines are lost.

l. 14 (ed. pr. l. 12): with the supplement of the editio princeps l. 14 contains 96 characters and thus is far too long. The editio princeps has taken over the clause which is in use in Pathyris (only). The will, however, is drawn up in Diospolis Mikra and undoubtedly employed another formula (see comm. on l. 14).

l. 10 and 11 (ed. pr. l. 8 and 9): we have made some minor changes to the supplements of these two lines, which fill the gaps more satisfactorily (see comm. on l. 10 and 11).

Contents (see in more detail §2-10). — We get acquainted with the first will of Dryton, which is, unfortunately, badly preserved. After a long dating formula with the titles and names of the eponymous priests (l. 1-12), the actual will starts in l. 12. Some clauses are difficult to identify. L. 20 and fragment 9, l. 3 are probably part of a penalty clause meant for those who do not adhere to the testamentary dispositions. Perhaps no part of the property could be pledged, as long as a future heir did not reach (wo)manhood (see comm. on l. 21). Possibly Dryton provides for the maintenance of his wife (see comm. on fragment 9, l. 2 and ?3). The will ends with a list of witnesses (l. 26-29 and fragment 10). In the lower margin the date is recorded (l. 30).

An agoranomic copy. — The will is written in a well-cared-for agoranomic handwriting. It is a copy (see §1), not the original deed, since the names of the witnesses are written in the same hand as the rest of the will and the résumé on the verso is written in demotic; it is probably from the hand of one of Dryton's descendants.

Text

Recto (fragments 1-5, 7, 12-14)

[Βασιλευόντων Πτολεμαίου καὶ Πτολεμαίου τοῦ ἀδελφοῦ καὶ Κλεοπάτρας τῆς ἀδελφῆς τῶν Πτολεμαίου καὶ Κλεοπάτρας θεῶν Ἐπιφανῶν ἔτους ς ἐφ' ἱερέως Πολυκρίτου τοῦ Ἀριστοδήμου Ἀλεξάνδρου καὶ θεῶν Σωτήρων καὶ θεῶν Ἀδελφῶν]
[καὶ θεῶν Εὐεργετῶν καὶ θεῶν] Φιλ[οπατόρων καὶ θεῶν Ἐπιφανῶν καὶ θεῶν Φιλομητόρων,]
[ἀθλοφόρου Βερενίκης Εὐεργ]ετίδος Ἀ[ριστονίκης τῆς *Nwl3ts* , κανηφόρου Ἀρσινόης Φιλαδέλφου]
[Ἑρμοκρατείας τῆς Ἑρμοκρά]του[ς, ἱερείας Ἀρσινόης Φιλοπάτορος Δημαρίου τῆς Μητροφάνους]
[τῶν οὐσῶν ἐν Ἀλεξανδρείαι· ἐν δὲ Πτολεμαίδι τῆς Θηβαίδος ἐφ' ἱερέων Πτολεμαίου μὲν Σωτῆρος]
[Νουμηνίου τοῦ Ἡρακλεοδώρου, βασιλέως δὲ Πτολεμαίου Φιλομήτορος - c. 10 - τοῦ Εὐρυμάχου,]
[Πτολεμαίου δὲ Φιλαδ]έλφου [Ἀρίστονος τοῦ Καλλικλέους, ἐφ' ἱερειῶν βασιλίσσης Κλεοπάτρας]
[Ἀγαθοκλείας τῆς Νουμ]ηνίου, Κ[λεοπάτρ]ας δὲ τῆς μη[τρὸς Πτολεμαίου Θεοῦ Ἐπιφανοῦς Εὐχαρίστου]
[Θαίδος τῆς *3pr*⌜ ⌝, καν]ηφόρου Ἀρ[σινόης Φιλ]αδέλφου Εὐχαρ̣[ίστης τῆς Πτολεμαίου τοῦ Πτολεμαίου τῶν οὐσῶν]
[ἐν Πτολεμαίδι, μηνὸ]ς Παχὼ[ν . . ἐ]ν Διὸς πόλει τῆ[ι μικρᾶι τῆς Θηβαίδος ἐπὶ Διονυσίου]
[ἀγο]ρ̣[ανόμου. *Vacat (?)* Τάδε διέθετο εὐαισθ]ητῶν νοῶν κα[ὶ φρονῶν Δρύτων Παμφίλου Φιλωτέρειος τῶν - c. 6 -]
ἱ̣π̣π̣έ̣ω̣[ν ὡς (ἐτῶν) . . μέ(σος) - c. 12 - οὐ(λὴ) παρ' ὀφρὺν ἀρι(στερὰν) ἄκρα]ν. Εἴ̣η μέμ μο[ι ὑγιαίνοντι τῶν ἐμαυτοῦ κύριον εἶναι. Ἐὰν δέ τι
ἀνθρώπ[ινον πάθω, καταλείπω καὶ δίδωμι - c. 40 -]
Σαραπιά̣[δ . . Ἐσθλάδου τοῦ Θέωνος ἀστη . ἧι σύνειμι γυναικὶ κατὰ νόμους - c. 16 -] . ου καὶ
δι' ἐμοῦ [- c. 22 -]ωι α̣ὐτ . [- c. 16 - ἄλλωι δὲ οὐθ]ενὶ οὐθὲν
καταλ[είπω οὐδὲ δίδωμι· ἐπίτροπον δὲ] καταλείπω [Ἑρμ.φιλον Παμφίλου - c. 10 - Δρύτ]ω̣ν̣ι̣
Παμφ[ίλου - χ. 25 - τῶ]ν μισθοφόρων ἱπ̣[πέων - c. 30 -]
[- c. 29 - τ]οῦ προγεγραμμέ[νου - c. 31 -]
[- c. 30 -] . ικωι μηθενὶ σ̣ . [- c. 34 -]
[- c. 30 -] . υτον ε̣ἰ̣ς ὑποθ̣ή̣[κην - c. 31 -]

22+/-x [- c. 72 -]. [. . .]
[- c. 72 -]νη αὐτῶι
[- c. 72 -] (τάλαντα) ρ
25+/-x [- c. 66 -]. ν διομολογουμένου
[- c. 68 -]αντινος
[- c. 72 -] οἱ δύο
[- c. 72 - ἱπ]πεῖς

Vacat

30+/-x [ ] (ἔτους) ς Παχὼ[ν . .]

For the new positioning of the fragments 5, 7 and 12 with repercussions for l. 15-17 and 25-26, see the introduction to the text. 1-2 [Βασιλευόντων Πτολεμαίου καὶ . . . θεῶν Ἀδελφῶν] supplevimus 10 Εὐχαρ[ίστης τῆς Πτολεμαίου τῶν οὐσῶν] ed., Εὐχαρ[ίστης τῆς Πτολεμαίου τοῦ Πτολεμαίου τῶν οὐσῶν] supplevimus 11-12 [Διονυ|[12]σίου ἀγορανόμου] ed. , [Διονυσίου |[12] ἀγο]ρ[ανόμου] legimus et supplevimus 12 [ ]ητων ed., [εὐαισθ]ητῶν ed. p. 434; [Δρύτων Παμφίλου Φιλωτέρειος τῶν - c. 6 -] supplevimus 13 ρ . [ ]. [ ] ed., ἱππέω[ν] legimus; [ὡς (ἐτῶν) . . μέ(σος) - c. 12 - οὐ(λὴ) παρ' ὀφρῦν ἀρι(στερὰν) ἄκρα]ν supplevimus 14 [καταλείπω καὶ δίδωμι τὰ ὑπάρχοντά μοι ἔγγαιά τε καὶ ἔπιπλα καὶ κτήνη καὶ ὅσα ἂν προσεπικτήσωμαι] ed., [καταλείπω καὶ δίδωμι - c. 40 -] supplevimus 15 Σαραπιά[δ . . Ἐσθλάδου τοῦ Θέωνος ἀστῆ . ἧι σύνειμι γυναικὶ κατὰ νόμους - c. 16 -] supplevimus 16 αι ἐμοῦ ed., δι' ἐμοῦ legimus 17 [οὐδὲ δίδωμι· ἐπίτροπον δὲ] καταλείπω [Ἑρμ.φιλον Παμφίλου] supplevimus; [Δρύτ]ωνι legimus et supplevimus 19 [ ]ου ed. , [τ]οῦ supplevimus 20 σο[ ] ed. , σ . [ ] legimus.

R e c t o (non-positioned fragments)

Fragment 6 (l. 2: is probably part of the epitropos-clause l. 17-18)

]αυτων . [
] συγγενῆ [
traces

συγγενηι ed. , συγγενῆ legimus

Fragment 8 (not identified)

]στον[
]. ισμου[

Fragment 9 (l. 3: probably part of the penalty clause l. 20)

]. [ ]. [
] . ημενουσα [
]ιου (δραχμὰς) κβ η[

ενμενουσα ed., . ημενουσα legimus; [ ]ιου, forsitan [ἀργυρ]ίου ed. p. 435

Fragment 10 (l. 2: part of the witness list l. 26-29)

] . . . [ ] . [

] Ἀ̣ντιοχ[

]π̣[

Fragment 11 (unidentified)

] ἀπὸ τῶ[ν

]των . . [

Translation

In the reign of Ptolemy (VI), Ptolemy (VIII), his brother, and Kleopatra (II), his sister, children of Ptolemy (V) and Kleopatra (I), the Gods Epiphaneis, year 6,

the priest of Alexander, the Gods Soteres, the Gods Adelphoi, the Gods Euergeteis, the Gods Philopatores, the Gods Epiphaneis and the Gods Philometores being Polykritos, son of Aristodemos,

the athlophoros of Berenike Euergetis being Aristonike, daughter of Nwl3ts,

the kanephoros of Arsinoe Philadelphos being **(5)** *Hermokrateia, daughter of Hermokrates,*

the priestess of Arsinoe Philopator being Demarion, daughter of Metrophanes: the priestesses who are (appointed) in Alexandria;

in Ptolemais in the Thebaid,

the priests of Ptolemy Soter being Noumenios, son of Herakleodoros,

of king Ptolemy Philometor being - - -, son of Eurymachos,

of Ptolemy Philadelphos being Ariston , son of Kallikles,

the priestesses of queen Kleopatra being Agathokleia, daughter of Noumenios,

of Kleopatra, the mother of Ptolemy the God Epiphanes Eucharistos, being **(10)** *Thais, daughter of 3pr⌜ ⌝,*

the kanephoros of Arsinoe Philadelphos being Euchariste, daughter of Ptolemaios, son of Ptolemaios: the priestesses who are (appointed) in Ptolemais,

in the month Pachon, the - - - day, in Diospolis Mikra in the Thebaid, before Dionysios, the agoranomos.

These are the testamentary dispositions of Dryton, son of Pamphilos, of the deme Philoteris, of the cavalrymen of - - - , about - - years old, of medium stature, - - -, with a scar at the top of his left eyebrow, having keen perceptions, being of sound mind and in possession of his wits.

«May it be granted to me to be master of my own property in good health. But if I suffer mortal fate, I bequeath and give - - - **(15)** *Sarapias, daughter of Esthladas, son of Theon, a citizen, the woman with whom I live according to the laws - - - and through me - - - . I neither leave nor give anything to anybody else. I leave as epitropos Herm[a/o]philos, son of Pamphilos, - - -, (a relative) of Dryton, son of Pamphilos, - - - of the misthophoroi of the cavalry - - -* **(19-29)** *- - - »*

(30) *- - - year 6, Pachon - - -*

V e r s o (of fragment 3)

[- - - i.ir Trwtwn s3 Pnphylw]⸢s⸣ n t3y=f sḥm.t [Srpy3s ta 3stlts]

- - - *which Dryton, son of Pamphilos, has drawn up for the woman Sarapias, daughter of Esthladas.*

Notes

9 [Ἀγαθοκλείας τῆς Νουμ]ηνίου: the father's name of the priestess of Kleopatra II was thus far unknown (see Pap. Lugd. Bat. XXIV, no. 126bis). G. Messeri Savorelli ('Frammenti del primo testamento' (1990), p. 433) demonstrated that the father's name, the ending of which is preserved, is most probably Noumenios: this man, son of Herakleodoros, is priest of Ptolemy I in Ptolemais (see l. 7; see also Mooren, *Prosopography* (1975), no. 024, 049 and 050). One year earlier, in 166/165 B.C., two of his daughters were eponymous priestesses, *viz.* Kleainete and a daughter whose name is lost. They were priestess of Arsinoe Philopator and athlophoros of Berenike Euergetis in Alexandria, respectively. G. Messeri Savorelli suggests that the Agathokleia of our text could be the daughter of Noumenios who was athlophoros in Alexandria the year before.

G. Messeri Savorelli specifies the problem of this interpretation: «nessun sacerdote di quelli finora noti, è stato ministro di culto in Alessandria in un certo anno per poi esserlo di nuovo l'anno dopo a Ptolemais; né viceversa». She proposes the following solution. The dynastic cult in Ptolemais was reformed in the year 165/164 B.C. (see Pap. Lugd. Bat. XV, p. 142). According to 'Bell's law', the daughter of Noumenios who was athlophoros in Alexandria in 166/165 B.C., should have become kanephoros in Alexandria in the next year; another kanephoros, however, comes to the fore: Aristonike, daughter of *Nwl3ts*. G. Messeri Savorelli concludes: «E possibile che quella figlia di Numenios fosse Agathokleia e che, invece di canefora ad Alessandria, fosse stata eletta sacerdotessa della regina a Ptolemais?».

10 [Θάιδος τῆς *3pr*⸢ ⸣]: the father's name of Thais is preserved in Text 10 descr.: *3pr*⸢ ⸣ (see Pap. Lugd. Bat. XXIV, no. 126bis); the Greek equivalent of this partly preserved name is unknown.

Εὐχαρ̣[ίστης τῆς Πτολεμαίου τοῦ Πτολεμαίου]: unlike G. Messeri Savorelli I supplement the grandfather's name as well; the lacuna is better filled that way. The grandfather's name and even the great-grandfather's name of Euchariste are recorded in the protocol of Text 10 descr. (see Pap. Lugd. Bat. XXIV, no. 126bis).

11-12 [ἐπὶ Διονυσίου |[12] ἀγο]ρ[ανόμου: G. Messeri Savorelli splits up the name of the agoranomos at the end of l. 11: [Διονυ|[12]σίου ἀγορανόμου]. I prefer to supplement the entire name of Dionysios at the end of l. 11 in order to fill the lacuna better. Moreover, there is a low trace visible at the beginning of l. 13 (see my commentary), undoubtedly belonging to the *rho* of [ἀγο]ρ[ανόμου at the beginning of l. 12.

12 [*Vacat (?)* Τάδε διέθετο εὐαισθ]ητῶν: the restoration [εὐαισθ]ητῶν is a proposal of G. Messeri Savorelli ('Frammenti del primo testamento' (1990), p. 434). This is indeed the only possible supplement. The introductory formula was possibly longer; in this case, the *Vacat* we have added in order to justify the lacuna and which is also attested in Dryton's second will Text 2 (l. 14) at the same place, should be omitted.

12-13 Δρύτων Παμφίλου Φιλωτέρειος τῶν - c. 6 -] |[13] ἱ̣π̣π̣έ̣ω̣[ν ὡς (ἐτῶν) . . μέ(σος) - c. 12 - οὐ(λὴ) παρ' ὀφρῦν ἀρι(στερὰν) ἄκρα]ν: G. Messeri Savorelli has supplemented these lines with few data on Dryton: [- - -] | ρ̣ [ ]̣ [ ] [- - -]ν. Let us start from the traces at the beginning of l. 13: 

The editor read ρ̣ [ ]̣ [ ]; finding a word beginning with a *rho* is problematic here. I think I can recognize ἱ̣π̣π̣έ̣ω̣[ν], with a trace of the *rho* of [ἀγο]ρ̣[ανόμου in the preceding line above the *omega* . For the writing of the *omega*, compare, for instance, the *omega* in νοῶν, l. 12: 

If we read ἱ̣π̣π̣έ̣ω̣[ν at the beginning of l. 13, the passage becomes clearer: the title(s) of Dryton are to be restored at the end of l. 12 and beginning of l. 13, followed by the age and the personal description. Although the description of Dryton's looks is well known (pros. 403), I have not supplemented it entirely: the lacuna does not offer place for the whole description; the last part of the description, however, can be added, since the *nu* of [ἄκρα]ν is preserved.

14 [καταλείπω καὶ δίδωμι - c. 40 -]: the editor supplements the overlong clause from Pathyris (see the introduction to this text). I have refrained from printing another formula, since the wording differs from town to town.

15 Σαραπιά̣[δ]: the most obvious supplement is the dative-ending of the name, which then depends on [καταλείπω καὶ δίδωμι - c. 40 -] in the preceding line. Here Dryton would bequeath (all or part of) his belongings to his wife Sarapias. It is, however, also possible that he wills his properties (in the lacuna of the preceding line) to a child who may be born of (ἐκ) him and Sarapias. If so, the genitive-ending Σαραπιά̣[δος] is to be added, depending on ἐκ.

The supplement of the lacuna after Σαραπιά̣[δ is based on the information on Dryton's first will offered by his third will (Text 4, l. 5-6).

15-16 [διὰ - c. 9 -]. ου καὶ |[16] δι' ἐμοῦ: 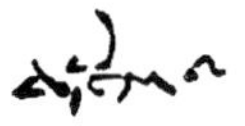 G. Messeri Savorelli read αι ἐμοῦ in l. 16. In my view, the traces better fit the reading δι' ἐμοῦ. Above this passage inexplicable ink traces can be seen.

17-18 [Ἑρμ. φιλον Παμφίλου - c. 10 - Δρύτ]ω̣ν̣ι̣ |[18] Παμφ[ίλου - c. 25 - τῶ]ν μισθοφόρων ἱ̣π̣[πέων]: fragment 6 with συγγενῆ (a relative) must be placed before or after Δρύτ]ω̣ν̣ι̣ |[18] Παμφ[ίλου, compare Text 2, l. 23 and Text 4, l. 6.

After [Ἑρμ. φιλον Παμφίλου - c. 10 - the demotic of Herm[a/o]philos in Text 2, l. 22, Φιλωτέρειον (of the deme Philoteris), may be supplemented.

20 [ ]. ικωι μηθενὶ σ̣ [ ]: this fragmentary formula apparently contained a prohibition, probably preceded by a clause such as μὴ ἐξέστω. According to G. Messeri Savorelli [ ]. ικωι can be the ending of the adjective ἐνήλικος or ἀφήλικος. The meaning of the clause is obscure. Fragment 9 (see below), containing a fiscal fine in silver coinage, must be part of a penalty clause following the prohibition in l. 20.

21 εἰ̣ς ὑποθή̣[κην]: this phrase is probably part of a clause whereby Dryton denies the possibility of pledging (one of) his belongings, presumably as long as his future heir is not grown-up. See Kreller, *Erbrechtliche Untersuchungen* (1919), p. 368: οὐκ ἐξό̣ν̣τ̣ο̣ς . . . πωλεῖν οὐδ' ὑποτίθεσθαι.

25 διομολογουμένου: τὰ διομολογηθέντα is a phrase frequently attested in wills meaning 'the things which are agreed on (in the will)', see Kreller, *Erbrechtliche Untersuchungen* (1919), p. 390, n. 5; διομολογουμένου, being a present participle singular, is rather a middle voice (the one who agrees, *viz.* the things which are stipulated in the will). The person who agrees could be the same as [τ]οῦ προγεγραμμέ[νου], l. 19.

26 [ ]αντινος: the two following (and last) lines of the will contain data on the witnesses. [ ]αντινος is most probably part of the witness list and could be the ending of an ethnic designation; ethnics ending on -αντινος are: Ταραντῖνος (from Tarentum; see P. Cair. Zen. III 59340, l. 20-21, 247 B.C.); Ἀκραγαντῖνος (from Agrigentum) and Μοργαντῖνος (from Morgantina).

Fr. 6 συγγενῆ: the editor reads συγγενηι̣. The *iota* is not at all certain.

Fr. 9 [ ]. ημενουσα̣:  The editor reads ε̣νμενουσα̣; I prefer the reading . ημενουσα̣. G. Messeri Savorelli suggests that the verb ἐμμένω (as the verb μένω) is related to the person who keeps to the contract (Berger, *Die Stafklauseln* (1911), p. 3 and Kreller, *Erbrechtliche Untersuchungen* (1919), p. 88-89; 372-373); the verb would be part of the penalty clause (see fragment 9, l. 3).

[ ].ημενουσα̣ is most probably the ending of a participle. It can be interpreted as ἡ μένουσα, followed by a phrase as ἐν τῶι οἴκωι or ἐν τῆι οἰκίαι of Dryton or of a third party, see, for instance, P. Freib. III 30, l. 32: καὶ μένουσα ἐν τῶι οἴκωι; P. Mich. IV 224, l. 2970: ἡ μ(ένουσα) ἐν τῆι οἰκίαι τοῦ Πτολεμ(αίου). Staying at the home of Dryton (or of another person), would then be the condition for the maintenance Sarapias receives from Dryton. A similar stipulation is to be found in Dryton's third will, with reference to his second wife Apollonia, see Text 4, l. 18.

[ ]ιου (δραχμὰς) κβ: G. Messeri Savorelli's proposal to supplement [ἀργυρ]ίου implies the phrase is part of a penalty clause, as in the second century B.C. only fiscal fines are still paid in silver coinage.

Fr. 10 Ἀ̣ντιοχ[ ]: can be the name Antiochos or the patronymic Antiocheus; it is part of the list of witnesses, l. 26-28.

Verso *[- - - i.ir Trwtwn s3 Pnphylw]⌜s⌝ n t3y=f sḥm.t [Srpy3s ta 3stlts], - - - which Dryton, son of Pamphilos, has drawn up for the woman Sarapias, daughter of Esthladas*: the ending of the ⌜*s*⌝ and the seated man determinative of the name of Dryton's father Pamphilos are still visible. For my supplement, compare the many demotic résumés, usually of the type: *p3/ t3* (+ type of document) *i.ir NN n NN, the (document) which NN has drawn up for NN* (for Pathyris, see Text 18; P. dem. *Enchoria* 7 (1977), p. 51-54).

One rather expects *ḥm.t, wife*, rather than *sḥm.t, woman*. Compare, however, Coptic ⲥϩⲓⲙⲉ, which can equally have the meaning of 'wife' (Crum, *Coptic Dictionary*, p. 385: ⲧⲉϥⲥϩⲓⲙⲉ, etc.).

2

The Second Greek Will of Dryton

Agoranomic copy

Plate II (recto)

[Collage by W. Clarysse]

Latopolis H. x W. = 31.5 x 18.5 cm [Width incomplete] 4 March 150 B.C.

Fragment A = Cairo, P. Gr. inv.no. 10349 [acquired before 1897] +
Fragments B, D, F, G = British Library, P. inv.no. 607 [bought on 9 Nov. 1895 from Grenfell] +
Fragments C and E = Heidelberg, P. Gr. inv.no. 1285 [date of acquisition unknown].

The fragments B, D, F and G from the British Library (London) were published for the first time as **P. Grenf. I 12**. G.A. Gerhard later joined these fragments with those from Heidelberg (fragments C and E): **G.A. GERHARD**, *Ein gräko-ägyptischer Erbstreit aus dem zweiten Jahrhundert vor Chr.* (Sitzungsberichte der Heidelberger Akademie der Wissenschaften 1911, 8. Abh.), p. 8-9 (l. 1-17 = **SB I 4637**). W. Clarysse discovered one more piece of the puzzle among the unpublished papyrus fragments from Cairo (fragment A), bearing on its back a Greek résumé: **W. CLARYSSE**, 'Le mariage et le testament de Dryton en 150 avant J.-C.', in *Chron. d' Ég.* 61 (1986), p. 99-103 (= **SB XVIII 13330**).

Photograph. — Plate II (recto); plate of the verso in W. Clarysse, in *Chron. d' Ég.* 61 (1986), p. 100. Plates of the fragments kept in Heidelberg are found on:
http://www.rzuser.uni-heidelberg.de/~gv0/Papyri/P.Heid._Uebersicht.html (see SB I 4637)

Description. — Compare the figure on the next page. The papyrus from Latopolis is of a better quality than those from the notary's office of Pathyris. The papyrus was rolled or folded from the right to the left, as the strips become broader to the left and thus contain more text. Only strip no. 8 was folded back. Subsequently the papyrus was folded double. The back of strips 7a-b formed the back of the document and on the verso of strip 7a a résumé was written. The papyrus got damaged along the horizontal and vertical folds. The strips 3a, 6b, 7b and 8a-b are entirely lost; the remaining strips are preserved to a greater or lesser degree. A sheet-join is clearly visible on strip 1b, near the right margin.

The *text upon the front* is written along the fibres, having a top margin of 2.5 cm, a bottom margin of 9 cm and a right-hand margin of c. 1 cm; the left-hand margin is lost with strip 8. Between the will proper (l. 1-24) and the witness list (l. 25-32) a space of approximately 1 cm has been left clear. The margin to the right of the witness list is somewhat wider than that of the will proper, *viz.* 2.5 cm. The text on the recto is written in a small agoranomic hand which from l. 20 onwards becomes slightly larger; this observation is of importance for the supplement of l. 20-24.

The Greek note *on the back* shows a larger and more cursive handwriting. The note is written at right angles to the text on the recto. It is difficult to identify the person who has written down this résumé.

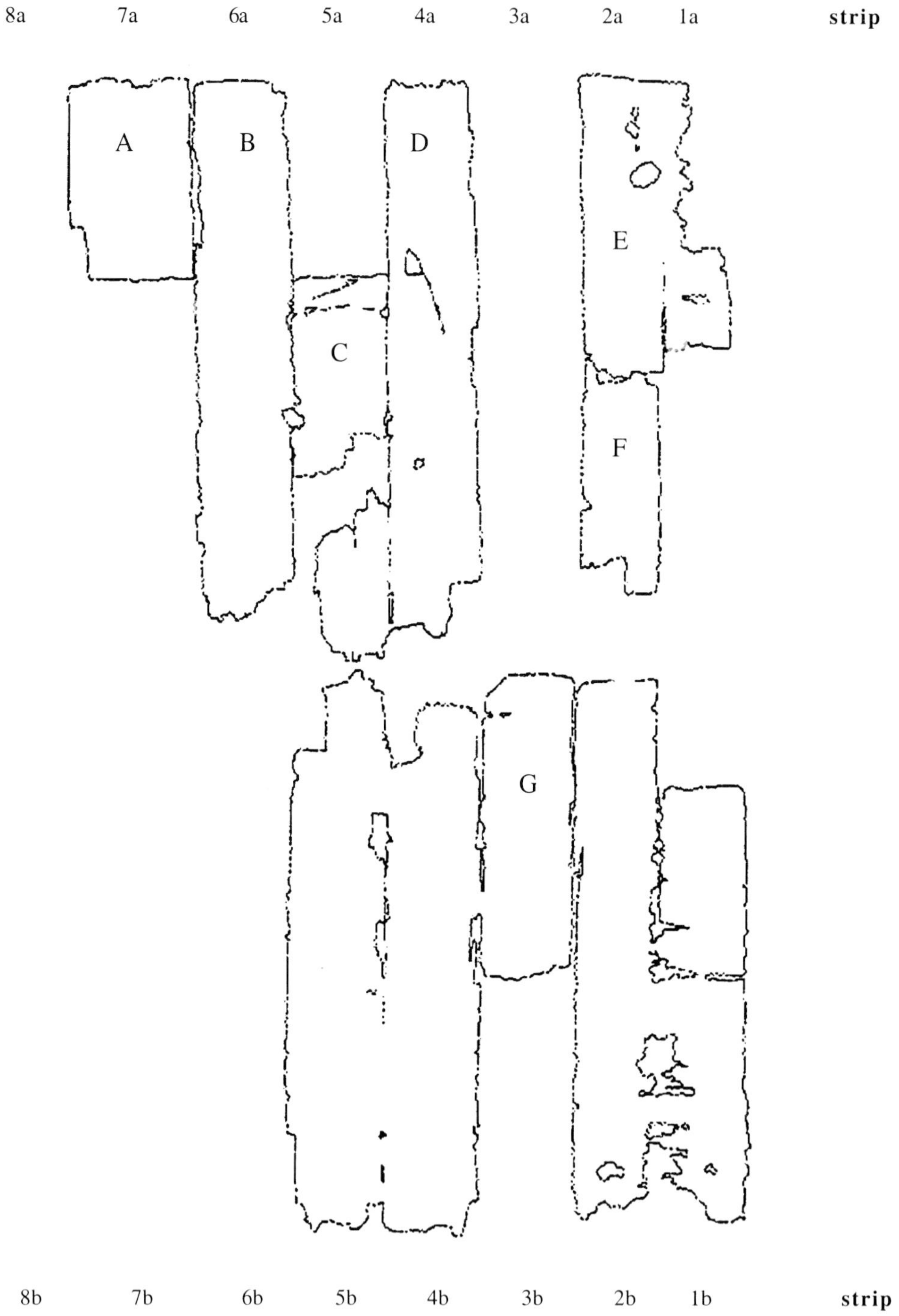
8a
7a
6a
5a
4a
3a
2a
1a
strip
A
B
C
D
E
F
G
8b
7b
6b
5b
4b
3b
2b
1b
strip

Introduction

Contents. — See §11-17.

An agoranomic copy. — The will is written in a small agoranomic hand. It is a copy, not the original deed (see §1), as the names of the witnesses are written in the same hand as the remainder of the will.

List of abbreviations

(1) Last letter (ρ or ι) drawn through the preceding letter:			(2) Last letter(s) written above the preceding letter:		
ρι		(l. 16) in ἀρι(στερός)	με		(l. 15) in μέ(σος)
ξι		(l. 26, cf. l. 29) in δεξι(ός)	τα		(l. 26, cf. l. 28) in τετα(νός)
χρ		(l. 15, cf. l.26) in μελίχρ(ως)	τρη		(l. 29) in τετρη(μένος)
			μεγ	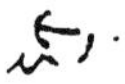	(l. 29) in εὐμεγ(έθης)
(3) ου		(l. 16, cf. l. 28) in οὐ(λή)			

Text

Recto

[Βασιλε]υόντων Πτολ̣εμαίου καὶ Κλ[εοπάτρας τ]ῆς ἀδελφῆς τ[ῶν Πτολε] μαίου κα[ὶ]
[Κλεοπ]άτρας θεῶν Ἐπ[ι]φανῶν ἔτο[υς λα ἐφ' ἱερέ]ως τοῦ ὄντος [ἐν Ἀλεξαν-] δρείαι Ἀλεξάνδρου
[καὶ θε]ῶν Σωτήρων καὶ [θ]εῶν Ἀδελφῶν [καὶ θεῶν Εὐ]εργετῶν καὶ [θεῶν Φιλο]πατόρων καὶ
[θεῶν Ἐ]πιφανῶν καὶ θε[ο]ῦ Εὐπάτορος κ[αὶ θεῶν Φιλομ]ητόρων ἀθλ[οφόρου Βερε]νίκης Εὐεργε-
[τίδος κα]ν̣ηφόρου Ἀρσινόης Φιλαδέλφου ἱ[ερείας Ἀρσινό]ης Φιλοπάτο[ρος τῶν οὐσ]ῶν ἐν Ἀλεξανδρε[ίαι,]
[ἐν δὲ Πτ]ολεμαίδι τῆς Θηβαίδος ἐφ' ἱερ[έων Πτολεμ]αίου μὲν Σωτ[ῆρος . . . .]ίου τοῦ Λυκόφρονος,
[βασιλέως δὲ Πτολεμαίο]υ Φιλομήτορος Ἀντιπάτρου τοῦ Ἀντιπά[τρου, Πτολε]μαίου δὲ Φιλαδέλφου
[- c. 10 - τοῦ - c. 5 -]ώρου, Πτολεμαίου δὲ Εὐεργέτου Πτο[λεμαίου τ]ο̣ῦ Πρωτάρχου,
[- c. 12 -, Πτολεμ]αίου δὲ Φιλοπάτορος Διοδώρου τοῦ Δι[- c. 7 -, Πτ]ολεμαίου δὲ θεοῦ
[Ἐπιφανοῦς Εὐχαρίστ]ου Νικίου τοῦ Δημητρίου, Πτολεμαίου [δὲ Εὐπ]άτορος Ζήνωνος
[τοῦ - c. 9 -, ἐφ' ἱερει]ῶν βασιλίσσης Κλεοπάτρας Θ[ε]οδώρ[ας τῆς - c. 4 -]α̣γρου, Κλεοπάτ[ρα]ς
[δὲ τῆς μητρὸς - c. 7 -]της τῆς Διογν̣ήτου, κανηφόρου Ἀρσινόης [Φιλαδέλφου . .]αιδος τῆς
[- c. 13 - τῶν οὐ]σῶν ἐν Πτολεμαίδι, μηνὸς Μεχεὶρ [ϛ̄ ἐν Λάτω]ν πόλει τῆ[ς]
[Θηβαίδος ἐπὶ Πτολεμ]αίου ἀγορανόμου. *Vacat* Τάδε διέθετο ὑ[γιαίνων ν]οῶν καὶ φρον[ῶν]
[Δρύτων Παμφίλου - c. 4 -] Φιλωτέρειος τῶν Διοδότου ἱππέ[ων ὡς ἐτῶν . .] μέ(σος) μελίχρ(ως) [τετα(νὸς)]
[μακροπρ(όσωπος) ἀνάσιλλος ἐπίγρυπος] οὐ(λὴ) παρ' ὀφρῦν ἀρι(στερὰν) ἄκρα[ν. Εἴη] μέμ με ὑγ[ιαίνοντα τ]ῶν ἐμαυτ[οῦ]
[κύριον εἶναι καὶ διοικ]εῖν τρόπωι̣ ὧ̣ι̣ ἂ̣ν̣ α̣ἱ̣[ρῶμαι.] Ἐὰν δέ τι ἀ[νθρώπινο]ν πάθω, κα[τα-]
[λείπω καὶ δίδωμι ἀπὸ τ]ῶν ὑπαρχόν[των μοι π]άν̣των ἐγγαί[ων καὶ ἐπίπ]λ̣ων Ἐσθλά[δαι τῶι]
[ἐξ ἐμοῦ καὶ Σαραπιάδ]ος τῆς Ἐσθλά[δου ἀστῆ]ς υἱῶι ἧι συνή[μην γυνα]ικί, Ἐσθλά[δαι]

[τῶι προγεγραμμ]ένωι υἱῶι τὸ ἥ[μισυ καὶ] τὰ ὅπλα καὶ τ[ὸν ἵππ]ον ἐφ' οὗ στ[ρατεύομαι,]
[τὰ δὲ λοιπὰ τοῖς] ἐπεσομένο[ις ἐ]ξ ἐμοῦ καὶ Ἀπολλωνί[ας τέκνοις.] Ἐπίτρο[πον]
[δὲ καταλείπ]ω Ἑρμ[.]φιλο̣[ν] Παμφίλου Φιλωτέρε[ιον Δρ]ύτωνι Πα[μφίλου]
[ὄντα συγγενῆ, ὁμ]οίως δὲ κ[αὶ Ἐ]σθλάδου τοῦ Ἐσθλάδ[ου.]
[Ἄλλωι δὲ οὐθενὶ οὐ]θ̣ὲν [καταλ]είπω οὐδὲ δί[δωμι. Μάρτυρ]ε[ς]

Vacat

[- c. 24 -]. . .[- c. 11 - δε]ξ[ι( ) - c. 12 -]
[- c. 22 - με]λίχρ(ως) τετα(νὸς) [- c. 3 - οὐ(λὴ) - c. 4 -] δεξι( ) οἱ δύ[ο] Πέρσαι
[- c. 23 -] Ἀπολλώ̣ν̣[ιος Ἀ]σκληπιάδου Ἀσπένδιος τῶ[ν
[- c. 21 - μελ]ίχρ(ως) τετα(νὸς) ἀ̣ν̣[αφ(άλαντος)] ο̣ὐ̣(λὴ) ὀφρύι δεξι(ᾶι)· Ἡρακλείδης
[- c. 9 - Πέρσης τῆς ἐπι]γονῆς ὡς (ἐτῶν) με εὐμεγ(έθης) μ[ελ]ίχρ(ως) τετα(νὸς) ὧς δεξι(ὸν) τετρη(μένος)·
[- c. 17 - τῶν Π]τολεμαίου τοῦ Πτολεμαίου ἱππέων ὡς (ἐτῶν)
[- c. 14 - οὐ(λὴ) ἐπ' ἀμφοτ]έρων ὀφρύω[ν]· Ἥροδος Ἀρσάκου Πέρσης
[- c. 22 -]

Vacat

[Π]τολεμαῖος κεχρη(μάτικα).

Recto 1 τ[ῶν ἐκ Πτολε]μαίου Grenfell, τ[ῶν Πτολε]μαίου supplevimus 2 [λα] suppl. Clarysse 6 ἐφ' ἱερ[έως] Grenfell, ἐφ' ἱερ[έων] supplevimus 13 [. ἐν Κροκοδίλω]ν πόλει Grenfell, [ϛ ἐν Λάτω]ν πόλει Clarysse 16 [- c. 16 -] οὐ(λὴ) παρ' ὀφρὺν φα<λα>κρό[ς Gerhard, [μακροπρ(όσωπος) ἀνάσιλλος ἐπίγρυπος] οὐ(λὴ) παρ' ὀφρῦν ἀρι(στερὰν) ἄκρα[ν] legimus et supplevimus 17 ὧ̣ι α̣ἱ̣ρο[ίμην] Gerhard , ὧ̣ι ἂ̣ν̣ α̣[ἱρῶμαι] Clarysse (*ZPE* 17 (1975), p. 253) 18 Ἐσθλά[δηι] Grenfell, Ἐσθλά[δαι] supplevimus 19 Ἐσθλά[δου ἀστῆ]ς suppl. Wilcken (BL I, p. 179); Ἐσθλά[δηι] Grenfell, Ἐσθλά[δαι] supplevimus 20 [- c. 5 - τῶι προγεγραμμ]ένωι Grenfell, [τῶι προγεγραμμ]ένωι supplevimus 20-21 στ[ρα |[21] τεύομαι - c. 7 - τοῖς] ἐπεσομένο[ις Grenfell, στ[ρατεύομαι· |[21] τὰ δὲ λοιπὰ τοῖς] ἐπεσομένο[ις supplevimus 21-22 ἐπιτρο[πευο-]|[22]μένοις 12]ω Grenfell, ἐπίτρο[πον |[22] δὲ καταλείπ]ω Clarysse (P.Petr.[2]. I The Wills, p. 41, n. 72). 22 Ἑρμ[ο]φιλ̣τ̣[. .] Παμφίλου Φιλωτερε[ί . .] Grenfell, Ἑρμ[ά]φ̣ι̣λο̣[ν] Παμφίλου Φιλωτέρε[ιον Schubart (*AfP* 5 (1913), p. 102, n.2), Ἑρμ[.]φ̣ι̣λο̣[ν] supplevimus 23 [συγγενῆ ὄντα (?)] suppl. Schubart (*AfP* 5 (1913), p. 102, n. 2), [ὄντα συγγενῆ] supplevimus 24 [- c. 28 -]ειπω οὐδὲ δι[ ]ε[ ] Grenfell, [ἄλλωι δὲ οὐθενὶ οὐ]θ̣ὲν [καταλ]είπω οὐδὲ δί[δωμι. Μάρτυρ]ε[ς] Wilcken et Hunt (BL I, p. 179) 25 [ ]ω̣ ἐπ[ ] Grenfell, [ ]. . .[- c. 11 - δε]ξ[ι( ) - c. 12 -] legimus et supplevimus 28 τετα(νὸς) α[. . .οὐ(λὴ)] ὀφρύι δεξι(ᾶι) Grenfell, τετα(νὸς) ἀ̣ν̣[αφ(άλαντος)] οὐ(λὴ) ὀφρύι δεξι(ᾶι) legimus et supplevimus 29 εὐμε(γέθης) Grenfell, εὐμεγ(έθης) legimus 30 [τῶν (?)] suppl. Hunt (BL I, p. 179); ὡς (ἐτῶν) [. .] Grenfell, ὡς (ἐτῶν) |[ ] supplevimus 31 [- c. 21 - ἀμφοτ]έρων ὀφρύω[ν] Grenfell, [- c. 14 - οὐ(λὴ) ἐπ' ἀμφοτ]έρων ὀφρύω[ν] supplevimus.

Verso

Ἐγενήθη ὁ γάμος Ἀ̣[πολλωνίας]
πρὸς Δρύτωνα ἐν Λάτ̣[ων πόλει]
ἐπὶ Πτολεμαίου ἀγο̣ρ[ανόμου]
(ἔτους) λα Μεχεὶρ ϛ̄.

Translation

Recto

In the reign of Ptolemy (VI) and Kleopatra (II), his sister, children of Ptolemy (V) and Kleopatra (I), the Gods Epiphaneis, year 31,

at the time of the office of the priest who is (appointed) in Alexandria, (viz. the priest) of Alexander, the Gods Soteres, the Gods Adelphoi, the Gods Euergetai, the Gods Philopatores, the Gods Epiphaneis, the God Eupator and the Gods Philometores;

(at the time of the office of) the athlophoros of Berenike Euerge- **(5)***tis;*

(at the time of the office of) the kanephoros of Arsinoe Philadelphos;

(at the time of the office of) the priestess of Arsinoe Philopator: the priestesses who are (appointed) in Alexandria;

in Ptolemais in the Thebaid,

the priests of Ptolemy Soter being - - - ios, son of Lykophron,

of king Ptolemy Philometor being Antipatros, son of Antipatros,

of Ptolemy Philadelphos being - - -, son of - - -oros,

of Ptolemy Euergetes being Ptolemaios, son of Protarchos - - -,

of Ptolemy Philopator being Diodoros, son of Di - - -,

of Ptolemy the God **(10)** *Epiphanes Eucharistos being Nikias, son of Demetrios,*

of Ptolemy Eupator being Zenon, son of - - - ;

the priestesses of queen Kleopatra being Theodora, daughter of - - -agros,

of Kleopatra, the mother, being - - -te, daughter of Diognetos;

the kanephoros of Arsinoe Philadelphos being - - -ais, daughter of - - -thwns, son of Tywgls (Diokles?): the priestesses who are (appointed) in Ptolemais,

in the month of Mecheir, the 6th day, in Latopolis in the Thebaid, before Ptolemaios, the agoranomos.

These are the testamentary dispositions of **(15)** *Dryton, son of Pamphilos, of the deme Philoteris, of the cavalrymen of Diodotos, about - - years old, of medium stature and honey-coloured complexion, with straight hair, a long face, hair brushed up, a hooked nose and a scar at the top of his left eyebrow, being healthy, of sound mind and in possession of his wits.*

«May it be granted to me to be master of my property in good health and to administer it the way I prefer. But if I should suffer mortal fate, I bequeath and give of my possessions in land and movables:

to Esthladas, my son by Sarapias, daughter of Esthladas, the woman together with whom I have lived, (so) to Esthladas **(20)**, *my above-mentioned son, the half share as well as my armour and the horse on which I serve in the army,*

the remaining to my children by Apollonia who may yet be born. As epitropos I leave behind Herm[a/o]philos, son of Pamphilos, of the deme Philoteris, a relative of Dryton, son of Pamphilos, equally of Esthladas, son of Esthladas. I neither leave nor give anything to anybody else.»

Witnesses:

(25) *NN, son of NN, - - - right - - -;*

NN, son of NN, - - -, of honey-coloured complexion, with straight hair, - - - with a scar on his right - - -, both Persians - - -;

Apollonios, son of Asklepiades, from Aspendos, of the - - -, of honey-coloured complexion, with straight hair, with bald forehead and a scar on his right eyebrow;

Herakleides, son of NN, Persian of the epigone, about 45 years old, tall, of honey-coloured complexion, with straight hair, his right ear being pierced;

(30) *NN, son of NN, - - - of the cavalrymen of Ptolemaios, son of Ptolemaios, about - - - years old, - - -, with a scar on both eyebrows;*

Herodos, son of Arsakes Persian - - -.

(33) *I, Ptolemaios, have dealt with the matter.*

Verso

The marriage of Apollonia with Dryton took place in Latopolis before Ptolemaios, the agoranomos, in year 31, 6 Mecheir.

Notes

1 [Βασιλε]υόντων: when fragment A was not yet known, the first editor supplemented [Βασιλεύοντος]. The new fragment A has the plural [Βασιλε]υόντων, as expected, since the joint reign of Ptolemy VI and Kleopatra II is described.

2 [λα]: the supplement of the year is based on l. 4 of the verso.

6-13 The names of the eponymous priests: these names are — also fragmentary— preserved in demotic, see P. dem. Cairo II 30650+30688+30800, see Pap. Lugd. Bat. XXIV, no. c. On the basis of this parallel text, most names of our text can be supplied.

6 ἐφ' ἱερ[έων] (Grenfell ἐφ' ἱερ[έως]): my supplement is paralleled by P. Grenf. I 25, col. II, l. 7; 27, col. II, l. 5 and P. Lond. III 879 (p. 5), l. 10.

8-9 Πτο[λεμαίου τ]ọῦ Πρωτάρχου | [- c. 12 -]: in the lacuna after the name of the priest Ptolemaios, son of Protarchos, the name of the grandfather is most probably missing. Another, but less probable supplement is the demotic, as, for instance, in P. Amh. II 45 (145-142 B.C.), where Lysimachos, son of Lysimachos, the priest of Ptolemy Eupator, is also called Φιλωτέρειος.

12-13 [.]αιδος τῆς | [- ca . 13 -]: the father's and grandfather's name of the priestess - - ais are missing; the demotic parallel text (see comm. on l. 6-13) has the ending of the father's name: - - - *thwns*, as well as the grandfather's name: *Tywgls* (presumably the transliteration of the Greek name Diokles).

13 [ς̄ ἐν Λάτω]ν πόλει: for the supplement of the precise day and the place of redaction, see the verso, l. 2 and 4. The note on the verso and the redaction of the will undoubtedly date to the same day, see §13.

15 [Δρύτων Παμφίλου - c. 4 -]: the lacuna of c. four characters either contained the ethnic Κρής or the word δῆμος (*deme*): δήμου Φιλωτερείου (pros. 403).

16 [μακροπρ(όσωπος) ἀνάσιλλος ἐπίγρυπος]: my supplement of Dryton's personal description is based on Text 11, l. 11; ἀνάσιλλος and ἐπίγρυπος are undoubtedly abbreviated, as are the remaining physical particularities. I have not, however, found parallels showing how these two words can be abbreviated.

οὐ(λὴ) παρ' ὀφρῦν ἀρι(στερὰν) ἄκρα[ν]: 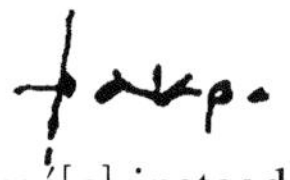

The first editor read and interpreted φα<λα>κρό[ς] instead of ἀρι(στερὰν) ἄκρα[ν]: the *iota* of ἀρι(στερὰν) is drawn through the *rho*, see the introduction to the text.

18 Ἐσθλά[δαι]: the first editor restores Ἐσθλά[δηι] (see also l. 19); as the other wills of Dryton always have Ἐσθλάδαι, I have opted for the Doric form (pros. 504).

20 [τῶι προγεγραμμ]ένωι: according to the first editor there are still about five characters missing before τῶι προγεγραμμ]ένωι. In my view, [τῶι προγεγραμμ]ένωι fills the entire lacuna: as the handwriting of the notary becomes larger from this line onwards, the supplements require less characters, see the description of the text.

20-21 στ[ρατεύομαι, |[21] τὰ δὲ λοιπὰ τοῖς] ἐπεσομένο[ις: the first editor supplied στ[ρα|[21] τεύομαι - c. 7 - τοῖς] ἐπεσομένο[ις; as hyphenation is rarely applied in this will (only attested in l. 4-5), I prefer to restore the entire στ[ρατεύομαι] at the end of l. 20. The lacuna in l. 21 is properly filled by the phrase τὰ δὲ λοιπά, which is attested in other wills, see, for instance, P. Petr.[2]. I. The Wills 3, l. 19; 25, l. 30.

21-22 ἐπίτρο[πον |[22] δὲ καταλείπ]ω: this supplement is tentatively suggested by W. Clarysse. The lacuna of l. 22 is not entirely filled with this proposal (two characters are still missing), but this can be attributed to the fact that the handwriting of the clerk or agoranomos is somewhat larger from l. 20 onwards.

There is still another possibility: in l. 21 the particle δέ can be added and in l. 22 the pronoun αὐτῶν or τούτων (*viz.* the children): ἐπίτρο[πον δὲ |[22] τούτων καταλείπ]ω, *as their epitropos I leave behind*; in this case, epitropos would have the meaning of 'guardian', not 'testamentary executor'; for this problem, see §6 and §15.

23 [ὄντα συγγενῆ]: Schubart's supplement [συγγενῆ ὄντα (?)] (in *AfP* 5 (1913), p.102, n. 2) is slightly changed by analogy with Text 4, l. 6.

23 ['Ε]σθλάδου τοῦ 'Εσθλάδ[ου]: for the dubious role of this person in the epitropos-formula, see §15.

25 [ ] ̣ ̣ ̣[- c. 11 - δε]ξ[ι( ) - c. 12 -] (Grenfell:]ω̣ ἐ̣π̣[ ): the traces read by B.P. Grenfell as επ, could stand for the beginning of ἀναφ(άλαντος) or ἀναφ(άλακρος), see comm. on l. 28.

Further on a broad horizontal line can be noted, undoubtedly part of the lower part of the ξ in [δε]ξ[ι( ); one does indeed expect here the description of the scar of the first witness.

26 [- c. 3 - οὐ(λὴ) - c. 4 -] δεξι( ): the lacuna contains data on the place of the scar; as a low trace is visible in the following line, οὐ(λή) must be preceded by another characteristic as, for instance, in l. 28: ἀν̣[αφ(άλαντος) οὐ(λὴ)] ὀφρύι δεξι(ᾶι), where this characteristic takes about as much space as [οὐ(λὴ) - c. 6 -] δεξι( ) in l. 26.

27 'Απολλώνι̣[ιος 'Α]σκληπιάδου 'Ασπένδιος: this person is otherwise unknown, see Pros. Ptol. II 3821. Aspendians are well represented among the military in Egypt already in the third century B.C., see L. Robert, *Noms indigènes dans l'Asie Mineure gréco-romaine* (Bibl. Archéol. et Histor. de l'Institut Français d'Archéologie d'Istanbul 13), 1963, p. 415-420; Launey, *Les armées hellénistiques* (1949-50), p. 1221-1225; H. Brandt, *Gesellschaft und Wirtschaft Pamphyliens und Pisidiens im Altertum* (Asia Minor Studien 7), Bonn 1992, p. 88.

28 τετα(νὸς) ἀν̣[αφ( )] (Grenfell τετα(νὸς) α[. . .):

These traces suggest αν̣, being the first two letters of ἀναφ(άλαντος) or ἀναφ(άλακρος), a characteristic which is often mentioned alongside τετα(νός), see, for instance, P. Petr.[2]. I. The Wills 23, l. 12.

[ ] οὐ̣(λὴ) ὀφρύι δεξι(ᾶι) (Grenfell [οὐ(λὴ)] ὀφρύι δεξι(ᾶι)): B.P. Grenfell supplies οὐ̣(λή) in the lacuna, but traces of this word are clearly visible.

29 εὐμεγ(έθης) (Grenfell εὐμε(γέθης)): the *gamma* is written, see the list of abbreviations in the introduction to the text.

30 [Π]τολεμαίου τοῦ Πτολεμαίου: this eponymous officer is otherwise unknown, see Pros. Ptol. II 1993.

31 [- c. 14 - οὐ(λὴ) ἐπ' ἀμφοτ]έρων ὀφρύω[ν] (Grenfell [- c. 21 - ἀμφοτ]έρων ὀφρύω[ν]): as the place where the scar is located, is recorded in the genitive (ἀμφοτ]έρων ὀφρύω[ν], *both eyebrows*) instead of the more common dative (see, for instance, l. 28), οὐ(λὴ) must have been followed by the preposition ἐπί: see, for instance, P. Petr.[2]. I. The Wills 24, l. 34-35: οὐλὴ ἐφ' ἑκατέρας [ὀφρύος].

31-32 Ἥροδος Ἀρσάκου Πέρσης [ ]: for this Persian [ ] from Latopolis, see Pestman, 'Pathyris II' (1963), in *Aegyptus* 43, p. 34, no. 21 (mentioned among the Persians from Krokodilopolis); as to the Persian father's name Arsakes, see Ph. Huyse, *Iranische Personennamenbuch. 5, Fasz. 6a. Iranische Namen in den griechischen Dokumenten Ägyptens*, Wien 1990, no. 13. The name Herodos is a hapax legomenon and, because of the ending, cannot be considered a variant of the Greek Ἡρώδης; possibly Herodos is equally a Persian name.

32 [- c. 22 -]: I add this extra line, which contained the further data on the last witness.

33 Π]τολεμαῖος κεχρη(μάτικα): for the meaning of χρηματίζω ('to deal with the matter'), see Pestman, 'Agoranomoi' (1985), in Pap. Lugd. Bat. XXIII, p. 33.

3

THE THIRD GREEK WILL OF DRYTON

Agoranomic copy

Plate III

[New collage]

Pathyris | H. x W. = 27.5 x 21 cm [Width incomplete] | 29 June 126 B.C.

Fragment A = British Library, P. inv.no. 687a [bought in June 1896 from Grenfell] +
Fragment B = British Library, P. inv.no. 640 [bought on 9 Nov. 1895 from Grenfell] +
Fragment C = British Library, P. inv.no. 687e [bought in June 1896 from Grenfell] +
Fragment D = Sorbonne Bouriant, P. inv.no. 46 [date of acquisition unknown].

Fragments B and D were at first published separately as **P. Grenf. I 44** and **P. Bour. 9**, respectively. The two fragments were joined by P.W. Pestman in **Pap. Lugd. Bat XIX 4**. I have found two more pieces among the unpublished fragments of the British Library: *fragments A and C* **ined.**

Photograph. — Plate III; Pap. Lugd. Bat XIX, pl. 6 and P. New Pap. Primer^2, p. 57 (col. II) (no photographs of the fragments British Library, P. inv.no. 687a and 687e).

Description. — The papyrus was rolled up from right to left and is damaged or broken off in the vertical folds. The left-hand side of the papyrus, being on the outside of the roll, is the most damaged: most of it is lost. On the right-hand side a small piece at the top is missing. The text has been written in two columns on the recto, along the fibres. The top margin measures 4 cm, the bottom margin of column I measures 3 cm, that of column II 6.3 cm. There is practically no margin to the right of column II. Between the two columns little space is left; the scribe starts writing further to the right from column II, l. 60 onwards.

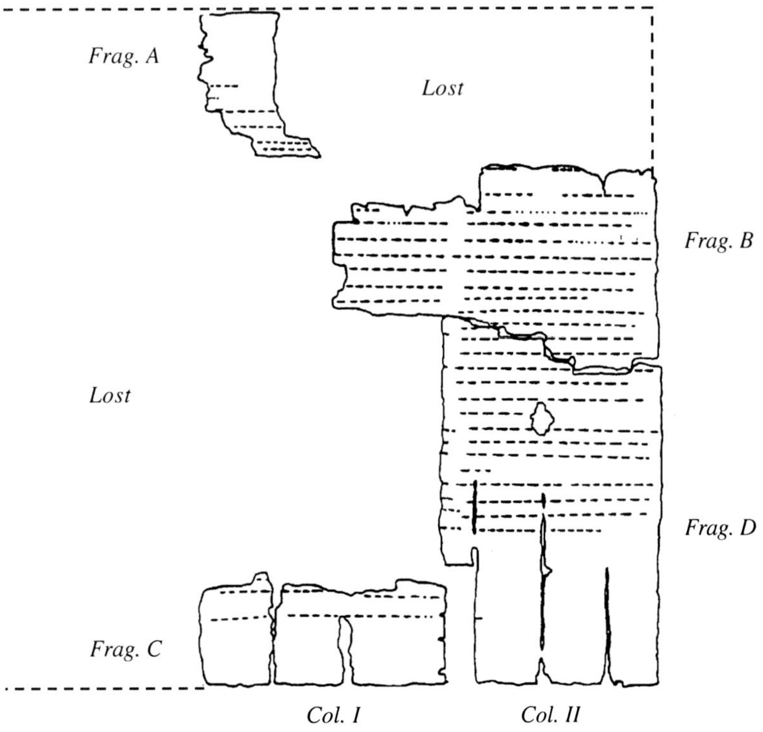

Introduction

Contents. — See §18-27.

New fragments and new supplements. — Until recently only fragments B and D were known. Consequently, it was not clear how many lines were lost at the top and bottom of column I nor how wide the lines of column I were. The only part preserved was the end of seven lines (l. 10-16). In the following lines (l. 17-30) only some faint traces of the final letters were visible. Despite the fact that the wording of column I was known thanks to the copy Text 4, the previous editor could not identify the traces, especially since the precise height of column I was unknown.

The new fragments A and C provide the upper and lower part of the first column. Fragment A contains part of the first six lines; the next three lines are missing (l. 7-9); lines 10-16 were already known (previous edition l. 1-7); traces at the end of lines 17-32 are sometimes visible, and these can now be deciphered by means of the copy Text 4, since the height of column I is known: formerly, column I appeared to contain 21 lines; now it is clear that column I numbers 35 lines. Fragment C preserves the remaining of l. 33-35, containing the last clauses of the will proper and the name of the testator.

The previous editor thought that no more than two lines were lost at the top of column II: this columns would then contain the names of five witnesses. As the discovery of fragment A shows that the papyrus was higher than initially thought, approximately five rather than two lines of column II are presumably missing.

Justification of the supplements in column I. — I have supplemented the lacunas of column I by means of the other copy of the will Text 4 and here, I reproduce the full text, apart from some orthographical particularities such as συγγενῆι for συγγενῆ (Text 4, l. 2). In the present Text 3 other abbreviations and some small variants were used, as shown by the comparison of the preserved passages of Text 3, column I and Text 4 (see Text 4, Introduction).

An agoranomic copy. — Text 3 is a copy (see §1), since the names of the witnesses are all written by the same hand. Moreover, four witnesses signed in demotic on the original deed according to col. II, l. 25-28. When copying this will, the scribe translated the testimonies into Greek.

• The original deed was drawn up in the notary's office of Pathyris. The witnesses are well-known individuals from Pathyris. The will was doubtless drawn up in the notary's office of Pathyris. It provides the same introductory clause as another will from Pathyris, drawn up three years later: *AfP* 1 (1901), p. 63-65: εἴη μέμ μοι ὑγιαίνοντι τῶν ἐμαυτοῦ κύριον εἶναι· ἐὰν δέ τι ἀνθρώπινον πάθω, καταλείπω καὶ δίδωμι τὰ ὑπάρχοντά μοι ἔγγαιά τε καὶ ἔπιπλα καὶ κτήνη καὶ ὅσα ἂν προσεπικτήσωμαι.

There are no other wills containing this exact wording. Text 2 from Latopolis, for instance, does not have this clause, nor does P. Grenf. I 24, though the latter will was written in the notary's office of Krokodilopolis[1], of which the notary's office of Pathyris was a branch. The wording is, thus, not typical of the Theban region, as suggested by H. Kreller.[2]

In Text 3 and *AfP* 1 (1901), p. 63-65, both (copies of) wills from Pathyris, the will proper is followed by the name of the testator and some data on him. This practice is not attested for Dryton's two other wills (from Diospolis Mikra and Latopolis, respectively), nor for other Ptolemaic wills.

• Text 3 is a copy written by an agoranomic hand; the name of the scribe is not recorded. P.W. Pestman[3] already noted that the will was probably written by Areios, who was in service as clerk of the agoranomos Asklepiades in the notary's office of Pathyris at that time (126 B.C.). Areios probably also wrote *AfP* 1 (1901), p. 63-65, a copy of a will of 123 B.C. Both handwritings show many similarities. Unfortunately, unlike the present text, few abbreviations are used in *AfP* 1 (1901), p. 63-65; consequently, we have hardly any reference material on this point.

List of abbreviations

δεξι( )		Text 3, col. II, l. 51	πρ(όσωπος)		Text 3, col. II, l. 24
		*AfP* 1 (1901), p. 63-65, l. 29			*AfP* 1 (1901), p. 63-65, l. 30
ευθυρ( )		Text 3, col. II, l. 55	μι(σθοφόρος)		Text 3, col. II, l. 55
	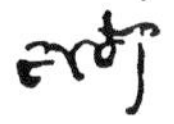	*AfP* 1 (1901), p. 63-65, l. 29			*AfP* 1 (1901), p. 63-65, l. 30

The present text has in addition the following abbreviations:

λι		(l. 66) in μελί(χρως)
ουλ		(l. 59) in οὐλή
θυ		(l. 49) in Παθύ(ρει)

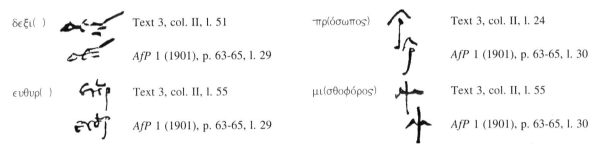

---

1 As shown by P.W. Pestman, P. Grenf. I 24 dates to the period 139-132 B.C., when Dioskourides was agoranomos (Pestman, 'Agoranomoi' (1985), in Pap. Lugd. Bat. XXIII, p. 16, no. 4 and note). This will ends after the introductory clause. The testamentary dispositions are lacking: P. Grenf. I 24 apparently served as a model for the scribe of the notary's office.

2 Kreller, *Erbrechtliche Untersuchungen* (1919), p. 345.

3 Pap. Lugd. Bat. XIX, p. 36, comm. on l. 18-21.

Text

Column I

1 [("Ετους) μδ Παῦνι θ ἐν Παθύρει ἐπ' Ἀσκληπιάδου ἀγορανό]μου τά̣δ[ε διέθετο ὑγιαίνων νοῶν φρονῶν Δρύτων Παμφίλου Κρὴς]

2 [τῶν διαδόχων καὶ τοῦ ἐπιτάγματος ἱππάρχης ἐπ' ἀνδρῶ]ν.

3 [Εἴη μέμ μοι ὑγιαίνοντι τῶν ἐμαυτοῦ κύριον] ε̣ἶναι. Ἐὰν δέ [τι ἀνθρώπινον πάθω, καταλείπω καὶ δίδωμι]

4 [τὰ ὑπάρχοντά μοι ἔγγαιά τε καὶ ἔπιπλ]α καὶ κτήν[η καὶ ὅσα ἂν προσεπικτήσωμαι, τὸν μὲν ἵππον]

5 [ἐφ' οὗ στρατεύομαι καὶ τὰ ὅπλα πάντα Ἐσθλ]ά̣δαι τῶι ἐ̣ξ [ἐμοῦ καὶ ἐξ Σαραπιάδος τῆς]

6 [Ἐσθλάδου τοῦ Θέωνος ἀστῆς ἧι συνῴ]ή̣μην γυν[αικὶ κατὰ νόμους καὶ κατὰ διαθήκην τὴν κεχρηματισμένην]

7-9 [διὰ τοῦ ἐν Διὸς πό(λει) τῆι μι(κρᾶι) ἀρχείου ἐπὶ Διονυσίου ἀγορανόμου ἐν τῶι ϛ (ἔτους) ἐπὶ τοῦ Φιλομήτορος ἣ διασαφεῖ τά τε ἄλλα καὶ ἐπίτροπον Ἑρμ.φιλον ὄντα συγγενῆ κατέστησεν καὶ ἀπὸ τῶν οἰκετικῶν σωμάτων δ̅ ὧν ὀνόματα Μυρσίνην καὶ ταύτης - c. 12 -· τὰ δὲ λοιπὰ θηλυκὰ β]

10 [αἷς ὄνομα Εἰρήνην καὶ Ἀμπέλιον Ἀπολλωνίαι καὶ ταῖς ἀδ(ελφαῖς) οὔσι ε̅ καὶ] τὸν ὑ[πάρχον]τά

11 [μοι ἐπὶ τοῦ Κόχλακος τῆς Ἀραβίας τοῦ Παθυρ(ίτου) ἔδαφος ἀμπελῶ(νος) κ]α̣ὶ̣ τὰ ἐν τούτωι

12 [φρέατα ἐξ ὀπτῆς πλί(νθου) καὶ τἄλλα συνκύροντα καὶ τὴν ἅμαξαν σὺν τ]ῆ̣ι ἐπισκευῆι καὶ

13 [τὸν περιστερῶνα - - - καὶ τὸν ἄλλον ἡμιτέ]λ̣εστον καὶ αὐλὴν

14 [ὧν γείτονες νό(του) ψιλοὶ τόποι τοῦ αὐ(τοῦ) Ἐσθλά(δου) βο(ρρᾶ) οἶκος κεκαμαρω]μένος Ἀπ[ολ]λωνίας

15 [τῆς νεω(τέρας) ἀπηλι(ώτου) τόπο̣ς - c. 6 - ς Πετρασ . . . τοῦ Ἐσθλά(δου) λι(βὸς) ψιλὸς τόπος Ἐσθλά(δου) ἕως τ]ῆς ἀνεῳγμ[έν]ης

16 [θύ(ρας) ἐπὶ λίβα· τοὺς δὲ λο(ιποὺς) οἴκους καὶ χρηστῆρας καὶ παλαιὰν - c. 5 - καὶ τὸν ψι]λὸν τόπον τὸν εἰς

17-18 [περιστερῶνα ἀποδεδειγμένον ὑποκάτω τῆς Ἐσθλά(δου) θύ(ρας) καὶ ἀπὸ λι(βὸς) τῆς καμάρας δίδωμι Ἀπολλωνίαι καὶ Ἀριστοῖ καὶ Ἀφροδισίαι καὶ Νικαρίωι καὶ Ἀπολλωνίαι νεωτέραι οὔσι ε̅ ταῖς ἐξ ἐμοῦ καὶ ἐξ Ἀπολλωνίας τῆς καὶ Σεμμώνθιος ἧι σύ]ν̣ει-

19-24 [μι γυ(ναικὶ) κατὰ νό(μους) καὶ τὰ θηλυκὰ β̅ σώματα καὶ τὴν βοῦν ἐξ ἴσου κυριευέτωσαν ταῖς οἰκίαις καθ' ὃν πεποίημαι μερισμόν· δότω δὲ Ἐσθλάδας ἀπὸ τοῦ δεδομένου αὐ(τῶι) ψιλοῦ τόπου ἀπέναντι τῆς θύ(ρας) αὐ(τοῦ) ἐπὶ λίβα πή(χεις) ἐμβαδοὺς δ̅ εἰς κλιβάνου τόπον· τὰ δὲ λο(ιπὰ) οἰκόπεδα καὶ ψιλοι τόποι ἐν Δι(ὸς) πό(λει) τῆι μεγά(ληι) ἐν τῶι Ἀμμωνι]είωι

25 [καὶ ἐν τοῖς Κεραμείοις ἐχέτω Ἐσθλάδας κατὰ τὸ (ἥμισυ) Ἀπολλω(νία)] δὲ

26-27 [καὶ ἀδελφαὶ κατὰ τὸ (ἥμισυ) καὶ τἆλλα ὑπάρχοντά μοι πάντα σύμβο(λά) τε σιτικὰ καὶ ἀργυ(ρικὰ) καὶ ἔπιπλα πάντα κατὰ τὸ (ἥμισυ)· δότω δὲ Ἐσθλά(δας) καὶ αἱ περὶ Ἀπολλωνίαν κατὰ κοινὸν εἰς οἰκοδομὴ]ν

28 [περιστερῶνος ἀνηλώματα εἰς τὸν ἀποδεδειγμένον περιστερῶνα ἕως ἂν ἐπιτελέσω]σι

29 [καὶ Ἀπολλωνίαι τῆι καὶ Σεμμώνθει τῆι ἐμῆι γυ(ναικὶ) ἐτῶν δ̄ ἐὰν παραμείνηι ἐν τῶι οἴκωι ἀν]έγκλη(τος)

30 [οὖσα εἰς τροφὴν αὐ(τῆς) καὶ ταῖς β̄ θυγατράσιν ἑκάσ(του) μηνὸς (πυροῦ) θ (ἥμισυ) κροτῶ(νος) ἱβ χα(λκοῦ) Σ καὶ μετὰ δ] (ἔτη)

31-32 [τὰ αὐτὰ μετρήματα δότωσαν ταῖς β̄ νεωτέραις ἐκ κοινοῦ ἕως ἐτῶν ια· δότωσαν δὲ Ταχράτει εἰς φερνὴν χαλκοῦ (τάλαντα) ιβ ἐκ τῶν] κọ[ινῶν· Ὅσα δ' ἂν φαίνηται]

33 [ἐπίκτη(τα) ἔχουσα ἡ Σεμμῶνθις ὄντα αὐτῆι σ]υνοῦσα Δ[ρ]ύτωνι κ̣[υ]ρ̣ι̣ε̣υ̣έ̣ṭ[ω] αὐṭῶν·

34 [-c. 3 - ἐπελεύσ -c. 5 - ἐπ' αὐτὴν περὶ τούτων -c. 4 -]

35 [Ἦν δὲ ὁ διατιθέμενος Δρύτων Παμφίλου Κρὴς τῶ]ν διαδόχων καὶ τῶν τοῦ ἐπιτάγματος ἱπ(πάρχης) ἐπ' [ἀνδρῶ]ν.

For the new restoration of column I, see Introduction to the text.

10 τὸν ὑ[πάρχον]τα Bingen (*Chron. d' Ég.* 53 (1978), p. 372) 14-15 Ἀπ[ολ]λωνίας \`ν(εωτέρας)´|15 [ed., Ἀπ[ολ]λωνίας |15 [τῆς νεω(τέρας) legimus et supplevimus.

Column II

[Μάρτυρες]
[Ἔγραψεν -]
[Ἔγραψεν -]
[ἱε]ρεὺς Ἀφρο[δ]ί̣τ̣η̣ς καὶ Σο̣ύχο̣υ̣
[τ]ῶν πρωτ̣[οσ]τ̣ολιστῶν καὶ
πτεροφόρ[ων ὡς] (ἐτῶν) λε εὐμεγέθ̣ης
μελί(χρως) τετανὸς πλατυπρ(όσωπος) εὐθύρ(ιν)
οὐλὴ κροτάφωι δεξ(ιῶι).
Ἔγραψεν Νεχούτης Θοτορταί<ου> ˋΠέρσηςˊ <ἱερεὺς> πρωτοστολιστὴς τοῦ ἐν Παθύ(ρει) ἱεροῦ ὡς (ἐτῶν) ν
μέσος μελί(χρως) τετανὸς μακροπρ(όσωπος) εὐθύρ(ιν)
οὐλὴ μετώπωι ἐγ δε(ξιῶν).
Ἔγραψεν Πατοῦς Ἑριέως Πέρσης ἱερεὺς
πρωτοστολιστὴς τοῦ αὐτ<οῦ> ἱεροῦ
ὡς (ἐτῶν) ν μέσος μελί(χρως) τετανὸς
πλατυπρ(όσωπος) εὐθύρ(ιν) οὐλ(ὴ) μετώπωι ἐξ ἀρ(ιστερῶν).
Ἔγραψεν Πατοῦς Ὥρου ὑπεπιστάτης
Παθύρεως Πέρσης τῶν πεζῶν
ὡς (ἐτῶν) μ μέσος μελί(χρως) τετανὸς μακρο-
πρ(όσωπος) εὐθύρ(ιν) οὐλ(ή).
οὗτοι οἱ τ[έσ]σαρες ⟦ . ⟧ τοῖς ἐγχωρίοις
⟦ ⟧ γράμμασιν διὰ τὸ μὴ εἶναι
ἐπι τῶν τόπων τοὺς ἴσους Ἕλλη-
νας.
Ἔγραψεν Ἀμμώνιος Ἀρείου Πέρσης
τῶν μι(σθοφόρων) ἱππέων ὡς (ἐτῶν) λ μέσος
μελί(χρως) ὑπόκλαστος μακροπρ(όσωπος) εὐθύρ(ιν)
οὐλ(ὴ) μετώπωι μέσωι.

---

48 ουτ in Νεχούτης corr. ex θμ 51 ἐγ δε( ) corr. ex ἐξ ἀρ( )
56 . . . ε . . . . . υ της ed., ὑπεπιστάτης Van 't Dack et Vandorpe 60 . . ed., ⟦ . ⟧ ed. pr.

Translation

Column I, l. 1-34

See Text 4.

Column I, l. 35

Testator was Dryton, son of Pamphilos, Cretan, of the diadochoi and cavalry officer over men, at the head of those of the epitagma-unit.

Column II

Witnesses:
[Has signed - - - - - - - - - - - - - - -]
Has signed NN, son of NN, priest of Aphrodite and Souchos, of the first stolistai and the pterophoroi, about 35 years old, tall, with a honey-coloured complexion, straight hair, a flat face, straight nose (and) a scar on his right temple.
Has signed Nechoutes, son of Thotortaios, Persian, priest, first stolistes of the temple in Pathyris, about 50 years old, of medium stature, with a honey-coloured complexion, straight hair, a long face, straight nose (and) a scar on his forehead on the right.
Has signed Patous, son of Herieus, Persian, priest, first stolistes of the same temple, about 50 years old, of medium stature, with a honey-coloured complexion, straight hair, a flat face, straight nose (and) a scar on his forehead to the left.
Has signed Patous, son of Horos, hypepistates of Pathyris, Persian, of the infantry, about 40 years old, with a honey-coloured complexion, straight hair, a long face, straight nose (and) a scar.
These four (witnesses have signed) in the native script because there was not the same number of Greeks on the spot.
Has signed Ammonios, son of Areios, Persian, one of the misthophoroi, about 30 years old, of medium stature, with a honey-coloured complexion, slightly curly hair, a long face, straight nose (and) a scar in the middle of his forehead.

Notes

Col. I For the commentary on col. I, l. 1-34, see Text 4.

42-47 P.W. Pestman argues that the first witness, who signs in demotic, is Schotes son of Phimenis. In P. dem. Cairo II 30704 of 157 B.C. he is called 'prophet of the *wrm.w*, prophet of the *sm.w*, servant of (followed by an enumeration of the Gods *Sunnaoi*)', which is according to P.W. Pestman an equivalent of the shortened Greek title [ἱε]ρεὺς Ἀφρο[δ]ί̣τ̣η̣ς καὶ Σο̣ύχο̣υ̣, recorded in the present text. Schotes, son of Phimenis, is said to be a lesonis-priest witnessing the swearing of an oath in the temple of Hathor in the same year as that of the present will (year 44, see O. dem. Tempeleide 180 and Pap. Lugd. Bat. XIX, p. 35 and n. 8). He is furthermore attested as scribe of a sale on a wooden tablet in 120 B.C. (*AcOr* 25 (1960), p. 296) and is found in the fragmentary list of names P. dem. Cairo II 30669. Schotes' family is well-known; a small archive of his son Harsiesis has survived (see Vandorpe, *Archives from Pathyris* (2001), §38). For Schotes and for his title, see Pros. Ptol. IX 5416a α; S.V. Wangstedt, in *AcOr* 25 (1960), p. 299-301; O. dem. Tempeleide, p. 300-301; Pap. Lugd. Bat. XIX, p. 35, n. l.1, p. 209 and 213; Lanciers, 'Priester des ptolemäischen Königskulte' (1991), in *Rd'É* 42, p. 133.

44 [τ]ῶν πρωτ̣[οσ]τ̣ολιστῶν: the *protostolistes* is at the head of the *stolistai*, priests who may enter the holy of holies in order to clothe the statues of the gods (see Otto, *Priester und Tempel I* (1905), p. 75, 77, 83, 97 and 380). The demotic equivalent is found in Text 43 appendix, l. 4: *[p3 ḥry] mnḫ.t.*

45 πτεροφόρ[ων]: the name of this priest is due to the two feathers worn on his head during ceremonies (see Otto, *Priester und Tempel I* (1905), p. 86-88). In demotic texts the title used is *sẖ mḏ3.t ntr* (*scribe of the holy book*), as shown by P.W. Pestman (see P. Mil. Vogl. III, p. 187, n. 20).

48 Ἔγραψεν: for the peculiar addition of Ἔγραψεν in the witnesses' list of a Greek will, see §27.

Νεχούτης Θοτορταί<ου>: the scribe first wanted to write the name Nechthminis, but noticed his mistake and corrected Νεχθμ- into Νεχουτ-. The reason for this mistake is mentioned by P.W. Pestman: «L' erreur est probablement la conséquence du fait que le nom se trouvait écrit en démotique sur l' original et que les deux noms commencent en démotique par le même signe.» (Pap. Lugd. Bat. XIX, p. 35, comm. on l. 6). Moreover, Nechouthes has a (well-known) brother called Nechthminis. Both are sons of Thotortaios, who was until 133 B.C. scribe of the temple. Nechthminis proper was supposedly also scribe of the temple for some time; only one attestation is preserved, dated to 125 B.C. Two years later, Nechouthes again acts as a witness in P. dem. Adler 2, verso l. 16 of 124 B.C. (Pros. Ptol. IX 5957 and Pap. Lugd. Bat. XIX, p. 211-212).

For Thotortaios, son of Nechthminis (scribe in the period 178-133 B.C.), see Pros. Ptol. III and IX 7746; 5392a; P. dem. Schreibertrad., p. 184, no. 47 (period: 163-136 B.C.)

addenda:

16 Sept. 178 B.C.: P. dem. Ackerpachtverträge, p. 34;

4 Aug. 161 B.C.: P. dem. Or. Inst. Chicago inv.no. 10551 (edition: Ritner, 'Property Transfer' (1984));

154 B.C.: P. dem. Strasb. Wiss. Ges. 8 ined. and the Greek translation P. Giss. I 37 + 36 + 108, col. I, l. 25 – col. II, l. 7;

c. 152 and c. 150 B.C.: ? P. dem. *FuB* 8 (1967), p. 80-86, no. 6, 7, 12 and Anhang;

133 B.C.: P. dem. Strasb. Wiss. Ges. dem. 7 ined.

For the scribe Nechthminis, son of Thotortaios (scribe in 125 B.C.), see Pros. Ptol. III and IX 7760; P. dem. Schreibertrad., p. 184, no. 48; ?addendum: Text 18 of 128 B.C, see Introduction to this text.

48 Πέρσης: for the addition of "Persian" to the titles of this and the other priests, see §27.

52 Πατοῦς Ἑριέως: for Patous, son of Herieus, who in my opinion is the priest Patous who has several contacts with the family of Dryton, see pros. 04.

56-57 Πατοῦς Ὥρου ὑπεπιστάτης Παθύρεως: Patous son of Horos is attested in several papyri from Pathyris. He acts as witness in a series of demotic documents in the period 137-113 B.C. (see Pros. Ptol. II and VIII 3532 = IV 10907; Pap. Lugd. Bat XIX, p. 36, comm. on l. 14). He is a soldier serving in the infantry and was appointed ὑπεπιστάτης of Pathyris.

The reading of the title as ὑπεπιστάτης was first proposed (with question mark) by E. Van 't Dack in a Dutch periodical: «men betreurt dat op r. 14 de titel van een functie onleesbaar is: zou men niet kunnen denken aan ὑπεπιστάτης . . . ? (*Tijdschrift voor Rechtsgeschiedenis* 49 (1981), p. 186).

I came, independently, to the same reading in my article 'Zwei Hypepistatai' (1988), in *ZPE* 73, p. 51-52, where more information on the title is to be found. The title of hypepistates was previously only once attested in a Hellenistic decree from Thessaloniki. In addition, it was recorded in another text from Pathyris, though in the form of a participle: a certain Hones is said to be ὁ ὑπεπιστάτησας; the latter held this office in 139/138 B.C., see Text 33, l. 19 and Introduction to this text.

59 εὐθύρ(ιν) οὐλ(ή): the place of the scar is not specified. P.W. Pestman notes that the same phenomenon is found in another will from Pathyris, *AfP* 1 (1901), p. 63-65, l. 23, probably of the hand of the same scribe Areios. I assume with P.W. Pestman that the scar was located on the part of the face that was mentioned just before, *viz.* the nose.

60 οὗτοι οἱ τ[έσ]σαρες ⟦ . ⟧ τοῖς ἐγχωρίοις: the first editor thinks that after τ[έσ]σαρες a *delta* was written, being either the cipher 4 or the beginning of διά, which he struck through and wrote down in the following line (l. 61: διὰ τὸ μὴ κτλ.). According to P.W. Pestman, on the other hand, it is not a «rature», but rather a later addition of the scribe, as, for instance, \`ἐν´.

64 Ἀμμώνιος Ἀρείου: see §27 and pros. 417.

4

THE THIRD GREEK WILL OF DRYTON
Copy by Esthladas

Plate IV

Pathyris	H. x W. = 23.5 x 36 cm [Width incomplete]	29 June 126 B.C.

British Library, P. inv.no. 617 [bought on 9 Nov. 1895 from Grenfell] = **P. Grenf. I 21** (= Chrest. Mitt. 302; Sel. Pap. I 83; C. Ptol. Sklav. 57).

Translations. — Bouché-Leclercq, *Histoire des Lagides* IV (1907), p. 113-114; Mélèze-Modrzejewski, 'Dryton le crétois' (1984), p. 375; Lewis, *Greeks in Ptolemaic Egypt* (1986), p. 100-101; Pomeroy, *Women in Hellenistic Egypt* (1990), p. 105-106; Rowlandson, *Sourcebook* (1998), no. 86.

Photograph. — Plate IV.

Description. — The papyrus was rolled from right to left. The right side of the text is thus hardly damaged. The left-hand side, on the other hand, being on the outside of the papyrus roll, is damaged in the vertical folds and the last strip, with the first letters of each line, is entirely lost. From lines 1 to 11 there is even a larger part missing. The text is written on the recto, along the fibres, and has a top margin of 1.5 cm and a bottom margin of 6 cm. The right margin measures up to 3.5 cm. The left-hand margin is lost. In the bottom margin there are traces of an older text which has been wiped out.

The papyrus is of a good quality; the fibres do not, however, always run parallel and in the bottom margin some horizontal fibres are lacking. Sheet-joins are visible at 2.5 cm from the right edge, in the middle and at 5 cm from the left edge.

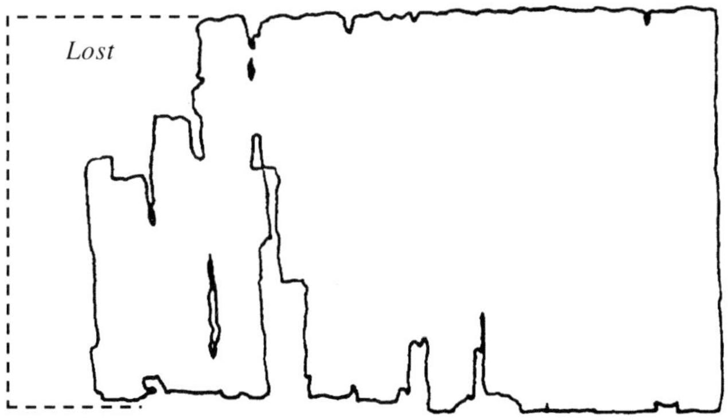

Introduction

Contents. — See §18-27.

A copy made by Esthladas. — Text 4 has always been considered a copy of Dryton's third will. It appears to be a copy made by Esthladas, Dryton's oldest son. The handwriting of Esthladas is discussed in §64-66.

Esthladas made the copy either from the original will kept at the notary's office (not preserved) or from the copy made at the notary's office and intended for Dryton and his family (Text 3). A short comparison between Texts 3 and 4 follows. Since the agoranomic copy Text 3 is fragmentary, there are few points of comparison. Nevertheless, Esthladas seems to have made an accurate copy. Only the following dissimilarities are to be indicated:

• *Writing variants*

Agoranomic copy Text 3, col. I, l. 1: τạ́δẹ
Esthladas' copy Text 4, l. 1: τάτε

Agoranomic copy Text 3, lost passage, but in a will probably from the hand of the same scribe Areios (*AfP* 1 (1901), p. 63-65, see Text 3) one can read in l. 2:
εἴη
Esthladas' copy Text 4, l. 2: εἴηι
(compare l. 6 συγγενῆι for συγγενῆ)

• *Different abbreviations*

Agoranomic copy Text 3, col. I, l. 24: [Ἀμμων]ιείωι
Esthladas' copy Text 4, l. 15: Ἀμμω(νιείωι)

Agoranomic copy Text 3, col. I, l. 29: [ἀν]έγκλη(τος)
Esthladas' copy Text 4, l. 18: ἀνέγκλητος

• *Careless copying*

The lacuna in the agoranomic copy Text 3, col. I, l. 13 [τὸν περιστερῶνα - - - καὶ τὸν ἄλλον ἡ̣μιτέ]λεστον is not entirely filled with the text found in Esthladas' copy; the original text by the agoranomos' scribe must have been more elaborate.
Esthladas' copy Text 4, l. 9: [καὶ τὸν περιστ]ερῶνα κ[α]ὶ̣ τὸν ἄλλον ἡ̣μιτέλεστον

Agoranomic copy Text 3, col. I, l. 16: [ψι]λὸν τόπον τὸν εἰς [περιστερῶνα]
Esthladas' copy Text 4, l. 11: ψιλὸν τόπον εἰς [π]εριστερῶνα (omission of τόν)

• *Passages not copied*

Esthladas has neither copied the name of the testator at the end of the will (Text 3, col. I, l. 35), nor the names and the details of the witnesses (Text 3, col. II).

The anacoluthon l. 7. — Dryton leaves

(a) his weaponry and his horse to Esthladas (l.3),

(b) "and of the four domestic slaves (I give to Esthladas) those named Myrsine and her (child - -); the remaining two female slaves called Eirene and Ampelion, (I leave) to Apollonia and her sisters, being five in number" (l. 6-7),

(c) "and the vineyard site ..." (l. 7-10).

This passage has led to the question whether the possessions which are listed in (c) are bequeathed to Esthladas or to the five daughters. In my view, they are left to Esthladas[1].

- Thus l. **3-10** contain the possessions to be inherited by Esthladas. The clause "the remaining two female slaves called Eirene and Ampelion, (I leave) to Apollonia and her sisters, being five in number" (l. 7) is only an insertion (in order to indicate what happened with the remaining two slaves) and is repeated in l. 13 among the belongings to be inherited by the daughters (τὰ θη[λ]υκὰ β̄ σώμα[τ]α). In addition, it is logical that the courtyard mentioned in l. 9, is bequeathed to Esthladas, since he owns most of the adjoining land.
- In l. **10-13** the inheritance of Dryton's daughters is listed, introduced by τοὺς δὲ λο(ιποὺς) οἴκους καὶ κτλ. and attributed explicitly to the daughters in l. 11-12.

List of abbreviations. —

Last letter (iota) written beneath or drawn through the preceding letter:

μι  (l. 5) in μι(κραῖ)

πλι 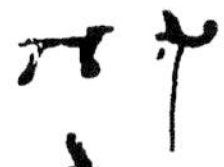 (l. 8) in πλί(νθου)

λι  (l. 10) in λι(βός)

Last letter (vowel) written above the preceding letter:

νο  (l. 9) in νό(του)

βο  (l. 9) in βο(ρρᾶ)

αυ  (l. 9, compare l. 14 and 18) in αὐ(τοῦ)

θυ  (l. 10) in θύ(ρας)

γυ  (l. 13, compare l. 18) in γυ(ναικί)

νο  (l. 13) in νό(μους)

πη  (l. 14) in πή(χεις)

1 *Pace* Pomeroy, *Women in Hellenistic Egypt* (1990), p. 105 (translation of the text).

εδα		(l. 8) in ἔδα(φος)
νεω		(l. 9) in νεω(τέρας)
μεγα		(l. 15) in Μεγά(λῃ)
εσθλα	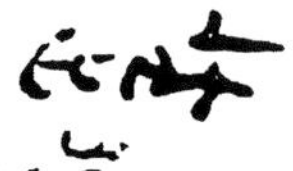	(l. 11, compare l. 15 and 16) in Ἐσθλά(δου)
αμμω		(l. 15) in Ἀμμω(νιείωι)
συμβο	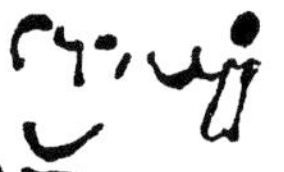	(l. 16) in σύμβο(λα)
αργυ		(l. 16) in ἀργυ(ρικά)
αμπελω	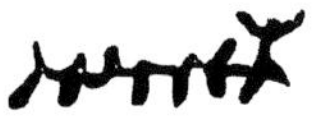	(l. 8) in ἀμπελῶ(νος)
απολλω	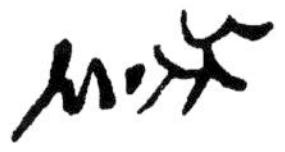	(l. 9) in Ἀπολλω(νίας)
επικτη		(l. 20) in ἐπίκτη(τα)

Special cases:

δι πο		(l. 15) in Δι(ὸς) πό(λει)
διοσπο		(l. 5) in Διὸς πό(λει)
αδ		(l. 7) in ἀδ(ελφαῖς)
εκασ		(l. 18) in ἑκάσ(του)

Symbol (borrowed from Demotic[1]):

(λοιποὺς)		(l. 10, compare l. 14)

Complete and abbreviated words in which letters are written one above the other:

διαθήκην	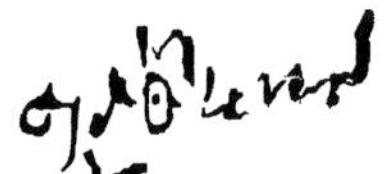	(l. 4)
χρηστῆρας	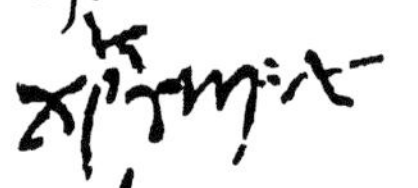	(l. 10)
φαίνηται	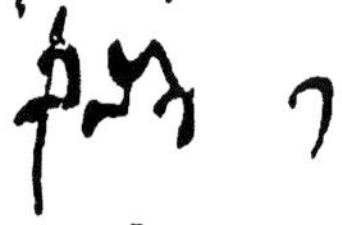	(l. 20)
κροτων		(l. 18) in κροτῶν(ος)

[1] See Pap. Lugd. Bat. XXI, p. 557.

Text

[Ἔτους μδ Παῦνι θ̄ ἐν Παθύρει ἐ]π̣' Ἀσκληπιάδου ἀγορανόμου. Τάτε διέθετο ὑγιαίνων νοῶν φρονῶν Δρύτων Παμφίλου Κρὴς τῶν διαδόχων καὶ

[τοῦ ἐπιτάγματος ἱππάρχη]ς ἐπ' ἀνδρῶν· ε̣ἴηι μέμ μοι ὑγιαίνοντι τῶν ἐμαυτοῦ κύριον εἶναι· ἐὰν δέ τι ἀνθρώπινον πάθω, καταλείπω καὶ

[δίδωμι τὰ ὑπάρχοντά μοι ἔγγαι]ι̣ά τε καὶ ἔπιπλα καὶ κτήνη καὶ ὅσα ἂν προσεπικτήσωμαι, τὸν μὲν ἵππον ἐφ' οὗ στρατεύομαι καὶ τὰ ὅπλα

[πάντα Ἐσθλάδαι τῶι ἐξ ἐμ]οῦ καὶ ἐξ Σαραπιάδος τῆς Ἐσθλάδου τοῦ Θέωνος ἀστῆς ἧι συνήμην γυναικὶ κατὰ νόμους καὶ κατὰ διαθήκην

[τὴν κεχρηματισμένην] δ̣ιὰ τοῦ ἐν Διὸς πό(λει) τῆι μι(κρᾶι) ἀρχείου ἐπὶ Διονυσίου ἀγορανόμου ἐν τῶι ς (ἔτους) ἐπὶ τοῦ Φιλομήτορος, ἣ διασαφεῖ τά τε ἄλλα

[καὶ ἐπίτροπον Ἑρμ.φιλο]ν ὄντα συγγενῆι κατέστησεν καὶ ἀπὸ τῶν οἰκετικῶν σωμάτων δ̄ ὧν ὀνόματα Μυρσίνην καὶ ταύτης

[- c. 12 - τὰ δὲ] λοιπὰ θη̣[λ]υκὰ β αἷς ὄνομα Εἰρήνην καὶ Ἀμπέλιον Ἀπολλωνίαι καὶ ταῖς ἀδ(ελφαῖς) οὔσι ε̄ καὶ τὸν ὑπάρχοντά μοι ἐπὶ τοῦ

[Κόχλακος τῆς Ἀραβία]ς τοῦ Πα̣[θυ]ρ̣(ίτου) ἔδα(φος) ἀμπελῶ(νος) καὶ τὰ ἐν τούτωι φρέατα ἐξ ὀπτῆς πλί(νθου) καὶ τἆλλα συνκύροντα καὶ τὴν ἅμαξαν σὺν τῆι

[ἐπισκευῆι καὶ τὸν περιστ]ερῶνα κ[α]ι̣ τὸν ἄλλον ἡ̣μιτέλεστον καὶ αὐλὴν ὧν γείτονες νό(του) ψιλοὶ <τόποι> τοῦ αὐ(τοῦ) Ἐσθλάδου βο(ρρᾶ) οἶκος κεκαμαρωμένος Ἀπολλω(νίας) τῆς νεω(τέρας)

[ἀπη]λ̣ι(ώτου) τόπο̣[ς - c. 6 -]ς Πετρασ[. .] . τοῦ Ἐσθλάδ̣[ο]υ̣ λι(βὸς) ψιλὸς τόπος Ἐσθλάδου ἕως τῆς ἀνεῳγμένης θύ(ρας) ἐπὶ λίβα· τοὺς δὲ λο(ιποὺς) οἴκους καὶ χρηστῆρας

[καὶ π]α̣λ̣αιὰν [- c. 5 -] καὶ ψιλὸν τόπον εἰς [π]εριστερῶνα ἀποδεδειγμένον ὑποκάτω τῆς Ἐσθλά(δου) θύ(ρας) καὶ ἀπὸ λι(βὸς) τῆς καμάρας δίδωμι

[Ἀπολ]λωνίαι καὶ Ἀριστοῖ καὶ Ἀφροδισίαι καὶ Νι[κα]ρίωι καὶ Ἀπολλωνίαι νεωτέραι οὔσι ε̄ ταῖς ἐξ ἐμοῦ καὶ ἐξ Ἀπολλωνίας τῆς καὶ Σεμμώνθιος

[ἧι σύ]νειμι γυ(ναικὶ) κατὰ νό(μους) καὶ τὰ θη[λ]υκὰ β̄ σώμα[τ]α καὶ τὴν βοῦν ἐξ ἴσου κυριευέτωσαν ταῖς οἰκίαις καθ' ὃν πεποίημαι μερισμόν·

[δότ]ω δὲ Ἐσθλάδας ἀπὸ τοῦ δεδομένου αὐ(τῶι) ψιλο[ῦ τ]όπου ἀπέναντι τῆς θύ(ρας) αὐ(τοῦ) ἐπὶ λίβ[α] πή(χεις) ἐμβαδοὺς δ̄ εἰς κλιβάνου τόπον· τὰ δὲ λο(ιπὰ) οἰκόπεδα [καὶ ψιλ]ọὶ τόποι ἐν Δι(ὸς) πό(λει) τῆι μεγά(ληι) ἐν τῶι Ἀμμω(νιείωι) [κ]α̣ὶ ἐν τοῖς Κεραμείοις ἐχέτω Ἐσθλάδας κατὰ τὸ (ἥμισυ) Ἀπολλω(νία) δὲ καὶ ἀδελφαὶ κατὰ τὸ (ἥμισυ) καὶ

[τἆλλα ὑ]πάρχοντά μοι πάντα σύμβο(λά) τε σιτικὰ [κ]αὶ ἀργυ(ρικὰ) καὶ ἔπιπλα πάντα κατὰ τὸ (ἥμισυ)· δότω δὲ Ἐσθλά(δας) καὶ αἱ περὶ Ἀπολλωνίαν κατὰ κοινὸν

[εἰς οἰκ]οδομὴν περιστερῶνος ἀνηλώματα ε[ἰς] τὸν ἀποδεδειγμένον περιστερῶνα ἕως ἂν ἐπιτελέσωσι καὶ Ἀπολλωνίαι τῆι καὶ Σεμμώνθει

[τῆι ἐ]μῆι γυ(ναικὶ) ἐτῶν $\overline{δ}$ ἐὰν παραμείνηι ἐ[ν τῶι] οἴκωι ἀνέγκλητος οὖσα εἰς τροφὴν αὐ(τῆς) καὶ ταῖς $\overline{β}$ θυγατράσιν ἑκάσ(του) μη(νὸς) (πυροῦ) θ (ἥμισυ) κροτῶ(νος) ἰβ χα(λκοῦ) Σ

[καὶ] μ̣ετὰ δ ἔτη τὰ αὐτὰ μετρήματα [δότ]ωσαν ταῖς $\overline{β}$ νεωτέραι<ς> ἐκ κοινοῦ ἕως ἐτῶν ια· δότωσαν δὲ Ταχράτει εἰς φερνὴν

[χαλκο]ῦ (τάλαντα) ιβ ἐκ τῶν κοινῶν· Ὅσα δ' ἂν φαίνη[ται ἐ]π̣ίκτη(τα) ἔχουσα ἡ Σεμμῶνθις ὄντα αὐτῆι συνοῦσα Δρύτωνι κυριευέτω αὐτῶν·

[οἱ δ' ἐπ]ελεύσοντες ἐπ' αὐτὴν περὶ τού[των - c. 4 -]

[(Ἔτους)] μ̣δ Παῦνι $\overline{θ}$.

---

1 τάδε ed., τάτε legimus, *l.* τάδε 2 [ἵππαρχο]ς ed., [ἱππάρχη]ς supplevimus; εἴ̣ηι, *l.* εἴη 4 Ἐσθλά[δηι] ed., Ἐσθλά[δαι] supplevimus 5 [- c. 19 - π]αρά ed., [τὴν ἀνακομισθεῖσαν π]αρά Mitteis, [τὴν κεχρηματισμένην] δ̣ιά Hunt-Edgar 6 [καὶ - c. 17 -]νοντα ed., [καὶ ἐπίτροπον - c. 8 -]ν ὄντα Hunt-Edgar, [καὶ ἐπίτροπον Ἑρμ. φιλο]ν ὄντα supplevimus; συγγενῆι, *l.* συγγενῆ 7 [- c. 9 -] ed., [τὰ $\overline{γ}$ παιδία] Hunt-Edgar, [- c. 12 -] supplevimus; ὄνομα ed., ὀνόματα Hunt-Edgar, ὄνομα legimus (cf. ed.); ταῖς $\overline{δ}$ ed., ταῖς ἀδ(ελφαῖς) Mitteis; οὖσι, *l.* οὔσαις 7-8 τὸν ὑπάρχοντά μοι . . . ἔδα(φος), *l.* τὸ ὕπαρχόν μοι . . . ἔδα(φος) 8 [- c. 14 -] τοῦ Πα̣[θυ]ρ(ίτου) ed., [Κόχλακος τῆς Ἀραβία]ς τοῦ Πα̣[θυ]ρ(ίτου) Montevecchi (*Aegyptus* 15 (1935), p. 92, n. 1) 9 [βοί - c. 5 - περιστ]ερῶνο ed., [ἐπισκευῆι καὶ τὸν περιστ]ερῶνα Mitteis; τόπο̣[ς ψιλὸ]ς ed., τόπο̣[ς - c. 6 -]ς supplevimus; Πετρασ[- c. 1-2 -]ι ed., Πετρασ[. .] . legimus; χρητῆρας ed., χρηστῆρας legimus 11 [ ] κ̣α̣ὶ αλ̣[ed.; [ ] . λλιαν Wilcken (apud Hunt-Edgar), [καὶ π]α̣λ̣αιάν Hunt-Edgar 12 οὖσι, *l.* οὔσαις 14 [ἐχέτ]ω ed.; [δότ]ω Mitteis 15 [ψι]λοὶ τόποι, *l.* [ψι]λοὺς τόπους; Διοσπό(λει) ed., Δι(ὸς) πό(λει) legimus 18 ἐτῶν δ ed, ἐτῶν $\overline{δ}$ legimus; [τῶι] οἴκωι ed., ἐ[ν τῶι] οἴκωι Wilcken (apud Mitteis); (πυροῦ) β ed, (πυροῦ) θ legimus 19 [ἐπὶ] δὲ τά ed., [καὶ] μ̣ετά Hunt-Edgar 20 (Ἔτους) ed.; [(Ἔτους)] legimus

Translation

Year 44, 9 Payni, in Pathyris, before Asklepiades the agoranomos.

These are the testamentary dispositions of Dryton, son of Pamphilos, Cretan, of the diadochoi and cavalry officer over men at the head of those of the epitagma-unit, being healthy, of sound mind and in possession of his wits.

«May it be granted to me to be master of my property in good health. But if I should suffer mortal fate, I bequeath and give all my immovable and movable property, cattle and everything I may acquire besides:

the horse on which I campaign and all my weaponry (I leave) to Esthladas, my son by Sarapias, daughter of Esthladas, son of Theon, a citizen, the woman with whom I have lived legally and in accordance with a will which was drawn up in the archeion of Diospolis Mikra, before the agoranomos Dionysios, in the 6th year of the reign of Philometor, and which records among its dispositions the appointment of Herm[a/o]philos as epitropos, being a relative;

of the four domestic slaves (I give to Esthladas) those named Myrsine and her (child) - - ; the remaining two female slaves called Eirene and Ampelion, (I leave) to Apollonia and her sisters, being 5 in number;

and (to Esthladas I leave) the vineyard site belonging to me on the Kochlax on the east bank of the Pathyrites, the wells in it made of baked brick and the other appurtenances; (I) also (leave to him) the wagon with its equipment, the dovecote, the other, half-finished dovecote, a courtyard of which the boundaries are, south: open lots of the said Esthladas, north: a vaulted room of Apollonia the younger, east: a lot - - of Petras- - son of Esthladas, west: an open lot of Esthladas, as far as the door opening to the west.

The remaining rooms with appurtenances, on old - -, an open lot intended for a dovecote down from the door of Esthladas and to the west of the vaulted room, I give to Apollonia, Aristo, Aphrodisia, Nikarion and Apollonia the younger, my 5 daughters by Apollonia alias Semmonthis, the woman together with whom I live in accordance with law. They are to possess the two female slaves and the cow in equal shares for their households according to the division I have made.

Esthladas shall give, from the open lot granted to him facing his door to the west, 4 square cubits for the site of an oven.

Of the remaining building(-site)s and open lots in the Ammonieion(-quarter) in Diospolis Megale and in the Kerameia, Esthladas is to have half, Apollonia and her sisters half. All my remaining belongings, my symbola for grain and cash as well as all my furniture, will be divided in half shares.

Esthladas, Apollonia and her sisters shall pay in common the expenses of building the dovecote, (that is) the intended dovecote until they have finished it.

(Esthladas, Apollonia and her sisters shall jointly give) to Apollonia alias Semmonthis, my wife, for (a period of) 4 years, if she stays at home irreproachably, for the maintenance of herself and her two daughters, every month 9.5 (artabas) of wheat,

1/12 (artaba) of kroton (and) 200 copper (drachmas). After 4 years they shall make the same provisions from common fund for the two younger daughters for 11 years. They (Esthladas and his sisters) shall give to Tachratis for a dowry **(20)** *12 copper talents out of the common fund. Whatever properties Semmonthis appears to have acquired as belonging to herself, while living with Dryton, she shall be the owner. Those who will proceed against her for these acquisitions,[- c. 4 -]».*

Year 44, 9 Payni.

Notes

The vocabulary relating to Dryton's movables and immovables is discussed in Vandorpe, *Archives from Pathyris* (2001), chapter V .

1 τάτε (ed. τάδε):  For the interchange of δ and τ, see Mayser, *Grammatik* I.1, p. 147.

2 εἴηι, *l.* εἴη: the writing ηι instead of η is already attested for the 3rd century B.C. and spread further in the 2nd and 1st centuries B.C. It is also found in otherwise correctly written texts, especially at the end of words: «sie setzt voraus dass für ηι der Lautwert η (=ē) an Stelle von ει (=i) restituiert worden war», see Mayser, *Grammatik* I.1, p. 106-108. Compare συγγενῆι, l. 6.

4 Ἐσθλάδαι: the editor supplemented Ἐσθλάδηι; since the other wills of Dryton have Ἐσθλάδαι, the latter form is to be preferred (see pros. 504).

6 [Ἑρμ.φιλο]ν: this supplement is based on Text 2, see §7.

συγγενῆι, *l.* συγγενῆ: see the commentary on l. 2.

6-7 τῶν οἰκετικῶν σωμάτων δ̄ ὧν ὀνόματα Μυρσίνην καὶ ταύτης [- c. 12 -]: the supplement [τὰ γ̄ παιδία] by Hunt-Edgar is due to a wrong interpretation of the passage (see §22). I return to the interpretation of Grenfell, the first editor (P. Grenf. I 21, note 7): he proposes the supplement [θυγατέρα - - -], but adds that, if ὄνομα is to be taken strictly, a personal name must also be supplied. Thus Mitteis wonders in his edition (Chrest. Mitt. 302) whether the abbreviation θυ(γατέρα) followed by a personal name is not to be preferred. This option does not take account of the possibility that Myrsine had a son. The lacuna doubtless contained a word such as 'child', 'daughter' or 'son', followed by the name of the child. For a nice parallel and for further comment, see §22.

τὸν ὑπάρχοντά μοι ... ἔδα(φος) ἀμπελῶ(νος), *l.* τὸ ὕπαρχόν μοι ... ἔδα(φος) ἀμπελῶ(νος): when he wrote τὸν ὑπάρχοντα, the writer doubtless had the masculine word ἀμπελών in mind rather than the neutral ἔδα(φος), to which it grammatically belongs.

8 ἐξ ὀπτῆς πλί(νθου): L.C. Youtie ('Lost Examples of ΕΞΟΠΤΟΣ', in *ZPE* 50 (1983), p. 59-60) proposes reading ἐξόπτης πλί(νθου), taking ἔξοπτος as an adjective. The main argument would be the use of an «unneeded preposition» in ἐξ ὀπτῆς πλί(νθου). The fact that the composite adjective ἔξοπτος carries a feminine ending, is, according to Youtie, due to a tendency in the koine to give feminine endings to adjectives ending on -ος, -ον; Youtie refers to grammars relating to later periods.

The prepostion ἐκ is, however, often used to denote the material of which something is made (see Mayser, *Grammatik* II.2, p. 345), in which case the article can be omitted. In addition, the simplex ὀπτός is attested, as pointed out by Youtie. In my view, there is no reason to interpret this example from the 2nd century B.C. as ἐξόπτης πλί(νθου), so accepting what in that period would be an unusual feminine ending for a composite adjective.

9 [ἐπισκευῆι]: the addition [ἐπισκευῆι] by Mitteis is assured by the other copy of the same will, Text 3, col. I, l. 12.

10 τόπο̣[ς - c. 6 -]ς: the editor supplied τόπο̣[ς ψιλό]ς. The normal expression is ψιλὸς τόπος. The unusual order τόπο̣[ς ψιλό]ς is not found elsewhere in the text and in general is rarely attested (it is found, for instance, in P. Tebt. III 870, l. 3, 8 and 10; 1070, l. 1, 7 and 10). In addition, the supplement [ψι.λό]ς does not fill the entire lacuna. Τόπος is here probably followed by another adjective, as, for instance, παλαιός.

Πετρασ[. .] . (ed. Πετρασ[. .]ι̣): one expects a name in the genitive. The reading by the editor of a *iota* at the end of the name, is not certain; the traces better fit an *upsilon*, which would point to the expected genitive ending. For commentary on the name, see pros. 612.

χρηστῆρας: -ησ- is written above the preceding characters (see the Introduction, List of Abbreviations); the editor read -η- instead of -ησ- and as a consequence, χρητήρ (ὁ) was recorded as a hapax legomenon in the lexicon of LSJ. For my reading χρηστῆρας, compare the -ησ- in χρηστῆρας with the -η- in, for instance, διαθήκην l. 4 (see the Introduction, List of Abbreviations).

The term χρηστήρ is attested, though not with the sense needed here («creditor, usurer»); χρηστῆρας is undoubtedly a mistake for χρηστήρια, "appurtenances".

11 [καὶ π]α̣λ̣α̣ιάν: the reading [ ] . λλιαν proposed by Wilcken is in theory possible, but does not fit a single word, except for κελλία, plural of κελλίον, which is a diminutive of κέλλα (Lat. cella) and is only found in the Roman period. The proposal [καὶ π]α̣λ̣α̣ιάν by Hunt-Edgar fits the traces well and makes more sense; the following lacuna probably contained a word like οἰκίαν, as also proposed by Hunt-Edgar.

15 Δι(ὸς) πό(λει): the editor read Διοσπό(λει); the *iota* is written below the *delta*; there is no space left for -ος. Compare on the other hand the writing of Διὸς πό(λει) in l. 5 (see the Introduction, List of Abbreviations).

18 (πυροῦ) θ (ed. (πυροῦ) β):  a *theta* is clearly written, compare the *theta* in the date l. 22:  ; compare on the other hand the *beta* l. 13: 

21 [οἱ δ' ἐπ]ελεύσοντες ἐπ' αὐτὴν περὶ τού[των - c. 4 -] : the penalty clauses following this expression are usually much longer than the four characters which are left in the lacuna. The other copy of the will Text 3, written by the scribe of the agoranomos, equally has little space left for this penalty clause (col. I, l. 34.). In addition, one expects a middle form of the participle of the verb (ἐπέρχεσθαι).

A possible explanation might be that the original will had the expression (καὶ) μὴ ἐπελεύσεσθαι / ἐπελεύσασθαι ἐπ' αὐτὴν περὶ τούτων ("and it is not allowed to proceed against her for these acquisitions", see Berger, *Die Strafklauseln* (1911), p. 125-126): in that case, there is nothing to be added in the small lacuna of four characters and the will ends with περὶ τού[των].

5

DEMOTIC DIVORCE AGREEMENT
for Aphrodisia alias Tachratis, daughter of Dryton

See facsimile below

[Pathyris]	H. x W. = 14.8 x 13.2 cm [Height incomplete]	25 March 123 B.C.

Heidelberg, P. dem. inv.no. 779a [In Heidelberg since 1898, acquired by Reinhardt] = **P. dem. Baden I 7**.

Description. — The upper part of the papyrus with the top margin and the first four lines is relatively well preserved. The fifth line is damaged along a horizontal fold. The remaining is broken off at the left and at the bottom. There is a sheet-join visible at 2 cm from the left-hand side. The papyrus is of a poor quality: between l. 8-9, for instance, the horizontal fibres are missing.

The text is written on the front along the fibres, with a top margin of 3 cm, a right-hand margin of c. 1 cm and a left-hand margin of at maximum 1.8 cm. The verso is blank.

Photograph and facsimile. — No photograph availabale; see my facsimile below.

Introduction

Contents. — Shortly after the redaction of her father's last will on 29 June 126 B.C., Tachratis alias Aphrodisia (pros. 510), daughter of Dryton and Apollonia, married the soldier Psennesis, son of P - - (pros. 511). The will of 126 B.C. made provision for a dowry for Tachratis (see §23). On 25 March 123 B.C., after barely three years of marriage, the couple divorced. See also §29.

The scribe. — The name of the scribe of the divorce agreements Text 5 and Text 6 is lost. Both agreements contain exactly the same fomulas as Text 8 of 100 B.C. from Pathyris and are undoubtedly written in the same temple notary's office. Text 5 dates from 123 B.C.; at that time Nechthminis, son of Nechthminis, was acting — since only one year — as temple notary or monographos in the Hathor temple of Pathyris (see Text 9, note 3). Since usually only one priest could be monographos at the same time (see §34), Text 5 is certainly written by Nechthminis. One can consult P. dem. Gebelein Heid. 17 (with facsimile) to compare the two handwritings. Also Text 6 can be attributed to Nechthminis in all probability. In Text 5, which dates from the beginning of his career as temple notary, his handwriting is still stiff and he uses a thicker pen; Text 6 shows a more practised hand and, finally, Text 8 of 100 B.C. reveals an experienced and facile hand.

To show the evolution of the handwriting of the monographos Nechthminis, I have chosen three words from the divorce agreements:

	Text 5 (123 B.C.)	**Text 6** (between 123-100 B.C.)	**Text 8** (100 B.C.)
ḥm.t.			
sḥm.t.		-	
rn			

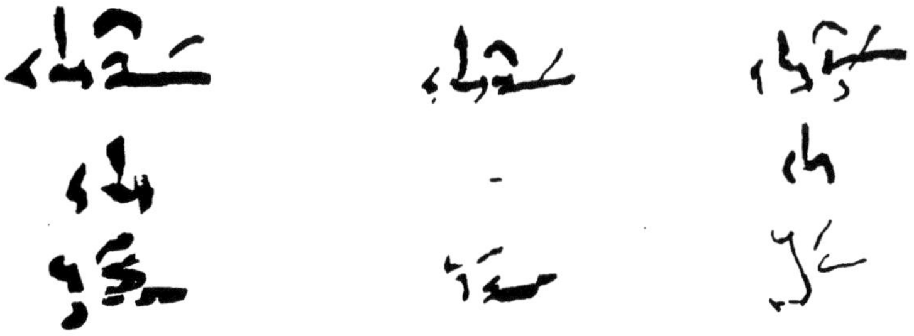

Facsimile

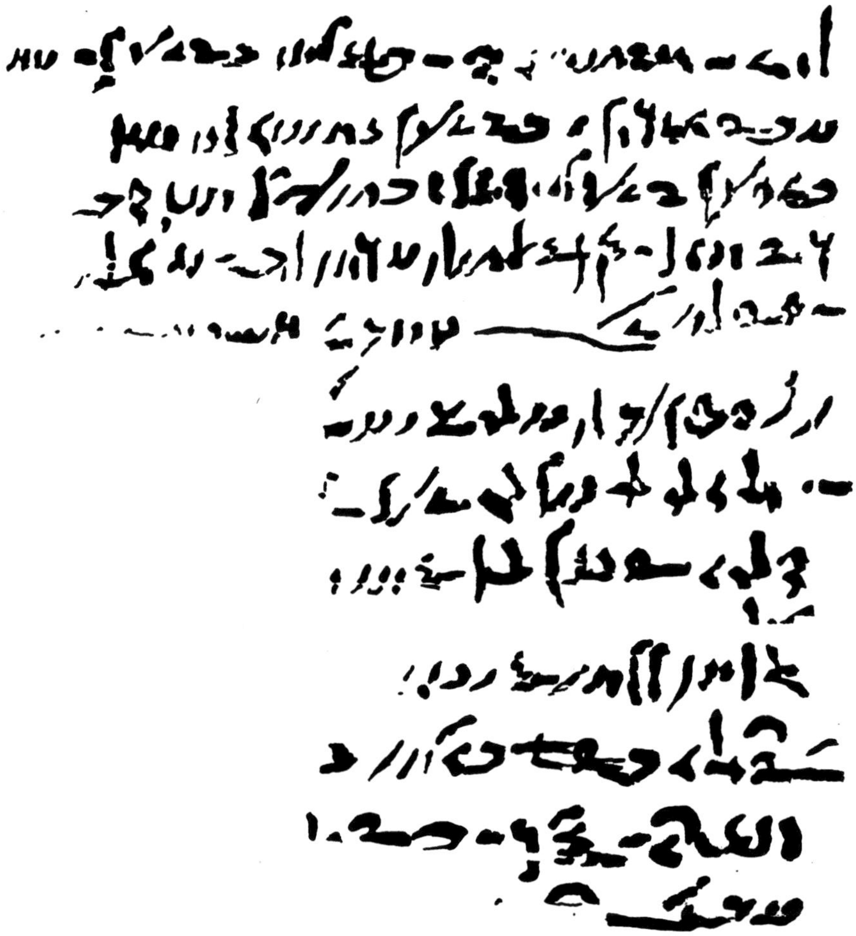

Text

Ḥ3.t-sp 47 ibd-3 pr.t ⸢sw⸣ 4 n Pr-ꜥ3ꜥws Ptlwmy⸢s⸣[ꜥws]
p3 mnḫ s3 Ptlwmysꜥws irm
Glwptr3ꜥws n3 ntr.w nty pr.w, irm n3 nty
smn.w n Rꜥ-qd P3-sy nty n p3 tš
n Nw.t. Ḏd rmt iw=f šp ⸢ḥbs⸣ [iw=f sẖ]
r 3mwr, P3-šr-Is.t s3 P3-⸢-⸣[- - - mw.ṱ=f - - -]
n sḥm.t Ta-ẖrd.ṱ ta Trw⸢t⸣[wn mw.ṱ=s]
T3-šr.t-Mnṱ. Ḫ3ꜥ=y ṱ[.t n ḥm.t.]
Tw=y wwy r.ḥr=⸢t⸣ n [rn n hp]
n ḥm.t. Mn mtw=y ⸢md⸣ [nb p3 t3]
i.ir.n=t n rn n hp [n ḥm.t. Ink]
p3 nty ḏd ⸢n⸣[=t]: ⸢i⸣. [ir n=t hy.]
. . . .

2 *p3 nty mnḫ* ed., *p3 mnḫ* legimus 5 *rmt iw=f šp ḥbs ꜥq (?)* ed., *rmt iw=f šp ⸢ḥbs⸣* Vleeming (Pap. Lugd. Bat. XXIII, p. 204-207) 6 *P3-šr-Is.t s3 [- - -]* ed., *P3-šr-Is.t s3 P3-⸢-⸣[- - -]* legimus 7 *Trw⸢t⸣[wn ṱs-ḥtr mw.ṱ=s]* ed., *Trw⸢t⸣[wn mw.ṱ=s]* supplevimus 10 *sḥm.t* ed., *ḥm.t* Pestman (*Marriage* (1961), p. 72, n. 5) 11 *[sḥm.t]* ed., *[ḥm.t]* Pestman (*Marriage* (1961), p. 72, n. 5)

Translation

Year 47, 4 Phamenoth, of king Ptolemy (VIII) Euergetes, son of Ptolemy (V) and Kleopatra (I), the Gods Epiphaneis, (and the year of the priests) who are appointed in Rakotis (Alexandria) (and) Ptolemais in the **(5)** *Thebaid.*
Has spoken the man receiving pay, registered at (the camp of) Krokodilopolis, Psennesis son of P - - -, his mother being - - -,
to the woman Tachratis, daughter of Dryton, her mother being Senmonthis:
«I have repudiated you as a wife. I am far from you on account of (the) right (to you) **(10)** *as (my) wife. I have nothing in the world to claim of you in the name of the right (to you) as (my) wife.*
I am the one who says to you: "take yourself a husband".»
- -

Notes

5 *rmt iw=f šp ⌜ḥbs⌝, man receiving pay*: for the reading of this military title as *rmt iw=f šp ḥbs* (and not *rmt iw=f šp ḥbs ʿq*), see Vleeming, 'The Title 'Man Receiving Pay'' (1985), in Pap. Lugd. Bat. XXIII, p. 204-207.

6 *P3-šr-Is.t s3 P3- ⌜-⌝[- - -], Psennesis son of P- - -*: although the beginning of the name of the father is clearly visible (), the first editor W. Spiegelberg did not interpret the traces (*P3-šr-Is.t s3 [- - -]*). Afterwards, the father's name has generally been taken to be *Iy-m-ḥtp* (Imouthes), see, for instance, Winnicki, 'Ein ptolemäischer Offizier' (1972), in *Eos* 60, p. 353.

The traces, however, hardly account for the name Imouthes. The name begins with the article *P3-* ; the horizontal line which follows, rules out a number of names, for instance, the names beginning with *P3-šr-* (Psen-) or *P3-dy-* (Pete-), as well as the name *P3-mr-iḥ* (Pelaias), frequently attested in Pathyris. A possible reading is *P3-m3y* (Pmois), see pros. 409.

6

DEMOTIC DIVORCE AGREEMENT
for a daughter of Dryton

See facsimile below

[Pathyris]	H. x W. = 9.4 x 7.4 cm [Fragment]	124-94, most probably between 123 and 100 B.C.

Heidelberg, P. dem. inv.no. 754c [In Heidelberg since 1898, acquired by Reinhardt] = **P. dem. Baden I 8**.
Photograph and facsimile. — No photograph available; see my facsimile below.

Description. — The papyrus is fragmentary: it is broken off at the right, at the top and at the foot. Thus the date and the end of the agreement, the name of the scribe and the names of the witnesses are lost. The text is written on the recto along the fibres, with a left-hand margin of at maximum 1.3 cm. The verso is blank.

Introduction

Contents. — One of the daughters of Dryton — her name is lost in the lacuna — is divorced by her husband Psenẹnoupis, son of the agoranomos Ammonios (pros. 514). Since he was around 110 B.C. an adult, he most probably was married to one of Dryton's youngest daughters: Nikarion (pros. 508) or Apollonia the younger (pros. 509). See also §29.

The scribe and the date. — The name of the scribe is lost, but the text can in all probability be ascribed to Nechthminis, son of Nechthminis, who was temple notary at Pathyris in the period 124-94 B.C. On palaeographical grounds, the text was written between 123 (Text 5) and 100 B.C. (Text 8. See for more details, Text 5, Introduction. The scribe).

Facsimile

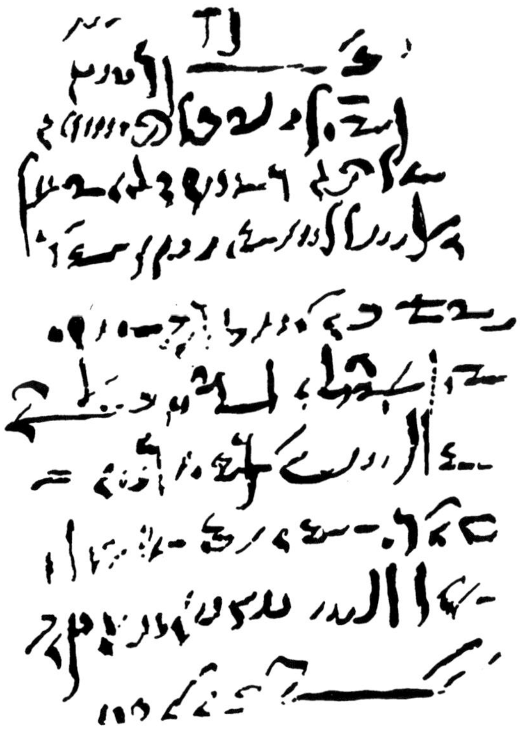

Text

. . . .

[irm n3 nty smn.w n] ⌜*Rꜥ-qd*⌝
[P3-sy nty n p3 tš n Nw.t.] Ḏd rmt ḥtr
[- - - P3-šr-]Inpw s3 3mwnys
[n sḥm.t - - - ta Trw]twn mw.ṱ=s T3-šr.t-Mnṱ.
[H̱3ꜥ=y ṱ.t n ḥm.t.] Tw=y wwy r.ḥr=t n rn
[n hp n ḥm.t.] Mn mtw=y md nb n p3 t3
[i-ir-n=t n rn h]p n ḥm.t. Ink p3 nty ḏd n=t:
[i.ir n=t hy.] Bn iw=y rḫ ꜥḥꜥ r-ḥ3.ṱ=t n
[ꜥ.wy nb nty ir=t] mr n šm r.r=w ⌜*ḏr.w*⌝
[r ir n=t hy] n.im=w. Iw=y gm.ṱ=t irm rmt nb
[p3 t3, bn iw=y rḫ] ḏd n=⌜*t*⌝*: mtw=t t3y(=y)*
[ḥm.t n ṯ3y p3 hrw r ḥry šꜥ ḏ.t. - - -]

. . . .

---

3 *[- - -]Inpw* ed., *[- - - P3-šr-]Inpw* supplevimus 4 *[mw.t=f- - - Trw]twn* ed., *[n sḥm.t - - - ta Trw]twn* supplevimus 5 et 6 *[sḥm.t]* ed., *[ḥm.t]* Pestman (*Marriage* (1961), p. 72, n. 5) 7 *n sḥm.t* ed., *n ḥm.t* Pestman (*Marriage* (1961), p. 72, n. 5) 9 *n dmy (?)* ed., *ḏr.w* legimus

Translation

- -

(and the year of the priests) who are appointed in Rakotis (Alexandria) (and) Ptolemais in the Thebaid.
Has spoken the cavalryman - - - Psenenoupis, son of Ammonios,
to the woman - - -, daughter of Dryton, her mother being Senmonthis:
« **(5)** *I have repudiated you as a wife. I am far from you on account of (the) right (to you) as (my) wife. I have nothing in the world to claim of you in the name of the right (to you) as (my) wife.*
I am the one who says to you: "take yourself a husband". I will not be able to stand in your way in any place to which you wish to go **(10)** *to take yourself a husband. If I find you together with any man in the world, I will not be able to say to you: "you are my wife", from this day on and afterwards, for ever.»*

- -

Notes

3 *[P3-šr-]Inpw s3 3mwnys, [Psen]enoupis, son of Ammonios*: the first editor supplemented the name of the husband in his translation as "Eri-]enupis". I suggest the name *[P3-šr-]Inpw*,"[Psen]enoupis" on the following grounds (compare P.W. Pestman, in *Chron. d'Ég.* 41 (1966), p. 315 and n. 4). Few inhabitants of Pathyris bear the Greek name Ammonios, recorded in Text 6 as father of the husband. An important person bearing this name is the agoranomos Ammonios, who also has an Egyptian name: Pakoibis. He was in office at least in the periods 114-109 and 98-97 B.C., which fits well with the date of the divorce agreement (124-94, most probably between 123 and 100 B.C.). The Ammonios mentioned here was doubtless agoranomos at that time, and it is thus not surprising that he is recorded here with his Greek name.

An additional argument is the fact that he had a son called Psenenoupis, who must have been of the age of the two youngest daughters of Dryton. Without doubt it is this Psenenoupis who is recorded in Text 6; of his name only the last element *Inpw* (–anoupis) has been preserved (see pros. 514).

4 *[n sḥm.t - - - ta Trw]twn, to the the woman - - -, daughter of Dryton*: there is no space left in the lacuna of l. 4 for the addition of the mother's name of the husband, as was suggested by the first editor (*[mw.t=f- - - Trw]twn*). The lacuna can only be filled with the expression *n sḥm.t* , "to the woman", followed by the name of this woman, as, for instance, in Text 5, l. 7 and Text 8, l. 4.

9 *ḏr.w*, (literally: *all*): the first editor, with due reservation, read *n dmy (?)*, "in (the) city"; this adverbial adjunct has a strange place in the sentence:[*ʿ.wy nb nty ir=t] mr n šm r.r=w n dmy*, "in any place to which you wish to go in (the) city". The traces interpreted by W. Spiegelberg as *n dmy* , are damaged.

My reading *ḏr.w*, "all", fits the traces well and finds its parallel in a Theban text of the same period, which at exactly the same place has *ḏr.w* (P. dem. Tor. Botti, l. 16); *ḏr.w* refers to *ʿ.wy nb* (each place) and is plural due to the preceding *r.r=w* (to them).

7

DEMOTIC MARRIAGE CONTRACT

of Senenouphis, granddaughter of Dryton

DESCRIPTION

Krokodilopolis 107-101 B.C.

Moskow, P. dem. inv.no. 431 = **unpublished**. The text will be published by V. Massa and U. Kaplony-Heckel. They kindly informed me of this text, a photograph of which was recently discovered by D. Devauchelle among photographs from the archives of M. Malinine.

Contents. — Dryton's granddaughter Senenouphis (pros. 604), daughter of Kaies and Senmouthis (alias Apollonia), marries Pates, son of Panebchounis (pros. 605). Pates is a soldier, a man receiving pay, while he is registered at the camp in Krokodilopolis.

The marriage contract is a *sẖ n ḥm.t*, a "deed concerning the wife" (see §31). The gift (*šp*) of Pates to his wife is lost in the lacuna. Several goods are listed which Senenouphis brings along with her, among them an *in-šn*-veil (see §31) worth 600 deben and a *swḥ3* (egg, see Text 45, l. 10) worth 50 deben. The total value of these goods amounts to 2140 deben or 42,800 drachmas.

The loan contract is written by Espnouthis, son of Teos[1], notary of the temple of Souchos in Krokodilopolis in the period 124-98 B.C.

[1] See Pros. Ptol. III and IX 7737; P. dem. Schreibertrad., p. 184, no. 45; addendum: Text 7.

8

DEMOTIC DIVORCE AGREEMENT

for Senmonthis, granddaughter of Dryton

See facsimile below

Pathyris	H. x W. = 17.5 x 16.2 cm [Height incomplete]	21 Sept. 100 B.C.

Heidelberg, P. dem. inv.no. 762 + 770a + 773 + 774 [In Heidelberg since 1898, acquired by Reinhardt].

The fragments no. 762, 770a and 774 were published by W. Spiegelberg as **P. dem. Baden I 6**. A large fragment has now been discovered in the collection of Heidelberg (no. 773), but has remained **unpublished**.

Photograph and facsimile. — No photograph available; see my facsimile below.

Description. — The papyrus has one vertical and four horizontal folds. It was apparently rolled from bottom to top (or vice versa) and subsequently folded double. The vertical fold does not run nicely in the middle, but is situated somewhat to the left. The papyrus was damaged or is broken off along the folds. Most fragments have been recovered, except for a small piece in the middle, from the bottom (with the name of the last two witnesses) and from the left lower part.

The text is written on the recto against the fibres, with a top margin of 2.2 cm, a right-hand margin of 1.2 cm and a left-hand margin of maximum 1.8 cm. There is a sheet-join between l. 1 and 2. It is clearly visible where the scribe took new ink, usually after half a line, sometimes already after one third of a line. The verso is blank.

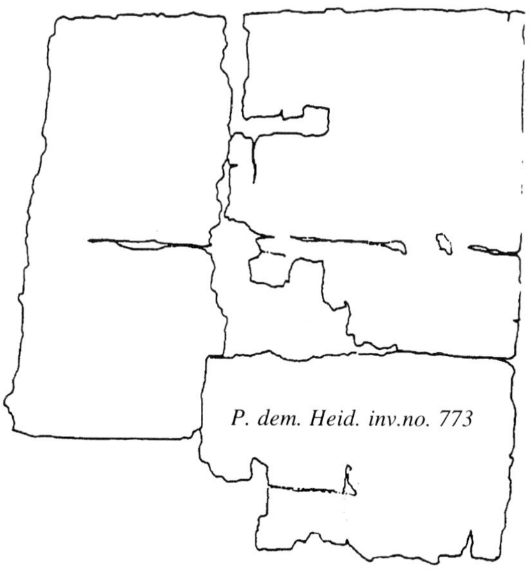

Introduction

Contents. — Senmonthis the younger (pros. 606), daughter of Kaies and Apollonia, granddaughter of Dryton, is divorced by Pamenos, son of Nechouthes and Senthotis. It is not known how long they were married. Four years after the divorce, Pamenos was married again (see pros. 607-608). See also §30.

The scribe and the witnesses. — The text is written by the temple notary, Nechthminis, son of Nechthminis (see Text 5. Introduction. The scribe). Of the four witnesses two names are preserved (see §32). They are written in different hands. Text 8 is thus the original divorce agreement, not a copy.

Facsimile

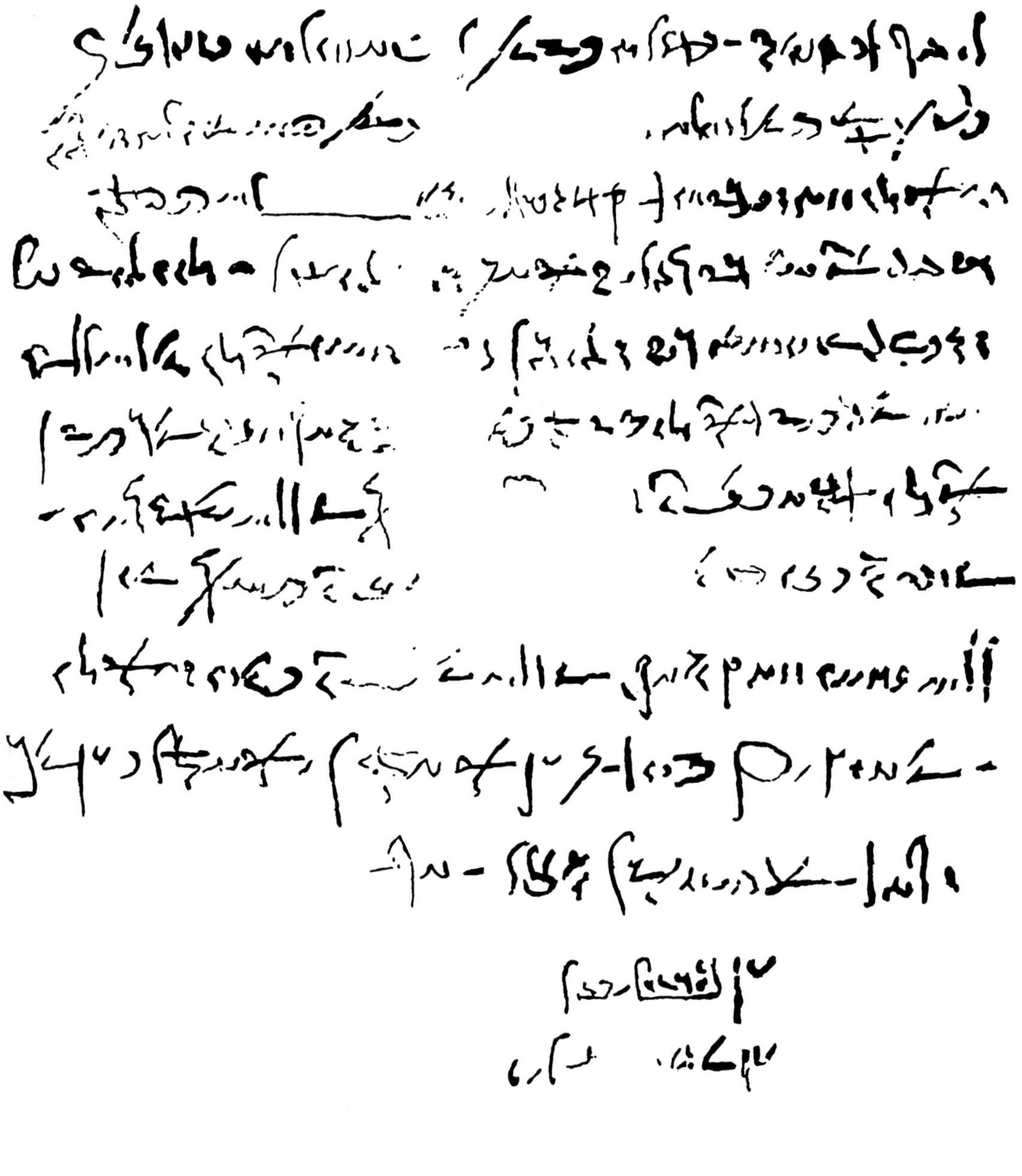

Text

Ḥ3.t-sp 15 ibd-1 3ḫ.t (sw) 5 n Pr-ʿ3ʿws Ptlwmys ʿws nty iw=w ḏd n=f
3lgsntrwsʿws [irm t3 Pr-ʿ3ʿws .t] Brnyg3ʿws t3y=f sn.t
t3y=f ḥm.t, irm n3 nty smn.w n ⸢Rʿ⸣-qd. Ḏd Wynn
ms n Kmy Pa-mnḥ s3 N3-nḫṯ=f mw.⸢ṯ⸣(=f) [T3-]šr.t-Ḏḥwṯ n sḥm.t T3-šr.t-Mnṯ
t3 ḫm(.t) ta Gʿy mw.ṯ=s T3-šr.t-Mw.t. ⸢Ḫ3ʿ=y⸣ ṯ.t n ḥm.t. Tw=y ww
⸢r.ḥr= t rn⸣ hp n ḥm.t. Mn mtw[=y] ⸢md⸣ nb p3 t3 i.ir.⸢n⸣=t rn hp
n ḥm.t. Ink p3 nty ḏd n=t: i[.ir] ⸢n⸣[=t] ⸢hy⸣. Bn iw=y rḫ ʿḥʿ ḥ3.ṯ=t r
ʿ.wy nb nty ir=t mr [n šm r.r=w ḏr.w] r ir n=t hy n.im=w.
Iw=y gm.ṯ=t irm rmt nb p3 t3, bn iw=y rḫ ⸢dd⸣ n=t: mtw=t t3y(=y) ḥm.t
n ṯ3y p3 hrw r ḥry šʿ ḏ.t. Sḫ Nḫṯ-Mn s3 Nḫṯ-Mn nty sḫ rn
n3 wʿb.w n Ḥ.t-Ḥr nb In.ty n p3 5 ⸢s3⸣[.w].
Sḫ ⸢Pa⸣-Sbk s3 Wn-nfr.
Sḫ ⸢Nḫṯ-Mn⸣ s3 - -[- - -].

. . . .

---

1 *sw 5* ed., *(sw) 5* legimus 6 *n sḥm.t* ed., *n ḥm.t* Pestman (*Marriage* (1961), p. 72, n. 5)
8 *[n ṯ3y p3 hrw r ḥry]* ed., *[ḏr.w]* supplevimus

Translation

Year 15, 5 Thot, of king Ptolemy (X), also called Alexander, and queen Berenike his sister (and) wife, (and the year of the priests) who are appointed in Rakotis (Alexandria).

Has spoken the Greek, born in Egypt, Pamenos, son of Nechouthes, his mother being Senthotis,

to the woman Senmonthis **(5)** *the younger, daughter of Kaies, her mother being Senmouthis:*

«I have repudiated you as a wife. I am far from you on account of (the) right (to you) as (my) wife. I have nothing in the world to claim of you in the name of the right (to you) as (my) wife.

I am the one who says to you: "take yourself a husband". I will not be able to stand in your way in any place to which you wish to go to take yourself a husband. If I find you together with any man in the world, I will not be able to say to you: "you are my wife", **(10)** *from this day on and afterwards, for ever.»*

Has written Nechthminis, son of Nechthminis, who writes in the name of the priests of Hathor, mistress of Inty, (priests) of the five phyles.

Has written Pasouchos, son of Onnophris.

Has written Nechthminis, son of - - -

- -

Notes

1 *ibd-1 3ḫ.t, first month of the 3ḫ.t-season, Thot*: the scribe has messed around when writing the name of the month, but the reading *3ḫ.t* by W. Spiegelberg is sure.

3 *irm n3 nty smn.w n ⌜Rʿ⌝-qd, and (the priests) who are appointed in Rakotis*: the scribe forgot to add the name of the city Ptolemais after Rakotis.

7-8 *r ʿ.wy*: one rather expects *n ʿ.wy* as found in parallel passages (see Pestman, *Marriage* (1961), p. 72 (Z§13)).

8 *[ḏr.w], all*: for this supplement instead of *[n ṯ3y p3 hrw r ḥry]* (ed.), compare the parallel passage Text 6, l. 9.

10 *šʿ ḏ.t., until eternity, definitively*: the vertical line between *šʿ* and *ḏ.t.* makes no sense here. Apparently, *šʿ ḏ.t.* and *ʿnḫ ḏ.t* (may he live forever) are contaminated.

11 For the reading of Hathor's epithet as *nb In.ty*, "mistress of Inty", see Vandorpe, *Archives from Pathyris* (2001), §2.

12 *⌜Pa⌝-Sbk, Pasouchos*: the reading *Sy-Sbk* (Sisouchos), a name more frequently attested in Pathyris than Pasouchos, is not excluded, but the traces better fit *Pa-Sbk.*

13 *⌜Nḫt-Mn⌝ s3 - -[- - -], Nechthminis, son of - - -*: a small trace of the father's name is visible and fits a name like *Ḥr* (Horos).

9

DEMOTIC MARRIAGE CONTRACT
of Tbokanoupis, granddaughter of Dryton

DESCRIPTION

Pathyris 16 March 95 B.C.

British Museum, P. dem. inv.no. 10514 [bought on 14 March 1899] = **unpublished**. The text will be published in P. dem. BM Shore (The publication was prepared by the late A.F.Shore and will be completed by C.A.R. Andrews). U. Kaplony-Heckel informed me of this text[1] and C.A.R. Andrews was so kind as to show me the original papyrus in the British Museum so that I could summarize the contents of the contract.

Contents. — Dryton's granddaughter Tbokanoupis (pros. 603), daughter of Kaies and Apollonia, marries Phagonis, son of Panebchounis and Kobahetesis, brother of the well-known Peteharsemtheus (see pros. 602). Phagonis is called a herdsman and servant of the god Harsemtheus (see pros. 602).

The marriage contract is a *sẖ n ḥm.t*, a "deed concerning the wife" (see §31). The gift (*šp*) of Phagonis to his wife consists of 100 deben of money (= 2000 drachmas) and 10 artabas of wheat. Among the goods which Tbokanoupis brings along with her are: probably an *in-šn*-veil (lost in the lacuna; see §31), a basin (*qnḏ*) worth 80 deben, a sieve (*mrḫ*) worth 60 deben and a *šš*-jar worth 50 deben[2].

The loan contract is written by Nechthminis, son of Nechthminis, notary of the temple of Hathor in Pathyris in the period 124-94 B.C.[3].

1 See also U. Kaplony-Heckel, in P. dem. Gebelein Heid., p. 11, n. 12.
2 For these goods, see E. Lüddeckens, in P. dem. Eheverträge, p. 289, 300, 294, 299.
3 Pros. Ptol. III and IX 7761; P. dem. Schreibertrad., p. 184, no. 49; addendum: 96-94 B.C.: P. dem. Ackerpachtverträge, p. 55; possible addendum: Text 18 of 128 B.C, see Introdution to this text; see also Text 5, Introduction. The scribe.

II

Loans and receipts

Loans from Pathyris : §33. Study of the loans from Pathyris.

The loans and receipts from the archive of Dyton and his family : §34. The various types of loans and receipts and the place where they were issued. — §35. Some stipulations of the loans: duration, repayment, fine and interest. — §36. Who kept the loans in his archive: creditor or debtor? — §37. Summaries on the back of the loans. — §38. Renewal of an old loan. — §39. Survey of the loans and receipts in the archive of Dryton and his family.

Loans from Pathyris

§33. *Study of the loans from Pathyris.* — A comprehensive study of the Greek and demotic loan contracts found in Pathyris is in course of preparation (Vandorpe, 'Greek and Demotic Loan Contracts from Pathyris' (2001)). In that study, I treat the following subjects:

- *where did the inhabitants of Pathyris negotiate their loans?*
- *a discussion and comparison of the contract clauses of the Greek and demotic loans*

  For the interest-clauses, see also Pestman, 'Loans Bearing no Interest?' (1971), in *JJP* 16-17, p. 7-29 and my article Vandorpe, 'Interest in Ptolemaic Loans' (1998).
- *the registration and the repayment of loans*
- *the summaries on the back*

  See also my article Vandorpe, 'Agoranomic Loans with Demotic Summary' (2000).
- *the size of the contracts and the place of the summary on the back.*

The loans and receipts from the archive of Dyton and his family

The following subjects are discussed in more detail in my comprehensive study of the loans from Pathyris, see §33.

§34. *The various types of loans and receipts and the place where they were issued.* — The loans which are under discussion are consumer loans: they deal with goods which are lost by consumption or use. At the end of the contract, the borrower has to return goods of the same quality and quantity, usually increased by interest. In the archive of Dryton's family the following goods are found: wheat (πυρός or *sw*), barley (κριθή or *it*), spelt (*hrn*), salt (ἅλς) and copper money (see §39).

- *Private arrangements: Greek or demotic acknowledgements of debt and receipts*

For smaller loans creditor and debtor could negotiate a private loan without the interference of a notary. The debtor himself wrote an acknowledgement of debt or, if he was illiterate, a third person did the writing for him; the name of the writer was explicitely mentioned at the end of the acknowledgement. The same goes for the self-written receipts, in which the creditor states that he has received the money or grain due (compare Text 21).

Such a private arrangement is called χειρόγραφον[1] in Greek and *bk* (document)[2] in demotic. It starts with the greeting formula found in letters: ὁ δεῖνα τῶι δεῖνι χαίρειν or *NN p3 nty d̠d n NN (NN is the one who declares to NN)*. Then, the writer of the document addresses himself in the first person to the other party.

The language in which the private arrangements were written depended on the native language of the writer. In Pathyris, the major part of the inhabitants were Egyptians or hellenized Egyptians, who were literate in Egyptian rather than in Greek. The acknowledgements of debt Text 15, 20, 24 and 28 were written by such people. Exceptions are the documents in the hand of the Greek Dryton and his son Esthladas, who wrote Greek well: thus, Esthladas penned the acknowledgement of debt Text 22 in Greek; the name of the writer of the Greek receipt Text 21 is lost in the lacuna. Dryton was asked to draw up the Greek cheirographon App. A.

- *Notarial deeds*

  Demotic notarial temple deeds, written by the temple notary (monographos) or his substitute

  Greek notarial deeds, written by the agoranomos or his substitute

When larger amounts of goods or money were lent, the contracting parties went to a notary. Such a loan contract could be drawn up by the notary of an Egyptian temple or by the Greek notary (agoranomos). For convenience I call both these types of contracts "notarial deeds", although the Egyptian notary is not a notary in the true sense of the word. The deeds he draws up are not automatically registered centrally in contrast with the contracts written in the Greek agoranomeion.

Among the notarial deeds two different types may be distinguished:

1) the deeds of the "long type" are juridically of high importance, such as the sale contracts which are proofs of ownership. For these acts a large sheet of papyrus is cut off and the text has long lines and large margins. The dating formula is comprehensive (with the names and/or titles of the eponymous priests) and the demotic notarial deeds are endorsed with the names of sixteen witnesses (on the verso).
2) the deeds of the "short type" are juridically of less importance, such as the loan contracts (they are valid for only one year on average). The size of the papyrus sheet is smaller and the text has shorter lines and small margins. The dating formula is compact and the demotic notarial deeds have the names of only four witnesses written on the recto of the papyrus.

A demotic notarial deed is called *sẖ*[3] or *smbwl*[4](= σύμβολον) in demotic (see Text 18, verso) and σύμβολον in Greek sources. It was written by the temple notary, called *sẖ* in demotic and

[1] Seidl, *Ptolemäische Rechtsgeschichte* (1962^2), p. 61.

[2] *E.g.*, in P. dem. *Enchoria* 7 (1977), p. 51-54, *bk* is clearly distinguished from *sẖ*, a notarial temple deed; for this type of document in epistolary style (*šʿ.t*), see Depauw, *Companion* (1997), p. 124.

[3] Seidl, *Ptolemäische Rechtsgeschichte* (1962^2), p. 5; Depauw, *Companion* (1997), p. 123-124.

[4] See Clarysse, 'Greek Loan-Words' (1987), no. 78.

monographos in Greek sources. The term monographos points to the fact that there was only one Egyptian notary in each temple who was authorized to issue *sẖ*-documents. Exceptionally, the monographos was replaced by a representative (*rd*), usually his son (see, for instance, Text 12, Introduction). This was often the case in the large temples of Thebes, but this procedure is not found in Pathyris and only once in Pathyris' twin sister Krokodilopolis (see Text 23, l. 24-25)[1]. The clauses of the loans written by the temple notary follow a rigorous scheme. The formulae in the loans of the temple of Pathyris and of Krokodilopolis are very similar, but differ in details which make it possible to identify the temple notary's office should the name of the notary be lost in the lacuna (see my forthcoming study, §33).

With the advent of the Greek agoranomoi who automatically register each contract in the registration office, things change. In the district of Thebes, for instance, the Egyptian notary may go to the registration office where his notarial temple deeds are filed from 145 B.C. onwards. The procedure to be followed for the registration of demotic contracts is described in P. Par. 65[2]. Further examples are to be found in the archive of Dionysios, son of Kephalas, from Akoris[3]: the registration is indicated by ἀναγέγραπται written beneath the document.

There are, however, no clear indications of the registration of notarial temple deeds in Pathyris. There is one text which may point to this practice. A Greek agoranomic deed of 110 B.C.[4] shows that a loan recorded in a notarial temple deed was partly paid off in the office of the Greek agoranomos together with another debt.

A Greek notarial deed is called *sẖ*[5] in demotic (as are the demotic notarial acts) and συγγραφή in Greek sources (a συγγραφὴ δανείου[6] is a Greek notarial loan contract); it is not clear whether *sẖ tnn* (*tnn* = δάνειον[7]) in P. dem. *Enchoria* 7 (1977), p. 51-54, points to a Greek or Egyptian notarial deed. The Greek notarial deeds were written by the Greek agoranomos or his substitute.

Pathyris' twin town Krokodilopolis had its own agoranomeion from c. 141 B.C.[8] onwards. In 136 B.C. at the latest a branch was established in neighbouring Pathyris, where subordinates of the agoranomos of Krokodilopolis were usually active[9]. The Greek notary's office (which was at the same time the registration office, see Vandorpe, *Archives from Pathyris* (2001), §28) was called ἀρχεῖον (*3rghn* in demotic, see Text 21, verso).

---

1 See P. dem. Schreibertrad., p. 3; 182-185; an up-to-date list of the temple notaries of Pathyris (temple of Hathor) and Krokodilopolis (temple of Souchos) is to be found in my forthcoming study, see §33.

2 P.W. Pestman, 'Registration of Demotic Contracts in Egypt. P. Par. 65; 2nd cent. B.C.', in J.A. Ankum *e.a.* (edd.), *Satura Roberto Feenstra*, Freiburg 1985, p. 17-25. In the metropolis of the Fayum, registered demotic contracts were stamped on the verso with red stamps in the late Ptolemaic period, see Vandorpe, 'Seals in and on the Papyri' (1997), p. 254-255.

3 Pap. Lugd. Bat. XXII, p. 25-28.

4 P. Grenf. II 22.

5 See, for instance, the verso of P. Lond. III 1209 and P. Baden II 4.

6 *E.g.*, Text 30, l. 1-2.

7 See Clarysse, 'Greek Loan-Words' (1987), no. 18.

8 The lists of G. Messeri Savorelli and P.W. Pestman (see next note) record a will (P. Grenf. I 12 + SB I 4637) of 151-145 B.C. as the first attestation of an agoranomos in Krokodilopolis. A new fragment of this will shows that it was drawn up in Latopolis and not Krokodilopolis (Text 2, 150 B.C.).

9 A list of the agoranomoi of Krokodilopolis and Pathyris is provided by Messeri Savorelli, 'Lista degli agoranomi' (1980), p. 185-271, and Pestman, 'Agoranomoi' (1985), in Pap. Lugd. Bat. XXIII, p. 9-27.

For additions to these lists of agoranomoi: see Vandorpe, 'Agoranomic Loans with Demotic Summary' (2000) , p. 195, n.4 and p. 199, n. 32.

The Greek notarial deeds were registered automatically. According to P. Adler 5[1] the archive in the registration office of Pathyris, called βιβλιοθήκη, kept copies of the contracts. Such copies are found among the unpublished papyri of the Cairo-collection: they are chronological lists of contracts and they show that the Greek notary makes a copy of the entire contract, except for the protocol (dating formula, place of redaction and name of the agoranomos) and the name of the scribe (mentioned at the end of the contract)[2].

• *The choice between the Greek and Egyptian notary*

Pathyris received a military camp at the end (186 B.C.) or after the rebellion of Hurgonaphor and Chaonnophris in Upper Egypt. As a result, many soldiers settled in this town, among them the grandparents and parents of Dryton's wife Apollonia. In this early period, there was only an Egyptian notary's office (attested from 176 B.C. onwards)[3] of which Apollonia's grandfather Panas (Text 10) and Apollonia herself (Texts 13 and 14) made use. In 141 B.C. at the latest a Greek agoranomos was installed in Krokodilopolis and in 136 B.C. at the latest a branch of the agoranomeion of Krokodilopolis was erected in Pathyris (see above). From then on, the inhabitants of Pathyris could appeal to the Greek notary. Apollonia, who especially after her marriage with Dryton wanted to profile herself as a Greek woman, preferred to go to the Greek notary[4] (Texts 16, 17, 19; exception: Text 18), whereas her son-in-law Kaies who had an Egyptian lifestyle, usually appealed to the Egyptian temple notary (Texts 23, 26, 27; exception: Text 25).

• *Place of redaction of the notarial deeds (Thebes, Pathyris and Krokodilopolis)*

The survey of the loan contracts in the archive of Dryton and his family (§39) show that the family members usually went to the Greek or Egyptian notaries of Pathyris. There are three exceptions. Texts 11 and 12 of 174 and 171 B.C., respectively, are drawn up in Thebes and were kept by Dryton, who at that time lived in or near Thebes (see p. 13). Text 23 is a notarial deed from Krokodilopolis and was added to the archive by Dryton's son-in-law Kaies: the reason why Kaies, who lived in Pathyris, went to the temple notary of Krokodilopolis is clear: he and the debtor both served as soldiers in the military camp of Krokodilopolis.

§35. *Some stipulations of the loans: duration, repayment, fine and interest.* —

• *Loans of corn (wheat and barley)*

Loans of corn from Pathyris are usually negotiated in the period between mid October and mid April, that is during the sowing and growing season. They have to be returned in the same year either in the month of Pachon or on 30 Pachon at the latest, that is mid June, when the corn is harvested.

The quality of the corn to be returned as well as the measure to be used are described. The debtor has to deliver the corn at the house of the creditor at his own expense.

If the loan is not returned in time, the debtor has to pay a fine. The notarial temple deeds and the acknowledgements of debt mention a fine of 50%, whereas the Greek notarial acts

---

1 See Pestman, 'Agoranomoi' (1985), in Pap. Lugd. Bat. XXIII, p. 43 §8.
2 See Vandorpe, *Archives from Pathyris* (2001), §28.
3 P. dem. Schreibertrad., p. 3; 217-222; Vandorpe, 'Outline of Greco-Roman Thebes' (1995), p. 231.
4 See Vandorpe, 'Apollonia, a Businesswoman' (2001).

demand a fine of either 50% or the current market price. Apparently, the price of the corn might fluctuate by more than 50%.

With few exceptions Greek loans drawn up by the agoranomos of Pathyris are ἄτοκα or ἄτοκος,"without interest": "NN has lent to NN *x* artabas of wheat ἄτοκα or ἀτόκους". The use of the adverb (ἄτοκα) or adjective (ἄτοκος) is misleading. Initially, scholars thought that such loans were loans on which no interest was paid[1]. Almost all Greek loans written in Pathyris or in neighbouring Krokodilopolis are, however, ἄτοκα or ἄτοκος loans, whereas the major part of the demotic loans stipulate that the interest is already included in the amount due: "I owe you *x* artabas of wheat, while their addition (*viz.* interest) is in them". Pestman[2] rightly pointed out that ἄτοκα loans were loans without interest only in the rarest of cases, the occasional act of kindness among friends or family[3], but that they were usually loans with interest included. In Pathyris the term ἄτοκα or ἄτοκος must be the Greek counterpart of demotic *iw p3j=w ḥw ẖn.w*, "while their addition (*viz.* interest) is in them".

It is generally assumed that the interest for loans in kind amounts to 50%.[4] This seems to be confirmed by the expression σὺν ἡμιολίᾳ, used in several loans chiefly of the Roman period.[5] In Ptolemaic Pathyris this phrase is, however, never used in loans made in kind. Moreover, some loans of seed-corn are, apparently, not issued with an interest of 50%, but rather with an (annually) varying interest, related to the harvest to be expected in a particular year (*e.g.*, Text 24). This practice is discussed in my article Vandorpe, 'Interest in Ptolemaic Loans' (1998).

• *Loans of copper money*

In the second century B.C. copper money became greatly devaluated in comparison to silver money[6] (which at that time was only recorded in fiscal fines). Therefore, it was advisable to state explicitly that copper money was lent: χαλκοῦ (Text 19; 21) or χαλκοῦ νομίσματος (Text 17) might be added in Greek loans. Demotic loans have *ḥd*, in origin a term for silver but in the second century B.C. used for (a deben) of copper money; *ḥḏ sp-sn* (real silver)[7] becomes the regular term for silver money.

Money loans from Pathyris were negotiated by the month (Text 19: 5 months), apparently since the interest rate was fixed by the month (see below). The loan does not, however, always last exactly one or more months: Text 19, for instance, is drawn up on 15 Phaophi (7 November), whereas the loan is valid "from Phaophi onwards".

---

1 See, for instance, the far-reaching conclusions drawn by E.N. Adler, who considers interest-free loans proof of Jewish influence (P. Adler, p. 5-6).

2 See Pestman, 'Loans Bearing no Interest?' (1971), in *JJP* 16-17, p. 7-29; see also Depauw, *Companion* (1997), p. 147.

3 In Pathyris this could be the case in agoranomic homologiai, where family members agree on an ἄτοκα-loan of money (*e.g.*, P. Lond. III 1203).

4 See Pestman, 'Loans Bearing no Interest?' (1971), in *JJP* 16-17, p. 9.

5 N. Lewis, 'The Meaning of σὺν ἡμιολίᾳ and Kindred Expressions in Loan Contracts', in *TAPhA* 76 (1945), p. 126-139.

6 See Reekmans, 'Ptolemaic Copper Inflation' (1951), p. 111; H. Cadell and G. Le Rider, *Prix du blé et numéraire dans l'Égypte lagide de 305 à 173* (Pap. Brux. 30), Bruxelles 1997.

7 See P.W. Pestman, in *Enchoria* 2 (1972), p. 33-36.

If the loan is not returned in time, a fine of 50% of the total amount lent is imposed. In addition, the customary interest of 2% (see below) is to be paid for each month that the loan is not paid off.

It is generally assumed that Ptolemy II introduced a maximum interest rate of 2% per month, that is 24% a year (250-245 B.C.)[1]. There are no exact data on the interest rate in money loans from Pathyris, since the interest is nowhere explicitely mentioned, but is always included in the sum to be returned. The high interest rate of 5% a month found in Text 19 according to the first editor[2], is based on a misreading: the text does not mention an interest rate of 5% a month, but a duration of 5 months. One may assume that in Pathyris the legal interest rate of 2% a month was valid. This may be confirmed by a loan from Pathyris referring to the above-mentioned ruling of Ptolemy II[3]. In addition, the penalty clause in Pathyris' money loans foresees a supplementary interest of 2% a month for each month that the loan is not paid off (*e.g.*, Text 19).

• *Loan of spelt and of salt*

For the loan of spelt, see Text 13. Only one loan of salt is found in Pathyris. For this type of loan, see Text 29.

§36. *Who kept the loans in his archive: creditor or debtor?* —

• *Greek notarial deeds*

The Greek notarial deeds were kept by the creditor as long as the loan was not paid off. What happened when the debt was repaid? First, the repayment was registered by the Greek notary. The archive of Dionysios, son of Kephalas[4], from Akoris, shows that the loan contract was then handed over to the debtor. In addition, the creditor might add a receipt acknowledging that the debt was paid off. In Pathyris, things went different. There are different possible scenarios.

The loan contract stays with the creditor

The preserved family archives, among them the archive of Dryton's family, show that Greek notarial deeds were kept by the creditor even after the repayment of the debt. One has to conclude that the debtor in turn received a receipt in which the creditor acknowledges that the debt has been paid off: the registration of the repayment (in the archeion) and the receipt were his guarantees.

The archive of Dryton's family contains one nice example illustrating this procedure: Text 21 is a private receipt, according to the demotic summary on the back, written in the archeion (*3rghn*, that is in the notary's office), undoubtedly on the occasion of the repayment of the debt. It was kept in the archive of the former debtor Esthladas, Dryton's son.

---

1 See Pestman, 'Loans Bearing no Interest?' (1971), in *JJP* 16-17, p. 7-9.

2 This reading has been taken over by Lewis, *Greeks in Ptolemaic Egypt* (1986), p. 96.

3 SB VI 9366.

4 Pap. Lugd. Bat. XXII 23-31.

The loan contract is handed over to the debtor

In a few cases the loan contract is handed over to the debtor. One such example from the archive of Dryton's family is Text 11, though this loan was negotiated in Thebes, not in Pathyris.

The loan contract is handed over to the debtor and a receipt is added

There are two examples from Pathyris where the creditor handed over the notarial deed to the debtor and added beneath the contract a receipt in which he acknowledges that the debt has been repaid. One example is Text 29 and the second example is discussed in the introduction to Text 29. In both cases the repayment of the loan took place in special circumstances which are clarified in the receipt: in one case the repayment was made not to the creditor but to a son of the creditor and in the other case the repayment was too late so that a fine was probably paid; in the latter case, the notarial deed was crossed out.

An new notarial deed is drawn up in which the repayment is confirmed

In exceptional cases, a new notarial deed was drawn up by the agoranomos confirming the repayment. Such a document is called an *epilysis* or *katabole* and is only issued in special cases, for instance when the loan is paid off too late or when only part of the loan is returned. Such notarial deeds are not found in the family archive of Dryton[1].

• *Demotic notarial temple deeds and acknowledgements of debt*

The notarial temple deeds and the private acknowledgements of debt were kept by the creditor or by a third person as long as the loan was not paid off. The notarial temple deeds record two possible scenarios once the loan was returned: either the contract was handed over to the debtor or the debtor receives a receipt recording that the debt is paid off. The major part of the notarial temple deeds in the family archive of Dryton are kept by the creditor (Texts 12, 13, 14, 18, 23, 26, 27); the debtor apparently received a receipt. There is one exception: Text 10 of 164 B.C. has been handed over to the debtor. Similar scenarios are to be assumed for the private acknowledgements of debt. The demotic acknowledgements of debt Texts 15, 20, 24 and 28 stayed with the creditor, whereas the Greek acknowledgement of debt Text 22 was returned to the debtor.

With the advent of the Greek agoranomoi, who automatically register each contract in the local registration office, things change. Since 145 B.C. the Egyptian temple notaries in, for instance, the district of Thebes might go to the registration office where their notarial temple deeds were filed. There are, however, no clear indications of the registration of these documents in Pathyris (see §34). If these types of loan and the returning of the loan were indeed registered, then the debtor had an extra guarantee to proof his repayment.

§37. *Summaries on the back of the loans.* — After loan contracts had been drawn up, the Greek notaries (or their subordinates) of Krokodilopolis and Pathyris usually wrote a Greek summary on the back, that is on one of the two sides of the rolled papyrus: this summary is

---

1 For examples from Pathyris, see my forthcoming study, see in §33.

usually written in two columns and records, among other things, the names of the creditor(s) and debtor(s) as well as the object loaned (Texts 16; 17; 19; 25; 29).

On the side of the verso which was left blank, the Egyptian holder of the contract (usually the creditor) might add a demotic summary containing the name of the debtor(s), the object loaned and the year in which the loan had to be paid off (no examples are found in the family archive of Dryton).

Both types of summary on the loan contracts of Krokodilopolis and Pathyris are discussed in my article Vandorpe, 'Agoranomic Loans with Demotic Summary' (2000).

The demotic notarial temple deeds do not contain a summary made by the Egyptian monographos. These temple deeds as well as the private arrangements may, however, contain a summary made by the keeper of the document, that is the creditor (who mentions the name of the debtor: Greek summary in Text 12 and Text 20; demotic summary in Text 24) or a third party (who mentions the names of the creditor and debtor: demotic summary in Text 18); in case of a receipt the debtor may have added a summary (demotic summary in Text 21).

§38. *Renewal of an old loan.* — A loan could be renewed when the debtor or creditor died before the debt was paid off. Examples from Pathyris are:

P. dem. Gebelein Heid. 24: renewal of an older loan negotiated by a (grand)father of the debtor .

P. dem. Ryl. 21 is a similar case: the loan is issued *n rn pr.w i.ir(=y) gm.t=w r NN p3y yt*, "in the name of the grains which I found with NN, my father".

P. Grenf. II 27 registers the renewal of a part (5,100 drachmas) of an old loan of 11,200 drachmas. The new loan contract is made with the father of the former creditor who is apparently deceased.

Finally, the fragmentary agoranomic contract Text 30 may record the renewal of (?a part of) an old loan (of ?200+x artabas, see comm. on l. 4) of wheat. The debtor of the old loan was a relative of the mother of the new debtors whose names are lost in the lacuna.

§39. *Survey of loans and receipts in the archive of Dryton and his family.* —

Loan involving Panas, grandfather of Apollonia

Text 10	is debtor	Wheat+barley	Dem. notarial temple deed	Pathyris	164

Loans involving Dryton

Text 11	is debtor	Wheat	Greek notarial deed	Thebes	10 Oct. 174
Text 12	is creditor	Money	Dem. notarial temple deed	Thebes	1 Sept. 171

Loans involving Apollonia
(in the period before 136 B.C., when no Greek notary's office was found in Pathyris)

Text 13	is creditor	Spelt	Dem. notarial temple deed	[Pathyris]	145-143/142
Text 14	is creditor	Corn	Dem. notarial temple deed	[Pathyris]	143/142-138/137
Text 15	is creditor	Wheat	Dem. acknowledgment of debt	-	6 Oct. 139

Loans involving Apollonia (in the period after 136 B.C., when a Greek notary's office was erected in Pathyris)

Text 16	is creditor	Wheat	Greek notarial deed	Pathyris	4 Jan. 131
Text 17	is creditor	Money	Greek notarial deed	Pathyris	14 May 129
Text 18	is creditor	?	Dem. notarial temple deed	[ ]	17 March 128
Text 19	is creditor	Money	Greek notarial deed	Pathyris	7 Nov. 127
Text 20	is creditor	Barley	Dem. acknowledgment of debt	-	after 150

Loans involving Esthladas

Text 21	is debtor	Money	Greek receipt	-	after 140
Text 22	is debtor	?	Greek acknowledgment of debt	-	after 140

Loans involving Kaies

Text 23	is creditor	Money	Dem. notarial temple deed	Krokodilopolis	124-116
Text 24	is creditor	Barley	Dem. acknowledgment of debt	-	12 Sept. 118
Text 25	is creditor	Wheat	Greek notarial deed	Pathyris	4 Jan. 117
Text 26	is creditor	Wheat	Dem. notarial temple deed	Pathyris	16 Oct. 116
Text 27	is creditor	Wheat	Dem. notarial temple deed	Pathyris	12 Febr. 112
Text 28	is creditor	Barley	Dem. acknowledgment of debt	-	after 135

Loan involving Phagonis

Text 29	is debtor	Salt	Greek notarial deed	Pathyris	12 Sept. 105

Renewal of a loan involving a descendant of Dryton?

Text 30	is debtor	Wheat	Greek notarial deed	Pathyris	131-113

10

DEMOTIC LOAN OF WHEAT AND BARLEY
to Panas, grandfather of Apollonia

DESCRIPTION

Pathyris 18 Jan. 164 B.C.

British Museum, P. dem. inv.no. 10515 [bought on 14 March 1899] = **unpublished**. The text will be published in P. dem. BM Shore (The publication was prepared by the late A.F.Shore and will be completed by C.A.R. Andrews). U. Kaplony-Heckel informed me of this text and C.A.R. Andrews was so kind as to show me the original papyrus in the British Museum so that I could summarize the contents of the loan.

Contents. — On 18 Jan. 164 B.C.[1] Panas (pros. 205), son of Nechthyris and Kalibis[2] (pros. 102-103), borrows 54 artabas of wheat and 14 artabas of barley together with four other people. The loan has to be repaid before 30 Pachon (mid-June) 164 B.C., after the harvest.

The Greek name of the lender is damaged; he is a son of Theon. He is a Greek, citizen of Ptolemais (in the Thebaid)[3], a man receiving pay among the cavalrymen. All these data make it possible to identify him with an inhabitant of Pathyris: Isidoros son of Theon, alias Paesis son of Teos[4], who bears the same titles. This Isidoros is possibly the father of Zois alias Onchasis, mentioned in Text 21 (after 140 B.C.)

The loan contract is written by [Thotortaios], son of Nechthminis, notary of the temple of Hathor in Pathyris at that time (see Text 3, comm. on l. 48). On the verso, the names of eight witnesses are preserved.

Part of the archive of Dryton, Apollonia and their offspring. — When the loan was repaid, the contract was most probably handed over to Panas, the debtor first named. The contract was kept in the archive of one of his descendants. Two of these archives are preserved: the archive of which the Erbstreit-dossier is part (see Vandorpe, *Archives from Pathyris* (2001), §37) and the archive of his granddaughter Apollonia, which was added to that of her husband Dryton. The museum archaeology strongly suggests that the loan is part if the latter archive. Thus, the loan first passed from Panas (pros. 205) to his oldest son Ptolemaios (pros. 304) and later from Ptolemaios, who did not have a son, to his oldest daughter Apollonia (pros. 404).

---

1 Compare P.W. Pestman, in Pap. Lugd. Bat. XV, p. 51.
2 This is the only text which mentions the name of the mother of Panas (see pros. 102).
3 Compare Text 12, where in a demotic loan Dryton is also called a Greek, citizen of Ptolemais; see also pros. 403.
4 Pros. Ptol. II and VIII 2215, 2549 and *4219 = IV 12371, *12377 and 12389; P.W. Pestman, 'Pathyris II' (1963), in *Aegyptus* 43, p. 15-33, no. 27; P.W. Pestman, in Pap. Lugd-Bat. XIX, p. 212.

11

GREEK LOAN OF WHEAT
to Dryton

Diospolis Megale	H. x W. = 16.5 x 17.8 cm [Width incomplete]	10 Oct. 174 B.C.

British Library, P. inv.no. 605 Recto [bought on 9 Nov. 1895 from Grenfell] = **P. Grenf. I 10**. For the literary text on the verso, see **Text 50**.
Photograph. — No photograph available.

Description. — After the redaction of the contract, the papyrus was rolled from the right to the left. As a consequence, the right part of the recto, which was on the inside of the roll, is well preserved. The vertical folds are barely visible. The left-hand side, on the contrary, which was on the outside of the roll, is either broken off and lost or badly damaged along the vertical folds.

The agoranomos of Diospolis Megale wrote the loan contract on the recto of the papyrus, along the fibres, with a top margin of 1.2 cm, a bottom margin of 2.3 cm and a right-hand margin of 6 cm; the left-hand margin is lost. Afterwards, Dryton copied a hellenistic poem on the back of the papyrus (Text 50), written against the fibres.

The papyrus is of poor quality: on the recto as well as on the verso the fibres do not always run perfectly parallel. On the back fibres are sometimes missing, as a consequence of which the underlying fibres of the recto are visible; when copying the poem Text 50 on the verso-side of the contract, Dryton has sometimes avoided writing on these underlying fibres, sometimes he did not.

Introduction

Contents. — The soldier Sosistratos, infantryman of the [- - -]τάξεως and taktomisthos (see comment on l. 8), lends the high amount of 100 artabas of wheat — either with or without interest (l. 10) — to Dryton, son of Pamphilos, and to another man whose name is lost in the lacuna of l. 12, but whose father is also called Pamphilos. Dryton was at the time at least 18 years old (pros. 403); the other debtor was 22 years old (l. 22). The latter could have been a brother of Dryton, belonging, however, to another deme of the city of Ptolemais: he is Σωστρατεύς (pros. 02), whereas Dryton belongs to the deme Philoteris. The loan begins on 10 Oct. and runs for nine months: after the harvest, in the month of Payni, the loan has to be returned.

The scribe. — The name of the agoranomos who drew up the contract or was assisted by one of his subordinates, is lost in the lacuna of l. 7. There was apparently only one Greek notary's office for the Perithebas and the Pathryites at that early date (174 B.C.), since the notary is called τοῦ πρὸς τῆ]ι ἀγορανομίαι τοῦ Περιθήβας καὶ Παθυρίτου[1]. See further below, The clauses of the contract (#6).

---

[1] See Pestman, 'Agoranomoi' (1985), in Pap. Lugd. Bat. XIII, p. 9 and n. 1.

The well-cared-for handwriting is very similar to the handwritings of the 3rd century B.C.: the scribe observes the tendency to horizontal distortion along the upper-line and does not yet link letters as much as is usual during the second half of the 2nd century B.C.

The clauses of the contract. — Text 11 will not be discussed in my study on the loan contracts from Pathyris or Krokodilopolis (see §33), since it is a contract from Thebes. A first important difference is that the loans from Pathyris are all contracts of the "short type", whereas Text 11 is of the "long type" (see §34): that implies that a different sheet format is used and that in Text 11 the protocol with the eponymous priests and the clauses of the contract are more elaborate. Other differences from the Pathyris-contracts are indicated below:

- *Clause #1: protocol* (l. 1-7)

  Text 11 does not only mention the date, the place of redaction and the name of the agoranomos, but also the names of the reigning kings and the titles of the eponymous priests in Alexandria and Ptolemais.

- *Clause #2*: *the actual acknowledgement of debt* (l. 8-13), with the names of the contractants, the mention of the loan object and the interest.

  Contrary to most documents from Pathyris, Text 11 records the physical description of the contractants and the loan object is mentioned before and not after the debtor's name. The duration of the loan of wheat is explicitely mentioned (9 months, l. 10), whereas in Pathyris this is only the case when a loan of money is dealt with. Data on the interest (included or excluded) are, unfortunately, lost in the lacuna of l. 10.

- *Clause #3: returning the loan* (l. 13-15), containing details on the time when and the condition in which the loan object has to be returned.

  This clause, which is partly lost in the lacuna, is very similar to that found in contracts from Pathyris, except for some details: instead of τὸ δὲ δάνειον τοῦτο ἀποδότωσαν it has τὸ δὲ δάν̣[ειο]ν τοῦτο τῶν πυρῶν ἀποδότωσαν, and it states that the wheat has to be [ἀκίνδυνον ἀ]πὸ παντὸς κινδύν̣[ου], which corresponds to the expression ἄδολον ἀπὸ παντός found in some deeds from Pathyris.

- *Clause #4 : penalty* (l. 15-18)

  The occasion on which a fine has to be paid is more elaborate in Text 11 in comparison to the deeds from Pathyris. The debtors have to pay the fine if they do not return the loan in time, or if they do not act nor measure the wheat as stipulated in the contract, or if they pledge things which were listed in the lacuna of l. 17. The amount of the fine is partly lost, but is most probably the same as that found in deeds from Pathyris: (1) the amount borrowed (*viz.* 100 artabas) with a surplus of 50% or (2) the valid market price (if higher than the amount borrowed increased by 50%).

- *Clause #5: sureties* (l. 18-19)

  The creditor can hold responsible (πρᾶξις) the debtor of his choice and can have a claim on the entire property of the debtors. The same πρᾶξις-clause is found in loans from Pathyris. In Text 11 there is, however, no space left to supplement the expression καθάπερ ἐγ δίκης, "as if there were a legal decision", a fixed part of the πρᾶξις-clause.

• *Clause omitted in deeds from Pathyris* (l. 19):
[καὶ μηθὲν] ἧσσον ἡ [συγγραφὴ ἥδε] κυρία ἔστω ἐφ' οὗ ἂν ἐπιφέρηται, "and nevertheless this contract shall be valid wherever it will be presented".

This so-called κυρία-clause ἡ συγγραφὴ ἥδε κυρία ἔστω, sometimes followed by an expression like ἐφ' οὗ ἂν ἐπιφέρηται, is often found in loan contracts and stipulates that the deed is valid wherever it is presented[1].

The first part μηθὲν ἧσσον (nothing less, nevertheless) causes some problems. The expression καὶ μηθὲν ἧσσον occurs in *loan contracts*, where it is part of clause #4, the penalty clause intended for the debtor: "the debtor has to pay (an amount) and nothing less"[2]. In *other types of contracts*, but not in loan contracts, it can introduce the κυρία-clause: καὶ μηθὲν ἧσσον ἡ συγγραφὴ ἥδε κυρία ἔστω. The expression than is preceded by a penalty clause which records that the person who does not keep to the stipulations of the contract, has to pay a fine[3]. Μηθὲν ἧσσον, "nevertheless", *viz.* although the stipulations of the contract are not observed, the contract remains valid because of the κυρία-clause. In the loan Text 11 μηθὲν ἧσσον is, however, preceded by the πρᾶξις-clause (clause #5), to which it cannot refer. In all probability the scribe made a slip of the pen and took over the μηθὲν ἧσσον in the κυρία-clause from other types of contracts.

• *Clause #6: name of the scribe and/ or agoranomos?* (l. 20)
In Pathyris the official who dealt with the deed wrote his name beneath the body of the contract. It is not sure whether this is also the case in Text 11. In any case, the contract ends in l. 19 with the appropriate clause ἡ [συγγρ(αφὴ) ἥδε] κυρία ἔστω ἐφ' οὗ ἂν ἐπιφέρηται. The last line of the recto (l. 20), of which only some letters are preserved, most probably contained the name of the scribe and/ or the agoranomos (Ammonios?). It was perhaps written by a second hand.

---

1 On the κυρία-clause, see P.W. Pestman, in Pap. Lugd. Bat. XXII, p. 28-30.

2 See Berger, *Die Strafklauseln* (1911), p. 49, n. 2; according to P.W. Pestman (in Pap. Lugd. Bat. XXII, p. 185) the expression μηθὲν ἧσσον. is wrongly used.

3 See Berger, *Die Strafklauseln* (1911), p. 47-50.

Text

[Βασιλεύοντος Πτολεμαίου τοῦ Πτολεμαίου καὶ Κλεοπάτρας θεῶν Ἐπι]φανῶν ἔτ̣ους ὀγδόου, ἐφ' ἱερέως τοῦ ὄντὸς
[ἐν Ἀλεξανδρείαι Ἀλεξάνδρου καὶ θεῶν Σωτήρων καὶ θεῶν Ἀδελφῶν κ]αὶ θεῶν Εὐεργετῶν καὶ θεῶν Φιλοπατόρων
[καὶ θεῶν Ἐπιφανῶν καὶ θεῶν Φιλομητόρων, ἀθλοφόρου Βερενίκης Εὐερ]γέτιδος, κανηφόρου Ἀρσινόης Φιλαδέλφου, ἱερείας
[Ἀρσινόης Φιλοπάτορος τῶν οὐσῶν ἐν Ἀλεξανδρείαι, ἐν δὲ Πτολεμαίιδι] τῆς Θηβαίιδος ἐ[φ' ἱ]ε̣ρέων Πτολεμαίου μὲν
[Σωτῆρος, Πτολεμαίου δὲ θεοῦ Ἐπιφανοῦς καὶ Εὐχαρίστου - 8 to 11 -]ου, βασιλέως δὲ Πτολεμαίου καὶ Κλεοπάτρας
[τῆς μητρὸς θεᾶς Ἐπιφανοῦς, κανηφόρου Ἀρσινόης Φιλαδέλφου τῆς ο]ὔσης ἐν Πτολεμαίιδι, μηνὸς Θωὺθ πέμ<π>τηι
[ἐν Διὸς πόλει τῆι μεγάληι τῆς Θηβαίιδος ἐπὶ - 8 to 11 - τοῦ πρὸς τῆ]ι ἀγορανομίαι τοῦ Περιθήβας καὶ Παθυρίτου.
['Εδάνεισεν Σωσίστρατος - 33 to 36 -]τάξεως πεζῶν τακτόμισθος, ὡς ἐτῶν
[- 48 to 51 - ἐ]πίγρυπος ὦτ' ἀπεστηκότα οὐλὴ καρπῶι δεξιῶι,
[πυροῦ ἀρτάβας ἑκατὸν - 23 to 26 - ἀπὸ] τοῦ̣ π̣ρογεγραμμένο[υ] χρόνου εἰς μ̣ῆνας ἐννέα, ⟦Δρύτωνι⟧
[Δρύτωνι Παμφίλου Φιλωτερείωι ὡς ἐτῶν .. μέσωι λευκ]όχρ[ωι] τετανῶι ⟦ . ⟧ μ[α]κροπροσώπωι ἀνασίλλωι ἐπιγρύ-
[πωι οὐλὴ παρ' ὀφρῦν ἀριστερὰν ἄκραν, καὶ - 10 to 13 - Πα]μφίλου Σωστρατεῖ [ὡ]ς ἐτῶν εἴκοσι δύο εὐμεγέθει μελίχρωι
[- 39 to 42 - κοιλο]γενείωι. Τὸ δὲ δάν̣[ειο]ν τοῦτο τῶν πυρῶν ἀποδότωσαν
[οἱ δεδανεισμένοι ἐν μηνὶ Παῦνι πυρὸν νέον ἀκίνδυνον ἀ]πὸ παντὸς κινδύν̣[ου] μ̣έτρωι ὧι καὶ παρειλήφασιν καὶ ἀπο-
[καταστησάτωσαν εἰς οἶκον πρὸς αὐτὸν τοῖς ἰδίοις ἀν]ηλώμασ[ιν]· ἐ̣[ὰν δὲ οἱ] περὶ τὸν Δρύτωνα μὴ ἀποκατασ-
[τήσωσι τὰς τοῦ πυροῦ ἀρτάβας ἐν τῶι ὡρισμένωι χρόνωι ἢ] μὴ π[οι]ῶσ[ι καθότι] γέγραπται ἢ παρὰ [τ]ὴν γεγενημέ-
[νην συγγραφὴν μετρῶσιν ἢ - 25 to 28 - ἐνεχυράσ]ωσιν, [ἀποτεισάτ]ωσαν οἱ περὶ τὸν Δρύτωνα τὰς ἑκατὸν
[ἀρτάβας ἡμιολίους ἢ τὴν ἐσομένην ἐν τῆι ἀγορᾶι τιμὴν] καὶ ἡ [πρᾶξις ἔστω Σ]ωσιστράτωι ἐξ ἑνὸς καὶ ἑκάστου
[αὐτῶν καὶ ἐκ τῶν ὑπαρχόντων αὐτοῖς πάντων καὶ μηθὲν] ἧσσον ἡ [συγγραφὴ ἥδε] κυρία ἔστω ἐφ' οὗ ἂν ἐπιφέρηται.
2nd H ?: [- 42 to 45 - Ἀμ]μ̣ωνίου̣[- c. 11 -] . ς

---

1 [Πτολεμαίου τοῦ ἐκ Πτολεμαίου] ed., [Πτολεμαίου τοῦ Πτολεμαίου] supplevimus 3 [θεοῦ Φιλομήτορος] ed., [θεῶν Φιλομητόρων] Kornemann (P. Giss. 2, p. 4) 4 [Πτολεμαίδι] ed., [Πτολεμαίιδι] supplevimus; Θηβαΐδος ed., Θηβαίιδος Hunt (BL I, p. 178) 5 [καὶ Πτολεμαίου Ἐπιφανοῦς Εὐχαρίστου] ed., [Πτολεμαίου δὲ θεοῦ Ἐπιφανοῦς καὶ Εὐχαρίστου] supplevimus 6 [θεᾶς Ἐπιφανοῦς] suppl. Hunt (BL I, p. 178); Πτολεμαίδι ed., Πτολεμαίιδι Wilcken (BL I, p. 178);

πέμπτηι ed., πέμ<π>τηι legimus 7 [ἐν - c. 15 - τοῦ Παθυρίτου ἐπί] ed., [ἐν Διὸς πόλει τῆι μεγάληι ἐπί] Gerhard (*Philologus* 64 (1905), p. 556); [ἐν Διὸς πόλει τῆι μεγάληι τῆς Θηβαίιδος ἐπί] supplevimus 8 [ ]τάξεως ed., [συν(?)]τάξεως Lesquier (*Institutions militaires* (1911), p. 92 et 99) 10 [πυροῦ ἀρτάβας ἑκατόν] supplevimus 11 [Φιλωτερείωι] suppl. Winnicki (*Eos* 60 (1972), p. 345, n. 10) 12 [οὐλὴ παρ' ὀφρὺν δεξιάν] ed., [οὐλὴ παρ' ὀφρὺν ἀριστερὰν ἄκραι] BL VIII, p. 140 14 [οἱ δεδανεισμένοι ἐν μηνὶ Παῦνι νέον] ed., [οἱ δεδανεισμένοι ἐν μηνὶ Παῦνι πυρὸν νέον] supplevimus; [καθαρὸν ἀ]πὸ παντὸς κ[αὶ ἀ]κινδύ[νου] ed., [ἀκίνδυνον ἀ]πὸ παντὸς κινδύν̣[ου] Wilcken et Hunt (BL I, p. 178); παρειλήφασι ed., παρειλήφασιν Wilcken (BL I, p. 178) 14-15 ἀπο|[καθεστάμενον] ed., ἀπο|[καταστησάτωσαν] Wessely (BL I, p. 178) 15 [τοῖς ἀν]ηλώμασ[ιν] ed., [τοῖς ἰδίοις ἀν]ηλώμασ[ιν] supplevimus 16 [τὰς τοῦ πυροῦ ἀρτ(άβας) ἐν τῶι ὡρισμένωι χρόνωι] suppl. Berger (*Die Strafklauseln* (1911), p. 108) 17 [συγγραφὴν μετρῶσιν ἢ - 25 to 28 - ἐνεχυράσ]ωσιν suppl. Wessely (BL I, p. 178); [ἀποτινέτ]ωσαν ed., [ἀποτεισάτ]ωσαν Witkowski (BL I, p. 178) 18 [ἡμιολίους ἢ τὴν ἐσομένην ἐν τῆι ἀγορᾶι τιμήν] suppl. Berger (*Die Strafklauseln* (1911), p. 108) 19 [καὶ ἐκ τῶν ὑπαρχόντων αὐτῶν πάντων καὶ μηδέν] suppl. Berger (*Die Strafklauseln* (1911), p. 108), [καὶ ἐκ τῶν ὑπαρχόντων αὐτοῖς πάντων καὶ μηθέν] supplevimus; ἥ[δε ἡ συγγραφή] suppl. Berger (*Die Strafklauseln* (1911), p. 108), ἡ [συγγραφὴ ἥδε] supplevimus 20 [- - - 'Αμ]μωνίου [- - -]ως, ed., [τόπου - - - 'Αμ]μωνίου [- - -]ως suppl. Wessely (BL I, p. 178), [- 41 to 43 - 'Αμ]μωνίου [- ± 11 -].ς legimus et supplevimus

Translation

In the reign of Ptolemy (VI), son of Ptolemy (V) and Kleopatra (I), the Gods Epiphaneis, year 8,

at the time of the office of the priest who is (appointed) in Alexandria, (viz. the priest) of Alexander, the Gods Soteres, the Gods Adelphoi, the Gods Euergetai, the Gods Philopatores, the Gods Epiphaneis and the Gods Philometores;

(at the time of the office of) the athlophoros of Berenike Euergetis;

(at the time of the office of) the kanephoros of Arsinoe Philadelphos;

(at the time of the office of) the priestess of Arsinoe Philopator: the priestesses who are (appointed) in Alexandria;

in Ptolemais in the Thebaid,

(at the time of the office of) the priests of Ptolemy Soter, Ptolemy the God Epiphanes and Eucharistos - - -, king Ptolemy, Kleopatra, the mother, the Goddess Epiphanes;

(at the time of the office of) the kanephoros of Arsinoe Philadelphos, the priestess who is appointed in Ptolemais,

in the month of Thoth, the 5th day, in Diospolis Megale in the Thebaid, before - - - , who is at the head of the agoranomia in the Perithebas and Pathyrite nome.

Has lent Sosistratos - - - of - - - ? troop, of the infantrymen, taktomisthos, about - - - years old - - - , with a hooked nose, a protruding ear (and) a scar on his right wrist, 100 artabas of wheat - - - from the above-mentioned time onwards for nine months, to Dryton, son of Pamphilos, of the deme Philoteris, about - - - years old, of medium stature, with fair complexion, with straight hair, a long face, hair brushed up, a hooked nose (and) a scar at the top of his left eyebrow, (and)

to - - - , son of Pamphilos, Sostrateus, about 22 years old, tall, with honey-coloured complexion - - - with a dimple in his chin.

The borrowers shall return this loan of wheat in the month of Payni, in wheat that is new, guaranteed against all risk, by the measure they have employed and they shall deliver it to him at his house at their own expense.

If Dryton and his companion(s) fail to return the artabas of wheat within the stated time and if they do not act as prescribed nor measure out as stipulated in the contract or pledge - - -, Dryton and his companion(s) shall return the 100 artabas increased by 50% or the market price valid at the time. Sositratos shall have the right of execution upon each and every one of them and upon all their property. This contract is nevertheless valid wherever it shall be presented.

2nd H?: - - - *? Ammonios - - -*

Notes

1 [Πτολεμαίου τοῦ Πτολεμαίου]: the editor supplies [Πτολεμαίου τοῦ ἐκ Πτολεμαίου]; our supplement without ἐκ finds its parallel in texts from the same period: BGU XIV 2382, P. Amh. II 43, P. Mich. III 190, P. Tebt. III 819 and P. Tebt. III 979.

4 [Πτολεμαίιδι] (ed. [Πτολεμαίδι]): I supply this etymological writing on the basis of l. 4 Θηβαίιδος and l. 6 Πτολεμαίιδι, see my comment on Θηβαίιδος, l. 4.

Θηβαίιδος: for the use of this etymological writing instead of the common form Θηβαίδος, see Mayser, *Grammatik* I.1, p. 85; a similar etymological writing is found in Πτολεμαίιδι, l. 6.

5 [Πτολεμαίου δὲ θεοῦ Ἐπιφανοῦς καὶ Εὐχαρίστου] (ed. [καὶ Πτολεμαίου Ἐπιφανοῦς Εὐχαρίστου]): for the addition δέ instead of καί, see Text 2, l. 9; for the supplement καὶ Εὐχαρίστου instead of Εὐχαρίστου, compare SB V 8876.

6 πέμ<π>τηι (ed. πέμπτηι): for the omission of the *pi* in the groop μπτ, see Mayser, *Grammatik* I.1, p. 152.

7 [ἐν Διὸς πόλει τῆι μεγάληι τῆς Θηβαίιδος ἐπὶ] (Gerhard [ἐν Διὸς πόλει τῆι μεγάληι ἐπὶ]): my additional supplement τῆς Θηβαίιδος, based on P. Stras. II 81, l. 16, fits into the lacuna perfectly well; only the name of the agoranomos is missing.

8 The creditor Sosistratos was an infantryman of the [- - -]τάξεως and taktomisthos (see Pros. Ptol. II 3588 = 4235). For the title of taktomisthos, see Vandorpe, *Archives from Pathyris* (2001), chapter V, pros. 205.

10 [πυροῦ ἀρτάβας ἑκατόν - 23 to 26-]: the lacuna doubtless contained the loan object (100 artabas of wheat, see l. 14 and 17), followed by stipulations on the interest.

⟦Δρύτωνι⟧: the scribe erased the name of the debtor Dryton at the end of l. 10 either because he wanted to begin a new line for the names of the debtors, or because of dittography.

11 ⟦ . ⟧: these traces of an erased letter were not observed by the editor.

12-13 For the supplement of the physical description of Dryton, see pros. 403.

14 [οἱ δεδανεισμένοι ἐν μηνὶ Παῦνι πυρὸν νέον]: the supplement proposed by the editor, is too short; the lacuna is filled perfectly by the addition of πυρόν.

15 [τοῖς ἰδίοις ἀν]ηλώμασ[ιν]: my additional supplement τοῖς fills the lacuna better. The article is often used in this expression, compare Pap. Lugd. Bat. XXII 23-27.

19 [ὑπαρχόντων αὐτοῖς] (Berger ὑπαρχόντων αὐτῶν): the verb ὑπάρχω is construed with the dative: parallel passages in texts from Pathyris always have αὐτῶι / αὐτοῖς or τούτωι / τούτοις (see §33).

20 This line is probably written by a second hand, see the Introduction to the text.

12

DEMOTIC LOAN OF MONEY
by Dryton

Plates V-VI (recto-verso); see facsimiles below

Thebes | H. x W. = 32.3 x 34.2 cm | 1 Sept. 171 B.C.

Louvre, P. dem. inv.no. E 10440 [gift of Lord de Grimberghe in 1890] = **unpublished**.

In 1987 U. Kaplony-Heckel was so kind as to inform me that the Louvre had among its papyrus collection a demotic contract mentioning Dryton, son of Pamphilos. The papyrus was damaged and broken off along several folds. The different strips had been mixed up and had to be rearranged; two strips were missing. I discovered the two missing pieces in an old envelope kept in a cupboard containing papyrus fragments of the Louvre. One of the two strips appeared to have a Greek résumé on the verso.

Photograph and facsimile. — Plates V-VI (recto-verso); see my facsimiles below.

Description. — The papyrus is complete. After the redaction of the loan, the papyrus was rolled from the left to the right and was then folded double. The papyrus became damaged along the horizontal and vertical folds.

The demotic loan contract is written upon the *recto* along the fibres, with a left- and right-hand margin of nearly 4 cm, a top margin of 4.2 cm and a bottom margin of 10.7 cm.

On the *verso* the twelve witnesses wrote their name against the fibres. The witness list is no longer complete, since it runs over the horizontal fold and was damaged: there are traces visible of the fourth name; the fifth name is lost and the sixth and seventh names are fragmentarily preserved. As is usual, the witness list on the verso starts under a long horizontal line with a small vertical stroke indicating where *ḏd* ("Has declared", l. 9) is written on the recto, «comme la signature de chaque témoin est censée confirmer le discours du déclarant»[1]. Dryton has made a Greek summary on the outside of the rolled and double-folded papyrus (verso of strip no. 8). The résumé is written along the fibres of the verso in two columns.

Verso

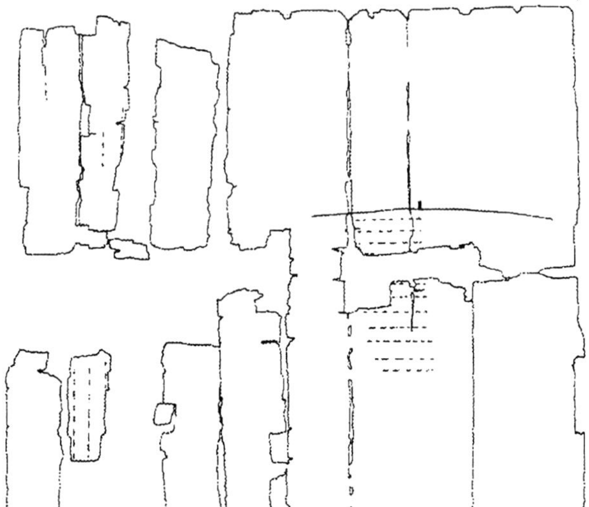

Strip 8

---

[1] P.W. Pestman, in P. dem. Tsenhor, p. 26; see also Pestman, 'L' agoranomie' (1978), p. 203 and Id., in P. dem. Tor. Amen., p. 161; Depauw, *Companion* (1997), p. 76.

Introduction

Contents. — In spite of the many lacunas, we possess all the necessary data. The preserved part on the recto and the résumé on the verso complement each other well. Dryton lends 261 deben, 5 kite (l. 11) or 5230 drachmas (verso col. I, l. 2), including interest (l. 11). The borrower is from Thebes; he is a shepherd and servant of Amon, called Pachnoubis (l. 10; verso col. II, l. 2), son of NN and Senatoumis (see comment on l. 10). The loan begins on 2 Mesore or 1 September 171 B.C. (l. 1) and runs for seven or eight months, until the beginning or end of Phamenoth (3 April-2 May 170 B.C., verso col. II, l. 3).

The Theban scribe and his family. — The text is written in a nice, well-cared-for and consistent hand. Note only the different writings *pr* (l. 1 and 17) and *pry* (l. 3 and 6). The scribe is called Kollouthes, son of Phabis. This Theban scribe and his family are well-known[1]:

- *Reconstruction of the family tree of the Theban scribes, descendants of Kollouthes.*

Possibility 1

PHABIS was monographos in the temple of the priests of Amonrasonther in Thebes from 185 until 170 B.C.; from the period 170-147 there is not a single testimony preserved; in 147 he again acts as monographos and in the period 145-140 he is found as scribe of ostraka.

HOROS succeeded his father Phabis and is attested as monographos from 146 until 141 B.C.

ZMINIS, another son of Phabis, was monographos in the period 137-118 B.C.; in 113 a representative of the latter is found.

KOLLOUTHES (II), a third son of Phabis, assisted his brother Zminis as monographos in **127/6-118** B.C.

In a recently published contract written by Phabis in **175** B.C. a Kollouthes son of Phabis is listed as first witness (see note 1). In Text 12 of **171** B.C. a Kollouthes son of Phabis is recorded in these early years and this time as scribe of the loan edited here, dated to 171 B.C. Consequently, Kollouthes (II) was already active in Thebes as scribe 45 years earlier than had been assumed thus far (*viz.* 127/6-118 B.C.). He was only known to have written an ostrakon in **153/52** or **142/41** B.C.[2].

1 See especially P.W. Pestman, J. Quaegebeur and R.L. Vos, in P. dem. Recueil I, p. 154-159; see also P. dem. Schreibertrad., index p. 313-315; Pros. Ptol. III and IX 7739+7766, 7751, 7773+7845, 7776, 7840; P. dem. Tor. Amen., p. 154-155; P. Choach. Survey, p. 310-311; R.K. Ritner, in *Enchoria* 22 (1995), p. 135, n.k.

To be added to the references in P. dem. Recueil are:

— Phabis (monographos): P. dem. BM Andrews 9 (182 B.C.)

— Phabis (monographos): P. dem. BM Andrews 10 (181 B.C.)

— Phabis (monographos): *Enchoria* 22 (1995), p. 130-137 (?181-180 B.C.)

— Phabis (monographos) and Kollouthes II (first witness): *Enchoria* 15 (1987), p. 97-146 (175 B.C.)

— Phabis (monographos) and Kollouthes II (representative scribe): Text 12 (171 B.C.)

— Phabis (monographos): P. dem. Brux. inv.no. E 8053 ined. (see *Enchoria* 8 Sonderband (1978), p. 27) + P. dem. BM Andrews 12; P. Brux. inv.no. E 8051 ined. (170 B.C).

— Zminis s.o. Phabis (monographos): P. dem. BM Andrews 21 (124 B.C.).

2 O. dem. Louvre inv.no. 9074.

How can this time span of 45 years be explained? When Kollouthes wrote the loan Text 12 in 171 B.C., he was not the monographos of the temple of Amonrasonther himself, but his representative (l. 16: *p3 rd*). His father Phabis was the actual monographos (l. 17). A similar case, where a son represents his father as scribe, is found within the same family: in P. dem. Tor. Amen. 10 and P. dem. Eheverträge 38 Osoroeris is *rd* of his father Kollouthes (II), the monographos (118-117 B.C.).

One can assume that Kollouthes II was an adult at the latest in 175 B.C. (when he acted as first witness in a contract written by his father, the monographos) and completed his training as scribe shortly before 171 B.C.; then he assisted his father in the notary's office of the temple, where he did a fine job. His status was that of representative (*rd*). Afterwards he perhaps became monographos in another temple, since he is an excellent scribe when he reappears at Thebes 45 years later.

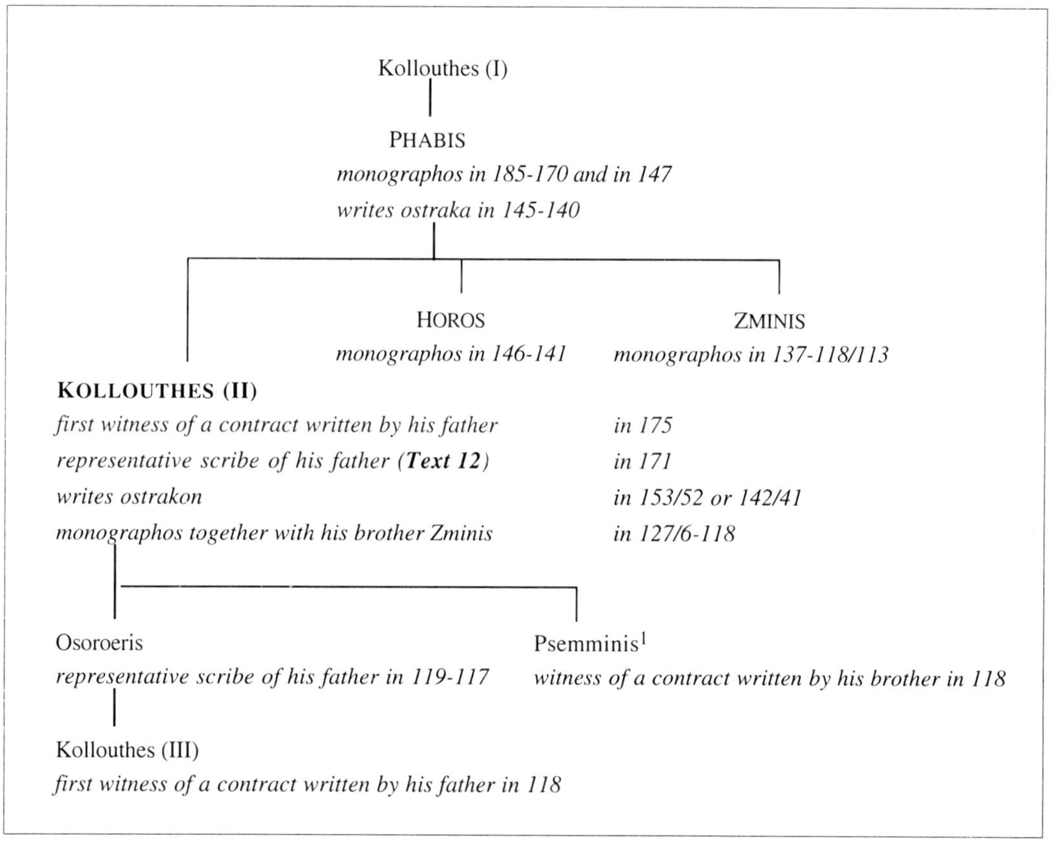

Family tree of the Theban scribes, descendants of Kollouthes I. Possibility 1

[1] For Psemminis, see P. dem. Tor. Amen., p. 155.

• *Reconstruction of the family tree of the Theban scribes, descendants of Kolluthes.*
Possibility 2

In opposition to this picture there is the possibility that the Kollouthes of 171 and the Kollouthes of 127/6-118 B.C. were two different persons, probably belonging to the same family[1]. A proposal along these lines was put forward by the editors of P. dem. Recueil, although they did not know Text 12. They admitted the possibility that between Phabis and his sons a double generation had to be inserted:

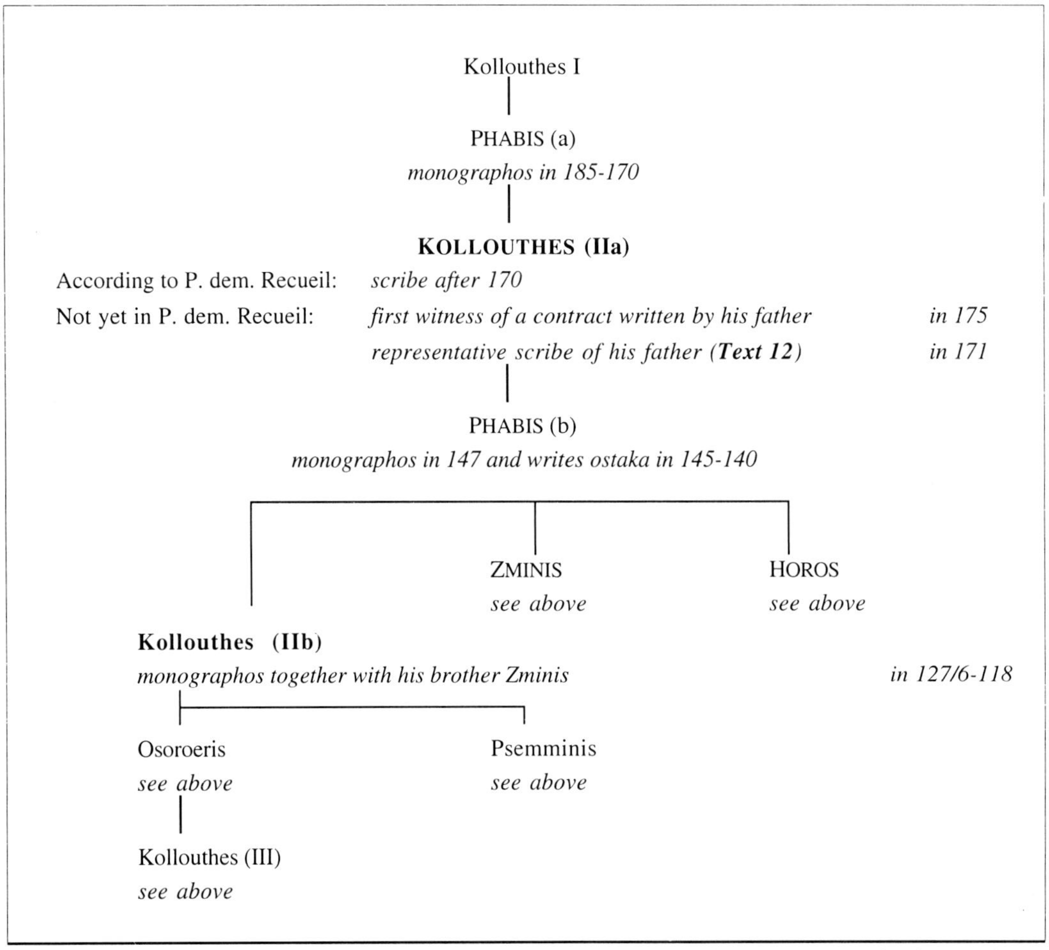

Family tree of the Theban scribes, descendants of Kollouthes I. Possibility 2

[1] See, for instance, G. Vittmann, who published the contract written by Phabis in 175 B.C. in which a Kollouthes son of Phabis is first witness: according to Vittmann «kann es sich aus chronologischen Gründen schwerlich um Pestmans Kollouthês II, den Sohn des Schreibers Phabis, handeln, da dieser Kollouthês erst zwischen 142 und 118 v. Chr. bezugt ist» (*Enchoria* 15 (1987), p. 138 (66)).

- *Arguments in favour of P o s s i b i l i t y 1*

The editors of the P. dem. Recueil consider the second family tree somewhat implausible: «Il y aurait trop de scribes dans cette période qui portaient le nom de Phabis, fils de Kollouthês, et de Kollouthês, fils de Phabis: cinq générations pour une période de moins de 90 ans, ce qui est seulement possible dans le cas où ils auraient tous vécu jusqu' à un age avancé et auraient seulement commencé à exercer la fonction de scribe passés la soixantaine.»[1].

I can only confirm their thesis and give an additional scientific underpinning for the first family tree. There are two facts which argue for the view that the Kollouthes of 171 and of 127/6-118 are one and the same person:

1. In 118 B.C. Kollouthes III, grandson of Kollouthes II, acts as witness in P. dem. Tor. Amen., verso l. 1, and was thus an adult. As a consequence the grandfather Kollouthes II must have been circa 60 years old in 118. The Kollouthes II of 127/6-118 B.C. had thus reached a respectable age, as expected if one identifies him with the Kollouthes of 171 B.C.
2. The handwritings of the Kollouthes of 171 and of 127/6-118 B.C. are very similar. One has of course to be cautious, since the handwritings of the members of this Theban family bear a close resemblance to each other.

As an example the writing of *ḥtr* is given:

	Phabis	*Horos*	*Zminis*	*Kollouthes 171*	*Kollouthes 127/6-118*
ḥtr	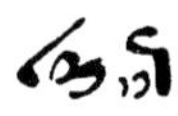		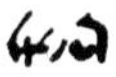	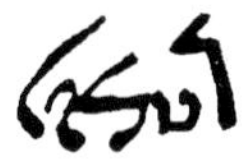	
P. dem.	Berl. Kaufv. 3140, 5	Berl. Spieg. 3119, 5	Tor. Botti 8B, 8	Text 12, 16	Nouv. Chrest., p. 87

On the other hand, the handwriting of these monographoi differ at certain points. Phabis and Zminis, for instance, usually write *Pṱlwmys* , Horos and Kollouthes always *Ptlwmys*.

Horos likes long strokes, for instance,
in P. dem. Berl. Spieg. 3119, l. 5: *mnḫ*

Zminis writes *mnḫ* in a compact way, for instance,
in P. dem. Tor. Botti 88, l. 1:

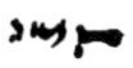

[1] See P.W. Pestman, J. Quaegebeur and R.L. Vos, in P. dem. Recueil I, p. 158.

The Kolluthes of 171 and the one of 127/6-118 have a very similar hand. The handwriting has, of course, evolved in the course of 45 years: the small dissimilarities consist either of simplifications of signs or of ligatures. I give below as an example *ntr.w* of which the plural signs in 127/6-118 are simplified and *tn* (in *tn nb*) is written with a ligature in 127/6-118:

	Kollouthes 171	*Kollouthes 127/6-118*
ntr.w	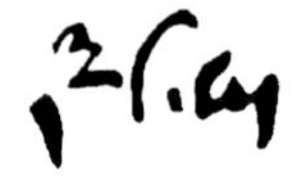 Text 12, 2	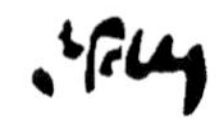 P. dem. Nouv. Chrest., p. 87
tn	 Text 12, 4	 P. dem. Nouv. Chrest., p. 87

- *Kollouthes II, oldest son of Phabis*

Before the discovery of Text 12 Kollouthes was attested later than his brothers Zminis and Horos and was considered the youngest son. Text 12 shows, however, that Kollouthes (II) is attested as scribe much earlier than his brothers and was undoubtedly the oldest son, named, as expected, after his grandfather.

The clauses of the contract. — Text 12 will not be discussed in my study on the loan contracts from Pathyris or Krokodilopolis (see §33), since it is a contract from Thebes. An important difference is the fact that loans from Pathyris are deeds of the "short type", whereas Text 12 is a deed of the "long type" (see §34; compare Text 11, Introduction). The clauses are otherwise similar to those used by the temple notary Thotortaios from Pathyris (see my study announced in §33).

- *Clause #1: Protocol* (l. 1-9)

  Text 12 does not only mention the date and the reigning kings, but also the names and the titles of the eponymous priests in Alexandria and Ptolemais (see comment on l. 2-9).
- *Clause #2: the actual acknowledgement of debt* (l. 9-11), with the names of the contractants, and mention of the loan object and the interest.
- *Clause #3: returning the loan* (l. 11-12), containing details on the time when and the condition in which the loan object has to be returned.
- *Clause #4 : penalty* (l. 12-14)

  The fine of 50% to be paid if the loan is not returned in time, is formulated in the following way: "I will give them to you" *tn (ḥḏ) 1 qd 5 ẖr.r=w*, "at the rate of 1 1/2 (deben of money) for them", that is 1 1/2 deben per 1 deben owed.
- *Clause #5: sureties and representative of the creditor* (l. 14-16).
- *Clause #6: name of and information on the scribe* (l. 16-18).

Facsimile

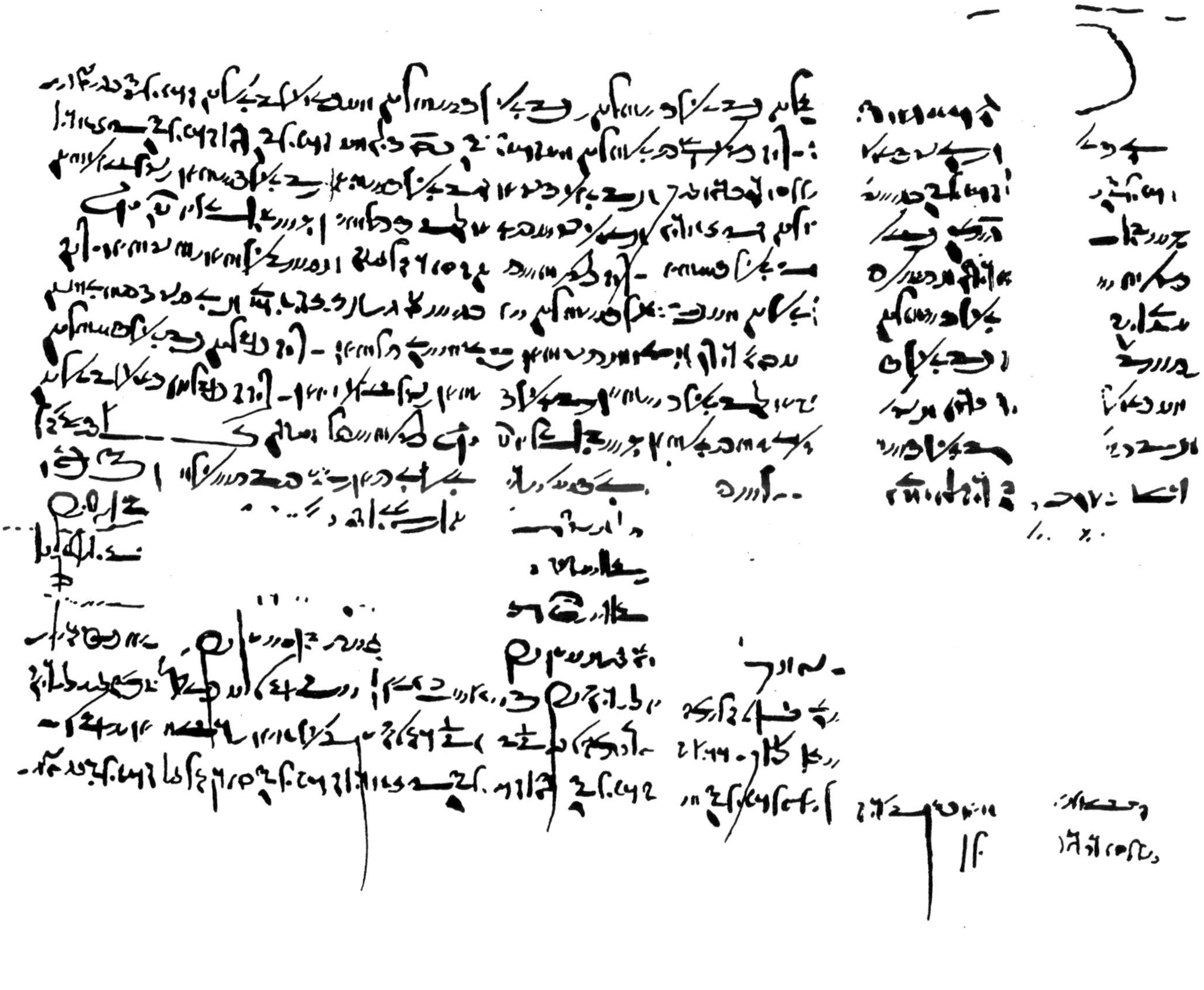

Text

R e c t o

Ḥ3.t[-sp] 10.t ibd-4 šmw sw 2 [n] Pr-ʿ3ʿws Ptlwmysʿws s3 Ptlwmysʿws irm Glwptrʿws n3 ntr.w nty pr
⌜iw⌝ Tmtr[ys] s3 T3mgl[s] n wʿb 3lgsntrsʿws irm n3 ntr.w nty nḥm irm n3 ntr.w sn.w n3 ntr.w mnḫ.w
[n3] ntr.w ⌜mr⌝ [it.ṯ]=w n3 ntr.w nty pry ⌜p3⌝ ntr mr mw.t.ṱ=f iw Ptwlm3 ta Ptlwmysʿws s3 Ptlwmys s3 3wbwlsʿws
f3y ⌜q⌝n n[ʿ]š Br[ny]⌜g⌝ʿws t3 mnḫ.t iw Gl3ynt ta Qmnws f3y tn nb m-b3ḥ
3rsy[nʿws t3] mr sn iw Hyrn[3] ⌜ta⌝ Ptlwmys n wʿb 3rsynʿws t3 mr it.ṱ=s iw Hyplws s3 S3s n wʿb
p3 tš Nw.t [P]tlwmysʿws [p3 S]⌜w⌝trʿws irm ⌜Pt⌝lwmysʿws p3 ntr nty pry i.ir ir n3 nfr.w iw Th3mnstsʿws
s3 Hypl⌜w⌝[s n] ⌜wʿb⌝ Ptlwm[ysʿws] p3 mr mw.t iw Gyn3s s3 Tsythws n wʿb Pr-ʿ3ʿws Ptlwmysʿws
irm Glw[ptr]⌜ʿws⌝ t3 mw.t iw 3r[syn]3 ta Ptlwmys s3 Ptlwm⌜y⌝s s3 3wbwls n wʿb t3 Pr-ʿ3.tʿws Glwptrʿws
iw Phy⌜l⌝[tr] ⌜ta⌝ Ptlwmy⌜s⌝ [s3] ⌜3⌝lgsntrs f3y tn nb m-b3ḥ 3rsyn[ʿws] t3 mr sn. Ḏd ʿ3m bk Imn
Pa-⌜H̱nm⌝ s3 ⌜- ⌝[- - -]⌜Is.t⌝ mw.t=f T3-šr.t-(n-)Itm n Wyn[n rmt n] dmy P3-s⌜y⌝ Trwtn s3 Pnphylws: wn-mtw=k
[ḥḏ 261 qd 5 r] ⌜sttr⌝ [1307 1/2 r ḥḏ 261 ḳd 5 ʿn iw p3y=w ḥw] ⌜ẖn⌝=w i-ir-n=y ⌜rn⌝ [n3] ⌜ḥḏ⌝.w r.dy=k n=y. ⌜M⌝tw=⌜y dy.t n=k⌝ [p3y=k ḥḏ 2]61qd 5 nty ḥry
[r-hn(-r) ḥ3.t-sp 11 ibd-3 pr.t ʿrqy. P3 ḥḏ n.im=w nty] ⌜iw⌝ bn iw=y dy.t s⌜t r-hn⌝ [(-r) ḥ3.t-sp 11 ibd-3 pr.t ʿrqy p3 ssw-hrw nty] ⌜ḥry⌝ [mtw=y dy.t st n=k] tn (ḥḏ) 1 qd 5 ẖr.r=w
[n ḥ3.t-sp 11 ibd-4 pr.t (ʿrqy) p3 ibd nty m-s3 p3 ibd rn=f n ḥtr.ṱ iwṱ mn.] Bn iw=y rḫ dy.t n=k [ky ssw-hrw (r.r=w) m-s3] ⌜p3 ssw⌝ [-hrw nty ḥry.] ⌜Bn iw=y rḫ⌝
[ḏd dy=y (n=k) ḥḏ pr nty nb n p3 t3 (n.im=w)] ⌜iwṱ⌝ iw iw=f ⌜ʿẖʿ⌝ [rd.]ṱ iw p3 sẖ nty ḥry [n dr.ṱ=k. I].ir p3 hp n p3 sẖ nty ḥry r ⌜ẖpr⌝ r ḏ3ḏ3=y
[ḥnʿ n3y=y ẖrd.w nty nb nkt nb nty mtw=y ḥnʿ n3 nty iw] ⌜=y⌝ r dy.t ẖpr.w n iwy.t md nb nty ḥry šʿ-tw=y mḥ=k n.im=w. P3y=k rd p3 nty nḥṱ r md nb
[nty iw=f r ḏd.ṱ=w irm=y rn md nb nty ḥry, mtw]=y ir=w r ẖrw=f n ssw nb n ḥtr.ṱ iwṱ mn iwṱ sẖ nb. Sẖ Qlwḏ s3 Pa=by p3 rd n
Pa=by [s3 Qlw]ḏ nty sẖ rn n3 ⌜wʿb⌝ [.w] ⌜Imn⌝-Rʿ-nsw-ntr.w irm n3 ntr.w sn.w n3 ntr.w mnḫ.w n3 ntr.w mr it.ṱ=w n3 ntr.w nty pr
p3 ntr mr mw.t.ṱ=⌜f⌝ [n p3 5] ⌜s3⌝.w.

Translation

Recto

Year 10, 2 Mesore, of king Ptolemy (VI), son of Ptolemy (V) and Kleopatra (I), the Gods Epiphaneis,

while Demetrios, son of Demokles, is priest of Alexander, the Gods Soteres, the Gods Adelphoi, the Gods Euergetai, the Gods Philopatores, the Gods Epiphaneis and the God Philometor;

while Ptolemais, daughter of Ptolemaios, son of Ptolemaios, son of Euboulos, is athlophoros of Berenike Euergetis;

while Kleainete, daughter of Komanos, is kanephoros of Arsinoe Philadelphos;

while Eirene, daughter of Ptolemaios, is priestess of Arsinoe Philopator;

while Hippalos, son of Sosos, is in the Thebaid priest of Ptolemy Soter and Ptolemy the God Epiphanes Eucharistos;

while Theomnestos, son of Hippalos, is priest of Ptolemy Philometor;

while Kineas, son of Dositheos, is priest of king Ptolemy and Kleopatra, the mother;

while Arsinoe, daughter of Ptolemaios, son of Ptolemaios, son of Euboulos,. is priestess of queen Kleopatra;

while Philotera, daughter of Ptolemaios, son of Alexander, is kanephoros of Arsinoe Philadelphos.

Has declared the herdsman and servant of Amon Pachnoubis, son of - -?esis, his mother being Senatoumis, to the Greek, citizen of Ptolemais, Dryton, son of Pamphilos:

«I owe you 261 (deben of) money and 5 kite — that is 1307 1/2 staters, being 261 deben and 5 kite again — interest included, in the name of the money you gave to me. I shall return to you your 261 (deben of) money and 5 kite above-mentioned by year 11, Phamenoth, last day. The money that I shall not have returned by the above-mentioned time — that is year 11, Phamenoth, last day — I shall give it back to you at the rate of 1 1/2 (deben of money) per deben in year 11, Pharmouthi (last day), that is the month following the month named, compulsorily, without delay.

I shall not be able to give to you another date for it except the above date. I shall not be able to say 'I have given to you money, corn or anything whatsoever' without a valid receipt, while the above deed is in your hand. The obligation (resulting from) the above-mentioned deed will be on my head and on that of my children. Everything, all that belongs to me and all that I shall acquire, are security for every word above until I have repaid them to you.

Your representative is the one who is authorized regarding every word which he will address to me in the name of every word which (is written) above. I shall execute them according to his instructions, always, compulsorily, without delay, withour any force.»

Has written Kollouthes, son of Phabis, representative of Phabis, son of Kollouthes, who writes in the name of the priests of Amonrasonther and of the Gods Adelphoi, the Gods Euergetai, the Gods Philopatores, the Gods Epiphaneis, the God Philometor, (priests) of the five phyles.

Text

Verso

Witness list

1 *P3-šr-⌜Imn⌝-Ipy s3 ⌜- - -⌝*
2 *Imn-ḥtp s3 Iy-m-ḥtp*
3 *Ḏḥwṯ-sḏm s3 Imn-p3-ym*
4 *[- - -]*
5 *[- - -]*
6 *⌜- - -⌝[- - -]*
7 *⌜Ḥr⌝ s3 P3-⌜ - ⌝[- - -]*
8 *P3-šr-Ḏḥwṯ s3 ⌜Twtw⌝*
9 *Sm3-t3.wy s3 Twtw*
10 *Nḫt.t-nb=f s3 Ḥr-Iy-m-ḥtp*
11 *P3-šr-Imn-Ip s3 P3-ḥtr*
12 *P3-šr-Imn s3 P3-šr-Ḏḥwṯ*

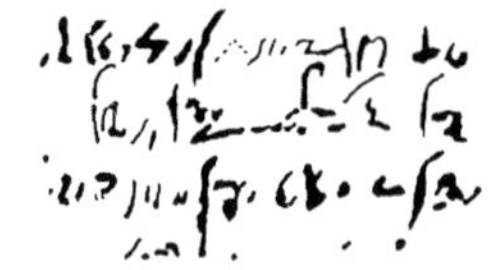

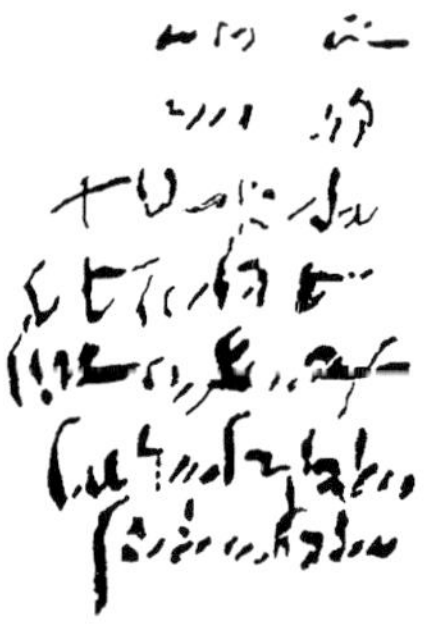

Greek summary

Col. I

1 . . [. . . .]ịος τọụ [- - -]
2 (δραχμὰς) Ἐσλ

Col. II

1 (Ἔτους) ị Μ̣ε̣σ̣[ορὴ β δάνειον]
2 Παχνούβιος τοῦ . ε[- - -]
3 ἕως Φαμενὼθ τοῦ [ια (ἔτους)]

Translation

Witness list

1 *Psenamenophis son of - -*
2 *Amenothes son of Imouthes*
3. *Thotsytmis son of Amphiomis*
4-6 - -
7 *Horos son of P- -*
8 *Psenthotes son of Totoes*
9 *Semtheus son of Totoes*
10 *Nechthnibis son of Horimouthes*
11 *Psenamenophis son of Phatres*
12 *Psenamounis son of Psenthotes*

Greek summary

Col. I: - - - *5230 drachmas.*

Col. II: *Year 10, 2 Mesore, (loan) to Pachnoubis, son of -e- - , until Phamenoth of the 11th year.*

Notes

Recto

2-9 The names of the eponymous priests of Text 12 were included in Pap. Lugd. Bat. XXIV (no. 119 and 119bis), although the text was not yet published at the time.

2 *Tmtr[ys] s3 T3mgl[s]*: there are traces of the seated man determinative visible at the end of both names.

3 *Ptlwmys*: the first *Ptlwmys*, like *3wbwls* in the same line and *Th3mnsts* in l. 6, did not receive a seated man determinative at the end, but the sign the scribe uses for *ʿws* (may he live prosperous and healthy) in case of pharaohs' names.

3wbwls: see preceding note.

6 *Th3mnsts*: see my comm. on l. 3.

9 *t3 mr sn*: is the last part of the protocol written in a small and compact way; compare, for instance, *mr* in l. 5.

10 *Pa-⸢Ḫnm⸣ s3 ⸢ - ⸣[- - -]⸢Is.t⸣*: the seated man determinative of *Pa-⸢Ḫnm⸣* is preserved, followed by *s3*, which may have run on beneath the following father's name, as is the case in l. 7 with *s3 Tsythws*.

The father's name is for the greater part lost. If my reading of the end of the name *-Is.t*, is correct, the name can be supplemented as, for instance, Psennesis, Peteesis, Harsiesis or Harpaesis. The traces of the name in the Greek summary on the verso (̣ ϵ[- - -]) rather suggest the name Psennesis (Ψ̣ϵ[ννήσιος]) or Peteesis (Π̣ϵ[τεήσιος]).

Verso : Witness list

9 *Sm3-t3.wy* (Semtheus): the reading *sm3* (without divine determinative) is to be preferred to *nsw*; see P.W. Pestman, in Pap. Lugd. Bat. XIX, p. 166-167 (d).

Verso : Greek summary

Col. I, 1 It is not clear what kind of information was given in this first line. Possibly Π̣α̣χ[νούβ]ιος τ̣ο̣ῦ̣ [- - -] stood in a clause as, for instance: *I have received from Pachnoubis, son of - - -, 5230 drachmas*. In this case, this part of the summary was annotated when the loan was returned, contrary to col. II, which was written when the loan was issued.

Col. II, 2 Παχνούβιος: probably depended on a word like δάνειον, *loan*. The name of the debtor Pachnoubis was followed by his father's name, introduced by τοῦ. The traces of the father's name are hardly legible (see also my comment on recto, l. 10).

13

DEMOTIC LOAN OF SPELT
by Apollonia

See facsimile below

[Pathyris] H. x W. = 13.5 x 3 cm [Fragmentary] 179-133, probably between 145 and 143/142 B.C.

Heidelberg, P. dem. inv.no. 749d [In Heidelberg since 1898, acquired by Reinhardt] = **P. dem. Gebelein Heid. 22**.

Photograph and facsimile. — No photograph available; see my facsimile below; facsimile in P. dem. Gebelein Heid., p. 101, no. 22.

Description. — The papyrus is very fragmentary. Since three-fours of the width and half of the height are lost the papyrus must have been folded from the right to the left (or the other way round), resulting in four vertical strips; it was subsequently folded double and became damaged along the horizontal and the vertical folds. Of the eight strips (1a-4a and 1b-4b) only one elongated strip is preserved containing part of the upper section of the text. On the basis of what is lost in line 1, one can conclude that two strips preceded the preserved fragment: P. dem. Heid. inv.no. 749d is strip 3a.

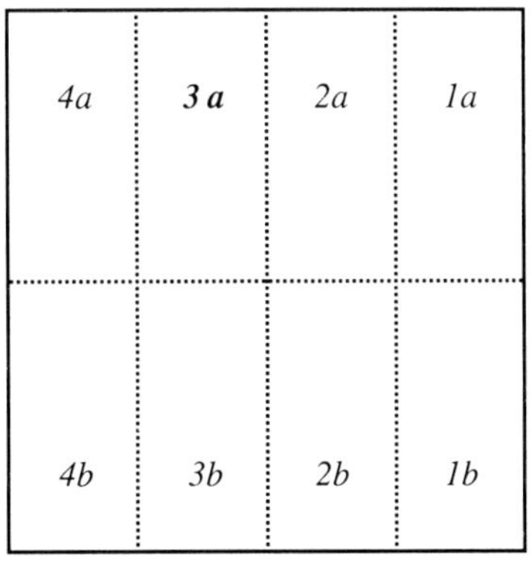

Introduction

Contents. — The preserved part in l. 6-7 led the editor to conclude that either two women act as creditors, or that in l. 6 a deceased woman is mentioned, on whose account the daughter (recorded in l. 7) is acting. The solution is more simple: the creditor is one woman, bearing a double name[1]. The woman mentioned in l. 6 is daughter of *Ptl[ ].* Only one woman from Pathyris is known to act as creditor and has a father with a Greek name (Ptolemaios): Apollonia, wife of Dryton. She is often attested with her double name "Apollonia alias Senmonthis, daughter of Ptolemaios alias Pamenos" and this double name should be supplied in l. 7. The last trace of the Egyptian father's name Pamenos is still visible.

Only the name of one of the three debtors is partly preserved: -esis, son of Harsiesis. He is possibly to be identified with Psennesis, son of Harsiesis, alias Apollonios, son of Apollodotos. This man is Apollonia's brother-in-law (pros. 408) and borrows wheat from her in 131 B.C. (Text 16). It is doubtful whether it is the same Psennesis, son of Harsiesis, who acts as witness in 115[2] and in 91/90[3] B.C.

The contract concerns a loan of *hrn* (spelt), a form of coarse wheat (*Triticum spelta*) with a small reddish brown grain giving fine flour.

The scribe and the date of the contract. — There are some minor [4] clues to date the text.

- The contractant Apollonia acts as creditor in several loans from the period 139-128 B.C.; she became an adult circa 150 B.C. and is attested for the last time in 126 B.C. (see pros. 404). Thus the present text most probably dates from the period **150-126** B.C.
- The way of rolling or folding the papyrus after it was written (rolling the papyrus from the right to the left, or the other way round, and then folding it double, see the description) is typical of the Egyptian scribe Thotortaios, son of Nechthminis, Pathyris' temple notary in the period 178-133 B.C. (see Text 3, comm. on l. 48). Since Apollonia was the creditor (preceding paragraph), the loan may be more closely dated to the period **150-133** B.C.
- The remaining part of the protocol is of importance for the further specification of the date: the length of the lacunae and the date proposed in the last paragraph (150-133 B.C.) suggest the following supplement[5]:

  n3 Pr-ʿ3 ʿws.w Ptlwmys ʿws irm Glwptr3 ʿws i.ir Ptlwmys ʿws irm Glwptr3 ʿws n3 ntr.w nty pr, the kings Ptolemy (VIII) and Kleopatra (II), children of Ptolemy (V) and Kleopatra (I), the Gods Epiphaneis.

  This protocol is attested in the period **145-143/142** B.C. One can assume with confidence that the contract dates more precisely from this period and is, consequently, the oldest loan contract of Apollonia.

---

1 For the proposal of P.W. Pestman, see comm. on l. 6-7.

2 Pap. Lugd. Bat. XIX 5, verso l. 3.

3 P. dem. Brux. inv.no. E 8442 ined., l. 25.

4 *Pace* the editor: «Für eine Datierung des Textes ist kein Anhaltspunkt vorhanden».

5 See Pap. Lugd. Bat. XV, p. 54.

*Facsimile and Text**

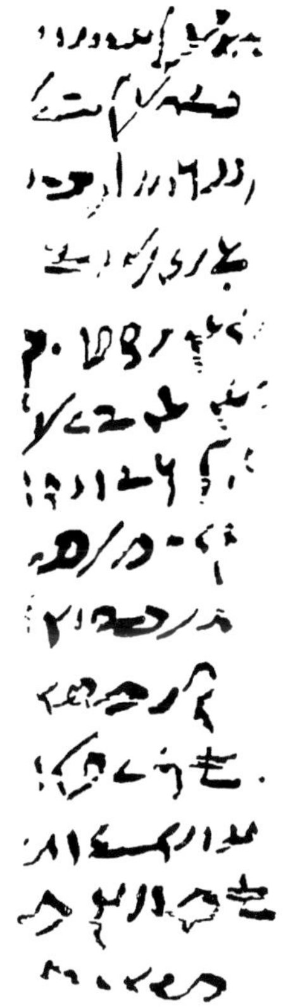

[Ḥ3.t-sp - - ibd - - sw - - n n3 Pr-ʿ3 ʿws .w] Ptlwmy⸢s⸣[ʿws irm Glwptr3ʿws]
[- - Ptlwmysʿws irm] Glwptr[3ʿws n3 ntr.w nty pr]
[irm n3 nty smn n Rʿ-qd] P3-sy nty n ⸢p3⸣ [tš n Nw.t.]
[Ḏd - - -]-Is.t s3 Ḥr-s3-Is.t [- - -]
[- - -] - r s 3 n ⸢wʿ⸣ [r3 n sḥm.t]
[Wynn.t 3pwlny]⸢3⸣ ta Ptl[wmys ḏd.ṱ n=s]
[T3-šr.t-Mnṱ ta Pa-mn]⸢ḥ⸣ mw.t.ṱ=s ⸢T3⸣[- - -]
[Wn-mtw=t] rdb n hrn [- - t3y=w pš.t - - r rdb n hrn - - ʿn]
[i-ir-n=n (n) rn n3] pr.w [r.dy=t n=n iw p3y=w]
[ḥw ẖn=w. Mtw=n dy.t st] n=t r-hn[(-r) ḥ3.t-sp - - ibd-1 šmw sw ʿrqy]
[n pr iw=f wʿb iwṱ sn.]⸢nw⸣ iwṱ stḥ ⸢iw⸣[=w ḫ3y.w iw=w f3y.w]
[iw=w swṱ.w r p3 ẖn (n)] p3y=t ʿ.wy [n Pr-Ḥ.t-Ḥr]
[n t3 mʿḏ.t r.ḫ3y=t n.im=s] iwṱ hy h[m.t . Iw=n]
[tm dy.t st n=t r-hn(-r) p3 ssw-]hrw ⸢nty ḥry⸣ [iw=n dy.t st irm - - - -]

- -

---

2 *Glwptr3* ed., *Glwptr[3 ʿws]* legimus 3 *P3-sy nty n [p3]* ed., *P3-sy nty n ⸢p3⸣* legimus 6 *[ ] ta Ptl[* ed., *[3pwlny]⸢3⸣ ta Ptl[wmys]* legimus (et supplevimus) 7 *]mw.t=s* ed., *[ta Pa-mn]⸢ḥ⸣ mw.t.ṱ=s ⸢T3⸣ [ ]* legimus (et supplevimus) 10 *r-hn-r* ed., *r-hn[(-r)]* legimus

---

* The identification of the creditor and consultation of similar loans made it possible for me to supplement more lacunae than in the first edition. These new supplements are not listed in the *apparatus criticus*, which only presents the new readings.

Translation

Year - - month - - day - - of the kings Ptolemy (VIII) and Kleopatra (II), children of Ptolemy (V) and Kleopatra (I), the Gods Epiphaneis, and the priests who are appointed in Alexandria (and in) Ptolemais in the Thebaid.

Have declared - - -esis, son of Harsiesis - - -, who are three persons speaking with one voice, to the Greek woman Apollonia, daughter of Ptolemaios, alias Senmonthis, daughter of Pamenos, her mother being T- - -:

«We owe you - - - artabas of spelt — their half is - - - being - - - artabas of spelt again — in the name of the grains which you gave to us, interest included.

We shall return it to you by - - - in grain that is pure, without adulteration (or) chaff, while they (viz. the grains) are measured, transported and consigned within your house in Pathyris, by the measure you employed, without expenses of freightage.

If we fail to return it within the stated time, we shall return it to you with - - - -»

- -

Notes

5 *[- - -] - r s 3, that are three persons*: the traces before *r s 3* show the last sign and the seated man determinative of the father's name of the third debtor.

6-7 P.W. Pestman (in *Chron. d'Ég.* 41 (1966), p. 318) supplies the lacuna with a double name as I do (see the introduction to the text), but he proposes to supply the name of a sister of Apollonia: Ammonia alias Senminis (pros. 405). Pestman's proposal, however, does not fill the entire lacuna of l. 7 and omits Pamenos, the Egyptian double name of the father: *3mny3] ta Ptl[wmys dd.ṯ n=s]* l. 7*[T3-šr.t-M]in mw.t.ṯ=s [- - -].* In addition, Ammonia alias Senminis is never attested as creditor in loan contracts.

8 *hrn, spelt*: the common writing is *hrnṯ*. The trace after *hrn* in the present text does not fit a *ṯ*, but a plant determinative which belongs to *hrn(ṯ)*.

14

DEMOTIC LOAN OF CORN
by Apollonia

See facsimile below

[Pathyris]	H. x W. = 12.5 x 7 cm [Fragmentary]	179-133, probably between 143/142 and 138/137 B.C.

Heidelberg, P. dem. inv.no. 739a [In Heidelberg since 1898, acquired by Reinhardt] = **P. dem. Gebelein Heid. 25**.

Photograph and facsimile. — No photograph available; see my facsimile below; facsimile in P. dem. Gebelein Heid., p. 102, no. 25.

Description. — The papyrus is very fragmentary: only two elongated strips are preserved. Taking account of the text which is lost but can be supplied, one can conclude that three-fifths of the width and half of the height are lost. The papyrus must have been folded or rolled from the right to the left (or the other way round) resulting into five vertical strips; it was subsequently folded double and became damaged along the horizontal and the vertical folds. Of the ten strips (1a-5a and 1b-5b) only two are preserved, containing part of the upper section of the text. The supplement in line 1 suggests that one strip preceded the two preserved fragments: P. dem. Heid. inv.no. 739a consists of strips 2a and 3a.

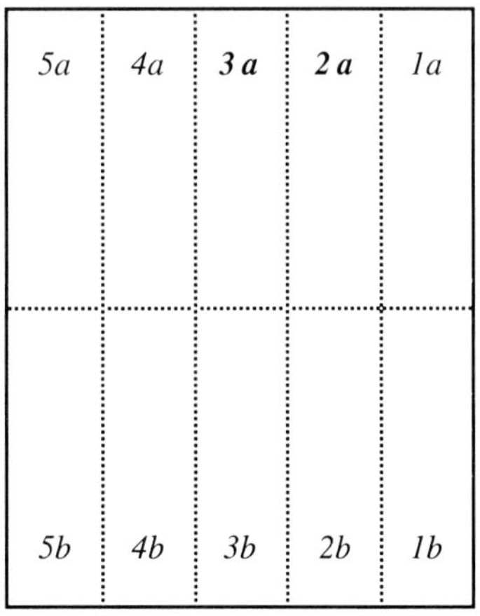

Introduction

Contents. — Apollonia lends corn (l. 7). It is not clear whether wheat, barley or spelt is involved, since the object of the loan and the number of artabas lent are missing. The debtor is a misthophoros and belongs to the company of the eponymous officer Diodotos, to which Apollonia's husband Dryton also belonged[1]. The debtor bears a double name: the Greek name starts with *Hr* (Hermokrates, Herakleides, etc.[2]). I read the Egyptian name as Harmais; the father's name is Panas. If the Egyptian name is correctly read, the debtor may be identified with the Harmais, son of Panas, the owner of a piece of land according to P. dem. Stras. Wiss. Ges. inv.no. 7 ined.[3] of 134 B.C.

The scribe and the date. — The name of the scribe is lost. The first editor dates the text to the reign of Ptolemy VIII, since the Goddess Euergetis is mentioned in l. 3, and prefers a date before 135 B.C. for prosopographical and palaeographical reasons: she identifies the handwriting as «der späteren Handschrift» of Thotortaios, son of Nechthminis, scribe of the Hathor temple in Pathyris in the period 178-133 B.C. (see Text 3, comm. on l. 48). This later handwriting of Thotortaios likes to connect successive signs, see, for instance, the writing of *Wynn.t* in l. 5, and of *iwṯ* in l. 8. I can only bring further evidence in support of her proposal:

• The contract is also for the following reasons to be attributed to the temple notary Thotortaios, son of Nechthminis. The way in which the papyrus is folded (rolled vertically and then folded double) is typical of Thotortaios. In addition, the clause recorded in l. 13 is only found for Pathyris in contracts written by Thotortaios (see my study announced in §33).

• The protocol (l. 1-3), which was not supplied by the first editor, suggests a more accurate date: the preserved text and the length of the lacunae only suit the following supplement[4]: *Pr-ʿ3 ⸢ʿws⸣ Ptlwmys⸢ʿws⸣ [p3 mnḫ s3 Ptlwmys ʿws irm Glw]ptr3 ʿws n3 ntr.w nty pr.w irm t3 Pr-ʿ3 ⸢ʿws⸣[.t Glwptr3 ʿws t3y=f sn.t t3y=f ḥm.t t3] ntr.t mnḫ[.t], king Ptolemy (VIII) Euergetes, son of Ptolemy (V) and Kleopatra (I), the Gods Epiphaneis, and queen Kleopatra (II), his sister (and) his wife, the Goddess Euergetis.* This is the protocol of the period **143/142 - 138/137** B.C.

---

1 Diodotos is dealt with in the prosopographical chapter *sub* Dryton (pros. 403).

2 See Pap. Lugd. Bat. XXIV, p. 113.

3 I owe this information to S.P. Vleeming.

4 See Pap. Lugd. Bat. XV, p. 56.

Facsimile

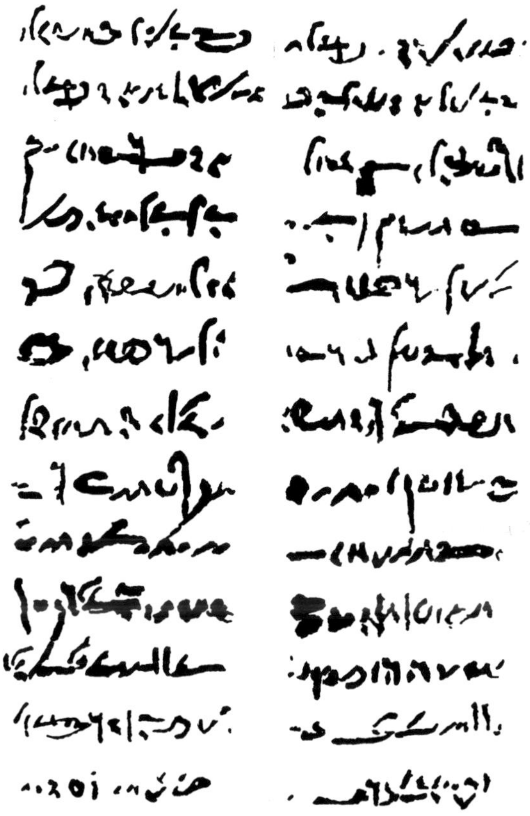

*Text**

[Ḥ3.t-sp - - - ibd - -] 3ẖ.t sw 18 n Pr-ʿ3 ⸢ʿws⸣ Ptlwmys ⸢ʿws⸣ [p3 mnẖ s3 Ptlwmys ʿws]
[irm Glw]ptr3 ʿws n3 ntr.w nty pr.w irm t3 Pr-ʿ3 ⸢ʿws⸣[.t Glwptr3 ʿws t3y=f sn.t]
[t3y=f ḥm.t t3] ntr.t mnẖ[.t] ⸢irm⸣ n3 nty smn n Rʿ-[qd P3-sy nty n p3 tš n Nw.t. Ḏd]
[rmt iw=f šp ḥbs] ẖn n3 rmt.w (n) T⸢y⸣[3]twtws Hr[- - - s3 - - -]
[ḏd.ṯ n=f] ⸢Ḥr-m-ḥb⸣ s3 Pa-n3 n ⸢sḥm⸣.t Wynn.t 3[pwlny3 ta Ptlwmys]
[ḏd.ṯ n=s] T3-šr.t-Mnṯ ta Pa-mn⸢ḥ⸣ s3 Pa-n3. Wn-[mtw=t rdb n - - t3y=w pš.t - -]
[r rdb n - - ʿn] i-ir-n=y (n) rn n3 pr.w r.tw=t n=y iw p3y=w ḥw [ẖn=w. Mtw=y dy.t st n=t r-hn(-r) ḥ3.t-sp - - ibd-1 šmw sw ʿrqy]
[n t3y=t] mḏʿ.t n pr iw=f wʿb iwṯ sn.nw ⸢iwṯ⸣ [sth iw=w ẖ3y.w iw=w f3y.w]
[iw=w swṯ.w r] ⸢p3⸣ ẖn (n) p3y=t ⸢ʿ.wy⸣ n Pr-Ḥ.t-⸢Ḥr⸣. [Iw=y tm dy.t st n=t r-hn(-r) p3 ssw-hrw nty ḥry]
[iw=y dy.t st] irm p3y=w 1 r 1 1/2 p3 ibd [nty] m-s3 p3 ibd (n) rn=f n ḥ[tr.ṯ iwṯ mn. Bn iw=y rẖ dy.t gr ssw-]
[hrw r.r=w] m-s3 p3 ssw-hrw nty ⸢ḥry⸣. Bn iw=y rẖ ḏd tw[=y n=t ḥḏ pr nty nb n p3 t3 iwṯ iw iw=f ʿḥʿ]
[rd.wy. Bn] iw=y rẖ ḏd ir⸢=y n=t⸣ p3 hp t3 smbw⸢l⸣ [iw t3 smbwl nty ḥry n-dr.ṯ=t]
[N3y=t pr.w nty ḥry] ḥnʿ p3y=w ẖl ẖpr r ḏ3ḏ3=y ⸢ḥnʿ n3y=y⸣ [ẖrd.w

---

1 *sw 16* ed., *sw 18* legimus 2 *nty pry* ed., *nty pr.w* legimus 3 *ntr.t mnẖt irm* ed., *ntr.t mnẖ[.t] ⸢irm⸣* legimus 4 *Tywtwtws* ed., *T⸢y⸣[3]twtws* legimus 5 *[ḏd.ṯ r=f]* ed., *[ḏd.ṯ n=f]* Zauzich (*ZDMG* 118 (1968), p. 377); . . . ed., *⸢Ḥr-m-ḥb⸣* legimus; *[ta Ptlwmys]* supplevimus 10 *Wynn* ed., *Wynn.t* legimus 5 *[swṯ.w] ẖn.* ed., *[swṯ.w r] ⸢p3⸣ ẖn* legimus (et supplevimus) 10 *ir=y [n=t] p3 hp n t3 smbwl* ed., *ir⸢=y n=t⸣ p3 hp t3 smbw⸢l⸣* legimus

---

* The consultation of similar loans made it possible for me to supplement more lacunae than in the first edition. These new supplements are not listed in the *apparatus criticus*, which only presents the new readings.

Translation

Year - - month of the 3ḫ.t-season, day 18, of king Ptolemy Euergetes (VIII), son of Ptolemy (V) and Kleopatra (I), the Gods Epiphaneis, and of queen Kleopatra (II), his sister, his wife, the Goddess Euergetis, and (the priests) who are appointed in Alexandria (and in) Ptolemais in the Thebaid.

Has declared the man receiving pay among the men of Diodotos, Hr- - -, son of - - - alias Harmais(?) -, son of Panas, to the Greek woman Apollonia, daughter of Ptolemaios, alias Senmonthis, daughter of Pamenos, son of Panas:

«I owe you - - - — their half is - - - being - - - again - - - — in the name of the grains which you gave to me, interest included.

I shall return it to you - - - in your measure, in grain that is pure, without adulteration (or) chaff, while they (viz. the grains) are measured, transported and consigned within your house in Pathyris.

If I fail to return it within the stated time, I shall return it to you increased by 50% in the month following the month named, compulsorily, without delay.

I shall not be able to give another date for it except the above date. I shall not be able to say 'I have given to you money, corn or anything whatsoever' without a valid receipt. I shall not be able to say 'I have performed for you the right of the symbolon', while the symbolon is in your hand. Your grains and their fine are at my expense and the expense of my children - - - »

- -

Notes

3 *mnḫ[.t], Euergetis*: there is an ink spot beneath the first sign *mn*.

5 *n ⌜sḥm⌝.t, to (the) woman*: the high ink trace between *n* and *⌜sḥm⌝.t*, cannot be explained.

5 *Wynn.t, Greek*: *Wynn* and the following foreign determinative, are written in ligature. *Wynn* is apparently given a feminine ending *.t* as it refers to *⌜sḥm⌝.t*, *woman*.

15

DEMOTIC ACKNOWLEDGMENT OF DEBT (WHEAT)
to Apollonia

Plate VIII; see scanned photograph below

Probably Pathyris | H. x W. = 4.7 x 14 cm [Fragmentary] | 6 Oct. 139 B.C.

British Museum, old inv.no. P. dem. 03 / on 11-6-1980 put under the same glass as inv.no. 69008 / registered on 12-7-1995 as inv.no. 74901 [date of acquisition unknown] = **unpublished**.

I discovered this papyrus fragment thanks to photographs U. Kaplony-Heckel put at my disposition during my stay at Marburg.

Photograph and facsimile. — Plate VIII; see scanned photograph below.

Description. — The papyrus is fragmentary. It was rolled or folded from the bottom to the top (or the other way round) resulting into horizontal folds, and is broken along one such horizontal fold. The upper part is preserved containing the first three lines and the beginning of the fourth line of the acknowledgement of debt. The verso is blank.

Introduction

Contents. — Apollonia, who is recorded with her Egyptian naam Senmonthis (l. 2), lends 4 artabas of wheat to Phibis, son of Thotortaios, who cannot be identified.

Scanned photograph

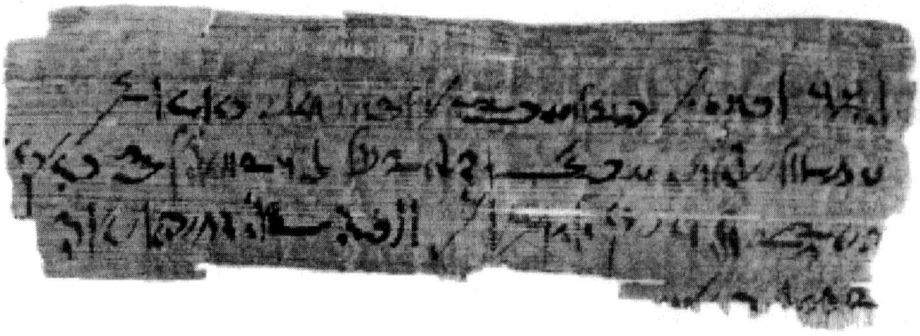

Text

1 *Ḥ3.t-sp 32 ibd-1 3ẖ.t sw 10 (n) Pr-ʿ3ʿws Ptlwmysʿws ʿnẖ ḏ.t.*
2 *P3-hb s3 Ḏḥwṯ-i.ir.dy-s p3 nty ḏd n T3-šr.t-Mnṯ ta Pa-mnḥ: wn-mtw<=t> rdb [sw 4]*
3 *t3y=w pš(.t) 2 r rdb sw 4 ʿn i-ir-n=y (n) rn n3 pr.w r.tw<=t> n=y [iw p3y=w ḥw]*
4 *ẖn.w. Mtw=y [dy.t st n=t- - -]*

- -

Translation

Year 32, 10 Thot, of king Ptolemy (VIII), may he live forever.
Phibis, son of Thotortaios, is the one who declares to Senmonthis, daughter of Pamenos:
«I owe you 4 artabas of wheat — their half is 2, being 4 artabas of wheat again — interest included.
I shall return it to you - - -»

- -

Notes

3-4 *[iw p3y=w ḥw] / ẖn.w, interest included*: the supplement *[iw t3y=w ms.t] / ẖn.w*, which has the same meaning, is possible as well (see §35; Vandorpe, 'Interest in Ptolemaic Loans' (1998); see also my study Vandorpe, 'Greek and Demotic Loan Contracts from Pathyris' (2001), announced in §33).

16

GREEK LOAN OF WHEAT
by Apollonia

Pathyris H. x W. = 30 x 11.5 cm 4 Jan. 131 B.C.

British Library, P. inv.no. 613 [bought on 9 Nov. 1895 from Grenfell] = **P. Grenf. I 18**.
Photograph. — No photograph available.

Description. — The papyrus is complete. The text on the recto is written along the fibres and has a top margin of 3.2 cm, a bottom margin of 5.5 cm and a left-hand margin of 2 cm. There is hardly any place left at the right side; the notary's scribe even began to write smaller at the end of several lines so as to end most words in the same line; this is clear, for instance, at the end of l. 8, where the last two letters of 'Αρσιήσιος are very small.

After the redaction of the loan, the papyrus was rolled vertically and then folded double. Consequently, the strips 2a and 2b were at the outside. On strip 2a a summary was recorded in two columns, at right angles to the text on the recto. The left column (verso l. 1a - 2a) is written against the left edge; l. 1b of the right column (verso l. 1b - 3b) runs until the right edge of strip 2a (see §37). The text is damaged along the horizontal and two vertical folds.

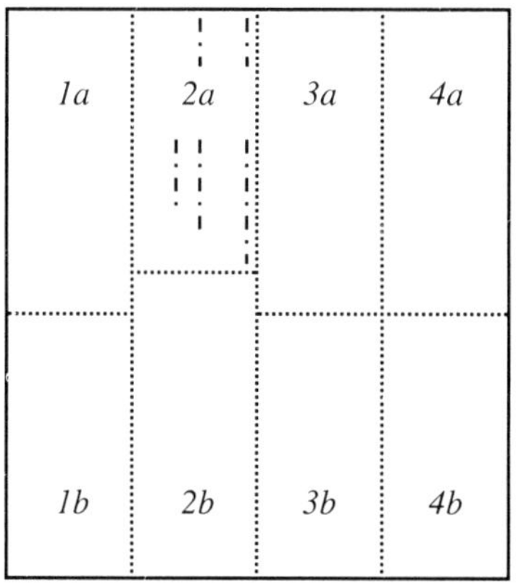

Verso

Introduction

Contents. — Apollonia lends 35 artabas of wheat, including interest, to her brother-in-law Apollonios alias Psennesis (pros. 408), son of Apollodotos alias Harsiesis, and her sister Herais alias Ti(e)sris (pros. 407).

The scribe Areios. — Areios, who represents the agoranomos Sarapion, is the writer of five loans which form part of the archive of Dryton and Apollonia (Texts 16, 17, 19, 25 and 30)[1]. A brief comparison of his handwriting is in order. The hand of Areios in this early text of 131 B.C. differs in many ways from his later contracts Texts 17, 19 and 25 (Text 30 is not dated). This difference was already noted by G. Messeri[2]. She divides the texts by Areios for palaeographical reasons into three periods: 1) Text 16 of 131, 2) the texts of 129[3]-123[4], 3) P. Lond. III 1203 of 113. Text 30 (not dated) rather belongs to the early period, as already suggested by Messeri[5]. In my opinion, Areios' handwriting of the earliest phase (Text 16) from 131 B.C. is much more elegant than his hand in later documents. From 129 B.C. onwards Areios' handwriting has widened and his *kappa's* and *eta's* are less high, see, for instance,

	in Text 16 of 131 B.C.		in Text 19 of 126 B.C.	
ἔκτεισιν		(l. 23)		(l. 15)
Ἄρειος	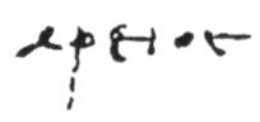	(l. 30)	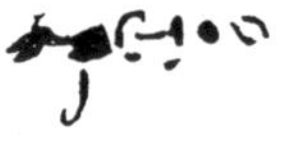	(l. 21)
δάνειον	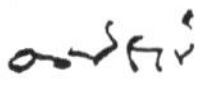	(verso)	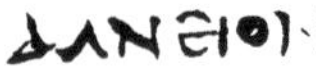	(verso)

---

1 For Areios, see Pros. Ptol. III 7687; Pestman, 'L' agoranomie' (1978), p. 205; Messeri Savorelli, 'Lista degli agoranomi' (1980), p. 208-210; Pestman, 'Agoranomoi' (1985), p. 13; addendum: Text 30. For Sarapion, agoranomos of Krokodilopolis, see Pros. Ptol. III 7680; Messeri Savorelli, 'Lista degli agoranomi' (1980), p. 208; Pestman, 'Agoranomoi' (1985), p. 12.

2 Messeri, 'P. Grenf. I 19' (1982), in *ZPE* 47, p. 276-277, n. 5.

3 Text 17.

4 *AfP* 1 (1901), p. 63-65.

5 Messeri Savorelli, 'Due Atti agoranomici' (1984), p. 524.

Text

Recto

Ἔτους λθ Χοίαχ ιβ ἐν Παθύρει ἐπὶ Σαραπίωνος ἀγορανόμου ἐδάνεισεν Ἀπολλωνίαι Πτολεμαίου τοῦ Ἑρμοκράτου Κυρηναίαι μετὰ κυρίου τοῦ ἑαυτῆς ἀνδρὸς Δρύτωνος τοῦ Παμφίλου Κρητὸς τῶν τοῦ ἐπιτάγματος ἱππάρχου ἐπ' ἀνδρῶν καὶ διαδόχων Ἀπολλωνίωι Ἀπολλοδότου τῶι καὶ Ψεννήσει Ἁρσιήσιος Πέρσηι τῆς ἐπι[γ]ονῆς καὶ Ἡραίδι Πτολεμαίου τῆι καὶ Τίσρει Παοῦτος Περσίνηι μετὰ κυρίου τοῦ ἑαυτῆς ἀνδρὸς Ἀπολλωνίου τοῦ προγεγραμμένου πυρῶν ἀρτάβας τριάκοντα πέντε ἄτοκα· τὸ δάνειον τοῦτο ἀποδότωσαν οἱ δεδανεισμένοι Ἀπολλωνίαι ἐμ μηνὶ Παχὼν [τ]οῦ λθ (ἔτους) πυρὸν νέον καθαρὸν ἄδολον ἀπ[οκ]αθεσταμένον εἰς οἶκ[ο]ν πρὸς αὐτ[ὴν] ἰδ[ί]οις ἀνηλώμασιν μέτρωι ὧι καὶ παρείληφαν πρὸς τὸ κθ-χ(οίνικον)· ἐὰν δὲ μὴ ἀποδῶσ[ι]ν ἐν τῶι ὡρισμένωι χρόνωι ἀποτεισάτωσαν παραχρῆμα ἡμι[ό]λιον τὴν ἐσο[μ]ένην ἐν τῆι ἀγορᾶι τιμήν· ἔγγυοι ἀλλήλων εἰς ἔκτεισιν τῶν διὰ τοῦ δανείου πάντων οἱ δεδανισμένοι· ἡ δὲ πρᾶξις ἔστω Ἀπολλωνία[ι] ἐξ ἀμφοτέρων τῶν δεδανισμένων καὶ ἐξ ἑνὸς καὶ ἑκάστου αὐτῶν καὶ ἐξ οὗ ἐὰν αἱρῆται καὶ ἐκ τῶν ὑπαρχόντων αὐτοῖς πάντων καθάπερ ἐγ δίκης.

Ἄρειος ὁ παρὰ Σαραπίωνος κεχρη(μάτικα).

Recto 3 Ἀπολλωνίαι, *l.* Ἀπολλωνία 4 Κυρηναίαι, *l.* Κυρηναία 12 ed.: αβ in ἀρτάβας corr. ex λε 19 κθ-χ(οίνικον),  papyrus 24 δεδανεισμένοι ed., δεδανισμένοι legimus, *l.* δεδανεισμένοι 26 δεδανεισμένων ed., δεδανισμένων legimus, *l.* δεδανεισμένων 27 ἐάν , *l.* ἄν

Verso

1a Ἀπόδοσις	1b Ἔτους λθ Χοίαχ ι̅β̅ δάνειον Ἀπολλωνίας
2a ἐν τῷ λθ (ἔτους)	2b πρὸς Ψεννῆσιν (πυρῶν) ἀρ(τάβας) λε
	3b καὶ Τίσριν γυ(ναῖκα) αὐ(τοῦ)

Verso 1b ιβ ed., ι̅β̅ legimus 3b γυ(ναῖκα) αὐ(τοῦ), papyrus

Translation

Recto

Year 39, 12 Choiak, in Pathyris before Sarapion, agoranomos.

Has lent Apollonia, daughter of Ptolemaios son of Hermokrates, Cyrenaean, having as kyrios her own husband Dryton, son of Pamphilos, Cretan, cavalry officer over men at the head of those of the epitagma-unit and one of the diadochoi,

to Apollonios, son of Apollodotos alias Psennesis, son of Harsiesis, Persian of the epigone, and to Herais, daughter of Ptole- maios, alias Tisris, daughter of Paous, Persian, having as kyrios her own husband, the above-mentioned Apollonios,

35 artabas of wheat without (further) interest (viz. with interest included).

The borrowers shall return the loan to Apollonia in the month of Pachon of the 39th year, in wheat that is new, pure, free from adulteration and delivered to her at her house at their own expense, according to the measure by which they received (it), (viz.) the 29-choinix-measure. If they fail to return it within the stated time, they shall immediately return (the 35 artabas) increased by 50% (or) the current market price.

The borrowers themselves are sureties for each other for the payment of all the liabilities of this loan. Apollonia shall have the right of execution upon both borrowers and on each and every one of them, and upon whomsoever she chooses and upon all their property, as if in accordance with a legal decision.

I, Areios, subordinate of Sarapion, have dealt with (this contract).

Verso

(1a) *Repayment* **(2a)** *in year 39.*

(1b) *Year 39, 12 Choiak, loan of Apollonia* **(2b)** *to Psennesis, of 35 artabas of wheat* **(3b)** *and to Tisris, his wife.*

Notes

Recto

12 ἀρτάβας : 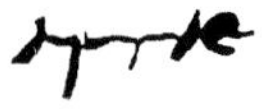 -αβ- is probably being corrected from λ̣ε̣. Apparently, Areios first wrote ἀρτ λε. It is, however, common in loan contracts to write the amount out in full (see Vandorpe, 'Greek and Demotic Loan Contracts from Pathyris' (2001)). Consequently, Areios corrected the passage and changed λε into -αβ- and added -ας, which results in ἀρτάβας, followed in the next line by the amount written in full: τριάκοντα πέν[τ]ε. See, for a similar case, Text 19, comm. on l. 7.

18 [π]α̣ρείληφαν: for [π]αρειλήφασι, see Mayser, *Grammatik* I.2, p. 85.

Verso

2b (πυρῶν): I prefer to supply the plural rather than the singular (πυροῦ), since Areios always uses the plural πυρῶν, see, for instance, recto l. 12; Text 25, l. 6; Text 30, comm. on l. 4; P. Grenf. II 18; see also Vandorpe, 'Greek and Demotic Loan Contracts from Pathyris' (2001).

3b καὶ Τίσριν γυ(ναῖκα) αὐ(τοῦ): is added later. It should have been inserted after πρὸς Ψεννῆσιν of l. 2b, *before* and not *after* the loan object (πυρῶν) ἀρ(τάβας) λε.

17

GREEK LOAN OF MONEY
by Apollonia

Plate VII (recto)
[Collage by P.W. Pestman]

Pathyris	H. x W. = 21 x 8.9 cm [Height incomplete]	14 May 129 B.C.

Fragment A = British Library, P. inv.no. 614 [bought on 9 Nov. 1895 from Grenfell] +
Fragment B = Cairo, P. Gr. inv.no. 10354 [acquired before 1897] +
Fragment C = lost +
Fragment D = British Library, P. inv.no. 614 addendum [bought on 9 Nov. 1895 from Grenfell] +
Fragment E = New York Pierpont Morgan Library, P. Gr. inv.no. 166 [bought in the period 1897-1899 from Grenfell & Hunt for Lord Amherst].

Fragment A and *Fragment E* were published for the first time as **P. Grenf. I 19** and **P. Amh. II 166**, respectively. G. Messeri discovered that both fragments and a third unpublished piece *Fragment D* belonged together: **G. MESSERI**, 'P. Grenf. I 19 + P. Amh. II 166', in *ZPE* 47 (1982), p. 275-280 (= **SB XVI 12716**).

Finally, **P.W. PESTMAN** found among the fragments of the Cairo Museum a fourth piece of the puzzle: *Fragment B*. I am grateful to him for giving me permission to publish his discovery[1] and to make use of his transcription.

Photograph. — Plate VII (recto); Messeri, 'P. Grenf. I 19' (1982), in *ZPE* 47, pl. 16, recto-verso (no photograph of Cairo, P. inv.no. 10354).

A

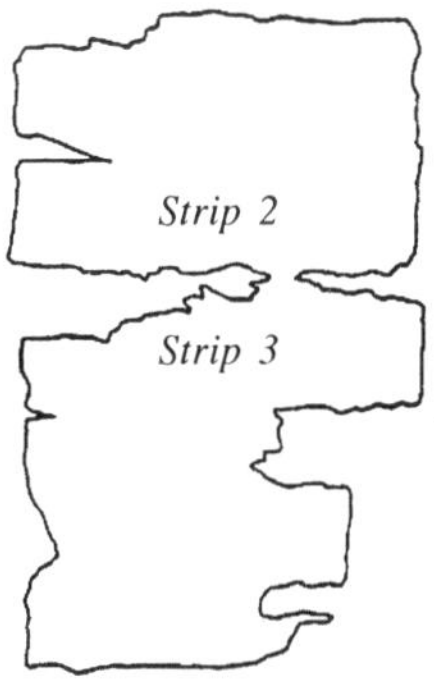

B

C = *lost*

D

E

F = *lost*

---

1 Compare Pestman, 'Agoranomoi' (1985), p. 13, n. b.

Description. — The papyrus is incomplete: parts are lost (Fragments C and F) in the middle and at the bottom. Fragments B and D are damaged at the right hand side and Fragment A is damaged along the horizontal fold. The contract is written on the recto, across the fibres: thus the scribe was able to use a small piece of papyrus with a height of c. 9 cm for an agoranomic contract. The text on the verso is written along the fibres.

After redaction, the papyrus sheet was folded horizontally; it is broken or damaged along the horizontal folds. The strips 2 and 3 (verso of Fragment A) came at the outside. On strip no. 2 a summary was written along the fibres (see above) in two columns: the left column (verso l. 1a-2a) is written against the left border, the right column against the right border.

Introduction

Contents. — Apollonia, having as kyrios her husband Dryton, lends 5,030 drachmas of copper ἄτοκα (that is with interest included, see §35). It is not clear for how long the money was loaned, since the duration of the loan is missing in the lacuna. Money was lent for a fixed amount of months: the loan was negotiated in the month of Pharmouthi of year 41 and was, according to the verso, to be returned in year 42, that is at least five months later (see also next subject: Later additions?).

The debtors are Aniketos, son of Ptolemaios, alias Nechoutes, son of Panobchounis, and his wife Nikaia, daughter of NN, alias Nechouthis, daughter of P - - ais, having as kyrios her husband Aniketos. The double names of the debtors are good equivalents: Aniketos (the invincible) is a translation of Nechoutes (*nḫt*, to be strong); Nikaia (the victorious) translates the feminine name Nechoutis, originating from the same stem as Nechouthes.

Aniketos acts here at the same time as agoranomos (l. 2) and as debtor (called a Persian, l. 10-12). More information on this individual and his family is to be found in other sources gathered by P.W. Pestman[1].

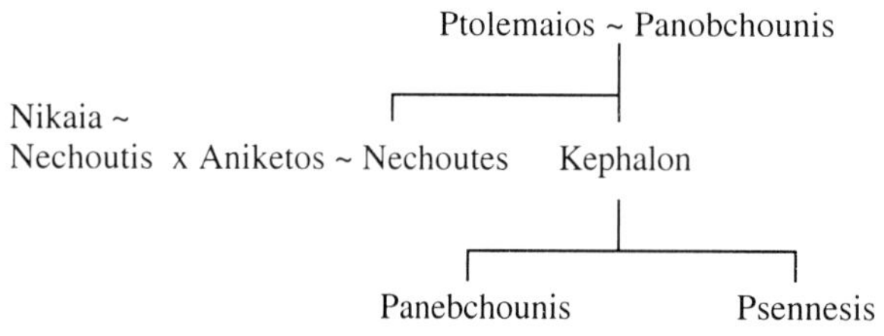

Later additions? — The agoranomic loan contract contains some cursive notes which may be remains of an old text or later additions. These cursive notes are found in the upper margin of the recto and in the left column of the verso:

The upper margin of the recto has:

'Ανίκη(τος) Πανοβχού(νιος) τῶι Κεφάλωνι Πανοβχούνιος

1 Pestman, 'Agoranomoi' (1985), p. 12-13; Id., 'L' agoranomie' (1978), p. 206; see also Pros. Ptol. III and IX 7651 = 7700.

The summary on the verso has:

	Left column	*Right column*
1a	'Α]πόδοσις	1b Δάνειον 'Απολλω-
2a		2b νίας πρὸς Νεχού(την) χα(λκοῦ) (τάλαντον) α 'Ελ
3a/b		

I n t e r p r e t a t i o n   o f   B . P .   G r e n f e l l : Grenfell, who knew only Fragment A, considered the cursive notes as remains of an older text: «The papyrus had been used before the contract between Apollonia and Nechouthes was recorded on it. At the top is written in very small letters 'Ανίκη(τος) Πανοβχού(νιος) τῶι Κεφάλωνι Πανοβχούνιος and on the verso

1a ἀ]πόδοσις
2a τό]πο̣υ̣ ω βL
3a]ος Κεφάλου »

I n t e r p r e t a t i o n   o f   G .   M e s s e r i : according to Messeri, the left column of the verso is related to the loan contract: «In realtà tutto ciò che è scritto sul verso [thus, also the left column] si riferisce al contratto del recto». Messeri did not yet know fragment B, according to which two debtors are involved: Aniketos alias Nechoutes and his wife Nikaia alias Nechoutis. The only information she had at the time was that several debtors were involved (see recto, l. 20+x - 23). The information on the verso led her to conclude that the debtors were Nechoutes (l. 2b) and Kephalon (l. 3a). She read the verso as follows, connecting l. 3b to the right column.

1a	ἀ]πόδοσις	1b δάνειον 'Απολλω-
2a	ἐ]ν̣ τῷ̣ μβ (ἔτει)	2b νίας πρὸς Νεχού(την) χα(λκοῦ) (τάλαντον) α 'Ελ
3b	κ(αὶ) π]ρὸς Κεφάλωνα	

In her view, the right column was written first, whereas the left column was penned in «una corsiva accurata, ma più piccola e veloce per il termine di restituzione (che è stato scritto subito dopo)». She assumes that the note in the upper margin does not necessarily belong to an older document: since it involves the same persons as the summary on the verso, it may have been added afterwards, «quando ormai il documento era in famiglia».

O u r   i n t e r p r e t a t i o n : thanks to the new fragment B discovered by Pestman, the names of the debtors are now known: Aniketos alias Nechoutes and his wife Nikaia alias Nechoutis. Thus, Kephalon was not a debtor, at least not in the initial contract. In addition, not the entire left column was written in a cursive hand, but only l. 3a/b; l. 2a was corrected on the same occasion.

I suggest the following interpretation, which is based on the view of Messeri. The scribe of the agoranomic contract wrote a summary on the verso in two columns: the right column referred to the loan object and the debtors, whereas the left column contained the date of return of the money, that is the year and/ or the month (money loans were negotiated for a fixed number of months). The original date of return is difficult to reconstruct and contained at least an *upsilon*:

1a	᾿Α]πόδοσις	1b	Δάνειον ᾿Απολλω-
2a	[ ] . . ῠ̣ . .	2b	νίας πρὸς Νεχού(την) χα(λκοῦ) (τάλαντον) α ᾿Ελ

Later, Kephalon, a brother of the debtor Aniketos, became involved for an unclear reason. He took over the debt or he became the third debtor alongside Aniketos and his wife. On that occasion, the name of Kephalon was added

1. to the contract in the form of a note in the upper margin:

   ᾿Ανίκη(τος) Πανοβχού(νιος) τῶι Κεφάλωνι Πανοβχούνιος

2. to the summary on the verso (l. 3a). On the same occasion, the date of return was probably changed in the summary into 'year 42' (l. 2a), that is at least five months after the redaction of the loan:

1a	᾿Α]πόδοσις	1b	Δάνειον ᾿Απολλω-
2a	{ [ ] . . ῠ̣ } μβ (ἔτους)	2b	νίας πρὸς Νεχού(την) χα(λκοῦ) (τάλαντον) α ᾿Ελ
3b	[π]ρ̣ὸς Κεφάλωνα		

Who made the additions? The additions are written in a cursive hand with letters above the preceding character not only *at the end* of a word (to denote an abbreviation), but also *within* a word (for instance, the *alpha* in Κεφάλωνα, verso, l. 3b). The latter phenomenon is rarely attested and I have only seen it on a regular basis in the handwriting of Dryton and his son Esthladas (see §65). Therefore, it is plausible that Dryton, who acted as kyrios for the creditor, his wife Apollonia, made the additions himself.

It is, however, not excluded that the notes are remains of an older text, as Grenfell already suggested (see above). The description has shown that the papyrus with its height of 9 cm was not suitable for an agoranomic contract. The agoranomos Aniketos may have torn it off a document in which his brother Kephalon and he himself were involved. The notes in the upper margin of the recto and in l. 2a and 3b of the verso are then remains of this older document.

The scribe Areios. — For the scribe Areios, who represents the above-mentioned agoranomos Aniketos, see Text 16, Introduction and note 1.

Recto

Text

Ἔτους μα Φαρμοῦθι κ̅γ̅ ἐν Παθύρει ἐπ' Ἀνικήτου ἀγορανόμου·
ἐδάνεισεν Ἀπολλωνία
Πτολεμαίου Κυρηναία
[μετὰ κυρίο]ụ [το]ῦ̣ ἑạ[υτ]ῆ̣[ς]
[ἀνδ]ρ̣[ὸ]ς Δρύτωνος τοῦ Παμφίλου Κρητὸς τῶν διαδόχων
καὶ τῶν τοῦ ἐπιτάγματος
ἱππάρχου ἐπ' ἀνδρῶν
Ἀνικήτωι Πτ̣[ολεμαίου]
τῶι καὶ Νιχούτ̣[ηι Πανοβ-]
χούνιος Πέρσηι̣ [τῶν ἐκ Πα-]
θύρεως καὶ Νικαία[ι - c. 6 -]
τῆι καὶ Νεχούτ̣ει Π[- c. 6 -]
` .αιτ̣ος´ Περσίνῃ̣ μετὰ κυρίο[υ τοῦ ἑαυ-]
τῆς ἀνδρὸς Νεχ[ο]ụ̣τ̣[ου τοῦ προ-]
γεγραμμένο[υ καὶ συνδεδανεισ-]
μένου χα(λκοῦ) νομ(ίσματος) (τάλαντον) [α (δραχμὰς) πεντακισ-]
χ[ιλίας τριάκοντα ἄτοκα·]
- [ἔγγυοι ἀ̣λ̣λήλων
εἰς ἔκτεισιν τῶν διὰ τοῦ δανείου πάντων]
[αὐτοὶ οἱ] δ̣εδ[ανεισμένοι. Ἡ δὲ
πρᾶ[ξις] ἔστ̣[ω] Ἀ̣π̣[ολλωνίαι ἐκ τῶν]
δεδανεισμένω̣[ν καὶ ἐξ ἑνὸς]
καὶ ἑκάστου αὐτῶν [καὶ ἐξ οὗ ἂν]
αἱρῆται καὶ ἐκ τῶṿ ụ̣π̣ạρχ[όν-]
των αὐτοῖς πάντων καθά[περ]
___ἐγ̣ δίκης.

Ἄρειος ὁ παρ' Ἀνική(του) κεχρη(μάτικα).

Recto 9 ἱππάρχου ed., -ου in ἱππάρχου corr. ex -ης 11 Νιχούτ̣[ηι] *l.* Νεχούτ̣[ηι] 12 -ρσηι̣ in Πέρσηι̣ corr. 18 χα(λκοῦ) νομ(ίσματος), papyrus  27 Ἀνική(του), papyrus 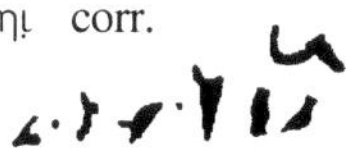

Translation

Year 41, 23 Pharmouthi, in Pathyris before Aniketos, agoranomos.

Has lent Apollonia, daughter of Ptolemaios, Cyrenaean, (5) *having as kyrios her own husband Dryton, son of Pamphilos, Cretan, cavalry officer over men at the head of those of the epitagma-unit and one of the diadochoi,*

(10) *to Aniketos, son of Ptolemaios, alias Nichoutes, son of Panebchounis, Persian, inhabitant of Pathyris, and*

to Nikaia, daughter of NN, alias Nechoutis, daughter of P - - ais, (15) *Persian, having as kyrios her own husband Nechoutes, mentioned above and joint borrower, one talent, 5,030 drachmas of copper, without (further) interest (viz. with interest included),*

- -

Sureties for each other for the payment of all liabilities described in this loan (20) *are the borrowers themselves.*

Apollonia shall have the right of execution upon the borrowers, upon each and every one of them and upon whomsoever she chooses and upon all their property, (20) *as if in accordance with a legal decision.*

I, Areios, subordinate of Aniketos, have dealt with (this contract).

Verso

Text and translation

1a	**1st H** 'Α]πόδοσις	1b	**1st H** Δάνειον 'Απολλω-
2a	{ [ ] . . ṿ } **2nd H** μβ (ἔτους)	2b	**1st H** νίας πρὸς Νεχού(την) χα(λκοῦ) (τάλαντον) α 'Ελ
3b	**2nd H** [π]ρ̣ὸς Κεφάλωνα		

2a [ἐ]ν̣ τῷ μβ (ἔτει) ed., { [ ] . . ṿ } μβ (ἔτους) legimus

2b Νεχού(την), papyrus  supplevimus

3b [κ(αὶ) π]ρ̣ὸς Κεφάλωνα ed., [π]ρ̣ὸς Κεφάλωνα

Return	*Loan of Apollonia*
- - - **2nd H** *year 42*	*to Nechoutes of 1 talent 5,030 (drachmas) of copper*
	2nd H *to Kephalon*

Upper margin recto

Text and translation

2ndH 'Ανίκη(τος) Πανοβχού(νιος) τῶι Κεφάλωνι Πανοβχούνιος

2ndH *Aniketos, son of Panobchounis, to Kephalon, son of Panebchounis.*

Notes

Recto

9 χου in ἱππάρχου: -  Areios wrongly used the nominative case and wrote ἱππάρχης; afterwards, he corrected this into a genitive depending on Δρύτωνος, l. 6. He made the same mistake in Text 19, l. 4, where he did not correct it.

12 Πέρσηι̣ : -  -ρσηι is corrected. It is not clear what was written originally.

12-13 Πέρσηι̣ [τῶν ἐκ Πα]|θύρεως: the lacuna can be filled with 8 to 11 characters. The supplement [τῶν ἐκ Πα]|θύρεως is confirmed by parallel constructions added to the name of the debtor(s) in P. Amh. II 50, P. Primer 10 and P. Adler 10. The debtors in loans from Pathyris are, however, always called Persians of the epigone. For an additional supplement of [τῆς ἐπιγονῆς] there is no room, unless ἐπιγονῆς is abbreviated as is done by Areios in Text 19, l. 5; a supplement Πέρσηι̣ [τῆς ἐπι(γονῆς) τῶν ἐκ Πα] | θύρεως of 12 characters is thus possible as well.

13-15 Νικαία[ι - 4 to 7 -] τῆι καὶ Νεχούτ̣ει Π[- 4 to 7 -]` .αιτ̣ος´ : the Greek patronymic of Nikaia is entirely lost in the lacuna, the Egyptian name partly; the latter name begins with a *pi* and ends on -ais. At first, Areios forgot to write the last part of the name when he started a new line, but he added it afterwards between l. 14-15: ` .αιτ̣ος´ ; before the *alpha* in ` .αιτ̣ος´ there is a high trace matching a *phi* or *psi*.

Verso

2a {[ ] . . υ̣ } μβ (ἔτους) : see Introduction: Later additions?

18

DEMOTIC LOAN
by Apollonia

See facsimile below

Pathyris or Krokodilopolis	H. x W. = 2.8 x 10.5 cm [Height incomplete]	17 March 128 B.C.

Heidelberg, P. dem. inv.no. 712a [In Heidelberg since 1898, acquired by Reinhardt] = **P. dem. Gebelein Heid. 18**.

Photograph and facsimile. — No photograph available; see my facsimile below; facsimile in P. dem. Gebelein Heid., p. 100, no. 18.

Description. — The papyrus is very fragmentary. After the redaction of the loan on the recto, the papyrus was rolled from the bottom to the top (or the other way round), resulting in horizontal strips, and was broken off along one of the horizontal folds. Only the upper strip is preserved with, on the *recto*, the first three lines of the loan contract written along the fibres. On the *verso* a summary of two lines is written against the fibres.

Introduction

Contents. — According to the few data provided by the summary on the verso, Senmonthis, daughter of Pamenos, lends corn or money to Senmouthis, daughter of Onnophris. The creditor Senmonthis, daughter of Pamenos, is undoubtedly to be identified with Dryton's wife Apollonia alias Senmonthis, daughter of Ptolemaios alias Pamenos[1]. The debtor Senmouthis, daughter of Onnophris, is not attested in other texts.

The scribe. — The name of the temple notary is lost and it is not clear whether the contract was drawn up in the temple of Pathyris or of Krokodilopolis. The first editor recognized the hand of Nechthminis, son of Nechthminis, notary in the temple of Pathyris in 124-94 B.C. (see Text 9, note 3). If this is correct, Text 18 of 128 B.C. would be the earliest testimony of this Nechthminis; the next testimony dates to 124 B.C.[2]. There is, however, another possible notary from Pathyris who may enter into account: Nechthminis son of Thotortaios, who is attested only once as temple notary in Pathyris in 125 B.C.[3] and whose handwriting too bears a close resemblance to that of Text 18.

---

1 *Pace* the first editor: «Die beide Kontrahenten . . . lassen sich aus anderen Texten bisher nicht nachweisen».

2 P. dem. Bürgsch. 9.

3 P. dem. BM Glanville 10500, with photograph pl. 13; see Text 3, comm. on l. 48.

Facsimile

Recto

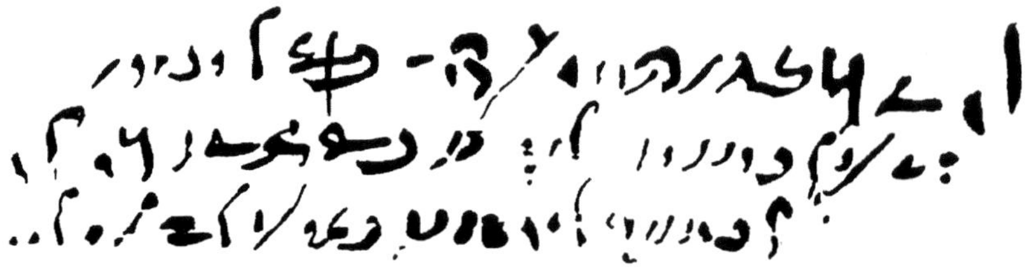

Verso

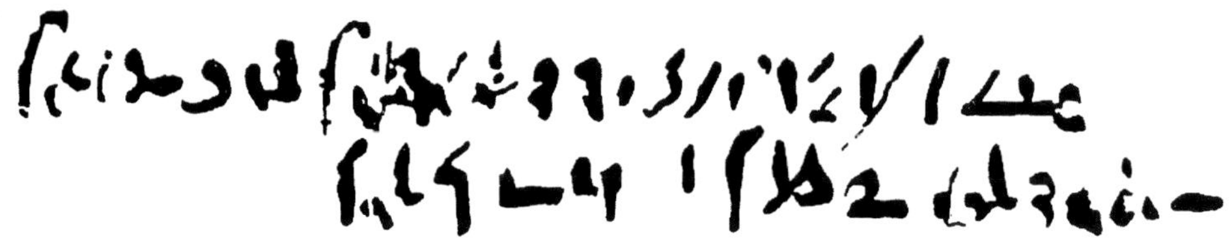

Recto

1 *Ḥ3.t-sp 42 ibd-2 pr.t sw 25 n Pr-ʿ3 ʿws*
2 *⸢P⸣tlwmys ʿws p3 mnḫ*
3 *[s3 Ptl]wmys ʿws irm Glwp[t]r3 ⸢ʿws⸣*

- -

Verso

1 *[T3 s]mbwl i.ir st T3-šr.t-Mw.t ta Wn-nfr*
2 *n sḥm.t T3-šr.t-Mnṯ ta Pa-mnḥ*

Recto 1 *sw 23* ed., *sw 25* legimus 3 *Glwptr3* ed., *Glwp[t]r3 ⸢ʿws⸣* legimus Verso 1 *[. . . s]mbwl* ed., *[T3 s]mbwl* supplevimus

Translation

Recto

Year 42, 25 Mecheir of king Ptolemy (VIII) Euergetes, son of Ptolemy (V) and Kleopatra (I)
- -

Verso

The symbolon which Senmouthis, daughter of Onnophris, has made for the woman Senmonthis, daughter of Pamenos.

Notes

Verso

1 *[T3 s]mbwl i.ir st, the symbolon which*: when the antecedent of a relative clause introduced by *i.ir*, becomes the direct object in the relative clause, it is usually not taken up by a resumptive pronoun (Spiegelberg, *Demotische Grammatik* (1925) §549 and 557); compare the verso of Text 21. Here, however, the direct object is taken up by *st*.

For the transcription of the Greek word σύμβολον in demotic contracts, see Clarysse, 'Greek Loan-Words' (1987), p. 30, no. 78; see also §34.

19

GREEK LOAN OF MONEY
by Apollonia

Pathyris | H. x W. = 15.8 x 10.7 cm [Width incomplete] | 7 Nov. 127 B.C.

British Library, P. inv.no. 616 [bought on 9 Nov. 1895 from Grenfell] = **P. Grenf. I 20**.
Photograph. — No photograph available.

Description. — The papyrus is broken off on the left side; consequently the beginning of each line (c. 9 characters) is missing. In addition, the text is badly damaged along the horizontal fold, between the second and the third strip, at the height of line 8 of the recto.

The text on the recto is written along the fibres and has a top margin of 0.7 cm and a bottom margin of 2.6 cm. The left-hand margin is lost and on the right side there is hardly any margin. After redaction the papyrus was rolled horizontally from bottom to top. The strips nos. 2 and 3 came on the ouside; in the middle of strip no. 2 a summary was written on the *verso* against the fibres. Strips nos. 1 and 7 have on the verso (with vertical fibres) an extra strip with horizontal fibres. Strip no. 4 contains ink traces of (an old?) Greek text on the verso.

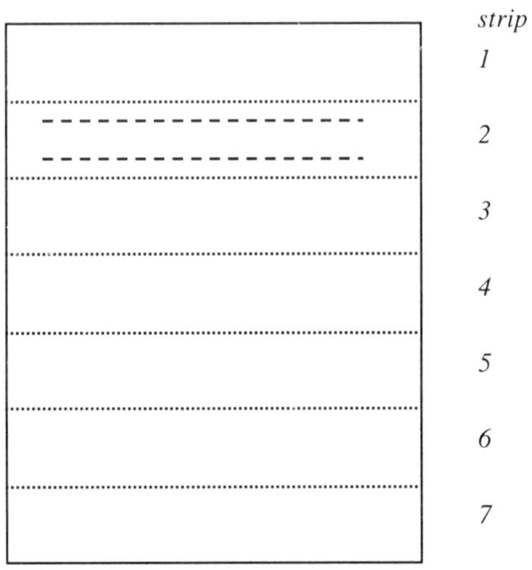

Verso

Introduction

Contents. — Apollonia, having as kyrios her husband Dryton, lends 10,000 drachmas of copper ἄτοκα (that is with interest included, see §35) for a period of five months, starting from 7 November 127 B.C. The debtors are Solon alias Sleis, and Harmais, both sons of Horos, as well as their mother Tebos, whose kyrios is her son Sleis. The family of Solon alias Sleis is well-known in Pathyris. I propose the following family tree:

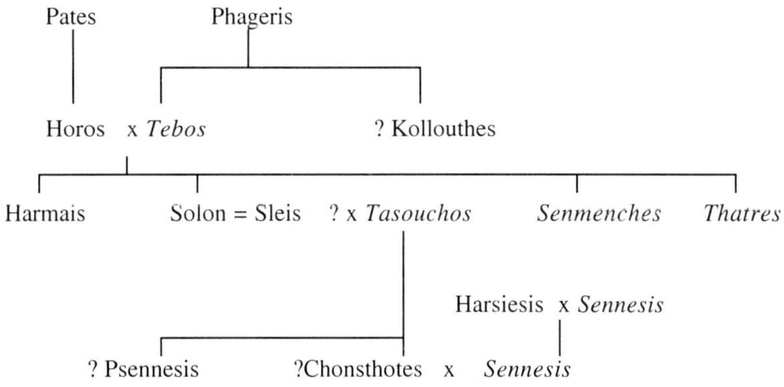

Sources: Text 19 of 127 B.C. (Solon and Harmais, sons of Horos and [Tebos]); P. dem. Ryl. 19 of 118 B.C. with receipt SB I 5107 of 113 B.C. (Harmais and Sleis, sons of Horos, son of Pates); P. dem. Ryl. 24 of 113 B.C. (Senmenches and Thatres, daughters of Horos and Tebos [ed.: *T3-ᶜq*], sisters of Harmais and Sleis).

Doubtful: P. dem. Cairo II 31028 descr. = Vandorpe, 'Agoranomic Loans with Demotic Summary' (2000) of 111 B.C. (Psennesis, son of Sleis); P. Adler 12 of 101 B.C. (Kollouthes, son of Phageris, 35 years old) and P. Adler 14 of 100 B.C. (Kollouthes, son of Phageris); P. dem. Eheverträge 48 of 92 B.C. (Chonsthotes, son of Sleis and Tasouchos, married to Sennesis, daughter of Harsiesis and Sennesis); in O. Stras. 312 of 157 B.C. a Sleis son of Harmais is mentioned [Ed.: Saisis].

For *Sleis alias Solon*, see Pros. Ptol. IV 11016; Pestman, 'Pathyris II' (1963), in *Aegyptus* 43, p. 46, no. 102; for *Harmais*, see Pros. Ptol. II and VIII 3838 = IV 10659; Pestman, 'Pathyris II' (1963), in *Aegyptus* 43, p. 31, no. 5.

The name *Šlḥ*, Σλῆις, has in old editons often been misread as Σαισις. Demotic evidence, which has *Šlḥ*, shows that the reading Σλῆις is certain. Sleis is apparently a Semitic name, compare the Hebrew name Šélaḥ (Gen. 10, 24; 11, 12-15). Solon must be a Greek translation.

The name of the mother of Harmais and Sleis is only found in P. dem. Ryl. 24, l. 5 and 7. It has been read by F.L. Griffith as *T3-ᶜq ?*, a name not otherwise attested. In the manuscript of my PhD (p. 231) presented in 1992, I suggested reading *T3-3b3*, Τεβῶς in Greek[1], a well-known name parallelled by *P3-3b3* [2], Πεβῶς. This mother's name is supplied in l. 6. The fascicle I 14 (p. 1050) of Lüddeckens, *Dem. Namenbuch*, published in 1996, also reads the name as *T3-3b3*.

The scribe Areios. — For the scribe Areios, who represents the agoranomos Asklepiades[3], see Text 16, Introduction and note 1.

---

1 Preisigke, *Namenbuch*, p. 425; Foraboschi, *Onomasticon*, p. 313.

2 Lüddeckens, *Dem. Namenbuch*, I.3, p. 154.

3 For Asklepiades, agoranomos of Krokodilopolis in 127-126 B.C., see Pros. Ptol. III 7661; Pestman, 'L' agoranomie' (1978), p. 205; Messeri Savorelli, 'Lista degli agoranomi' (1980), p. 208-210; Pestman, 'Agoranomoi' (1985), p. 12.

Text

Recto

[Ἔτους μδ] Φαῶφι $\overline{\text{ιε}}$, ἐν Παθύρει ἐπ' Ἀσκληπιάδου ἀγορανόμου·
[ἐδάνεισεν] Ἀπολλωνίαι Πτολεμαίου Κυρηναίαι, μετὰ κυρίου τοῦ
[ἑαυτῆς ἀνδ]ρὸς Δρύτωνος τοῦ Παμφίλου Κρητὸς τῶν τοῦ ἐπ[ι-]
[τάγματος ἱπ]πάρχης ἐπ' ἀνδρῶν καὶ διαδόχων, Σόλωνι
[τῶι καὶ Σλ]ήει Ὥρου καὶ Ἁρμάει Ὥρου Πέρσαις τῆς ἐπι(γονῆς)
[καὶ Τεβῶτι] Φαγήριος Περσίνηι μετὰ κυρίου τοῦ προ-
[γεγραμμέ]νου Σλήιος υἱοῦ αὐτῆς χα(λκοῦ) ⟦(τάλαντον)⟧ τάλαντον ἓν
[δραχμὰς τετ]ρα[κισχιλίας ἄτοκ]α εἰς μῆνας πέν-
[τε ἀπὸ Φαῶ]φι ἕως Μεχεὶρ λ τοῦ μδ (ἔτους)· τὸ δὲ δάνειον
[τοῦτο ἀποδό]τωσαν οἱ δεδανεισμένοι Ἀπολλωνίαι
[ἐν μηνὶ Με]χεὶρ $\overline{\lambda}$· ἐὰν δὲ μὴ ἀποδῶσιν ἐν τῶι
[ὡρισμέν]ωι χρόνωι, ἀποτεισάτωσαν παραχρῆμα
[ἡμιόλιον] καὶ τοῦ ὑπερπεσόντος χρόνου τόκους
[διδράχμο]υς τῆς μνᾶς τὸν μῆνα ἕκαστον· ἔγγυοι
[ἀλλήλω]ν εἰς ἔκτεισιν τῶν διὰ τοῦ δανείου
[γεγραμμ]ένων πάντων αὐτοὶ οἱ δεδανεισμένοι·
[ἡ δὲ πρᾶ]ξις ἔστω Ἀπολλωνίαι ἐκ τῶν δεδα-
[νεισμέν]ων καὶ ἐξ ἑνὸς καὶ ἑκάστου αὐτῶν καὶ
[ἐξ οὗ ἂν αἱ]ρῆται καὶ ἐκ τῶν ὑπαρχόντων αὐτοῖς
[πάντω]ν καθάπερ ἐγ δίκης.

Ἄρειος ὁ παρ' Ἀσκλη(πιάδου) κεχρη(μάτικα).

Recto 1 ιϵ ed., $\overline{\text{ιϵ}}$ legimus 2 Ἀπολλωνίαι, *l.* Ἀπολλωνία ; Κυρηναία ed., Κυρηναίαι legimus, *l.* Κυρηναία 4 [ἱπ]πάρχης *l.* [ἱπ]πάρχου 5 [Σαή]ει ed., [Σλ]ήει supplevimus; ἐπ(ιγονῆς) ed., ἐπι(γονῆς) legimus, papyrus 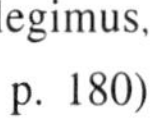 6 [Τεβῶτι] supplevimus 7 Σαήιος ed., Σλήιος Wilcken (BL I, p. 180) et Grenfell & Hunt (P. Grenf. II, p. 216); χα(λκοῦ) τάλαντον ed., χα(λκοῦ)  τάλαντον Wilcken (BL I, p.180); χα(λκοῦ) ⟦(τάλαντον)⟧ τάλαντον legimus 8-9 [δραχμὰς τετρακισχιλίας . . .]α ϵ[. . . μ]νᾶς πέν| [τε δραχμάς (a break in the papyrus) | [. . . . . ἀπὸ Φαῶ]φι ed., [δραχμὰς τετρακισχιλίας ἄτοκ]α ϵ[ἰς μῆ]νας πέν| [τε ἀπὸ Φαῶ]φι Meyer (P. Meyer, p. 14 and 34) 14 [. . . . .]υς ed., [διδράχμο]υς Grenfell & Hunt (P. Grenf. II, p. 216) 16 [κειμ]ένων ed., [γεγραμμ]ένων supplevimus 21 Ἀσκληπιάδου ed., Ἀσκλη(πιάδου) Hunt (BL I, p. 180), papyrus 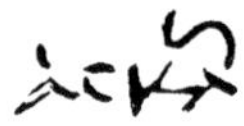

Verso

Δάνειον Ἀπολλωνίας πρὸς
Σλῆιν καὶ ἄλλους χα(λκοῦ) (τάλαντον) $\overline{\alpha}$ ͵Δ

Verso 2 Σαῆιν ed., Σλῆιν Wilcken (BL I, p.180) et Grenfell & Hunt (P. Grenf. II, p. 216)

Translation

Recto

Year 44, 12 Phaophi, in Pathyris before Asklepiades, agoranomos.

Has lent Apollonia, daughter of Ptolemaios, Cyrenaean, having as kyrios her own husband Dryton, son of Pamphilos, Cretan, cavalry officer over men at the head of those of the epitagma-unit and one of the diadochoi,

to Solon alias Sleis, son of Horos, and to Harmais, son of Horos, Persians of the epigone, and to Tebos, daughter of Phageris, Persian, having as kyrios her own son, Sleis mentioned above,

one talent, 4000 drachmas of copper, without (further) interest (viz. with interest included), for a period of five months, from Phaophi onwards until 10 Mecheir of the 44th year.

This loan the borrowers shall return to Apollonia in the month of Mecheir, (before) the 30th day. If they fail to return it within the stated time, they shall immediately return (it) increased by 50% and for the overtime interest (they shall pay) at the rate of 2 drachmas the mina each month.

Sureties for each other for the payment of all liabilities described in this loan are the borrowers themselves. Apollonia shall have the right of execution upon the borrowers, upon each and every one of them and upon whomsoever she chooses and upon all their property, as if in accordance with a legal decision.

I, Areios, subordinate of Asklepiades, have dealt with (this contract).

Verso

Loan of Apollonia to
Sleis and others of 1 talent, 4000 drachmas in copper.

Notes

Recto

2 Ἀπολλωνίαι and Κυρηναίαι (ed. Κυρηναία): Areios wrongly uses a dative instead of a nominative. He makes the same mistake in exactly the same passage of Text 16, l. 4.

4 [ἱπ]πάρχης: Areios writes a nominative instead of the genitive [ἱπ]πάρχου depending on Δρύτωνος l. 3. He made the same mistake in Text 17, l. 9, where later he corrected ἱππάρχης into ἱππάρχου.

5 ἐπι(γονῆς): the editor reads  as ἐπ for ἐπ(ιγονῆς); the *epsilon* is, however, followed by a ligature of *pi* and *iota*: I read ἐπι for the abbreviation of ἐπι(γονῆς).

7 χα(λκοῦ) ⟦ (τάλαντον) ⟧ τάλαντον: after χα(λκοῦ) traces are visible of a word or a sign:  ; they were not read by the editor. Wilcken (BL I, p. 180) proposed  . In my view, the traces fit the symbol for talent: $\overline{\Lambda}$; the writer Areios erased this symbol since he wished to write the word out in full, which is usual in a loan contract (Vandorpe, 'Greek and Demotic Loan Contracts from Pathyris' (2001)). Areios made a similar correction in the loan Text 16, where he corrected ἀρτ λε into ἀρτάβας τριάκοντα πέν[τ]ε (see comm. on l. 12).

9 Μεχεὶρ λ: the figure λ was probably marked by a supralinear line (as, for instance, in l. 1 and 11), but this is lost in the lacuna.

16 [γεγραμμ]ένων: the editor supplied [προκειμ]ένων; my proposal [γεγραμμ]ένων is based on a parallel passage in P. Grenf. II 18 of the same scribe Areios.

20

DEMOTIC ACKNOWLEDGEMENT OF DEBT (BARLEY)
to Apollonia

Plate VIII (recto-verso)

Probably Pathyris	H. x W. = 5.3 x 5.4 cm [Fragmentary]	Probably after 150 B.C.

Heidelberg, P. Gr. inv.no. 313 [acquired by Reinhardt in 1897] = **unpublished**.
Photograph and facsimile. — Plate VIII (recto-verso) and see my facsimile below.

Description. — The papyrus used for the loan Text 20 was apparently torn from an older document, since the self-written acknowledgement of debt is written on the recto, but against the fibres. The verso has a Greek summary written along the fibres. The papyrus is now fragmentary: it is broken off at the right and at the foot.

Introduction

Contents and date. — The name of the debtor is preserved on the recto and in part on the verso: the priest Peteharsemtheus, son of Patous. A man with the same name and father's name is found in the fragmentary P. dem. Cairo II 30794 (not dated) and in a receipt for wheat from the temple of Pathyris (109 B.C.)[1]. It is not clear whether he can be identified as a son of the Patous who is often attested in this archive and who is also a priest (pros. 04).

Peteharsemtheus borrows 1 1/3 artabas of barley from a daughter of Pamenos. The only daughters of a Pamenos in Pathyris are Apollonia alias Senmonthis (Dryton's wife) and her sisters. That Apollonia alias Senmonthis is most probably the creditor, is suggested by museum archaeology (see Vandorpe, *Archives from Pathyris* (2001), §22-27): this text was bought together with Texts 43 and 44, both accounts from the archive of Dryton and Apollonia. Assuming the three texts originally belonged together, the text dates after 150 B.C. when Apollonia married Dryton and attained the age of majority.

1 O. dem. *Enchoria* 19/20 (1992/1993), no. 13.

Recto

Facsimile and text

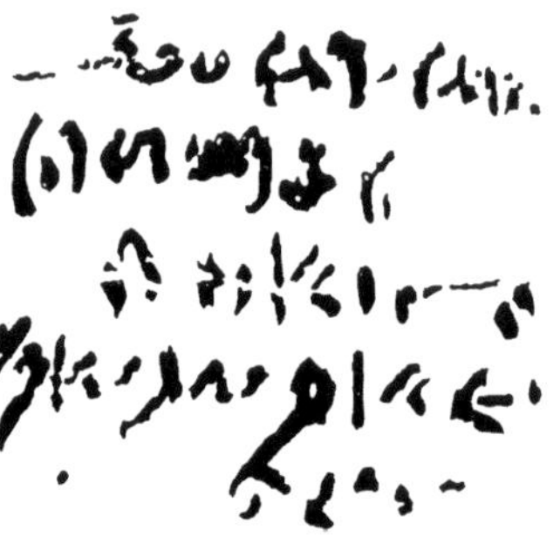

[P3-dy-]⌜Ḥr-sm3⌝-t3.wy s3 Pa-t3.wy p3 nty ḏd
[n T3-šr.t-Mn]⌜ṯ⌝ ta Pa-mnḥ
[- - -] ⌜ - - - ⌝ (r.)tw<=t> s n=y
[- - -] ⌜ - - - ⌝ it 1 1/3 r it 2/3 r it 1 1/3 ͨn.
[Mtw=y] ⌜dy.t st⌝ n=⌜t⌝ [r-hn-r] ⌜ḥ3.t-sp⌝ [- -]

- -

Verso

Facsimile and transcription

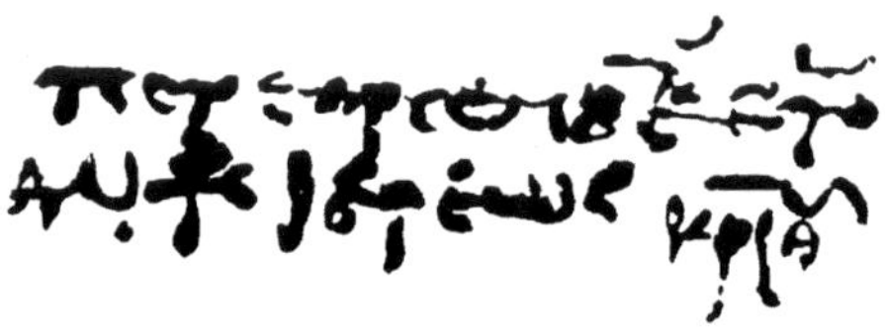

ω υ
]πετεαρσεμθε cτο
υ οc η
].τοτ ιερεωc κριθ
] . . .

Text

[. .] Πετεαρσεμθέως τοῦ
[Π]ạτοῦτος ἱερέως κριθῆ(ς)
[. .] . . .

Translation

Recto

Peteharsemtheus, son of Patous, is the one who declares to Senmonthis, daughter of Pamenos:
« - - - which you gave to me - - - 1 1/3 (artaba) of barley — (their half is) 2/3, being 1 1/3 (artaba) of barley again. I shall return it before year - - -»
- - - - - - - - - - - - - -

Verso

(Loan of) Peteharsemtheus, son of Patous, priest, barley - - -

Notes

Recto

3-4 The formula used by temple notaries (*Wn-mtw=t* + loan object *i-ir-n=y n rn n3 pr.w r.tw=t s n=y*) does not seem to be maintained in this self-written acknowledgement of debt. The same elements are found, but in another order. For the absence of the feminine pronoun *t* in *(r.)tw*<*=t*> , compare Text 15, l. 3.

Verso

1 [. .] Πετεαρσεμθέως: the lacuna before Πετεαρσεμθέως probably contained δά(νειον).

21

GREEK RECEIPT
for Patous on behalf of Esthladas

See facsimile of the verso below

Probably Pathyris	H. x W. = 10.5 x 11.5 cm [Height incomplete]	After 140 B.C.

British Library, P. inv.no. 889a [bought on 8 July 1901 from C. Murch]. The *recto* is published as **P. Lond. III 889a** (p. 22); the *verso* with a demotic note has remained unnoticed and is **unpublished**.
Photograph and facsimile. — No photograph available; see my facsimile of the verso below.

Description. — The papyrus is fragmentary. The papyrus is broken off at the foot, probably in a horizontal fold, and is of inferior quality; on the verso, several fibres are missing. The papyrus is probably torn from an older document, since the Greek receipt on the recto is written against the fibres. After redaction, the papyrus was rolled from right to left and a demotic summary was written on the outside.

Introduction

Contents. — Text 21 is a self-written receipt. Zois alias Onchasis acknowledges having received 12 talents of copper from the priest Patous who represented Esthladas (pros. 504), son of Dryton. Since she could not write Greek, a representative whose name is lost in the lacuna wrote the Greek acknowledgement. The receipt was issued in the Greek notary's office or archeion (see the verso), where the repayment of the loan had to be registered (see §34).

The Greek double name Ζωίς (from ζωή, *life*) is a translation of the Egyptian name *ʿnḫ=s*/ Onchasis[1] (from *ʿnḫ, life*). She is the daughter of Isidoros; only one Isidoros is known in Pathyris and he had contacts with Esthladas' step-family (see Text 10). The priest Patous who acts on behalf of Esthladas is probably to be identified with the Patous who is an acquaintance of Esthladas and of the other family members (see pros. 04).

The role of Esthladas. — The loan is repaid ὑπὲρ Ἐσθλάδου τοῦ Δρύτωνος (l. 6); in receipts and acknowledgements of debt ὑπέρ[2] can mean «für Rechnung des Zahlers» as well as «für Rechnung des Empfängers». N. Lewis formulated the problem as follows[3]: does Zois receives the money on behalf of Esthladas (= creditor), or does Patous gives it back on behalf of Esthladas (= debtor)?

N. Lewis adhered to the first possibility; the reason why Zois received money for Esthladas is clear: she was his wife. This interpretation causes several problems. An unpublished demotic ostrakon (see App. C) informs us that Esthladas was married to and in

---

1 Lüddeckens, *Dem. Namenbuch* I.2, p. 104.
2 Preisigke, *WB*, *s.v.*; Mayser, *Grammatik* II.2, p. 459.
3 Lewis, 'Dryton's wives' (1982), in *Chron. d' Ég.* 57, p. 320-321 (Who was Zois alias Onchasis?).

124 B.C. was divorced from a woman called Tagombes (pros. 503) and not Zois alias Onchasis. Esthladas could, of course, have married Zois in an earlier or later period of his life.

There is a more serious problem: why was the receipt found in the archive of Esthladas' family, if Esthladas was the creditor? The receipt would be a proof of repayment, to be kept by the debtor Patous. Patous must indeed have received the document and kept it in his archive, since the demotic summary on the verso contains only the name of Zois (*[The Greek document] which Onchasis has made in the archeion*). If the summary was made by Zois, not her name but that of Patous would have been recorded and if a third person had composed the summary, the name of Patous would have been added.

I have another proposal, which is in accord with the view of the first editor[1] and of J.K. Winnicki[2]: Patous repaid the money on behalf of Esthladas, who was probably on campaign. Patous made a summary on the verso in his native language and when Esthladas came home, the receipt was given to him and became part of the archive of Dryton and his family.

Date[3]. — A *terminus post quem* is 140 B.C.[4], when Esthladas attained the age of majority. N. Lewis[5] suggests 131-130 B.C. «when Esthladas is known to have been away from home on active service» (see Text 36). This is possible, but Esthladas was a soldier and must have been on campaign fairly often. A more general date (after 140 B.C.) is to be preferred.

1 Introduction to the text: «the priest is said to make payment on behalf of Esthladas, son of Dryton».
2 Winnicki, 'Ein ptolemäischer Offizier' (1972), in *Eos* 60, p. 351-352.
3 First editor: «2nd cent. B.C.»; Pros. Ptol. III 6440: «fin 2e s.».
4 See also Winnicki, 'Ein ptolemäischer Offizier' (1972), in *Eos* 60, p. 344: «nach 140».
5 Lewis, 'Dryton's wives' (1982), in *Chron. d' Ég.* 57, p. 321.

Text

Recto

Ζωὶς ἡ καὶ Ὀγχᾶσις Ἰσιδώρου
Πατοῦτι ἱερεῖ τῶι παρὰ τῶν
ἱερέων τοῦ ἐν Κροκοδίλων
πόλει καὶ Παθύρει ἱερῶν
χαίρειν. Ἔχω παρὰ σοῦ
ὑπὲρ Ἐσθλάδου τοῦ Δρύτωνος
χαλ[κ]ọῦ τάλαντα δεκάδυο
δρα[χ]μὰς τρισχιλίας, κοὐθέν
[σοι ἐγ]ḳαλῷ. Ἔγ[ρα]ψεν
- -

---

3 τοῦ, *l.* τῶν 9 ε[. . . .]εν ed., ἔγ[ρα]ψεν Grenfell-Hunt (*AfP* 4, p. 530)

Verso

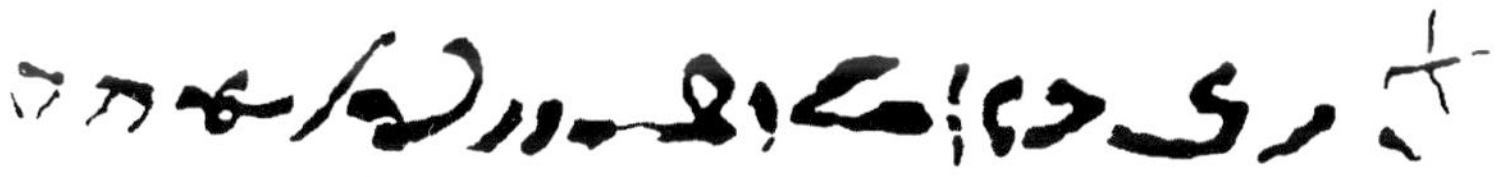

- - - - - - - - *[wynn] r.ir ʿnḫ=s n p3 3rghn.*

Translation

Recto

Zois alias Onchasis, daughter of Isidoros, to Patous, one of the priests of the temples in Krokodilopolis and Pathyris, (5) *greetings.*
«I have received from you on behalf of Esthladas, son of Dryton, 12 talents of copper, 3000 drachmas and I bring no accusation against you.»
Has written - - - .

Verso

[The Greek document] which Onchasis has made in the archeion.

Notes

Recto

5 Ἔχω παρὰ σοῦ: this formula can introduce either an acknowledgement of debt or a receipt (beside ἀπέχω, see, for instance, Pap. Lugd. Bat. XXII, p. 280-281). The addition of κοὐθέν [σοι ἐγ]κ̣αλῶ̣, l. 8-9, rules out any doubt: the document is a receipt by which the former creditor can bring no accusation against the debtor.

9 Ἔγ[ρα]ψεν: the receipt is a χειρόγραφον (see §34) and has to be written by the creditor himself/ herself. If he/ she cannot write (Greek), a third person writes the document by order of the creditor. At the end of the document he usually records his name and explicitly mentions that he acts on behalf of the creditor because he/ she cannot write (the latter part is here lost in the lacuna).

Verso

1 *- - - [wynn] r.ir ꜥnḫ=s n p3 3rghn*: the beginning of the summary is lost. The first visible sign is the foreign determinative, commonly used with the word *wynn* (*Greek*).

Similar summaries usually have "the document that NN has made (*i.ir*)". As a private and not a notarial receipt is involved, it must have been labelled *bk* (document). The summary probably had: *[p3 bk wynn] r.ir NN, the Greek document which NN has made.*

1 *3rghn*: this Greek loan word, often attested in Pathyris, stands for ἀρχεῖον (Greek notary's office and registration office, see §34), see Clarysse, 'Greek Loan-Words' (1987), p. 21, no. 9.

22

GREEK ACKNOWLEDGEMENT OF DEBT
by Esthladas

See scanned photograph p. 418

Probably Pathyris — H. x W. = 5.6 x 10.6 cm [Width incomplete] — After 140 B.C.

Heidelberg, P. Gr. inv.no. 1291 [date of acquisition unknown] = **P. Baden II 6**.
Photograph. — See p. 418 and see http://www.rzuser.uni-heidelberg.de/~gv0/Papyri/P.Heid._Uebersicht.html (see VBPII 6)

Description. — The papyrus is broken off on the right side. The papyrus is probably torn from an older document, since the acknowledgement of debt on the recto is written against the (vertical) fibres. The text has a top margin of 1 cm and a bottom and left margin of 1.5 cm. The papyrus is of a rather poor quality: some vertical fibres of the recto are missing. In l. 1 and 2 the scribe avoided writing on the underlying horizontal fibres, whereas in l. 3 and 4 he did so.

Introduction

Contents and date. — The acknowledgement of debt is written by Esthladas (for his handwriting, see §64-66) and dates to the period after 140 B.C., when Esthladas was an adult (see pros. 504). The creditor's name and the loan object are lost.

Text

1 Ἐσθλάδας Δρύτωνος Κρὴς τῶν δ̣[ιαδόχων - - - Πέρσηι]
τῆς ἐπιγονῆς· ὁμολογῶ ἔχειν π[αρὰ σοῦ - - -]
σομαι αὐτὸν̣ προσδε̣χο̣μενον . [- - - - - ἡ δὲ πρᾶξις ἔστω σοι]
ἐκ τ' ἐμοῦ καὶ ἐκ τῶν ὑπαρχόντ̣[ων μοι πάντων πράσσοντι καθάπερ ἐγ
δίκης]

---

1 [Πέρσηι] supplevimus 2 σοῦ supplevimus 3 o ed., legimus

Translation

Esthladas, son of Dryton, Cretan, one of the diadochoi, - - - to - - - Persian of the epigone: «I acknowledge having received from you - - - . I shall - - - him, guaranteeing- - - . You shall have the right of execution upon me and upon all my property, as if in accordance with a legal decision.»

Notes

1 χαίρειν and the name of the creditor are expected in the lacuna. χαίρειν usually comes after the name of the addressee, which cannot be the case here.

2 ὁμολογῶ ἔχειν π[αρὰ σοῦ - - -]: this clause can introduce an acknowledgement of debt as well as a receipt (see Text 21, l. 5). The praxis-formula in l. 3-4 makes clear that an acknowledgement of debt is involved.

3 σομαι αὐτὸν̣ προσδε̣χ̣όμενον: this clause is problematic. Judging by the meaning of προσδέχεσθαι ("accept", here rather: "guarantee, credit a sum"), αὐτόν must refer to a person.

23

DEMOTIC LOAN OF MONEY
by Kaies

Plate IX; see facsimile below

[New collage]

Krokodilopolis

H. x W. =
Fragment A : 8.5 x 7.5 cm
Fragment B: 21.5 x 12.5 cm
Total: 30 x 12.5 cm
[Height incomplete]

124 - 116 B.C.

Fragment A = Heidelberg, P. dem. inv.no. 770b [in Heidelberg since 1898, acquired by Reinhardt] +
Fragment B = Louvre, P. dem. inv.no. E 10595 [in the Louvre since 1891 or 1892, bought by an intermediary of Lord Wilbour].

Fragment A was published as **P. dem. Gebelein Heid. 30**. During my stay in Paris, I discovered that the large Louvre-fragment B, which has remained **unpublished**, joins the Heidelberg-fragment perfectly.

Photograph and facsimile. — Plate IX and see my facsimile below; facsimile in P. dem. Gebelein Heid., p. 104, no. 30 (no facsimile of Frag. B = Louvre, P. dem. inv.no. 10595).

Description. — The upper part of the papyrus (fragment A) is incomplete: the upper margin, the first line and the right part of lines 2 to 11 are missing; faint traces of the second line are visible. At the height of l. 6 to 8 a small piece is missing on the left side. The two fragments A and B are broken off in a horizontal fold. The vertical tear responsible for the missing right part of fragment A continues in the first four lines of fragment B. Fragment B is complete, but is damaged along the horizontal folds, especially in the lower part. For the way in which the papyrus was folded, see Vandorpe, 'Greek and Demotic Loan Contracts from Pathyris' (2001).

The papyrus is of an inferior quality: the fibres on the recto do not always run parallel; in the beginning of l. 14 the horizontal fibres are missing; consequently, the scribe had to write on the underlying fibres. It is not clear whether or not the verso contained a summary, since the large fragment B is glued on paper.

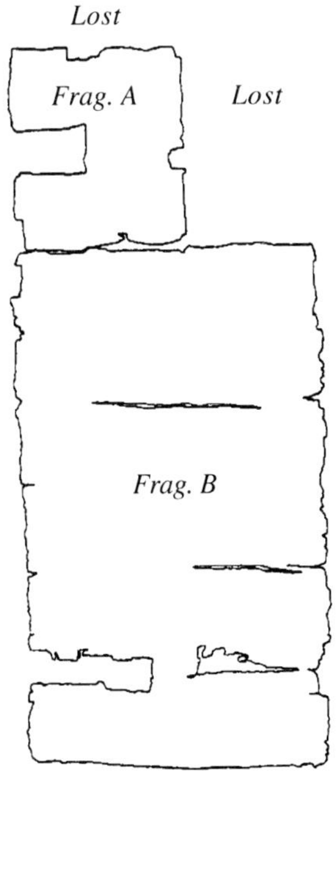

Introduction

Contents. — The name of the lender is lost; he is a son of Pates. There are several reasons to identify him with Dryton's son-in-law Kaies, son of Pates (pros. 505), who is creditor in several loans (Texts 24 to 28); this identification was already proposed by P.W. Pestman[1]. The lender is a soldier, a "man receiving pay" among the men of the officer Lochos and registered at the camp of Krokodilopolis, as was Kaies. In addition, museum archaeology strongly suggests that the loan was part of the archive of Dryton and his family (see p. 9-11; Vandorpe, *Archives from Pathyris* (2001), §25, 3).

The debtor Nechouthes, son of Nechouthes, is a colleague: he is also a "man receiving pay", registered at the camp of Krokodilopolis. He is otherwise unknown. Nechouthes borrows 450 deben, which is 9000 drachmas, interest included, until 30 Phamenoth (mid-April). It is not clear when the loan was negotiated, probably a few months before.

Date. — The date is lost. The remainder of the protocol and the name of the temple notary suggest the period 124-116 B.C.

The protocol is problematic, since the representative of the temple notary did not write down all the titles of the rulers. The mention of the Gods Euergetai (l. 4) shows that the loan was issued in the reign of Ptolemy VIII; the Gods Euergetai are[2]:

from 143/142 to 138/137 B.C. Ptolemy VIII and Kleopatra II
from 138/137 to 132/131 B.C. Ptolemy VIII, Kleopatra III and Kleopatra II
from 132/131 to 125/124 B.C. Ptolemy VIII and Kleopatra III
from 125/124 to 116 B.C. Ptolemy VIII, Kleopatra III and Kleopatra II.

The titles of king Ptolemy VIII can be supplied in the lacuna of l. 1-3. There is not, however, enough space left for the title of the queen(s) in l. 4; the protocol usually has[3]:

during the reign of Ptolemy VIII and the queen Kleopatra II, his sister (and) his wife, the Goddess Euergetis (t3 Pr-ʿ3 ʿws.t Glwptr3 ʿws t3y=f sn.t t3y=f ḥm.t t3 ntr.t mnḫ.t).

or

during the reign of Ptolemy VIII and the queen Kleopatra II, his sister, and the queen Kleopatra III, his wife, the Goddess Euergetis (t3 Pr-ʿ3 ʿws.t Glwptr3 ʿws. t3y=f sn.t irm t3 Pr-ʿ3 ʿws.t Glwptr3 ʿws t3y=f ṣhm.t t3 ntr.t mnḫ.t).

The lacuna of l. 4, however, can only contain *t3 Pr-ʿ3 ʿws .t*, *the queen* (that is, Kleopatra II or Kleopatra III) or *n3 Pr-ʿ3 ʿws.wt*, *the queens* (Kleopatra II and Kleopatra III).

The name of the temple notary (l. 25) is of further help: Espnouthis, son of Teos, is active in the period 124-98 B.C. (see below).

In conclusion, the mention of the Gods Euergetai and the name of the temple notary suggest that the loan was negotiated in the period 124-116 B.C. Consequently, the lacuna of l. 4 has to be supplied with *n3 Pr-ʿ3 ʿws .wt, the queens* (Kleopatra II and Kleopatra III).

Scribe. — The man who acts as scribe in the name of Espnouthis, son of Teos, temple notary of Krokodilopolis in the period 124-98 B.C. (see Text 7, note 1), is called Pakoibis, son of

1 P.W. Pestman, in *Chron. d'Ég.* 41 (1966), p. 319 and n. 6.
2 See Pap. Lugd. Bat. XV, p. 62.
3 See Pap. Lugd. Bat. XV, p. 56.

Schotes. His family is well-known[1]. A small archive of his brother Harsiesis is preserved[2]. Pakoibis is attested as scribe of other documents: another temple deed from Krokodilopolis (112 B.C.)[3], an ostrakon (108/107 B.C.)[4] and an oath sworn in the temple of Souchos (in Krokodilopolis or Pathyris; 90 B.C.)[5]. Furthermore, he acts as a witness for the temple notary of Pathyris in the period 124-89 B.C.[6]. He is found in two tax receipts[7] and in two accounts[8]. Finally, he is known to have leased temple land together with his companions in 116/107[9] and in 100 B.C.[10].

Witnesses. — The loan is the original deed, since the names of the four witnesses (l. 27-30) are written in their own handwriting beneath the contract. These witnesses from Krokodilopolis are otherwise unknown. The third witness Harsiesis, son of Spemminis, is most probably a son of the preceding witness Spemminis, son of Teos.

---

1 See Pap. Lugd. Bat. XIX, p. 213 g.
2 Vandorpe, *Archives from Pathyris* (2001), §38.
3 P. dem. BM inv.no. 10570A ined., see P. dem. Gebelein Heid., p. 16, comm. on no. 1 verso l. 9.
4 O. dem. BM inv.no. 30249 ined., see P. dem. Gebelein Heid., p. 16, comm. on no. 1 verso l. 9.
5 O. dem. Tempeleide 172a.
6 P. dem. Bürgsch. 9, verso l. 5 (124 B.C.); P. dem. Gebelein Heid. 1, verso l. 9 (115-100 B.C.); P. dem. Ryl. 23, verso l. 3 (115-108 B.C.); P. dem. Ryl. 24, verso l. 2 (113 B.C.); P. dem. Adler 4, verso l. 4 (110 B.C.); P. dem. Ryl. 29, verso l. 8 (91 B.C.); P. dem. Ryl. 30, verso l. 6 (89 B.C.).
7 O. dem. Mattha 242 = O. dem. *Enchoria* 19/20 (1992/1993) no. 3 (issued in Pathyris, payment for Krokodilopolis; 108 B.C.) and O. dem. *MDAIK* 21, 1966, p. 160, no. 30 (s.d.).
8 O. dem. *MDAIK* 21, 1966, p. 163, no. 32 (s.d.).
9 P. dem. Gebelein Heid. 13 (Pathyris).
10 P. Grenf. II 33 (Pathyris; see Pros. Ptol. IV 10861).

Facsimile

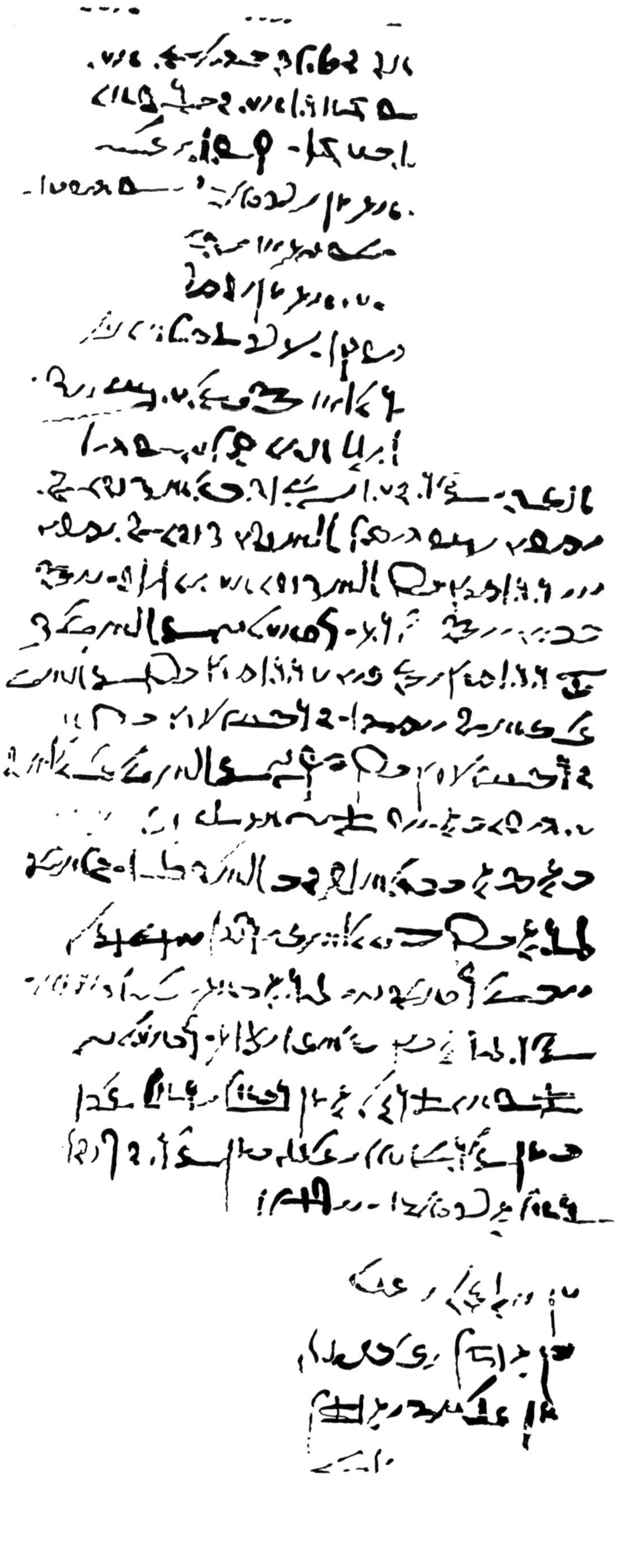

Text

[Ḥ3.t-sp - - ibd - - sw - - n Pr-ʿ3ʿws Ptlwmysʿws]
[p3 ntr mnḫ s3 Ptlwmysʿws] ⸢irm⸣
[Glwptr3]ʿws n3 ntr.w nty pr.w irm
[?n3 ?Pr-ʿ3ʿws .wt n3 ntr.w] mnḫ.w irm n3 nty smn
[n Rʿ-qd P3-s] ⸢y⸣ nty p3 tš n Nw.t. Ḏd
[rmt iw=f šp ḥbs] iw=f sḫ r 3mwr ḫn n3 rmt.w ⸢n⸣
[- - -] ⸢N3⸣-nḫṯ=f s3 N3-⸢nḫṯ⸣[=f]
[n rmt iw=f šp] ⸢ ḥbs⸣ iw=f sḫ r t3 h⸢3⸣[pytrs]
[n 3mwr] ⸢ḫn⸣ n3 rmt.w L3qhws
[Gʿy] ⸢s3⸣ Pa-tw. Wn-mtw=k ḥḏ 400 + 50
[- - tbʿ 2]⸢4⸣ qd 2.t iw p3y=w ḥw ḫn=w
i-ir-n=y n rn n3 ḥḏ.w r.dy=k n=y. Mtw=y dy.t st n=k
r-hn-r ibd-3 pr.t sw ʿrq. Iw=y tm dy.t st n=k r-hn-
r p3 ssw-hrw nty ḥry, iw=y dy.t st irm p3y=w 1 r 1 1/2 n p3 ibd
nty m-s3 p3 ibd ⸢rn⸣ =f n ḥtr.ṯ. Bn iw=y rḫ dy.t
ky ssw-hrw r-r=w m-s3 p3 ssw-hrw nty ḥry. Bn iw=y rḫ
ḏd ir=y n=k p3 hp n t3 smbwl3 nty ḥry iw
t3 smbwl3 nty ḥry n dr.ṯ=k. Bn iw=y rḫ ḏd tw=y n=k
ḥḏ pr nty nb n p3 ⸢t3⸣ iwṯ iw iw=f ʿḥʿ ⸢rd.ṯ⸣.
Nty nb nkt nb nty mtw=y ḫnʿ n3 nty iw=y dy.t ḫpr=w n iwi
md nb nty ḥry šʿ-tw=y ir r-ḫ.ṯ=w. P3y=k rd
p3 nty nḥṯ r md nb nty iw=f r ḏd.ṯ=w irm=y n
rn md ⸢nb⸣ nty ⸢ḥry. M⸣tw=y ir=w r-ḫrw=f n ḥtr.ṯ
iwṯ mn iwṯ sḫ nb. Sḫ Pa-Gbk s3 Sbk-ḥtp
nty sḫ rn Ns-p3-ntr s3 Ḏd-ḥr nty sḫ rn n3 wʿb.w
Sb⸢k⸣ nb 3mwr n p3 5 s3.w.
Sḫ P3-šr-mwt s3 Ḥr.
Sḫ Sp-Min s3 Ḏd-ḥr.
Sḫ Ḥr-s3-Is.t s3 Šp-Min.
[Sḫ - - - s3 - - -]ʿnḫ.

---

2 *Spuren* ed., *⸢irm⸣* legimus 3 *[. . .] irm n3 ntr.w nty pry* ed., *[Glwptr3]ʿws n3 ntr.w nty pr.w* legimus et supplevimus 5 *P3-]sy* ed., *P3-s]⸢y⸣* legimus 6 *rmt.w* ed., *rmt.w ⸢n⸣* legimus 8 *[rmt iw=f šp ʿq ḥ]bs* ed., *[rmt iw=f šp] ⸢ḥbs⸣* legimus; *t3 h3py / [trs]* ed., *t3 h⸢3⸣[pytrs]* legimus et supplevimus 10 *[Gʿy]* supplevimus; *400 qd 50* ed., *400 'und' 50* Zauzich 11 *[i-ir-n=y ḥḏ ḥmt 24 qd] 2.t* ed., *[- - tbʿ 2]⸢4⸣ qd 2.t* legimus et supplevimus

Translation

Year - - month - - day - - of king Ptolemy (VIII) Euergetes, son of Ptolemy (V) and Kleopatra (I), the Gods Epiphaneis, and the queen(s ?), the Gods Euergetai, and of those who are appointed (priests) in Alexandria (and) Ptolemais in the Thebaid.

Has declared the man who receives pay, while he is registered at the camp in Krokodilopolis among the men of - - -, Nechouthes, son of Nechouthes, to the man who receives pay, while he is registered at the camp in Krokodilopolis among the men of Lochos, [Kaies], son of Pates:

«I owe you 450 (deben of copper) money, at the rate of 24 obols to 2 kite, interest included, in the name of the money you gave to me.

I shall return it to you before 30 Phamenoth. If I fail to return it to you within the stated time, I shall return it at the rate of 1 1/2 (deben of money) per 1 (deben) in the month following the month named, under compulsion.

I shall not be able to give to you another date for it except the above date. I shall not be able to say: 'I have performed for you the right of the symbolon' while the above symbolon is in your hand. I shall not be able to say: 'I have given to you money, corn or anything whatsoever' without a valid receipt.

Everything, all that belongs to me and all that I shall acquire, are security for every above word until I have acted accordingly.

Your representative is the one who is authorized in respect to every word which he will address to me in the name of every word which (is written) above; I shall execute them according to his instructions, under compulsion, without delay, without any force.»

Has written Pakoibis, son of Schotes, who writes in the name of Espnouthis, son of Teos, who writes in the name of the priests of Souchos, lord of Krokodilopolis, (priests) of the five phyles.

Has written Psemmous, son of Horos.

Has written Spemminis, son of Teos.

Has written Harsiesis, son of Spemminis.

Has written - - -, son of - - - ʿnḫ.

Notes

3 *[Glwpr3] ʿws n3 ntr.w nty pr.w, Kleopatra, the Gods Epiphaneis*: the editor read the first traces of l. 3 as *irm*. This reading is problematic for supplementing the protocol. In my view, not *irm* is to be read (compare the *irm* at the end of the line), but ʿ*ws*, preceded by traces which fit the divine determinative. Undoubtedly, the name of Kleopatra (I) is to be supplied, the female half of the Gods Epiphaneis mentioned at the end of l. 3.

10 *400 + 50*: the sign read by the editor as *qd* (kite), appears to be a demotic symbol for "and". It is not clear how the sign has to be read (? *ḥn*ʿ, ? *irm*), see K.-Th. Zauzich, in *ZDMG* 118 (1968), p. 380 and P.W. Pestman, in Pap. Lugd. Bat. XIX, p. 220 and n. g.

11 *ḥḏ 400 + 50 [- - tb*ʿ *2]⸢4⸣ qd 2.t* : the most plausible supplements are either *ḥḏ 400 + 50 [tn tb*ʿ *2]⸢4⸣ qd 2.t, 450 deben each time 24 obols to 2 kite, 450 deben at the rate of 24 obols to 2 kite*, or *ḥḏ 400 + 50 [(n) ḥm̱t tb*ʿ *2]⸢4⸣ qd 2.t, 450 copper deben at the rate of 24 obols to 2 kite*. This formula shows that no agio is to be charged on sums paid in copper (2 kite or 1/5 of a deben = 24 obols or 1 stater = 4 drachmas), see R.H. Pierce, 'Notes on Obols and Agios in Demotic Papyri', in *JEA* 51 (1965), p. 155-159.

24

DEMOTIC ACKNOWLEDGMENT OF DEBT (BARLEY)
to Kaies

See scanned photograph below

Probably Pathyris	H. x W. = 17 x 6 cm [Width incomplete]	12 Sept. 118 B.C.

Berlin, P. dem. inv.no. 13388 ['Ersatz Ehnas'] = **U. Kaplony-Heckel**, 'Die demotischen Gebelên-Papyri der Berliner Papyrussammlung', in *FuB* 8 (1967), p. 76-77, no. 2.

Photograph and facsimile. — No photograph available; see scanned photograph below; facsimile in Kaplony-Heckel, 'Gebelên-Papyri' (1967), p. 76-77.

Description. — Approximately one third of the papyrus is lost on the right side. The acknowledgement of debt is written on the recto and has a top and bottom margin of circa 2 cm. After redaction the papyrus was rolled horizontally. On the outside the lender has noted the name of the debtor.

Introduction

Contents. — The acknowledgement of debt records a loan of barley (the exact amount is lost). The debtor is called Harpaesis, son of Portis. He is also found as debtor one year later (Text 25 of 117 B.C.). In 102 B.C. he leases land from Peteuris, son of Pates[1]. It is not sure whether or not he is a son of the well-known Portis alias Gounsis, son of Thotomous[2] alias Thotortaios[3], who has several sons (see Vandorpe, *Archives from Pathyris* (2001), §44).

The name of the lender is lost; he is a son of Pates. There are several reasons for identifying him with Dryton's son-in-law Kaies, son of Pates (pros. 505). Museum archaeology strongly suggests that the loan was part of the archive of Dryton and his family (see p. 9-11; Vandorpe, *Archives from Pathyris* (2001), §25, 3). In addition, Kaies, son of Pates, is a lender in several loans (see survey §39); in Text 25 of the next year he negotiates a loan with the same debtor Harpaesis, son of Portis.

Scribe. — The scribe (*[S]gn*, l. 11) is attested in other texts, which have been collected by P.W. Pestman[4]. *Sgn* is a son of Paos and appears as witness in four demotic contracts in the period 118-104 B.C. Here, he is the scribe of the acknowledgement of debt and acts on behalf

1 P. dem. Ryl. 26, recto = P. dem. Ackerpachtverträge, p. 55; for Peteuris, son of Pates, see Pros. Ptol. IV 10666.
2 Pros. Ptol. IV 11311 = IX 7188a.
3 Pros. Ptol. III and IX 7188a.
4 Pap. Lugd. Bat. XIX, p. 48, n. cc.

of the debtor Harpaesis, who apparently cannot write Egyptian. *Sgn* may be a transcription of the Greek name Sogenes[1].

Scanned photograph and facsimile[2] and Text

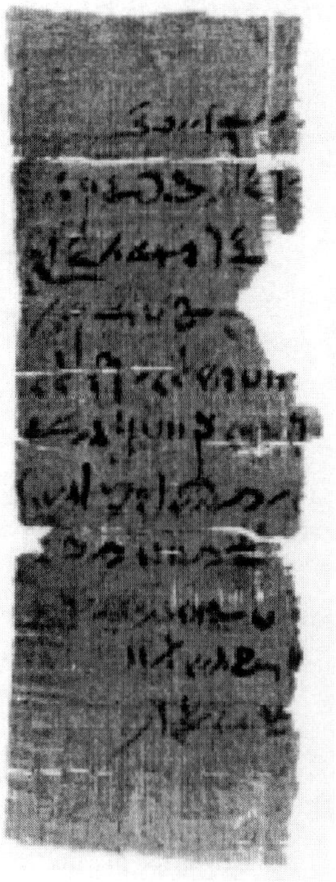

R e c t o

[Ḥr-pa-Is.t s3] P3-wr-dy.w p3 nty ḏd
[n Gʿy] s3 Pa-tw: wn-mtw=k rdb it
[- - - i-ir-n=y n] rn n3y=k it(.w)
(r.)tw=k n=y.
[Mtw=y] ⸢dy.t⸣ n=k p3y=k rdb it
[- - -] irm t3y=w ms.t r-ẖ t3 ms.t
[nty iw=s r] smn (n) wʿ irm 2 Pr-Ḥ.t-
[Ḥr] r-hn(-r) ḥ3.t-sp 53 ibd-1 šmw sw
ʿrq
[- - -] iwṯ hy hm.t
[- - - n] p3 qs 29 n Ḥr-pa-Is.t.
[Sẖ n ḥ3.t-sp 5]2 ibd-4 šmw sw 26.
[Sẖ S]gn r-ḫrw=f.

Recto 2 *[Gʿy]* supplevimus 2 *n3 it* ed., *n3y=k it(.w)* legimus 4 *[. . . Mtw=y dy.t]* ed., *[Mtw=y] ⸢dy.t⸣* legimus 6-7 *(n) pr [iw=f wʿb. . .]* ed., *Pr-Ḥ.t-[Ḥr]* legimus et supplevimus 7 *r-hn-r* ed., *r-hn(-r)* legimus; *ʿrq* ed., *sw ʿrq* legimus 9 *p3 mn* ed., *p3 qs 29* legimus 10 *[ḥ3.t-sp 5]2* ed., *[Sẖ n ḥ3.t-sp 5]2* supplevimus

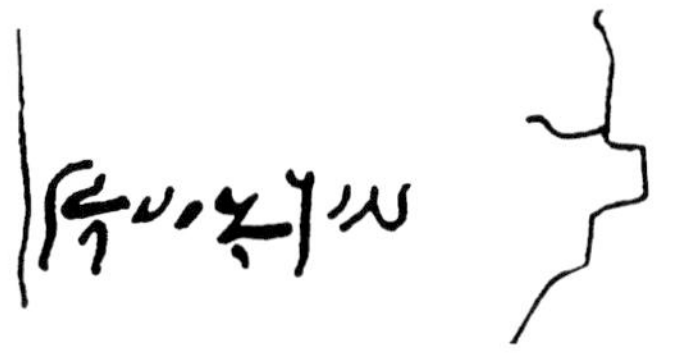

V e r s o

Ḥr-pa-Is.t s3 P3-wr-dy.w

---

1 Bogaert, 'Banques et banquiers' (1998), p. 195.
2 The facsimile of the verso is taken from the edition by U. Kaplony-Heckel.

Translation

Recto

Harpaesis, son of Portis, is the one who declares to [Kaies], son of Pates:
«I owe you - - - artabas of barley in the name of the barley you gave to me.
I shall return your - - - artabas of barley **(5)** *together with their interest according to the interest to be established for each and everyone of Pathyris, before year 53, 30 Pachon, (while they are consigned) without expenses of freightage, (while they are measured in) the 29-choinix measure of Harpaesis.»*
(10) *Written in year 52, 26 Mesore.*
Has written Sgn (? Sogenes) to his (Harpaesis') dictation.

Verso

Harpaesis, son of Portis.

Notes

Recto

6-7 *Pr-Ḥ.t-[Ḥr]*: the editor read *pr* (corn), followed by an unusual determinative. In my view, *pr* is followed by *ḥw.t*, the beginning of the place name *Pr-Ḥ.t-[Ḥr]* or Pathyris. The remaining part of the place name has to be added in the lacuna of the next line (l. 7); traces of the end of the place name (with the city determinative) are still visible in l. 7.

A parallel construction for the interest-clause of l. 6-7 is found in the Greek loan P. Grenf. I 31, the only difference being that the interest in the Greek loan is already established:

Text 24
irm t3y=w ms.t r-ẖ t3 ms.t [nty iw=s (r)] smn w ͨ irm 2 *(n) Pr-Ḥw.t-[Ḥr]*
with their interest according
to the interest to be established for each and everyone of Pathyris

P. Grenf. I 31
[σὺν] τῶι σταθέντι τόκωι ἑνὶ καὶ ἑκάστωι τῆς Παθύρεως
with the interest established for each and everyone of Pathyris

For the interpretation of this interest-clause, see Vandorpe, 'Interest in Ptolemaic Loans' (1998).

8 *[- - -] iwṱ hy hm.t, without expenses of freightage*: apparently, a clause such as *iw=w swṱ.w, while they are consigned*, is to be supplied.

9 *[- - - n] p3 qs 29, in the 29-choinix measure*: the editor read *p3 mn* and added in her commentary: «Was *p3 mn* (?) "der Rest" (?) hier bedeutet, ist unklar». I prefer to read *qs (measure)*, followed by a number: the first part of the number is clearly 20, the second part must be a 9: *p3 qs 29, the 29-choinix measure*, attested in Pathyris (see Vandorpe, 'Greek and Demotic Loan Contracts from Pathyris' (2001)).

p3 q(w)s 29 is shortened for *p3 qws n* **2** *29*, an equivalent of the Greek μέτρωι ὧι καὶ [πα]ρείληφεν πρὸς τὸ κθ-χ(οίνικον). The sign **2** , sometimes read as the feminine article *t3*, points to a measure and must be a feminine word since the number which follows may have the feminine ending *.t*. According to P.W. Pestman, this measure may be the Greek (ἡ) χοῖνιξ or a sign for *mḥ, capacity* (the measure with a capacity of 29, that are choinikes)[1]. In any case, the expression denotes a measure which corresponds to the artaba of 29 choinikes, that is c. 30 litres.

The lacuna of l. 9 may have contained a clause such as *iw=w ẖ3y, while they are measured.*

[1] See Pap. Lugd. Bat. XX, p. 69, n. *n*.

25

GREEK LOAN OF WHEAT
by Kaies

Pathyris | H. x W. = 20.3 x 8.25 cm [Height incomplete] | 4 Jan. 117 B.C.

British Library, P. inv.no. 619 [bought on 9 Nov. 1895 from Grenfell] = **P. Grenf. I 23**.

Description. — The papyrus seems to be complete but the last strip with the name of the scribe (l. 24) is missing. The text on the recto is written along the fibres and has a top margin of circa 3.6 cm and a left-hand margin of 2.3 cm. On the right side there is hardly any margin. After the redaction the papyrus was rolled horizontally. The strips no. 2 and 3 came on the outside. On the right side of strip no. 2 a summary of two lines was written on the verso against the fibres (see §37).

The papyrus is of a bad quality: on the recto some horizontal fibres are missing; consequently, the text has in a few cases been written on the underlying fibres (for instance, in l. 2, 16 and 21). Also on the verso fibres are missing and other fibres run at an angle.

Introduction

Contents. — On 4 January 117 B.C. Kaies, son of Pates, (pros. 505) lends 25 artabas of wheat (probably interest included), to Harpaesis, son of Portis. The same debtor is found in Text 24.

Scribe. — The name of the scribe is lost, but the loan is undoubtedly written by Areios, subordinate of the agoranomos Heliodoros[1], who was still active in 117 B.C., see Text 16, Introduction and note 1.

[1] For Heliodoros, agoranomos of Krokodilopolis in 124-111 B.C., see Pros. Ptol. III 7673; Messeri Savorelli, 'Lista degli agoranomi' (1980), p. 210-212; Pestman, 'Agoranomoi' (1985), p. 12; addendum of 111 B.C.: P. dem. Cairo 31208, see Vandorpe, 'Agoranomic Loans with Demotic Summary' (2000).

Text

Recto

Ἔτους νγ Χοίαχ ι̅ε̅ ἐν Παθύρει
ἐφ' Ἡλιοδώρου ἀγορανόμου·
ἐδάνεισεν Καίης Πατῆτος
Πέρσης τῆς ἐπιγονῆς
Ἁρπαήσει Πόρτιτος Πέρσῃ
τῆς ἐπιγονῆς πυρῶν ἀρ(τάβας) κε·
τὸ δὲ δάνειον τοῦτο ἀπο-
δότω ὁ δεδανεισμένος
Καίητι ἐν μηνὶ Παχὼν
τοῦ νγ (ἔτους) νέον καθαρὸν
ἀποκαθεστάμενον εἰς οἶκον
πρὸς αὐτὸν ἰδίοις ἀνηλώ-
μασιν μέτρωι ὧι καὶ
παρείληφεν· ἐὰν δὲ μὴ
ἀποδῶι ἐν τῶι ὡρισμένωι
χρόνωι, ἀποτεισάτω παρα-
χρῆμα ἡμιόλιον τὴν
ἐσομένην ἐν τῆι ἀγορᾶι
τιμήν· ἡ δὲ πρᾶξις ἔστω
Καίητι ἐκ τοῦ Ἁρπαήσιος
καὶ ἐκ τῶν ὑπαρχόντων
αὐτῶι πάντων καθάπερ
ἐγ δίκης.

24 [Ἄρειος ὁ παρ' Ἡλι(οδώρου) κεχρη(μάτικα).]

Verso

Δά(νειον) Καίητος πρὸς
Ἁρπαῆ(σιν) (πυρῶν) κε.

Recto 24 [Ἄρειος ὁ παρ' Ἡλι(οδώρου) κεχρη(μάτικα).] supplevimus Verso 1 Δά(νειον), papyrus 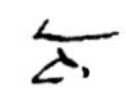 2 Ἁρπαῆ(σιν), papyrus 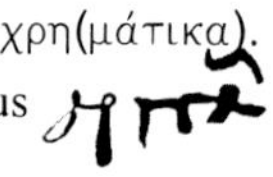 ; (πυροῦ) ed., (πυρῶν) supplevimus

Translation

Recto

Year 53, 15 Choiak, in Pathyris before Heliodoros, agoranomos.

Has lent Kaies, son of Pates (and) Persian of the epigone, to Harpaesis, son of Portis (and) Persian of the epigone, 25 artabas of wheat.

This loan the borrower shall return to Kaies in the month of Pachon of the 54th year, in wheat that is new, pure and delivered to him at his house at his (= Harpaesis') own expense, according to the measure by which he received (it). If he fails to return it within the stated time, he shall immediately return (the 25 artabas) increased by 50% (or) the current market price.

Kaies shall have the right of execution upon the (above) Harpaesis and upon all his property, as if in accordance with a legal decision.

---

(24) *[I, Areios, subordinate of Heliodoros, have dealt with (this contract).]*

Verso

(1) *Loan of Kaies to*
(2) *Harpaesis of 25 (artabas) of wheat.*

Notes

Verso

2 (πυρῶν): the editor renders the Greek symbol for wheat as (πυροῦ), which is commonly used. Here, I prefer the plural (πυρῶν), since Areios always uses the plural instead of the singular, see, for instance, the recto, l. 6 and see Text 16, comm. on verso, l. 2b.

26

DEMOTIC LOAN OF WHEAT
by Kaies

DESCRIPTION

Pathyris 16 Oct. 116 B.C.

British Museum, P. dem. inv.no. 10484 [bought on 13 May 1893] = **unpublished**. The text will be published in P. dem. BM Shore (The publication was prepared by the late A.F.Shore and will be completed by C.A.R. Andrews). U. Kaplony-Heckel informed me of this text and C.A.R. Andrews was so kind as to show me the original papyrus in the British Museum so that I could summarize the contents of the loan.

Contents. — Kaies (pros. 505), son of Pates, man receiving pay, registered at the camp of Krokodilopolis, lends 15 7/12 artabas of wheat, interest included, to two brothers: Panebchounis and Horos, sons of Psennesis and *T3y-T3*[1]; these people are further unknown. The loan is negotiated on 16 October 116 and is to be repaid before 30 Pachon (mid-June 115), after the harvest.

Scribe and witnesses. — The loan is written by Nechthminis, son of Nechthminis, notary in the temple of Hathor in Pathyris (see Text 9, note 3). The clauses of the contract are identical to those of other loans in the hand of Nechthminis. The loan is the original deed, since the names of the four witnesses are written in their own handwriting beneath the contract; each name is preceded by *sẖ* (has written).

---

1 For this name, also attested in Thebes, see Lüddeckens, *Dem. Namenbuch* I.16, p. 1242 (second name).

27

DEMOTIC LOAN OF WHEAT
by Kaies

See facsimile below

Pathyris H. x W. = 32.5 x 12.5 cm 12 febr. 112 B.C.

Heidelberg, P. dem. inv.no. 724 [In Heidelberg since 1898, acquired by Reinhardt] = **P. dem. Gebelein Heid. 16**.

Photograph and facsimile. — No photograph available; see my facsimile below; facsimile in P. dem. Gebelein Heid., p. 98, no. 16.

Description. — The papyrus is complete. The text on the recto is written along the fibres. It has a top and right-hand margin of 1 cm and a bottom margin of 5 cm. On the left side there is hardly any margin. After redaction the papyrus was rolled horizontally from bottom to top; at the bottom the horizontal folds are just visible, whereas at the top, which was at the oustide of the rolled papyrus, the folds are damaged.

The papyrus is of inferior quality: the fibres on the recto do not always run horizontally and in some cases the horizontal fibres are missing; consequently, the scribe had to write on the underlying fibres. In l. 17 the scribe has apparently left some space blank because of the poor quality of the papyrus.

On the right-hand side of the verso, at right angles to the text of the recto, the remainder of an older document is visible: traces of two lines are preserved, of which only the name Psenapathes (*[P3-šr-]ʿ3-pḥṯ*) can be read. Psenapathes is also the father's name of one of the contractants of the recto (l. 5). One might assume that the text on the verso is a summary of the loan on the recto. This assumption is problematic, since the summary is written in a vertical direction, whereas the papyrus was rolled horizontally. In addition the summary is incomplete, whereas the loan on the recto is completely preserved. I rather assume with the first editor that the verso contains traces of an older document. A similar case is the temple deed P. dem. Gebelein Heid. 24, which has on the verso the Greek characters [- - -]ριος, whereas the recto is complete; these may also be traces of an older document.

Introduction

Contents. — On 12 February 112 B.C. Kaies, son of Pates, lends 15 artabas of wheat, interest included, until 30 Pachon (mid-June), that is after the harvest. The debtor is Siepmous the younger, son of Psenapathes, who is a collegue of Kaies: he is a "man receiving pay", registered at the camp in Krokodilopolis. Siepmous is otherwise unknown.

Witnesses. — At least two of the four witnesses are priests. The first witness, Peteharpres, son of Pakoibis, belongs to the second phyle[1]. He acts also as witness in a deed of 118 B.C. in Krokodilopolis[2] and probably in a contract from Pathyris[3]. The last witness Sto(to)etis[1] is a

---

1 P. dem. Ryl. 25, col. II, l. 6 (113/112 B.C.), for the date see Pros. Ptol. IX 6460.

2 P. dem. Ryl. 17, verso l. 13.

3 P. dem. Adler 26, l. 7 (*P3-dy-Ḥr-p3-Rʿ s3 Pa-[Gbk]*; 124-94 B.C.).

priest of Souchos and Aphrodite. He is a son of Peteharoeris and Senminis and was married to Nahomsesis, daughter of Onnophris, a well-known business woman of the period 114-96/95 B.C.[2]. Sto(to)etis acts as witness in two further demotic deeds from Pathyris[3].

The second witness is called Peteharsemtheus, son of Dryton, otherwise unknown; for this son of (a?) Dryton, see pros. 504.

The third witness Mesoeris, son of Harekysis, acts as witness in three further deeds from Pathyris and Krokodilopolis in the period 116-104 B.C.[4]

Scribe. — For Nechthminis, son of Nechthminis, scribe of the temple of Hathor in Pathyris in the period 124-94 B.C., see Text 9, note 3.

---

1 Variant forms of Egyptian names with or without the article occur indifferently alongside each other. The alternation Stoetis - Stotoetis is a typical example of this: Sto(to)etis, son of Peteharoeris, is usually called Stoetis in demotic and Stotoetis in Greek sources, see W. Clarysse, in *Enchoria* 8.2 (1978), p. 5-6.

2 Pestman, 'Nahomsesis' (1981); see also Vandorpe, *Archives from Pathyris* (2001), §40.

3 **1)** P. dem. Gebelein Heid. 6, verso l. 5 (115-100 B.C.). **2)** P. dem. Stras. 9, verso l. 3 (104 B.C.; recto = P. dem. Ackerpachtverträge, p. 49; verso = N. Reich, in *RecTrav* 33 (1911), p. 149-150).

For further data on Stotoetis, see Pros. Ptol. III and IX 6519 = IX 5818b; P. dem. Gebelein Heid., p. 26, II; Vandorpe, 'Paying taxes to the thesauroi of the Pathyrites' (2000).

4 **1)** P. dem. Ryl. 20, verso l. 6 (recto = P. dem. Eheverträge 39) (Krokodilopolis; 116 B.C.): for the reading of the name *Ms-wr*, see U. Kaplony-Heckel, in *FuB* 8 (1967), p. 75. **2)** P. dem. Adler 5, l. 21 (Pathyris; 108/107 B.C.). **3)** P. dem. *FuB* 8 (1967), p. 74, verso l. 6 (recto = P. dem. Ackerpachtverträge, p. 52) (103 B.C.).

Facsimile

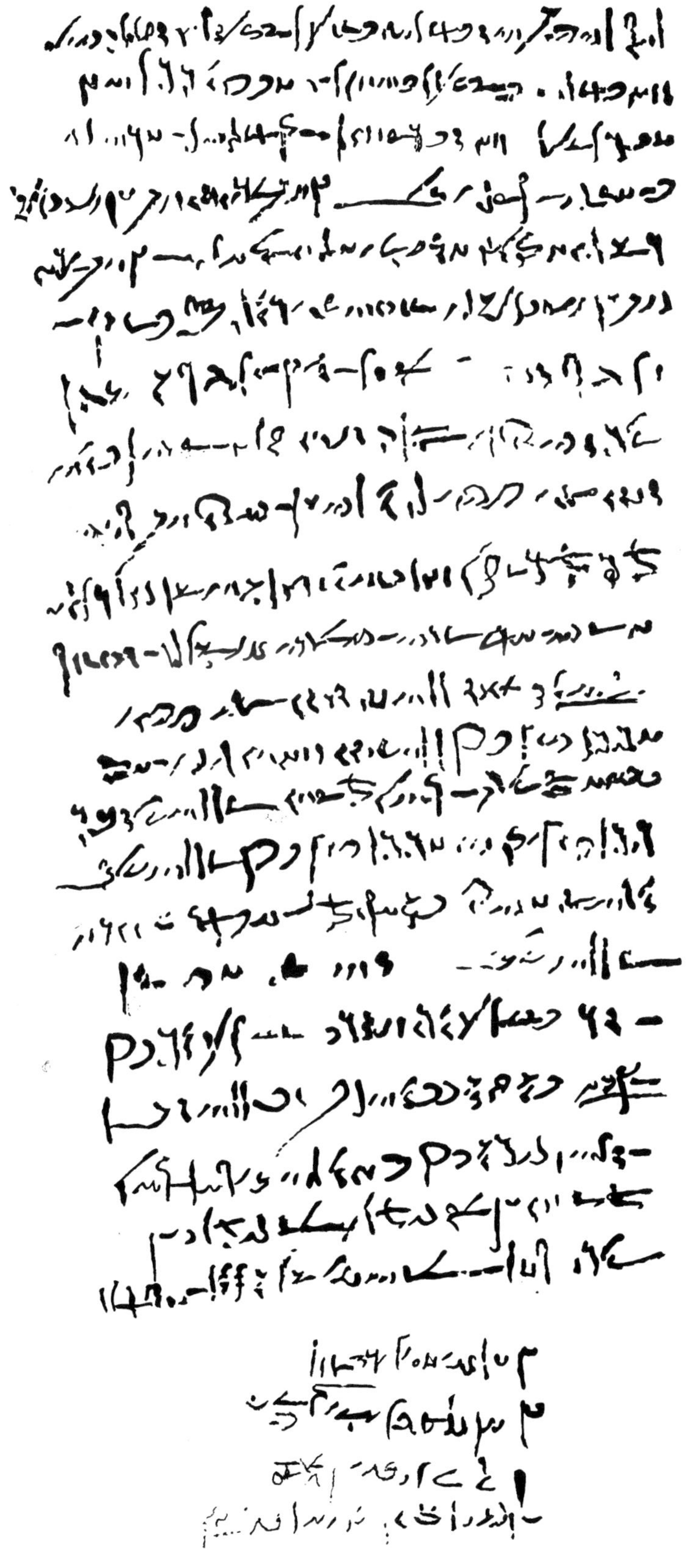

Text

Ḥ3.t-sp 5.t ibd-1 pr.t sw 26 n t3 Pr-ʿ3ʿws.t Glwptr3ʿws n3 ntr.w nty pr irm Pr-ʿ3ʿws Ptlwmysʿws p3 nty mr mw.t p3 Swtr irm n3 nty smn.w n Rʿ-qd P3-sy nty n p3 tš n Nw.t. Ḏd rmt iw=f šp ḥbs iw=f sẖ r 3mwr S3y-p3-mw.t p3 ḫm s3 P3-šr-ʿ3-pḥṱ n rmt iw=f šp ḥbs iw=f sẖ r 3mwr Gʿy s3 Pa-tw. Wn-mtw=k rdb n sw 15 t3y=w pš 7 1/2 (r) rdb n sw 15 ʿn ⸢i⸣-ir-n=y (n) rn n3 pr.w r.dy=k n=y iw p3y=w ḥw ẖn=w. Mtw=y dy.t st n=k r-hn-r ḥ3.t-sp 6 ibd-1 šmw ʿrq n pr iw=f wʿb iwṱ sn.nw iwṱ stḥ iw=w ḫ3y iw=w f3y iw=w swṱ p3 ẖn n p3y=k ʿ.wy n Pr-Ḥ.t-Ḥr n t3 mʿḏ r.ḫ3y=k n=y n.im=s. Iw=y tm dy.t st n=k r-hn-r p3 ssw-hrw nty ḥry, iw=y dy.t st irm p3y=w 1 r 1 1/2 n p3 ibd nty m-s3 p3 ibd n rn=f n ḥtr iwṱ mn. Bn iw=y rḫ dy.t gr ssw-hrw r-r=w m-s3 p3 ssw-hrw nty ḥry. Bn iw=y rḫ ḏd tw=y n=k ḥḏ pr nty nb (n) p3 t3 iwṱ iw iw=f ʿḥʿ rd.ṱ Bn iw=y rḫ ḏd Vacat *ir=y n=k* Vacat *p3 hp n t3 smbwl.t iw t3 smbwl.⸢t⸣ nty ḥry n dr.ṱ=k. Nty nb nkt nb nty mtw=y ḥnʿ n3 nty iw=y dy.t ḫpr=w n iwy.t md nb nty ḥry šʿ-tw=y ir r-ẖ.ṱ=w n ḥtr iwṱ mn. Sẖ Nḫṱ-Mn s3 Nḫṱ-Mn nty sẖ rn n3 wʿb.w n Ḥ.t-Ḥr nb In.ty n p3 5 s3.w. Sẖ P3-dy-Ḥr-p3-Rʿ s3 Pa-Gbk. Sẖ P3-dy-Ḥr-sm3-t3.wy s3 Trwtn. Sẖ Ms-wr s3 Ḥr-igš. Sẖ Sṯ3=w-wṱ s3 P3-dy-Ḥr-wr.*

---

1 *t3 Pr-ʿ3ʿws.t* ed., *n t3 Pr-ʿ3ʿws.t* legimus 2 *p3 mr mw.t* ed., *p3 nty mr mw.t* Lüddeckens (*OLZ* 65 (1970), p. 27) 5 *rmt iw=f šp ʿq ḥbs* ed., *rmt iw=f šp ḥbs* Vleeming (Pap. Lugd. Bat XXIII, p. 204-207) 7 *r.ir.n=y* ed., *⸢i⸣-ir-n=y* legimus 10 *iw=w ḫ3yw iw=w f3yw* ed., *iw=w ḫ3y iw=w f3y* legimus 11 *mʿḏt* ed., *mʿḏ* legimus 16 *rdwy* ed., *rd.ṱ* legimus 18 *t3 smbwl iw t3 smbwl* ed., *t3 smbwl.t iw t3 smbwl.⸢t⸣* Clarysse (‘Greek Loan-Words’ (1987), p. 30) 23 *Pa-Gb* ed., *Pa-Gbk* legimus 26 *Sṯ3-w-t3-wtyt* ed., *Sṯ3=w-wṱ,* Lüddeckens (*OLZ* 65 (1970), p. 22) et Zauzich (*ZDMG* 118 (1968), p. 378)

Translation

Year 5, 26 Tybi, of queen Kleopatra (III), (granddaughter of) the Gods Epiphaneis, and king Ptolemy (IX) Soter and (the priests) who are appointed in Alexandria (and in) Ptolemais in the Thebaid.

Has declared the man receiving pay, while he is registered at Krokodilopolis, Siepmous the younger, son of Psenapathes, to the man receiving pay, while he is registered at Krokodilopolis, Kaies, son of Pates:

«I owe you 15 artabas of wheat — their half is 7 1/2, being 15 artabas of wheat again — in the name of the grains which you gave to me, interest included.

I shall return it to you before year 6, 30 Pachon, in grain that is pure, without adulteration (or) chaff, while they (viz. the grains) are measured, transported and consigned within your house in Pathyris according to the measure which you used for me.

If I fail to return it within the stated time, I shall return it to you increased by 50% in the month following the month named, under compulsion, without delay.

I shall not be able to give another date for it except the above date. I shall not be able to say 'I have given to you money, corn or anything whatsoever' without a valid receipt. I shall not be able to say 'I have performed for you the right of the symbolon' while the symbolon is in your hand.

Everything, all that belongs to me, all that I shall acquire, are security for every above word until I have acted accordingly, under compulsion, without delay.»

Has written Nechthminis, son of Nechthminis, who writes in the name of the priests of Hathor, mistress of Pathyris, (priests) of the five phyles.

Has written Peteharpres, son of Pakoibis.

Has written Peteharsemtheus, son of Dryton.

Has written Mesoeris, son of Harekysis.

Has written Stoetis, son of Peteharoeris.

Notes

11 *mʿḏ, measure*: the scribe has forgotten the first part of the *ayin*, probably misled by the similarity with the preceding *m*.

28

DEMOTIC ACKNOWLEDGEMENT OF DEBT (BARLEY)
to Kaies

See scanned photograph below

Probably Pathyris	H. x W. = 5 x 8.5 cm [Height incomplete]	after 135 B.C.

Berlin, P. dem. inv.no. 13385 [from the 'Ersatz Ehnas'] = **U. Kaplony-Heckel**, 'Die demotischen Gebelên-Papyri der Berliner Papyrussammlung', in *FuB* 8 (1967), p. 77, no. 3.

Photograph and facsimile. — No photograph available; see scanned photograph below; facsimile in Kaplony-Heckel, 'Gebelên-Papyri' (1967), p. 77.

Description. — The papyrus is fragmentary. After redaction the papyrus was rolled from bottom to top (or the other way round), resulting in horizontal folds. The papyrus broke off along one of these folds. Only the upper part has been preserved with the first four lines of the acknowledgement of debt. The text has a top margin of 2 cm. On the right and left side there is hardly any margin. On the preserved part of the verso no traces of a summary are found.

Introduction

Contents and date. — Kaies, son of Pates, lends 3.5 artabas of barley to Pmois, son of Nechouthes. A Pmois, son of Nechouthes, is attested, together with his brothers, in an oath, sworn in the temple of Souchos (compare App. C) in 111 B.C. concerning a large amount of wheat[1].

The date is lost. As Kaies is an adult, the text may be dated after 135 B.C. (see pros. 505).

---

1 O. dem. *Enchoria* 21 (1994), no. 40, recto.

Scanned photograph

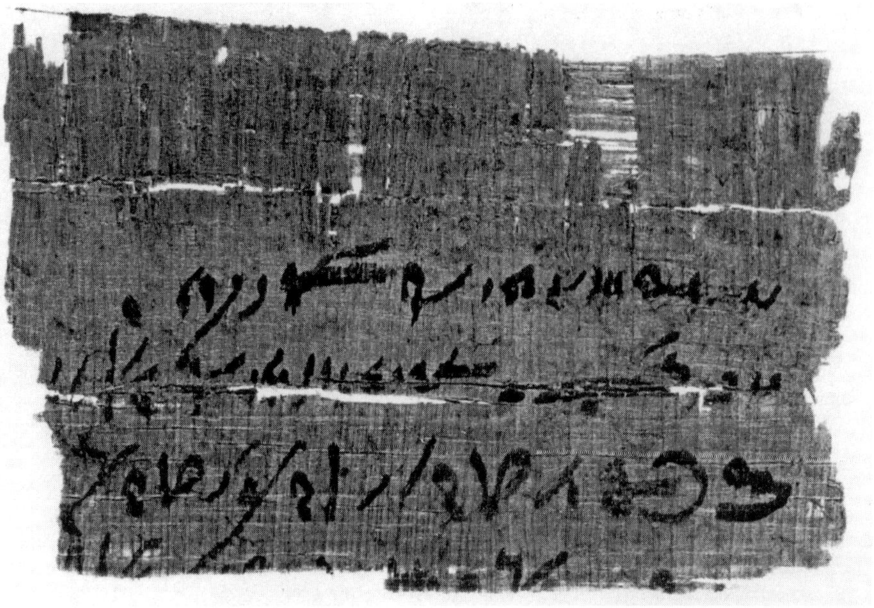

Text

1 *P3-m3y s3 N3-nḫṯ=f*
2 *p3 nty ḏd n Gʿy s3 Pa-tw:*
3 *wn-mtw=k it 3 1/2 r 1 1/2 1/4 r 3 1/2 ʿn*
4 *[i-ir-]⸢n=y⸣ [n] ⸢rn n3y=k pr(.w) (r.)tw⸣[=k] n=y.*

- -

---

4 *Spuren* ed., *[i-ir-]⸢n=y⸣ [n] ⸢rn n3y=k pr(.w) (r.)tw⸣[=k] n=y* legimus

Translation

Pmois, son of Nechouthes is the one who declares to Kaies, son of Pates:
«I owe you 3 1/2 (artabas) of barley — (their half is) 1 1/2 1/4, being 3 1/2 again — in the name of your grains which you gave to me.»

- -

Notes

4 I was able to supply l. 4 on the basis of the clauses known from other acknowledgements of debt; the supplement fits the traces.

29

Greek Loan of Salt with Demotic Receipt
for Phagonis

Plate X (recto-verso); see facsimile of the demotic receipt below

Pathyris	H. x W. = 17.8 x 12.7 cm	12 Sept. 105 B.C.

British Library, P. inv.no. 625 [bought on 9 Nov. 1895 from Grenfell] = the *Greek text* is published as **P. Grenf. I 29**; the *demotic receipt* is **unpublished**.

Photograph and facsimile. — Plate X (recto-verso) and see my facsimile of the demotic part below.

Description. — The papyrus is complete. The text on the recto is written along the fibres and has a top margin of 2.5 cm, a bottom margin of 3 cm and a left-hand margin of 0.5 cm. The margin on the right side is irregular (maximum 2 cm). The bottom margin of the Greek loan was afterwards used for a demotic receipt, confirming the repayment of the loan.

After redaction the papyrus was rolled horizontally from top to bottom; the strips nos. 2 and 3 came on the outside. The text on strip no. 3 and on two horizontal folds (between strip no. 1 and 2 and between no. 2 and 3) is damaged. On the back of strip no. 2 a summary of two lines was written, against the fibres (see §37).

Introduction

Contents. — On 12 September 105 B.C. Sennesis, daughter of Patseous, lends 6 artabas of salt, interest included, to Phagonis. He has to return the salt in the month of Choiak (mid-January). If he fails to return the loan in time, he has to pay in addition some artabas of wheat in the month of Phamenoth (end of the month = mid-April), after the harvest. This is a deviant clause. Usually, the fine has to be paid immediately (παραχρῆμα), that is immediately after the last day on which the loan could be repaid. Here, the fine has to be paid three months later. The reason is obvious. The salt has to be returned in the month of Choiak, that is at the latest on 30 Choiak (mid- January). If the debtor cannot return the salt at that time, he has to pay in grain instead of in salt and the grain has to be given back after the harvest, that is in the month of Phamenoth (end of the month = mid-April).

Later a demotic receipt was added beneath the Greek contract, confirming that the loan was repaid by Phagonis. The receipt was not issued by Sennesis, but by one of her sons; possibly, Sennesis was deceased. After the repayment Phagonis could take home the loan contract containing the receipt.

Sennesis, daughter of Patseous (l. 3-4), was married to a man called Pates and had at least one son (demotic receipt, l. 1). It is not possible to identify her with certainty. A Sennesis the younger, daughter of Patseous, is known from a temple oath of 103/102 B.C.[1], from three

[1] O. dem. Tempeleide, p. 403.

years after this loan. If one assumes that Sennesis died shortly after 105 B.C. (date of the loan Text 29), the identification is not possible.

It is interesting to note that in 98/97 B.C. a man called Phagonis is accused of having stolen 1/2 artaba of salt; he has to swear a temple oath in order to proof he is innocent[1]. Considering that Text 29 is the only loan of salt in Pathyris (loan made to Phagonis son of Panebchounis) and the theft is the only theft of salt attested in Pathyris (theft by a Phagonis), it is tempting to identify both individuals called Phagonis.

Scribe. — Hermias (I)[2], the subordinate of the agoranomos Paniskos in the period 106-98 B.C.[3], is notorious for his mistakes of spelling, case and construction. In Text 29 the "damage" is limited, since most clauses are standard. When he has to form cases himself, he makes blunders. In l. 4-5, for instance, he writes Φαγώνιος . . . Πέρσης instead of the dative Φαγῶνι . . . Πέρσῃ. The verso contains his biggest mistake. The correct construction is used for the summary (Δά(νειον) + name of creditor πρὸς + name of debtor, *Loan of NN to NN*), but the scribe switches the names of the creditor and of the debtor: Δά(νειον) Φαγώνιος πρὸς Σεννῆσιν, *Loan of Phagonis to Sennesis.*

Demotic receipt. — Only in two cases is a demotic receipt added beneath a Greek agoranomic loan contract from Pathyris; both receipts have remained unpublished. In addition, a demotic receipt is found beneath a demotic acknowledgment of debt.

In **Text 29** a son of the creditor Sennesis issued the receipt, confirming that the loan has been repaid.

P. Grenf. I 28 is an agoranomic loan of wheat; after the repayment, the lender wrote a receipt beneath the contract and stroke through the Greek loan. In the receipt the lender acknowledges having reveived *t3 ms.t, the interest* (probably the fine of 50% to be paid in case the loan was not returned in time).

Finally, the demotic acknowledgement of debt **P. dem. *Enchoria* 7 (1977), p. 51-54** is followed by a receipt recording that the old loan is cancelled and has been replaced by a new loan contract.

The three demotic receipts have a similar structure:

1. *The names of the contractants*:
NN p3 nty ḏd n NN, NN (viz. the creditor or family member) is the one who declares to NN (viz. the debtor)

2. *The creditor acknowledges that the debtor has observed the stipulations of the contract*: he has fulfilled (*mḥ*) *p3 hp n p3 sẖ, the right of the loan.* The terminology is similar to that found in temple deeds, where the debtor (and not the creditor as is the case

---

1 O. dem. Tempeleide 125 = O. dem. *OrSu* 8 (1959), p. 49.

2 For Hermias (I), see Pros. Ptol. III 7689; Pestman, 'L' agoranomie' (1978), p. 205; Messeri Savorelli, 'Lista degli agoranomi' (1980), p. 220-232; Pestman, 'Agoranomoi' (1985), p. 13; addendum: SB XX 14198 (104 B.C.: Hermias, subordinate of Paniskos).

3 For Paniskos, see Pros. Ptol. III 7678; Messeri Savorelli, 'Lista degli agoranomi' (1980), p. 220-232; Pestman, 'Agoranomoi' (1985), p. 12; addenda: SB XVIII 13846 (107 B.C.: Paniskos); SB XX 14198 (104 B.C.: Hermias, subordinate of Paniskos)

here) declares: "I shall not be able to say 'I have performed for you the right of the deed' while the above deed is in your hands" (see, *e.g.*, Text 14, l. 12). In the following examples the Greek agoranomic loan contract is called a *sẖ, deed.*

Text 29: *Tw=y mḥ n p3 hp n p3 sẖ r.ir=k n T3-šr.t-Is.t t3y=n mw.t, I am fulfilled of the right of the deed which you made for Sennesis, our mother.*

P. Grenf. I 28: *tw=y [mḥ n p3 hp n] p3y sẖ irm t3y=w ms.t, I am fulfilled of the right of this deed and their (viz. of the artabas of wheat) interest.*

P. dem. *Enchoria* 7 (1977), p. 51-54: this clause is missing, since the loan has not yet been repaid.

3. *The creditor declares that he cannot bring any accusation against the debtor on the basis of the loan contract:*

Text 29: *Tw=y wwy r.ir=k n.im=⸢f⸣, I am far from you in respect to it.*

P. Grenf. I 28: *Mn md [n p3 t3 iw=y ˁš m-] ⸢s3=k⸣ n.im=s ẖr-r=f, There is nothing in the world which I claim against you concerning it (viz. the above document).*

P. dem. *Enchoria* 7 (1977), p. 51-54: *Tw=y wy=k r.ir=k r p3y bk r.ir=k n=y nty ḥry rn p3y sẖ tnn r.ir=k n=y. Mn md n p3 t3 iw=y ˁš m- s3=k n.im=s ẖr p3 bk nty ḥry, I am far from you in respect to the above document which you have made for me in the name of this (new) loan contract which you have made for me. There is nothing in the world which I claim against you concerning the above document.*

4. *The name of the scribe and/ or the date of redaction:*
The receipt is written by the creditor himself, or, if he could not write Egyptian, by a representative whose name is explicitly mentioned (see P. dem. *Enchoria* 7 (1977), p. 51-54). The date of redaction is recorded in P. Grenf. I 28 (introduced by *sẖ, has written in*), and in P. dem. *Enchoria* 7 (1977), p. 51-54 (introduced by *sẖ, has written in*).

Text

Recto

Ἔτους ιβ τοῦ καὶ θ Μεσορὴ λ
ἐν Παθύρει ἐφ' Ἑρμίου τοῦ παρὰ Πανίσκου
ἀγορανόμου· ἐδάνεισεν Σεννῆσις
Πατσεοῦτος Περσίνη Φαγώνιος
Πανοβχούνιος Πέρσης τῆς ἐπιγονῆς
ἁλὸς ἀρτάβας ἓξ ἄτοκα· τὸ δὲ δάνειον
τοῦτο ἀποδότω ὁ δεδανεισμένος
Φαγῶνις Σεννήσει ἐν μηνὶ Χοίαχ
τοῦ ιγ τοῦ καὶ ι (ἔτους)· ἐὰν δὲ μὴ ἀποδῶι
ἐν ṭῷ ὡṛισμένọι χρόνωι καθότι πρό-
κειται, ἀ̣[ποτεισ]άτωι ἐṇ ṭῷ Φạμ̣ενὼθ
πυροῦ ἀρ[τάβας - c. 5 -]· ἡ̣ δ̣ὲ πρᾶξεις ἔστω
Σεννήσ̣[ει ἐκ τοῦ Φαγώ]νιος καὶ ἐκ τῶν
ὑ̣[παρ]χό̣[ντων αὐτῶι π]ά̣ντων πράσσοντι καθάπ̣ε̣ρ̣ ἐγ δ̣ί̣κ̣ης.

Ἑρμίας ὁ παρὰ Πανίσκου κεχρη(μάτικα).

Verso

Δά(νειον) Φαγώνιος πρὸς Σεννῆσιν
ἁλὸς ἀρ(ταβῶν) ϛ.

Recto 4 Παπεοῦτος ed., Πατσεοῦτος Hunt et Wilcken (BL I, p. 181) 4 Φαγώνιος, *l.* Φαγῶνι 5 Πέρσης, *l.* Πέρση 11 ἀ[ποτισ]άτωι ed., ἀ[ποτεισ]άτωι Witkowski (BL I, p. 181) 12 πρᾶξεις, *l.* πρᾶξις 14 πράσσοντι *l.* πρασσούση 16 παρά, papyrus 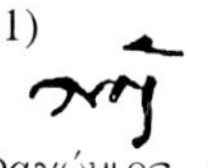
Verso 1 Δά(νειον), papyrus  ; παρά ed., πρός legimus; Δά(νειον) Φαγώνιος πρὸς Σεννῆσιν, *l.* Δά(νειον) Σεννήσιος πρὸς Φαγῶνιν 2 ζ ed., ϛ Hunt (BL I, p. 181)

Translation

Recto

In year 12 which is also year 9, 30 Mesore, in Pathyris before Hermias, subordinate of Paniskos, agoranomos.

Has lent Sennesis, daughter of Patseous, Persian, to Phagonis, **(5)** *son of Panobchounis (and) Persian of the epigone, 6 artabas of salt, without (further) interest.*

This loan the borrower shall return to Sennesis in the month of Choiak of year 13 which is also year 10. If he fails to return it **(10)** *within the stated time mentioned above, he shall pay - - - artabas of wheat in the month of Phamenoth. Sennesis shall have the right of execution upon the (above) Phagonis and upon all his property, exacting (payment)* **(15)** *as if in accorcance with a legal decision.*

---

(16) *I, Hermias, subordinate of Paniskos, have dealt with (this contract).*

Verso

(1) *Loan of Phagonis to Sennesis (* read: *Loan of Sennesis to Phagonis)*
(2) *of 6 artabas of salt.*

Notes

Verso

1 πρός : 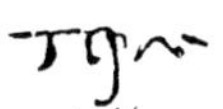 the first editor read παρά, probably because this reading makes more sense: Δά(νειον) Φαγώνιος παρὰ Σεννῆσιν, *Loan by Phagonis (viz. the debtor) from Sennesis (viz. the creditor)*; the reading πρός is, however, to be preferred for palaeographical reasons; in addition, παρά is never attested in the summaries of loan contracts. In Δά(νειον) Φαγώνιος πρὸς Σεννῆσιν, *Loan of Phagonis (viz. the debtor) to Sennesis (viz. the creditor)*, Hermias has mixed up the names of the creditor and of the debtor (see Introduction to the text. Scribe).

DEMOTIC RECEIPT

Facsimile

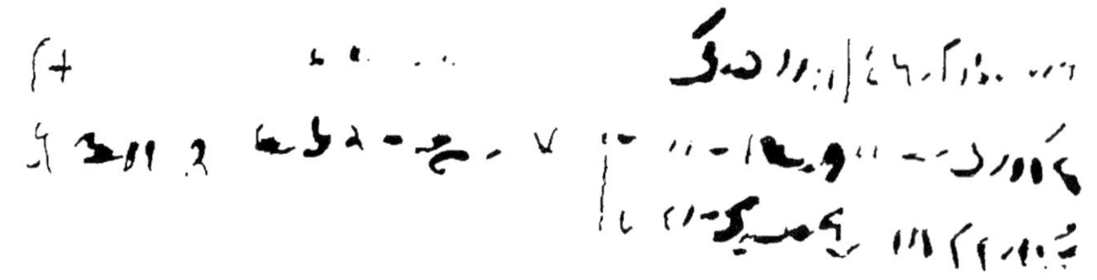

Text

1 *⸢P3- ⸣ s3 Pa-tw p3 nty ḏd ⸢n⸣ [Pa-wn s3] ⸢Pa-nb-ẖnw⸣. ? Traces*
2 *Tw=y mḥ n p3 hp n p3 sẖ r.ir=k n T3-šr.t-Is.t t3y=n mw.t.*
3 *Tw=y wwy r.ir=k n.im=⸢f⸣.*

Translation

1 *⸢P- ⸣, son of Pates, is the one who declares to Phagonis, son of Panobchounis.*
2 *I am fulfilled of the right of the deed which you have made for Sennesis, our mother.*
3 *I am far from you in respect to it.*

Notes

1 *⸢P3- ⸣*: the name has the divine determinative (? *P3-i.ir-...*).

2 *sẖ, deed*: the determinative of the scribe's outfit, which is hardly visible, is also found in the unpublished receipt of P. Grenf. I 28 (see Introduction to the text).

t3y=n mw.t, our mother: the author of the receipt, a son of Sennesis, changes from the first person singular to the first person plural. Apparently, he acts on behalf of his brother(s) and/or sister(s).

3 *n.im=⸢f⸣*: the masculin suffix *=f* is hardly visible, but is required since it refers back to *sẖ, deed*, l. 2.

30

GREEK LOAN OF WHEAT

by a descendant of Dryton?

Pathyris | H. x W. = 13.8 x 5.4 cm [incomplete] | 131-113 B.C.

Cairo, P. Gr. inv.no. 10357 [acquired before 1897] = **G. Messeri Savorelli**, 'Due Atti agoranomici di età tolemaica: SB III 7204, P. Cairo 10357', in *Studi in onore di A. Biscardi* V, Milano 1984, p. 522-525 = **SB XVI 12986**.

Photograph. — Messeri Savorelli, 'Due Atti agoranomici' (1984), p. 523.

Description. — The papyrus is broken off at the top; consequently the first half of the text is lost. Of the preserved part, the papyrus is broken off on the right side; thus, the end of each line (c. 23 characters, that is approximately two thirds of the lines) is missing. The text is written on the recto across the fibres and has a left margin of c. 2.5 cm and a bottom margin of c. 4 cm.

Introduction

Contents. — The present loan is a renewal of an old loan.

Loan A — 136-134 B.C. The old loan may have involved 200+x artabas of wheat (l. 4, see comm.). The name of the creditor is apparently Dryton (l. 1: Δρύ[?των]). The debtor may have been a family member of the mother of the debtors of the new loan (l. 4-5). The loan was issued by Dioskourides, agoranomos in the period 136-134 B.C.[1].

Loan B— 131-113 B.C. The new loan does not necessarily concern the same amount of wheat. Part of the loan may have been repaid. The loan is written by Areios, subordinate of the agoranomos in Pathyris in the period 131-113 B.C. The names of the contracting parties are lost:

- the creditor may still be Dryton; in this case the loan was issued in the period 131-126 B.C., since Dryton died in or shortly after 126 B.C. (see pros. 403). The text dates rather to this early period for paleographical reasons. Or Dryton is already dead and the loan is renewed by a family member in or after 126 B.C.
- the debtors are family members of the debtor(s) of Loan A (l. 4-5), who probably died before the loan was returned.

The scribe and date. — The scribe is Areios, subordinate of the agoranomos in the period 131-113 B.C.[2]. For paleographical reasons, the contract Text 30 belongs rather to the early

[1] For Dioskourides, see Pros. Ptol. III 7664, 7665; Messeri Savorelli, 'Lista degli agoranomi' (1980), p. 206-208; Pestman, 'Agoranomoi' (1985), p. 12; addendum: Text 30.

[2] See Text 16, Introduction and note 1.

period of his career (see Text 16, Introduction), that is before 126 B.C., when Dryton was still alive.

Text

καὶ .[. .] . Δρύ[?των - - - κατὰ συν-] γραφὴν δανε[ίου - - - ἐπὶ] Διοσκουρίδου [ἀγορανόμου - - -] πυρ. . δ̣ιακ.[- - - τῶι τῆς] μητρὸς αὐτ[ῶν - - -] ἐὰν δὲ μὴ ἀπ[οδῶσιν ἐν τῶι ὡρισμένωι] χρόνωι ἀποτ[εισάτωσαν παραχρῆμα] ἡμιόλ̣ι̣ο̣ν τ[ὴν ἐσομένην ἐν τῆι ἀγορᾶι τιμήν·] ἔγγυοι ἀλλή[λων εἰς ἔκτεισιν τῶν διὰ τοῦ] δανείου πάν[των αὐτοὶ οἱ δεδανεισμένοι·] ἡ δὲ πρᾶξις [ἔστω - - - ἐκ τῶν] δεδανεισμέν[ων καὶ ἐξ ἑνὸς καὶ ἑκάστου αὐτῶν] καὶ ἐξ οὗ ἂν αἱρῆτ̣[αι καὶ ἐκ τῶν ὑπαρχόντων αὐτοῖς] πάντων πρά[σσοντι καθάπερ ἐγ δίκης.]

Ἄρειος [ὁ παρὰ - - - κεχρη(μάτικα).]

---

4 πυρὸν̣ δ̣ιακε̣ ed., πυρ . δ̣ιακ. legimus

Translation

- - - - - - - - - - - -

and - - - ?Dryton - - - according to a loan contract - - - before Dioskourides, agoranomos, - - - wheat - - - to the - - - of their mother - - -

If they fail to return it within the stated time, they shall immediately return (the artabas) increased by 50% (or) the current market price.

The borrowers themselves are sureties for each other for the payment of **(10)** *all the liabilities of this loan. NN shall have the right of execution upon both borrowers and on each and every one of them, and upon whomever he/she chooses and upon all their property, as if in accordance with a legal decision.*

(15) *I, Areios, subordinate of NN, have dealt with (this contract).*

Notes

1-2 κατὰ συν]γραφὴν δανε[ίου - - - ἐπὶ] Διοσκουρίδου [ἀγορανόμου: a possible addition proposed by Messeri Savorelli is κατὰ συν]γραφὴν δανε[ίου τὴν τεθεῖσαν ἐπὶ] Διοσκουρίδου [ἀγορανόμου ἐν τῶι .. (ἔτει)]. The clause with τὴν τεθεῖσαν is usually found in combination with ἐπὶ τοῦ ἀρχείου and not with the name of the agoranomos and refers to the submission of the contract in the archeion, the Greek notary's office which is at the same time the registration office (see §34). For examples from Pathyris with τὴν τεθεῖσαν ἐπὶ τοῦ ἀρχείου, see P. Grenf. I 26; P. Grenf. II 19 and 30.

4 πυρ . . δ̣ιακ .[: Messeri Savorelli suggested to read πυρὸν̣ δ̣ιακε̣[; a possible supplement she proposed is: πυρὸν̣ δ̣ιακε[ίμενον ἐν ὀνόματι; for the use of the verb διάκειμαι in a similar context she refers to Roman papyri.

Another possible reading, in my view, is πυρῶ̣ν̣ δ̣ιακο̣[σίας: in this case the amount of the old loan is mentioned here (200+x artabas). The subordinate of the agoranomos, Areios, usually writes πυρῶν rather than πυροῦ (see Text 16, comm. on verso, l. 2b); one does, however, expect ἀρτάβας after πυρῶν.

III

PETITIONS

Survey of the petitions in the family archive of Dryton : §40. Survey.
Means used to impress or to raise compassion : §41. Personal data. — §42. Stressing the unjustice. — §43. Syntax and language.

Survey of petitions in the family archive of Dryton

§40. *Survey.* — Four petitions are found in the family archive of Dryton: two from Dryton, one from his wife Apollonia and her sisters and one from their daughters.

Petition from	*Addressed to*	*Date*	*Original or copy*	*Text*
[Dryton ?]	Epimeletes Hermias	140-131/130	copy	31
Dryton	Epistrategos Boethos	137-130	original	32
Apollonia and sisters	Epistrategos Boethos	136	original and draft	33 + 33bis
Daughters of Dryton	Epistrategos Phommous	115-110	original or copy	34

The elements required in the structure and phrasing of petitions have been studied by A. Di Bitonto, 'Le Petizione ai funzionari' (1968), in *Aegyptus* 48, p. 53-107, and these may be found in the petitions of the family archive of Dryton.

Means used to impress or to raise compassion

§41. *Personal data.* — Emphasizing the Greek origin appears to be important to impress the Greek authorities to whom the petition is addressed. Dryton explicitely mentions his Greek origin, his important function in the army, his aulic titulature and his citizenship of the Greek polis of Ptolemais. Apollonia and her sisters use their Greco-Egyptian double name (the Greek name is listed first) and refer to their Cyrenaean origin, although their family has already lived in Egypt for four generations. They add that their father, who is deceased, was a soldier and only mention his Greek name and father's name (Ptolemaios, son of Hermokrates).

Women appear to be in a strong position to raise compassion. Apollonia and her sisters, as well as Dryton's daughters, are wronged by a man. They state emphatically that this man despises them, in the case of Apollonia and her sisters because they have been left as orphans (ὑπερισχύων καταφρονήσας τῶι νεωτέρας ἀπολελεῖφθαι, Text 33, l. 6), in the case of Dryton's daughters simply because they are women (κατεγνωκὼς τῶι γυναῖκας ἡμᾶς εἶναι, Text 34, l. 22-23).

§42. *Stressing the injustice.* — Dryton(?) relates in Text 31 that the man who wrongly (παρὰ τὸ [καθῆ]κον, l. 3) registered him, acted out of personal animosity (καθ' ἰδίαν μῆνιν, l. 3).

A topic which is often found in the statement of women is the violence used against them (βίαι, Text 33, l. 9 and 19; βιαιότερον, Text 34, l. 18 and βίας, l. 30)[1]. Dryton's daughters explicitely ask the epistrategos to condemn, as one who hates wickedness (μισοπονήρως), their waylayer in respect of the violence he has committed (περὶ δὲ ἧς πεπόη[τα]ι βίας) (Text 34, l. 29-30).

§43. *Syntax and language.* — The complaints in Texts 31-34 show in general a long and complicated syntax, evidence of a profound knowledge of the Greek language. The petitions are a sequence of independent genitives, participles and subordinate clauses. Somewhere in between the principal verb is hidden. In Text 32 the main verb is even lacking. The long petition Text 33 + 33bis is split up in a few sentences, whereas in Text 34 the writer manages to formulate the complaint of 20 lines in one long sentence.

Sometimes words are used which are attested nowhere else in the papyri. They are in most cases taken over from literary works. Μῆνις (Text 31, l. 3), for instance, is undoubtedly borrowed from the Iliad (*e.g.*, Iliad 5.34). A rare expression such as οὐ μετρίως σκύλλω is to be read in a rhetorical circular of a dioiketes, copied and kept in the Memphite archive of the Katochoi (UPZ I 110). W. Clarysse[2] already suggested in 1983 that this expression would be perfect for use in a petition, and οὐ μετρίως ἐσκυλμένος is indeed found in the petition Text 31, l. 4, from Pathyris, published here for the first time.

---

1 Compare di Bitonto, 'Le petizioni ai funzionari' (1968), p. 79.

2 W. Clarysse, 'Literary Papyri in Documentary «Archives»', in E. Van 't Dack and P. Van Dessel (edd.), *Egypt and the Hellenistic World. Proceedings of the International Colloquium, Leuven 24-26 May 1982* (Studia Hellenistica 27), Leuven 1983, p. 59-60: «A schoolboy copied a very long and strongly rhetorical circular of a dioiketes (UPZ I 110 [from the katochoi-archive, Memphis]). A few of the technical terms in this letter are almost hapax legomena in documentary papyrology, e.g. the words (...) οὐ μετρίως σκύλλω. And it can hardly be mere chance that they recur in some of the petitions of Ptolemaios.»

31

GREEK DIAGRAPHE AND PETITION

Copy perhaps by Dryton

Plate XI

[New collage]

? H. x W. = 6 x 26 cm 140 - 131/130 B.C.
[Fragmentary]

Fragment A = John Rylands Library, P. inv.no. 67 [date of acquisition unknown] +
Fragment B = British Library, P. inv.no. 686f [bought in July 1897 from Grenfell] +
Fragment C = British Library, P. inv.no. 687b [bought in July 1897 from Grenfell] +
Fragment D = Heidelberg, P. Gr. inv.no. 1301 [date of acquisition unknown].

Fragment A was published as **P. Ryl. II 67**. I discovered fragments B and C in London and fragment D in Heidelberg among the **unpublished** fragments of the respective collections.

Photograph. — Plate XI.

Description. — The fragments A-D are broken off along the vertical folds. A kollesis is visible at the right-hand side and another at 2cm from the left edge. The upper part and a small part at the right-hand side are missing. At the left-hand side one character at the maximum is lost. Between l. 1 and 2 of fragment A the horizontal fibres are missing and the text is written on the underlying fibres. Of l. 1-5 of fragment D only the vertical fibres of the verso are preserved.

The text is written on the recto along the fibres. The handwriting has a peculiar characteristic, found only in texts written by Dryton or his son Esthladas (see §64-66): characters are often written above or beneath the preceding character not only at the end of a word (as is often attested), but also within one word (see the bold characters in the text edition, below).

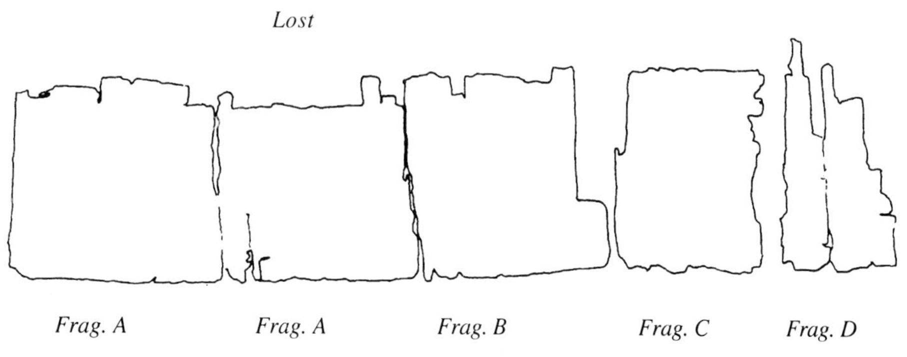

Introduction

Copy of a diagraphe and of a petition. — The text is a copy since several characters are written above or beneath other characters within one word in order to save space (see description of the text), a practice which is not usual in official documents; in addition, the papyrus contains two different documents written by the same hand:

Document 1. A document of which only the end is preserved (l. 1). It may have been a diagraphe (see below, Contents).

Document 2. A petition which starts in l. 2 with the name of the official to whom the petition is addressed. The list of objects declared τῶν ὑπογεγραμμένων μοι ἐγγαίων, *my plots of land listed below* (l. 7) is not found on this papyrus, apparently because this is only a copy. The original petition undoubtedly listed these plots of land at the end of the text.

Date. — The dates of the original documents are not preserved. Prosopographical data are of some help and suggest 140 B.C. as *terminus post quem* and 131/130 B.C. as *terminus ante quem.*

As *terminus post quem* I propose 140 B.C., since Esthladas is already of age according to the petition. Esthladas was born c. 158 B.C. (pros. 504).

The *terminus ante quem*: the petition is addressed to Hermias[1], τῶν διαδόχων καὶ ἐπιμελητής[2] (l. 2). The epimeletes is regularly attested only until c. 140 B.C. After that date, he is gradually replaced by the στρατηγός, the head of the civil administration, who now also becomes the head of the financial department and is called ὁ ἐπὶ τῶν προσόδων[3]. E. Van 't Dack[4] pointed out that the epimeletes Hermias must have assumed his aulic title of τῶν διαδόχων before 131/130 B.C., since at that date a vice-Thebarch had already been promoted to the category of the archisomatophylakes.

If the petition is written by Dryton, as I believe (see below), then it should have been presented before 126 B.C., when Dryton made his last will; he died shortly afterwards (see §19). The *terminus ante quem* suggested by E. Van 't Dack is thus confirmed.

A final person recorded in the petition is Patseous, komogrammateus of Pathyris. He cannot be identified with the Patseous who was komogrammateus of Pathyris some 30 years later. He may be identical with Patseous alias Asklepiades, who was agoranomos in Pathyris in 127-126 B.C. (see comm. on l. 3).

---

1 Hermias may be identified with the Hermias from the Thebaid who in 112 B.C. was ὁ ἐπὶ τῶν προσόδων and in 110 *p3 ḥrj Nw.t* (*the chief of Thebes*) (Pros. Ptol. I and VIII 979; see also Van 't Dack, *Ptolemaica Selecta* (1988), p. 299-302). Van 't Dack is, however, dubious about this identification (*Ptolemaica Selecta* (1988), p. 279, n. 28.; p. 30).

2 Pros. Ptol. I and VIII 940; Mooren, *Prosopography* (1975) no. 0187; Id., *La hiérarchie de cour* (1977), p. 160, n. 5.

3 Van 't Dack, *Ptolemaica Selecta* (1988), p. 250.

4 Van 't Dack, *Ptolemaica Selecta* (1988), p. 279, n. 28; *pace* Mooren, *La hiérarchie de cour* (1977), p. 160-161.

Contents. — The petition is not clear in every particular. A first problem is the identity of the petitioner. L. 2 shows the petitioner was a Cretan, belonging to a deme, probably Philoteris (a deme of the city of Ptolemais), and, according to l. 3, living in Pathyris. These data perfectly fit the profile of Dryton. In addition, the traces in l. 2 fit the supplement [πα]ρ[ὰ Δ]ρ[ύτωνος]. One does not, however, expect Dryton to have had financial problems, as suggested by this petition.

Assuming that Dyton presented the petition, we may reconstruct the events that led up to it: Patseous, komogrammateus of Pathyris, registers Dryton among those who are able (?to pay a large sum of money) (l. 3), in my view on the basis of the plots of land owned by Dryton (l. 7), but according to Dryton 'out of personal wrath'. Consequently, Dryton is required to pay the large sum of 5 talents and 1000 drachmas minimum (l. 4), apparently to an association of ἄνδρες (see below). Dryton is unable to do so and is mistreated by Patseous (l. 4). He is removed from the τόπος συν[όδου?] or meeting place of the association (l. 4) and is transferred from one place to another under (police) surveillance (l. 5) and, probably since he cannot make a living in this situation, he is afraid that he will not be able to keep afloat (l. 5). Thus forced to give in, he pays part of the sum demanded (l. 6). But as financial means are lacking for what remains, he again runs into trouble: when he is brought before the ἄνδρες, he cannot discharge his debt (l. 6).

A solution is found: Dryton sells (all or part of) his plots of land to his son Esthladas, probably for a fictitious sum. The latter now takes over and will pay the outstanding debt (l. 7). Dryton cannot be registered among the well-to-do any more. The plots are now administered (ἐποικονομ[ ) by Esthladas; the verb ἐποικονομέω, composed with ἐπι- ("besides"), could suggest that Esthladas has become joint and not full owner of his father's plots (see comm. on l. 7); this seems to be confirmed by a fragmentary agreement between Dryton and, probably, Esthladas concerning some property (see below, Relation to Text 47).

Dryton's request is somewhat unexpected. One might expect Dryton to request investigation of the injustice done to him, but instead he asks Hermias, the financial officer (called epimeletes), to hand over the proper diagraphe for the plots which have been bought by and are now administered by Esthladas; these plots of land were listed below the original petition. Such a diagraphe was necessary for Esthladas if he was to become the owner of these plots.

The diagraphe[1] is here a bank-diagraphe or report in which the immovables that are sold are accurately described and in which the taxes related to the sale are established, among them the enkyklion-tax or sales-tax[2]. The enkyklion-receipts from Pathyris make clear that the amount and the payment of this tax to the banker is based on such a diagraphe-report. The payment of the enkyklion-tax is important because the seller becomes the legal owner of the property only if he has paid this tax.

The report can take the form of a letter written by the farmer of taxes or by a financial official and addressed to the banker: *e.g.*, «Hermias to Dionysios, greeting . (...) Please receive at the bank of Hermonthis (...) the 1200 copper drachmae (...). Receive also the usual taxes

---

1 See U. Wilcken, UPZ I 114, scr. ext. comm. on l. 10; Seidl, *Ptolemäische Rechtsgeschichte* (1962), p. 67 and 127 and see especially P.W. Pestman, in Pap. Lugd. Bat. XIX, p. 215-217.

2 Pestman, 'L' impôt-ἐγκύκλιον' (1978), in Pap. Lugd. Bat. XIX, p. 214-218.

and any other charge that is usual. Farewell.»[1]. An additional clause may specify that nothing should be overlooked by the responsible officials: *e.g.*, «Receive (the money), on the condition that the topogrammateus adds a statement, signed by himself, of the measurements and adjoining areas and further declares that nothing in this case has been overlooked ».

A similar expression is found in Text 31, l. 1: [- - - ἵνα μηθὲν] ἐ̣ν̣ τ̣ο̣ύτοις ἀγν[ο]ηθῆι [- - -], "in order that nothing in this case should be overlooked". That is the reason why I assume that the (copy of the) petition was preceded by a (copy of the) diagraphe-report. Furthermore, the diagraphe is actually mentioned and asked for in the petition (l. 8).

I assume that Dryton could not obtain this report in Pathyris because of his troubles with the komogrammateus and has to write a petition to the head of finances in person, that is the epimeletes, who can give the necessary orders. P. Amh. II 31 shows that a bank-diagraphe could even be issued by the head of the financial department, who at that time (112 B.C.) was the ὁ ἐπὶ τῶν προσόδων or overseer of the revenues.

A final problem: why or for what reason does Dryton, registered among the well-to-do, have to pay a large amount of money? Our only guide comes in the recurrent ἄνδρες. The ἄνδρες are the able-bodied men in army terms. As they are demanding money from Dryton as a group, they must form an association to which Dryton belonged. Associations of contemporaries are well-known in Egypt: clubs of ephebes, νέοι, ἄνδρες and γέροντες are commonly found[2]. The reference to 'the τόπος σ̣υ̣ν̣[-]' in l. 4, may confirm that an association is involved: τόπος is often used to denote the meeting place of the members of an association; it is likely that it is here followed by σ̣υ̣ν̣[?όδου] (see comm. on l. 4).

F. Poland observed of the members (like Dryton) of this type of association: "Sie bezweckten fast alle die Phlege gymnastischer Übungen, und ihr Mittelpunkt ist daher ein Gymnasium"[3]. The gymnasium was the ideal place for their physical training. Which gymnasium was frequented by Dryton when he lived in Pathyris, is not clear. Text 39 (see Introduction) shows that there was a gymnasium at Thebes, with which Dryton's son Esthladas had contacts. Hermonthis probably had its own gymnasium by 103/102 B.C. at the latest[4].

There was not only a link between the associations of contemporaries and the gymnasium, but also between Greek soldiers (like Dryton) and the gymnasium[5]. According to M. Launey, soldiers founded and maintained the gymnasia and thus frequented these establishments. He continues: "La marque la plus nette d'intérêt que puisse donner un soldat est d'accepter une

---

[1] Diagraphe preserved in P. Amh. II 31, l. 5-19, by Hermias, head of the financial department in the Thebaid (112 B.C.).

[2] See F. Poland, *Geschichte des griechischen Vereinswesens*, Leipzig 1909, p. 94 and 98 (Altersgenossen); Launey, *Les armées hellénistiques* (1949-50), p. 1001.

[3] F. Poland, *Geschichte des griechischen Vereinswesens* , Leipzig 1909, p. 88; see also M. San Nicolò, *Ägyptisches Vereinswesen zur Zeit der Ptolemäer und Römer* (Münchener Beiträge zur Papyrusforschung und antiken Rechtsgeschichte 2), München 1972^2, p. 30-31.

[4] Launey, *Les armées hellénistiques* (1949-50), p. 844.

[5] For the group of ἄνδρες within the gymnasium, see Launey, *Les armées hellénistiques* (1949-50), p. 817, 825-826, 829, 833, 873 (Les armées et le gymnase).

liturgie ou une fonction dans le gymnase"[1]. Such a liturgy could be imposed by the association to which the soldier belonged. An example may make this clear.

According to BGU VI 1256 the cavalryman Hermon is chosen as λαμπαδάρχης or superintendent of the torch-race against his will (Philadelphia, first half of the 2nd century B.C.). Consequently, he has to defray the costs involved. He complains to the komogrammateus and asks him to hand over a report to the gymnasiarch and the νεανίσκοι (a class of young soldiers) of the gymnasium, as if "à côté du gymnasiarque, le groupe des *néaniskoi* constituait une sorte de commission administrative de l'établissement, dotée d'une pleine autorité en matière de liturgie"[2].

What happens to Dryton? He has to pay a sum of money, imposed by an association of ἄνδρες. What the money was for is not clear: was it for a liturgy like the superintendence of a torch-race or was it money for, *e.g.*, the supply of oil or for the restoration of the buildings of the gymnasium[3]?

The only fact which is clear is the reason why he was chosen to pay the sum: the komogrammateus registered him among those who could pay a large amount of money. The involvement of the komogrammateus in matters of a private association seems at first sight strange. However BGU VI 1256 mentioned above confirms this involvement. There, Hermon, who is chosen as λαμπαδάρχης, asks the komogrammateus to write a report for the gymnasiarch and the νεανίσκοι stating that he is not wealthy and has barely enough to provide for himself, his wife and his children. Such a report could free him from the λαμπαδαρχία. The komogrammateus is qualified to assess the financial situation of an individual, since he lists all the property and the yield of the land in an annual survey. Dryton has indeed several plots of land and was thus registered among the well-to-do. The editors of BGU VI 1256 explain the involvement of the komogrammateus: "Die Beteiligung von Staatsbeamten an rein gymnasialen Fragen wird am ehesten verständlich, wenn der Staat darauf bedacht war, die Gymansion-Hellenen durch gymnasiale Leistungen nicht übermäßig belasten zu lassen, um dem Staate ihre Wirtschafts- und Steuerkraft zu erhalten."

Relation to Text 47? — The very fragmentary Text 47 is an agreement between Dryton and a second person. The appearance of the words]τῆς διαγραφ[in l. 2 makes it plausible that the agreement is related to the events described in the petition published here. If this is correct, then Esthladas, who has bought some plots of land from his father, agrees not to [alienate] certain goods without the permission of his father, goods of which Esthladas is the owner (together with his father?). Among these "goods" are the male slaves. Compare also Text 46.

Relation to Text 32? — Text 32 is another petition by Dryton, dated to the same period (137-130 B.C.). Dryton complains that he constantly runs risks on the road from Diospolis Mikra, where he is stationed, to his plots of land in Diospolis Megale and in the Pathyrites. It is unlikely that Dryton is here referring to the acts by the komogrammateus of Pathyris who is maltreating him. I prefer to link this danger with the unrest in the south of Egypt at that time due to dynastic troubles and an internal revolt.

1 Launey, *Les armées hellénistiques* (1949-50), p. 849.
2 Launey, *Les armées hellénistiques* (1949-50), p. 859.
3 Compare Launey, *Les armées hellénistiques* (1949-50), p. 850.

Relation to Text 50? — Text 50 is a poem, a lyric monody which Dryton may have copied from an original used by Dionysiac artists for a performance (see Text 50, Introduction). Thus the synodos mentioned in Text 31, ?l. 4, could have been an association of Dionysiac artists in the Greek city of Ptolemais, of which Dryton was a citizen.

Text

The characters marked in ***bold*** *are written above or beneath the preceding character in the original text (see description of the text).*

Doc. 1 -

traces [- - - ἵνα μηθὲν]

ἐ̣ν̣ τ̣ο̣ύτοις ἀ̣γν[ο]ηθῆι ̣ [- - -]

Doc. 2 Ἑ̣ρμίαι τῶν διαδ**ό**χ**ων** καὶ ἐπιμε̣λ̣ητ̣ῆ̣ι̣, [πα]ρ̣[ὰ ?Δ̣]ρ̣[ύτωνος τοῦ ?Παμφίλου

- c. 2 to 6 - παρεφεδρε]ύ̣οντος Κρ**η**τ**ὸς** δήμ**ου** Φ̣[?ιλωτερείου - - -].

Ἐ̣πεὶ Πατσεο̣ῦ̣τος κ**ω**μ**ο**γρ(αμματέως) Παθ̣**ύ**̣ρ(εως) καθ' ἰδίαν μῆνιν

ἀναγράψαντός με παρὰ τὸ [καθῆ]κ̣ον ἐν τοῖς δυνα[μένοις - - -

(τάλαντα)]

ε̣ (δραχμὰς) ᾿Α καὶ περὶ τῆς τούτων ἀπαιτήσεως οὐ μετρίως ἐσκυλμένος

ὑπ' [αὐτοῦ], ἀπὸ το**ῦ** τ**ό**π**ου** συ̣ν̣[?όδου - -]

μ̣ετὰ φυλακῆς τόπον ἐκ̣ τόπου μεταγειοχότων καὶ ἐκ το**ῦ** τοιο**ύ**τ**ου** π̣ρ**α**[

. . . .]η̣σ̣ων ἀπ' ὀλίγων [- - -]

καὶ διαγεγραφὼς εἰς ταῦτα μέρος τι· τὸ δὲ λοιπὸν διασυνεσταμένος

[τοῖς ἀ]ν̣δράσιν καὶ ἀ̣δ̣υ̣[νατ]ῶ̣ν τάξασθα̣[ι - -]

[ὠ]νητὴν τ̣ῶν ὑπ**ο**γεγρ**α**μμένω̣ν μοι ἐγγαίων Ἐσθλάδαν Δρύτωνος

διαγράφε̣[ιν] τ̣οῖς ἀνδρ**ά**σι· τὰ δ[ὲ νῦ]ν̣ ἐποικον**ο**μ[- - -]

Διὸ ἀξιῶ, ἐὰν φαίνηται, συντάξαι ἐγδοθῆναι **α**ὐ**τ**ῶι τὴν κ**α**θ**ή**κο**υ**σαν

διαγρ**α**[φὴ]ν̣. Οὗ καὶ γεν**ο**μέν**ου**, ἔσ̣[ομαι] πεφιλανθρ**ω**πημ̣[ένος].

[Εὐ]τύχει.

---

1 [ ] ̣ ̣ τ̣ο̣ύτοις ἀγν[ο]ηθῆι α̣[ ] ed., [ἵνα μηθὲν] ἐ̣ν̣ τ̣ο̣ύτοις ἀγν[ο]ηθῆι ̣ [ ] supplevimus et legimus 2 διαδόχω(ν) ed., διαδόχων legimus; [. .] ̣ ̣ [. .] ̣ ̣ ̣ ̣ [ ] ed., [πα]ρ̣[ὰ ?Δ]ρ̣[ύτωνος] legimus et supplevimus 3 [ ]ε̣πει ed., [Νεχθανο]ῦ̣πει Pestman (*Aegyptus* 43 (1963), p. 13), Ἐ̣πεί legimus; Παπεῦ̣τος ed., Πατσεο̣ῦ̣τος Pestman (*Aegyptus* 43 (1963), p. 13); πατ̣ρ(ί) ed., Παθ̣ύ̣ρ(εως) legimus 4 χα̣(λκοῦ) ed., ε̣ (δραχμάς) legimus 7 [ὠ]νητήν supplevimus; ποιεῖται ων ed., μοι ἐγγαίων legimus; Ἐσθλάδας ed., Ἐσθλάδαν legimus 8 αὐ(τ) τ ̣ [ed., αὐτῶι legimus 7 κ in ἐποικονομ[- - -] corr.

Translation

\- Doc. 1

in order that nothing in this case should be overlooked - - -

To Hermias, one of the diadochoi and epimeletes, Doc. 2

from ?Dryton, son of ?Pamphilos, who keeps guard in - - - , Cretan, of the deme ?Philoteris - - -.

Since, out of personal animosity, Patseous, komogrammateus of Pathyris, has wrongly registered me among those who are able to - - (x+)5 talents, 1000 drachmas and since I have been excessively maltreated by him concerning the claim for this (sum), - - - away from the (meeting) place of the ?association, **(5)** *they had me transferred from one place to another under surveillance, and as a consequence I - - - with few means and I paid a part of these dues. Then I was brought before the men and since I was not able to pay - - - that Esthladas, son of Dryton, buyer of my plots of land listed below, pay to the men. They are now managed besides - - -.*

Therefore, I ask, if it seems good to you, that you order the proper diagraphe to be handed over. Once this has happened, I will have obtained redress.

May you prosper.

Notes

1-7 *The lacuna at the end of the lines*: it is not clear how long this lacuna was. L. 8 can certainly be supplemented as πεφιλανθρωπημ̣[ένος], but as this is the last sentence of the text, the lacunae at the end of the previous lines may have contained more than four characters.

1 [ἵνα μηθὲν] ἐ̣ν̣ τ̣ο̣ύτοις ἀγν[ο]ηθῆι . [ ]: my supplement and reading [ἵνα μηθὲν] ἐ̣ν̣ finds its parallel in UPZ II 208, l. 7: [ ] ἵνα δὲ μηθὲν ἐν τούτοις [ἀγνοη]θῆι. For similar expressions, see P. Amh. II 31, l. 15; UPZ I 114, l. 8; UPZ II 218, col. I l. 22; 220, II l. 24; 223A, l. 12.

2 Ἑρμίαι τῶν διαδόχων καὶ ἐπιμελητῆι: see the introduction to the text (Date).

διαδόχων (ed. διαδόχω(ν)): the *nu* is clearly written, compare -ων in ὑπογεγραμμένω̣ν, l. 7.

2 [πα]ρ̣[ὰ ?Δ]ρ̣[ύτωνος τοῦ ?Παμφίλου - c. 2 to 6 - παρεφεδρε]ύ̣οντος: the composite verb παρεφεδρε]ύ̣οντος is also found in another petition of Dryton from the same period (Text 32, l. 8). The length of the remaining lacuna (2 to 6 characters) depends on how many letters were written above others (see the description of the text); one can fill in the place where Dryton keeps guard as, for instance, ἐν **Παθύρ**(ει) or ἐν Δι(ὸς) Π**ό**(λει) Μι(κρά), where Dryton served as guard in 137-130 B.C. (see Text 32): the characters marked in bold may be written above or through the preceding character, compare the writing of Δι(ὸς) Π**ό**(λει) Μ**εγ**(άλῃ) in Text 39, l. 24.

3 Ἐ̣πεὶ Πατσεο̣ῦτος . . . ἀναγράψαντος: P.W. Pestman (*Aegyptus* 43 (1963), p.13) suggested reading [Νεχθανο]ῦ̣πει Πατσεο̣ῦτος . . . ἀναγρα[ ]. The first visible trace does indeed fit an *upsilon*. If this were correct, the petition should be dated to a later period, between 118 and 92 B.C., when Nechthanoupis was active.

The new fragments show, however, that the verb is a participle in the genitive case (ἀναγράψαντος) and thus goes with Πατσεο̣ῦτος. The dative [Νεχθανο]ῦ̣πει no longer makes sense. I therefore suggest following the first editor in reading ε̣πει. Ἐπεί often introduces petitions and can be immediately followed by a genitive case, see, for instance, BGU VI 1256, l. 6-8.

Πατσεο̣ῦτος κωμογρ(αμματέως) Παθ̣ύρ(εως): Patseous (Pros. Ptol. I and VIII 822: Pathyris? - fin 2e s.), is doubtless the komogrammateus of Pathyris (read Παθ̣ύ̣ρ(εως) instead of πατ̣ρ(ί)) some time between 140 and 130 B.C. This Patseous may be identified with the well-known Patseous alias Asklepiades, son of Phibis, who in 127-126 was agoranomos in Krokodilopolis and in 118 became basilikogrammateus: see Pros. Ptol. I and VIII 460 = III and IX 5704 and 7661; Van 't Dack, *Ptolemaica Selecta* (1988), p. 364; Pap. Lugd. Bat. XIX, p. 209-210; Pestman, 'L' agoranomie' (1978), p. 205, 208-209.

An identification with the Patseous who was komogrammateus of Pathyris in 94-92 B.C., is unlikely because of the great difference in time. For this later Patseous, see Vleeming, 'Village Scribes' (1984), p. 1053-1056.

καθ' ἰδίαν μῆνιν: the word μῆνις, wrath, is not found elsewhere in the papyri, except in a magical text of the 4th century A.D. (BGU IV 1026, col. XXII, l. 14). It is probably borrowed from the Iliad (see §43). For the use of ἴδιος rather than ἴδιος, see E. Mayser, *Grammatik* I.1, p. 175.

ἐν τοῖς δυνα[μένοις - - - (τάλαντα)]: the expression οἱ δυνάμενοι is usually followed by an infinitive, see, for instance, P. Tebt. I 61, B, col. XIII, l. 371, and UPZ I 110, col. IV, l. 122-123. The lacuna presumably contained a verb such as ἀποτεῖσαι.

4 ε̣ (δραχμάς): the first editor read χα̣(λκοῦ) instead of ε̣ (δραχμάς). The *epsilon* is joined to the symbol for drachmas by a long line.

4 ἀπὸ τοῦ τόπου συ̣ν̣[?όδου - -]: the general term τόπος is often found in connection with associations and denotes the meeting place of the association (σύνοδος): *e.g.*, τόπος συνόδου χηνοβοσκῶν (Inscr. Fay. II 109), τόπος συνόδου γεωργῶν ἰδίων (Inscr. Fay. II 134). See M. Launey, *Armées hellénistiques*, p. 858: «topos est le lieu de réunion et d'exercices (...) il désigne même parfois le gymnase»; A. Bernand, in Inscr. Fay. II 202, notes that: «topos est utilisé pour désigner les biens-fonds des associations».

5 τόπον ἐκ̣ τόπου μεταγειοχότων: the direct object of μετάγω (transfer) is undoubtedly the petitioner Dryton. The verb is construed with an internal accusative (τόπον) which makes up one expression with ἐκ̣ τόπου. The phrase τόπον ἐκ τόπου is often found in (especially later) Greek literature in combination with verbs composed with μετα-: *e.g.*, with μεταβάλλειν (Hesychius, *s.v.* πάππος), μετέρχεσθαι (Meletius, *De natura hominis*, 21.1), μεταβαίνειν (Simplicius, *In Aristotelis Physica commentaria*, 10. 1260.15).

ἐκ τοῦ τοιούτου π̣ρα[. . . .]η̣σων ἀπ' ὀλίγων: the use of ἀπ' ὀλίγων, "with few means", leads one to suspect that Dryton could no longer make a living and thought that he would no longer be able to keep afloat. A similar expression is found in the petition BGU VI 1256, where a man hoping to be exempted from a liturgy imposed by an association of the gymnasion, argues that he has to make a living with few means (διαζῶντος ἐξ ὀλίων (*sic*)).

Which verb (probably a future participle ending on -ησων) is to be supplemented in the lacuna, is not clear. I cannot find a verb starting with π̣ρα- which suits the meaning needed here (πραγματεύεσθαι, "to be engaged in business", is middle voice).

Maybe one should supply: ἐκ τοῦ τοιούτου π̣ρά[γματος ζ]ή̣σ̣ων ἀπ' ὀλίγων, *as a consequence of such a practice I should have to live with few means*. For the expression ζῆν ἀπ' ὀλίγων, see, for instance, Strabo 7.3.4.8 and *Socratis et Socraticorum epistulae* 6.3.9.

7 [ὠ]νητὴν τῶ̣ν ὑπογεγραμμένω̣ν μοι ἐγγαίων Ἐσθλάδαν . . . διαγράφε̣[ιν]: the reading by the first editor ποιεῖται ων (instead of μοι ἐγγαίων) is meaningless. The reading Ἐσθλάδαν (and not Ἐσθλάδας) is paleographically and grammatically preferable.

Τὰ δ[ὲ νῦ]ν̣ ἐποικονομ[- - -]: the lacuna may have contained Τὰ δ[ὲ νῦ]ν̣ ἐποικονομ[ούμενα ὑπ' Ἐσθλάδου ἔγγαια -], *the plots of land which are now managed by Esthladas*. The composite verb ἐποικονομέω is a hapax (ἐπικονωνεῖται is to be read rather than ἐποικονομεῖται in Aristoteles, *Oeconomica*, 1346a. 14). The term ἐποικονομητέον ("one must treat") is attested. The addition of the prefix ἐπι-, "besides", may denote that the plots of land are now managed by Esthladas besides his other plots of land or that the plots are now administered by Esthladas besides Dryton, that is that both men have control.

32

GREEK PETITION
from Dryton

?	H. x W. = 11 x 10 cm [Height incomplete]	3 July 137 - 15 Jan. 130 B.C.

New York Pierpont Morgan Library, P. Gr. inv.no. 36 [acquired in 1912] = **P. Amh. II 36**.
Photograph. — No photograph available.

Description. — After completion the papyrus was folded vertically and then folded double. As a consequence, it has been damaged along the vertical folds and broken off along the horizontal fold: only the upper part is preserved. The papyrus is of inferior quality: the horizontal fibres are missing on two spots (l. 4 and 7) and, consequently, the text was written on the underlying fibres. A kollesis is probably visible at the left-hand side.

The text is written on the recto, along the fibres. There is a left-hand and top margin of 1.5 cm and a right-hand margin of 0.9 cm at the maximum. The petition is written in the same hand as Text 33 of 136 B.C., most probably the hand of Dryton, who is the petitioner (for his handwriting, see §64-66). The writer has rewritten some characters (compare Text 43): he wrote the same letter(s) over the original character(s):

νγ in συνγενεῖ (l. 1)
σ in στρ[α]τηγῶι (l. 2)
ος in Δ[ρ]ύτωνος (l. 3)
part of the ν in διαδόχων (l. 5)
ον in παρεφεδρεύοντος (l. 8)

Introduction

Contents. — Dryton is a cavalry officer in the military camp of Ptolemais, the Greek city of which he is a citizen; he belongs to the deme Philoteris. When he writes this petition (between 137 and 130 B.C.), he is on guard-duty in Diospolis Mikra. The motivation for his request to the epistrategos is briefly formulated: he constantly runs risks on the road from (probably) Diospolis Mikra to his plots of land in Diospolis Megale and in the Pathyrites. These possessions are also found in other texts of the archive and are discussed in Vandorpe, *Archives from Pathyris* (2001), chapter V.

The reason why Dryton runs risks on the road from Diospolis Mikra to Thebes and the Pathyrites is not explicitely stated, but may be connected with the troubles in the south around 132-129 B.C.: Thebes and environment became involved in the dynastic troubles between Ptolemy VIII and Kleopatra II (132-130 B.C.) and the situation was worsened by a rebellion under the command of Harsiesis (132-129 B.C.)[1].

---

[1] See the introduction to Text 36; Vandorpe, 'Outline of Greco-Roman Thebes' (1995), p. 233-234; McGing, 'Revolt Egyptian Style' (1997), in *AfP* 43, p. 273-314, esp. p. 296-299; Veïsse, *Les «révolutions égyptiennes»* (2000).

The request of Dryton to the epistrategos is lost in the lacuna. He probably asked to be posted from Diospolis Mikra to Pathyris or Krokodilopolis, where he had been living since he married his second wife in 150 B.C. and where he had part of his belongings.

For another interpretation of the petition, which is less plausible, see the Introduction to Text 31.

Date. — The petition is not dated. Since it is addressed to Boethos, who was at the time sungenes, epistrategos and strategos of the Thebaid, the request must have been presented between 3 July 137 and 15 January 130 B.C.[1]

Text

Βοήθω[ι] συνγενεῖ κα[ὶ ἐπιστρ]ατήγωι̣
καὶ στρ[α]τηγῶι τῆς Θηβ[αίδ]ος·
παρὰ Δ[ρ]ύτωνος τοῦ Πα[μ]φίλου
Κρητὸς δήμου Φιλωτ[ερ]είου
τῶν διαδόχων καὶ το[ῦ ἐ]πιτά-
γματος ἱππάρχων ἐπ' ἀνδρῶν
ἀπὸ τῶν ἐκ τοῦ ἐν Πτολεμαίδι
ὑπαίθρου, νυνὶ δὲ παρεφεδρεύοντος
ἐν Διὸς πόλει τῆι μικρᾶι. Ὑπαρχόντων γάρ μοι ἐν Διὸς πόλει τῆι μεγάληι
καὶ ἐν τῶι Παθυρίτηι ἐγγαιδίων,
δι' ἣν α[ἰ]τίαν, λείπω τε τὴν
ὑπερβολὴν, διοδεύων κιν-
δυν[εύω π]αρ' ἕκαστον. Διὸ ἀξιῶ
- -

---

11 ἐπαρδίων ed., ἐγγαιδίων Clarysse (*ZPE* 41 (1981), p. 256)

---

[1] For 3 July 137 B.C., see H. Heinen, in *AfP* 43 (1997), p. 341 and 346-347; for 15 January 130 B.C., the date when Boethos was succeeded by Paos as strategos of the Thebaid, see L. Mooren, in *Ancient Society* 5 (1974), p. 140 and note 17.

Translation

To Boethos, kinsman (of the King), epistrategos and strategos of the Thebaid.

From Dryton, son of Pamphilos, Cretan, of the deme Philoteris, **(5)** *one of the diadochoi and cavalry officer over troops of the epitagma-unit, now on guard-duty in Diospolis Mikra.*

(10) *I own small plots of land in Diospolis Megale and in the Pathyrite nome, and for this reason — and I do not exaggerate — I constantly run risks on the road (to them).*

Therefore, I ask - - -

\- -

Notes

1 Βοήθω[ι]: for the epistrategos Boethos and his titulature, see Text 33, comm. on l. 1*.

10 γάρ: in petitions, the explicative γάρ may introduce the complaint, whether or not preceded by ἀδικοῦμαι, see Mayser, *Grammatik* II.3, p. 122.

12 δι' ἣν α[ἰ]τίαν: for this expression with the meaning "for which reason, and for this reason", see Mayser, *Grammatik* II.2, p. 427.

12-13 λείπω τε τὴν ὑπερβολήν: for this expression, compare the passage in Isocrates 4. 5.110: λείπειν οὐδεμίαν ὑπερβολήν.

13 διοδεύων: the verb is usually further defined by the area through which the travel takes place (in the genitive, accusative or διά with the genitive). Here the verb stands alone, but l. 8-11 show that Dryton travelled from Diospolis Mikra (where he served) to Diospolis Megale and the Pathyrites (where he had plots of land).

14 [π]αρ' ἕκαστον: for the meaning "on every occasion, constantly", see Text 33, comm. on l. 11.

33

GREEK PETITION

from Apollonia and her sisters

Plates XII (recto)-XIII (verso)

[Collage]

? | H. x W. = 15.2 x 28.9 cm [Height incomplete] | 20 June 136 B.C.

Fragment A = Heidelberg, P. Gr. inv.no. 1280 [acquired between 1897 and 1899] +
Fragment B = British Library, P. inv.no. 612 [bought from Grenfell on 9 Nov. 1895].

First edition of fragment B = **P. Grenf. I 17**; first edition of fragment A and second edition of fragment B in **G.A. GERHARD**, *Ein gräko-ägyptischer Erbstreit aus dem zweiten Jahrhundert vor Chr. (Sitzungsberichte der Heidelberger Akademie der Wissenschaften*, 8. Abh.), Heidelberg 1911 (= **SB I 4638**, l. 1-27 and 39-41, with some corrections, mainly taken from U. Wilcken, *AfP* 6 (1920), p. 274-5).

Translation. — Rowlandson, *Sourcebook* (1998), no. 85.

Photograph. — Plates XII-XIII (recto-verso); photograph of fragment Heidelberg, P. Gr. 1280, and of the verso in R. Seider, *Paläographie der griechischen Papyri* III.1, Stuttgart 1990, p. 394-395 (with transcription) and on http://www.rzuser.uni-heidelberg.de/~gv0/Papyri/P.Heid._Uebersicht.html (see SB I 4638)

Description. — Text 33 consists of two fragments. Fragment A is the left half, fragment B the right half of a petition of which the lower part is lost. Fragment B has six lines more than fragment A (l. 22-27). Text 33bis contains the lost end of Text 33, but this was part of another version of the petition, apparently a draft or a copy.

Fragment A has a left-hand margin of 2.3 cm and a top margin of 1.2 cm, fragment B a top margin of 0.7 cm. The text is written on the recto along the fibres in a small, partly cursive hand, here and there leaving a large space before a new episode is recorded (l. 4, 13, 20, 25). A small space is sometimes left at the end of a sentence or clause (passim). One can see clearly where the writer has taken new ink.

The verso contains annotations from the office of the epistrategos (see Introduction), showing that Text 33 is the original petition.

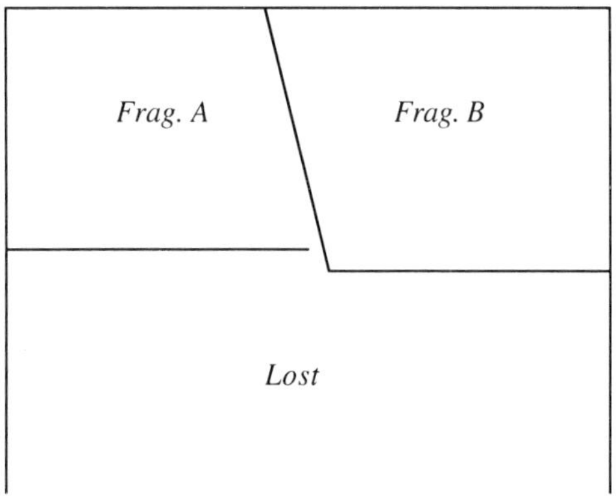

Introduction

Contents. — Text 33 is a petition from the four daughters of Ptolemaios alias Pamenos (pros. 304): Apollonia alias Semmonthis (pros. 404), Ammonia alias Senminis (pros. 405), Herakleia alias Senapathis (pros. 406) and Herais alias Tasris (pros. 407). They act without a kyrios: like Egyptian women, Greek women were able to petition the king or an official without the assistance of a guardian[1].

The four girls have been wronged by their uncle Kallimedes (pros. 308), his wife Kalibis (pros. 307) and their sons Panobchounis (pros. 414) and Orses (pros. 415).

I. *What happened before the petitioners addressed their final request to the epistrategos?*

Ia. *What happened when the petitioners were minors?*

When Ptolemaios alias Pamenos died (some years before 141-140 B.C.), he left behind four orphan daughters: Apollonia and her three sisters. A mother is never referred to; she was probably already dead. As the four girls were still minors, a guardian or ἐπίτροπος had to be appointed.

Statutory regulations undoubtedly defined who became guardian when the father died. Relatives on the maternal and paternal side were appealed to in a fixed order which can no longer be retrieved. In addition, guardians could be appointed by the will of the father or by a stipulation recorded in his marriage contract. But if an orphan did not have relatives and if the father did not leave behind a will in which a non-relative was left as guardian, a request had to be presented to the government for the appointment of a guardian[2].

As Ptolemaios alias Pamenos did not leave behind a will, there was no testamentary guardian for the four orphans (l. 5). They did have relatives. Consequently, their uncle on father's side Kallimedes alias Patous (pros. 308), his wife Kalibis (pros. 307) and their sons took on the role of guardians, appealing to the rights provided by kinship: ὡς δὲ κατὰ τὸ συνγενικόν, "as in accordance with kinship" (l. 6-7). But the uncle did not have the welfare of the orphans in mind, as is clearly shown in the petition. His attitude towards the orphans is depicted as overbearing and contemptuous of the orphans since they had been left as minors (l. 6). At all times, the uncle has actually been the guardian par excellence and through the ages his wickedness has become legendary[3].

According to the orphans, uncle Kallimedes, his wife and sons were, however, *unlawful* guardians (l. 7-8). Statutory regulations (see above) stipulate that they might become guardians

1) if they were left as guardians in the father's will, but the father did not write a will;
2) if they were relatives; in this case, they apparently had to register themselves as guardians according to the rights they held as next-of-kin, but they neglected to do this. The same obligation is found in Athenian law: a next-of-kin might claim the guardianship, but had to register himself as such[4].

---

1 Wolff, *Justizwesen* (1970^2), p.135 and note 41.

2 See Taubenschlag, *Law* (1955^2), p. 159-61.

3 See H.P. Jolowicz, 'The Wicked Guardian', in *JRS* 37 (1947), p. 82-3.

4 A.R.W. Harrison, *The Law of Athens. 1. The Family and Property*, Oxford 1968, p. 103.

As long as the girls were minors, none of their acquaintances reacted against this unlawful situation and the girls were often intimidated.

The second point of controversy between the orphans and their (unlawful) guardians was the inheritance of their father Ptolemaios alias Pamenos, which was not covered by any will. This inheritance consisted of immovables (a house and plots of land) and movables (furniture, etc.). As long as the orphans were minors, the (unlawful) guardians managed this property. They took possession of the house and dwelled in it (l. 8-9). In addition, they appropriated to themselves goods which were kept in the house: furniture and old title-deeds for plots of land (l. 9-10)[1].

Ib. *The petitioners became of age* *in or shortly before 141/140 B.C.*

According to the petition, the orphans became of age in or shortly before 141/140 B.C. (l. 11-12). It is not clear whether girls in Ptolemaic Egypt became an adult when they married, as was usual in Roman Egypt[2].

Apollonia, who was the oldest sister, already attained the age of majority in 150 B.C., when she married Dryton (pros. 403). Her three younger sisters must have become of age between 150 and 141/140 B.C. Now the four girls, who were the legal heirs, could take the necessary measures in order to inherit their father's belongings which were administered by the guardians as long as they were minors. Thus, they paid the succession taxes to the Goddess Berenike (see comm. on l. 12) and became the legal owners of their father's inheritance.

Ic. *Complaint to Herakleides, archiphylakites of the Pathyrites* *141/140 B.C.*

As the former guardians were, however, not willing to return the inheritance, the four orphans filed a complaint to Herakleides (l. 13-14), the archiphylakites of the Pathyrites, in 141/140 B.C. The former guardians reached an agreement in the presence of the chief of police, but they did not fulfil their promises. Contracts, acknowledgements of personal debt as well as other papers were given back, but they were spoiled and the profits realisable through them were destroyed (l. 14-15). The furniture was not returned at all. The guardians were able to keep it by committing perjury (l. 16-17). What happened with the house is not recorded. Some passages in the petition strongly suggest that the orphans got possession of it (l. 18-20).

Id. *Petitions again and again*

The girls presented several petitions in order to get back that part of the inheritance which was not returned (l. 17-18). To whom these were addressed is not made explicit. In any case, their attempts were unsuccessful.

Ie. *Petition to the strategos Santobithys* *in or shortly after 139/8 B.C.*

In 139/8 B.C. the four girls were surrounded by their former guardians, who carried off 13 artabas of wheat; in this they were assisted by Hones, the former hypepistates, who stole 3

---

1 See P.W. Pestman, 'Some Aspects of Egyptian Law in Graeco-Roman Egypt. Title-Deeds and ὑπάλλαγμα', in E. Van 't Dack *e.a.* (edd.), *Egypt and the Hellenistic World* (Studia Hellenistica 27), Leuven 1983, p. 293-4.

2 Taubenschlag, *Law* (1955^2), p. 167.

artabas of barley from the house (l. 18-20). This theft, as well as their uncle's new claim to the house of the girls, are the immediate cause for a new complaint, submitted to the strategos Santobithys. The latter had the uncle Kallimedes arrested (l. 20-21).

If. *Request to Ptolemaios, strategos of the Pathyrite nome, and settlement*

What happened afterwards, is for the main part lost in the lacuna. A partial reconstruction of events is possible. After his arrest, Kallimedes makes a request "on the grounds that [he would do] justice to everyone after his release" (l. 21). Apparently, Kallimedes asks for a settlement which would lead to his release, promising that he would do justice to everyone, including the orphans.

The girls turned to Ptolemaios, strategos of the Pathyrite nome, probably to establish a settlement for the inheritance (l. 22-23). This probable settlement, by which the remaining part of the inheritance and a written contract of their father are returned, was signed by Kallimedes (l. 24-25).

Ig. *Appeal by Kallimedes?* *137/6 B.C.*

But the agony went on. Kallimedes probably entered an appeal in 137/6 B.C.; what part was played by the Egyptian notary (monographos) Thot(or)taios (l. 26-27), is not clear; a possible explanation is given below. According to G.A. Gerhard, Kallimedes wanted to take the affair to the court of the Laokritai, the Egyptian judges[1]. He is probably right, since the girls ask at the end of the petition (preserved in a draft or copy version, Text 33bis), not to be judged before the "incompetent courts". As they are of Greek (that is Cyrenaean) origin, they do not want to be judged by an Egyptian court, which passes judgement according to the indigenous laws (κατὰ τοὺς τῆς χώρας νόμους[2]).

From 118 B.C. onwards, this court could only judge cases between Egyptians or cases in which an Egyptian contract lay at the basis of the dispute[3]. Maybe the settlement of l. 24-25, signed by Kallimedes, was an Egyptian contract written by the Egyptian notary Thot(or)taios and it was for this reason that Kallimedes turned to the Egyptian judges.

---

1 Gerhard, *Ein gräko-ägyptischer Erbstreit* (1911), p. 14 and comm. on l. 33, p. 34.

2 For the court of the Laokritai, see Seidl, *Ptolemäische Rechtsgeschichte* (1962²), p. 74-77.

3 See J. Modrzejewski, 'Chrématistes et Laocrites', in *Hommages à Cl. Préaux*, Bruxelles 1975, p. 699-708; P.W. Pestman, 'The Competence of Greek and Egyptian Tribunals according to the Decree of 118 B.C.', in *BASP* 22 (1985), p. 265-269. See in general, Wolff, *Justizwesen* (1970²), p. 48-53 (Laokriten) and p. 64-89 (Chrematisten).

II. *Final request to the epistrategos Boethos*

(20 June 136 B.C.)

The girls submitted their final complaint to the most important authority in Upper Egypt, the epistrategos, on 20 June 136 B.C. In support of their request, they gave a detailed account of the events and portrayed their former guardians as scoundrels. The fact that orphans are the victim of unlawful practises, is put forward as a question of awkward circumstances (l. 17).

The final request to the epistrategos is not preserved in the original petition Text 33, but in the draft version Text 33bis. The four girls ask that their case should not be judged before the "incompetent courts", undoubtedly the court of the Laokritai (see above), but before (the court presided over by) the strategos Santobithys, who was already concerned with the case in an earlier phase (see above Ie).

The epistrategos Boethos complied with their request, since a note on the verso of the petition preserves the phrase "To Santobithys". The notes on the verso were made in the office of the epistrategos and contain 1) the date of the submission of the petition, 2) the names of two of the four petitioners (the date and the names are written in a very cursive hand), and 3) the name of the addressee ("To Santobithys"), written in a clear and large uncial.

Dates. — The petition was submitted under the reign of Ptolemy VIII and the dates mentioned in the petition (year 30, 32 and 34) are also to be situated during the reign of Ptolemy VIII, see Text 33bis, Introduction.

Text

Recto

1* Βοήθωι συγγενεῖ καὶ ẹπιστρατ̣ή̣γωι

παρ' Ἀπολλωνίας τῆς καὶ Σεμμώνθιος κα[ὶ] Ἀμμωνί̣α̣ς τῆς καὶ Σεμμίνιος καὶ Ἡρακλείας ἣ Σεναπᾶθις
καὶ Ἡραΐδος ἣ Τάσρις τῶν Πτολεμαίου Κυρηναίων καταγινομένων ἐν Παθύρει. Ἀδικούμεθ' ὑπὸ Καλλιμήδου
τοῦ Ἀπολλωνίου ὃς Πατοῦς Ψεμμώνθου τῶν πεζῶν καὶ Καλίβιος γυναικὸς αὐτοῦ καὶ τῶν τούτων
Ia υἱῶν Ὀρσέους καὶ Πανοβχ<ο>ύνιος. *Vac.* Τοῦ προγεγραμμένου πατρὸς ἡμῶν Πτολεμαίου τοῦ Ἑρμοκράτου ὃς ἦν
τῶν Διοδότου πεζῶν μεταλλάξαντος τὸν βίον καὶ ἀπ[ο]λιπόντος ἡμῖν τὰ ὑπάρχοντ' αὐτῶι ἀδιάθετα
ὁ ἐνκεκλημένος ὑπερισχύων καταφρονήσας τῶι νε[ω]τέρας ἀπολελεῖφθαι, ὡς δὲ κατὰ τὸ συνγενικὸν ἐπελ-
θὼν σὺν τοῖς ἐνκαλουμένοις καὶ ἄλλοις οὔτε κατ' ἀνχιστείαν ἀπογραψάμενοι οὔτε κατὰ διαθήκην ἀπολελειμμένοι ἐπίτροποι κατὰ τὸ σιωπώμενον ἐμβατεύσαντες εἰς τὴν ὑπάρχουσαν ἡμῖν οἰκίαν ἐν τῆι Παθύρει
ἐνώικησαν βίαι οἳ ἐπανοίξαντες τὸν οἶκον καὶ τὰ ἀπολειφθένθ' ἡμῖν ὑπὸ τοῦ πατρὸς ἡμῶν ἔπιπλα
τάς τε προκτήσεις τῶν ἐνγα`ι̣´δίων ἐξιδιασάμενοι ἀπηνέγκαντο καὶ ἀπ' ἐκείνου διὰ παρευρέσεως ἀεί ποτε
Ib ἀντιποιούμενοι τῶν ἡμετέρων παρ' ἕκαστον καταβλάπτοντες διασείουσιν. *Vac.* Ἐνήλικοι δὲ
γενόμεναι κατὰ τὸ ἀναγκαῖον κληρονομήσασαι ταξάμεναι τὰ καθήκοντα τέλη θεᾶι Βερενίκηι κυρι-
Ic εύομεν. *Vac.* Ὅθεν οὐκ ἀποδιδόντων τὰ ἡμέτερα ἐπεδώκαμεν ἐν τῶι λ (ἔτει) προσανγελίαν
Ἡρακλείδει γενομένωι ἀρχιφυ(λακίτηι) τοῦ Παθ`υ´ρίτου ἐφ' οὗ ἀνομολογη-σάμενοι μόλις ἀπέδωκάν τινα. Συναλλά-

---

1* [καὶ στρατήγωι τῆς Θηβαΐδος] suppl. Gerhard, nihil supplevimus 7 ἀγχιστείαν Gerhard, ἀνχιστείαν legimus 10 ἐνγαα̣ίων Gerhard, ἐνγα`ι̣´δίων Clarysse; ἐξιθιασάμενοι Gerhard, ἐξιδιασάμενοι legimus

Translation

R e c t o

To Boethos, kinsman (of the King) and epistrategos.

From Apollonia alias Semmonthis, Ammonia alias Senminis, Herakleia alias Senapathis and Herais alias Tasris, daughters of Ptolemaios, Cyrenaean, living in Pathyris.

We are wronged by Kallimedes alias Patous, son of Apollonios alias Psenmonthes, belonging to the infantry regiment, and by his wife Kalibis and by their sons Orses and Panobch<o>unis.

When our before-mentioned father Ptolemaios, son of Hermokrates, who belonged to the I a
infantry regiment of Diodotos, died and left us his property without a will, the accused,
behaving in an overbearing and contemptuous manner since we had been left as minors, attacked (us) together with the accused and others, on the grounds of kinship, although they had not registered themselves as guardians according to their rights as next-of-kin nor were left as guardians in accordance with a will; they secretly entered into possession of the house that belongs to us in Pathyris and forcibly took up occupation there; they opened the house and appropriated to themselves the furniture left to us by our father as well as the old title-deeds for the small plots of land, and carried them away and from then on they always lay claim to our things under false pretences and causing damage on every occasion they intimidate (us).

After we came of age, we necessarily entered into possession of our inheritance, paid the Ib
proper taxes to Goddess Berenike and (now) are in control.

Therefore, when they did not give back our property, we submitted a complaint in the 30th Ic
year to Herakleides, who was (at that time) archiphylakites of the Pathyrite nome. In **141/40**
his presence they came to an understanding and scarcely returned anything.

γμαθα δὲ καὶ συμβόλαια ἰδιόχρεα καὶ ἕτερα γράμματα λοιμανάμενοι ἔβλαψαν τὰ δι' αὐτῶν διάφορα
τά τ' ἔπιπλα ταξάμενοι ἀποδοῦναι οὐκ ἐποίησαν, οἰόμενοι ὅρκωι ἀποκλύσαντες ἡμᾶς
στερέσειν, προφανῶς ἔνοχοι ὄντες φωρᾶι λείας ἐφημμένοι ἀλλοτρίων καὶ
Id ταῦτ' ὀρφανικῶν. Ὑπὲρ ὧν
Ie πλειονάκι ἐντετευχυιῶν ὑπερέχων ἡμᾶς ἀπράκτους καθίστησι. Καὶ ἐν τῶι δὲ λβ (ἔτει) καταπερι-
στάντες ⟦ . . . . ⟧ σὺν Ὀνῆι τῶι ὑπεπιστατήσαντ[ι] τῆι βίαι ἀπηνέγκαντο (πυροῦ) ἀρ(τάβας) ιγ̅ καὶ ἐξ οἴκου
Ὀνῆς κριθῆς ἀρ(τάβας) γ̅, ἀντιποιοῦνται δὲ καὶ τῆς προγεγραμμένης οἰκίας. Διὸ καὶ ἐπὶ Σαντοβίθυος
[τοῦ στρατηγοῦ - c. 13 - συ]νσχεθεὶς ἠξίωσεν ὡς μετὰ τὴν δίεσιν παντὶ δίκαιον
If [- c. 39 -]ου. Ὡσαύτως ἐπὶ Πτολεμαίου τοῦ ἐπὶ τοῦ Παθυρ(ίτου)
[- c. 39 -]ṃων κληρονομίαν καὶ συγγραφὴν πατρικῆς
[- c. 38 - ὑ]πογράφει ἐν τοῖς μάρτυσι ὁ Πατοῦς συνορῶν
Ig [- c. 37 - τὴ]ν ὑπογραφήν. Οὕτως ἑκουσίως ὁ Καλλιμήδης
[- c. 42 -]α διὰ μον[ο]γράφου Θορ[τ]αίου ἔφεσιν λαβόν-
[- c. 66 -] τοῦ λδ (ἔτους)

II The end of the petition is preserved in a draft or copy version, see Text 33bis.

14-15 Συναλλάγμαθα *l.* Συναλλάγματα 15 λοιμανάμενοι *l.* λυμανάμενοι 17 στερέσειν corr. ex ⟦ ⟧ 18 πλειονάκι *l.* πλεονάκις 21 [τῶν πρώτων φίλων καὶ στρατηγοῦ] suppl. Henne, [τοῦ στρατηγοῦ] supplevimus; ιν in δίεσιν corr. ex ⟦ ⟧

Verso

[(Ἔτους) λ]δ̣ Παχὼν κη̅
Ἀπολλωνίας καὶ ΣΑΝΤΟΒ[ΙΘΥΙ]
Ἀμμωνίας

---

1 Ἡρακλ(είας) καί ed., [(Ἔτους) λ]δ̣ Παχὼν κη̅ legimus

But they spoiled the contracts, acknowledgements of personal debt as well as other papers and destroyed the profits realisable through them.

They agreed to give back the furniture, but they did not do it, thinking that they could wash away (the agreement) by an oath and deprive us, although obviously guilty of theft of stolen property, since they had claimed property of others, even of orphans.

Although we have petitioned several times on these matters, he prevents us achieving Id
anything, as he is too strong for us.

In the 32nd year they surrounded (us) together with Hones, the former hypepistates, and Ie
forcefully carried away 13 artabas of wheat and Hones carried off 3 artabas of **139/8**
barley from (our) house. They even lay claim to the afore-mentioned house.

Therefore, [when we applied] to Santobithys [the strategos], he was kept under arrest and asked, as if [he would do] justice to everyone after his release, - - -.

[When we applied] in like manner to Ptolemaios, strategos of the Pathyrite nome, - - - If
inheritance and a written contract of - - - of our father - - - Patous, comprehending - -, signs among the witnesses - - - the hypographe.

Thus Kallimedes voluntarily - - - through the monographos Thortaios an ?appeal in the 34th Ig
year. **137/6**

- -

The end of the petition is preserved in a draft or copy version, see Text 33bis. II

V e r s o

Year 34, 28 Pachon.
From Apollonia and *to* SANTOBITHYS
Ammonia

Notes

Recto

1* Βοήθωι συγγενεῖ καὶ ἐπιστρατήγωι [ ] : in my article *Der früheste Beleg eines Strategen der Thebaïs als Epistrategen,* in *ZPE* 73 (1988), p. 47-50, I stated that the lacuna after ἐπιστρατήγωι is not large enough to contain the supplement proposed by Gerhard [καὶ στρατήγωι τῆς Θηβαίδος]. I suggested reading and/or supplying

either συγγενεῖ καὶ ἐπιστρατήγωι [τῆς Θηβαίδος]
or συγγενεῖ καὶ ἐπιστρατήγωι [ ], without supplying anything in the lacuna.

New evidence shows that the reading συγγενεῖ καὶ ἐπιστρατήγωι (without supplement) is to be preferred, since Boethos appears to be epistrategos of a larger area than the Thebaid. Papyri from Trier and Yale also record the title of συγγενής καὶ ἐπιστράτηγος (without mention of the area), see H. Heinen, in *AfP* 43 (1997), p. 341 and 346-347.

The text published here dating to June 136 B.C. no longer contains the oldest reference to Boethos as epistrategos, as suggested in my article *Der früheste Beleg eines Strategen der Thebaïs als Epistrategen* (see above). The above-mentioned Yale papyri are earlier (3-8 July 137 B.C.).

For the career of Boethos, see Kramer and Heinen, 'Der κτίστης Boethos' (1997), Teil I, in *AfP* 43, p. 315-339, Teil II, p. 340-363; H. Heinen, 'Boéthos, fondateur de *poleis* en Égypte ptolémaïque (*OGIS* I 111 et un nouveau papyrus de la collection de Trèves)', in L. Mooren (ed.), *Politics, Administration and Society in the Hellenistic and Roman World. Proceedings of the international colloquium, Bertinoro 19-24 July 1997* (Studia Hellenistica 36), Leuven 2000, p. 123-153.

6 τὸ συνγενικόν: this term is here distinguished from ἀγχιστεία, see the next comment.

7 ἡ ἀγχιστεία: the terms ἀγχιστεία, deriving from the superlative of ἄγχι, and συγγένεια «embrace relatives other than ascendants or descendants. (...) The former was the narrower and the more technical. It denoted all those who were related to the deceased, whether on the father's or the mother's side, down to and including sons of cousins (...), or possibly down to and including second cousins. (...) The term συγγένεια on the other hand had no such restrictive use and would apply to relatives beyond this limit. Thus all ἀγχιστεῖς were συγγενεῖς, but not all συγγενεῖς were ἀγχιστεῖς.» (A.R.W. Harrison, *The Law of Athens.* 1. *The Family and Property*, Oxford 1968, p. 143-9).

An extended meaning of ἡ ἀγχιστεία is "the rights of next-of-kin", thus opposed to the more general τὸ συγγενικόν, "the rights of kinship".

ἀπογράφομαι: means in the first place "Vermelden unter Einreichung einer ἀπογραφή, i.e. die schriftliche Vermeldung über Bewohner oder Besiß zur Festlegung, ständischer oder steuerlicher Tatsachen" (Kiessling, *Wörterbuch* IV, *s.v.* ἀπογράφομαι and ἀπογραφή).

The verb usually has an object: "register a person or property"; thus the tax assessment on this person or property could be established. In Text 33 ἀπογράφομαι, however, has no object. How is ἀπογράφομαι to be interpreted?

The uncle and his accomplices imposed themselves as guardians

(1) οὔτε κατ' ἀγχιστείαν ἀπογραψάμενοι
(2) οὔτε κατὰ διαθήκην ἀπολελειμμένοι ἐπίτροποι.

These two denying participles with concessive meaning, contain the reasons why the uncle and his accomplices did not have the right to act as guardians:

(2) they were not left as guardians in the father's will
(1) being relatives, they did not "ἀπογράψασθαι according to the right of next-of-kin".

According to Gerhard (*Ein gräko-ägyptischer Erbstreit* (1911), p. 19, comm. on l.7) κληρονομίαν, "inheritance", is implied; the expression ἀπογράφομαι κληρονομίαν is indeed attested (see UPZ II 162, col. VII, l. 10-11).

Others suppose that ἐπιτροπήν is to be understood as the object of ἀπογραψάμενοι: "to register the guardianship" (see, for instance, J.C. Naber, 'Observatiunculae ad papyros iuridicae', in *Mnemosyne. Nova Series* 57 (1929), p. 80, note 2).

I agree with this interpretation, but, in my view, no implied object needs to be assumed with ἀπογραψάμενοι: the clause with the two denying participles has a parallel construction:

οὔτε +	κατά with accusative +	participle:	
(1) οὔτε	κατ' ἀγχιστείαν	ἀπογραψάμενοι	
(2) οὔτε	κατὰ διαθήκην	ἀπολελειμμένοι	ἐπίτροποι

ἐπίτροποι is added at the end and is to be interpreted as a predicative adjunct not only of the second participle ἀπολελειμμένοι, but also of the first participle ἀπογραψάμενοι; οὔτε κατ' ἀγχιστείαν ἀπογραψάμενοι ἐπίτροποι thus means "although they had not registered themselves as guardians according to the rights of next-of-kin", ἀπογράφομαι being a direct reflexive middle voice.

10 πρόκτησις: πρόκτησις (see also UPZ II 162, col. IX, l. 5) or προκτητικὸν βιβλίον (see BGU VIII 1827, l. 27) is a title-deed showing previous ownership. It corresponds to demotic *sẖ* (or *qnb.t* or *ḏm*^{c}) *is*, "old document". It involves a type of title-deed which is kept by the new owner, but is issued in the name of the previous owner. This "old document" is opposed to the "new document" which is issued in the name of the new owner. The latter is entitled to both types of title-deed as is often explicitly stated in demotic papyri: "they belong to you, your fields (...) together with their old and new title-deeds".

These title-deeds were important because they proved the origin of one's title of property. Consequently, they were carefully kept in family-archives (see P.W. Pestman, 'Some Aspects of Egyptian Law in Graeco-Roman Egypt. Title-Deeds and ὑπάλλαγμα', in E. Van 't Dack *e.a.* (edd.), *Egypt and the Hellenistic World* (Studia Hellenistica 27), Leuven 1983, p. 281-94).

10 ἐνγαίδιον (and not ἐνγααι̣ον): this diminutive of ἔγγαιον is also found in Text 32, l. 11. The diminutive has a more emotive sound to it than has the neutral ἔγγαιον and is therefore preferred in petitions (see W. Clarysse, ' Ἐπάρδιον and ἐγγαίδιον, delendum and addendum lexicis', in *ZPE* 41 (1981), p. 256).

ἐξιδιασάμενοι: Gerhard read ἐξιθιασάμενοι (= ἐξιδιασάμενοι). The interchange of *delta* and *theta* is, however, rare, except in οὐδείς (μηδείς) (see Mayser, *Grammatik* I.l, p. 148). In addition, the reading with the *delta* is palaeographically to be preferred.

11 παρ' ἕκαστον: παρ' ἕκαστον or παρ' ἕκαστα means "at every occasion" and not "against every right", see Kiessling, *Wörterbuch* IV, *s.v.* ἕκαστος.

διασείω: the verb usually denotes extortion by officials (see di Bitonto, 'Le petizioni ai funzionari' (1968), in *Aegyptus* 48, p. 78). Here, intimidation by private persons is involved.

11-12 Ἐνήλικοι δὲ γενόμεναι κατὰ τὸ ἀναγκαῖον κληρονομήσασαι: when the father died, minor children fell under the supervision of a guardian (Taubenschlag, *Law* (1955^2), p. 157-170). One of the latter's tasks was the management of the inheritance until the orphans came to age (di Bitonto, 'Le petizioni ai funzionari' (1968), in *Aegyptus* 48, p.78).

12 ταξάμενοι τὰ καθήκοντα τέλη Βερενίκηι: in order to enter on the possession of the inheritance the heir had to prove his kinship. According to the πολιτικοὶ νόμοι and ψηφίσματα, he/she had to pay inheritance taxes to the deified queen Berenike, wife of Ptolemy III. Here, this tax is called τὰ καθήκοντα. The usual expression is ἀπαρχή (Bouché-Leclercq, *Histoire des Lagides* (1903-1907) III, p. 333 and note 4; Préaux, *L'économie royale* (1939), p. 337). According to the same πολιτικοὶ νόμοι and ψηφίσματα, the heir finally had to declare the inheritance (κληρονομίαν ἀπογράψασθαι) (see Taubenschlag, *Law* (1955^2), p. 212-4).

13 προσαγγελία: the terms προσαγγελία or προσάγγελμα and the verbs προσ-, εἰσ- and παραγγέλλειν denote a declaration of an unlawful action either to the archiphylakites or his policemen, or to the komogrammateus. Semeka distinguishes between προσαγγελία and προσάγγελμα:

«Der Unterschied zwischen προσαγγελία und προσάγγελμα liegt darin, daß προσαγγελία ausschließlich Strafanzeige bedeutet, προσάγγελμα dagegen im wesentlichen den amtlichen Bericht zu bedeuten scheint, so z.B. den Bericht eines Komogrammateus über seine Einnahmen aus der Verwaltung des königlichen Landes usw.» (Semeka, *Ptolemäisches Prozessrecht* (1913), p. 266 and 276-7; compare Seidl, *Ptolemäische Rechtsgeschichte* (1962^{2}), p. 65, who only mentions the term προσάγγελμα; Wolff, *Justizwesen* (1970^{2}), p. 163).

14 Ἡρακλείδης γενόμενος ἀρχιφυλακίτης: for the archiphylakites Herakleides, see Pros. Ptol. II 4578.

14-15 Ἡρακλείδει ... ἐφ' οὗ ἀνομολογησάμενοι ... διάφορα: G.A. Gerhard proposed the following reading and translation: Ἡρακλείδει ... ἐφ' οὗ ἀναμολογησάμενοι μόλις ἀπέδωκάν τινα συναλλάγμαθ'. ἃ δὲ καὶ συμβόλαια ἰδιόχρεα καὶ ἕτερα γράμματα λοιμανάμενοι ἔβλαψαν τὰ δι' αὐτῶν διάφορα *(«Herakleides ...; vor diesem verpflichteten sie sich (zur Zurückgabe), gaben aber mit knapper Not einige Kontrakte zurück; bei den gleichfalls zurückgegebenen, sie selber belastenden Schuldscheinen und anderen Papieren verletzten und beschädigten sie die (Zahlen der) darin enthaltenen Summen»).*

In this reading ἃ δὲ καὶ συμβόλαια ἰδιόχρεα καὶ ἕτερα γράμματα can be interpreted in two ways.

1. ἅ is a relative (or pseudo-relative) pronoun with συναλλάγμαθ' as antecedent;
2. or a verb such as ἀπέδωκαν is implied: ἃ δὲ καὶ συμβόλαια . . . καὶ . . . γράμματα (ἀπέδωκαν), that is τὰ δὲ καὶ συμβόλαια ... καὶ ... γράμματα ἃ καὶ (ἀπέδωκαν).

In both suggestions the syntax is unusual and laboured. Alternative punctuation can avoid this contrived construction: ... μόλις ἀπέδωκάν τινα. Συναλλάγμαθα (*l.* συναλλάγματα) δὲ καὶ συμβόλαια ... καὶ ... γράμματα λοιμανάμενοι . . . For the interchange of *tau* and *theta,* see Mayser, *Grammatik* I.1, p.147.

Both συναλλάγματα and συμβόλαια have a general meaning. They include both written and unwritten contracts (Taubenschlag, *Law* (1955^{2}), p. 292-4; for συμβόλαιον, see also Wolff, *Recht der griechischen Papyri* (1978), p. 141). In this Text 33 συμβόλαια has a restricted meaning since it is further specified as ἰδιόχρεα, "carrying a personal obligation": συμβόλαια ἰδιόχρεα are acknowledgments of personal debt.

15 λοιμανάμενοι (*l.* λυμανάμενοι): in documentary papyri verbs on -αίνω usually have an aorist on -ανα, see Mayser, *Grammatik* I.2, p.132-133.

16 ἀποκλύσαντες: Grenfell wrongly read ἀποκλήσαντες (see Mayser, *Grammatik* I.2, p. 132-3 and Mandilaras, *The Verb* (1973), §304). Kenyon proposed reading ἀποκλήαντες or ἀποκλύσαντες (see Gerhard, *Ein gräko-ägyptischer Erbstreit* (1911), p. 24, comm. on l. 16): in ἀποκλήαντες the *sigma* would have disappeared; ἀποκλύσαντες is the reading taken over by Gerhard in his edition and assumed that there was a «seltene (itazistische?) Verwechslung von η mit υ». Thus, ἀποκλύσαντες is according to Gerhard a mistake for ἀποκλήσαντες. Wilcken suggested yet another possible reading: ἀποκλίσαντες for ἀποκλείσαντες, in which case the *jota* was joined with the *sigma* by a «Ligaturstrick» (U. Wilcken, in *AfP* 6 (1920), p. 275).

The photograph clearly shows that ἀποκλύσαντες must be read. It is not, however, necessary to take ἀποκλύσαντες as a mistake for ἀποκλήσαντες. It may be an aorist of ἀποκλύζω, "wash off". The compound ἀποκλύζω is rarely attested, but so is ἀποκλάω. In addition, Text 33 has several rare compounds, such as ἐπανοίγνυμι (l. 9), καταπεριίσταμαι (l. 18-9), ὑπεπιστατέω (l. 19).

18 πλειονάκι (= πλεονάκις): for ει instead of ε before a sound, see Mayser, *Grammatik* I.1, p. 41; for the disappearance of the end-*sigma*, see Mayser, *Grammatik* I.l, p. 180-1.

19 Ὀνῆς: Pros. Ptol. I 695. The edition of G.A. Gerhard wrongly reads Ὀνῆς. The name is derived from demotic *Ḥwn* and is thus aspirated (see Lüddeckens, *Dem. Namenbuch* I.11, p. 778).

ὑπεπιστατέω: see Text 3, l. 56.

ἐξ οἴκου: for the absence of the article after a preposition, see Mayser, *Grammatik* II.2, p. 35, l. 36.

20-21 ἐπὶ Σαντοβίθυος [τοῦ στρατηγοῦ]: Pros. Ptol. I and VIII 326 and Mooren, *Prosopography* (1975), no. 0119; Van 't Dack, *Ptolemaica Selecta* (1988), p. 258, 310, 322 and 346.

H. Henne (in *REA* 42 (1940) (= *Mélanges G. Radet*), p. 175, n. 13) proposed the supplement [τῶν πρώτων φίλων, etc. (*i.e.* καὶ στρατηγοῦ)]. Henne's addition is not entirely taken over in the BL III, p. 171: [τῶν πρώτων φίλων].

Santobithys may indeed have borne the aulic title τῶν πρώτων φίλων (see Mooren, *La hiérarchie de cour* (1977), p. 116 and note 1) when this petition was submitted (June 136 B.C.) and when the case was put before him.

This passage (l. 18-21), however, where Santobithys' titulature is missing in the lacuna, relates to year 32 (l. 18) of Ptolemy VIII (= 139/8 B.C.). In year 32 the daughters of Ptolemaios again have troubles with their uncle. For that reason, they petition Santobithys (l. 20: Διὸ καὶ ἐπὶ Σαντόβίθυος), that is in year 32 or perhaps the beginning of year 33 (= 138 B.C.). In 139/8 B.C. Santobithys could not yet have the title of τῶν πρώτων φίλων, since he was still an ἀρχισωματοφύλαξ in Febr./March 137 B.C. (BGU VI 1247, l. 1: Σαντοβίθυι ἀρχισωματοφύλακι καὶ στρατηγῶι; for the date, see Mooren, *La hiérarchie de cour* (1977), p. 115).

He presumably acquired this title in 139/8 B.C. (compare the remark by Mooren, *La hiérarchie de cour* (1977), p. 116, note 1). L. 21 may have contained: [ἀρχισωματοφύλακος καὶ στρατηγοῦ]. This supplement of 29 characters is, however, somewhat long (c. 25 letters are needed).

To solve this problem, one might abbreviate the aulic title. But there is another difficulty: the lacuna also needs a verb on which ἐπὶ Σαντοβίθυος depends, such as ἡμῶν καταστασῶν (proposal by Gerhard, *Ein gräko-ägyptischer Erbstreit* (1911), p. 26, comm. on l. 20-22).

Omitting the aulic title is the only solution; this is not unusual, especially since the aulic titles for all officials are missing, except, of course, in l. 1* (see l. 14, 19 and 22). One may supply [τοῦ στρατηγοῦ ἡμῶν καταστασῶν], making 27 characters.

Santobithys is a strategos, not of one, but of several nomes in the Thebaid, among them the Pathyrite and Ombite nomes and the nome of Syene (see Mooren, *Prosopography* (1975), no. 0119).

22 ἐπὶ Πτολεμαίου τοῦ ἐπὶ τοῦ Παθυρ(ίτου): the governor of a single nome is never called a strategos before the 1st century B.C. He is named ἐπιστάτης or ὁ πρὸς τῆι στρατηγίαι τοῦ..., ὁ ἐν τῶι..., ὁ ἐπὶ τοῦ... (plus the name of the nome, see L. Mooren, in *Ancient Society* 3 (1972), p. 130, note 19 and id., *La hiérarchie de cour* (1977), p. 122); for Ptolemaios, see Pros. Ptol. I 385 and Van 't Dack, *Ptolemaica Selecta* (1988) , p. 322 and 355.

23-24 συνγραφὴν πατρικῆς [ ]: Gerhard proposed adding συνγραφὴν πατρικῆς [ὠνῆς] or [οἰκίας]; for the last supplement, compare l. 20: ἀντιποιοῦνται δὲ καὶ τῆς προγεγραμμένης οἰκίας. Gerhard preferred the former, since in the latter case the article is expected (p. 28-29, comm. on l. 23).

25 ὑπογραφή: the hypographe or subscription mentioned here in a fragmentary context may be either a subscription on a contract by Kallimedes himself or a decision of an official on a petition handed to him (P. Tebt. I 45, l. 28).

26 μονογράφος Θορταῖος: Tho(to)rtaios was the Egyptian notary of the temple of Pathyris in the period 178-133 B.C., see Text 3, comm. on l. 48.

27 ἔφεσις: this term is well-known in Attic law, but is hardly found in Egypt. It is attested in an inscription from Theadelphia of 70 B.C. with the meaning "permission" (SB III 6236, l. 28). It is more frequently found in the Roman period with a meaning which is accurately defined by Harpokration: ἡ ἐξ ἑτέρου δικαστηρίου εἰς ἕτερον μεταγωγή. Thus, ἔφεσις appears to be an equivalent for the modern concept of "appeal". Whether ἔφεσις already had this meaning in Ptolemaic Egypt, is not clear (see Seidl, *Ptolemäische Rechtsgeschichte* (1962), p. 99, note 4; see also Taubenschlag, *Law* (1955^{2}), p. 521, n. 13).

20-27 From l. 21 onwards, the left half of the text is lost. It is not possible to fill the lacunae of c. 40 characters. Gerhard makes several propositions in his comment on the text.

Verso [(Ἔτους) λ]δ Παχὼν κη̅ Ἀπολλωνίας καὶ Ἀμμωνίας (= παρ' Ἀπολλωνίας . . .) (ed. pr.: Ἡρακλ(είας) καὶ Ἀπολλωνίας καὶ Ἀμμωνίας): the left column of the verso contains the date and the Greek names of two of the four petitioners-sisters; Apollonia and Ammonia are also first mentioned at the beginning of the petition (recto, l. 1-2: παρ' Ἀπολλωνίας τῆς καὶ Σεμμώνθιος κα[ὶ] Ἀμμωνί̣α̣ς τῆς καὶ Σεμμίνιος καὶ Ἡρακλείας ἣ Σεναπᾶθις καὶ Ἡραίδος ἣ Τάσρις).

The previous editions read Ἡρακλ(είας) instead of the date [(Ἔτους) λ]δ Παχὼν κη̅. Thus, according to Gerhard, three of the four petitioners-sisters were mentioned on the verso («Unter den überaus kursiv und flüchtig geschriebenen und nahezu unleserlichen Namen der Petentinnen, deren Reihenfolge auffällt, vermißt man die Herais»,Gerhard, *Ein gräko-ägyptischer Erbstreit* (1911), p. 35). As Gerhard noted («Namen der Petentinnen, deren Reihenfolge auffällt »), it was odd that Herakleia was mentioned first on the verso, whereas at the beginning of the petition her name was recorded after those of Apollonia and Ammonia. The new reading with the date instead of the name of Herakleia is paleographically certain and was suggested to me by W. Clarysse.

33bis

GREEK PETITION

from Apollonia and her sisters
(draft or copy)

Plate XVII

? | H. x W. = 15.2 x 10.8 cm [Fragmentary] | 20 June 136 B.C.

British Library, P. inv.no. 611 recto a [bought on 9 Nov. 1895 from Grenfell].
First edition = **P. Grenf. I 15**; second edition (together with Text 33) in G.A. **Gerhard**, *Ein gräko-ägyptischer Erbstreit aus dem zweiten Jahrhundert vor Chr.* (Sitzungsberichte der Heidelberger Akademie der Wissenschaften, 8. Abh.), Heidelberg 1911, l. 28-38 (= **SB I 4638**, l. 28-38, with some corrections, mainly extracted from U. Wilcken, in *AfP* 6 (1920), p. 274-5).
Photograph. — Plate XVII.

Description. — The papyrus is broken off at the top and at the left-hand side. The recto has two different documents. The older document is a draft or copy of a petition and is lost for the greater part (= Text 33bis). It is written along the fibres on the recto in a medium-sized and partly cursive hand. At right angles to it comes a completely preserved account of Dryton (= Text 40). On the verso lies a third document: an account of Dryton's wife Senmonthis (= Text 41). Since Texts 40 and 41 are complete, the papyrus was in its present fragmentary state before it was used for the two accounts.

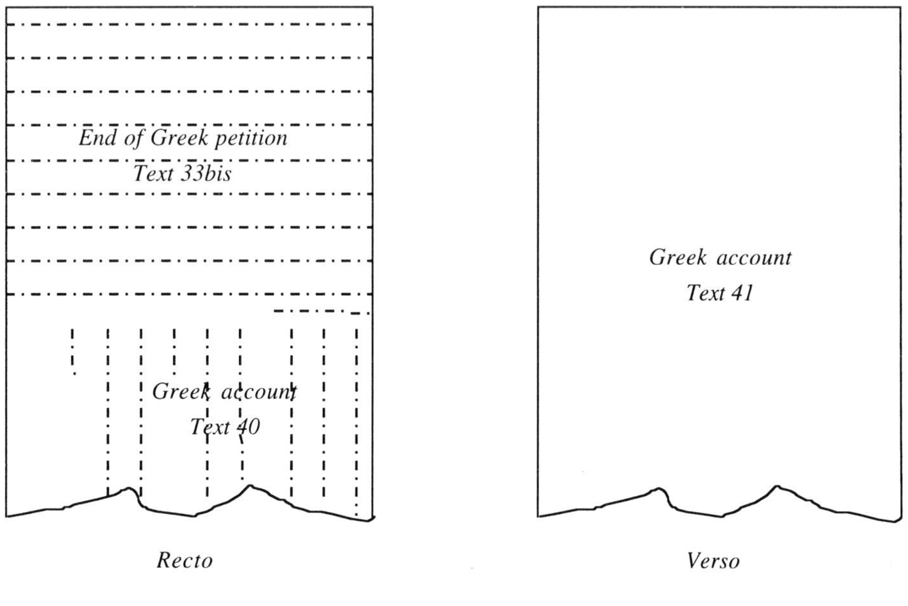

Introduction

Relation to Text 33 — Text 33bis contains the lost end of Text 33, as convincingly shown by Gerhard[1]. But Text 33bis does not belong to the same document as Text 33: it is written in another hand on a papyrus of inferior quality and with a different line width[2]; Text 33 is the original petition, whereas Text 33bis is apparently a draft or copy. Arguments in support of Gerhard's proposal that Text 33bis is the continuation of Text 33, are:

A Both petitions are addressed to the epistrategos:
- Text 33 is an appeal to the epistrategos.
- The formulae in Text 33bis are stereotypical for the end of a petition[3]. The expression τὴν ἐπὶ σὲ καταφυγὴν πεποιημένος (l. 29) is only found in petitions addressed either to the epistrategos or the strategos[4]. In case of Text 33bis, the petition was presented to the epistrategos according to the information provided by l. 35-36: the petitioners ask that their case be dealt with by Santobithys. Consequently, the appeal must have been addressed to a superior of Santobithys who was strategos of several nomes (see Text 33, comm. on l. 20-21) and subordinate only to the epistrategos.

B Both petitions were submitted by the same women:
- The petition Text 33 was made by the four daughters of Ptolemaios (l. 1-2).
- Text 33bis was also submitted by several female petitioners (see l. 29 πεποιημέναι and l. 37 [ἀντειλημμέ]ναι). In addition, Text 33bis was kept by Apollonia alias Senmonthis, one of the daughters of Ptolemaios, and by her husband Dryton, as shown by two accounts written on the same papyrus (Texts 40 and 41).

C In both petitions the opponent is male:
- in Text 33 Patous alias Kallimedes is accused of unlawful practices (l. 2-3, 21, 24-6).
- in Text 33bis a male opponent is mentioned (see l. 30 ὑπ' αὐτοῦ).

D According to both petitions the strategos Santobithys will deal with the case:
- the verso of Text 33, l. 2 (ΣΑΝΤΟΒ[Ι ΘΥΙ]), shows that the case has been handed over to Santobithys.
- In Text 33bis the petitioners ask that their case be handled by Santobithys (see l. 33-6 ὅπως ... εἰ δέ τι οἴεται [ἐπὶ τοῦ Σαντο]βίθυος τὰ καθ' ἡμᾶς διεξα[χθῆι]).

Text 33bis clearly contains the end of the same petition as Text 33, but belonged to another document. Text 33 is the original petition (as shown by the verso with a note from the bureau of the epistrategos). Text 33bis is undoubtedly a copy or a draft: it was written on a papyrus of inferior quality and the last four lines are carelessly written.

---

1 Gerhard, *Ein gräko-ägyptischer Erbstreit* (1911), p. 3-4. His view is generally accepted, see Plaumann, *Ptolemais* (1910), p. 67 n.4; U. Wilcken, in *AfP* 6 (1920), p. 274; F. Preisigke, SB I 4638.

2 G. Plaumann (see previous note) unjustly assumed that Texts 33 and 33bis belong to the same specimen.

3 See di Bitonto, 'Le petizioni ai funzionari' (1968), in *Aegyptus* 48, p. 53-107.

4 See di Bitonto, 'Le petizioni ai funzionari' (1968), in *Aegyptus* 48, p. 70-71.

Date of the petition of Texts 33 and 33bis. — The date of the petition is damaged (see below), but in the course of the petition three dates are mentioned: years 30, 32 and 34. It is not made clear whether the regnal years of Ptolemy VI or Ptolemy VIII are involved.

		Ptolemy VI	*Ptolemy VIII*	*Boethos as epistrategos*
Previous actions	Year 30	152/151	141/140	
	Year 32	150/149	139/138	
				July 137
	Year 34	148/147	Sept. 137/136	↓
Petition submitted	In year 34			
				January 130

The petition is addressed to Boethos. The latter's titles (sungenes and epistrategos) in Text 33, l. 1*, are important: Boethos became sungenes and epistrategos on 3 July 137 B.C. at the latest[1]. Thus, the petition appears to have been submitted under Ptolemy VIII and the previous actions in years 30, 32 and 34 are undoubtedly also to be situated under this Ptolemy; otherwise the period between the last action (year 34) and the submission of the petition (June 136 B.C.) would be too long.

A *terminus ante quem* until recently stood at 15 January 130 B.C., when Paos replaced Boethos. Text 33bis offers a more precise *terminus ante quem*: the date of the accounts written 1) on the recto, across the fibres and at right angles to the petition and 2) written on the verso. Since the petition is fragmentary and the accounts are complete, the accounts were written at a later date (see the description of the papyrus). One of these accounts is dated to the month of Mesore of year 35 (Text 40). In theory, the 35th year of Ptolemy VI and Ptolemy VIII could be considered. But since the petition Text 33 + 33bis is to be dated to the reign of Ptolemy VIII, so is the account which must date to the period of 22 August to 20 September 135 B.C., a *terminus ante quem* for the petition.

In conclusion: the four daughters of Ptolemaios submitted their complaint to the epistrategos Boethos between Sept. 137/136 (= year 34, period of the last action) and 22 Aug./ 20 Sept. 135 B.C. (= Mesore of year 35, date of the account Text 40). A new reading of the verso of Text 33 with notes from the office of the epistrategos Boethos provides an exact date: the first line does not contain the name of one of the petitioners, but the date. The year is badly damaged, but the traces perfectly fit a *delta*: [(Ἔτους) λ]δ̣ or year 34. The reading of the month is clear: 28 Pachon, that is 20 June 136 B.C.

The dating proposed is contrary to Gerhard's conviction that the petition is to be dated to the reign of Ptolemy VI. The titles of Boethos caused no problems at that time[2]. Gerhard appealed to arguments based on content[3]: the petition was submitted by the four daughters of Ptolemaios alias Pamenos in or after year **34**[4] (of Ptolemy VI, 148/7 B.C., or of Ptolemy VIII,

---

1 H. Heinen, in *AfP* 43 (1997), p. 340-349.
2 Gerhard, *Ein gräko-ägyptischer Erbstreit* (1911), p. 10-11.
3 Gerhard, *Ein gräko-ägyptischer Erbstreit* (1911), p. 7-10.
4 See Text 33, l. 27.

137/6 B.C.). One of the daughters was Apollonia alias Senmonthis, who married Dryton. The fact that Dryton is not mentioned in the petition shows — according to Gerhard — that *Apollonia was not yet married* when she submitted the petition together with her sisters.

Dryton's second will (Text 2, verso) shows that he married Apollonia shortly before the redaction of the will, which dates to the end of the reign of Ptolemy VI, at the latest to year **36** of his reign (= **146/145** B.C.). Since Apollonia and her sisters become of age in or shortly before year 30 and since their petition was submitted in or after year 34, these years 30 and 34 have to be situated before Apollonia's marriage to Dryton, that is before 146/5 B.C., in the reign of Ptolemy VI.

Gerhard's argumentation may be refuted by the following reasoning: the exact date of Apollonia's marriage now appears to be 6 Mecheir of year **31** of Ptolemy VI (= 4 March **150** B.C., see Text 2). Whether the petition was handed in in year 34 of Ptolemaios VI (= 148/7 B.C.) or of Ptolemy VIII (= 137/6 B.C.), *in either case Apollonia was already married.*

Facsimile
(for the justification of the supplements, see below)

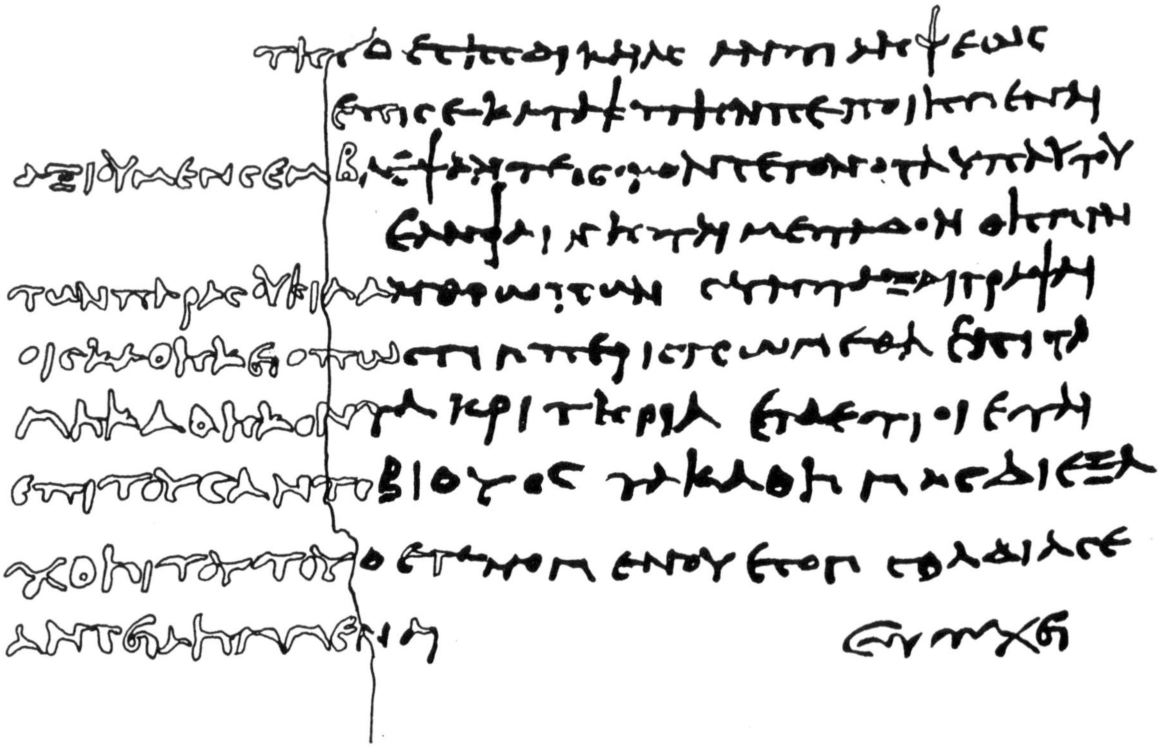

Text

Lines 1-27 are preserved in the original version, see Text 33.

[- c. 10 - Τῆ]ς δὲ σῆς δικαίας ἀντιλήψεως
[- c. 9 - τὴν] ἐπὶ σὲ καταφυγὴν πεποιημέναι
[ἀξιοῦμεν σ' ἐμ]βλέψαντ' εἰς τὸν γεγονότα ὑπ' αὐτοῦ
[- c. 12 -] *Vac.* ἐὰν φαίνηται μεταδόνθ' ἡμῖν
[τῶν παρὰ σοῦ φι]λανθρώπων συντάξαι γράψαι
[οἷς καθήκει ὅπ]ως μὴ περισπώμεθα ἐπὶ τὰ
[μὴ καθήκον]τα κριτήρια, εἰ δέ τι οἴεται
[ἐπὶ τοῦ Σαντο]βίθυος τὰ καθ' ἡμᾶς διεξα-
[χθῆι. Τούτου] δὲ [γ]ενομένου ἐσόμεθα διὰ σὲ
[ἀντειλημμέ]ναι. Εὐτύχει.

---

28 [τευξόμεναι] Gerhard; [Τῆ]ς δὲ σῆς Wilcken (*AfP* 6 (1920), p. 275) 30 [ἀξιοῦμεν ἐμ] Gerhard, [ἀξιοῦμεν σ' ἐμ] supplevimus 31 [διασεισμὸν] Gerhard 32 [τῶν παρὰ σοῦ] supplevimus 33 [οἷς καθήκει] supplevimus 35 [- c. 2 - ἐπὶ Σαντο] Gerhard, [ἐπὶ τοῦ Σαντο] supplevimus 36 [γεσθαι. Τούτου] Gerhard, [χθῆι. Τούτου] supplevimus 37 [βεβοηθημέ]ναι Gerhard, [ἀντειλημμέ]ναι supplevimus

Text as edited by G.A. Gerhard

[τευξόμεναι] δὲ σῆς δικαίας ἀντιλήψεως
[- c. 6 - τὴν] ἐπὶ σὲ καταφυγὴν πεποιημέναι
[ἀξιοῦμεν ἐμ]βλέψαντ' εἰς τὸν γεγονότα ὑπ' αὐτοῦ
[διασεισμὸν] ἐὰν φαίνηται μεταδόνθ' ἡμῖν
[- c. 7 - φι]λανθρώπων συντάξαι γράψαι
[- c. 7 - ὅπ]ως μὴ περισπώμεθα ἐπὶ τὰ
[μὴ καθήκον]τα κριτήρια, εἰ δέ τι οἴεται
[- c. 2 - ἐπὶ Σαντο]βίθυος τὰ καθ' ἡμᾶς διεξά-
[γεσθαι. Τούτου] δὲ [γ]ενομένου ἐσόμεθα διὰ σὲ
[βεβοηθημέ]ναι.

Εὐτύχει.

Translation

Lines 1-27 are preserved in the original version, see Text 33.

Having fled to you [out of need of] your just support, we ask that you investigate the former - - - by him (and), if it (seems good to you), that you let us participate in your benefactions and give orders to write to the proper authorities so that we are not dragged before unauthorized tribunals and so that, if he is up to something (?), our case is conducted before Santobithys.

If this happens, we shall have received help from you. *May you prosper.*

Justification of the above supplements

For his edition G.A. Gerhard did not have a photograph of the text nor did he see the original papyrus. He had to rely on the edition by Grenfell and on his correspondence with F.G. Kenyon, the director of the British Museum at that time, who provided information on P. Brit. Libr.inv.no. 612[1].

A study of the photograph led to the following conclusions:

- from l. 32 onwards the lacuna becomes wider: an extra character can be added.
- in l. 33-6, on the other hand, the scribe used larger characters and wrote in a more careless way. As a consequence, the lacunae of l. 33-36 contained fewer characters than other lines.
- there is no l. 38, as suggested by Gerhard; εὐτύχει is part of the same line as [ἀντειλημμέ]ναι, l. 37.

G.A. Gerhard assumed that the lacuna contained 9 to 10 letters. U. Wilcken (*AfP* 6 (1920), p. 275) on the other hand, thought that the lacunae were larger, since in his view the lacuna of l. 33 following συντάξαι γράψαι must have contained the name of an official and a verb such as προνοηθῆναι on which ὅπως ... περισπώμεθα depended. Wilcken's suggestion was adopted by F. Preisigke (SB I 4638).

Considering that the text can be understood quite easily in spite of the lacunas, I assume that not much can be lost. Wilcken's argument about l. 33 can be refuted: ὅπως ... περισπώμεθα (l. 33) does not necessarily depend on a verb such as προνοηθῆναι, but can be construed with γράψαι, found in l. 32[2]. Examples of a similar construction are:

SB I 4309, l. 26-28: δεόμεθα ... γράψαι ... ὅπως ἐκεῖνοι παρα[δῶσι], not παρα[δοῦναι] (Mayser, *Grammatik* II 1, p. 251)
P. Grenf. I 40, l. 6: ἔκρινον γράψαι σοι ὅπως ... παραγγείλῃς.
Similar construction with ἵνα instead of ὅπως: P. Tebt. I 30, l. 19-20: ἀξιῶ συντάξαι γράψαι ... ἵνα ... ἀναγράφηι.

If my suggestion is correct, then in l. 35-36 one has to supply διεξα[χθῆι], a subjunctive dependent on ὅπως instead of the infinitive διεξά[γεσθαι] as suggested by Gerhard.

---

1 Gerhard, *Ein gräko-ägyptischer Erbstreit* (1911), p. 4.

2 See Mayser, *Grammatik* II 1, p. 251-2: «ὅπως und ὅπως μή + Konjunktiv im Begehrungs- und Inhaltssatz an Stelle des Infinitifs».

Conclusion:

- in my view, in l. 33 the supplement [οἷς καθήκει ὅπ]ως μὴ περισπώμεθα is sufficient with only 12 characters.
- For l. 28-33 I propose a supplement of 11 to 12 characters, and
- for l. 34-37 (the text is written with larger characters and in a more careless way, see above) a supplement of 10 to 11 characters.

Notes

Recto

28 Gerhard's supplement of 10 characters, [τευξόμεναι] δε σῆς δικαίας ἀντιλήψεως, has been refuted by U. Wilcken (*AfP* 6 (1920), p. 27) for the following reason: σῆς ... ἀντιλήψεως needs an article: τῆς δὲ σῆς ... ἀντιλήψεως. In addition, the *sigma* of τῆς is still visible, as noted by F.G. Kenyon (see Gerhard, *Ein gräko-ägyptischer Erbstreit* (1911), p. 32, comm. on l. 28).

Since the use of δέ points to a new sentence, a verb such as τευξόμεναι can no longer preceed τῆς δὲ σῆς ... ἀντιλήψεως, but has to be supplied after it, in the lacuna of l. 29.

29 The lacuna was partly supplemented by Gerhard: [- c. 6 - τὴν] ἐπὶ σὲ καταφυγὴν πεποιημέναι. The article with καταφυγήν is indeed usual (see Pap. Lugd. Bat. XXII 9, l. 6; UPZ I 8, l. 6-8; UPZ II 191, l. 5-6).

In the lacuna a verb or adjective is missing on which the genitive τῆς δὲ... ἀντιλήψεως (l. 28) depends (see comm. on !. 28). The usual verb is τυγχάνω and the usual form in similar passages of petition is the subjunctive in a final clause (see UPZ II 191, l. 5-6).

A final clause is unlikely, as the conjunction must be at the beginning of the clause, before τῆς δὲ ... ἀντιλήψεως (l. 28), which is impossible because of the position of δέ (δέ always takes the second position in a new sentence).

Another possibility is the future participle of τυγχάνω, as suggested by Gerhard. The future participle is, however, rarely used in the papyri (see Mayser, *Grammatik* II 1, p. 220). In addition, the supplement τευξόμεναι for l. 29 is too long.

τῆς ... ἀντιλήψεως may also be dependent on a verb composed with δέομαι, that is προσδέομαι (BGU VIII 1767, l. 5). But προσδέομαι is too long to be supplied in addition.

30 Gerhard's supplement of 10 characters [ἀξιοῦμεν ἐμ]βλέψαντ' εἰς τὸν γεγονότα ὑπ' αὐτοῦ, is correct, but , in my view, too short. Therefore, σέ may be added.

The explicit mention of the object σέ is not necessary, but grammatically more logical, as the participles ἐμβλέψαντ' and μεταδόνθ' (l. 31) depend on it. For ἀξιῶ or ἀξιοῦμεν σέ, see P. Mert. I 5, l. 29; P. Petr. III 29e, l. 9-10; g, l. 2-3; h, l. 4-5; P. Petr. III 780, l. 15; UPZ I 2, l. 24; 7, l. 18; 8, l. 28; 13, l. 30.

31 Gerhard's supplement of 10 characters [διασεισμὸν] - - ἐὰν φαίνηται μεταδόνθ' ἡμῖν, is based on the verb διασείουσιν which is found earlier in the petition (Text 33, l. 11).

According to my calculations, the supplement is somewhat short. There are two possibilities: either another word has to be added or the space (of 2 characters) before ἐάν already began in the lacuna, which may have contained: [διασεισμὸν *vac.*] *vac.* ἐάν.

32 Gerhard does not supplement the lacuna in his edition, but proposes in his commentary: [τῶν σῶν φι]λανθρώπων συντάξαι γράψαι. This supplement of the article and possessive pronoun is possible (see P. Ryl. IV, 578, l. 14-5), but is less frequent that my proposal [τῶν παρὰ σοῦ φι]λανθρώπων (see PSI V 502, l. 18). This supplement of 12 characters fits the lacuna perfectly.

33 For the supplement [οἷς καθήκει], already proposed by Gerhard in his commentary, see UPZ II 191, l. 12; 192, l. 21; 193, l. 21.

34 εἰ δέ τι οἴεται: Gerhard proposed in his commentary: εἰ δέ τι οἴεται/ 35 [βλάψειν (sc. ἡμᾶς)] and added: «Wenn die vorgeschlagene Ergänzung scheinbar den am Zeilenanfang verfügbaren Raum überschreitet, so hilft hier vielleicht die Annahme eines außergewöhnlichen Herausragens aus der Kolumne» .

Such a supllement is, however, not necessary: οἴεται already has an object (τι) and can have the meaning of "but if he is up to something", compare the expression εἰ δέ τι ἀντιλέγῃ or ἐὰν δέ τι ἀπειθῇ, also often found in petitions (see M. T. Cavassini, 'Exemplum vocis ἐντεύξεις', in *Aegyptus* 35 (1955), p. 319). What is meant by εἰ δέ τι οἴεται, is not clear since the expression is related to a part of the petition which is very fragmentary (Text 33, l. 20-27).

35 In order to fill the lacuna of 10 to 11 characters, I suggest adding the article to Gerhard's text: [ἐπὶ τοῦ Σαντο]βίθυος instead of [... ἐπὶ Σαντο]βίθυος. Moreover, the article is expected since Santobithys has already been mentioned before (Text 33, l. 20-21) as well as has his official position. Here, in l. 35, the petitioners refer to the above-mentioned Santobithys and omit his post.

36 Gerhard proposed for l. 35-6 διεξά[γεσθαι. Τούτου] δὲ ..., a supplement of 12 characters, which is too long. Gerhard interpreted διεξάγεσθαι as an infinitive dependent on γράψαι. As it is probable that γράψαι in l. 32-33 is to be construed with ὅπως + subjunctive (see above, justification of the above supplements), it would be illogical to construe γράψαι with an infinitive in l. 35-36. One rather expects a subjunctive (aorist): διεξαχθῆι, in which case only a supplement of 10 characters is needed (διεξα[χθῆι. Τούτου] δὲ ...).

37 Gerhard's proposal [Βεβοηθημέν]αι, a supplement of 9 characters, is possible, but my addition of 10 characters fits the lacuna better: [ἀντειλημμέ]ναι, see, for instance, Pap. Lugd. Bat. XXII 11, l. 36 and 12, l. 20.

34

GREEK PETITION
from Dryton's daughters

? H. x W. = 29 x 16.5 cm 115-110 B.C.

British Library, P. inv.no. 401 [acquired between 1891 and 1895] = **P. Lond. II 401**, p. 12-14 (= Chrest. Mitteis 18).

Translations. — Lewis, *Greeks in Ptolemaic Egypt* (1986), p. 102; Rowlandson, *Sourcebook* (1998), no. 87.

Photograph. — No photograph available.

Description. — The papyrus is complete. After redaction the text was folded vertically and then folded double. The papyrus is slightly damaged along some vertical folds; the horizontal fold caused even more damage. The fibres do not always run parallel and in one spot (c. 2.2 cm from the right-hand margin, at the level of l. 8-11) the horizontal fibres are missing; as a result the text was written on the underlying fibres.

The petition is written on the recto *across* the fibres and has a top margin of 4 cm, a bottom margin of 4.5 cm, a left-hand margin of 3.5 cm on average and a right-hand margin of 2 cm at the maximum.

Introduction

Contents. — Dryton's two oldest daughters Apollonia (pros. 506) and Aphrodisia (pros. 510) address a petition to Phommous, epistrategos of the Thebaid. They act also in the name of their three younger sisters Aristo (pros. 507), Nikarion (pros. 508) and Apollonia the younger (pros. 509). They record at length how their father left them half of his immovable property in the Peritheban and Pathyrite nomes, as well as a half share of the domestic slaves. Among the immovables was a vineyard with appurtenances on the Kochlax, on the east bank (Arabia) of the Pathyrite nome, of which they had inherited a half share. For a detailed description of the vineyard, see Vandorpe, *Archives from Pathyris* (2001), chapter V.

Dryton's last will (Text 4) does indeed record the inheritance of his five daughters of a half share of most of his belongings. The vineyard is, however, an exception. It was left entirely to his son Esthladas (l. 7-8). But this petition shows that the girls nevertheless own half of the vineyard, probably after a settlement with their half-brother Esthladas (see §21).

Problems arose over their share in the vineyard. The sisters live in Pathyris and cannot often travel to the vineyard on the other side of the Nile. In addition, there has been a period of unrest or ἀμιξία, when it was safer to stay at home. A man from Diospolis Megale, called Ariston, son of Athenodotos, took advantage of this situation: he violently occupied the vineyard plot and planted part of it.

The sisters ask the epistrategos Phommous to summon Ariston and to investigate the matter. If they tell the truth, they should re-claim that share of the vineyard with appurtenances and the plants growing in it. Ariston should also pay for the crops he has harvested, since they belong to the girls. At the end of the petition they once again emphasize that Ariston has used violence and they hope that Phommous will do justice.

The period of unrest[1]. — After the death of Dryton, on 29 June 126 B.C. at the earliest, an outsider from Diospolis Megale takes possession of the share of a vineyard, belonging to Dryton's daughters. This happens in times of unrest (ἐν τοῖς τῆς ἀμειξίας καιροῖς, l. 20). The term ἀμιξία/ ἀμειξία[2] is usually related to dynastic troubles and the accompanying civil wars in the country, in contrast to πόλεμος, referring to battles abroad[3]. Dynastic troubles are attested here and elsewhere for the period 126 (last attestation of Dryton) and 110 B.C. (last possible date of this petition).

R. Scholl[4] refers to the renewal of dynastic hatred in 124-122 B.C.[5] and the troubles which eventually led to the amnesty of 118 B.C. What information do we have for Upper-Egypt? In 123 B.C. friction is observed between the inhabitants of Krokodilopolis and Hermonthis[6]. In the Thinite nome a man takes advantage of the ἀμειξία in 123/122 B.C. to appropriate a palm grove surrounded by a mud wall[7]. R. Scholl identifies the ἀμειξία of the petition published here with these troubles attested for the period 123/122 B.C. Consequently, Dryton died between 126 and 123/122 B.C. and the girls lost part of their inheritance in these times of unrest. Seven years later at the earliest (115 B.C.), they hand in a petition.

The argumentation of R. Scholl is plausible. Nevertheless, one has to take account of another possible date. In 116/115 B.C. there are further dynastic troubles as a result of the succession[8]. This period is nowhere labelled as a period of ἀμιξία, but UPZ II 196 of Nov./Dec. 116 clearly shows that there was unrest. If Ariston from Diospolis Megale appropriated the vineyard in 116/115 B.C., then the girls handed in their petition soon afterwards.

Date. — The petition is not dated. It was addressed to Phommous, who was epistrategos of the Thebaid between 17 Aug./15 Sept. 115 and 6 February 110 B.C. (see comm. on l. 1).

J.K. Winnicki proposes a more precise date. The petition is handed in sometime after the death of Dryton. The exact day of death is not known (on or after 29 June 126 B.C., see Text 4). As Winnicki identifies Dryton with the eponymous officer called Dryton in P. Ross. Georg. II 6 (l. 34) from 113 B.C., he dates the petition to the period 113-111 B.C.

The identification of Dryton with the homonymous officer in P. Ross. Georg. II 6 is very uncertain (see pros. 403); Dryton's last will from 126 B.C. shows that Dryton had not long to

---

1 For the civil wars of the 2nd century B.C. in general, see Vandorpe, 'Outline of Greco-Roman Thebes' (1995), p. 232-234; Veïsse, *Les «révolutions égyptiennes»* (2000); Lewis, *Greeks in Ptolemaic Egypt* (1986), p. 102 interprets the expression ἐν τοῖς τῆς ἀμειξίας καιροῖς in his translation «at a time when travel between the two banks [of the river] was interrupted».

2 See P. Collart and P. Jouguet, in *Ét. de Pap.* 2 (1933), p. 33; L. Mooren, in *Ancient Society* 5 (1974), p. 139 and the bibliography cited in note 13.

3 L. Mooren, in *Ancient Society* 5 (1974), p. 137-146.

4 Scholl, 'Drytons Tod' (1988), in *Chron. d' Ég.* 63, p. 141-144.

5 See also Otto and Bengtson, *Geschichte* (1938), p. 108.

6 Chrest. Wilcken 11.

7 PSI III 171, l. 33-34.

8 Compare the translation of this petition in Rowlandson, *Sourcebook* (1998), no. 87, p. 112, note 2.

live (see §19). In addition, times of unrest (ἀμιξία) are not attested for the period 113-111 B.C., as R. Scholl already noted.

A date between 115-110 B.C. is preferable.

Scribe. — The petition is written in a facile, but not always easily legible hand, which becomes more cursive towards the end of the text. The scribe often leaves space between words and hyphenates at the end of a line (l. 9, 10, 14, 25, 26 and 27). He uses only one abbreviation (for ἥμισυ: l. 11, 12, 21 and 27). His vocabulary is extensive and he likes variation. He uses, for instance, for 'above-mentioned': δηλούμενος (l. 19), σημαινόμενος (l. 24) and διασαφούμενος (l. 27).

The text contains few mistakes and the writer has corrected two of them himself, that is ʼΑπολλωνίας τῆς `καὶ´ Σενμούθεως (l. 3) and γυναῖκα`ς´ (l. 23); other mistakes slipped his notice: ἐπο<ι>κίων (l. 13), φο<ρο>λογίας (l. 14) and ἀντειλημ<μέ>ν̣αι (l. 30). For other small aberrations, see the comm. on l. 16, l. 23 and l. 26.

Text

Φομμοῦτι συνγενεῖ καὶ ἐπιστρατήιγωι καὶ στρατηιγῶι τῆς Θηβαίδος, παρὰ Ἀπολλωνίας τῆς \`καὶ´ Σενμούθεως καὶ Ἀφροδισίας τῆς καὶ Ταχράτιος ἀμφοτέρων Δρύτωνος θυγατέρων κατ[οι]κουσῶν ἐν Παθύρει. Ὑπάρχοντος ἡμῖν τε καὶ ταῖς ἑαυτῶν ἀδελφαῖς Ἀριστοῖ τῆι καὶ Σενμώνθει καὶ Νικαρίωι τῆι [καὶ] Θερμούθει καὶ Ἀπολλωνίαι νεωτέραι τῆι καὶ Σενπελαίαι, μέρ[ους] ἡμίσους τῶν πατρικῶν ἐγγαίων ὄντων Δ ἔν τε τῶι Περ[ι]θήβας καὶ Παθυρίτηι, ὁμοίως δὲ καὶ τῶν οἰκετικῶν σω-μάτ[ων], ἐν οἷς καὶ ἐπὶ τοῦ Κόχλακος τῆς Ἀραβίας τοῦ δηλου-μένο[υ] Παθυρίτου νομοῦ μέρους (ἡμίσους) ἀπὸ ἐδάφους ἀμπελῶνος ἀρουρῶν β (ἡμίσους) ἢ ὅσον ἂν ἦι ἐπὶ τὸ πλεῖον καὶ τοῦ ἀπὸ ἀπηλιώτου αὐτοῦ παραδείσου καὶ φρεάτων καὶ ἐπο<ι>κίων καὶ ληνῶνος καὶ γῆς χέρσου καὶ ἄλλης γῆς ἐκτὸς φο<ρο>λογίας καὶ τῶν συνκυ-ρόντων πάντων ὧν κεκράτηκεν ὁ πατὴρ ἡμῶν ἐφ' ὅσον [π]εριῆι χρόνον, ἡμῶν δὲ μετὰ τὴν ἐκείνου [τελευτὴν] τῶν λοι[πῶν κρατουσῶν], Ἀρίστω[ν Ἀ]θηνοδότου τῶν ἀ[πὸ] Διὸς πόλεως τ[ῆς με]γάλης βιαιότερον ἐμβατεύσ[α]ς εἰς τὸ δη[λούμενο]ν ἔδαφος τοῦ ἀμπελῶνος καὶ εἰς τὰ συνκύροντα [τ]ούτωι ἐν τοῖς τῆς ἀμειξίας [κ]αιροῖς, ἀντιποιεῖται ἀδίκως τοῦ ἐπιβάλλοντος ἡμῖν μέρους (ἡμίσους) καὶ μέρος τι καταπεφύτευκεν ἀμπέλωι, κατεγνωκὼς τῶι γυναῖκα\`ς´ ἡμᾶς εἶναι καὶ ἑτέρωι τόπωι κατοικούσας μὴ εὐχερῶς δύνασθαι ἐπιβαλεῖν ἐπὶ τὴν σημαινομένην κτῆσιν. Διὸ καταπεφευγυῖαι ἐπὶ σέ, ἀξιοῦμεν, ἐὰν φαίνηται, μετα-πεμψάμενον αὐτὸν ἐπισκέψασθαι καὶ ἐὰν ἦι <οἷ>α γράφομεν ἐπαναγ-κάσαι ἐκστῆναι τοῦ διασαφουμένου ἡμῖν μέρους (ἡμίσους) τοῦ ἐδάφους τοῦ ἀμπε-λῶνος καὶ τῶν ἐν αὐτῶι πεφυτευμένων καὶ τῶν προσκυρόντων τόπων καὶ ἐκτεῖ[σ]αι ἃ ἀπενήνεκται ἐξ αὐτῶν γενήματα, περὶ δὲ ἧς πεπόη[τα]ι βίας, διαλαβεῖν μισοπονήρως, ἵν' ὦμεν ἀντειλημ<μέ>ναι.

Εὐτύχει.

---

1 ἐπιστρατήιγωι καὶ στρατηιγῶι, *l.* ἐπιστρατήγωι καὶ στρατηγῶι 3 φ in Ἀφροδισίας corr. ex. π 6 ἑαυτῶν, *l.* ἡμῶν αὐτῶν 7 Σενπελαίδι ed., Σενπελαίαι Wilcken apud Mitteis 13 ἐποικίων ed., ἐπο<ι>κίων legimus 14 φολογίας ed., φο<ρο>λογίας ed. (p. 14, n. l. 14) 17 τῶν λοι[πῶν – c. 10 -], τῶν λοι[πῶν κρατουσῶν] Witkowski et Schubart (BL I, p. 244; BL II.2, p. 80) 20 ἀμειξίας, *l.* ἀμιξίας 26 ἐὰν ἦι ἃ γράφομεν ed., ἐὰν ἦι <οἷ>α γράφομεν Bickermann (BL II.2, p. 80) 30 πεπόη[κεν] ed., πεπόη[τα]ι Mitteis; πεπόη[τα]ι, *l.* πεποίη[τα]ι; ἀντειλημέναι ed., ἀντειλημ<μέ>ναι legimus

Translation

To Phommous, sungenes, epistrategos and strategos of the Thebaid.

From Apollonia alias Senmouthis and Aphrodisia alias Tachratis, both daughters of Dryton, living in Pathyris.

There belongs to us and to our sisters Aristo alias Senmonthis, Nikarion alias Thermouthis and Apollonia the younger alias Senpelaia, a half share of our father's plots of land, being four in number, in the Peritheban and Pathyrite nomes, and similarly (a half share) of the domestic slaves; among the plots of land: there is on the Kochlax on the east bank (of the Nile) in the said Pathyrite nome, a half share of a vineyard plot of more or less 2 1/2 arouras and to the east of this a garden, wells, farm buildings, a wine press, a plot of dry land, another plot of non-revenue yielding land and all the appurtenances that our father owned as long as he lived.

After his death, we were owners of the rest (of the inheritance), (but) Ariston, son of Athenodotos, from Diospolis Megale, forcefully occupied the said vineyard and its appurtenances in times of unrest and he unjustly lays claim to the half share that belongs to us. He has planted a certain part with vines, despising us because we are not able easily to go to the property referred to, since we live in another place.

Therefore, having fled to you, we ask, if it seems (good to you), that you summon him and investigate, and, if things are as we write, that you compel him to vacate the half share of the vineyard described by us and the plants growing in it and the adjoining places, and also to compensate for the crops he has removed therefrom. As regards the violence he has committed, (we ask that you), as one who hates wickedness, condemn him so that we may obtain redress.

May you prosper.

Notes

1 Φομμοῦτι: Phommous is attested as epistrategos (?of the Thebaid) for the period 17 Aug./ 15 Sept. 115 to 6 February 110 B.C., see Pros. Ptol. I and VIII 202; Mooren, *Prosopography* (1975), no. 058; Id., in *Ancient Society* 4 (1973), p. 130-131, no. 10.

ἐπιστρατήιγωι καὶ στρατηιγῶι, *l.* ἐπιστρατήγωι καὶ στρατηγῶι: for the use of ηι instead of η in the middle of a word, see Mayser, *Grammatik* I.1, p. 107 and Text 4, comm. on l. 2.

3 'Αφροδισίας: the first editor did not notice that the φ in 'Αφροδισίας is corrected from π. Presumably, the scribe started to write Απολλωνίας again, but noticed his mistake in time.

8-15 Vocabulary: l. 8-15 gives us information on the possessions of Dryton, for which see Vandorpe, *Archives from Pathyris* (2001), chapter V.

13 ἐπο<ι>κίων: the editor read ἐποικίων, as is expected, but the scribe missed the *iota*.

16 ἐφ' ὅσον̣ [π]εριῆι χρόνον: one rather expects ἐφ' ὅσον̣ ἂν [π]εριῆι χρόνον.

17 'Αρίστω[ν 'Α]θ̣ηνοδότου: this man from Diospolis Megale cannot be identified.

19 ἐμβατ̣ε̣ύσ̣[α]ς ε̣ἰ̣ς: for the meaning of ἐμβατεύω, compare Text 33, l. 8.

20 ἐν τοῖς τῆς ἀμειξίας [κ]αιροῖς: for the interpretation, see the introduction to the text. A similar expression is found in UPZ I 19, l. 8-9: ἐν ἀμείκτοις καιροῖς, treating the troubles of 165 B.C.

22 καταπεφύτευκεν ἀμπέλωι: one rather expects the plural ἀμπέλοις.

23 ἑτέρωι τόπωι κατοικούσας: κατοικέω is usually followed by an accusative or a construction with a preposition (Mayser, *Grammatik* II.2, p. 312-313). Here the scribe uses a dative (without preposition), whereas in l. 5 he correctly writes κατ[οι]κουσῶν ἐν Παθύρει.

26 ἐὰν ἦι <οἷ>α γράφομεν: the emendation of ἅ (if things are what we write) into <οἷ>α makes the sentence clear (if things are as we write).

28 τῶν προσκυρόντων τόπων: the expression refers to the places which adjoin to the vineyard, such as a garden, the buildings etc. (see l. 12-14). It is a more precise expression than τὰ συνκύροντα (l. 14-15 and l. 20), the 'appurtenances'.

29-30 περὶ δὲ ἧς πεπόη[τα]ι βίας (= περὶ τῆς βίας ἣν πεπόηται): the expression ποιέομαι βίαν is an equivalent for βιάζομαι.

30 πεπόη[τα]ι: for the frequently attested form πεπόηται alongside the usual form πεποίηται, see Mayser, *Grammatik* I.1, p. 87.

IV

LETTERS

§44. *Classification of letters.* — §45. *The epistolary formulae.* — §46. *Seals on the back of letters.*

§44. *Classification of letters.* — Only two private letters are preserved in the family archive of Dryton and Apollonia:

Text 35 = a demotic letter from an unknown person, Onnophris, son of Sisouchos, addressed to Dryton
Text 36 = a Greek letter from Dryton's son Esthladas to his parents.

An exhaustive survey of the demotic letters from Pathyris is to be found in Kaplony-Heckel, 'Gebelein-Briefe und -Verwaltungsschreiben' (2000).

The letters which are found in the archives from Pathyris, can be classified as follows[1]:

A. Official correspondence

This subdivision contains letters from officials, usually written in Greek, the language of the administration[2]. Among the official correspondence I classify the letters by the strategos Platon, written in 88 B.C., when Pathyris was to be seized by rebels. Platon addressed these letters to the inhabitants, the priests and the epistates of town. The Platon-letters are briefly discussed in Vandorpe, *Archives from Pathyris* (2001), §29.

B. Temple correspondence

The letters addressed to the temple are usually written in demotic, see the above-mentioned article by U. Kaplony-Heckel. Compare the temple archive of Pathyris, discussed in Vandorpe, *Archives from Pathyris* (2001), §30.

---

1 This survey does not contain an exhaustive list of letters from Pathyris.
2 *E.g.*, P. Giss. I 37+36+108, col. IV, l. 12-17 (copies of letters); P. Grenf. I 22; P. Grenf. I 40 to which the unpublished fragment P. Heid. Gr. inv. no. 1304 belongs; P. Grenf. II 37.

C. Military correspondence

A well-known example of letters written by and to soldiers (on campaign) is the correspondence edited by W. Clarysse in P. War of Sceptres and dating to the period 103-101 B.C. It is described as «the correspondence between groups of soldiers from Pathyris, all addressed to a company headed by the hegemones Pates and Pachrates»[3]. See also Vandorpe, *Archives from Pathyris* (2001), §29.

D. Private letters

Letters by soldiers
The family archives contain several letters written home by soldiers on campaign, in Greek[4] or demotic[5]. In such letters usually several military men greet their family and acquaintances.

Other letters
Few letters reporting facts from daily life are preserved in Pathyris' family archives. P. Grenf. I 43[6] is an example of a Greek letter in which a man called Menon writes to his brother Hermokrates concerning a mare which had not been delivered to him by a Jew called Daniel.

§45. *The epistolary formulae.* — The epistolary formulae in Greek papyrus letters are discussed by H. Koskenniemi, *Studien zur Idee und Phraseologie des griechischen Briefes bis 400 n. Chr.*, Helsinki 1965; F.X.J. Exler, *The Form of the Ancient Greek Letter of the Epistolary Papyri (3rd c. B.C. - 3rd c. A.D.)*, Chicago 1976; R. Buzón, *Die Briefe der Ptolemäerzeit. Ihre Struktur und ihre Formeln*, Inaugural-Dissertation, Buones Aires 1984 (p. 3, no. 108 = Text 36).

The epistolary formulae in demotic papyri are briefly discussed by M. Depauw, 'The Demotic Epistolary Formulae', in *Acta Demotica. Acts of the Fifth International Conference for Demotists (Pisa 1993) = EVO* 17 (1994), p. 87-94.

§46. *Seals on the back of letters.* — The verso of the two letters Text 35 and Text 36 contains the address: part of the address is written to the right-hand side, the remaining part to the left-hand side; in the middle a blank space is left for the seal, which is now lost in both cases.

The practice of putting clay seals on the back of a letter is discussed by Vandorpe, 'Seals in and on the Papyri' (1997), p. 241 and 267-268.

---

3 P. War of Sceptres, p. 37.

4 *E.g.*, from the Peteharsemtheus archive (see Vandorpe, *Archives from Pathyris* (2001), §41): P. Grenf. II 36 (= Sel. Pap. I 103; Witkowski, *Epistulae* 64); P. Lips. 104 (= Witkowski, *Epistulae* 63).

5 *E.g.*, from the Peteharsemtheus archive (see Vandorpe, *Archives from Pathyris* (2001), §41): P. BM dem. 10498 ined.

6 = CPJ I 135.

35

DEMOTIC LETTER
to Dryton

Plate XIII (recto-verso); see facsimile below

Pathyris [place of receipt]	H. x W. = 7 x 9.4 cm [Height incomplete]	150 - 126/115 B.C.

Heidelberg, P. dem. inv.no. 742a [In Heidelberg since 1898, acquired by Reinhardt] = **W. Spiegelberg**, 'Papyrus Erbach. Ein demotisches Brieffragment', in *ZÄS* 42 (1905), p. 51 (with facsimile and translation).

Photograph and facsimile. — Plate XIII (recto-verso); see my facsimile below; facsimile in editio princeps.

Description. — The papyrus is fragmentary: only the two upper horizontal strips are preserved. The text is written on the recto along the fibres, with a top margin of 3 cm. There is only a narrow margin to the right and the left of the letter.

The verso of the second strip contains the address, written across the fibres. The address is split up: the first part is written on the right-hand side and is continued on the left-hand side; in the middle a blank space is left for the seal, which is now lost (for seals put on the back of a letter, see §46).

Introduction

Contents and date — The letter is not informative, since the text breaks off where the actual communication starts. The writer of the letter, Onnophris son of Sisouchos, cannot be identified with certainty (see comm. on l. 1). It is not clear where the letter was sent from; the god Souchos before whom the proskynema by the writer takes place (see comm. on l. 1-3), is worshipped in several towns.

Dryton bears the title *p3 ṯs-ḥtr*, an equivalent of his Greek title ἱππάρχης (pros. 403). Since Dryton did not yet have this title in 150 B.C. (see Text 2), the letter should be dated after 150 B.C. The *terminus ante quem* is 126/115 B.C., the period in which Dryton died.

Recto

Facsimile

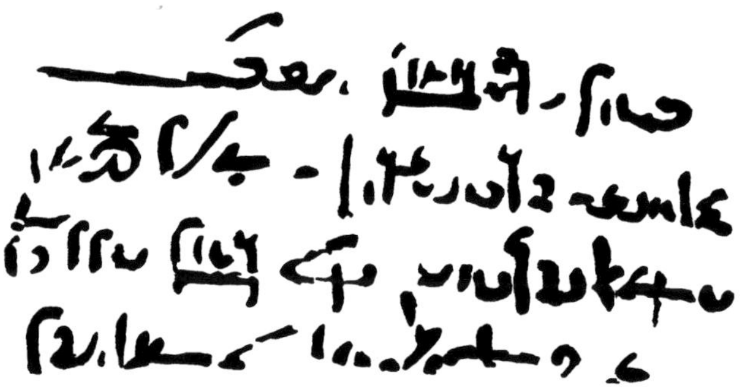

Text

1 *Wn-nfr s3 Sy-Sbk p3 nty ḏd:*
tw=y ir n n3 sm.w n Trwtn
p3 ṯs-ḥtr m-b3ḥ Sbk p3 nṯr ʿ3
[iw=f] ⌜ir n=k⌝ s3 nb n ʿnḫ. Iy-m-ḥtp

- -

Verso

Facsimile

Text

1 *r dy.t s n* *Trwtn*

---

1 *Gb* ed., *Wn-nfr* legimus et supplevimus 4 *[Wsir?] p3 nṯr ʿ3 nb n ʿnḫ* ed., *[iw=f] ⌜ir n=k⌝ s3 nb n ʿnḫ* legimus

Translation

Recto

Onnophris, son of Sisouchos, is the one who says:
«I make obeisance for Dryton, hipparches, before Souchos, the great god, while he offers you all protection for life. Imouthes - - - »

Verso

To give it to *Dryton.*

Notes

Recto

1 *Wn-nfr s3 Sy-Sbk, Onnophris son of Sisouchos*: it is not clear whether or not Onnophris lives in Pathyris nor whether he is to be identified with Onnophris son of Sisouchos who is a priest of the second phyle in Pathyris in 113/112 B.C. (Pros. Ptol. III and IX 6417). The latter probably also acts as a witness in contracts from the temple notary's office in the period 110-89 B.C. (P. dem. Adler 4, verso l. 2; 20, verso l. 3; 25, l. 27).

1-3 *NN p3 nty ḏd: tw=y ir n n3 sm.w n NN m-b3ḥ, NN is the one who says: I greet NN before the god NN* : the formula in its simple form has *NN sm (r) NN m-b3ḥ, NN makes obeisance for NN before* (see, *e.g.*, from Pathyris: P. War of Sceptres 5, l. 1-4); *sm* can also be a substantive construed with the verb *ir* : *ir (n3) sm.w n NN m-b3ḥ.* The more elaborate formula beginning with *NN p3 nty ḏd, NN is the one who says*, followed by a direct speech *tw=y ir n3 sm.w n, I make obeisance for NN before the god NN,* is found in, *e.g.*, P. dem. Loeb 5 and 11; P. dem. Oxford 13 and 17.

W. Spiegelberg has shown that this greeting formula in combination with *m-b3ḥ, before*, followed by the name of a god, is an equivalent of the Greek proskynema-formula: τὸ προσκύνημα σοῦ ποιῶ παρά + name of the god (Spiegelberg, 'Papyrus Erbach' (1905), in *ZÄS* 42, p. 53-54; W. Clarysse, in P. War of Sceptres, p. 67, comm. on l. 4-5).

4 *[iw=f] ⸢ir n=k⸣ s3 nb n ʿnḫ, while he offers you all protection for life*: W. Spiegelberg read *[Wsir?] p3 ntr ʿ3* instead of *[iw=f] ⸢ir n=k⸣ s3*. The remaining traces do not, however, fit *p3 ntr*, but rather *ir* and *n=k*.

My reading of the protection formula is confirmed by P. dem. Oxford 13, l. 6-7 and 17, l. 5, where it is found in the same form and the same place, but the proskynema takes place before two or respectively, three gods (*iw=w ir n=k s3 nb n ʿnḫ, while they offer you all protection for life*). Finally, a letter found in Pathyris (P. dem. Louvre inv.no. E 10596 ined., l. 6) contains the same protection clause: *iw=w ir n=tn s3 nb n ʿnḫ* :

s3 (protection) is here followed by a god determinative, which is not the case in Text 35.

For other "wishing formulae", see M. Depauw, 'The Demotic Epistolary Formulae', in *Acta Demotica. Acts of the Fifth International Conference for Demotists (Pisa 1993) = EVO* 17 (1994), Pisa 1995, p. 93.

Iy-m-ḥtp : with the personal name Imouthes the actual communication starts.

36

GREEK LETTER
from Esthladas to Dryton and Apollonia

Plate XIV[1] (recto)

Pathyris [place of receipt] | H. x W. = 19.5 x 12 cm | 15 January 130 B.C.

Louvre, P. inv.no. E 10594 [Bought by an intermediary of Wilbour in 1891 or 1892] = M. Révillout, *Mélanges sur la métrologie, l'économie politique et l'histoire de l'ancienne Egypte avec de nombreux textes démotiques, hiéroglyphiques, hiératiques ou grecs inédits ou antérieurement mal publiés*, Paris 1895[4], p. 295; **S. de Ricci**, 'Papyrus de Pathyris au musée du Louvre', in *AfP* 2 (1903), p. 517-518 (= Chrest. Wilcken 10 = Sel. Pap. I 101 = J.L. White, *Light from Ancient Letters*, Philadelphia 1986, no. 43.)

Compare for the epistolary formulae R. Buzón, *Die Briefe der Ptolemäerzeit. Ihre Struktur und ihre Formeln*, Inaugural-Dissertation, Buones Aires 1984, p. 3, no. 10.

Translations. — Sel. Pap. I 101; J.L. White, *Light from Ancient Letters*, Philadelphia 1986, no. 43.

Photograph. — Photograph of the recto: Plate XIV; no photograph available of the verso.

Description. — The papyrus is complete, but is damaged along the horizontal folds. It is of inferior quality: in two spots the horizontal fibres are missing so that the text is written on the underlying fibres of the verso (l. 3 and 14). The letter is written on the recto along the fibres, with a top margin of 1.1 cm, a bottom margin of 6.1 cm, a left-hand margin of 1.8 cm and a right-hand margin of 2.1 cm at the maximum.

The verso contains the address: after redaction the papyrus was rolled from bottom to top and at the top two strips were turned back. Thus, there are eight strips of which no. 5 and 6 are at the outside. Strip no. 6 contains the address in two parts: part is written to the right-hand side, the remaining part to the left-hand side; in the middle a blank space is left for the seal, which is now lost (for seals put on the back of a letter, see §46).

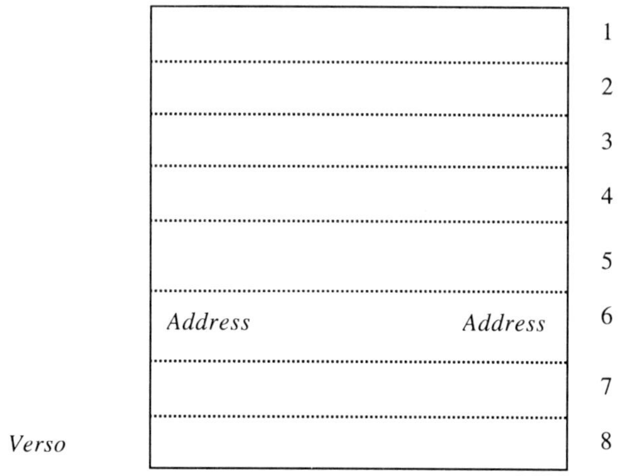

1 The papyrus is from l. 9 onwards moved too much to the right, as can be seen on the photograph.

Introduction

Contents. — Esthladas (pros. 504) writes this letter to his parents when he is on campaign in 130 B.C. The text informs us of the dynastic troubles between Ptolemy VIII and Kleopatra II (132/131-124 B.C.). It is a period of unrest. Therefore, Esthladas advises caution to his parents until the situation is back to normal. He greets his (half-)sisters, as well as Pelops and Stachys, who are often mentioned in the archive of Dryton and Apollonia (pros. 10 and 09) and, finally, Senathyris, otherwise unknown (pros. 11).

Esthladas serves in a troop which is loyal to the king Ptolemy VIII. On 23 Choiak of year 40 (15 January 130 B.C.) he informs his parents of the approaching troop movements: in the month of Tybi, that is the following month, Paos, strategos of the Thebaid, will attack the inhabitants of Hermonthis with a large military force, since they are rebellious (ἀποστάται, l. 12). Hermonthis, a town near Pathyris, had chosen the side of Kleopatra II. Pathyris, however, remains loyal to the king[1].

Corrections by Esthladas. — Esthladas wrote his letter in a well-cared-for hand[2]. On rereading, he made several corrections.

First, he realized that he would be treating his stepmother Apollonia, second wife of Dryton, in a step-motherly way if he did not address the letter also to her. W. Peremans[3] remarks «D' une façon tout à fait naturelle, poussé par son amour filial, Esthladas a écrit à son père. Car bien que Dryton se soit remarié, Esthladas n'a plus de mère. Seulement en relisant sa lettre, il se rend compte de son impolitesse vis-à-vis de celle qui remplace sa mère et il lui cède une place dans la formule initiale de la lettre sans recopier toutefois celle-ci entièrement». Esthladas corrects the introductory formula in the following way:

in 1 Ἐσθλάδας τῶι πατρὶ χαίρειν καὶ
2 ἐρρῶσθαι

he wipes χαίρειν καὶ and replaces it by καὶ τῆι μητρὶ. The *chi* of the first χαίρειν is still visible under the *kappa* of καί; for the new χαί(ρειν) he had not enough place at the end of the line and had to abbreviate it; the new καί is added before the beginning of the second line. The introductory formula now runs as follows:

1 Ἐσθλάδας τῶι πατρὶ καὶ τῆι μητρὶ χαί(ρειν)
2 \`καὶ´ ἐρρῶσθαι

He returns, however, to the singular with σοι in l. 2.

The sentence which begins in l. 8 with προσπέπτωκεν Παῶν, is afterwards provided by Esthladas of a particle, as is expected in a good Greek text: between προσπέπτωκεν and Παῶν Esthladas was able to insert γάρ. The particle γάρ is, however, written in a smaller hand. In the next line Esthladas has inserted μ(ηνὶ) after ἐν τῶι Τῦβι. Perhaps also the particle δ̣[ὲ] after ἐπισκοποῦ was added later, since it is written very closely to the right-hand side.

---

1 For the troubles between Ptolemy VIII and Kleopatra II, see Introduction to Text 32 and Vandorpe, 'Outline of Greco-Roman Thebes' (1995), p. 233-234; McGing, 'Revolt Egyptian Style' (1997), in *AfP* 43, p. 273-314, esp. p. 296-299; Veïsse, *Les «révolutions égyptiennes»* (2000).

2 For the handwriting of Esthladas, see §64-66.

3 Peremans, 'Wilck. Chrest. 10' (1953), p. 83.

In two cases a word is struck through and replaced by a new word written above the line: ἀ̣ποκαταστῆναι in l. 5 and ὄχλους in l. 11.

Finally, in l. 13 Esthladas discovered a dittography: ἀδελφὰς ἀδ(ελφὰς): the second, abbreviated form is struck through (see comm. on l. 13). However, he missed another dittography: αὐτοῖς at the end of l. 11 and at the start of l. 12.

Text

Recto

Ἐσθλάδας τῶι πατρὶ καὶ τῆι μητρὶ χαί(ρειν)
\`καὶ´ ἐρρῶσθαι· ἐπεὶ πλειọνάκις σοι γρά-
φω περὶ τοῦ διανδραγαθήσαντα
σαυτοῦ ἐπιμέλεσθαι μέχρι τοῦ
τὰ πράγματα ἀ̣ποκαταστῆναι·
ἔτι καὶ νῦν καλῶς ποιήσεις παρα-
καλῶν σαυτὸν καὶ τοὺς παρ' ἡμῶν·
προσπέπτωκεν \`γὰρ´ Παῶν ἀνα-
πλεῖν ἐν τῶι Τῦβι \`μ(ηνὶ)´ μετὰ δυνάμεων
ἱκανῶν πρὸς τὸ καταστεῖσαι τοὺς
ἐν Ἑρμώνθει ὄχλους, χρήσασθαι δ' αὐτοῖς
{αὐτοῖς} ὡς ἀποστάταις· ἐπισκοποῦ δ̣[ὲ]
καὶ τὰς ἀδελφὰς ⟦ἀδ(ελφὰς)⟧ καὶ Πέλοπα
καὶ Στάχυν καὶ Σεναθῦριν.
Ἔρρωσο, (ἔτους) μ Χοίακ κ̅γ̅.

Verso

ἀπόδος [ε]ἰς
Παθῦρ(ιν)
τῶι πατρί.

---

1 καὶ τῆι μητρὶ corr. ex χαίρειν καί 5 ἀ̣ποκαταστῆναι corr. 8 πρ in προσπέπτωκεν corr. ex πα 9 ἐν τῶι Τῦβι . . ed., ἐν τῶι Τῦβι μ(ηνὶ) Wilcken, ἐν τῶι Τῦβι \`μ(ηνὶ)´ legimus 10 καταστεῖσαι, *l.* καταστεῖλαι 11 ὄχλους corr. 12 ἐπισκοποῦ ed., ἐπισκοποῦ δ[ὲ] Wilcken 13 ⟦α̣ . .⟧ ed., ⟦αδ⟧ Wilcken, ⟦ἀδ(ελφὰς)⟧ interpretamur

Translation

Recto

Esthladas to his father and mother, greetings and good health.

As I often write you to be of good heart and to look after yourself until things get back to normal, it would be good if you put heart into yourself and our family. For it has come to our ears that in the month of Tybi Paos is sailing up the Nile with sufficient forces to suppress the rabble in Hermonthis (and) that he will treat them as rebels.

Greetings to my sisters and to Pelops, Stachys and Senathyris.

Farewell. Year 40, 23 Choiak.

Verso

Bring (this letter) to Pathyris, to my father.

Notes

Recto

2 πλειọνάκις (for πλεονάκις): for the ει instead of ε before a vowel, see Mayser, *Grammatik* I.1, p. 41.

3 διανδραγαθήσαντα: the verb διανδραγαθέω ("to remain courageous") is also found in the letter BGU IV 1204, l. 6 (28 B.C.): καὶ σὺ δὲ διανδραγάθει ἕως.

7 τοὺς παρ' ἡμῶν: S. de Ricci considers ἡμῶν a mistake for ὑμῶν. Esthladas, however, addresses his father with the informal pronoun (l. 2, 4, 6, 7, 12). Here, in l. 7, he now changes to a plural. In my view, Esthladas uses τοὺς παρ' ἡμῶν because the family he left in Pathyris are not only relatives and housemates of Dryton, but also of himself. For the expression οἱ παρ' ἡμῶν with the meaning of "housemates, family members", see Mayser, *Grammatik* II.1, p. 17-18.

8 προσπέπτωκεν: the *rho* in προσπέπτωκεν is corrected from an *alpha*. Probably, Esthladas planned to start his sentence with Παῶς, but changed into an impersonal verb.

Παῶν: in the period 137/136 to 15 January 130 B.C. (date of Text 36) Paos belonged to the πρῶτοι φίλοι and was a strategos, probably of several nomes in the Thebaid. Thereafter, he was promoted to sungenes and strategos of the Thebaid. This promotion is presumably related to his achievements in the struggle of the king against Kleopatra II. Between 4 October 130 and 28 July 129 he is even promoted to epistrategos of the Thebaid, see Pros. Ptol. I and VIII 197 and 302; Mooren, *Prosopography* (1975), no. 054; Thomas, *The Epistrategos* I (1975), p. 94-96.

10 καταστεῖσαι: could be a mistake for καταστῆσαι, or, as proposed by Wilcken, for καταστεῖλαι (see also Mayser, *Grammatik* I.1, p. 49, 40-41). The latter verb, having the meaning of "suppress", fits the context better.

11 ὄχλους: Esthladas first writes another word instead of ὄχλους, which he later struck through. Only traces of the last letter of this word are visible, probably a *iota*.

In Esthladas' letter, the word ὄχλος has undoubtedly a negative undertone: in military language ὄχλος, an undisciplined crowd, is opposed to στρατός, army (Herodian 6.7.1), whereas in a civilian context ὄχλος, mob or rabble, is opposed to δῆμος, the people (Thucydides 7.8).

χρήσασθαι: this infinitive still depends on προσπέπτωκεν, l. 8; one rather expects a future infinitive.

12 ἐπισκοποῦ: Text 36 is the oldest text in which ἐπισκοπέομαι (first meaning "to take care of") is used in the greeting formula as synonymous with the more regular ἀσπάζομαι ("to greet"). In Ptolemaic examples the imperative mood ἐπισκοποῦ is always used, whereas in the Roman period the first person singular ἐπισκοποῦμαι is usually found (for the 1st century both forms are attested). The use of a verb which originally means 'to take care of' in the greeting formula finds its parallel in Egyptian *nḏ-ḥr* ("to greet"), derived from *nḏ* ("to ask, to examine someone's face") and in Coptic ϢΙΝЄ (= *šnj*, "to inquire"). See W. Clarysse, 'An Epistolary Formula', in *Chron. d' Ég.* 65 (1990), p. 103-106.

Otherwise, Esthladas uses good Greek expressions, such as

χαίρειν καὶ ἐρρῶσθαι (l. 1-2, a combination of the greeting formula and the wishing of a good health, a combination frequently attested from the mid-2nd century B.C., see F.X.J. Exler, *The Form of the Ancient Greek Letter of the Epistolary Papyri (3rd c. B.C. - 3rd c. A.D.): a study in Greek epistolography*, Washington 1923 [= Chicago 1976], p. 32),

or ἐπεί (l. 2, introducing the explanation of a request).

13 ⟦ἀδ(ελφάς)⟧: ἀδ(ελφάς) is abbreviated in the same manner as in Dryton's third will, copied by Esthladas (Text 4, l. 7).

Verso

2 τῶι πατρί: as Dryton's name is not mentioned on the back of the letter, it may have been sent with someone who knew Dryton personally.

V

Lists and Accounts

Introduction : §47. Lists and accounts in the archives from Pathyris. — §48. Which lists and accounts belong to the archive of Dryton's family? — §49. Second-hand papyri as writing material. — §50. Survey of the lists and accounts of the family archive of Dryton.
The lists of goods and vocabulary : §51. Structure. — §52. Vocabulary.
The accounts : §53. Structure. — §54. Trade. — §55. Deposit and transport of goods.

Introduction

§47. *Lists and accounts in the archives from Pathyris.* — The archive of Dryton's family contains nine lists and accounts written on papyrus; eight of these are in Greek. They represent almost one fifth of the total family archive. Similar numbers of lists and accounts on papyrus are not found in the other family archives from Pathyris[1]; there are only a few private accounts, written on ostraka in demotic[2]: these are called *ip* (*account*), as is our Text 45. Once more the Dryton archive appears as an unusual archive.

There are, however, several accounts preserved on papyrus which were part of an official archive of the town. A fragmentary Greek text[3], which clearly once consisted of several columns, records 225 wagon loads of barley (1350 artabas) and 200 wagon loads of wheat (1000 artabas), of which a large part was transported to Pathyris. Another fragmentary Greek account of 103 B.C.[4] deals with the payment of the soldiers who are stationed in Krokodilopolis and the delivery of grain to the granary of Krokodilopolis between 7 and 9 May.

Finally, the temple archive of Pathyris has several, demotic accounts on papyrus[5] dealing with the revenues and expenditure, the distribution of bread, the construction of chapels, etc.

§48. *Which lists and accounts belong to the archive of Dryton's family?* — Modern editions and studies attribute three accounts to the archive of Dryton's family: Texts 40, 41 and 45.

---

1 There are, however, some dubious cases among the unpublished papyri from Cairo; as no photographs are availabale or as the texts are too fragmentary, it is not clear whether they are private accounts or accounts of the temple.

2 O. dem. *MDAIK* 21 (1966), no. 2; O. dem. *OrSu* 30 (1981), p. 10-12; O. dem. *MIO* 13 (1967), p. 184-186; O. dem. Zürich 31 and 32); O. dem. *MDAIK* 21 (1966) no. 32. Compare the introduction to Text 45.

3 P. Grenf. I 39 with BL I, p. 182 and III, p. 70.

4 P. Baden II 9 with BL II.2, p. 173. The Greek account is written on the verso, probably above a washed-off demotic text; to the right of the Greek account the end of a demotic text is still visible. The recto contains three columns of demotic text (for bibliography, see Pap. Lugd. Bat. XXIII, p. 217, n. 73).

5 *E.g.*, P. dem. Cairo II 30801; 30965; 31011; P. dem. Ryl. 35 (see also *Enchoria* 12 (1984), p. 54).

These texts record explicitly that they are accounts of Dryton or his wife Apollonia. There are six more accounts and lists which I would attribute to the same archive: two are published (Texts 37 and 38); four other ones I have found among the *inedita* of the collections of Heidelberg and the British Library (Texts 39, 42, 43 and 44). Why do they belong to the family archive of Dryton? I appeal to several criteria; usually there are at least three criteria valid for each text, which makes it highly probable that these lists and accounts belong to the family archive of Dryton.

• **Prosopography** : In almost all of the new lists and accounts persons are mentioned who are connected to the family archive of Dryton.

In Text 39 Dryton's son Esthladas is found twice. In addition, Pelops (pros. 10) and Stachys (pros. 09) are involved, two persons who are closely connected to Dryton's family; Pelops is also recorded in the account Text 40.

According to the list in Text 42 the writer gives several goods to Senmonthis. Few women in Pathyris bear this name. In view of other features I assume that this Senmonthis is Dryton's wife, Apollonia alias Senmonthis.

Texts 43 and 44 mention Myrsine several times. Only one woman in Pathyris is known to bear this Greek name; she is a household slave of Dryton (pros. 05).

For the lists Texts 37 and 38, which contain many names, we have little convincing prosopographical data. In Text 37 goods are delivered to the temple to a "priest Patous". In Text 21 a lady called Zois receives money from "priest Patous" who acts on behalf of Dryton's son Esthladas. According to Text 20 Dryton's wife Apollonia lends barley to a man called Peteharsemtheus, son of "priest Patous". Presumably, in these three cases the same man is found (pros. 04).

• **Handwriting**: It is clear that the lists Texts 37 and 38 are written in the same hand. After careful examination I would conclude that the list Text 42, written 5 years later and having more abbreviations, was written by the same man, Dryton's son Esthladas, whose handwriting is well-known (see §64-66).

Dryton's private accounts are written more cursively than these in the hand of his son: Text 40 is an account on his name. The accounts Texts 43 and 44 are written in a similar hand.

• **Museum archaeology** (compare p. 9-10) : the nine lists and accounts belong to collections where several Dryton papyri are kept: the papyrological Institute of Heidelberg, the British Library and the museum of Cairo.

The list Text 38 has the inventory number Brit. Libr., P. Gr. 402 and was acquired together with Brit. Libr., P. Gr. 401, a petition of Dryton's daughters, Text 34. Together with Brit. Libr., P. Gr. 218[1], they are the first papyri from Pathyris that were bought by the British Library. The list Text 37 or Brit. Libr., P. Gr. 609 and the account Text 39 or Brit. Libr., P. Gr. 641, are registered among Dryton papyri which were acquired through Grenfell in 1895.

The private accounts Texts 43 and 44 (Heid., P. Gr. 314 and 315) arrived in Heidelberg together with a loan by Dryton's wife, Text 20 (Heid., P. Gr. 313), through Reinhardt in 1897.

---

1 P. Lond. II 218 (p. 15-16).

• **Language and milieu** : the lists and accounts are written by someone who knows the Greek language and script very well. In addition, someone who writes his private notes in Greek must be someone with a Greek background and a Greek education. This is also confirmed by the fact that the writers of the accounts and lists have contacts with the gymnasium of Thebes (Text 39, l. 7). Several specific data clearly point to Dryton and his son Esthladas: the writers of the accounts and lists were Greeks living in Pathyris (there were not many Greeks who lived in Pathyris apart from Dryton and Esthladas), at least one of them possessed an expensive horse equipment (Text 38 and 42; Dryton and Esthladas were cavalrymen) and at least one of them travelled to the Greek polis Ptolemais (Text 43; Dryton was a citizen of this polis).

§49. *Second-hand papyri as writing material.* — It may be interesting to have a look at the material used by Dryton and his family for their private accounts and lists. The other inhabitants used ostraka for their private notes. Dryton and his family apparently could afford to use papyri, though second-hand papyri. There is only one ostrakon with an account of a daughter of Dryton and her cousin (Text 58).

Papyri that had lost their value could be recycled by re-using the blank spaces (the margins and a blank verso); sometimes the old text was washed off in order to have more space for a new text; in exceptional cases, the new text was written above the older one although the latter was not washed off[1]. In all these cases, the second-hand papyrus might be torn apart before it was re-used.

Dryton and his family made use of the first described process. They used second-hand papyri, tore them apart or bought them in pieces (Texts 37, 38, 43, 44) or re-used their own old papers (Texts 40, 41). They wrote either on the blank verso (Texts 37, 38) or on the blank verso and in the margins of the recto (Texts 40, 41, 43, 44). The old text was not washed off, except in one case (Text 37).

There are two special cases: the two tiny pieces of papyrus on which Texts 42 and 45 are written, are the right-hand and left-hand margin, respectively, of an old papyrus and, consequently, they no longer contain traces of the older text. Thus, the left-hand side and right-hand side, respectively, have straight borders, whereas the other side, which has been torn off, is irregular.

It seems odd that both accounts begin on the verso, although the recto is blank. There is a reasonable explanation. As Greeks write from the left to the right, they prefer to have a straight left-hand side, which Text 42 had on the verso. As Egyptians write from the right to the left, they prefer to have a straight right-hand side, which Text 45 had on the verso.

Only the account Text 39 is problematic. The long account is written on the rough and dark verso, whereas the recto only contains the last two lines of the text. There are no traces of an

[1] *E.g.*, the unpublished fragments P. dem. Cairo inv.no. 31030, 30815, P. dem. Heid. inv.no. 667 and P. dem. Brit. Mus. inv.no. 34 which are, according to information provided by U. Kaplony-Heckel, part of the same text. Above and at right angles to a Greek contract, which has not been washed off, two columns of demotic text are written. Both texts are legible.

older document visible on the recto, which might have explained the use of the verso. Nevertheless, a substantial part of the papyrus is missing, and this may once have contained an older text on the recto side.

Parallels for the use of second-hand papyri for private ends (though not for accounts or lists) are encountered in the archive of Horos (Pathyris, see Vandorpe, *Archives from Pathyris* (2001), §39). P. dem. Adler 3[1] is a demotic self-written acknowledgement of debt. It is found on the verso of a piece of papyrus which has been torn off; the recto still contains part of the old demotic contract[2]. There is no proof that the latter contract was originally part of the archive of Horos.

For the family arrangement P. dem. Adler 9[3], Horos made use of the verso of a papyrus containing accounts; the last two lines of the arrangement are written on the recto. A similar case is P. dem. Adler 12[4], an acknowledgement of debt, written on the verso of a papyrus with two columns of old accounts, probably originating from the temple of Pathyris.

Among the unpublished fragments of Cairo and the British Library, several papyri contain text on the recto and verso side. As they are all fragmentary it is often difficult to know whether re-used papyri are involved or documents which continue on the verso. Only when a Greek text is written on the recto and a demotic one on the verso, or the other way round, there is a fair chance that the papyrus has been re-used. Such an example is P. Heid. Gr. inv. no. 1290 ined. which, in my view, forms part of the same document as P. Cairo dem. inv. no. 31024 ined.: the recto shows a demotic loan and has been re-used for a copy of a petition, written in a very cursive hand.

1 P. Adler, plate 6.
2 P. dem. Adler 1 and plate 6.
3 P. Adler, plate 9.
4 P. Adler, plate 10.

§50. *Survey of the lists and accounts of the family archive of Dryton.*

Text	*Date (B.C.)*	*Language*	*Type*	*Writer*
37	18 Nov. 139	Greek	List of goods	?Esthladas
38	after 153/152 or 142/141	Greek	List of goods	?Esthladas
39	circa 137/136	Greek	Account	?Dryton
40	Aug.-Sept. 135	Greek	Account	Dryton
41	10 Sept. 135	Greek	Account	Dryton for Apollonia
42	26 July 134	Greek	List of goods	?Esthladas
43	after 154/153-143/142	Greek	Account	?Dryton
44	after 154/153-143/142	Greek	Account	?Dryton
45	after 141/140	Demotic	Account	NN for Apollonia

The lists of goods and vocabulary (Texts 37, 38 and 42)

§51. *Structure.* —

- Introduction to the list
  in case of a simple inventory: a title,
  γραφὴ σκευῶν *(list of goods)*[1] in Text 38
  in case of goods which are handed over to another person: date, a verb which denotes that goods are handed over and the name of the person to whom the goods are given,
  see Texts 37 and 42
- List

Some goods are transported separately, other items are put in a receptacle (*e.g.*, σάκκος ἐν ὧι *or* ἐν ἄλ(λωι) μώϊωι + list of goods in it[2]). In both cases the goods are listed in the nominative case[3] and usually without the conjunction καί. The goods may be followed by an adjective and/ or by a figure denoting the number involved. If an object has just been mentioned, in the following entry it is replaced by ἄλ(λος).

In Texts 37 and 38 short lines are used to denote the several subdivisions of the list[4]. These lines usually stand either before a new receptacle which contains a number of objects or before an item which is transported separately. Text 42 has only one long line before a new receptacle (recto, l. 8-9).

Text 38		*Text 37*	
l. 2-5 =	loose objects	l. 3-7 =	loose objects
l. 6-8 =	bag with objects	*line*	
l. 9-10 =	shoulder bag with objects	l. 8-10 =	several receptacles
line		*line*	
l. 11-14 =	another bag with objects	l. 11-12 =	two baskets with objects
line		*line*	
l. 15 =	mattress (loose piece)	l. 13-17 =	list of objects from the city
line			
l. 16-31 =	travelling sack with objects		
line			
l. 32-33 =	three bags with objects		

§52. *Vocabulary.* — In contrast with accounts, lists of goods comprise a wide vocabulary. I have chosen to arrange the goods by topic: receptacles, equipment of horse and cavalryman, tableware, sleeping requirements, writing and reading materials, miscellanea.

Several objects listed are typical of a traveller and/ or military and/or cavalryman, which very well suits the profile of Esthladas, a cavalryman often on campaign.

---

1 Compare γραφὴ σκευῶν in P. Oxy. X 1269, l. 5; σκευογραφία in P. Lond. II 191 (p. 264), l. 1.

2 The verb is recorded in UPZ I 6, l. 20 (163 B.C.): στάμνον ἐν ὧι καὶ ἐνῆσαν χαλκοί.

3 In two cases, the accusative is wrongly employed: λυχνίαν (Text 38, l. 17) and βάσιν (Text 37, l. 15).

4 For the use of short or long lines in accounts, compare P. Cair. Zen. I 59054 and several accounts in UPZ I 82-105.

Several objects in Esthladas' lists are rarely attested in the papyri, but are frequently found in Greek authors or in Greek inscriptions, such as the inventory lists of Delos. Esthladas' horse equipment can be compared to that in Xenophon's *De equitum ratione*. Some of Esthladas' drinking cups are extensively described in Athenaeus' *Deipnosophistai*. When the objects are found in papyri, then these texts usually originate from a Greek environment, such as the Zenon papyri and P. Col. Youtie I 7, where women from the Greek bourgeoisie have been robbed. The nature and the value of some of these objects imply that Esthladas belongs to the rich Greek class. Only a few objects are Egyptian, such as the receptacles in which goods are kept: θῖβις (*basket*), μώϊον (*receptacle*), μώστιον (*basket*), and the Egyptian *hin*-jar (ἵνιον).

RECEPTACLES
(**§52** continued)

Goods that have to be transported are usually put away in a chest, a bag or a similar receptacle. The following receptacles are found in Esthladas' lists.

ἀσφαλιὼν Ἀττικός (ὁ): *Attic safe* (Text 37, l. 8)
The hapax ἀσφαλιών[1] is undoubtedly derived from the adjective ἀσφαλής. The use of the suffix -ών, -εών and ιών may refer, among other things, to a place[2]: ἀσφαλιών denotes a safe storage room, a safe[3]. In Text 37, myrrh is kept in two Attic safes.

βῖκος (ὁ): *jar* (Text 37, l. 4)
This receptacle is usually found with the meaning "jar"[4], which, in Text 37, contains resin of pine.

γλωσσόκομον (τό): *casket* (Text 37, l. 3; 42, l. 12)
Originally, a γλωσσόκομον was a case to keep the reeds or tongues (γλῶσσαι) of fleetes. It has become a general term for a casket, probably made of wood. It is not always clear what is kept in it, but it is probably a casket for «valuables, money and jewellery»[5]. According to Text 42, papyrus sheets have been put in a small (μικρὸν) γλωσσόκομον; compare P. Oxy. LIX 4005, l. 6, which mentions a μικρὸν γλωσσοκομεῖον. P. Tebt. II 414, l. 21, records a large one: τὸ γλωσ<σ>όκομον τὸ μέγα.

---

1 For the reading ἀσφαλιῶνες instead of ἀσφαλῶνες, see comment of Text 37, l. 8. The lexicon of LSJ lists ἀσφαλών instead of ἀσφαλιών.

2 See P. Chantraine, *La formation des noms en Grec Ancien* (La société de linguistique de Paris. Collection linguistique 38), Paris 1933 [=1979], § 123.

3 Reil, *Kenntnis des Gewerbes* (1913), p. 77, with the old reading ἀσφαλών: «safe?».

4 Reil, *Kenntnis des Gewerbes* (1913), p. 43.

5 E.M. Husselman, in *Tapha* 92 (1961), p. 263 (compare SB VIII 9834); see also Reil, *Kenntnis des Gewerbes* (1913), p. 77; H.C. Youtie, in *Tapha* 98 (1967), p. 8; P. Oxy. XII 1449, col. I, l. 15; P. Oxy. LIX 4005, comm. l. 6; SB VIII 9834, B verso, l. 46.

θῖβις (ἡ): *basket* (Text 37, l. 10)
Θῖβις is a loan word[1]. It is found in the Septuagint (where θῖβις is the papyrus basket in which Moses was left behind), in Hesychius, in the Suda and in the papyri. Hesychius describes the θῖβις as πλεκτόν τι κιβωτοειδές, ὡς γλωσσοκομεῖον (*a kind of basket which resembles a chest, as a case to keep reeds* (see γλωσσόκομον)). According to the papyri this basket could contain silver money[2], loaves of bread[3], or several sealed bags[4]. Esthladas used two such baskets for different kinds of papers, such as accounts, hereditary documents, books and wooden tablets.

κίστη (ἡ): *chest* (Text 37, l. 3 and 9)
A κίστη is made, according to Theophrastus[5], of the bark of lime[6]. A list of goods from the Zenon archive[7] records a κίστη ἰτεΐνη (*of willow*) and Text 37 mentions a chest which is ξυ(λίνη) (*wooden*). According to a memorandum from the Zenon archive[8] large chests were used for transporting stones; according to a second-century letter[9] papers were put away in κίσται; Esthladas filled a large wooden κίστη with myrrh (Text 37).

μώϊον (τό): *receptacle* (Text 37, l. 13 and 16; Text 42, l. 14-15 and 19-20)
Μώϊον is a loan word from Egyptian: *mjḥ* [10], Coptic ⲘⲞⲈⲒϨ [11], is the name of a measure especially for hay or chaff; *mjḥ tḥ 14* are, for instance, 14 measures of chaff[12]. The Greek equivalent μώϊον is similarly used as a measure of capacity, usually for ἄχυρον (*chaff*) as well[13]. A second-century text[14] shows that 80 μώϊα correspond to one ἀγώγιον, that is one wagon load[15]. The Greek term μώϊον is also found in the more general meaning of receptacle[16], used for poppy[17], olives[18], loaves of bread[19] and even for non-food goods such as bronze objects[20]. In Esthladas' lists, several μώϊα are found: one for six wooden tablets, another small receptacle for papyrus sheets, one for asphalt and still another for a bronze object. Two μώϊα in Text 37 (l. 16) are made of Parian marble.

---

1 For the Hebrew equivalent and for the discussion on the Egyptian equivalent of θῖβις, see P. Grelot, 'Les textes Araméens d' Eléphantine', in *Revue Biblique* 78 (1971), p. 519; Vycichl, *DELC*, p. 212.
2 P. Petr. IIIA 51, l. 4.
3 UPZ I 149, l. 21.
4 P. Cair. Zen. I 59069, l. 5.
5 Theophrastus, *Historia Plantarum* 5.7.5.
6 See especially, Brümmer, 'Griechische Truhenbehälter' (1985), p. 16-20.
7 PSI VII 858 with PSI IX, p. x.
8 P. Cair. Zenon III 59518, l. 5.
9 P. Tebt. II 414, l. 16-17.
10 Äg. Wb. II, p. 31 (*m3ḥ*); Erichsen, *Glossar* , p. 153.
11 Crum, *Coptic Dictionary*, p. 208a; Vycichl, *DELC*, p. 109-110.
12 O. dem. Mattha 261, l. 3.
13 *E.g.*, P. Heid. III 18 and 25; P. Oxy LXIV 4441, l. 25, 26, 31 with comment; P. Rein. II 138; O. Bodl. I 231.
14 P. Heid. III 18 and comm.
15 For a discussion of the capacity of the measure, see P. Kell. IV, p. 49-50.
16 G. Husson, 'P. Giss. Univ. 10, II 13: ἐν μωείῳ', in *Chron. d'Ég.* 57 (1982), p. 118-119.
17 P. Cair. Zen. IV 59627, l. 8.
18 P. Hib. I 49, l. 8.
19 SB XVI 12468, Fr. 1, l. 7.
20 PSI IV 428, l. 78.

μώστιον (τό): *basket (or bag)* (Text 37, l. 5)
In the lexicon of LSJ μώστιον was considered a diminutive of τὸ μώϊον, a well-known Egyptian loan word (see above). In my opinion, however, μώστιον is not to be connected with μώϊον, but should be connected with the Egyptian word *mstj* for phonetic and semantic reasons which I hope to develop in a future article. The Egyptian *mstj* is a kind of basket or bag[1] for fruit (such as grapes and figs), herbs, fish, etc.

The μώστια are found in three Greek texts. In Text 37 the μώστια are sealed. In the letter Pap. Lugd. Bat XX 54 (246 or 245 B.C.; Philadelphia (Arsinoites)) different kinds of receptacles are recorded for transporting goods, among them τὰ ὀνικὰ μώστια δύο in l. 29 (two mostia for donkey-transport, that is fit for being carried by a donkey). The editor explains mostion as a "kind of jar which can be sealed". The ostrakon BGU VII 1523 (3rd cent. B.C.; Philadelphia (Arsinoites)) shows that μώστια are used to transport linseed and shallots.

σακκοπήρα (ἡ): *knapsack, travelling sack* (Text 38, l. 16)
The term σακκοπήρα is rarely found in papyri[2]. It is usually interpreted as a knapsack or wallet. In view of the context of the σακκοπήρα in Text 38, I prefer the translation "travelling sack": according to the latter text (l. 16-25), one such travelling sack contained a whole list of objects needed by a cavalryman on campaign: a Lacedaemonian drinking-vessel (κώθων), a coat, a short mantle, a lamp stand, a small red carpet, 3 new cloths for wiping perspiration, 6 other old ones, 4 weapons, 2 sabres with wavy blades, a horse muzzle(?), a leather bag holding wine, a stand for vessels, a drinking-cup, a nose-bag for horses, a vinegar-cruet, an inkstand, 2 oil-flasks, a scraper.

σάκκος (ὁ): *bag, sack* (Text 38, passim)
Σάκκοι or bags, made of rough cloth (especially of goats' hair), are often used by Esthladas for holding travelling goods. Σάκκος is a Semitic word, transliterated into demotic as *sq*[3].

χιλωτήρ (ὁ): *fodder bag* or *nose-bag for horses, bag* (Text 38, l. 9 and 24)
A χιλωτήρ is a fodder bag for horses, derived from χιλός, the fodder for cattle and horses. According to Text 38, l. 24, Esthladas has such a nose-bag among other equipment for his horse. In l. 9 a χιλω(τήρ) is mentioned which hangs from the shoulder and which contains papyrus sheets; apparently, the χιλω(τήρ) is used here as an ordinary bag.

---

1 According to I. Grumach-Shirun the translation of *mstj* as 'basket' is correct and suggests the definition «die auf Seilbasis geflochtene Tasche» (LÄ III, col. 741).
2 P. Enteux. 32, l. 7; P. Wisc. I 30, col. II, l. 5 ([σακκοπ]ήρα α̅).
3 See Clarysse, 'Greek Loan-Words' (1987), p. 32, no. 11.

EQUIPMENT OF HORSE AND CAVALRYMAN
(**§52** continued)

The results of my study on the equipment of horses and cavalrymen in the accounts and lists of the archive of Dryton's family were presented at the 21st International Congress of Papyrologists (Berlin, 13-19 August 1995), see my article ' "When a Man has found a horse to his mind" (Xen., *De equitandi ratione*, IV.1)". On Greek horsemanship in Ptolemaic Egypt', in B. Kramer *e.a.* (edd.), *Akten des 21. internationalen Papyrologenkongresses Berlin 13-19.8.1995* (AfP, Beiheft 3), Stuttgart-Leipzig 1997, p. 984-990 and 10 fig.

ἀγωγεύς (ὁ): *leading rein* (Text 38, l. 28)
The reins proper are to be distinguished from the leading rein or ἀγωγεύς[1]. The latter is a long cord or rope used to lead out (ἄγειν) the horse by hand, for instance at a drinking-place or when walking[2]. The leading rein can be useful in several circumstances. In his *De equitandi ratione* (8.3), Xenophon records that a man who has problems getting his horse over a ditch must get over the ditch himself first, holding the horse loosely by the leading rein and then give him a pull with the leading rein to make him leap over the ditch. Thus the leading rein can be used in combination with the bridle and the reins. In Text 38 two leading reins are listed.

ἐφίππιον (τό): *saddle* (Text 38, l. 5; Text 42, l. 6)
According to Xenophon, the horseman sat either on the bare back of the horse or on an ἐφίππιον. The word ἐφίππιον is used for the first time by Xenophon: he records that it is not just a blanket or saddle-cloth, nor a pile of coverings[3], but that it contained filling material and was stitched (ἐρράφθαι) in such a way that the horseman had a safer seat, without hurting the horse's back[4]. The saddle had to be large enough to protect the belly of the horse.

In Esthladas'(?) lists saddles are mentioned twice. In Text 42 ἐφίππια συνερραμμένα (*saddles stitched together*) are listed. They are probably saddles with filling material. The same verb ῥάπτω (*to stitch*) is used by Xenophon to point to the filling material of the saddles (see above). The κασ(ῆς) ἐφίππι(ος) φοινι(κοῦς) of Text 38 may be either a real purple-red saddle or rather a blanket used as horse-cloth[5] (see κασῆς). According to Xenophon, such κασᾶς ἐφιππίους were donated by Cyrus to the cavalrymen[6].

The saddle was fastened by means of a girth or belly band (see ζωστήρ). The sweat cloths (see ἱδρῶιον) undoubtedly were placed beneath the saddle to protect it against the impact of sweat.

---

1 See also P. Cair. Zen. IV 59781, l. 10 and 16.
2 Vigneron, *Le cheval dans l' Antiquité* (1968), p. 55 and 68-71; Delebecque, *Xénophon. De l'art équestre* (1978), p. 82-83; Spence, *Cavalry* (1993), pl. 15.
3 Xenophon, *Cyropaedia* 8.8.19.
4 Xenophon, *De equitandi ratione* 12.9; see also Vigneron, *Le cheval dans l' Antiquité* (1968), p. 81-84; according to the latter, the filling material was not part of the saddle itself, but was fastened to the saddle; Delebecque, *Xénophon. De l'art équestre* (1978), p. 77-81; for ἐφίππιον in the papyri, see, *e.g.*, P. Oxy. XLII 3060, l. 2 (2nd cent.); SB XVI 12628, col. III, l. 54 (c. 329-331): see note on l. 54: «The Harris-text implies that ἐφίππια came in pairs (ζ(εύγους))» (*ZPE* 37 (1980), p. 232-233; BL IX).
5 See U. Wilcken, in *AfP* 1 (1901), p. 135; compare J. Kramer, in *AfP* 45 (1999), p. 193-194.
6 Xenophon, *Cyropaedia* 8.3.6; see Spence, *Cavalry* (1993), pl. 16.

ζωστὴρ ἱππικός (ὁ): *horse girth* (Text 38, l. 8)
The ζωστῆρες ἱππικοί are horse's girths or belly bands. Another word for girth, mentioned in a Zenon papyrus, is ζώνη, listed together with the saddle (ἀστράβη) of a donkey; in the same text a double ζώνη is recorded, used to fasten the load of a pack mule[1].

θώραξ (ὁ): *breastplate* (Text 38, l. 6)
To face danger on horseback, Xenophon recommends among the defensive arms a θώραξ or breastplate that fits the body[2]. In the papyri, the breastplate is mentioned casually. In a letter from the Zenon archive, the writer wants a breastplate and a nice coat[3]. In a will from the 3rd century B.C. a man leaves behind his breastplate and cuirass-belt (ζώνη θωρακῖτις)[4]. A document from Hadrian's reign records a breastplate of fine brass and cloth, as quite light in relation to its size[5].

ἱδρῶιον (τό): *sweat cloth* (Text 38, l. 18-20)
The papyri record sweat cloths for donkeys, to be put under the saddle or under the load of a pack mule[6]. The sweat cloths from Text 38 are undoubtedly meant to be put under the saddle of the horse, to protect the saddle against sweat (see ἐφίππιον); among the sweat cloths of Text 38, there are three new (καινά) and six old ones (παλαιά), of which two are round (στρογγύλα). The round shape is undoubtedly due to the shape of the saddle proper. Compare BGU VII 1515, an "Abrechnung über ausgegebene Schweißtücher", which also records an old and new sweat cloths; these are τρίχινα *(of hair)*.

ἱμὰς ἱππικός (ὁ): *horse chain or bar* (Text 42, l. 17)
A ἱμάς is a leather strap, used for all kinds of purposes. For horses, there are the ἱμάντες (always plural) or the reins[7]. Leather straps were, furthermore, used for the horse's bridle (see χαλινός) and to fasten the saddle (see ἐφίππιον)[8]. A ἱμάς can, finally, denote a whip[9]. In Text 42 the ἱμάς is of iron (σιδηροῦς). This iron horse object is probably a chain or bar to be attached to the bronze cavesson, listed in the preceding line (see περιστομίς).

κασῆς ἐφίππιος (ὁ)[10] : horse-cloth (Text 38, l. 5)
For my reading κασ(ῆς) ἐφίππι(ος) and not κὰς ἐφίππι(ον), see Text 38, comm. on l. 5.

Besides Text 38, three attestations of κασῆς (= κασᾶς) are found in the papyri. The term is discussed in depth by J. Kramer, 'Warm und wollig, dick und rauh: κάς, κασῆς und κάσ(σ)ος in den Papyri', in *AfP* 45 (1999), p. 192-204, see especially p. 194-195. Kramer informs us that «Die antiken Lexikographen stimmen mit Xenophon und Agatharchides darin

1 P. Cair. Zen. IV 59659, l. 13-14, 18 and 22; PSI V 527, passim; ? P. Lond. VII 2180, l. 9 and note.
2 Xenophon, *De equitandi ratione* 12.1.
3 P. Lond. VII 1932, l. 10.
4 P. Petr. I^2. The Wills. 3, l. 75-76.
5 P. Giss. I 47, l. 6.
6 P. Cair. Zen. IV 59659, l. 13 and 16; P. Cair. Zen. IV 59720, col. I, l. 4; P. Lond. VII 2180, l. 3 (12 new sweat cloths, of four different colours); PSI V 527, passim (ἱδρῶια ὀνικά).
7 Vigneron, *Le cheval dans l'Antiquité* (1968), p. 56.
8 Xenophon, *De equitum magistro* 8.4.
9 Vigneron, *Le cheval dans l'Antiquité* (1968), p. 86.
10 Text 38, l. 5.

überein, daß unter κασᾶς eine Decke oder ein Tuch zu verstehen ist; sie bieten die zusätzliche Information, daß von einer haarigen, wolligen oder filzigen Oberfläche auszugehen ist.».

See also ἐφίππιον.

μάχαιρα (ἡ): *sabre* (Text 38, l. 21)

A μάχαιρα is a short sword or sabre[1]. As the word is here accompanied by σπειραντική (*curved*), it must point to the Persian sabre: a single-edged, slightly curved short sabre, carried in a sheath on the left side; it was regularly used in a downward slash, brought from far behind the left shoulder. It is to be distinguished from the sword or ξίφος, which has a double-edged, straight and broad blade. To harm the enemy from horseback, Xenophon recommends the Persian sabre or μάχαιρα[2], rather than the sword or ξίφος, because "the rider will find the cut with the Persian sabre more efficacious than the thrust with the sword"[3].

The two Persian sabres or μάχαιραι mentioned in the list Text 38 are called σπειραντικαί. This adjective is a hapax legomenon, but as the verb σπειράομαι has the meaning "to be coiled or folded round", σπειραντικός must point to the curve of the Persian sabre. A similar term is found in a fifth-century text: μάχερα στρογ<γ>ύλα[4].

Sword

Persian sabre

---

1 Compare μάχαιρας σιδηροκολέους (*iron-sheathed*) and σκυτοκολέους (*leather-sheathed*) in P. Cair. Zen. I 59054, col. II, l. 41-42.

2 Xenophon, *De equitandi ratione* 12.11; Xenophon, *Hellenica* 3.3.7; *Cyropaedia* 1.2.13.

3 Xenophon, *De equitandi ratione* 12.11, translation by E.C. Marchant (Loeb-edition); see also A.M. Snodgrass, *Arms and Armour of the Greeks*, London 1967=1982, p. 97; Spence, *Cavalry* (1993), p. 54-56.

4 P. Oxy. X 1289, l. 4, see also l. 7.

ὅπλα (τά): *weapons* (Text 38, l. 20)
What is meant in Text 38 by the "four weapons", is not specified. A ὅπλον is in the first place a shield, but ὅπλα can, by extension, be used for all kinds of weapons, defensive and offensive[1]. Xenophon[2] lists among the defensive arms of the cavalryman: the breastplate (see θώραξ) and other body-protecting pieces, such as the helmet and high boots; cavalrymen did not, however, carry shields[3]. Xenophon furthermore recommends, as offensive arms, the Persian sabre (see μάχαιρα) and two Persian javelins of cornel wood (κρανέινα παλτά), light spears which were shorter than the Greek spear.

περιστομίς (ἡ): *cavesson* (Text 42, l. 16)
Περιστομίς is never attested with horses, but its diminutive περιστόμιον is[4]. The περιστόμιον is part of the bridle: it is the strap around the mouth or nose, the nose band. Like the other bands, it is usually, made of leather and is only a small part of the bridle, not even an indispensable part (see χαλινός). In Text 42, however, only this part is listed; the remaining straps of the bridle are lacking. Furthermore, the περιστομίς is made of bronze (χαλκῆ), not of leather as usual. So the bronze περιστομίς cannot be a simple part of the bridle. It must be a piece of equipment of which the bronze nose piece is the most important part. Such an object is known: the cavesson (French *caveçon*, Italian *cavezzone*)[5].

The cavesson is a form of bridle, but without a bit[6]. The figure below shows a Greek cavesson of the fifth century B.C., probably made of leather. Control is achieved by pressure on the nose; the cavesson can, however, be used together with or as an accessory to the bit, its purpose then being to keep the mouth closed, so the animal cannot get away from the bit.

The metal cavessons shown below could be our περιστομίς of bronze: the front part is put on the horse's nose, the upper part under its neck. The cavesson is especially used when the horse is fastened in the stable or led by the hand with the leading rein (see ἀγωγεύς).

The ἱμὰς σιδηροῦς ἱππικός (see ἱμάς) mentioned in the next line of Text 42 must be an iron chain, attached to the rings of the cavesson, thus replacing the leather strap(s) that kept the cavesson in place or serving as a kind of ἀγωγεύς or leading rein. The two pieces, cavesson and chain, were sufficient to keep the horse under control.

What is the usual Greek word for cavesson? The only word known until now that might point to the cavesson is the ψάλιον; about this term P. Vigneron writes: «De tous les termes techniques de la langue hippique grecque, aucun n'a été interprété de manière plus contradictoire que le mot ψάλιον». The περιστομίς of Text 42 is apparently a new and plausible Greek word for cavesson.

---

1 See A.M. Snodgrass, *Arms and Armour of the Greeks*, London 1967=1982, passim; for the weaponry and protection of the cavalryman, see Spence, *Cavalry* (1993), p. 49-65.
2 Xenophon, *De equitandi ratione* 12.
3 See Spence, *Cavalry* (1993), p. 60-65.
4 Compare the equivalent στομίς - στόμιον.
5 Vigneron, *Le cheval dans l' Antiquité* (1968), p. 58-62 (le licou et le caveçon); the remark of Vigneron, *Le cheval dans l' Antiquité* (1968) p. 71, note 2 supports my theory: «...il suffit que la muserolle soit de cuir épais et garni de piquants, ou qu' elle soit remplacée par un demi-cercle de métal pour qu' on ait un caveçon».
6 Examples in M.A. Littauer, 'Bits and Pieces', in *Antiquity* 43 (1969), p. 291-292, esp. fig. 3 and pl. 41c.

Greek cavesson (5th cent. B.C.)

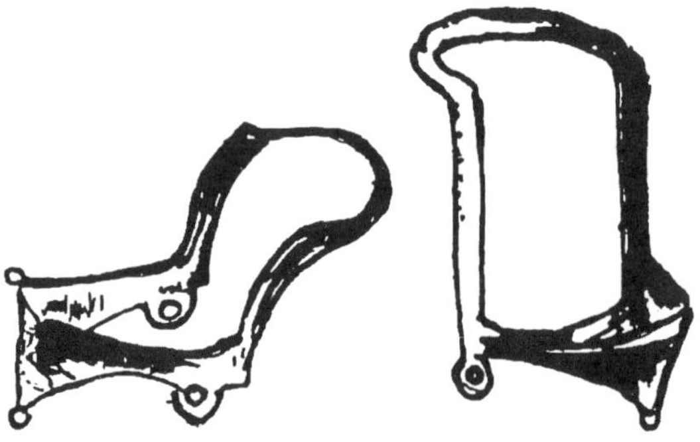

Metal cavessons . The forward part had to be put on the nostrils, the upper part behind the ears of the horse. A rope or a strap was fixed to the rings.

σῦστρον ἱππικόν (τό): *curry-comb* (Text 42, l. 18)
The σῦστρον (for ξῦστρον) is a scraper or a polishing instrument. The word is used here for the first time in relation to horses, and must point to a curry-comb, the usual Greek word being ψῆκτρον[1]. Xenophon depicts in detail how the cavalryman has to groom the horse and where he must stand while doing so to avoid accidents[2].

σφαίρω(μα) ἱππικόν (τό): *horse muzzle* ? (Text 38, l. 22)
Text 38 has σφαιρω( ). The first editor thought this was an abbreviation of σφαιρω(τήρ ?), a proposal taken over in the Greek-English Lexicon of LSJ. Σφαιρωτήρ is mentioned only by Hesychius, according to whom it is a variant of the uncommon σφυρωτήρ (*leather tong* or *shoe-latchet*). I prefer to take σφαιρω( ) as the abbreviation of σφαίρωμα, since here it is defined by ἱππικόν and since this word is listed in a Zenon papyrus in a similar context as in Text 38[3]. According to the Zenon papyrus, a mule that carries a person has a horse-bridle with reins, five sweat cloths, a mule-saddle as well as a σφαίρωμα; the second mule, used to transport goods, has also a σφαίρωμα, this time an Egyptian one.

The exact meaning of σφαίρωμα is not clear from the context: the editor of the Zenon papyrus proposes in a footnote: "collar or round pectoral". The lexicon of LSJ put "dub. sens.". In any case, the object must be something round or rounded that is part of the equipment of the horse and of the mule. In my opinion σφαίρωμα is a muzzle. The Greek author Lucian informs that the muzzle was used for mules or asses to prevent them from

1 The word ψῆκτρον is also attested in a Zenon papyrus: PSI IV 430, l. 5.
2 Xenophon, *De equitandi ratione* 5.5-10; 6.1-3; see Vigneron, *Le cheval dans l' Antiquité* (1968), p. 25-26 and pl. 7d.
3 P. Cair. Zen. IV 59659, l. 12 and ? 17 with BL VI.

grazing on the way[1]. According to Xenophon, the muzzle was also used for horses: "the horseman must always put the muzzle on when he leads the horse anywhere (ἄγειν, see ἀγωγεύς) *without* bridle. For the muzzle prevents him from biting without hampering his breathing"[2], for instance, when the horse has to be groomed. The muzzle can also be put on *together with* the bridle. The figure below is a well-preserved bronze muzzle, found in a Boeotian tomb of the fourth century B.C., together with a flexible bit.

The normal Greek word for muzzle is φιμός or κημός[3]. I suggest, however, that σφαίρωμα is another Greek word for the same object. The muzzle is indeed rounded or σφαιρικός, as is shown in the right-hand figure below. Furthermore, Xenophon records that the muzzle is περικείμενος, that is put or laid round (περι-) the nose and mouth of the horse, which also points to a rounded shape of the muzzle. One could object that the muzzle is not entirely globular, but this objection can be put aside easily, as the Greek word σφαιρίον means, among other things, "end of the nose"; this σφαιρίον or "end of the nose" has the same shape as the muzzle.

P. Col. X 290, verso, l. 15-16, even suggests that also σφαιρίον, "end of the nose", may have the meaning of "muzzle": one such σφαι̣[ρί]ον is listed together with two cog-wheels (of the saqiya gear drive). The editor remarked that «both meaning and supplement to our instance must remain uncertain». In my view, the σφαι̣[ρί]ον may be a muzzle for a draught animal of the saqiya.

1 Lucian, *Asinus* 17.
2 Xenophon, *De equitandi ratione* 5.3.
3 Vigneron, *Le cheval dans l' Antiquité* (1968), p. 77.

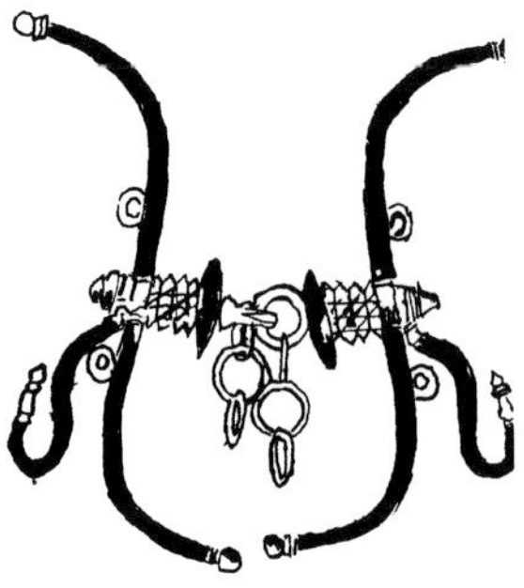

χαλινός (ὁ)/ **χαλινόν** (τό): *bit, bridle* (Text 38, l. 7 and 33) In ancient Greece[1] the bridle was made of a bit or mouthpiece (χαλινός), to which the reins (ἡνία, ῥυτῆρες) were fastened. Xenophon recommends a flexible bit in preference to a stiff bit for several reasons. Most bits from Antiquity are, indeed, flexible ones, Such a flexible bit consists of two axles joined in the middle by two links. Xenophon advises the use of at least two bits: this advice is followed by Dryton (or Esthladas) and, for instance, by the owner of two flexible bits found in a Boeotian tomb and kept in the Berlin Museum until 1945 [see figure]. A silver χαλινός is recorded in a Zenon-text[2].

The bit had to be kept in place by leather straps, among them the head-stall (κορυφαία)[3], the browband (κεκρύφαλος) and two cheekpieces (τὰ κατατείνοντα). Two bands, however, were not essential: the nose band (περιστόμιον), girding the mouth above the nostrils, and the throat band (γενειαστήρ). The term χαλινός (*bit*) is also used by classical authors and in the papyri to denote the complete bridle — the bit with leather straps, with or without reins. It is used in that sense in the above-mentioned Zenon text[4], which has χαλινὸν ἱππικὸν ἔχον ῥυτῆρας, "a horse bridle with reins". The χαλινά of Text 38 (for the neuter, see comm. on Text 38, l. 7-8) probably have this broader sense; in l. 7-8, they are defined by ταύρεα which undoubtedly refers to the leather straps of the bridle.

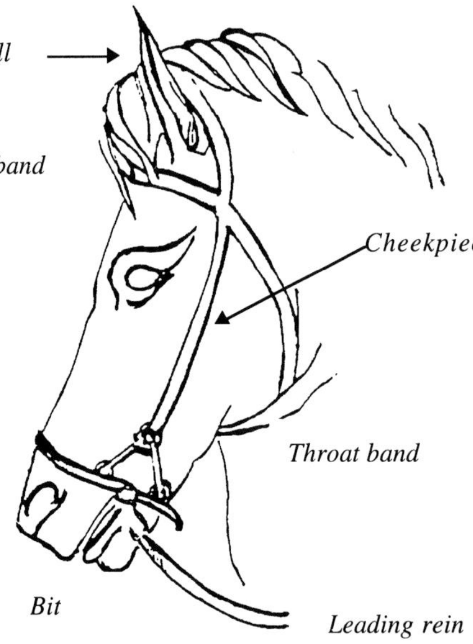

---

1 See Vigneron, *Le cheval dans l'Antiquité* (1968), p. 52-58; Delebecque, *Xénophon. De l'art équestre* (1978), p. 81-82.

2 PSI V 543, l. 50; see also P. Cair. Zen. IV 59782a, l. 9 note: probably χαλινοί, «each bit having two τρίβολοι».

3 *E.g.*, in P. Cair. Zen. IV 59781, l. 9 and 12 (head-stall of flax or hemp fibre).

4 P. Cair. Zen. IV 59659, l. 11.

χιλωτήρ (ὁ) : *fodder bag* or *nose bag for horses, bag*
See above, Receptacles.

TABLEWARE
(§52 continued)

ἄβαξ (ὁ): *dining plate* (Text 38, l. 29)
An ἄβαξ or ἀβάκιον (Latin *abacus*) is a slab or a board, such as a «reckoning-board, a board sprinkled with sand or dust for drawing geometrical diagrams, a dice-board or a plate» (LSJ). The term is occasionally found in the papyri, but the meaning is never clear. Kiessling[1] preferred the meaning reckoning-board. The editor of P. Cair. Zen. I 59071 translates ἀβάκεια, in my view correctly, as «dishes»; they were probably even silver dishes[2]. The meaning of dish or dining plate is confirmed by the fact that in Text 38 ἄβαξ and κελλίβας (*portable dining table*, see below) are listed together; the same combination is found in a petition on objects which have been stolen in a house[3]: κελλίβας καὶ ἄβαξ α (*portable dining table and one dining plate*). The ἄβαξ μέγας of P. Alex. 31, l. 9, is probably also a dining plate, since the text is "un inventaire d'ustensiles de cuisine". In addition, ἄβαξ is found with the same meaning in an inventory list from Delos[4]. Finally, the term is apparently transliterated into demotic as *3bgs* and is recorded among stolen furniture in a second-century text[5].

ἀλαβαστροθήκη (ἡ): *case for alabaster ornaments, small box, casket* (Text 38, l. 28)
Pliny[6] compared an ἀλάβαστ(ρ)ος with a pearl tapering lengthwise and with a rose bud because of its form; it was a long, oval bottle with a narrow neck, without a base or handles. It was often made of alabaster, but also of glass or clay. Because of its form, it was suitable for keeping perfume or certain oils. As the bottles could not stand without a base, they were put in a purpose-made case: an ἀλαβαστροθήκη[7]. The ἀλαβαστροθήκη is rarely attested in the papyri, where it apparently has the general meaning of small box or casket. It is found in the Zenon-archive[8], where it is used in a strange way: it is listed alongside baskets, large chests, sacks and other objects needed to transport stones. Furthermore, it is mentioned among goods stolen from some well-to-do women[9]; this casket contained myrrh. In Text 38 it is not clear what exactly was kept in the casket.

---

1 Kiessling, *Wörterbuch*, *s.v.*
2 See the introduction to the text.
3 P. Tebt. III 793, col. VI, l. 4.
4 *BCH* 29 (1905), p. 510, l. 151.
5 See Clarysse, 'Greek Loan-Words' (1987), p. 21, no. 1.
6 Plinius, *Naturalis Historia* 9.113 and 21.14.
7 For the term -θήκη, see Brümmer, 'Griechische Truhenbehälter' (1985), p. 15.
8 P. Cair. Zen. III 59518, l. 6; see also P. Cair. Zen. I 59015, col. I, l. 11.
9 P. Col. Youtie I 7, l. 12.

ἀριστοφόρον (τό): *breakfast-tray* (Text 37, l. 7)
Breakfast-trays are found in the Zenon-archive: in a list of travelling goods (ἀριστοφόρον μεῖζον)[1], in a list of varied objects[2] and in a list of foods and other articles (breakfast-trays and silver ware which are kept in a chest)[3].

δέρμα οἰνοφόρον (τό): *leather bag for holding wine* (Text 38, l. 22)
Δέρμα (*skin, hide* or *leather bag*) is often attested in the Zenon-archive and implies the skin of an animal: young and full-grown goats[4] or an onager[5]. The δέρμα οἰνοφόρον in Text 38 is a leather bag for keeping wine.

ἐγγυθήκη (ἡ): *stand for vessels* (Text 38, l. 23)
Ἐγγυθήκη is not found elsewhere in the papyrological evidence[6].

ἵνιον (τό): *hin-jar* (Text 38, l. 14)
The Egyptian hin-jar[7], originally pot-bellied, lacking handles or a base, was used already in the Middle Kingdom as a measure of capacity of c. 0.456 l. for liquids and dry products. The hin-jar is sporadically found in Greek papyri transcribed as ἵνιον: a Zenon-papyrus[8] mentions 10 ἵνια of sweet oil put into alabaster jars which are to be sealed. In Text 38 ἵνιον or hin-jar is recorded not as a measure but as an object.

κελλίβας (ὁ): *portable dining table* (Text 38, l. 30)
Κελλίβας or κιλλίβας, often plural, was a tripod used as a support for several objects. It is found in this meaning in a sale of a goldsmith's workshop, which lists built-in supports for kettles (18 B.C.)[9]. The word is taken over in Latin as *cilliba.* Varro[10] describes this object as a dining table, which is among other things used in the army camp. Κελλίβας (singular) undoubtedly has this meaning of dining table when it is mentioned together with ἄβαξ, dining plate (as in Text 38, see above), or with furniture such as ποτήρια κασειδέρια (*tin drinking cups*)[11].

κόνδυ (τό): *drinking-cup* (Text 38, l. 13)
Nothing has come down to us about the form of the κόνδυ. It may have been a round drinking-vessel without base[12]. In Athenaeus[13] a κόνδυ is described as an Asiatic drinking-cup which, according to Menander, could contain 10 kotylae, that are 2.7 l. The κόνδυ is sporadically found in the papyri: three bronze κόνδυα are listed among the possessions of

1 P. Cair. Zen. I 59054, l. 39.
2 P. Cair. Zen. IV 59776, l. 8.
3 PSI IV 428, l. 47.
4 P. Cair. Zen. I 59060, l. 8; 59061, l. 4; P. Cair. Zen. III 59429, l. 13; P. Mich. Zen. 67, l. 26; P. Wisc. II 78, l. 6-14.
5 P. Cair. Zen. IV 59692, l. 17.
6 For the term -θήκη, see Brümmer, 'Griechische Truhenbehälter' (1985), p. 15.
7 S.P. Vleeming, in LÄ III, col. 1210-1211.
8 PSI IV 333, l. 6; see also P. Cair. Zen. IV 59545, l. 7.
9 BGU IV 1127, l. 11.
10 Varro, *De Lingua Latina* 5.118.
11 P. Ryl. II 136, l. 10.
12 RE, *s.v.* Kondu.
13 Menander apud Athenaeus 11.477.

some well-off ladies[1] and stolen κόνδυα are recorded in notifications of loss or burglary[2]. These texts date to the third and second centuries B.C. Finally, the κόνδυ is found in Greek inscriptions, such as the inventory lists of Delos[3].

κώθων (ὁ): *Lacedaemonian drinking-cup* (Text 38, l. 23)
According to Critias, the Lacedaemonian κώθων is a drinking-cup «most suitable for military service and most easily carried in a knapsack. It is adapted to military purposes for the reason that it is often necessary to drink water that is not pure. In the first place it was useful in that the water drunk could not be too clearly seen; and in the second place, since the kothon had inward-curving edges, it retained a residue of the impurities inside it»[4]. The κώθων is mentioned by ancient authors and in Greek inscriptions, but is rarely found in the Greek papyri: the examples date from the third and second centuries B.C.[5]. In Text 38 The κώθων is listed among military equipment and kept in a knapsack (see l. 16) as advised by the above-mentioned Critias. In addition, three demotic ostraka of the Ptolemaic and Roman period deal with *qwtn*, an object which appears to be used for wine[6]. E. Van 't Dack was able to identify this demotic term with the Greek κώθων[7]. The relation between κώθων and wine is affirmed by a third-century text where a woman is described as being κωθωνική (*drunk*)[8], undoubtedly by the drinking of wine and not of water. Finally, the diminutive κωθώνιον is occasionally attested in the papyri.

λεκάνη (ἡ): *pot* (Text 37, l. 5; Text 38, l. 32; Text 42, l. 11)
Λεκάνη is a kind of pot in the first place destined for foods. The term is often found in the papyri and appears to be a valuable object: for instance, a bronze λεκάνη for a goddess[9], or a bronze λεκάνη among the furniture which a man left to his wife[10], another bronze λεκάνη mentioned in an inventory of property[11] and a λεκάνη of which the value is indicated (the actual value is lost in the lacuna)[12]. In Text 38, l. 32 the value of the λεκάνη is also stated: 3,200 drachmas, that is one to four monthly wages of an Egyptian employee[13].

λήκυθος (ἡ): *oil-flask* (Text 38, l. 25)
In current archaeological usage a λήκυθος is a well-defined type of tableware. In ancient Greece λήκυθος was rather a general term for jars or bottles in which especially oil[14], but also other liquids such as wine[15] were kept. In the papyri λήκυθος as well as the diminutive

---

1 P. Col. Youtie I 7, l. 8-9.
2 P. Tebt. III 794, l. 6-7; 12; 14; SB XVIII 13160, l. 13.
3 *E.g.*, IG XI.2 226, B l. 24.
4 Critias apud Athenaeus XI 483b; Loeb-translation by Ch.B. Gulick.
5 P. Heid. VI 385, l. 8 (with comment); P. Mich. III 173, l. 20; Text 38.
6 Pap. Lugd. Bat XXIII, p. 160-166.
7 Apud Clarysse, 'Greek Loan-Words' (1987), p. 25, no. 45a.
8 P. Vind. Tand. 2, l. 9.
9 UPZ I 6, l. 24.
10 P. Heid. IV 336, l. 32.
11 P. Tebt. II 406, col. II, l. 13.
12 P. Rain. Cent. 50, l. 5.
13 See Reekmans, 'Ptolemaic Copper Inflation' (1951), p. 109.
14 P. Cair. Zen. IV 59627, l. 8; P. Tebt. I 221.
15 P. Cair. Zen. IV 59741, l. 31.

ληκύθιον are attested; they are usually earthenware, but bronze[1] and tin[2] lekythoi were also found. The lekythoi did not have a standard measure of capacity. Thus, the capacity is sometimes added: in an account of the second century B.C.[3] a λήκυθος holding 15 kotylae (c. 4 l.) of kiki-oil is recorded, whereas a papyrus of the fourth century[4] mentions two tin ληκύθια with a capacity of half a kotyle each (c. 0.13 l.). It is not clear whether ληκυ( ) in Text 38 is an abbreviation of λήκυθος or ληκύθιον.

μελίεφθον (τό)[5] : *honey-jar* (Text 38, l. 32)
Μελίεφθον is a rare word and in the papyri is only attested in Text 38.

ὀξίς (ἡ): *vinegar-cruet* (Text 38, l. 24)
An ὀξίς is usually earthenware, but can exceptionally be made of bronze or silver.

ποτήριον (τό): *drinking-cup* (Text 38, l. 12)
Earthenware, silver, bronze or tin ποτήρια are frequently attested in the papyrological material[6]. The drinking-cup of Text 38 is made of bronze.

σκάφιον (τό): *a small bowl* (Text 38, l. 13)
Σκάφιον is the diminutive of σκάφη, a trough or bowl.

SLEEPING REQUIREMENTS
(§52 continued)

ἐντύλη (ἡ): *mattress* (Text 38, l. 15)
Ἐντύλη is a hapax; the simple term τύλη is more frequently attested and is often equated with προσκεφάλαιον (*pillow*)[7]. In several cases, however, two different items are involved. Προσκεφάλαιον and τύλη often appear alongside one another[8]. A προσκεφάλαιον is usually a pillowcase, whereas a τύλη denotes the pillow itself: a τύλη σὺν πλήσματι[9] is a pillow with stuffing, τύλη μεστή[10] is a stuffed pillow, a τύλη κενή[11] is an empty pillow, τύλη ἐριδίων ἐσφραγισμένη[12] is a sealed pillow filled with sheep's wool. The pillow which

---

1 *E.g.*, P. Ifao I 30, l. 19; P. Wash. Univ. I 58, l. 21 and 23.
2 *E.g.*, P. Oxy. I 114, l. 9; X 1269, l. 27.
3 UPZ I 104, col. II, l. 15.
4 SB VIII 9834b, l. 30.
5 Text 38, l. 32.
6 See Reil, *Kenntnis des Gewerbes* (1913), p. 45, 58, 67 and 71.
7 See Reil, *Kenntnis des Gewerbes* (1913), p. 119 and 121, *s.v.*; Wipszycka, *L' industrie textile* (1965), p. 119-120 and n. 46.
8 *E.g.*, P. Lond. VII 1979, l. 6; P. Meyer 62, l. 6-7; P. Oxy. I 109, l. 14-15; XXIV 2424, l. 36 and 38; Ed. Diocl. 28, 46: τύλη μετὰ προσκεφαλαίου.
9 P. Wisc. I 30, col. III, l. 2.
10 Stud. Pal. XX 67, l. 31.
11 P. Hamb. I 10, l. 38; P. Oxy. I 109, l. 4.
12 P. Wisc. I 30, col. II, l. 18 with *ZPE* 5 (1970), p. 23-24.

is filled, is usually made of linen, as suggested by the profession of τυλυφάντης, but may also be of leather[1].

Τύλη may, by extension, also denote the mattress; it is not surprising that in a list of bedding 77 προσκεφάλαια (pillowcases) are recorded as opposed to only 4 τύλαι (mattresses or pillows?)[2].

The hapax ἐντύλη is translated by the first editor of Text 38[3] as «wrapper or rug», by Reil[4] as «Decke, Überwurf» and in the lexicon of LSJ as «rug or cushion». In my view, ἐντύλη is rather a mattress: the term is defined as an ἐριᾶ ἐντύλη πό(κων) λε, "a woollen mattress made of 35 fleeces". Information about the amount and the weight of a πόκος is found in the Zenon-archive. One πόκος is the fleece provided by one sheep every eight months[5]. The weight if one πόκος corresponds to 2 minas or c. 714 grammes[6]; consequently, an ἐντύλη of 35 fleeces weighs almost 25 kilogram. That is too heavy for a cushion or a blanket or a rug, but is normal for a woollen mattress. In addition, mattresses of 40, 50 and 60 minas (14, 18 and 21.5 kilogram, respectively) are found in the Zenon-archive, as well as a στρωμάτιον, a small and lighter mattress made of 25 minas (9 kg.) of wool[7].

ἐπικρεμασ(τὸς) ταρσ(ός) (ὁ): *hammock* (Text 42, l. 5)
Ταρσός (*mat*) is preceded here by a hapax, not yet listed in the lexicon of LSJ. The verb ἐπικρεμάννυμι (*hang over*) and the simple adjective κρεμαστός (*hung, suspended*) are well-known. The papyri mention a λ[ύχνος κρε]μαστός (*hanging lamp*)[8], a οὐηλάρ(ιον) (=*velarium*) ἐρειν(οῦν) κρεμ(αστόν) (*a suspended, woollen velarium*) and a στρῶμ(α) κρεμ̣α̣σ̣τ(όν); both these items were, according to the editor, part of the decoration of the Episcopal throne (5th-6th century)[9]. An ἐπικρεμασ(τὸς) ταρσ(ός) is undoubtedly a hammock.

κασῆς (ὁ): *horse-cloth*
See above, the equipment of horse and cavalryman.

πόδες κλίνης (οἱ): *legs of a bed* (Text 37, l. 7; 38, l. 27 and 30-31)
Bed legs are rarely mentioned in the papyri[10]. It is odd that in the list of travelling goods (Text 38) and in the list of goods delivered to the temple (Text 37), legs of a bed are recorded, but not the other components of the Greek bed: four or six legs bore a rectangular frame of four planks (ἐνήλατα or -ον[11]) over which ropes (κειρία[12], τόνοι or σπάρτα[1]) were stretched; on top of that a mattress was laid; mattresses are listed in Text 38.

1 P. Ryl. IV 627, col. II, l. 28.
2 P. Meyer 62, l. 6-7.
3 P. Lond. II p. 11, n. line 15.
4 Reil, *Kenntnis des Gewerbes* (1913), p. 117.
5 PSI IV 377, l. 7 with Pap. Lugd.-Bat XXIA, p. 141.
6 P. Cair. Zen. IV 59774.
7 P. Cair. Zen. II 59241.
8 P. Ryl. IV 627, col. III, l. 55.
9 P. Grenf. II 111, l. 16-17.
10 *E.g.*, P. Oxy. III 520, l. 17: 6 legs of a bed.
11 For the papyri, see, for instance, PSI VI 616, l. 16-17 of the Zenon-archive: τὸ τῆς κλίνης ἐνήλατον.
12 See ibidem, l. 33: τῆς κιρίας; P. Freib. IV 53, col. II, l. 35: κιρίας κλινῶν δύο.

Texts 37 and 38 mention four bed legs, furthermore box-wood legs and turned bed legs (πόδες κλίνη(ς) τορνευτοί) with a value of 1,000 drachmas[2], which remind of the κλίνη τορυνευτή in a Greek will from Pathyris[3].

προσκεφάλαιον (τό): *pillowcase* (Text 38, l. 3; Text 42, l. 3-4)
In contrast with τύλη (*pillow*, see above, ἐντύλη) προσκεφάλαιον usually denotes a pillowcase. Often a pair (ζεῦγος) of pillowcases is recorded[4]. Together with the περιστρώματα (*sheets*) they are part of the linen[5]; they may be made of the finest linen[6] or they may be embroidered[7]. Among the pillowcases handed over to Dryton's wife in Text 42, seven are flowered and one is white. The pillowcases were sometimes made of wool[8] or, exceptionally, of leather[9].

στρῶμα (τό): *mattress*, in plural also: *bedding* (Text 38, l. 2)
A στρῶμα or mattress appears to be made of wool and can weigh up to 21.5 kg.; a στρωμάτιον, a small mattress, weighs c. 9 kg. (see above, ἐντύλη). Sometimes a double (διπλοῦν) mattress is mentioned[10]. If the term is used in the plural, it can denote bedding. Thus, under the title Λόγος στρωμάτων, sheets, pillowcases and ?mattresses are listed[11]. In a list of goods of the early fourth century the στρώματ(α) appear to be (ὁμοί(ως)) cushions, sheets, a bedspread, pillows and so on[12]. A third-century papyrus mentions a τρίκλινον, a three-sided couch with linen coverings (στρώματα), embroidered throughout[13].

---

1 For the papyri, see, for instance, P. Tebt. III 793, col. VI, l. 3: κλίνη σπαρτότονος μυρικίν[η (*bed slung on ropes made of tamarisk*); P. Univ. Giss. 10, col. II, l. 6.
2 1,000 drachmas is the wage of an Egyptian employee for 12 to 50 days of work, see Reekmans, 'Ptolemaic Copper Inflation' (1951), p. 109.
3 P. Cairo Gr. 10388, l. 5 (in *AfP* 1 (1901), p. 63-65); τορυνευτός is a variant of τορνευτός.
4 *E.g.*, P. Cair. Zen. I 59092, l. 22.
5 P. Lond. VI 1942, l. 5; προσκεφάλαια and περιστρώματα are often recorded together, for instance, in P. Cair. Zen. I 59060, l. 9; P. Lond. VII 2159, l. 26-27; PSI IV 391, l. 35-36; VI 616, l. 9; VII 858, l. 33-34.
6 Ibidem; P. Hamb. I 106, l. 6.
7 P. Oxy. X 1277, l. 8.
8 P. Col. Youtie 1, l. 7.
9 P. Lond. VII 1979, l. 6.
10 PSI VII 858, l. 32.
11 P. Meyer 62.
12 P. Ryl. IV 627, col. II, l. 27.
13 P. Oxy. X 1277, l. 7.

WRITING AND READING MATERIALS
(§52 continued)

ἀναγνωστικά (τά): *reading matter* (Text 37, l. 12)
The adjective ἀναγνωστικός has an active and passive meaning: "capable of reading", or "suitable for reading". The ἀναγνωστικοί mentioned by Aristotle in his *Rhetorica*[1] are poets of whom the writings are readable and widespread. The term ἀναγνωστικά is only found in the list Text 37 among accounts and hereditary documents and probably indicates regular reading matter, such as popular literary works.

βυβλίον (τό) and **βυβλιοθήκη** (ἡ): *papyrus sheet, document* (Text 38, l. 9; Text 42, l. 12, 13 and 20) and *book-case* (Text 38, l. 8)
A βυβλίον is a strip of a βύβλος (papyrus roll) or, if it is written on, a document. In Texts 38 and 42 it is abbreviated as βυβλί(α) or βυ(βλία); I prefer to interpret the abbreviations as being plural, since this form is more frequently attested (for instance in the Zenon-archive[2]) and since the chest or bag in which βυ(βλία) are kept, undoubtedly contained more than one sheet of papyrus. In Text 42 βυ(βλία) in l. 12 and 13, probably blank sheets, are opposed to βυ(βλία) γεγρα(μμένα), written sheets, in l. 20.

κληρ( ): *hereditary documents*? (Text 37, l. 11)
Κληρ( ) in Text 37 is recorded among documents such as accounts, reading matter and wooden tablets, which are put away in baskets. In his commentary, the first editor Grenfell[3] solved the abbreviation as κλῆρ(οι); as a consequence, the lexicon of LSJ listed among the meanings of κλῆρος that of «title-deeds». As κλῆρος is nowhere else attested with this meaning, I prefer to take κληρ( ) as an abbreviation of κληρ(ονομικά), documents related to the inheritance, a word formation similar to the following ἀναγνωστικά (see above).

λόγος (ὁ): *account* (Text 37, l. 11)
The term λόγος is well-attested with the meaning "account". In Text 37, these accounts are stored in baskets together with other documents (see above, κληρ( )).

λυχνία (ἡ): *lamp stand* (Text 37, l. 6 and 15; 38, l. 17)
Λυχνία, a lamp stand with one or more λύχνοι, lamps, is frequently attested in the papyri. In Text 37, two iron lamp stands and a base of a lamp stand are listed.

πύξινον (τό): *wooden tablet* (Text 37, l. 12 and 14)
The term πύξινον is problematic. In Text 37 the adjective πύξινος is found in connection with legs of a bed and points to box-wood legs; box-wood is a very hard type of wood which scarcely splits. In the same text, some ξύ(λινα) πύξινα[4] are mentioned and, at the end of the

---

1 Aristoteles, *Rhetorica* 1413b 12.
2 See Pap. Lugd. Bat. XXI B, index *s.v.*
3 P. Grenf. I 14, comm. on l. 11.
4 In theory, ξυ( ) πύξινα may be an abbreviation of ξύ(λα) πύξινα with ξύ(λα) as substantive (*wooden tablets*; ξύλον is not attested with this meaning) and πύξινα the adjective (*of box-wood*); this interpretation is unlikely, since the text further on reads πύξινα ξενικῶν ξύ(λων), which clearly shows that πύξινα is the substantive.

list, six πύξινα are recorded, of which four are of a foreign type of wood (πύξινα ξενικῶν ξύ(λων). These πύξινα are apparently wooden tablets. Πύξινον is, however, never attested with this meaning .

MISCELLANEA
(§**52** continued)

ἄσφαλτος (ἡ): *asphalt* (Text 42, l. 15)
Terminology: the ancient Greek word ἄσφαλτος has a broader meaning than the modern technical term. The terminology concerning petroleum and its derivatives was not clear in ancient times. In order to understand what is meant by asphalt in the ancient world, it is necessary to distinguish between several modern products which are distilled from petroleum. They are classified in increasing order of carbon grade: the higher the carbon grade, the higher the boiling point is and the less volatile and the more solid the products are (from gasiform through liquid to half-solid and solid). The main products are:

1. petroleum gas **2.** crude petrol (supplies several types of petrol, also called naphtha) **3.** crude petroleum (supplies kerosene and lamp petroleum) **4.** gas oil (or diesel oil) **5.** residue oil (supplies lubricant, wax and paraffin, as well as asphalt bitumen; asphalt bitumen mixed with mineral material such as clay, stone or sand, results in **asphalt**).

In Antiquity[1] the deep and rich oil wells had not yet been struck. Only the surface sources were explored. As no distillation techniques were known, petroleum was used in the form in which it was discovered. The different forms of petroleum in Antiquity are classified here in increasing order of carbon grade (from gasiform through liquid to half-solid and solid); the term **asphalt** in Antiquity appears to correspond to what we call petroleum in modern times and is defined as being liquid (no. 2) or solid (no. 4):

1. gas: in Mesopotamia **2.** liquid: Strabo[2] records ἄσφαλτος ὑγρά or νάφθα (*bitumen liquidum* in Pliny[3]), which may be black or light-coloured and highly inflammable. The black "liquid asphalt" or νάφθα is petroleum with a higher grade of solid components rich in carbon, whereas the white and inflammable "liquid asphalt" or νάφθα is petroleum with a higher grade of volatile components poor in carbon (compare our crude petrol). The term naphtha is generally used in Antiquity for the liquid form of petroleum. **3.** oleaginous: sporadic[4] **4.** half solid to solid: Strabo[5] calls the (half) solid form of petroleum ἄσφαλτος ξηρά, Diodorus Siculus[6] ἄσφαλτος στερεᾶ (*dry* or *solid asphalt, bitumen durum*). When **asphalt** is mentioned in ancient texts, this solid form of petroleum (and not the liquid form) is usually meant. It is found on the surface of salt water, where it is usually mixed with water and mineral material such as sand or stone; this muddy pulp is called *limus* by Pliny. Well-known in Antiquity was the ἀσφαλτῖτις λίμνη[7] or *lacus asphaltites*[1], that is

---

1 See the profound discussion by R.J. Forbes, *Studies in Ancient Technology*, I, Leiden 1964, p. 1-124: Bitumen and Petroleum in Antiquity; see also RE, *s.v.* Asphalt.
2 Strabo 16.1.15.
3 *Naturalis Historia* 35.178.
4 See, for instance, Plinius, *Naturalis Historia* 35.178 (*bitumen pingue oleique liquoris*).
5 Strabo 16.1.15.
6 Diodorus Siculus 19.98.
7 Diodorus Siculus 19.98; Josephus, *Bellum Judaicum* 1.657; 3.515; Idem, *Antiquitates Judaicae* 17.171 (λίμνη ἀσφαλτοφόρος); Stephanus Byzantius, *s.v.* Ζόαρα (ἀσφαλτῖτις θάλασσα).

the Dead Sea, where asphalt appeared on the surface. Further solid forms of petroleum were found in porous stones (stone asphalt or *terra* [2]). These solid forms of petroleum, called asphalt in Antiquity, were particularly multi-purpose.

Find spots in Antiquity: surface oil wells were found especially in Iraq and Iran, but also in Syria and Palestine, where the Dead Sea was called the "Asphalt Lake" (see above). Africa was and still is poor in oils wells. The petroleum products which were used in Egypt were imported from Syria and Palestine (especially the Dead Sea)[3].

Use in Antiquity: the solid form of petroleum was used in Ancient Mesopotamia as mortar or as an impervious substance for building constructions, ships, basket work or mats; roads, embankments, quays, floors and bridges were made of this solid petroleum. It served, furthermore, as paint and/ or a protective layer for outside walls, doors, woodwork, and so on, and was a suitable binder for all kinds of materials, for instance, for fixing the blade of a knife in its handle. Petroleum was used for lighting to a lesser degree; according to Strabo[4], the black liquid asphalt or naphtha (see above) was sometimes burnt in lamps. There were several other applications; petroleum is, for instance, found in medicines for external and internal use.

Egypt and the papyri: information on the use of imported petroleum in Ancient Egypt is scarce[5], especially since it is not clear what term was used in Egyptian for petroleum or asphalt. It is possible that it occurs in pharmaceutical prescriptions. It may also have been used as a binder for wooden objects such as coffins. It is doubtful whether petroleum products were used in the mummification process before the Ptolemaic period.

The papyri give more information on the use of petroleum in Greco-Roman Egypt. It is called asphalt in Greek texts, which apparently points to the solid form of petroleum (see above). In the Zenon archive (third century B.C.) asphalt is recorded in two accounts concerning costs of paint work: P. Cair. Zen. IV 59763 records that all requirements for the paint work are available, except for the pitch and asphalt (l. 12); P. Cair. Zen. V 59847 calculates the expenses for the painting of the windows: alongside red and dark blue paint, asphalt is needed for the "ears"[6] of windows, undoubtedly because of its impervious quality. Text 42 shows a last Ptolemaic example of asphalt, transported in a small receptacle, but the context does not make clear what purpose the asphalt was kept for.

In a letter from the second century[7] κῦφι, a kind of incense, is mentioned which is compounded, among other things, of resin and asphalt; it is to be burnt before the god Herpebekis. In a prescription of a μάλαγμα or salve, asphalt appears to be one of the ingredients[8]; according to Dioscorides[9] asphalt is indeed emollient, suppressing inflammations and healing wounds. Finally, in a third-century letter a merchant from Coptos lists "asphalt

---

1 Pliny, *Naturalis Historia* 2.226; 5.71; 7.65
2 Pliny, *Naturalis Historia* 35.178.
3 The wells of the Red Sea were used on a modest scale not until Roman times.
4 Strabo 16.1.15.
5 See R.J. Forbes, *Studies in Ancient Technology*, I, Leiden 1964, p. 7-12, 25-26, 96 and 103.
6 The term "ears" is still used to denote the protruding parts of buildings constructions.
7 Pap. Lugd. Bat. I 13, l. 6.
8 PSI Congr. XVII 19, 5, and see *BASP* 18 (1981), p. 16-19.
9 Dioscorides 1.73.

from Syria" among products which are commonly used in drugs. Thus, the papyrological documents affirm what we already knew about the use of asphalt from ancient Mesopotamia.

The accounts

§53. *Structure.* —

• Introductory part

If the beginning is preserved, the account may be dated (Texts 40 and 41); the remaining part of the introduction:

- may refer to the private account of the person who records his receipts and expenditure. In Texts 40 and 41 the private account is called ἴδιος λόγος, a term which is rarely used for accounts of private people[1]; it usually refers to the special governmental account of that name[2]. In other private accounts, for instance that of the twins in the Serapeum of Memphis[3], a private account is simply called λόγος, account. The demotic accounts on ostraka from Pathyris have *p3 ip NN* (*the account of NN*)[4].

- may contain a heading; the list of goods in Text 37 is followed by a short account, called λό(γος) (πυροῦ). The demotic account Text 45 bears the title *p3 ip n n3 sw.w r.tw NN* (*the account of wheat which NN has given to*)[5].

• the account

The accounts of the archive of Dryton and his family have the regular constructions:

- *to receive* : ἔχειν or προέχειν (*to receive in advance*), *from* : παρά with genitive, *through the agency of* : διά with genitive.

- *to give* : δίδωμι, *to* : dative, πρός with accusative or ὥστε with dative; *through the agency of*: διά with genitive.

- *to deposit* : παρατίθεμαι, for this verb, see Text 37, comm. on l. 1.

- in Texts 39 and 40, lines are drawn before a new subdivision; parallels for this practice are found in the archive of the twins in the Serapeum at Memphis: a line is usually drawn before each new date.

§54. *Trade.* — The accounts mainly register the trade of products in kind, especially wheat, but also barley, kroton or castor-oil (for a woman when she was pregnant and when she gave birth, see Introduction to Text 44), green fodder (γράστις) for cattle, jars of wine and the spice kardamon (Text 41 reveals that the ratio wheat : kardamon is 1 : 1.5, see Introduction to Text 41).

According to Texts 39 and 45, objects are sold or purchased and in Text 39 loans with interest are recorded.

---

1 On the private account (ἴδιος λόγος) of the ruler, see P. Bingen 45 and P. Van Minnen, in *Ancient Society* 30 (2000), p. 33, comm. on l. 8.

2 See Swarney, *Idios Logos* (1970), p. 7-40.

3 UPZ I.

4 See, for instance, O. dem. Zürich 32.

5 For parallel constructions, see Text 45, Introduction.

Another source of income appears to be the lease of a plot of newly-gained land (νῆσος) and the rent of a wagon. According to Text 40 Dryton leases both a νῆσος and a wagon, whereas according to Text 44 he appears earlier to have leased out both a νῆσος and a wagon (see below). A νῆσος, called in demotic *t3 m3j* (*the newly-gained land*), is land which came into being when the Nile deposited silt either in the Nile resulting in an island which could become attached to the riverside later on, or which resulted in a peninsula on the bank of the Nile. This newly-gained land could easily be irrigated and was thus suitable for cultivation[1].

For the lease of the new land of Lamenthis (Text 40) Dryton pays "14 artabas of wheat, 2 artabas of barley, as embadikon 30 drachmas [- -]", and for the leasing out of his plot of new land he receives "[- -] as embadikon for the new land 60 artabas of wheat". Several Ptolemaic ostraka from Thebes[2] and Coptos[3] inform us on the embadikon. When someone leased a plot of land such as an orchard of fig trees, a vineyard, a vegetable garden, a kleros, he not only had to pay a rent (ἐκφόριον) but also the ἐμβαδικόν to the owner: to enter on the property of the creditor (ἐμβαδεύει)[4] and to come (temporarily) into possession of it (ἐμβαδεία: entering into possession), the lessee had to pay the ἐμβαδικόν (*sc.* τέλος) [5], the "Übernahmesteuer"[6] or the takeover tax. As suggested by B. Kramer, the ἐμβαδικόν may be identical to the newly-attested ἐμβαδόν-tax[7].

In some ostraka the rent and the embadikon are paid together[8]; the total amount is not always recorded. Three ostraka only mention the embadikon: in O. Wilcken 1358 from 130 B.C. the amount is 5 artabas of wheat, in BGU VI 1458 from 124 B.C. 1 artaba of wheat; O. Wilcken 1080 from 134 B.C. does not mention the amount to be paid. When the rent and the embadikon are paid together, the amounts appear to be much higher: 8000 drachmas for an orchard of fig-trees[9] or 13 talents for a vegetable garden in Thebes[10]. The embadikon is thus relatively low in comparison to the rent, which is confirmed by Text 40: the 14 artabas of wheat and the 2 artabas of barley are undoubtedly the rent, worth c. 3000 drachmas, whereas the embadikon amounts to only 30 drachmas. The 60 artabas of wheat in Text 44 are apparently the total of rent and embadikon.

The embadikon is paid in kind or in cash: in kind when grain-bearing land is involved, in cash when orchards or vineyards are leased. This resembles the tax system: the tax on grain land is regularly paid in kind[11], whereas the tax on orchards or vineyards (the apomoira) is charged in cash in the second century B.C.[12]

The rent and embadikon are paid between June and September, that is after the harvest and at the termination of the lease contract. The demotic lease contracts from Pathyris[13] show that

1 See, *e.g.*, Bonneau, *Le fisc et le Nil* (1971), p. 70, 79, 115, 117, 193.
2 O. BGU VI 1458; O. Cambr. 17; O. Wilck. 1024; 1237; 1358.
3 O. Wilck. 1080.
4 On the writings with δ instead of τ, see B. Kramer, in *AfP* 43 (1997), p. 325, n. 43.
5 See Mommsen apud O. Wilck. I, p. 190-191.
6 Translation by B. Kramer, in *AfP* 43 (1997), p. 324-325.
7 Ibidem.
8 O. Wilck. 1024; 1237; 1262.
9 O Cambr. 17.
10 O. Wilck. 1237.
11 Vandorpe, 'The Ptolemaic Epigraphe' (2000), in *AfP* 46, p. 165-228.
12 Vandorpe and Clarysse, 'The Ptolemaic Apomoira' (1998).
13 See Felber, *Demotische Ackerpachtverträge* (1997), p. 34-60; 125-129.

land was leased for the period of one year, that is from the inundation in August/ September until the inundation of the following year. According to Text 40, Dryton also paid the rent and the embadikon in August/ September; in Text 44, the date is missing. Only in O. Wilcken 1358 is the embadikon paid in January.

§55. *Deposit and transport of goods.* — The depots recorded in the accounts are the ταμιεῖον or magazine[1], the δῶμα or housetop[2], the κλῖμαξ or staircase[3] and, for products in kind, the κυψάλη or receptacle[4].

A δῶμα is the housetop, the roof garden surrounded by a balustrade. It could be closed off and served, among other things, as a depot for goods[5].

The deposit ἐπὶ κλίμακος (*on the staircase*) seems odd. Papyrological evidence informs us that such a staircase had an own door and thus functioned as a separate room of the house. Excavations in Karanis show that a staircase could even be a separate structure in the form of a tower[6]. The use of the staircase as depot is also found in other texts: according to a Ptolemaic inventory five jars with wheat are put ἐπὶ τῆς κλίμακος[7].

Apart from in the archive of Dryton's family, there is only one attestation of the Greek word κυψάλη (= κυψέλη, a *receptacle* or *reservoir*). A text of the Zenon archive mentions 300 l. of kroton deposited in a κυψάλη[8]. In the demotic version of the text the κυψάλη is called *šꜥ.t n ꜥm* (*a receptacle of clay*) and appears to be rectangular according to the determinative of *šꜥ.t*. The same κυψάλη, too large to be transported, is said to be lying in the granary (κεῖται ἐν τῶι σιτοβολῶνι); this parallel text makes my amendment to Text 44, l. 6-7, ἐν μεγ(άληι) κυψά(ληι) ἔξω [κειμέ]ν̣η̣ι very probable. In a comedy by Aristophanes[9] a κυψέλη with corn is further mentioned with a capacity of 6 medimni, that is c. 312 l., a capacity similar to that of the reservoir of the above-mentioned Zenon papyrus (300 l.).

In Dryton's account Text 44 a μεγάλη κυψάλη is twice recorded; the κυψάλη is rightly called "large", since its capacity is two to three times larger than the κυψάλαι known up to date: one μεγάλη κυψάλη contains 40 artabas of wheat (c. 1200 l.), the other 37 artabas (c. 1110 l.)[10].

For the transport of goods[11] two special wagons were in use: the ἅμαξαι and the ἀπῆναι, which were probably smaller. Both vehicles had four wheels, in contrast to the passenger wagons such as the ἅρματα, which had only two wheels and could sporadically be used for the

---

1 Text 39, l. 10.
2 Text 44, recto l. 1.
3 Text 39, l. 17; Text 43, verso l. 4.
4 Text 44, verso l. 6-7.
5 See Husson, *Oikia* (1983), p. 63-65.
6 See Husson, *Oikia* (1983), p. 150-151.
7 P. Giss. Univ. 10, col. III, l. 9.
8 Pap. Lugd. Bat. XX 13.
9 Aristophanes, *Pax* 631.
10 The capacity of the artaba in Pathyris is not fixed, but usually amounts to c. 30 l., see Vleeming, 'The Artabe in Pathyris' (1979), in *Enchoria* 9, p. 93-100.
11 Vigneron, *Le cheval dans l' Antiquité* (1968), p. 150-153.

transport of goods as well. The ἅμαξαι and the ἀπῆναι were usually pulled by cattle[1], but also by horses[2]. The ἅμαξα was also used as a unit of measure, a "wagon load"; such a wagon load might consist, for instance, of 15 artabas[3] or of 5 to 6 artabas[4]. Owners of a transport wagon have to pay a tax: the τέλος ἁμάξης[5].

According to Text 40, Dryton rents a ἅμαξα and according to Text 44, he hires out his own ἅμαξα. Text 43, verso l. 2, shows that the wagon was used for transport (ἐφ' ἁμάξης) and Dryton's will of 126 B.C. (Text 4, l. 8-9) informs us that Dryton owned indeed a ἅμαξα with its equipment (ἐπισκευή). ἅμαξαι are often rented according to the papyri. The common term μισθός[6] is used to denote the rent, as, for instance, in Text 40, whereas in Text 44, verso l. 1, the term κάτεργον (*use, service*) is found.

In both accounts Texts 40 and 44 the rent of the wagon is more or less the same: in Text 40 it amounts to 10.5 artabas of barley (= 6.3 artabas of wheat) and 15 artabas of wheat, a total of 21.3 artabas of wheat; Dryton pays part of it in copper drachmas. In Text 44 Dryton asks a rent of 25 artabas. Converted into copper drachmas[7], the rent comes to 4260 and 5000 drachmas, respectively; this is a high price, considering the fact that a workman earned 20 to 120 drachmas a day at that time[8]. The period during which the wagon was rented, is not recorded. According to the date of the account Text 40, the lease of the land and the rent of the wagon ended in August/ September. Land was leased for a year (see above), from the inundation in August/ September until the inundation of the next year. The wagon was possibly rented during the harvest period (May/ June until July/ August).

---

1 Vigneron, *Le cheval dans l' Antiquité* (1968), p. 153-155; P. Panop. Beatty 2, col. VI, l. 153; SB VIII 9699, col. XXIII and XXVI; SB VIII 10204, l. 7-8.

2 P. Hib. II 211, col. II, l. 16.

3 See L.S.B. MacCoull, in *ZPE* 25 (1977), p. 157, comm. on l. 8.

4 P. Grenf. I 39.

5 See O. Wilck. I, p. 145-146: the tax on wagons is often mentioned in connection with the tax on the driving of donkeys, see also O. Ont. Mus. II 160, introduction.

6 *E.g.*, in P. Oxy. XX 2272, recto col. II, l. 63 and 68; SB VIII 9699, col. XXIII, l. 500; col. XXVIII, l. 615-6, 623.

7 In Text 40, l. 8, 1 artaba of wheat is worth 200 drachmas of copper.

8 Reekmans, 'Ptolemaic Copper Inflation' (1951), p. 109.

37

GREEK LIST OF TEMPLE GOODS AND ACCOUNT
Written by ?Esthladas

? H. x W. = 28.5 x 8.3 cm 18 Nov. 139 B.C.

British Library, P. inv.no. 609 Verso [purchased from Grenfell on 9 Nov. 1895] = **P. Grenf. I 14**.
Photograph. — No photograph available.

Description. — The recto contains traces of a Greek text written along the fibres; 10 lines are preserved; this text is presumably broken off at the top and at the right-hand side. At the foot, a margin of 10.5 cm is visible. Between lines 4 and 5 the horizontal fibres are missing; they undoubtedly once carried another line of Greek text. At the top and bottom, some more horizontal fibres are missing. Once the text was no longer useful, it was washed off and the papyrus was torn into pieces in order to serve as second-hand paper (see §49).

The verso shows traces of an older Greek text as well, written along the fibres and washed off. The older text only takes up a small part of the verso. The verso has been re-used for a list of goods and for an account (Text 37). The writer left a top margin of 4 cm before he wrote down the list of goods. Below the list a blank space has been left since part of the older text was still clearly visible at that spot. After these traces of the older text the writer continued and wrote down an account which is less wide than the list of goods, since vertical fibres were missing on the right-hand side. The list and the account are both complete.

Introduction

Text belonging to the archive of Dryton, Apollonia and their offspring. — See §48. The handwriting can be attributed to Esthladas and is very similar to that in Text 38, see §64-66.

Contents and structure. — The text contains A. a list of goods and B. an account.

A. Lines 1-17 contain a list of goods which have been deposited (παρατίθεσθαι, see comm. on l. 1) in the temple with the priest Patous. The latter is closely connected to the family of Dryton (see pros. 04).

B. Lines 18-22 contain an account of wheat: Harekysis, who cannot be identified with certainty since his father's name is missing, has further (συν-) deposited goods with the priest Patous: 30.5 artabas of wheat during the last six months (see comm. on l. 21).

Text and Translation

*The characters marked in **bold** are written above or beneath the preceding character in the original text (see also §64-66).*

("Ετους) λβ Φαῶφι κγ̄ παρεθέμεθα	*Year 32, 23 Phaophi. We have deposited*
ἐν ἱερῶι παρὰ Πατοῦτι ἱερεῖ·	*in (the) temple with the priest Patous:*
γλωσσόκομα γ̄, ἄ**λ**(λο) μ**ι**(κρὸν), κίσται	*3 caskets, another small casket, two chests,*
δύο, βῖκος ἐσφ**ρ**(αγισμένος) ῥητίνης,	*a sealed jar (filled) with resin of pine,*
λεκάνη, μώστια β ἐσφ**ρ**(αφισμένα),	*a pot, 2 sealed baskets,*
ἐπίστατον, λυχνίαι β σιδ**η**ρ(αῖ),	*a support, 2 iron lampstands,*
ἀριστοφόρον, πόδες κλ**ί**(νης) π**ύ**ξ**ι**(νοι),	*a breakfast-tray, box-wood legs of a bed;*
———	———
ἀσφαλιῶνες β 'Αττικοὶ ἐν ὧι	*2 Attic safes in which*
ζμύρνα, κίστη μ**ε**(γάλη) ξ**υ**(λίνη) μεστὴ	*myrrh (is kept), a big wooden chest full of*
ζμύρνης, θιβεῖς β̄	*myrrh; 2 baskets*
———	———
ἐν αἷς λόγοι καὶ κλ**η**ρ( ) καὶ	*in which accounts, hereditary documents (?),*
ἀναγνωστικὰ καὶ ξ**ύ**(λινα) πύξινα·	*reading matter and wooden tablets (are kept);*
———	———
\`τὰ´ ἀπὸ π**ό**(λεως)· μώϊον μ**ι**(κρὸν) ἐν ὧι	*objects from the city: a small receptacle in which*
πύξινα ϛ̄ ἀφ' ὧν πύξινα	*6 tablets (are kept) of which 4 tablets*
ξενικῶν ξ**ύ**(λων) δ̄, βάσιν λ**υ**χνί(ας),	*are made of foreign woods, a base of a lamp stand,*
< ? >ἐν ὧι μώϊα Παρίου λ**ί**θου	*< a ? > in which 2 receptacles of Parian marble (are kept).*
β.	

Vacat

18 Λό(γος) (πυροῦ)·
ἀπὸ Φαρμοῦθι τοῦ λα (ἔτους)
20 ἕως Φαῶφι λβ (ἔτους)
συνυπέδω(κε) Ἁρεκῦσις
22 (πυροῦ) λ∠ τὸ πᾶν.

Account of wheat:
from Pharmouthi of the 31st year
until Phaophi year 32,
Harekysis has made a further deposit
of wheat, (making) 30 1/2 (artabas) in total.

4 ρητι in ῥητίνης corr. 6 ἔτι στατόν ed., ἐπίστατον Wilamowitz (P. Grenf. II, p. 211) 7 κα ed., κλί(νης) Wilamowitz (P. Grenf. II, p. 211) 8 ἀσφαλῶνες ed., ἀσφαλίωνες Wilcken (BL I, p. 180); ἐν ὧι, *l.* ἐν οἷς 11 αἷς corr. ex ὧι, Wilcken (BL I, p. 180) 13 τά ed., \`τά´ Wilcken (BL I, p. 180); ἀπόλο(ιπα) ed., ἀπὸ πό(λεως) legimus 14 ϛ ed., ϛ̄ legimus 15 δ ed., δ̄ legimus; βάσιν, *l.* βάσις 21 συνεπιέδω ed., συνυπέδω(κε) Wilcken (apud Otto, *Priester und Tempel* (1905-08), I, p. 320).

Notes

The vocabulary is discussed in §52.

1 Παρεθέμεθα: the verb παρατίθεσθαι has frequently the meaning of "to deposit (what belongs to one in another's hands)" in the papyri. According to W. Otto, on the other hand, the verb may have the meaning of "to give in pledge" (*Priester und Tempel* (1905-08), p. 320); he refers to CPR I 12, l. 3. In the latter text, however, it is explicitely recorded that the goods are given in pledge (ἐνέχυρα) and the end of the contract stipulates that the debtor looses the goods which he gave in pledge in the event that he does not return the loan on time. As in the list Text 37, no similar clause or pledge is mentioned, Otto's suggestion is unlikely. In addition, the same verb παρεθέμεθα is clearly used in the meaning "we have deposited" in the account Text 44, recto l. 1.

8 ἀσφαλιῶνες: the editor read ἀσφαλῶνες (a hapax) which has justly been corrected by Wilcken (BL I, p. 180) into ἀσφαλιῶνες (a further hapax). The lexicon of LSJ still lists ἀσφαλών rather than ἀσφαλιών.

21 συνυπέδω(κε): the compound verb συνυποδιδόναι is a hapax. The use of συν- suggests that the verb has the same meaning as παρατίθεσθαι in l. 1 and should be translated as "to deposit also" (as already suggested in LSJ). W. Otto, on the other hand, proposes taking the verb as a variant of ὑποτιθέναι, "to pledge", thus confirming his suggestion about παρατίθεσθαι (see comm. on l. 1).

38

GREEK LIST OF TRAVELLER'S ITEMS

Written by ?Esthladas

Plate XV

? H. x W. = 31 x 10.8 cm after 153/152 or 142/141 B.C.

British Library, P. inv.no. 402 Verso [bought between early 1891 and mid 1895] = **P. Lond. II 402 Verso** (p. 11-12).
Photograph. — Plate XV.

Description. — The text on the recto, written along the fibres, is an official account of which only a small part is missing. It may have been part of an official register which was later used as second-hand paper. The verso contains a list of goods which is complete, but is damaged along the folds in two spots (l. 7 and l. 13-14). To the left of the list a *kollesis* is visible, at circa 3.5 cm from the left-hand edge.

Introduction

Papyrus belonging to the archive of Dryton, Apollonia and their offspring. — See §48. The handwriting can be attributed to Esthladas and is very similar to that in Text 37, see §64-66.

Text on the recto . — The recto contains an official account registering the payment of taxes in kind (wheat). The editor notes that several readings are doubtful because of the very cursive hand[1]. In addition, several passages are damaged; the writer erased some lines and then rewrote them between the lines, which complicates the reading of the text (l. 6-7, 18-24). As the editor noted, the document is to be dated to year 29 (l. 20, 21, 22 and 24), that is 153/152 or 142/141 B.C., a *terminus post quem* for the list on the verso.

The tax list on the recto was undoubtedly part of an official register. It is not clear to which town it should be attributed. The names of the taxpayers are not typical of Pathyris. Names such as Psenamounis and Poöris rather suggest a Theban origin; there are also some Jewish names; ostraka from Thebes (East Bank) show that several Jews lived in that region[2].

Text on the verso. — The back of the official account described above has been re-used by a private individual for a list of traveller's items of the type needed by a cavalryman on campaign.

---

1 P. Lond. II 402 recto (p. 10-11) with BL I, p. 243; l. 9-12 = C. Pap. Jud. I 42.

2 See, for instance, U. Kaplony-Heckel, 'Theben-Ost II', in *ZÄS* 126 (1999), p. 41-54, no. 8 and 9 (for Isakis son of Straton, compare O. Bodl. 164).

Text and Translation

The characters marked in **bold** *are written above or beneath the preceding character in the original text (see also §64-66).*

Γρα̣(φὴ) σκε**υ**(ῶν)·	*List of (traveller's) items :*
στρ**ώ**(ματα) β,	*mattresses: 2,*
προσκεφ**ά**(λαια) δ,	*pillowcases: 4,*
κασ̣αὶ γ,	*horse-cloths: 3,*
ἄ**λ**(λος) κασ(ῆς) ἐφίππ**ι**(ος) φοιν**ι**(κοῦς),	*another purple horse-cloth;*
σά̣κκος ἐν ὧι θώραξ,	*bag containing a breastplate,*
λεκάνη ‵Μενδη̣[σία]′, χαλιν[ὰ]	*a pot from Mendes, bridles*
ταύρεα, ζωστ**ῆρ**(ες) **ἱ**π(πικοί), β**υ**βλ**ιο**θ(ήκη),	*from bull's hide, horse girths, a book case,*
κατωμηλ( ) χιλ**ω**(τὴρ) ἐν ὧι β**υ**βλ**ί**(α),	*a shoulder bag containing sheets of papyrus,*
ὑποδήμα(τα), μ**έ**(γας) ἀσκός·	*sandals (and) a big leather sack;*
———	———
ἄ**λ**(λος) σάκκος ἐν ὧι ὀθόνια	*another bag containing*
καινὰ καὶ παλαι(ά), ποτήριον	*new and old linen, a drinking-cup*
χ**α**λκ(οῦν), σκ[ά]φιον, κόνδυ,	*of bronze, a small bowl, a drinking-cup,*
ἵνιον, χιτ**ῶ**[**ν**] παιδικ̣[ός,]	*a hin-jar, a boy's tunic;*
———	———
ἐριᾶ ἐντύλη π**όκ**(ων) λε,	*a woollen mattress made of 35 fleeces;*
———	———
σακκοπήρα ἐν ἧι ἱμ**ά**(τιον), χλ**α**(μύς),	*a travelling sack containing a coat, a short mantle,*
λυχνίαν, ταπίδιον πυρρὸν	*a lamp stand, a small red carpet*
καὶ ἱδρῶια καινὰ γ,	*and 3 new sweat cloths,*
ἄ**λ**(λα) ἱδρῶια παλ**αι**(ὰ) ς (ὧν)	*6 other old ones of which*
στρογγ**ύ**(λα) β, ὅπλα δ,	*2 are round, 4 weapons,*
μάχαιραι β σπειραντικαί,	*2 sabres with curved blades,*
σφαίρ**ω**(μα) **ἱ**π(πικὸν), δέρμ**α** οἰνοφόρον,	*a horse muzzle(?), a leather bag holding wine,*
ἐγγ**υ**θήκη, ποτ**ήρ**(ιον), κώθων,	*a stand for vessels, a drinking-cup, a Lacedaemonian drinking-cup,*
χιλωτήρ, ὀξίς,	*a horse's nose-bag, a vinegar-cruet,*
μελανοδόκον, λήκ**υ**(θοι) β, ξύστρ**α**,	*an inkstand, 2 oil-flasks, a scraper,*
ἄ**λ**(λοι) σάκκοι κενοὶ β,	*2 other, empty bags,*
πόδες κλίνης δ̅,	*4 legs of a bed,*
ἀγωγεῖς β, ἀλαβαστροθ**ή**κη	*2 leading-reins, a small box,*

ἄβαξ παρ' Ἰναρῶτι κείμενος, κελλίβας, ἄλ(λοι) πόδες κλίνη(ς) τορνευτοὶ Ἀ	*a dining plate kept by Inaros, a portable dining table, other turned legs of a bed, (worth) 1000 (drachmas);*
———	———
ἄλ(λος) λεκάνη Ἐσ, ἄλ(λος) μελίεφθα ˋφˊ,	*another (bag containing) a pot (worth) 3200 (drachmas), another (bag containing) honey-jars (worth) 500 (drachmas),*
ἄλ(λος) μι(κρὸς) κόνδυ Ṫ χαλινὰ Ṫ (γίνονται) χ	*another small (bag containing) a drinking-vessel (worth) 300 (drachmas and) bridles (worth) 300 (drachmas), total 600 (drachmas).*

---

1 γραμ[ed., Γρα(φὴ) σκευ(ῶν) legimus 4 καλαι ed., κλιναι BL I, p. 243, κασαί legimus 5 κασεφιππι ed., κας εφιππι(ον) BL I, p. 243, κασ(ῆς) ἐφίππι(ος) supplevimus; φαινι ed., φαινι(κικον) = φοινι(κικον) BL I, p. 243, φοινι(κοῦς) legimus et supplevimus 6 θωρα = ed., θωρα(ξ) = BL I, p. 243, θώραξ legimus 7 λεκανης ed., λεκάνη legimus; ˋΜενδη[ ]ˊ ed., ˋΜενδη[σία]ˊ supplevimus; χαλιν[ ] ed., χαλιν[ά] supplevimus 8 ζωστη(ρια) ed., ζωστῆρ(ες) legimus; πρ ed., ἱπ(πικοί) legimus et supplevimus; βυ q λι θ ed., βυβλιοθ(ήκη) legimus et supplevimus 9 εν ηι ed., ἐν ὧι legimus; βυ β λι ed., βυ(σσοι) βλι(ναι) BL I, p. 243, βυβλί(α) legimus et supplevimus 12 παλαι ed., παλαι(ον) BL I, p. 243, παλαι(ά) supplevimus 13 υαλας ed., <γ>υαλας BL I, p. 243, χαλκ(οῦν) legimus; σκ . . . ον ed., σκ[ά]φιον BL I, p. 243 14 χιτω ed., χιτώ[ν] legimus; παιδα[ ] ed., παιδικ[ός] legimus et supplevimus 16 ι μαχαια ed., ἱμά(τιον) χλα(μύς) BL I, p. 243 17 λυχνίαν, *l.* λυχνία; ταγειδιον ed., ταπίδιον BL I, p. 243 19 παλ' ed., παλαι(ά) legimus et supplevimus; ϛι ed., ϛ (ὧν) legimus 22 «the meaning of the symbol following σφαιρω(τήρ?) is doubtful. It can hardly be the numeral = 900» ed., μι(κρός) BL I, p. 243, ἱπ(πικόν) legimus 23 κηθιυ ed., κώθων legimus 25 μελανδοκον ed., μελανοδόκον BL I, p. 244 28 αλαβαστρουθηκαι ed., ἀλαβαστροθή(κη) καί BL I, p. 244, ἀλαβαστροθήκη legimus 29 παριναρ . . κ . μνος ed., παρ' Ἰναρῶτι κείμενος BL I, p. 244 30 κελλι β̄ ιασο ed., κελλί(βας) β̄ ιασο Husson (BL VIII, p. 178), κελλίβας legimus 31 Ἀ φ ed., Ἀ legimus (cf. l. 32) 32 μελι εφ . . ed., μελίεφθα ˋφˊ legimus 33 χαιον ed., χαλινά legimus

Notes

The vocabulary is discussed in §52.

1 Γρα̣(φὴ) σκευ(ῶν) (γρα̣μ̣[ed.): the following traces are visible: 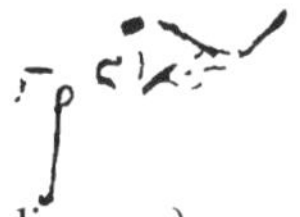

4 κασ̣αί (καλα̣ι̣ ed., κλιναι BL I, p. 243): 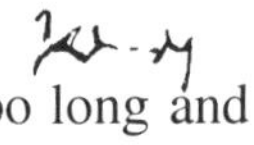 : for the reading καλα̣ι̣, which is senseless, the right part of the *labda* is too long and too flat; there is not enough space for the reading κλιναι; my reading κασ̣αί fits perfectly and is confirmed by the addition of ἄλ(λος) to κασ(ῆς) in the following line.

5 ἄλ(λος) κασ(ῆς) (κάς BL I, p. 243): I prefer κασ(ῆς) to κάς for two reasons: 1. the preceding line has κασ̣αί, the plural of κασῆς; therefore, l. 5 has ἄλ(λος) κασ(ῆς), another κασ(ῆς); 2. κάς is only attested in Hesychius (see Kramer, 'κάς, κασῆς und κάσ(σ)ος' (1999), in *AfP* 45, p. 192), whereas κασῆς is well-attested (see, *e.g.*, P. Tebt. I 38, l. 22).

φοινι(κοῦς) (φαινι ed., φαινι(κικον) = φοινι(κικον) BL I, p. 243, φοινι(κοῦς) legimus et supplevimus): the additions φοινί(κικος) (purple-red, red) and φοῖνι(ξ) (intense red) are less probable, see Kramer, 'κάς, κασῆς und κάσ(σ)ος' (1999), in *AfP* 45, p. 193-194.

6 θώραξ (θωρα = ed., θωρα(ξ) = BL I, p. 243): the editor and later correctors saw two lines following θωρα, but did not connect them with a ξ. In addition, the beginning of the third, lower line of the ξ is visible.

7-8 χαλιν[ὰ] ταύρεα: in my view, ταύρεα depends on χαλιν[ὰ]: χαλινός (heteroclite) may be neuter in the plural (see the lexicon of LSJ) and even in the singular: see P. Cair. Zen. IV 59659, l. 11, which has χαλινὸν ἱππικὸν ἔχον ῥυτῆρας (*a horse bridle with reins*). Otherwise, ταύρεα has to depend on the following ζωστηρ( ) ἱπ( ). ζωστήρ is, however, a masculine word; ζωστήριον would be a hapax legomenon.

8 βυβλιοθ(ήκη) (βυ q λι θ ed.): 

9 βυβλί(α) (βυ β λι ed., βυ(σσοι) βλι(ναι) BL I, p. 243):  the reading βυβλί(α) is confirmed by βυβλιοθ(ήκη) of the preceding line.

10 με(γάς): με( ) could, in theory, depend on the preceding word ὑποδήμα(τα).

19 παλαι(ά) (παλ' ed.):  compare the writing of παλαι(όν) in Text 42, l. 4 and 7 (with facsimile)

(ὢν) (ι ed.): 

23 κώθων (κηθιυ ed.): 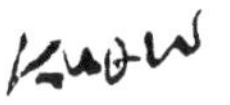 The word κήθιν in the lexicon of LSJ, based on the wrong reading of the first editor, should be deleted.

28 ἀλαβαστροθήκη (αλαβαστρουθηκαι ed., ἀλαβαστροθή(κη) καί BL I, p. 244) : the reading ἀλαβαστροθή(κη) καί (instead of ἀλαβαστροθήκη) has been suggested since the *êta* was written above the *thêta* which usually implies an abbreviation; in Esthladas' and Dryton's hands, however, characters are often written above another character in the middle of a word (see §64-66).

30 κελλίβας (κελλ̣ι̣ β̄ ̣ιασο ed., κελλ̣ί(βας) β̄ ̣ιασο Husson (BL VIII, p. 178)) :

κελλίβας and not κελλ̣ι(βας̣) β̄ ̣ιασο; the alleged *omikron* is a dark spot on the papyrus.

31-2 ἄλ(λος) <σάκκος ἐν ὧι> : I interpreted ἄλ(λος) as ἄλ(λος) <σάκκος ἐν ὧι> and not as an adjunct of the goods mentioned in l. 31-32. μελίεφθα̣, for instance, is not yet mentioned in the list and thus cannot be referred to by ἄλ(λος), whereas χαλινά has already been recorded (l. 7) and is not referred to by ἄλ(λοι); ἄλ(λος) has to be connected with a named receptacle, that is σάκκος.

Compare the construction of l. 32: ἄλ(λος) <σάκκος> μι(κρὸς) <ἐν ὧι> κόνδυ ͞τ χαλινο̣ὶ ͞τ (γίνονται) χ.

31 μελίεφθα̣ `φ´ :

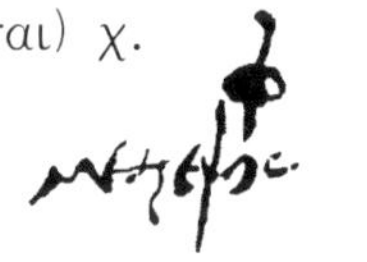

there was just enough place to write μελίεφθα̣, whereas the value of this object, φ or 500 drachmas, had to be written above the line. That is the reason why the editor took the 500 drachmas with the preceding line where legs of a bed of a value of 1000 drachmas are recorded. There is, however, a large blank spot between 1000 and 500 drachmas; for this reason I prefer to take the 500 drachmas with μελίεφθα̣.

32 χαλινά̣ (χαι̣ο̣ν̣ ed.) :

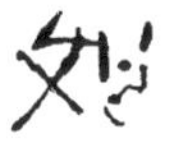

for the writing of χαλ-, compare χαλκῆ in Text 42, recto l. 17 (with facsimile).

39

GREEK ACCOUNT

written by ?Dryton

Plate XVI (verso-recto); see facsimile below

[Collage]

? *fragment A* H. x W. = 31.6 x 13.3 cm *fragment B* H. x W. = 3 x 1.5 cm circa 137/136 B.C.

Fragment A = British Library, P. inv.no. 641 [bought on 9 Nov. 1895 from Grenfell] +
Fragment B = British Library, P. inv.no. 686e [bought in July 1896 from Grenfell] = **unpublished**.
Photograph. — Plate XVI (verso-recto); see my facsimile below.

Description. — The account has been written on the dark, rough verso of the papyrus, and is continued on the recto (2 lines); the major part of the recto has remained blank. In addition, the text is broken off on the left-hand side: from l. 1 to l. 20 two thirds of the account and from l. 21 to 26 one third is missing. The text is full of abbreviations and of characters which are written above another character in the middle of a word (see §64-66).

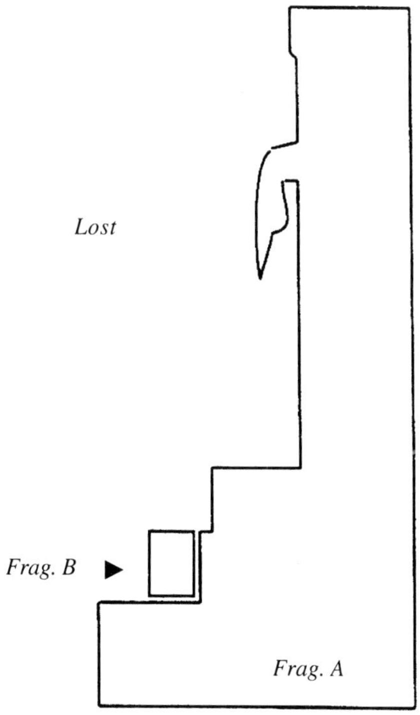

Verso

Introduction

Text belonging to the archive of Dryton, Apollonia and their offspring. — See §48.

Contents. — Text 39 is an account written in Dryton's hand. As the papyrus is broken off on the left-hand side, only a few provisional conclusions may be drawn:

A. *Receipts and expenditure*: contrary to the other accounts, Text 39 deals with the expenditure and the receipt of large sums of money (l. 3, 4, 8-9, 11-14, 25, 26), as a result of the sale or purchase of objects or the lending of money at interest (l. 8-9). The following wares are recorded: sealed alabaster jars (?) (l. 1-2), an Egyptian bed worth 1000 drachmas (l. 3), κύαθοι or jars worth 500 drachmas (l. 4), a sabre with belt (l. 5) and a bronze drinking-cup (l. 24).

B. *The towns where and the people with or through the agency of whom business is done*: business is done with the help (διά or ἔχει) of people who are closely connected with Dryton's family: Dryton's son Esthladas (l. 3 and 29; pros. 504) and Stachys and Pelops (l. 10, 18, 22, 24, 26; pros. 09-10).

Some people, with whom dealings are done, may be identified with people known from Pathyris (see comm.): Didymos (l. 18), Sentotoes (l. 20), Phibis son of Patseous (l. 23), Taimouthis (l. 25), Mr. X son of Psemmonthes (l. 26), Thaibis (l. 27) and Choreris (l. 30). Finally, an embalmer from Hermonthis is mentioned (l. 21).

Dryton and his entourage do not only trade in Pathyris (explicitely mentioned in l. 25), but also in Thebes (Diospolis Megale, l. 7 and 24). Of importance is the mention of the gymnasium of Diospolis Megale (l. 7). Three gymnasiarchs are attested for Thebes and ostraka record the payment of a contribution for oil for the gymnasium (the evidence dates from the second century B.C.)[1]. A gymnasium is known to have existed in Karnak[2].

Date. — In l. 24 a year 34 is recorded[3]. This may be the reigning year of Ptolemy VI ((148/7 B.C.) or Ptolemy VIII (137/6 B.C.). As the other (dated) accounts and lists are to be situated in the period 139-134 B.C. and as Esthladas (mentioned in l. 3 and 29) was still a young boy in 148/7, a date under Ptolemy VIII (137/6 B.C.) is to be preferred.

---

1 See W. Clarysse, 'Greeks in Ptolemaic Thebes' (1995), in Pap. Lugd. Bat. XXVII, p. 7 and note 17.

2 Th. A. Brady, 'The Gymnasium in Ptolemaic Egypt', in *The University of Missouri Studies. A Quarterly Research* 11 (1936), p. 10 and n. 6: inscription probably to be dated in the period 116-108 B.C.

3 L. 29 has year 30 + x (L λ[ ]).

Facsimile and transcription

Verso

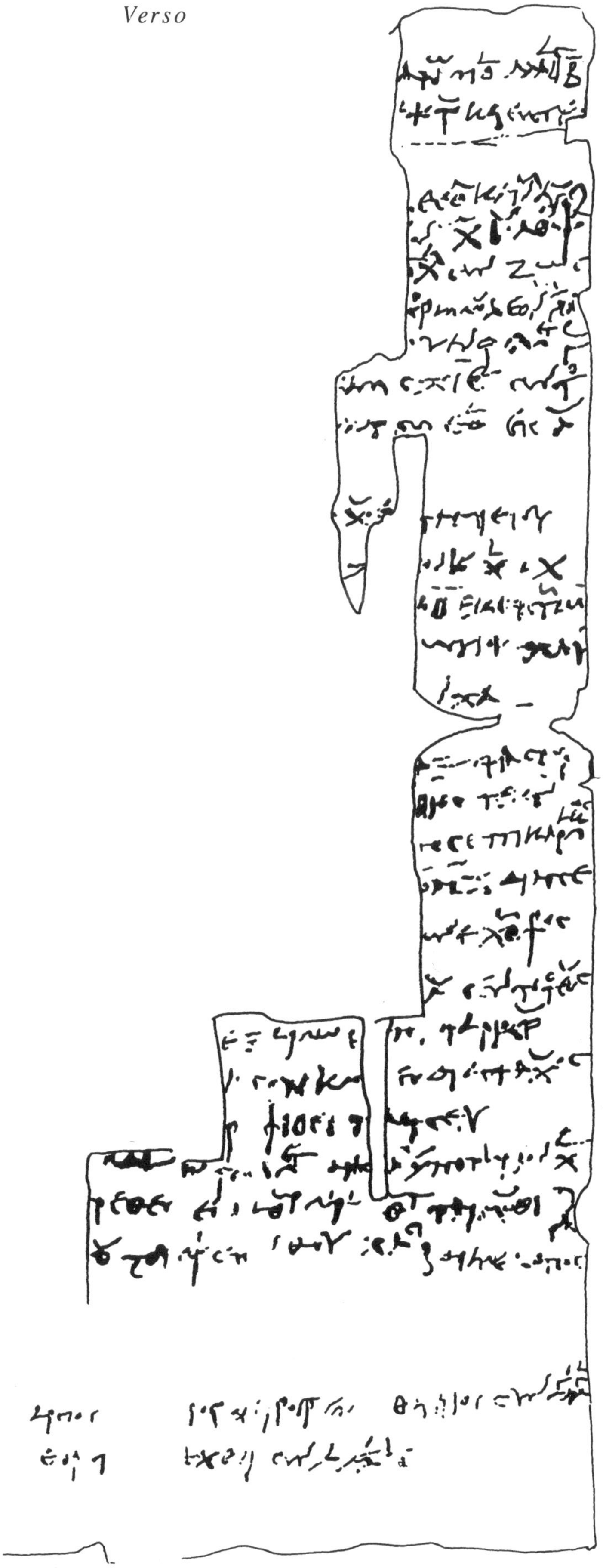

ω α ας
1]αν πιθ αλαβ β̄
υ
2]ακτ και ε . . . .
λ η υ
3]εςθ κλιν αιγ ʼΑ
α υ οι
4].ν .χ καθ ψ
ααι
5]μχ ϲυν ζωϲ
υ α
6]χραμμολεοννν.
εγ υ
7]ουεν Δ̣ρ̣μ γ
ο
8].αϲτ ϲ Λ̄ ῑε ϲυντ
α υ
9]ϲυντοκωι εδ ειϲ α
υ
10]χοε[ ]ταμιειου
α
11] Λ̄ [ ]ον. . χ ∠ χ
η
12] β̄ εκκιϲτϲ η
13]ωϲυιου Λ̄ α Ί
14]/ Λ̄ α.
15].ξ.ταϲι..
ων
16]βιοϲ τεκν
οϲ
ακ
17].οϲεπικλιμ
υ
18].διδ διαπε
η ρ
19]ηνεχθπ^οϲ^
υ ο υ
20]α ϲεντοτεοϲ
υ
21]εξερμωνθ . . . ταριχε
υ
22]μονκα[ ]εν διαϲταχ^οϲ^
23]ρα̣ φιβει πατϲε$_{ο}$υ
εγ υ α
24]λδ L εν Δ̣ρ̣μ δια ϲ[ ]αχποτηριονχ
υρ υγ υ
25]υρεθεν εν π̣αθ παρα θ ταιμοθι ʼΑ
υ
26]ο τουψεμμωνθου Λ̄ αʼΒ διαπελοποϲ
μα
αγ
27 αρ . ο̣υ̣ [- - -]ιοϲχε̣ιρογρ. . θαιβιοϲ ϲυναλλ
αγμα
28 θορτ [- - -]εχθ . . ϲυναλλ

Interpretation

Verso

1 [- - -]α̣νω( ) π̣ιθά(κναι) ἀλαβάσ(τριναι) β̄
2 [ἐσφραγισμέναι τῶι - δ]ακτυ(λίωι) καὶ ε. . . .

---

3 [- - -] Ἐσθλ(άδ -) κλίνη Αἰγυ(πτία) ᾿Α
4 [- - -] . ν.χα̣( ) κύαθοι ψ
5 [- - -] μ̣ά̣χαι(ρα) σὺν ζωσ(τῆρι)
6 [- - -]χραμμου( ) Λεοννα.( )
7 [- - - τ]οῦ ἐν Δι(ὸς) πό(λει) μεγ(άληι) γυ(μνασίου)
8 [- - -] . ασ̣τ̣ο̣ς (τάλαντα) ιε σὺν τό(κωι)
9 [- - -] σ̣ὺ̣ν̣ τ̣ό̣κ̣ωι ἐδά(νεισ) εἰς αὐ(τ)

Vacat

10 [- - - διὰ Στά]χυ(ος) ἐ[κ] ταμ̣ιείου
11 [- - -] (τάλαντα) [ ]ον . . χα(λκοῦ) (δραχμὰς) χ
12 [- - -]. β̄ ἐκ κίστης η̣
13 [- - -]ως υἱοῦ (τάλαντον) α ᾿Γ̣
14 [- - -] (γίνονται) (τάλαντον) α.
15 [- - -] . ξ . τα̣σ̣ι̣ . .
16 [- - - ι]βιος τέκνω̣ν̣
17 [- - -] . ος ἐπὶ κλίμακος
18 [- - -]. Διδ̣υ̣(μ) διὰ Πέ(λοπος)
19 [- - -]η̣νέχθη πρὸς
20 [- - -] αὐ(τ) Σεντοτοέους
21 [- - -] ἐξ Ἑρμώνθ̣. . . ταριχευ(τ..)
22 [- - -]μονκα[μ]εν διὰ Στάχυος
23 [- - - πα]ρ̣ὰ̣ Φίβει Π̣α̣τ̣σεο̣ῦ(τος)
24 [- - - τοῦ] λδ (ἔτους) ἐν Δι(ὸς) πό(λει) μεγ(άληι) δια̣ Σ[τ]άχυ(ος) ποτήριον χα(λκοῦν)
25 [- - - ε]ὑ̣ρεθὲν ἐν̣ Π̣αθύρ(ει) παρὰ θυγ(ατρὶ) Ταιμούθι(ος) ᾿Α
26 [- - παρὰ -]ο̣υ̣ τοῦ Ψεμμώνθου (τάλαντον) α ᾿Β διὰ Πέλοπος

Vacat

27 Αρ. . ο̣υ̣ [- - -]ιος χε̣ιρόγρ(αφον). . Θαίβιος συνάλλαγμα
28 Θορτ̣[- - -]εχθ . . συνάλλαγ(μα)

Recto

(continues the account of the verso):
facsimile, transcription and interpretation

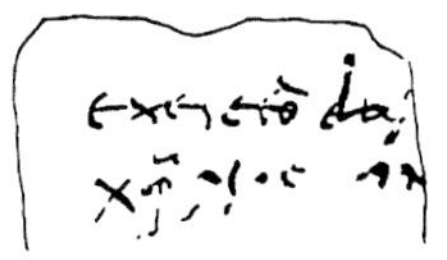

λ
εχειεcθ Lλ[
η
χορριοc ..[

Ἔχει Ἐσθλ(άδας) (ἔτους) λ[- - -]
Χορήριος . .

---

29 (ἔτους) corr. ex ἐκ

Notes

The vocabulary is discussed in §52.

18 Διδυ(μ): a Didymos, son of Menon, a soldier from the town Itou, is recorded in a papyrus from Pathyris of 128 B.C. (*YCS* 28 (1985), p. 79-83 = SB XVIII 13848).

20 Σεντοτοέους: a Sentotoes, daughter of Thotsytmes, is found in P. dem. Gebelein Heid. 2 of 180-170 B.C.

21 ἐξ Ἑρμώνθ. . . ταριχευ(τοῦ): for "embalmers of the persons of Hermonthis", see P.W. Pestman, in P. Choach. Survey, p. 230, note b.

23 Φίβει Πατσεοῦ(τος): a witness called Phibis, son of Patseous, is found in P. dem. Adler 8, verso l. x+5 (104 B.C.) ; P. dem. Ryl. 17, verso l. 3 (118 B.C.).

27 Θαίβιος: the mother of the well-known Horos, son of Nechouthes (see Vandorpe, *Archives from Pathyris* (2001), §39), is called Thaibis; she is a relative of Dryton: she is a sister of Thrason, uncle of Dryton's wife Apollonia (pros. 305).

30 Χορήριος: a Choreris is named as owner of a piece of land in Pathyris in P. Stras. II 81, col. II, l. 23 (115 B.C.).

40

GREEK ACCOUNT
written by Dryton

Plate XVII (recto); see facsimile below

? H. x W. = 15.2 x 11.1 cm 22 Aug. /20 Sept. 135 B.C.

British Library, P. inv.no. 611 Recto b [purchased from Grenfell on 9 Nov. 1895] = **P. Grenf. I 16.**
Photograph. — Plate XVII (recto); see facsimile below.

Description. — The accounts Texts 40 and 41 have been written by Dryton on a piece of papyrus torn off a draft or copy of a petition. This piece of papyrus thus contains **1.** the end of a petition, written on the recto along the fibres (see description of Text 33bis). The large margin of 7 cm below the petition and the blank verso have been re-used for two private accounts: **2.** Text 40 on the recto written at right angles to the petition and across the fibres (with a bottom margin of 2.5 cm), and **3.** Text 41 on the verso and across the fibres. Both accounts Text 40 and 41 are complete. The papyrus is damaged in two spots along the folds: at the height of l. 4 and l. 8 of Text 40.

The papyrus is of a poor quality, since both on the recto and the verso fibres are missing. In one spot there is even a hole in the papyrus. As a consequence Dryton had to stop writing in the middle of a name: δι' Ἀλύ *vacat* κιος (Text 40, l. 4).

Introduction

Contents. — Text 40 is a private account, called ἴδιος λόγος in l. 1 (see §53), of Dryton recording several costs. The account dates from the period after the harvest (August-September) when taxes and rents had to be paid. See also the Introduction to this chapter, §53-55.

A. L. 2-3 show that Dryton has leased a plot of newly-gained land (νῆσος) from a man called Lamenthis (see comm. on l. 2). Dryton pays a rent of 12 artabas of wheat and 2 artabas of barley and a takeover tax (ἐμβαδικόν) of 30 drachmas; then the text breaks off. See furthermore §54.

B. According to l. 4-6 Dryton pays through the agency of Alukis (see comm. on l. 4) 7 artabas of barley — it is not clear why — in addition to 60 artabas of wheat to a man called (?)Andreias[1] in accordance with a contract (συνγραφή), probably a loan-contract.

C. L. 7-9 treat the rent for a wagon (ἅμαξα, see §55). Dryton has to pay 10.5 artabas of barley and 15 artabas of wheat. The barley and 5 of the 15 artabas of wheat are paid in kind, whereas the remaining 10 artabas of wheat are paid in cash, that is at the rate of 200 drachmas per artaba, in total 2000 drachmas. The payment in cash has been

[1] No Andreias is attested in Pathyris.

undertaken through the agency of Pelops, often attested in relation to Dryton's family (pros. 10); Pelops has retained 200 drachmas out of the total of 2000 drachmas.

RENTAL PRICE FOR THE WAGON	°10.5 art. of barley
	°15 art. of wheat, of which
	— 5 art. in kind
	— 10 art. in cash = 2000 drachmas, of which
	Pelops still owns 200 drachmas.

Facsimile and transcription

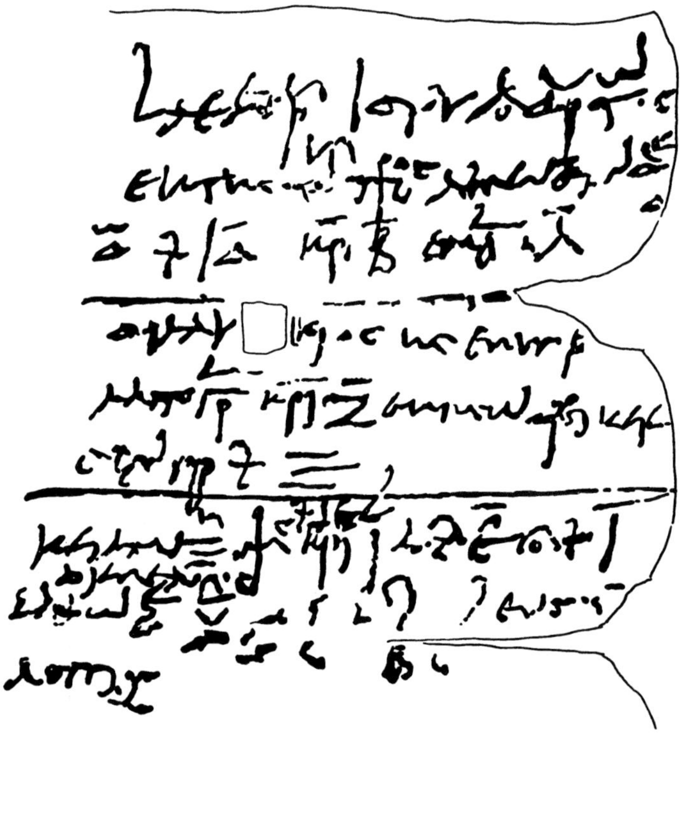

ϵcoη υ ων
Lλϵμ ρ ιδιου λ̣δρτοc
η ροc ϵ
ϵκτηcν π λαμϵνθινδ
ω α . δ
δ Ɨ ιδ̄ κρ̄ι̅ β̄ ϵμβ ∠ λ̄ [ ]

ϵ
διαλυ κιοc ωcϵπ. . γ[ ]
α
λατογρ κρ̄ι̅ ζ̄ αιπροcανδρϵι κατα
συνγρ Ɨ ξ

η c Ɨιϵ *l*
καιαμαξ μ κρ̄ι̅ ῑ∠ Ɨϵ̄ ͡ Ɨῑ
διαπϵλοποc
ϵ α
ανθων δ χ αν c∠ ʼΒ *l* ϵνπ[ ]
λοπι∠c

Interpretation

1 (Ἔτους) λε Μεσ̣ο̣ρὴ ἰδίου λό(γου) Δρύτωνος.
2 Ἐκ τῆς νή(σου) πρὸς Λαμένθιν δέ-
3 δω(κα) (πυροῦ) ιδ̅ κ̅ρ̅ι̅(θῆς) β̅ ἐμβα(δικὸν) (δραχμὰς) λ̅ [- -] . δ̣[- -]·

---

4 δι' Ἀλύ *Vacat* κιος ὡ̣ς ἐπη̣γγε[ί-]
5 λατο γρα(?μματεὺς) κ̅ρ̅ι̅(θῆς) ζ̅, αἳ πρὸς (?)Ἀνδρεί(αν) κατὰ
6 συνγρ(αφὴν) (πυροῦ) ξ

---

7 καὶ ἁμάξη(ς) μισ(θὸς) κ̅ρ̅ι̅(θῆς) ι̅∠̅ \`(πυροῦ) ιε (ὧν)ʹ (πυροῦ) ε̅ (λοιπὸν)
(πυροῦ) ι̅
8 ἀνθ' ὧν δέ(δωκα)\`διὰ Πέλοποςʹ χα(λκοῦ) ἀ̣ν̣(ὰ) σ (δραχμὰς) Ἐ (ὧν) ἐν Π[έ-]
9 λοπι (δραχμαὶ) σ.

---

2 λα . άνειν ed., Λαμένθιν legimus 3 ἐμβα . λ̅ ed., ἐμβα(δικὸν) (δραχμὰς) λ̅ legimus et supplevimus 4 διὰ Λύκιος ed., δι' Ἀλύκιος interpretamur; ἐπη̣νγε[ed., ἐπη̣γγε[ί-] legimus 5 εκ̣ησ̣ ανδρει ed., αἳ πρὸς (?) Ἀνδρεί(αν) legimus et supplevimus 7 ἁμάξη μι(κρὰ) \`σ (πυροῦ) ιε∠ʹ ed., ἁμάξη(ς) μισ(θὸς)\`(πυροῦ) ιε (ὧν)ʹ legimus; κρι(θῆς) ια ed., κ̅ρ̅ι̅(θῆς) ι∠ legimus 8 χα(λκοῦ) νΣ (δραχμὰς) Ἐυ ed., χα(λκοῦ) ἀ̣ν̣(ὰ) σ (δραχμὰς) Ἐ (ὧν) legimus 8-9 ἐν π[ ] | λοιπο Σ ed., ἐν Π[έ] | λοπι (δραχμαὶ) σ legimus

Translation

1 *Year 35, Mesore. From the private account of Dryton:*
2 *because of the newly-gained land I gave to Lamenthis:*
3 *14 (artabas) of wheat, 2 (artabas) of barley, as embadikon 30 drachmas - - - ;*

---

4 *through the agency of Alukis, as (the) grammateus ordered:*
5 *7 (artabas) of barley; intended for (?)Andreias according to*
6 *contract: 60 (artabas) of wheat;*

---

7 *and the rent of a wagon: 10.5 (artabas) of barley, 15 (artabas) of wheat, of which 5 (artabas) of wheat (in kind); there remains: 10 (artabas) of wheat*
8 *in exchange for which I gave, through the agency of Pelops, 200 copper (drachmas per artaba, that is) 2000 drachmas, of which Pelops has 200 drachmas.*

Notes

The contents and the vocabulary are discussed in the Introduction to this chapter, see §53-55.

1 ἰδίου λό(γου): a nominative is expected (Mayser, *Grammatik* II.2, p. 185), as in Text 41, l. 1; perhaps the simple genitive is used instead of περὶ ἰδίου λό(γου) or instead of ἐξ ἰδίου λό(γου), since the account only deals with expenditure.

2 Λαμένθιν (ed. λα. άνειν): the name Lamenthis is not often attested in the papyri, but is found twice in Pathyris: Lamenthis, father of a Horos who negotiates a loan (P. Adler 6; 106 B.C.) and a *Lmnt s3 Pa- ?* (P. dem. Cairo II 30669, p. 101). *Lmnt* is undoubtedly the Egyptian counterpart of Greek Λαμένθις (see also Lüddeckens, *Dem. Namenbuch* I, p. 725 and G. Vittmann, in *Or* 58 (1989), p. 225).

2-3 πρὸς Λαμένθιν δέδω(κα): δίδωμι is usually construed with the dative, exceptionally also with πρός + accusative (Mayser, *Grammatik* II.2, p. 241).

4 δι' Ἀλύκιος: the editor suggested a division as: διὰ Λύκιος; rather than Lukis, the name of Alukis is found in the Ptolemaic period, even in Pathyris: Psenthotes, son of Alukis, borrows wine in 105 B.C. (P. Amh. II 48).

4-5 ὡ̣ς ἐπη̣γγε[ί-]λατο γρα(?μματεύς): the reading and interpretation of this passage, which is very cursively written, is problematic. The reading, suggested to me by W. Clarysse, is the only proposal which makes sense and is paleographically justified. It is not clear what kind of grammateus ordered the payment of the barley.

5-6 αἳ πρὸς . . (πυροῦ) ξ: the reading αἳ (ed.: ει) is to be preferred, in my view, both palaeographically and for reasons of contents. The destination of the wheat is explained by a relative clause introduced by a relative pronoun: αἵ (*sc.* ἀρτάβαι of (πυροῦ) ξ).

7 ἁμάξη(ς) μισ(θός): the editor read ἁμάξη μι(κρά) `σ´, but could not explain the remaining *sigma*. For the renting of a wagon, compare Text 44, l. 1-2: κάτερ[γον ἁμ]άξης.

(πυροῦ) ιε (ὧν): the editor read (πυροῦ) ιε (ἥμισυ). If the reading of 15 1/2 artabas of wheat is accepted, the following addition of 10+5 = 15 is not correct. Also for palaeographical reasons, the reading (ἥμισυ) is undesirable: compare the symbol for (ἥμισυ) in κρι(θῆς) ι (ἥμισυ), l. 7.

8 ἀ̣ν̣(ὰ) σ (δραχμὰς) ˏΒ (ὧν): the reading of the editor νΣ (δραχμὰς) ˏΒυ (*? 50, 200, drachmas 2400*) causes serious problems of interpretation. I prefer to read the damaged characters before σ as the common ἀν(ά) (1 artaba of wheat at 200 drachmas), that is for 10 artabas of wheat the sum of 2000 drachmas; ˏΒ is not followed by υ, but by the symbol for (ὧν): of these 2000 drachmas, 200 drachmas are kept by Pelops.

8-9 ἐν Π[έ-]λοπι (δραχμαὶ) σ (ed. ἐν π[ ] | λοιπο Σ): in accounts, the construction ἐν + person in the dative points to the debt of that person (Mayser, *Grammatik* II.2, p. 396). Pelops is often found in Dryton's accounts and in other texts of the archive (pros. 10).

41

GREEK ACCOUNT

Written by ?Dryton on behalf of Apollonia

Plate XVIII (verso); see facsimile below

? H. x W. = 15.2 x 11.3 cm 10 Sept. 135 B.C.

British Library, P. inv.no. 611 Verso [purchased from Grenfell on 9 Nov. 1895] = **unpublished**; a short description is found in P. Lond. II, p. xx.
Photograph. — Plate XVIII (verso); see facsimile below.

Description. — Text 41 is written on the back of Texts 33bis and 40 (see the description of these texts). The account has remained unpublished; it was, according to Grenfell, «hopelessly illegible». P. Lond. II, p. xx describes the account as «Complete, but defaced by rubbing». The ink has indeed disappeared in many places, especially in the middle and at the bottom. Nevertheless, the text can to some degree be deciphered.
The account is complete and has a small margin on the left- and right-hand sides, and a bottom and top margin of 1.9 cm.

Introduction

Contents. — The text is a private account (λό(γος) ἴδιος) of Dryton's wife Senmonthis (see §53), but it is written by Dryton (for his handwriting, see §64-66). As a consequence, the account starts with Ἔ̣χει, third person ("Senmonthis has"), instead of the more usual first person singular.

The account is apparently an account of wheat, since the products which are mentioned besides wheat are always converted to wheat. I propose — with reservations — the following structure (compare the scheme of the translation):

A. + *12 artabas of wheat:*

according to l. 2 Senmonthis receives 12 artabas of wheat through the agency of a person whose name is difficult to read. These 12 artabas of wheat come from several people listed in l. 3-5; the sum of the artabas of wheat mentioned in l. 3-5 is 11 3/4; thus 1/4 artaba has to be added to one of the figures of l. 3-5.

B. + *1 1/6 artabas of wheat:*

according to l. 6 two people bring in 2 artabas of barley which are to be equated with 1 1/6 artaba of wheat; this conversion of barley into wheat is lost in the lacuna of l. 7, but is paralleled in other texts.

C. + *21 1/2 1/6 artabas of wheat:*

in l. 7-9 Senmonthis receives kardamon, a spice with the Latin name *Lepidium Sativum*, the seed of which is eaten as mustard. This spice is rarely attested in the papyri[1]. The kardamon is converted to wheat, which is important since the ratio wheat : kardamon was previously unknown. The reading of the amounts is difficult, but they appear to be:

2 1/4 art. kardamon = 1 1/2 art. wheat and

30 1/4 art. kardamon = 20 1/6 art. wheat;

Thus the ratio wheat : kardamon is 1: 1 1/2 artaba.

D. *[total 34 1/2 1/3 artabas of wheat] - [31] 1/3 artabas of wheat, remains 3 1/2 artabas of wheat:*

in l. 10 something is apparently bought for [31] 1/3 artabas of wheat.

E. + *3 artabas of wheat, total 6 1/2 artabas:*

in l. 11 a certain number of wine jars are valued at 3 artabas of wheat.

F. *[- 3 1/2 artabas of wheat], remains 3 artabas:*

in the last line 3 artabas of wheat are spent for an object which cannot be read. Senmonthis has left: 3 artabas of wheat.

Some of the people with whom Apollonia alias Senmonthis is doing business may be identified. Senenouphis, daughter of Thrason, is a cousin of Apollonia (pros. 411); for Stachys, see pros. 09. It is not clear whether Senminis, wife of Psenmonthes, is Apollonia's sister (pros. 405), or whether the daughter of Herieus is a sister of Patous, son of Herieus, who is closely connected to the family of Dryton (pos. 04). The other individuals recorded in the account cannot be identified; they are: Taremphis and Tapeëis.

---

1 *E.g.*, P. Oxy. XII 1429, l. 5 of 300 A.D.

Facsimile and transcription

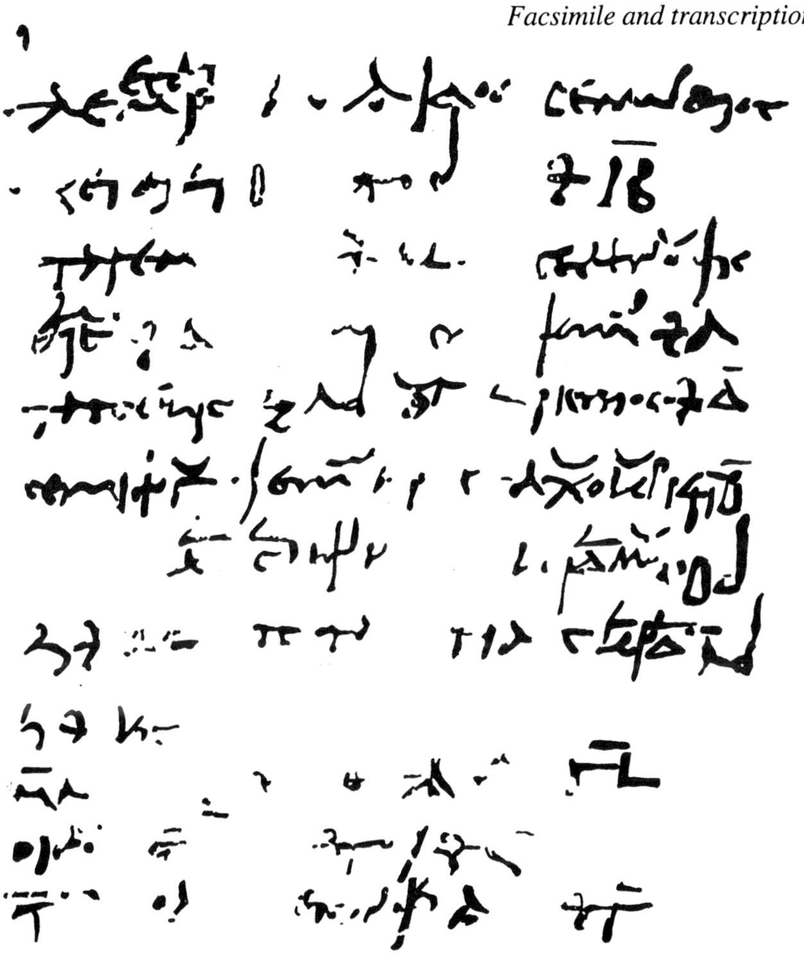

ϵco η
1 Lλϵ μ ρ κ λ̣ ιΔoc cϵμμωνθιoc
2 ϵχϵι δια..[ ].oc Ɨ ι̅β̅
υ
3 Ταρϵμ- - - Ɨ α∠ cϵνϵνoφιc
αωṿ ων
4 Θρc Ɨδ - - - Ψϵμμ Ɨα
υγ
5 ταπϵηιc Ɨ ad θ ..ριϵυτoc Ɨ δ̅
c υ ων υ υρ
6 cϵμμι ν γ Ψϵμμ κ[ ]ι σ.αχo κ κρ̅ι̅
d α α υ
7 - - - ..c ν - - - καρδμo αρ βd
αρα
8 αι Ɨα∠ π.τα- - - . .λ. .σ κ δ λ̅d
9 αι Ɨ κϛ́
10 μ̣̅α - - - Ɨ ..γ́Λ̣ Ɨ γ̅∠
α
11 oινoυ [ ]ϵ[ ] Ɨ γ /Ɨ ϛ
αι
12 τ̅[ ]oλ[ ]ϵισoνφ Λ̣ Ɨ γ̅

Interpretation

1 (Ἔτους) λε Μεσορὴ κ̣ λό(γος) ἴδιος Σεμμώνθιος.
2 Ἔ̣χει διὰ . .[. .]τ̣ος (πυροῦ) ι̅β̅,
3 Ταρέμ[φις] (πυροῦ) α̣∠, Σενενοῦφις
4 Θράσωṿ(ος) (πυροῦ) δ, - - - Ψεμμών(θου) (πυροῦ) α,
5 Ταπεῆις (πυροῦ) αd, θυγ(άτηρ) Ἐ̣ριεῦτος (πυροῦ) δ̅,
6 Σεμμῖνις γυ(νὴ) Ψεμμών(θου) κ̣[α]ὶ̣ Σ̣τ̣άχυ(ς) ὁ κύρ(ιος) κρι(θῆς) β̅,
7 . . . . . .α.σα.νι.[ ] κα̣ρδάμου (ἀρτάβαι) βd,
8 αἳ (πυροῦ) α̣∠, Π. τα̣[ ]. . λ̣ι̣ο̣ς καρδά(μου) λ̣̅d
9 αἳ (πυροῦ) κϛ́,
10 μ̣̅α̣ . . . . (πυροῦ). . γ́, λο(ιπὸν) (πυροῦ) γ̅∠,
11 οἴνο̣υ [κ]ε[ρ]ά(μια). . (πυροῦ) γ̅ (γίνονται) (πυροῦ) ϛ[∠],
12 τ̣̅. . . ο̣λ̣. . .ε̣ι̣σ̣ο̣νφαι, λο(ιπὸν) (πυροῦ) γ̅.

Translation

		Products other than wheat	Wheat or value in wheat + / -	Wheat *total*
1	*Year 35, Mesore 20. Private account of Senmonthis.*			
2	*She has (received) through the agency of . . . 12 (artabas) of wheat, (originating from)*		+12, that is:	
3	*Taremphis 1 1/2 (artaba) of wheat, Senenouphis*		+1 1/2	
4	*daughter of Thrason 4 (artabas) of wheat, . . . of Psenmonthes 1 (artaba) of wheat,*		+4 +1	
5	*Tapeëis 1 1/4 (artaba) of wheat, daughter of Herieus 4 (artabas) of wheat,*		+1 1/4 +4	12[1]
6	*Senminis wife of Psenmonthes and the guardian Stachys 2 (artabas) of barley,*	barley +2	[+1 1/6]	
7	*. . . 2 1/4 artabas of kardamon,*	kardamon + 2 1/4		
8	*which (are worth) 1 1/2 (artaba) of wheat, . . . 30 1/4 (artabas) of kardamon,*	kardamon +30 1/4	+ 1 1/2	
9	*which (are worth) 20 1/6 (artabas) of wheat;*		+ 20 1/6	[34 1/2 1/3]
10	*. . . [31] 1/3 (artabas) of wheat, remains 3 1/2 (artabas) of wheat,*	[?]	- [31] 1/3	**remains** 3 1/2
11	*jars of wine . . . 3 (artabas) of wheat, total 6 [1/2] (artabas) of wheat;*	wine	+ 3	6 [1/2]
12	*. . ., remains 3 (artabas) of wheat.*	[?]	[- 3 1/2]	**remains** 3

Notes

The contents and the vocabulary are discussed in the Introduction of this chapter, see §53-55.

1 The addition of the artabas of wheat in l. 3-5 amounts to 11 3/4; the missing 1/4 artaba is probably to be added to one of the amounts listed in l. 3-5, but has become illegible.

42

GREEK LIST OF TRAVELLER'S ITEMS
Written by ?Esthladas

Plate XXI (verso-recto); see facsimile below

?	H. x W. = 8 x 4.5 cm [Height incomplete]	26 July 134 B.C.

Heidelberg, P. inv. no. Gr. 1320 [date of acquisition unknown] = **unpublished**.

Photograph. — Plate XXI (verso-recto); see facsimile below.

Description. — The small piece of papyrus, merely 4.5 cm wide, has clearly been torn off an old text, probably from one of its margins since the top and right-hand edge are very straight. The piece of papyrus has been re-used for a personal list of traveller's items and is broken off at the bottom.

The list starts on the verso and is written across the fibres over the vertical *kollesis*. It continues on the recto along the fibres. The writer probably started on the verso since this has a straight left-hand border against which the Greek lines could be started. Compare Text 45 and §49.

Introduction

Text belonging to the archive of Dryton, Apollonia and their offspring. — See §48. The handwriting can be attributed to Esthladas.

Contents. — The papyrus contains a list of traveller's items which are given to Dryton's wife Senmonthis (l. 2).

Facsimile and transcription

Verso

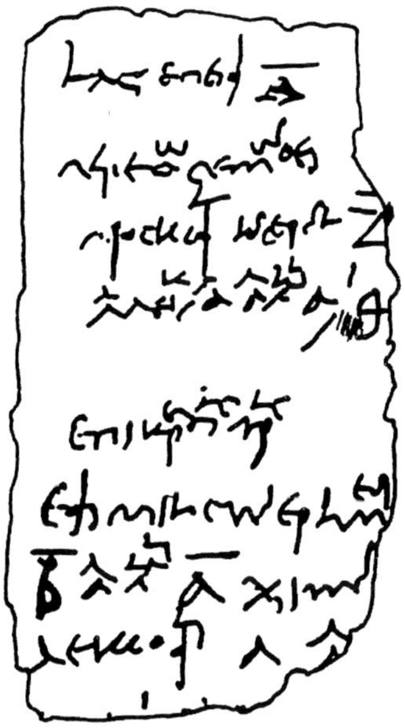

Lλς επειφ δ̄

ω ων
παρεδ cεμμ θει
α
προσκεφ ανθεινα ζ̄
αι
λ κ _ λαλ
αλευ ᾱ απ α/θ

εας ας
επικρμ τρ
ενα
εφιππια cυνεραμμ
αι
λ αλ
β̄ α π ᾱ χιτων
αι λ
λευκοφ α α

- - - - - - - - - - -

Recto

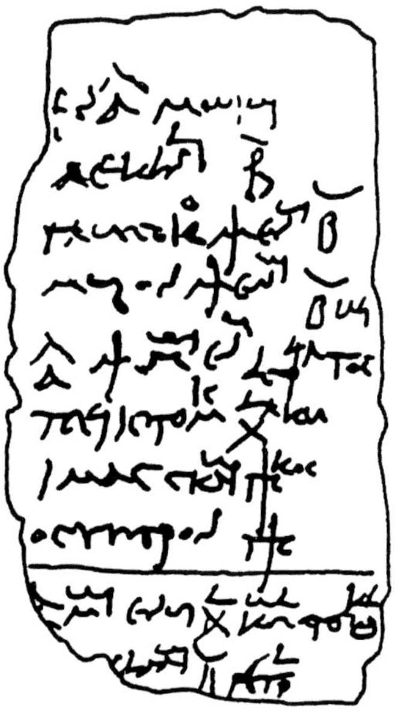

λ
ενα μωιωι
αι
λεκαν β̄
ο ωι υ
γλωccοκ|μεν β
ωι υ
μωιον |μεν β και
λ ωι ωι αλ
α |μμ εν αcφ τοc
ιc α
περιcτομ χ^λκη
ηρ κοc
ιμαc cιδ |κ
οcυcτρον |κ
λ ωι αωα κα
α μ ενωι χκμ το.θ
ωι υ α
]ναλλ β γεγρ

Interpretation and translation

Verso

(Ἔτους) λϛ Ἐπεὶφ δ̅.	*Year 36, 4 Epeiph.*
Παρέδω(κα) Σεμμώνθει·	*I have given to Semmonthis:*
προσκεφά(λαια) ἀνθεινὰ ζ̅,	*flowered pillowcases: 7,*
ἄλ(λον) λευκ(ὸν) α̅, ἄλ(λον) παλαι(ὸν) α (γίνονται) θ,	*another, white (pillowcase): 1, another, old (pillowcase): 1, total: 9,*
vacat	
ἐπικρεμασ(τὸς) ταρσ(ός),	*a hammock,*
ἐφίππια συνερ<ρ>αμμένα̣	*horse-cloths stitched together:*
β̅, ἄλ(λον) παλαι(ὸν) α̅, χιτὼν	*2, another, old (horse-cloth): 1, a tunic*
λευκόφαι(ος) α, ἄλ(λος)	*ash-coloured: 1, another, . . .*
traces	
- -	

Recto

ἐν ἄλ(λωι) μωΐωι	*in another box:*
λεκάναι β̅,	*2 pots,*
γλωσσόκο(μον) μι(κρὸν) ἐν ὧι βυ(βλία),	*another small casket containing sheets of papyrus,*
μώϊον μι(κρὸν) ἐν ὧι βυ(βλία) καὶ	*a small receptacle containing sheets of papyrus and*
ἄλ(λον) μι(κρὸν) μώϊ(ον) ἐν ὧι ἄσφαλτος,	*another small box containing asphalt,*
περιστομὶς χαλκῆ,	*a bronze noseband,*
ἱμὰς σιδηρ(οῦς) ἱπ(πι)κός,	*an iron horse chain,*
{ο} σῦστρον ἱπ(πικόν)·	*a curry-comb;*
ἄλ(λον) μώϊ(ον) ἐν ὧι χά<λ>κωμα το.καθ	*another receptacle containing a bronze item - - -,*
[- , ἐ]ν̣ ἄλλωι βυ(βλία) γεγρα(μμένα)	*. . ., in another (box) are written sheets of papyrus, . . .*
- -	

Notes

The vocabulary is discussed in §52.

18 {ο} σῦστρον: σῦστρον is preceded by an *omikron* which I cannot explain. There is no room for the article [τ]ό.

19 το.καθ: at first sight, the reading τὸ καθ' (ἕν) (*e.g.*, P. Tebt. I 47, l. 34) seems obvious, but this expression is usually followed by a detailed list of goods, which is lacking here. In addition, there is a trace of a character after the *omikron*, which I cannot explain.

43

GREEK ACCOUNT
written by ?Dryton

Plate XIX (recto-verso); see facsimile below

? | H. x W. = 17 x 8.5 cm [Width incomplete] | after 154/3 - 143/2 B.C.

Heidelberg, P. inv. no. Gr. 314 [bought by Reinhardt in 1897] = **unpublished**.
Photograph. — Plate XIX (recto-verso); see facsimile below.

Description. — Texts **43** and **44** originally belonged to the same piece of papyrus containing, on the recto, a demotic loan of corn. Since this loan apparently does not belong to the archive of Dryton and his family, it has not been published here as a separate text. The edition of the loan is added as an **appendix** to Text 43. The loan is important for the date of the Greek accounts on the recto and on the verso: it offers a *terminus post quem* for Texts 43 and 44, that is 154/3 - 143/2 B.C.

Dryton probably acquired this old loan as second-hand paper, tore it into pieces and re-used it for his private accounts Texts 43 and 44. The margin on the recto as well as the blank verso were most suitable for writing down some small private notes.

Both accounts Text 43 and 44 contain part of the old demotic loan contract. Text 43 shows the middle part of the first seven lines of the loan, Text 44 the end of the first three lines. As l. 7 of the loan records one of the last or the last contract clause, only followed by the name and title of the scribe, the loan may have counted eight or nine lines.

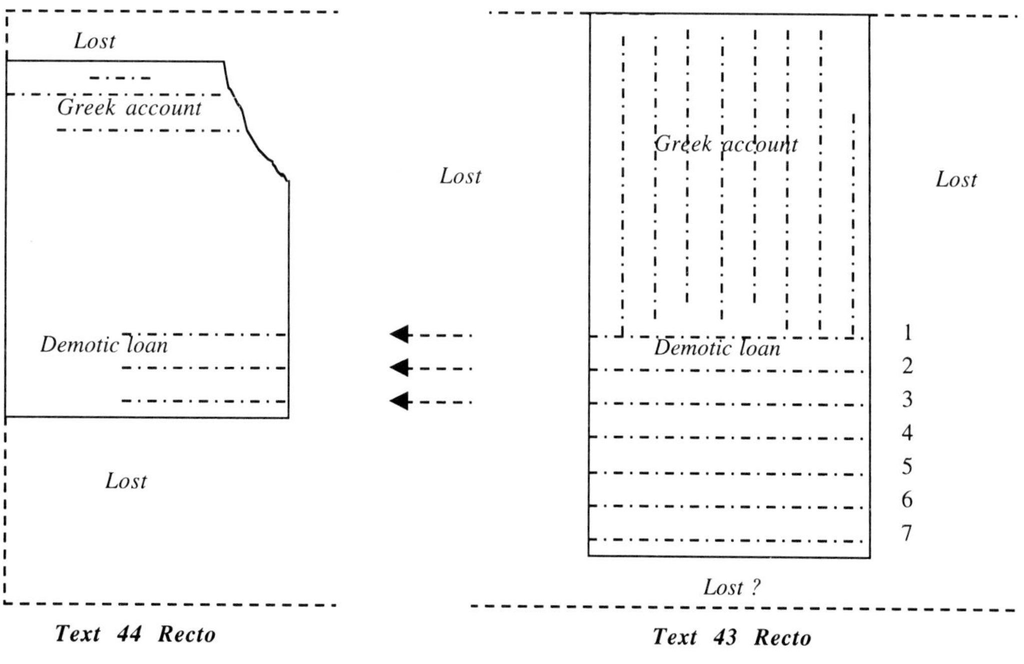

On the recto of Text 43 a Greek account is written in the top margin, at right angles to the old loan. Some lines of the account end in the middle of the first line of this loan (see plate). The first three lines of the account (l. 1b-3) were at first written with watery ink and were difficult to read. Later, Dryton wrote over them with black ink of a better quality. The same effect is created when one writes a text with pencil and writes over it in ink. Of course, the first version with the watery ink often comes from below the second version which renders the reading more difficult. The remaining part of the account was written at a later date and has not been written over.

The account on the verso of Text 43 is written across the fibres, having a top margin of 2.3 cm and two blank spaces of 2 and 2.3 cm, respectively.

This piece of papyrus is not complete: the account of the recto is broken off at the top and bottom; the account of the verso is broken off on the left- and right-hand sides and may be broken off at the bottom.

Introduction

Text belonging to the archive of Dryton, Apollonia and their offspring. — See §48. The handwriting can be attributed to Dryton, see §64-66.

Contents. — The account on the **recto** records the expenditure of artabas. Which product was traded is not clear. The account is divisible into three parts, written at different times, as suggested by the dates[1] and the changing hand[2].

A. 10 Choiak, or the beginning of January (l. 1- middle l. 3)

This first part is somewhat problematic, since it is not clear what preceded. In l. 1 the remaining amount appears to be 40 artabas, but above it something is written which I cannot decipher (see the facsimile). One expects **44** artabas[3].

- Dryton gives part of these 40+x (= ? 44) artabas to his cattle from 15 Phaophi onwards (beginning of November).
- From 21 Hathyr onwards (middle of December) another 2 artabas are spent (also for the cattle?) by Dryton's female household slave Myrsine (pros. 05).
- On 10 Choiak (beginning of January) someone, probably Dryton himself, spends another 2 artabas.

On 10 Choiak Dryton totals the expenditure to date: 20 artabas have been spent. At first, Dryton was mistaken about the date: in l. 2 and 3 he corrected 8 Choiak into 10 Choiak.

B. 2 Pachon, or end of May (end l. 3 - beginning l. 7)

Dryton is absent from the beginning of January until the end of May. He was staying in the Greek polis of Ptolemais of which he is a citizen (see pros. 403). When he returns after five months, he rereads the first three lines of the account and overwrites with his pen these lines which had been written with a watery ink (see description of the text). He concludes that there remain **24** artabas. During his absence his household slave Myrsine gave 0.5

---

[1] The dates (day and month) cannot be converted since the exact year is not known.

[2] Compare the scheme of the translation.

[3] According to l. 3, 20 artabas are spent and 24 artabas are left; consequently one expects a total of 44 artabas in l. 1 at the start.

artaba to a banker Hermokrates. Dryton spends 4 artabas on 2 Pachon. There remain 19.5 artabas. When deducting (24 - 4.5 artabas) Dryton made a mistake: his first result was 14.5 artabas, which he corrected into **19.5** artabas.

C. 28 Pachon, or end of June (remaining part of l. 7)

At the end of June, Dryton spends another 2 artabas; there remain **17.5** artabas. The remaining part of the account is lost.

It is not possible to make a scheme of the account on the **verso**, since the text is broken off on the left- and right-hand sides. Two products are traded: green fodder (γράστις, l. 1) for the cattle and wheat. A wagon is used for transport (ἐφ' ἁμάξη(ς), l. 2) and a staircase (κλῖμαξ) is mentioned as depository. The names of the people with whom Dryton does business are all fragmentary, except for Onthonmouthis (l. 8), who cannot be identified. The (Egyptian) name Onthonmouthis is attested here for the first time; it is not found in demotic documents. Other names compounded with Ὀνθον-[1] are however known.

Date. — The accounts Texts 43 and 44 are written on second-hand paper containing fragments of an old loan (Text 43 appendix). This old loan offers a *terminus post quem* for Texts 43 and 44, that is 154/3 - 143/2 B.C.

---

[1] P. Bad. IV 95, col. II, l. 35: Ὀνθ(ονόβεως); P. Oxy. IV 815: Ὀνθονοβει; P. Princ. III 130, l. 20: Ὀνθον[.

Recto

Facsimile and transcription

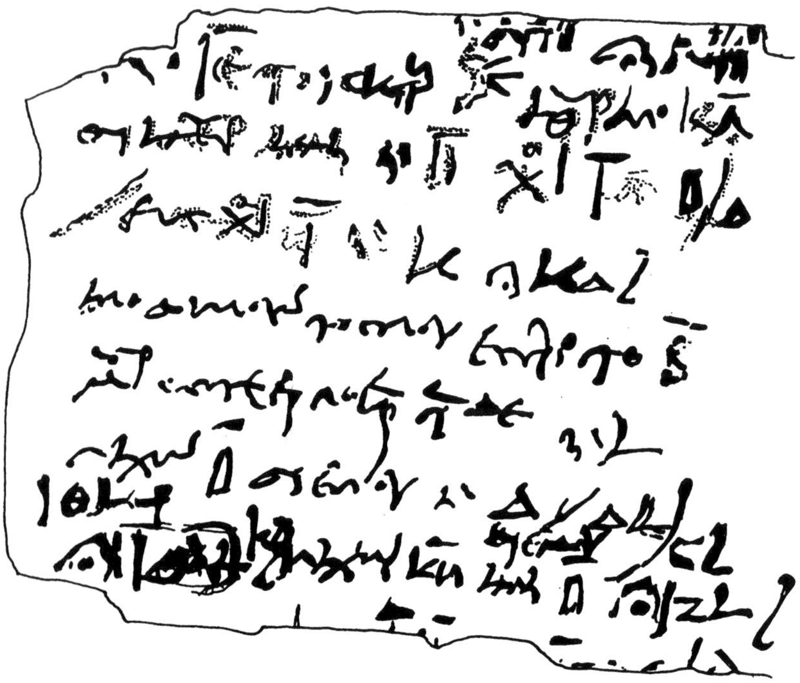

˙˙
αρ απο ◠̣ Μ
η ϵ υρ
1 απο ι̅ϵ̅ τοιcκτν δ αθ απο κα̅
υρ οι .
2 διαμ αλλαι αρ β̅ χ ι̅ꟻ β/δ
οι *corr.*
3 /ϵωc χ ι̅ αρ κ ◠̣ κδ *l*
το
4 αποδημουντοcμου ϵιcπ το β̅
υρ α α
5 μ ωcτϵϵρμοκρ τρ δϵ αρ ∠

6 παχων β̅ διϵμου αρ δ/δ∠
ιθ∠ *corr.* διϵμου /c∠
7 ◠̣ ~~ιδ∠~~ και παχων κη̅ αλλαι β̅ ◠̣ ιζ∠*l*

Recto

Interpretation

\- -

1+x α̣π̣ὸ ι̅ε̅ τοῖς κτήν(εσι) δ̣έ̣(δωκα) \`(ἀρτάβας) ἀπὸ (λοιποῦ) μ . .', Ἁθὺρ ἀπὸ κ̣̅α̣̅
2 διὰ Μυρ(σίνης) ἄλλαι (ἀρτάβαι) β̅, Χοί(ακ) ι̅ ⟦η̣⟧ β (γίνονται) δ,
3 (γίνονται) ἕως Χοί(ακ) ι̅ (ἀρτάβαι) κ, (λοιπὸν) κδ (ὧν)
4 ἀποδημοῦντός μού εἰς Πτο(λεμαίδα) τὸ β̅
5 Μυρ(σίνη) ὥστε Ἑρμοκρά(τει) τρ̣α(πεζίτηι) δέ(δωκεν) (ἀρτάβας) ∠,
6 Παχὼν β̅ δι' ἐμοῦ (ἀρτάβαι) δ (γίνονται) δ∠,
7 (λοιπὸν) ⟦ιδ∠⟧ ιθ∠ καὶ Παχὼν κ̅η̅ \`δι' ἐμοῦ' ἄλλαι β̅,
\`(γίνονται) ϛ∠', (λοιπὸν) ιζ∠ (ὧν)
traces

\- -

---

3 ι̅ corr. ex η̣̅ 7 καί corr. ex (ὧν)

Translation

		+ / -	Sub-totals	Total
	. . . .			
1	*from 15 (Phaophi) onwards I gave for the cattle - - -*			
	artabas of the remaining 40 [+ x = ?44] (artabas),	- ?		4[?4]
	in Hathyr from the 21st day onwards			
2	*through the agency of Myrsine another 2 artabas,*			
	on 10 Choiak 2 (artabas), total 4,	-4		
3	*total until 10 Choiak 20 (artabas),*		-20	
	remains 24, of which			24
4	*when I was away to Ptolemais for the second time*			
5	*Myrsine gave to the banker Hermokrates: 1/2*	-1/2		
	artaba,			
6	*on 2 Pachon by me 4 artabas, total 4 1/2,*	-4	-4 1/2	-4 1/2
7	*remains 19 1/2 and on 28 Pachon by me*			19 1/2
	another 2, total 6 1/2,	-2	-6 1/2	-2
	remains 17 1/2, of which			17 1/2
	. . . .			

Verso

Facsimile and transcription

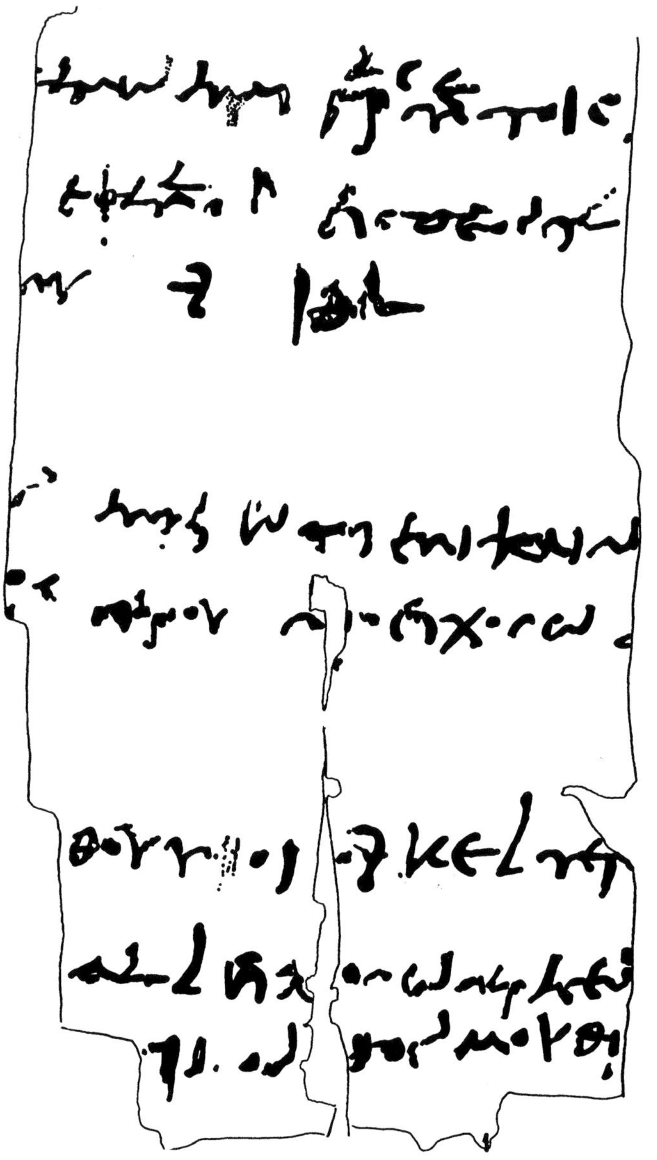

αϲ ϵ
]καμϵναυτωι γρ τ τοιϲ[

αη
] ϵφαμξ ϵιϲδϵοντα[

]που ł ιθ∠

corr.
] . . αυται ϵν τωι ϵπι κλιμα[

] . . παρου προϵιχομϵν . [

]θουυιοι ł κϵ *l* τϵρ.[

]δ∠*l* ϵιχομϵνπαραϲϵν[

]ιαονθονμουθι[

Verso

Interpretation

Vacat

1 [- - - ἐδώ]κ̣αμεν αὐτῶι γράστε(ως) τοῖς [κτήνεσι]

2 [- - -] ἐφ' ἁμάξη̣(ς) εἰς δέοντα [- - -]

3 [- - -]που (πυροῦ) ιθ∠

Vacat

4 [- - -]. . αὐταὶ ἐ̣ν̣ τῶι ἐπὶ κλίμα[κος - - -]

5 [- - -]. . πα̣ρ̣' οὗ προείχομεν . [- - -]

Vacat

6 [- - -]θου υ̣ἱοὶ (πυροῦ) κε (ὧν) Τερ.[- - -]

7 [- - -] δ∠(ὧν) εἴχομεν παρὰ Σεν[- - -]

8 [- - - δ]ιὰ Ὀνθονμούθι[ος - - -]

---

4 κλίμα[κος, κ corr. ex τῶι

Translation

1 . . . *we gave him green fodder for the cattle . . .*

2 . . . *on the wagon for the necessary . . .*

3 . . . *19 1/2 (artabas of) wheat . . .*

4 . . . *these in the . . . on the staircase. . .*

5 . . . *from whom we received beforehand . . .*

6 . . . *sons of . . . -thes: 25 (artabas of) wheat, of which Ter- . . .*

7 . . . *4 1/2 (artabas) of which we had from Sen- . . .*

8 . . . *through the agency of Onthonmouthis . . .*

Notes

The contents and the vocabulary are discussed in the Introduction of this chapter, see §53-55.

Recto

1 \`(ἀρτάβας) ἀπὸ (λοιποῦ) μ . .´ : I assume that this phrase was added to l. 1 later. It is also possible that this group of words is the end of the preceding line which ran very obliquely.

Above the letter *mu* a further letter is added which cannot be read; one expects a *delta* (see Introduction to the text).

4 εἰς Πτο(λεμαίδα): the *iota* of εἰς coincided with the lower part of the *sigma*. A similar writing for πτο( ), here an abbreviation of Πτολεμαίς, is found in a text of 78 B.C.[1]: the *pi* is written above the *tau* and the *omikron* is added to the right of the *tau*.

τὸ β̄: I translate this neuter accusative as "for the second time".

5 τρα(πεζίτηι) δέ(δωκεν): at first sight τάδε seems to be written. This demonstrative pronoun is senseless in the context. I suggest reading τρ̣α(πεζίτηι) δέ(δωκεν) with a ligature of *tau* and *rho* in τρ̣α(πεζίτηι).

Verso

1 γράστε(ως): is perhaps a partitive genitive of ἐδώ]κ̣αμεν.

4 αὐταὶ ἐ̣ν̣ τῶι ἐπὶ κλίμα[κος: the receptacle, in which the products are stored, is lost in the lacuna; this receptacle is kept on the staircase.

8 For the name Onthonmouthis, see the Introduction to this text.

---

[1] Pap. Lugd. Bat. XXV 21, l. 2 with commentary and reference to P. Mich. V 235, 3.

43 Appendix

DEMOTIC LOAN OF CORN

Plates XIX-XX; see facsimile below

? H. x W.: see Text 43 154/3 - 143/2 B.C.

Description. — See Text 43.

Introduction

Contents. — The demotic contract which is partly preserved on the papyri of Texts 43 and 44, is a grain loan (see l. 5). The data on the amount and the type of grain are lost.

The names of both contractants are missing. The *debtor* is a *[ḥry] mnḫ.t n p3 hb p3 bk t3 šd.t ⸢rsy⸣*; this title is found in an another text from Pathyris of c. 180-179 B.C.[1]. A *ḥry mnḫ.t* is a priest who is at the head of the *mnḫ.t* or στολισμός; the title *mnḫ*, derived from *mnḫ.t*, is known as the equivalent of the Greek title στολιστής; a *ḥry mnḫ.t* is undoubtedly the counterpart of the πρωτοστολιστής still attested in Pathyris in the second half of the 2nd century B.C.[2]. This priestly office is rarely found in connection to the cult of the ibis and the falcon[3]. The priest in Text 43 Appendix held his office in *t3 šd.t ⸢rsy⸣* or "the southern district", a controversial term, in my view an old-Egyptian term for the south of Egypt or the Thebaid[4] or the southern part of the Thebaid. The *creditor* appears to be a man, since in l. 5 *n t3j=k mḏ.t* (*in your* [= masculine form] *measure*) is mentioned.

---

1 U. Kaplony-Heckel, 'Woher kommen die Zeugen?', in *Intellectual Heritage of Egypt. Studies presented to L. Kákosy* (Studia Aegyptiaca 14), Budapest 1992, p. 326 (P. dem. Heid. inv.no. 714 + P. dem. Berlin inv.no. 23841).

2 See Text 4 of 126 B.C. and comm. on l. 44.

3 See K.A.D. Smelik, *The Cult of the Ibis in the Graeco-Roman Period,* in M.J. Vermaseren (ed.), *Studies in Hellenistic Religions* (EPRO 78), Leiden 1979, p. 239. For the joint cult of ibis and falcon, see ibidem, p. 240-241; J. Quaegebeur, in *Enchoria* 5 (1975), p. 23, n. 36; J.D. Ray, *The Archive of Hor* (Texts from Excavations 2), London 1976, no. 19, l. 5-6 and comm. p. 136-144; S. Cauville, in *BIFAO* 89 (1989), p. 63-64.

4 See my article'Horos son of Amenothes' (1997), in *JJP* 27, p. 75, n. 3.

Date. — The date of the loan is missing, but the remaining part of the protocol (l. 1-3 or 4) is helpful and shows the loan was issued between 154/3 and 143/2 B.C.:

- L. 1 shows that the kings were children of Ptolemy V and Kleopatra I, the *Gods Epiphaneis*. The kings may be either Ptolemy VI and Kleopatra II (163-145 B.C.) or Ptolemy VIII and Kleopatra II (145-**143/2**[1]).
- A priest of Ptolemy IV Philopator (l. 3) is only found in the papyri from 158/7 B.C. onwards[2].
- The man named after the priest of Ptolemy IV Philopator, can only be the priest of Ptolemy V Epiphanes. His priestly title is attested from **154/3** B.C. onwards[3].

Facsimile

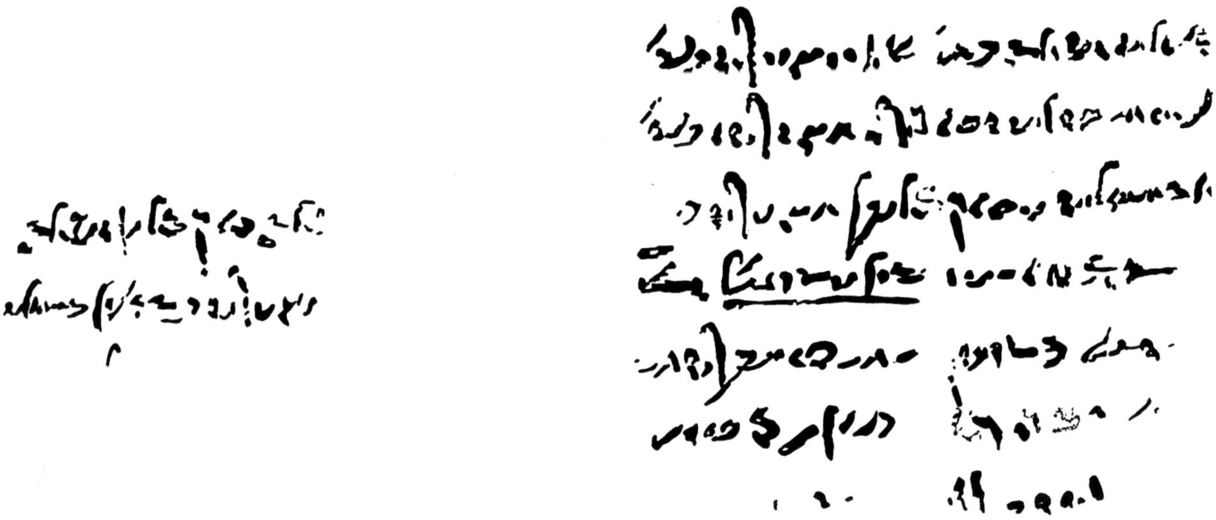

[1] After 143/2 B.C. the royal titulature changes, see Pap. Lugd. Bat. XV, p. 56.

[2] See Pap. Lugd. Bat. XV, p. 143.

[3] Ibidem.

Transcription

(the underlined part is preserved)

1 *[Ḥ3.t-sp - - - ibd - - - n3 Pr-ʿ3ʿws.w Ptlwmysʿws irm Glwptr3ʿws (? t3y=f sn.t [1]) n3 ẖrd.ṱ.w n Ptlwmysʿws irm Glwp]tr3ʿws n3 ntr.w nty pr.w irm p3 wʿb 3l[gsntrsʿws irm n3 ntr.w nty nḥm n3 ntr.w sn.w n3 ntr.w mnḫ.w n3] ntr.w mr it.ṱ=w n3 ntr.w*

2 *[nty pr.w - - - [2] n3 ntr.w mr mw.t=w irm t3 f3y qn n ʿš Brnyg3ʿws t3 mnḫ.t irm t3 f3y tn nb m-b3ḥ 3]rsyn3ʿws t3 mr sn irm t3 wʿb.t 3r[syn3ʿws t3 mr it.ṱ=s irm p3 wʿb Ptlwmysʿws p3 Swtr] irm p3 wʿb Ptlwmysʿws*

3-4 *[- - - [3] irm p3 wʿb Ptlwmysʿws p3 mr sn irm p3 wʿb Ptlwmysʿws p3 mnḫ irm p3 wʿb Pt]lwmysʿws p3 mr it.ṱ=f irm p3 wʿb [Ptlwmysʿws p3 ntr pr i.ir ir n3 nfr.w - - - [4] irm t3 wʿb.t t3 Pr-ʿ3.t Glwptr3ʿws irm t3 f3y tn nb m-b3ḥ 3rsyn3ʿws t3 mr sn irm t3 wʿb.t Glwptr3ʿws t3 mw.t t3 ntr.t nty pr. Ḏd NN s3 NN ḥry] mnḫ.t n p3 hb p3 bk t3 šd.t ⸢rsy⸣ [- - - n NN s3 NN - - - Wn mtw=k - - -]*

5 *[- - - i.ir.n=y n rn n3 pr.w r.dy=k n=y - - - Mtw=y dy.t st n=k r-hn-r - - -] n t3y=k md.t n pr iw=f wʿb [iwṱ sn.nw iwṱ sth - - -]*

6 *[- - - Bn iw=y] ⸢rḫ⸣ dy.t gr sw-hrw r.r=w m-s3 ⸢p3⸣ [sw=hrw nty ḥry - - -]*

7 *[- - - Nty nb n nk.t nb nty mtw=y] ⸢hnʿ n3 nty⸣ iw=⸢y dy.t ẖpr=w⸣ [n iwy.t md.t nb nty ḥry šʿ-tw=y ir r-ẖ.ṱ=w - - -]*

- -

Translation

Year - month - day of the kings Ptolemy (VI or VIII) and Kleopatra (II) (his sister?)[1], *children of Ptolemy (V) and Kleopatra (I), the Gods Epiphaneis,*

and (the year of) the priest of Alexander and the Gods Soteres, the Gods Adelphoi, the Gods Euergetai, the Gods Philopatores, the Gods Epiphaneis, - - - [2], *the Gods Philometores;*

and (the year of) the athlophoros of Berenike Euergetis, the kanephoros of Arsinoe Philadelphos and the priestess of Arsinoe Philopator;

and (the year of) the priest of Ptolemy Soter, the priest of Ptolemy - - - [3], *the priest of Ptolemy Philadelphos, the priest of Ptolemy Euergetes, the priest of Ptolemy Philopator, the priest of Ptolemy Epiphanes Eucharistos, - - -* [4];

and (the year of) the priestess of the queen Kleopatra, the kanephoros of Arsinoe Philadelphos and the priestess of Kleopatra, the mother, the goddess Epiphanis.

---

1 *t3j=f sn.t (his sister)* should be added if the contract dates from the reign of Ptolemy VI, see Pap. Lugd. Bat. XV, p. 50.

2 If the contract dates from 153/2 B.C. or later, Ptolemy Eupator should be added, see Pap. Lugd. Bat. XV, p. 143.

3 The epithet of the reigning king should be added here.

4 If the contract dates from 153/2 B.C. or later, the priest of Ptolemy Eupator should be listed, see Pap. Lugd. Bat. XV, p. 143.

Has declared NN, son of NN, - - - protostolistes of the ibis (and) the falcon in the Southern District - - - , to NN, son of NN, - - -:

(5) *«I owe you in the name of the corn you gave to me - - - I shall return it to you before - - - in your measure, in corn that is pure, without adulteration (or) chaff - - - I shall not be able to give another date for it except the above date - - - Everything, all that belongs to me and all that I shall acquire, are security for every word above until I have acted accordingly - - -».*

- -

44

Greek Account
written by ?Dryton

Plate XX (verso-recto); see facsimile below

[Pathyris]	H. x W. = 10.4 x 9.3 cm [Fragmentary]	after 154/3 - 143/2 B.C.

Heidelberg, P. inv. no. Gr. 315 [bought by Reinhardt in 1897] = **unpublished**.
Photograph. — Plate XX (verso- recto); see facsimile below.

Description. — On the verso a Greek account is written across the fibres over a kollesis. When the account was written down, a strip of vertical fibres was missing on the verso. Consequently, a small part of the text was written on the underlying horizontal fibres (see photograph). The account on the verso is broken off at the top, bottom and left-hand side.

The recto contains part of a Greek account, probably the end of the account on the verso, written along the fibres and broken off at the top and at the right-hand side. After a blank space of 5.5 cm traces are visible of an older demotic contract (see the description of Text 43). A kollesis is visible near the left-hand edge of the recto.

It is not clear how wide or how high the papyrus was at the time of the redaction of the account(s).

Introduction

Text belonging to the archive of Dryton, Apollonia and their offspring. — See §48. The handwriting can be attributed to Dryton, see §64-66.

Contents. — The writer started the account on the verso of the second-hand papyrus and continued on the recto. As the papyrus is broken off at the top, the beginning of the account (on the verso) is missing. The remaining part of the account registers :

A. Revenues (verso l. 1-2):

- an unknown number of artabas of kroton (lost in the lacuna)
- 85 artabas of wheat of which
  - — 60 artabas are paid as rent and as takeover tax (ἐμβαδικόν) for newly-gained land to ?Dryton (see §54).
  - — 25 artabas are paid, probably by the same person, for the use of the wagon (ἅμαξα) of ?Dryton.

B. Expenditure of the above-mentioned revenues (verso l. 3-9):

- Dryton's female slave Myrsine (pros. 05) receives, before and on the occasion of the birth of her child, 1 1/2 artabas of kroton, respectively. Kroton, Egyptian kiki, is used for making castor-oil[1] commonly used in lamps. The reason why a pregnant woman receives castor-oil before and on the occasion of the birth may be that the oil was used to prepare a soap or a salve[2].
- of the above-mentioned 85 artabas of wheat:

  — a person whose name is lost, receives 1/2 1/4 artaba of wheat, Myrsine 1 1/2 1/12 artabas;

  — 40 artabas (c. 1200 l.) are kept in a large receptacle outside (μεγ(άλη) κυψά(λη) ἔξω) and further 37 artabas (c. 1100 l.) in "the large receptacle" (ἡ με[γάλ]η κυψά(λη)). For the discussion of the term ἐν τῆι με[γάλ]ηι κυψά(ληι), see §55;

  — the remaining 5 1/2 1/12 artabas are delivered to Thotortaios, son of Nechthminis, in his pastophorion. P. Grenf. II 34 informs us that a Thotortaios, son of Nechthminis, indeed possessed a pastophorion within the walls of the temple of Pathyris (ἐντὸς τοῦ ἐν Παθύρει ἱεροῦ)[3], which he sold in 99 B.C. If he is to be identified with the well-kown Egyptian temple notary (μονογράφος) of the temple of Hathor in Pathyris in the period 178-133 B.C. (see Text 3, comm. on l. 48), then he must have been circa 100 years old in 99 B.C. It is more probable that the owner of the pastophorion is a grandson of the temple notary.

The addition is correct except for 1/12 artaba: 1/2 1/4 + 1 1/2 1/12 + 40 + 37 + 5 1/2 1/12 = 84 11/12, whereas the account starts with 85 artabas of wheat.

C. Deliveries (recto, l. 1-2):

The recto contains the last two lines of an account recording that goods (presumably artabas of wheat; only the relative ἅς is preserved) are deposited (παρατίθεσθαι)[4] ἐπὶ τοῦ δώμ[ατος] ("on the housetop"; see §55). Another total of artabas is lent to a man.

Date. — See Text 43, Introduction.

---

1 See Sandy, *Vegetable Oils* (1989), p. 35-54.

2 See, for instance, Sandy, *Vegetable Oils* (1989), p. 53 §14.

3 In Pathyris, all pastophoria, houses of the pastophoroi-priests, were located within the walls of the temple of Hathor, see Pestman, 'Pétéharsemtheus' (1965), p. 54; on pastophoria in general, see Husson, *Oikia* (1983), p. 221-222.

4 For the meaning of this verb, see Text 37, comm. on l. 1.

Facsimile and transcription

Verso

Traces

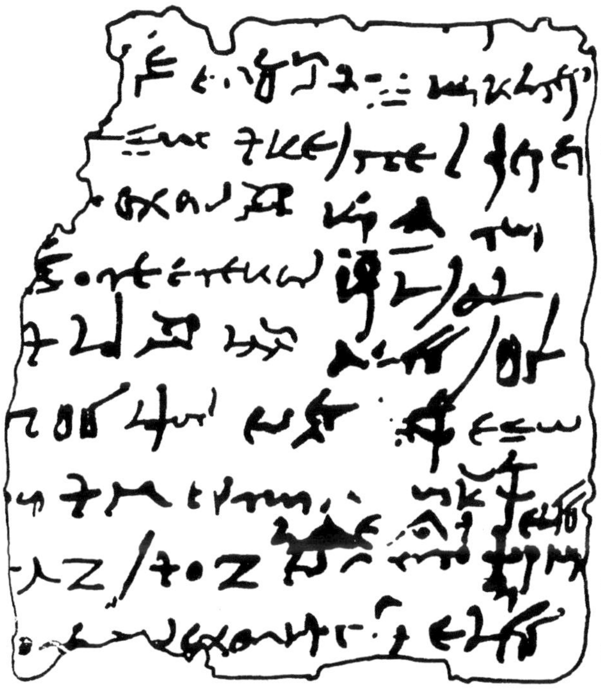

ϵ α η
]. γ ϵμβ ν Ɫ Ξ καικατϵρ

]αξηϲ Ɫ κϵ / πϵ *l* φϵρϵι

υρ ο
]οϵχϵιν μ κρ α τηι

ϵ ō
]δ οτϵ ϵτϵκϵν κρ Z̄ / α∠

υρ η
] Ɫ ∠d μ αλλ α∠ίβ́ / βγ́

ϵγ υα
]π ββ́ αφων ϵν μ κψ ϵξω

υα
]νηι Ɫ μ ϵν τηι μϵ[ ]ηι κψ́

αιδϵ ̣ Ɫ ϵ∠ίβ́
]Ɫλζ / Ɫ οζ ϵν παϲτοφοριωι

α.δϵαλλαι
]ρταιωινϵχθμινιοϲ Ɫ ϵ∠ίβ́

Recto

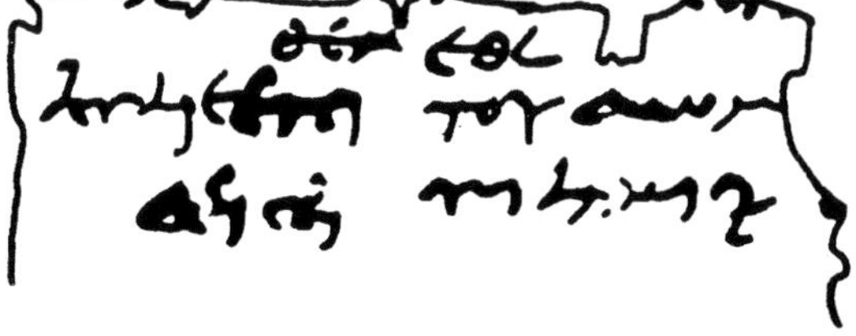

θϵμϵθα
αϲπαρϵϵπι του δωμ[

. . .ιϲαι τωι αλλωι Ɫ.[

Interpretation

Verso

\- -

Traces

1+x [- - -] . γε( ) ἐμβα(δικὸν) νή(σου) (πυροῦ) ξ καὶ κάτερ-
2 [γον ἁμ]άξης (πυροῦ) κε (γίνονται) πε (ὧν) φέρει
3 [- - - πρ]οέχειν Μυρ(σίνην) κρο(τῶνος) α, τῆι
4 [αὐτῆι] δέ(δωκα) ὅτε ἔτεκεν κρο(τῶνος) Ζ̄ (γίνεται) α∠,
5 [- - -] (πυροῦ) ∠d, Μυρ(σίνηι) ἄλλη α∠ίβ́ (γίνονται) βγ́,
6 [(λοιπὸν) (πυροῦ)] πβ́β́ ἀφ' ὧν ἐν μεγ(άληι) κυψά(ληι) ἔξω
7 [κειμέ]νηι (πυροῦ) μ, ἐν τῆι με[γάλ]ηι κυψά(ληι)
8 [- - -] (πυροῦ) λζ (γίνονται) (πυροῦ) οζ, `αἱ δὲ (λοιπαὶ) (πυροῦ) ϵ∠ίβ́ ´ ἐν παστοφορίωι
9 [Θοτο]ρταίωι Νεχθμίνιος `αἱ δὲ ἄλλαι ´ (πυροῦ) ϵ∠ίβ́

Traces

\- -

Recto

\- -

1+x `ἃς παρεθέμεθα´ ἐπὶ τοῦ δώμ[ατος,]
2 δανῖσαι τῶι ἄλλωι (πυροῦ) [- - -]

Verso 8 αἱ δέ: δ corr. ex (λοιπαί)   Recto 2 δανῖσαι, *l.* δανεῖσαι

Translation

Verso

		Kroton	Wheat +/-	*Totals*
	- -			
1	*. . . embadikon on newly-gained land: 60 (artabas) of wheat and the use*		+60	
2	*of the wagon: 25 (artabas) of wheat, makes 85 of which NN records*		+25	85
3	*that Myrsine already has (received) 1 (artaba) of kroton, to the*	-1		
4	*same (Myrsine) I gave when she gave birth 1/2 (artaba) of kroton,*	-1/2		
	which makes 1 1/2 (artabas),	-1 1/2		
5	*. . . 1/2 1/4 (artaba) of wheat, to Myrsine another*		-1/2 1/4	
	1 1/2 1/12 (artaba), which makes 2 1/3 (artabas);		-1 1/2 1/12	-2 1/3
6	*remains: 82 2/3 (artabas) of wheat, of which are kept in a large receptacle lying outside*			82 2/3
7	*40 (artabas) of wheat, in the large receptacle*		-40	
8	*. . . 37 (artabas) of wheat, which makes 77 (artabas);*		-37	-77
	(as to) the remaining 5 1/2 1/12 (artabas) of wheat, in the pastophorion			5 1/2 1/12
9	*to Thotortaios, son of Nechthminis, the remaining 5 1/2 1/12 (artabas) of wheat*		-5 1/2 1/12	
				[0]
	- -			

Recto

- -

1 *which we have deposited on the housetop,*

2 *to have lent to the other person x (artabas) of wheat.*

Notes

The contents and the vocabulary are discussed in the Introduction of this chapter, see §53-55.

Verso

1 . γε( ) ἐμβα(δικὸν) νή(σου): the abbreviation γε( ) is problematic: it may be a participle of γίγνομαι or the abbreviation of a word such as γένη, γένημα or γεωργός; the letter which preceeds γε( ) may be a *nu* or *upsilon*.

I consider ἐμβα(δικόν) as an accusative case, but a genitive depending on a lost preposition is also possible.

4 κρο(τῶνος): in contrast with l. 3, the abbreviation $\overline{\text{κρο}}$ has a supralinear horizontal stroke.

6 μεγ(άλῃ): it is not clear whether μεγ(άλῃ) is abbreviated; there is place enough to write the word in full, but there are no traces of the remaining part of the adjective visible.

6-7 κυψά(λῃ) ἔξω [κειμέ]ṇῃ: the preposition ἔξω is construed with a genitive; as the ending of the word following ἔξω does not match a genitive case, ἔξω must here be used as an adverb, probably depending on [κειμέ]νῃ ("lying outside").

8-9 The construction in l. 8-9 seems odd, but is the result of several additions. At first, there was written:

8 ἐν παστοφορίωι | 9 [Θοτο]ρταίῳ̣ι̣ Νεχθμίνιος (πυροῦ) ϵ∠ίβ

This phrase did not make it clear that the remaining artabas of wheat were in question; thus, the writer added above l. 9 \`α̣ἱ̣ δ̣ὲ̣ ἄλλαι ´ to (πυροῦ) ϵ∠ίβ; this addition apparently still did not make things clear enough and the writer added above l. 8 \`αἱ δὲ (λοιπαὶ) (πυροῦ) ϵ∠ίβ´.

Recto

2 δα̣ṿῖσαι: infinitive depending on a verb lost in the lacuna, compare φέρει ("he records", with infinitive) on the verso l. 2. The reading of δα̣ṿῖσαι is doubtful: θεῖσαι is also possible.

45

DEMOTIC ACCOUNT
of Apollonia

See facsimile below

?	H. x W. = 11 x 5 cm [Height incomplete]	after 141/ 140 B.C.[1]

Cairo, P. inv.no. 30674 [acquired during the excavations of the 1890'] = **P. dem. Cairo II 30674**, p. 104-105; second edition by **U. Kaplony-Heckel**, 'Soll und Haben in Pathyris', in *Festschrift J. von Beckerath* (HÄB 30), Hildesheim 1990, p. 139-146.

Photograph and facsimile. — Photograph in P. Cairo dem. II, plate 50, and Kaplony-Heckel, 'Soll und Haben' (1990), plate 8b. See my facsimile below.

Description. — The narrow strip (width: 5 cm) used for this account can be compared to the strip on which the account Text 42 (width: 4.5 cm) is written. Like Text 42, the account published here has undoubtedly been torn from an old text, probably from one of its margins since the top and left edges are neatly bordered. The piece of papyrus has been re-used for an account and is broken off at the bottom.

The account is written on the verso across the fibres. The writer probably used the verso because it has a straight right-hand border against which the demotic lines could be started (compare Text 42). The recto probably did not contain text since this side of the papyrus has been glued on cardboard.

Introduction

Contents. — The account consists of two parts:

a) *account of wheat* (l. 1-6)

The account is introduced by *P3 ip n n3 sw.w r.tw T3-šr.t-Mnṯ n* (*the account of wheat which Senmonthis has given to*)[2].

Senmonthis gives artabas of wheat to two of her sisters: 13 1/2 1/4 artabas to Senapathis (pros. 406) and 2 artabas to Tiesris (pros. 407).

b) *purchase of goods* (l. 7-12)

Without a new subtitle the account goes over to the purchase of kitchen utensils by Senmonthis; the purchase price is introduced by *n swn wᶜ* (*as price for one*), followed by the object. A possible subtitle is found in an ostrakon from Pathyris: *P3 ip n n3 ḥḏ.w r.tw , . . ., swn wᶜ iḫ r* (*the account of the money which NN gave to, ..., the price for one cow amounts to*)[3].

The utensils bought by Senmonthis are found among the goods which women bring with them when they marry and which are listed in demotic marriage contracts.

[1] In year 141/140 B.C. Apollonia and her sisters became adults, see Text 32, l. 12-13.

[2] Compare the introduction to similar accounts from Pathyris: O. dem. *Or Su* 30 (1981), p. 10-11 and p. 11-12.

[3] O. dem. *OrSu* 30 (1981), p. 11-12.

Senmonthis buys from her sister Senapathis a bronze stove for 150 deben (3000 drachmas) and a bronze egg-shaped pot for cooking for 50 deben (1000 drachmas). From another sister Tiesris she buys another bronze stove for 100+x deben (2000+x drachmas).

Facsimile and transcription

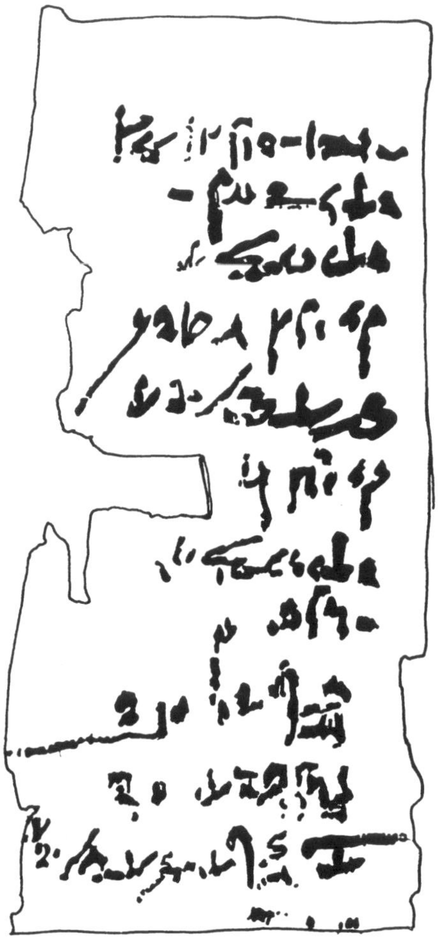

1 *P3 ip n n3 sw.w r.tw*

2 *T3-šr.t-Mnṯ n*

3 *T3-šr.t-ʿ3-pḥ(ṯ)*

4 *rdb sw 13 1/2 1/4*

5 *T3y-Isr*

6 *rdb sw 2*

7 *T3-šr.t-ʿ3-pḥ(ṯ)*

8 *n swn wʿ*

9 *ʿš ḥḏ 150*

10 *wʿ.t swḥ(.t) ḥḏ 50*

11 *kj ʿš n T3y-Isr*

12 ⌜*ḥḏ 100 +* ⌝

5, 11 *T3y-Isr3* ed., *T3y-Isr* legimus

Translation

1 *The account of the wheat which has been given by*
2 *Senmonthis: to*
3 *Senapathis*
4 *13 1/2 1/4 artabas of wheat,*
5 *Tiesris*
6 *2 artabas of wheat;*
7 *Senapathis*
8 *the price for one*
9 *(bronze) stove: 150 deben,*
10 *(for) one (bronze) egg-shaped pot for cooking: 50 deben;*
11 *(for) another (bronze) stove*
to Tiesris:
12 *100 +x deben*

Notes

3 *T3-šr.t-ˁ3-pḥ(ṯ), Senapathis*: after *ˁ3-pḥ(ṯ)* (*Great of strength*), an epithet for several gods (compare H.S. Smith, in *Serapis* 6 (1980), p. 147), the scribe initially wrote the determinative of a person. According to the first editor U. Kaplony-Heckel the determinative of a god, the usual determinative for this name[1], was added afterwards; the determinative of a god was, however, not added to the same name in l. 7 (with determinative of a person).

9 *ˁš, stove, furnace*: the ancient Egyptian word *ˁẖ* is a fireplace for burnt offerings[2]. The term is found in demotic texts as *ˁẖ*, *ˁš* or in Roman times as *3š*[3]. It appears to be one of the objects which a woman brings with her into the house of her husband[4]. The word is accompanied by the fire determinative, as is the case in Text 45. It is usually made of metal: in Text 45 *ˁš* is indeed followed by the bronze determinative.

---

1 See Lüddeckens, *Dem. Namenbuch*, I 15, p. 1092.

2 Äg. Wb. I, p. 223; Coptic ⲁϣ, Crum, *Coptic Dictionary*, p. 22.

3 See O. dem. Wangstedt 64, l. 5.

4 E. Lüddeckens, in P. dem. Eheverträge, p. 293; see also the "Frauensachen-Listen" on ostraka from Pathyris: O. dem. *Enchoria* 21 (1994), p. 45-47, no. 46, l. 21 (value: 250 deben) and p. 53-54, no. 52, l. 4 (value: 250 deben); see furthermore the list O. dem. Wangstedt 64, 5, where the stove is mentioned among goods such as cloths and a kettle.

This fireplace is not a real oven, as it is often translated. An oven was built into a corner of the house. An *ʿš* is rather a stove or furnace made of clay; the more expensive types were made of metal. They had a cavity in which a fire could be lit for cooking[1]. My interpretation may be confirmed by the mention of an egg-shaped cooking pot, called *swḥ(.t)* (see below) together with the stove. The prices of the stove vary from 100 to 250 deben (2000 to 5000 drachmas)[2] in the second half of the 2nd century and the beginning of the 1st cent. B.C.

A stove with cooking pot. Representation from the Middle Kingdom [3]

10 *swḥ(.t), an egg-shaped cooking pot*: the ancient Egyptian word *swḥ.t* means "egg" and is in the first place determined by an egg. The word is found a few times in the demotic material, among other things as an object which a woman brings into the house of her husband or in accounts and lists of goods. The additional determinatives in Text 45 are that for metal and that for bronze. Other texts show similar determinatives: bronze and even silver. Lüddeckens[4] interprets the object as a «Kegel» or as «eine Art Ball oder Kugel»; P.W. Pestman *e.a.*[5] describes it as «un objet en bronze ou en argent, peut-être une écuelle ayant la forme de la moitié d' un oeuf d' autruche»; U. Kaplony-Heckel, the first editor of Text 45, translates it as «ein *swḥ(.t)* -Ei».

1 See Vandier, *Manuel* IV, p. 262-263.

2 Text 45: 150 deben; E. Lüddeckens, in P. dem. Eheverträge, p. 293: 30 to 100 deben; O. dem. *Enchoria* 21 (1994), p. 45-47, no. 46, l. 21: 250 deben, and p. 53-54, no. 52, l. 4: 250 deben.

3 Vandier, *Manuel* IV, p. 261.

4 E. Lüddeckens, in P. dem. Eheverträge, p. 298.

5 P. dem. Recueil I, p. 63, n. 9.

In my view, it is a metal cooking pot, rather than a metal bowl (see P.W. Pestman), which could be put on the above-mentioned *ʿš* (*stove*). In addition, it is not necessary to interpret this cooking-pot as a half egg, since it needs a lid: the whole looks like an egg. I found a stove with such an egg-shaped cooking pot in kitchen scenes from Deir el-Bahri[1].

Griffith[2] connects the *swḥ(.t)* with the κῶνος pledged according to the Pathyris text P. Grenf. II 17 (see App. A). This "cone" made of iron has in 134 B.C. a value of 8000 copper drachmas, which is quite high in comparison with the bronze and silver *swḥ(.t)*-cooking pots with an average value of 50 to 60 debens or 1000 to 1200 drachmas[3].

11 *kj ʿš n T3j-Isř, (for) another (bronze) stove to Tiesris*: *n T3j-Isř, to Tiesris,* was added afterwards. Due to lack of space, the scribe had to put the person determinative above the water determinative. The name had to be written at the beginning of the line, before *kj ʿš*.

1 Vandier, *Manuel* IV, p. 261.
2 P. dem. Ryl., p. 270, n. 10.
3 Text 45: 50 deben; E. Lüddeckens, in P. dem. Eheverträge, p. 298: 50 to 60 deben; O. dem. *Enchoria* 21 (1994), p. 49-52, no. 49, verso l. 26: 50 deben.

VI

Varia

§56. *Survey*. —

46 Gr.	Greek fragment of a division or an agreement	after 150
47 Gr.	Greek fragment of an agreement made by Dryton	s.d.
48 Gr.-Dem.	Greek fragment with a royal oath made by Esthladas	145-116
49 Dem.	Demotic deed of partnership of Phagonis	94
50 Gr.	The 'Alexandrian Erotic Fragment' or 'Maedchens Klage'	after Oct. 174

46

GREEK FRAGMENT OF A DIVISION OR AN AGREEMENT

? H. x W. = 12.3 x 5.5 cm after 150 B.C.
[Fragmentary]

Heidelberg, P. Gr. inv.no. 1316 [date of acquisition unknown] = **P. Baden II 5** = C. Ptol. Sklav. 56.
Photograph. — Photograph available on
http://www.rzuser.uni-heidelberg.de/~gv0/Papyri/P.Heid._Uebersicht.html (see VBPII 5)

Description. — The papyrus is broken off at the left-hand side and at the foot. Only a small fragment containing the end of the first eleven lines is preserved.

The text is written on the recto along the fibres, with a top margin of 4 cm and a right-hand margin of at maximum 4.3 cm. The text has not been written in an agoranomic hand nor does it resemble the handwriting of Dryton or Esthladas, compare §64-66.

Introduction

Contents. — See §1 and 11.

Date and identification of the fragment. —

(1) *Not a fragment of Dryton's second will.* This tiny fragment has caused problems. The mentioning of σωμάτων (l. 6) and [- -]εστω Ἐσθλάδαι (l. 7) has led scholars to conclude that it is part of one of Dryton's wills. Since in l. 5 Dryton's second wife Apollonia is recorded, but not her children, it is generally considered — with some reservations — to be a copy of the second will (see §11)[1]. The reservations are due to the fact that the few remains of the text do not correspond with the clauses known from the second will of 150 B.C. (Text 2).

That this fragment contained another version of the second will, is contradicted by the title mentioned in l. 3. On the redaction of his second will, Dryton was still τῶν Διοδότου ἱππέ[ων], and only later became τῶν διαδόχων καὶ τοῦ ἐπιτάγματος ἱππάρχης ἐπ' ἀνδρῶν (see pros. 403). Consequently, the fragment is to be dated after 150 B.C.[2].

S.B. Pomeroy[3] thinks that Text 46 was drawn up shortly after Dryton's second marriage to Apollonia «He immediately wrote a short will [Text 46], now fragmentary, . . . By 146 B.C., he had written a much more elaborate will [Text 2] . . .». This viewpoint cannot be maintained, since a new fragment of the second will Text 2 shows that that will was drawn up in 150 B.C. on the occasion of his marriage with Apollonia.

---

1 Lewis, *Greeks in Ptolemaic Egypt* (1986), p. 169 («exiguous fragment»); P.W. Pestman, in Pap. Lugd. Bat. XIX, p. 33 («? petit fragment»); R. Scholl, in C. Ptol. Sklav., p. 227.

2 J.K. Winnicki, who assumed that the second will dated to 148 B.C., proposes as the date for this fragment «nach 147/146», without adding an explicit reason (Winnicki, 'Ein ptolemäischer Offizier' (1972), in *Eos* 60, p. 344).

3 Pomeroy, *Women in Hellenistic Egypt* (1990), p. 105.

(2) *Fragment of a will ?* There remain two possibilities: either it is indeed a will, which would be Dryton's fourth will, drawn up between 150 [Text 2, second will] and 126 B.C. [Texts 3-4, third will], or it may be some other kind of text.

There are no certain indications that it is a will at all[1]. In the case of a will, the long introductory testamentary clause has to be supplied in l. 5 (compare Text 2, l. 15-17). As a consequence, the first four lines, which would then refer to the testator, are already long, so causing problems when they are to be filled with the titles and physical description of the testator Dryton.

It could, however, be another form of contract, for instance, a division (compare §21, where a division of parts of Dryton's house is discussed, a division which predates his last will of 126 B.C.) or an agreement between Dryton and Esthladas (compare Text 47). The city designation [Πτο]λεμαιεὺς in l. 1 can either refer to Dryton or to Esthladas. In the first two lines Esthladas could be recorded as the first contractor, while in l. 3-4 Dryton would appear with his title and physical description as second contractor.

Text

[- - - Πτο]λεμαιεὺς
[- - -]σ̣μίωι
[- - - τῶν διαδόχων καὶ] τοῦ ἐπιτάγματος
[ἱππάρχης ἐπ' ἀνδρῶν - - - οὐ(λὴ) παρ' ὀφρῦν ἀρι(στερὰν) ἄ]κ̣ραν
[- - - γυναικὸ]ς ἧι ὄνομα \` Ἀπολλωνία{ι} ἣ´
[\`καὶ´ Σεμμῶνθις - - -] κ̣αὶ σωμάτων
[- - -]εστω Ἐσθλάδαι
[- - - Δρ]ύτωνι
[- - -]ηται
[- - -] ̣ των
[- - - α]ὐ̣τῶι
- -

2-3 [- - -] τοῦ ἐπιτάγματος | [- - -]κ̣ραν ed., [- - - τῶν διαδόχων καὶ] τοῦ ἐπιτάγματος | [ἱππάρχης ἐπ' ἀνδρῶν - - - οὐ(λὴ) παρ' ὀφρῦν ἀρι(στερὰν) ἄ]κ̣ραν supplevimus
5 Ἀπολλωνίαι καί ed., \` Ἀπολλωνία{ι} ἥ´ legimus; ἥ corr. ex καί

[1] Compare W. Clarysse, in P. Petr. I². The Wills, p. 12 («I am not certain that it is part if one of Drutôn's wills»).

Notes

4]κ̣ραν: this is undoubtedly the end of the physical description of Dryton as known from other texts (see pros. 403): οὐ(λὴ) παρ' ὀφρῦν ἀρι(στερὰν) ἄ]κ̣ραν.

5-6 ἧι ὄνομα \` Ἀπολλωνία{ι} ἡ´ | [\`καὶ´ Σεμμῶνθις]: the writer had at first just written Semmonthis, the Egyptian name of Dryton's second wife; he later added her Greek name in the right-hand margin after l. 5, which had to be followed by ἡ καί (alias).

7 [- - -]εστω Ἐσθλάδαι: can be supplemented as ἔστω Ἐσθλάδαι or μὴ ἐξέστω Ἐσθλάδαι.

47

GREEK FRAGMENT OF AN AGREEMENT
made by Dryton

Plate XXI

?	H. x W. = 6 x 7.2 cm [Fragmentary]	s.d.

Cairo, P. Gr. inv.no. 10355 [bought on 9 Nov. 1895 from Grenfell] = **unpublished**.
Photograph. — Plate XXI.

Description. — The papyrus is fragmentary; only part of the last seven lines and of the bottom margin (c. 1.5 cm) is preserved. On the basis of what is missing at the end of l. 6 and at the start of l. 7 (see comm. on l. 6-7), one can calculate that approximately one third of the width is preserved. The text is written on the recto along the fibres.

Introduction

Contents. — Only a tiny fragment of the text is preserved. Nevertheless, several deductions can be made.

The contract is an agreement between two parties: it is called a homologia in the last line (l. 7) and the clauses in the last three lines (l. 5-7) indeed fit the structure of a homologia (see comm. on l. 5-7). The body of the contract must have started with the verb ὁμολογεῖ. One of the parties is undoubtedly Dryton (l. 5 and see comm. on l. 5).

The most important question is: what kind of homologia is involved here? There are agreements for all types of contracts (sale, loan, marriage, parachoresis, ...). The words γνώμης (l. 3) and κυρι̣[εύ - - -] (l. 3) might suggest that a marriage agreement is involved. This would be the first marriage-agreement for Dryton and his first or second wife. Few Greek marriage contracts are preserved for Ptolemaic Egypt; in Pathyris all marriage contracts are Egyptian (see §31). Some Greek marriage contracts contain similar clauses at the end of the contract:

- the woman may not leave the house without the knowledge (γνώμη) of the husband[1] and one contract adds that the woman may not alienate the property without the permission of her husband[2].

---

1 CPR XVIII 18 (Kalliphanous, 231 B.C.); P. Freib. III 30 (Philadelpheia, 179/178 B.C.); P. Giss. I 2 (Krokodilopolis, Arsinoite nome, 173 B.C.); P. München. III 62 (?; 2nd cent. B.C.); P. Tebt. I 104 (Tebtynis, 92 B.C.); P. Yale I 26 (Hibeh, 3rd cent. B.C.); SB XII 11053 (Tholtis, 267 B.C.?).

2 P. Freib. III 30 (Philadelpheia, 179/178 B.C.).

• some contracts have a clause which records that the woman is in control of (κυριεύουσα) all the property together with the husband (μετ' αὐτοῦ κοινῆι τῶν ὑπαρχόντων)[1]. L. 3-4 may have contained such a clause, adding explicitly the possession of the household slaves.

This interpretation causes some problems. First of all, the order of the above-mentioned clauses at the end of the agreement is nowhere found in a marriage-agreement: two marriage contracts do contain both clauses, but in the reverse order[2]. Secondly, the term τ̣ῆς διαγραφ[- - -] in l. 2 cannot be explained.

Another view is possible: the term τ̣ῆς διαγραφ[- - -] recalls the bank-diagraphe of Text 31, a petition according to which Dryton(?), who has financial problems, sells some of his plots of land to his son Esthladas. At the end of this petition, Dryton asks the epimeletes to ordain that the proper (bank-)diagraphe in which the plots are described and which establishes the tax on sales to be collected by the banker, be handed over to Esthladas.

The agreement edited here may be an agreement between Esthladas and Dryton, stipulating that Esthladas agrees to having received property of Dryton as well as the proper bank-diagraphe (l. 2: τ̣ῆς διαγραφ[- - -]). Esthladas, however, is not free to do certain things (for instance, to alienate the property?) without the approval of Dryton (l. 3: [ἄνευ τῆς Δρύτων]ος γνώμης), but he is master of the property as well as of the ?male household slaves (l. 3-4: κυρι̣[εύ - - - τῶν] οἰκετικῶν σωμάτων ἀν̣δ[?ρείων - - -]). For the mentioning of slaves next to immovable property, compare Text 34, l. 8-10, where the daughters of Dryton record that they have inherited half of their father's plots of land as well as a half share of the household slaves (μέρ[ους] ἡμίσους τῶν π̣α̣τρικῶν ἐγγαίων ... ὁμοίως δὲ κ̣αὶ τῶν οἰκετ̣ικῶν σωμάτων).

This kind of agreement between father and son reminds of the Egyptian deed of division (*sẖ dny.t pš*), a form of *donatio inter vivos*: the testator divides his belongings between his children, who become joint owners of their part while the testator lives and owners on his or her death. Two Greek counterparts are found in Pathyris: the παραχώρησις or cession and the δόσις or donation (see §1). They usually have the form of a homologia[3]. Is the agreement published here also a παραχώρησις or δόσις in the form of a homologia? An additional argument for this view is provided by Dryton's third will of 126 B.C. where indirect reference is made to an earlier division (see §21).

According to the end of the agreement Esthladas is not allowed to enter into dispute with Dryton, otherwise this action will be invalid and he will have to pay a fine, whereas the homologia remains valid.

Scribe. — The agreement is written in an agoranomic hand and contains formulas typical of agoranomic homologiai (see comm. on l. 5-7).

---

[1] P. Freib. III 30 (Philadelpheia, 179/178 B.C.); P. Giss. I 2 (Krokodilopolis, Arsinoite nome, 173 B.C.); P. Tebt. III 974 (Tebtynis, 2nd cent. B.C.).

[2] P. Freib. III 30 (Philadelpheia, 179/178 B.C.); P. Giss. I 2 (Krokodilopolis, Arsinoite nome, 173 B.C.).

[3] παραχώρησις: P. Cairo Goodsp. 6; P. Grenf. I 27; P. Grenf. II 33; P. Lond. VII 2191; δόσις: BGU III 993; P. Lond. III 880 (p. 8-9); P. Stras. II 83 and 85.

Text

[- - -] ̣ ̣ ̣ [- - -]
[- - -]τ̣ῆς διαγραφ[- - -]
[- - - ἄνευ τῆς Δρύτων]ος γνώμης ἀλλὰ κυρι̣[εύ - - -]
[- - - τῶν] οἰκετικῶν σωμάτων ἀν̣δ̣[?ρείων - - -]
[- - -]οι ὑπὲρ αὐτῶν Δρύτωνι ἢ τοῖς̣[- - -]
[- - - τὰ - - -] ̣ ἄκυρα ἔστω καὶ προσαποτε̣[ισάτω - - -]
[- - - ?καὶ μηθὲν] δ̣' ἧττον κυρία ἔστω ἡ δὲ ὁμολ̣[ογία - - -]

Notes

2-3 See the introduction to the text.

4 τῶν] οἰκετικῶν σωμάτων ἀν̣δ̣[?ρείων: the genitive depends on κυρι̣[εύ - - -]; ἀνδρεῖοι is often used in relation to slaves as a counterpart of γυναῖκες/ θηλυκαί (opposite sex) or of υἱοί (opposite age), see R. Scholl, in C. Ptol. Sklav., p. 720.

5-7 The clauses of l. 5-7 are typical of the end of a homologia, compare the formulas of the agoranomeion of Pathyris (*e.g.*, P. Grenf. I 27; P. Lond. VII 2191; Pap. Lugd. Bat. XIX 7A-B; P. Stras. II 85) and of Hermoupolis (Pap. Lugd. Bat. XXII 28-31):

A it is not permitted to take action against Dryton or his relatives;

B if someone takes action against Dryton or his relatives (Δρύτωνι ἢ τοῖς̣[- - -]), the action will be invalid (ἄκυρα) and the claimant must pay (προσαποτε̣[ισάτω]) a fine;

C nevertheless (μηθὲν] δ̣' ἧττον) the agreement remains valid (κυρία).

5 [- - -]οι ὑπὲρ αὐτῶν Δρύτωνι ἢ τοῖς̣[- - -]: this fragmentary clause could be part of formula A or B (see preceding comment). If it is part of formula A, the dative Δρύτωνι is dependent on a verb as μὴ ἐπικαλεῖν, see, *e.g.*, P. Lugd. Bat. XIX 7A, l. 11-12; one does, however, expect μὴ ἐπικαλεῖν Δρύτωνι *μηδὲ* τοῖς̣[- - -] rather than μὴ ἐπικαλεῖν Δρύτωνι *ἤ* τοῖς̣[- - -]. Therefore, I prefer the clause to form part of fomula B.

ὑπὲρ αὐτῶν: dispute with Dryton is not permitted ὑπέρ (concerning) αὐτῶν: αὐτῶν probably refers to the property mentioned in the previous line (? plots of land and slaves). Compare P. Lugd. Bat. XIX 7B, l. 12-13 (with comment): μὴ ἐπικαλεῖν Ναομσήσι ὑπὲρ αὐτῆς (that is, the τιμή).

Δρύτωνι ἢ τοῖς ̣[- - -]: the dative is dependent on a verb such as ἐπικαλεῖν, see, *e.g.*, P. Lugd. Bat. XIX 7A, l. 11-12. τοῖς may have been followed by παρ' αὐτοῦ.

6 ἄκυρα ἔστω: it is not clear what the subject (neutral plural) may have been. Other homologiai from Pathyris often have ἡ ἔφοδος (the action) ἄκυρος ἔστω, see, *e.g.*, P. Lugd. Bat. XIX 7A, l. 13-14.

7 μηθὲν] δ̣' ἧττον: the superfluous δέ is also found in other homologiai from Pathyris, see P. Stras. II 83 (114 B.C.; name of the scribe not mentioned) and P. Lugd. Bat. XIX 7A (109 B.C.; written by Ammonios).

ἡ δὲ ὁμολ̣[ογία - - -]: it is not clear whether another superfluous δέ should be assumed (see preceding note) or a new clause begins, such as ἡ δὲ ὁμολογία ἥδε κυρία ἔστω πανταχοῦ οὗ ἂν ἐπιφέρηται, see P. Adler 2, l. 18-19 and BGU III 998, l. 13.

48

GREEK FRAGMENT WITH A ROYAL OATH
made by Esthladas

See scanned photograph of the demotic note below

?	H. x W. = 13.2 x 8.4 cm [incomplete]	Between 145 and 116 B.C.

Cairo, P. Gr. inv.no. 10343 [bought before 1897] = the Greek text has remained **unpublished**, see P. dem. Cairo II, p. 45. The demotic note below the Greek text was published in P. dem. Cairo II, p. 337.

Photograph and facsimile. — Photograph of the Greek and demotic text in P. dem. Cairo II, plate 146; see scanned photograph of the demotic note below.

Description. — The papyrus is irregularly broken off at the top and on both the left-hand and right-hand sides. To judge from the supplement in l. 11-12, there are 2 to 7 characters lost in the lacuna at the left-hand side and c. 27 characters lost in the lacuna at the right-hand side. The Greek text is written on the recto along the fibres. Below the Greek text a demotic note of one line has been written upside down.

Introduction

Contents and date. — The context is not clear. An Esthladas, probably Dryton's son, disclaims (l. 3, ἐ]ξεχώρησεν) certain properties; in l. 6 προσγένημα is recorded: such a προσγένημα is the pincipal bone of contention in a long-standing dispute between the priests of Hermonthis and the priests of Pathyris[1]. According to D. Bonneau[2], προσγενήματα (literally "additions") are deposits of silt whereby new islands in the Nile are joined to the mainland[3].

The text ends with a king's oath[4] (l. 7-12), sworn by the ruling pharaoh (Ptolemy VIII, see below) and the dynasty of the Ptolemies.

In the fragmentary text the grandfather of the king (probably Ptolemy IV, l. 4) is recorded as well as the 25th year of the reigning king (l. 5), undoubtedly Ptolemy VIII, who regains control in his 25th year (145 B.C.). A later date under Ptolemy X is palaeographically improbable. If the Esthladas mentioned in the text is to be identified with Dryton's son, who became an adult c. 140 B.C. (pros. 504), the text may date from the period 140-116 B.C.

It is not clear whether the demotic text is connected to the Greek text.

---

1 P. Lond. VII 2188 (148 B.C.), passim.
2 Bonneau, *Le fisc et le Nil* (1971), p. 168.
3 For further commentary, see P. Lond. VII 2188, introduction.
4 For Greek oaths in the name of the king(s), see Seidl, *Der Eid* (1929); Depauw, *Companion* (1997), p. 138.

Text

Greek text

[- c. 7 -] . [- c. 44 -]
[- c. 5 -]. τα ⟦ . ⟧ τὴν προσγεγ[ενημένην - c. 18 -]
[- c. 3 - ἐ]ξεχώρησεν Ἐσελάδας τῷ[ν - c. 27 -]
[- c. 2 -] τοῦ πάππου τοῦ βασιλέως [- c. 28 -]
[- c. 2 -]ζ καὶ ἀπὸ τοῦ κε (ἔτους) μη[νὸς - c. 28 -]
[- c. 2 -]ς ἄλλο δὲ προσγένημα . [- c. 30 -]
[τ]οῦ προκειμένου πλήθους [- c. 4 - Ὀμνύω βασιλέα Πτολεμαῖον]
[τὸ]ν ἐγ βασιλέως Πτολεμαίου [καὶ - c. 27 -]
[- c. 4 -] καὶ τοὺς τούτων προγόνους [- c. 27 -]
[- c. 4 -] εἶναι ταῦτα κατ' ἀλήθειαν [- c. 27 -]
[- c. 2 -]εν προσγεγονέναι. Εὐορκοῦ[ντι μέν μοι εὖ εἴη, ἐφιορκοῦντι δὲ]
[τἀν]αντία.

---

3 Ἐσελάδας, *l.* Ἐσθλάδας

Demotic note (written upside down)

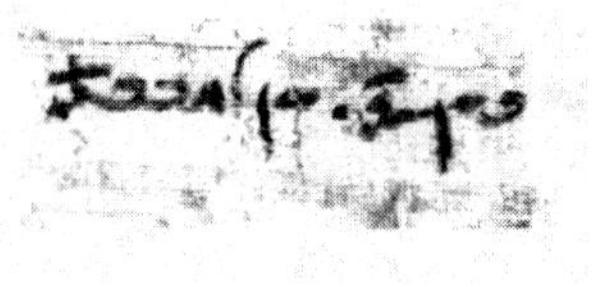

[- - -] *nty sẖ n bnr n sẖ wynn*

which is written alongside the Greek document.

49

DEMOTIC DEED OF PARTNERSHIP
of Phagonis

Probably Pathyris H. x W. = 21.5 x 13 cm 21 September 94 B.C.

Heidelberg, P. dem. inv.no. 725 [in Heidelberg since 1898, acquired by Reinhardt] = **P. dem. Gebelein Heid. 11**. This text was discussed in a seminar on Pathyris under the supervision of S.P. Vleeming in 1987 (Leiden). On this occasion some minor corrections to the previous edition were proposed; they are incorporated in the edition below. Other corrections are to be found in the BL dem.

Photograph and facsimile. — No photograph available; facsimile in P. dem. Gebelein Heid., p. 92-93, no. 11.

Translations. — Ed. pr.; Seidl, 'Bilaterale Urkunde' (1980), in *Serapis* 6, p. 117-118; S. Grunert, *Der Kodex Hermopolis und ausgewählte private Rechtsurkunden aus dem ptolemäischen Ägypten* (Reclams Universal-Bibliothek 909), Leipzig 1982, p. 105.

Description. — The text on the recto is written across the fibres and has a top margin of 1.7 cm, a bottom margin of 1.1 cm and a right-hand margin of 1 cm. There is one kollesis visible on the verso (at c. 4 cm from the top). After redaction the papyrus was rolled horizontally from bottom to top. The text on the verso is written along the fibres and consists of 1) a summary written on the second last strip which was on the outside of the rolled papyrus (verso, l. 1-2); 2) a later addition to the agreement which was on the inside (l. 3-4).

Introduction

Contents. — The document is a demotic deed of partnership (verso, l. 1: *bk n ḫbr*) in which two individuals take each other as partner (*ḫbr*) in a common project. This type of document is an example of a bilateral document, whereas most demotic deeds are unilateral[1]. Such deeds of partnership are not commonly attested; most parallels date from the pre-Ptolemaic period[2]. Besides the example published here (94 B.C.), there is one more reference to such a deed of partnership in Pathyris: P. dem. Ryl. 33, verso, records a cession of the rights of a *bk n ḫbr* (95 B.C.)[3]. It may be a coincidence, but both deeds of partnership date from a period in which the Greek institutions in Pathyris, such as the Greek notary's office, apparently did not function (c. 100-90 B.C.)[4]: people had to fall back on Egyptian types of documents for, among other things, their private agreements (compare comm. on l. 5).

The document is a *bk* (private document), not a *sẖ* (notarial deed), see §34. Such a private arrangement was written down by one of the parties or by a third person. Here, a third person

---

1 See Seidl, 'Bilaterale Urkunde' (1980), in *Serapis* 6, p. 117-120.

2 See Depauw, *Companion* (1997), p. 145.

3 *ḫbr* was not read by the editor; for the reading, see Ch. F. Nims, in *JNES* 7 (1948), p. 252, and BL dem., p. 316.

4 See Vandorpe, 'Paying Taxes to the Thesauroi of the Pathyrites' (2000), p. 415.

called Nechouthes, son of Peteharsemtheus, penned the document: he took dictation from the two partners. The stipulations of the agreement have thus been established by the partners themselves. Consequently, the agreement is not well structured: some stipulations are (partly) repeated (l. 7 and 13: payment to Pharaoh and to the god; l. 3-4 and 7-10: division of the land), other clauses were added later (l. 17 and verso l. 3-4).

The two partners are Peteharsemtheus, son of Psennesis, and Phagonis, son of Panebchounis (pros. 602). The former can be identified with the Peteharsemtheus, son of Psennesis, who acts as a witness in a demotic marriage contract of 92 B.C. (P. dem. Eheverträge 48, verso, l. 12), in a demotic purchase contract from 91 B.C. (P. dem. Ryl. 29, verso, l. 4) and in a purchase contract of 88 B.C. (P. dem. Strasb. 8, verso l. 6).

The common project involves the cultivation of a piece of land and is agreed at the end of September (21 September), that is immediately after the inundation and at the beginning of the agricultural season.

The land to be cultivated is owned by Peteharsemtheus and the cattle that will work on the land (according to verso, l. 3: a pair of cows) belong to Phagonis. Peteharsemtheus will take two thirds of the land: one third because he owns the land and one third because of the farm work which he will undertake. Phagonis will take the remaining one third because of the cattle that he will bring in. The land or at least part of the land is located on Temrauthis and on newly gained land. This area is to be located to the north of the town of Pathyris, close to the Nile, and consists, in general, of corn land and vineyards (see comm. on l. 11-12).

The cultivation consists of *sk3*, that is ploughing, sowing and harvesting (see comm. on l. 2) and of "filling the land with cattle, corn and all the equipment of a farmer" (see comm. on l. 6). Thus, the land will be sown with corn. There is, however, one strange clause: the *sm* (grass or hay) is to be divided among the two partners (l. 17).

It is well-known that grass is planted to allow the land to recuperate. One may plant his land one year with wheat, the other year with grass. Here, the agreement involves the cultivation of land during only one year. It is not likely that the grass or hay meant here is the grass of the past year that would still be on the land after the inundation. There are two alternative interpretations. Part of the land may be planted with grass, part with corn[1]. Another possibility has been suggested in the commentary on the lease contract P. dem. Bürgsch. 9 (2 Sept. 124 B.C.) from Pathyris, where l. 10 has «wir werden Wasser auf sie geben und werden sie bestellen mit Zwiebeln und Gras (*sm*) als Ruhe. Und wir werden sie pflügen und werden sie füllen mit Rindern, Saatkorn, ...». The editor comments: « Zwiebeln und Gras sind hier und in der ... Parallelurkunde Kairo 31012 augenscheinlich als Pflanzen genannt, mit denen der Acker nach der Aberntung des Getreides, resp. vor der Bestellung damit bestellt werden soll, um ihm Erholung zu gewähren»; thus we are dealing here with «Fruchtwechsel schon in demselben Jahre vorgesehen, wie das in Oberägypten auch heute vielfach geschieht.»[2].

---

1 Schnebel, *Die Landwirtschaft* (1925), p. 221.

2 P. dem. Bürgsch. 9, p. 169 (§39b) and p. 169-170 (§40); compare Schnebel, *Die Landwirtschaft* (1925), p. 155-156; according to H. Felber «Eine Zweierntenwirtschaft ist aus den Pachtverträgen nicht zu belegen» (P. dem. Ackerpachtverträge, p. 138).

The cattle of Phagonis are to work in the germination and harvest season (*n pr.t šmw*; see comm. on l. 12-13), as expected: to plough the land and to harvest the grain.

The costs are paid by the two men together:
- — 10 artabas of wheat for the yoke tax on the cattle (see comm. on l. 5);
- — the taxes of Pharaoh and of the god (probably Hathor, as the major part of the land in Pathyris is part of the endowment of Hathor) (see comm. on l. 7);
- — the fodder for the cattle and the seed for sowing.

The fines to be paid by the partner who breaks the contract are stipulated in l. 14-16 (see also comm. on l. 14-16):
- — a fiscal fine of 5 deben of real silver to the Crown for burnt offerings;
- — a contractual fine of 5 deben of real silver to the other partner.

The scribe. — The demotic deed of partnership of 94 B.C. was written by a man called Nechouthes, son of Peteharsemtheus. For paleographical reasons, he can be identified with Nechouthes, son of Peteharsemtheus, who is found as witness in two demotic contracts (98 and 92 B.C.). He may be the topogrammateus of the southern toparchy of the Pathyrites, of whom a report has been copied in an important tax list of the period 94/93-91/90 B.C. On this person, see U. Kaplony-Heckel, in P. dem. Gebelein Heid., p. 36 and Ead., 'Demotische Verwaltungsakten aus Gebelein: der große Berliner Papyrus 13608', in *ZÄS* 121 (1994), p. 75-91, esp. p. 88.

Text

Recto

P3-dy-Ḥr-sm3-t3.wy s3 P3-šr-Is.t Pa-wn s3 Pa-n3-bẖn.w
n3 nty ḏd. Mtr=n p3 s 2 r sk3 ẖn p3 3ḥ
n P3-dy-Ḥr-sm3-t3.wy. Mtw P3-dy-Ḥr-sm3-t3.wy s3 P3-šr-Is.t ṯ3y dny.t 2.[t]
mtw Pa-wn ṯ3y dny.t wʿ.t. Mtw=n dy.t rdb n sw 10 n t3 iḥ.t
n Pa-wn s3 Pa-n3-bẖn.w (n-)mtr t3y=s nḥb mtw=n
sk3 mtw=n mḥ=w n iḥ.t pr stbḥ nb n wyʿ
mtw=n mḥ Pr-ʿ3ʿws p3 ntr n-mtr. I.ir P3-dy-Ḥr-sm3-t3.wy (s3)
P3-šr-Is.t ṯ3y n t3 wʿ.t n3 dny.wt nty sẖ ḥry ḥr p3y=f 3ḥ iw=f ṯ3y n t3 kṱ.t dny.t
ẖr t3y=f wp.t n wyʿ 3ḥ nty i.ir P3-dy-Ḥr-sm3-t3.wy r tw-s.
Mtw=n sk3=f. Mtw P3-dy-Ḥr-sm3-t3.wy (s3) P3-šr-Is.t ṯ3y dny.t 2.t
n-im=f mtw Pa-wn ṯ3y wʿ.t ḥr T3-mrwṱ.t
irm t3 m3y r-ḏb3 t3 iḥ.t. I.ir=w <ir> wp.t n pr.t
šmw. Mtw<=n> mḥ Pr-ʿ3ʿws p3 ntr n-mtr.
P3 rmt mtw=f st3.ṱ=s r tm ir r-ẖ md ⸢nb⸣ nty sẖ ḥry
mtw=f dy.t ḥḏ sp-sn n ḏnf (dbn) 5 r n3 grly n Pr-ʿ3ʿws
mtw=f dy.t ky ḥḏ sp-sn n ḏnf (dbn) 5 ⸢n⸣ p3y=f iry n-im=n.
Vacat
P3 sm mtw=f pš r-ẖ(?) t3 pš.
Sẖ N3-nḫt=f s3 P3-dy-Ḥr-sm3-t3.wy r-ḫrw=w n p3 s 2
n ḥ3.t-sp 21 ibd-1 3ẖ.t sw 6.

Verso

P3 bk n ẖbr r.ir P3-dy-Ḥr-sm3-t3.wy (s3) P3-šr-Is.t
irm Pa-wn s3 Pa-n3-bẖn.w.
Vacat
Mtw=n mḥ t3 ẖr.t syẖ n t3 iḥ.t n-mtr
t3 pr-sẖ.t.

---

1 *Pa-t3-bẖn.t* ed., *Pa-n3-bẖn.w* Lüddeckens (*OLZ* 65 (1970), p. 23) 3 *2.t* ed., *2[.t]* legimus 5 *Pa-t3-bẖn.t* ed., *Pa-n3-bẖn.w* Lüddeckens (*OLZ* 65 (1970), p. 23) 8 *kt* ed., *kṱ.t* legimus 9 *wyʿ p3y=f 3ḥ* ed., *wyʿ 3ḥ* Pestman (*Chron. d'Ég.* 41 (1966), p. 316); *r ṯ3y-s* ed., *r tw-s* Zauzich (*ZDMG* 118 (1968), p. 379) 10 *P3-dy-Ḥr-sm3-t3.wy* ed., *P3-dy-Ḥr-sm3-t3.wy (s3) P3-šr-Is.t* Pestman (*Chron. d'Ég.* 41 (1966), p. 316, n. 6) et Zauzich (*ZDMG* 118 (1968), p. 379) 11 *t3 mrwṱ* ed., *T3-mrwṱ.t* legimus 12 *r-ḏb3(?)* ed., *r-ḏb3* Lüddeckens (*OLZ* 65 (1970), p. 23) 13 *mtw-w* ed., *mtw<=n>* legimus 14 *st3tj* ed., *st3.ṱ=s* legimus; *r-ẖ mdw* ed., *r-ẖ mdw ⸢nb⸣* Zauzich (*ZDMG* 118 (1968), p. 379) 15 *gllw* ed., *grly* legimus 16 *n n3y=f iryw* ed., *⸢n⸣ p3y=f iry* aut *[n] n3y=f iry.w* legimus 17 *r t3 pš* ed., *r-ẖ(?) t3 pš* Pestman (*Chron. d'Ég.* 41 (1966), p. 316, n. 6) 19 *sw 16* ed., *sw 6* legimus Verso 3 *t3 ẖrrt(?)* ed., *t3 ẖr.t* BL dem., p. 198

Translation

Recto

Peteharsemtheus, son of Psennesis, (and) Phagonis, son of Panebchounis, are the ones who declare:

«We, being two men, agreed to plough on the land of Peteharsemtheus. Peteharsemtheus, son of Psennesis, will take two parts, whereas Phagonis will take one part. We will give, together, 10 artabas of wheat for the cattle of Phagonis, son of Panebchounis, for its yoke tax. We will plough and fill them (the land) with cattle, corn and all the equipment of a farmer. We will pay Pharaoh and the god, together. Because of his land, Peteharsemtheus, son of Psennesis, takes one of the above-mentioned parts (and) because of his farm work on the land which he will undertake, he takes the other part. We will plough the land. Peteharsemtheus, son of Psennesis, will take two parts of it, whereas Phagonis will take one part on Temrauthis and on the newly gained land because of (his) cattle. They (the cattle) will work in the germination and harvest season. We will pay Pharaoh (and) the god, together.

The man who refuses to act in accordance with all the stipulations mentioned above, will pay 5 (deben) of real silver for the burnt offerings of Pharaoh and another 5 (deben) to his companion among us.

The hay, it will be divided in two parts.»

Nechouthes, son of Peteharsemtheus, has taken dictation from the two men in year 21, 6 Thoth.

Verso

Document of partnership which Peteharsemtheus, son of Psennesis, and Phagonis, son of Panebchounis, have made.

«We will pay the fodder for the pair of cattle, together, and the seed corn.»

Notes

Recto

2 *sk3, to plough*: for the meaning of *sk3*, see S.P. Vleeming, in P. dem. Hou, p. 79, where he points to the use of the verb *sk3* «in its widest sense to include all agricultural activities from ploughing until harvesting. In fact, ploughing itself comprised the twin activities of ploughing and sowing. To the Egyptian mind, the one who ploughed a field, and who sowed it subsequently, derived therefrom the right to harvest its crop.». For a similar view, see H. Felber, in P. dem. Ackerpachtverträge, p. 125.

4 *iḥ.t, the cattle*: in l. 4, 5 and 12 the word *iḥ.t* (cow) is written with the feminine ending *.t* before the skin determinative. There are no plural signs. The plural verb *i.iry=w* in l. 12 and the expression *syḫ n t3 iḥ.t* (pair of cattle) on the verso, l. 3, however, show that not one but two cows are involved. Therefore, I prefer to translate *iḥ.t* by cattle throughout the text.

For the expression *syḫ n t3 iḥ.t* (pair of cattle), compare Pap. Lugd. Bat. XXII 4, l. 9 (*syḫ n iḥ.t*).

5 *nḥb, yoke tax*: the nature of the yoke tax is not clear. The text makes clear that the tax is related to the cattle used for the cultivation of land and supports the view of S.P. Vleeming that it may be a tax on transport animals (or transport vehicles) (O. dem. Varia, p. 14-15; see also D. Devauchelle, in O. dem. Louvre I, p. 39-43 and Depauw, *Companion* (1997), p. 134). Except for two examples from Pathyris, the tax is only attested in the early Ptolemaic period (reign of Ptolemy II and III) and, according to S.P. Vleeming, «the virtually complete silence of the Greek sources seems to suggest that this tax was typical of the Egyptian milieu, but, unfortunately, we cannot draw such a conclusion from our limited material» (O. dem. Varia, p. 15). Alongside the example of the text published here (of 94 B.C.), there may be one more piece of evidence for the yoke tax in Pathyris, recorded in the fragmentary text P. dem. Adler 12, verso, l. 10, of ?100/99 B.C. (see P. dem. Gebelein Heid., p. 36 IV (5)). The fact that this tax surfaces again in the late Ptolemaic period may be related to the particular situation of Pathyris at that time: apparently, almost no Greek institutions were functioning at the time (period c. 100-90 B.C.), see above, Contents.

6 *mtw=n mḥ=w n iḥ.t pr stbḥ nb n wyᶜ, we will fill them (the three thirds of land) with cattle, corn and all the equipment of a farmer*: for this and similar formulas, often attested in lease contracts, see H. Felber, in P. dem. Ackerpachtverträge, p.135.

7 *mtw=n mḥ Pr-ꜥ3 p3 ntr, we will pay Pharaoh and the god*: for the interpretation "Pharaoh (and) the god" rather than "den König, den Gott" (apposition, suggested by Seidl, 'Bilaterale Urkunde' (1980), in *Serapis* 6, p. 117 and 119), see the ed. pr. and BL dem., p. 197.

The payment of taxes to Pharaoh as well as to the god is rarely attested in Pathyris (see ed. pr., p. 36 (7), with reference to P. dem. Ryl. 34 and P. dem. BM 10516 ined.). The lease contracts usually mention only taxes to be paid to Pharaoh (see P. dem. Ackerpachtverträge, p. 142-150). The most important tax on land in Upper Egypt was the epigraphe or harvest tax, which was indeed to be paid to the Crown at the latest in the second century B.C. However, part of it flowed back (indirectly or directly) to the temples and thus the god was paid after all. See Vandorpe, 'The Ptolemaic Epigraphe' (2000).

n-mtr, together: the translation "together", rather than "ordnungsgemäß" (ed. pr.) or "voraus" (Seidl, 'Bilaterale Urkunde' (1980), in *Serapis* 6, p. 117-118), is suggested by the BL dem. (p. 197) after P.W. Pestman, in P. dem. Tor. Choach., p. 17, n. o (*n t3 mtr.t*, "insieme": «una locuzione avverbiale costruita con il sostantivo *t3 mtr.t*, "la comunione", "la cosa comune"»).

9 *ẖr t3y=f wp.t n wyꜥ 3ḥ, because of his farm work on the land*: the ed. pr. has *ẖr t3y=f wp.t n wyꜥ p3y=f 3ḥ* (because of his farm work on his land). According to P.W. Pestman (*Chron. d'Ég.* 41 (1966), p. 316), the signs read as *p3y=f* constitute the determinative of the preceding word *wyꜥ* (farmer).

11-2 *ḥr T3-mrwṯ irm t3 m3y, on Temrauthis and on the newly gained land*: at least part of the land is located on *T3-mrwṯ*, which is not to be interpreted as "fertile land" (see ed. pr. and Seidl, 'Bilaterale Urkunde' (1980), in *Serapis* 6, p. 117), but as a toponym because of the house determinative. It is well known also in Greek texts from Pathyris where it is transliterated as Temrauthis. The area is located by Pestman to the north of the town of Pathyris and to the west of *m3y*-land or island-land, that is newly gained land next to the Nile. This is confirmed by this passage in l. 11-12 according to which Temrauthis borders newly gained land (see Vandorpe, *Archives from Pathyris* (2001), §4 and Pestman, 'Pétéharsemtheus' (1965), p. 79-80 and map p. 78; P. dem. Ackerpachtverträge, p. 122). For the meaning of *m3y* (newly gained land), translated in Greek as νῆσος (island), see Vandorpe, *Archives from Pathyris* (2001), §4.

12-3 *n pr.t šmw, in the germination and harvest season*: the cattle are said to be available in the *pr.t*- and *šmw*–seasons. At the end of the second and in the beginning of the first centuries B.C. these seasons correspond to the period mid-January until mid-September, whereas the cattle are expected to help for the ploughing and sowing already in October-November. A similar clause is found in several lease contracts from Pathyris which stipulate that the lessee will cultivate the land in the *pr.t*- and *šmw*–seasons as well. H. Felber interprets it as the «Winter, d.h. eigentlich für den Herbst und Winter, die Zeit der Aussaat, des Aufgehens und Wachsens der Anbauprodukte, genauso aber auch für die gesamte Erntezeit».

The unusual determinatives of *pr.t* and *šmw* in this expression, however, suggest that these periods are not to be interpreted as well-defined periods of the year, that are winter until summer in 94 B.C., but as general indications within the agricultural season (as they originally were): *pr.t* always has the determinative of the legs walking, *šmw* always that of the corn-measure with grain pouring out. H. Felber already concluded as to the *šmw*-season: «somit ist deutlich die Zeit der Ernte gemeint, nicht die *šmw*-Jahreszeit» (P. dem. Ackerpachtverträge, p. 135). Thus, it is more correct to translate *šmw* here as the harvest season than as the summer season. For the *pr.t*–season, I propose a similar interpretation: the determinative of the legs walking refers to the verb *pr*, "emerge": either the emergence of the fields from the water or the emergence of the plants is meant. In both cases, we are dealing with the period immediately after the inundation, that is the germination season.

Seidl suggested still another interpretation. Because of the above-mentioned determinatives he interpreted *pr.t* as the verb *pr* ("Herauskommen") and *šmw* as "Getreideernte" and translated the clause as "Die Kuh soll Arbeit zum Herauskommen (einer) Getreideernte tun" (Seidl, 'Bilaterale Urkunde' (1980), in *Serapis* 6, p. 117). I prefer the more simple explanation of the preceding paragraph.

15-6 *ḥḏ sp-sn, real silver*: *ḥḏ* was in origin a term for silver but in the second century B.C. it was used for (a deben) of copper money; *ḥḏ sp-sn* (real silver) became the regular term for silver money (see P.W. Pestman, in *Enchoria* 2 (1972), p. 33-36).

Fines in demotic contracts are often set in real silver and not in copper because of the increasing copper inflation in the second and first centuries B.C. (see Reekmans, 'Ptolemaic Copper Inflation' (1951)).

Fines l. 15-16: the penalty clause records the fines to be paid by the partner who breaks the contract (see Berger, *Die Strafklauseln* (1911)): 1) a fiscal fine of 5 silver deben to the Crown for the burnt offerings of the kings, 2) a contractual fine of another 5 silver deben to the other partner. The demotic papyri which contain this penalty clause are private or notarial contracts (for the lease contracts, see H. Felber, in P. dem. Ackerpachtverträge, p. 186-187). The penalty clause, however, is found especially in Greek agoranomic papyri from Pathyris, but in reverse order: first the contractual fine is mentioned, then the fiscal fine.

The amount to be paid is the same for the two types of fine (for one exception, see below). There is again a difference between the demotic and the Greek documents. In demotic deeds the value of both fines is expressed in the same currency (real silver or copper money), whereas the Greek papyri record the fiscal fine in silver drachmas, the contractual fine in copper money.

The fine of twice 5 silver deben (or 100 silver drachmas) mentioned here is not high in comparison with similar fines recorded in other (usually agoranomic) contracts from Pathyris and Krokodilopolis:

AfP 1 (1901), p. 62-65, of 123 B.C.:	twice (60?) copper talents or 1200 silver drachmas
P. dem. Erbstreit, p. 39-46 and Greek translation: P. Giss. I 37 + 36 + 108, III 7-IV10, of 136 B.C.:	twice 50 copper talents or 1000 silver drachmas
P. dem. Erbstreit, p. 49-57, of 133 B.C.:	twice 500 silver drachmas
P. Adler 2 of 124 B.C.:	twice 20 copper talents or 300 silver drachmas
P. Lond. VII 2191 of 116 B.C.:	twice 20 copper talents or 300 silver drachmas
P. Strasb. II 83 of 114 B.C.:	twice 15 copper talents or 300 silver drachmas
P. Grenf. I 27 of 109 B.C.:	twice 10 copper talents or 200 silver drachmas
P. Grenf. II 25 of 103 B.C.:	twice 10 copper talents or 200 silver drachmas
P. Grenf. II 28 of 103 B.C.:	twice 10 copper talents or 200 silver drachmas
BGU III 998 of 101 B.C.:	twice 8 copper talents or 160 silver drachmas
P. Grenf. II 30 of 102 B.C.:	twice 5 copper talents or 100 silver drachmas
P. Grenf. II 33 of 100 B.C.:	twice 5 copper talents or 100 silver drachmas
Pap. Lugd. Bat. XIX 7 of 109 B.C.:	twice 5 copper talents or 100 silver drachmas
P. dem. Adler 27 (date unknown):	twice 5 copper talents
This Text 49 of 94 B.C.:	twice 100 silver drachmas
P. dem. Bürgsch. 9 of 124 B.C.:	twice 3 copper talents

In most cases, 1 copper talent corresponds to 20 silver drachmas, except for two cases where 1 copper talent corresponds to 15 silver drachmas (P. Adler 2; P. Lond. VII 219); see P.W. Pestman, in Pap. Lugd. Bat. XIX, p. 66, n. w.

There is one example where the amount of the fiscal and contractual fine is not the same: P. dem. Gebelein Heid. 14 of 114 B.C. records a fiscal fine of 5 copper talents and a contractual fine of 2 copper talents.

16 *⌜n⌝ p3y=f iry n-im=n, to his companion among us* (ed. pr.: *n n3y=f iryw n-im=n*): I prefer the reading *⌜n⌝ p3y=f iry n-im=n* to *[n] n3y=f iry.w n-im=n*, since parallel texts from Pathyris all have the former clause (P. dem. Bürgsch. 9, l. 23; P. dem. Cairo II 30702 + 30703, l. 5; P. dem. Gebelein Heid. 14, l. 23). After *p3y=f* there is an ink line which cannot be explained.

Verso

3 *t3 ẖr.t, the fodder*: for the reading *ẖr.t* (food), with the food determinative, rather than *ẖr* ("Geldbuße", suggested by Seidl, 'Bilaterale Urkunde' (1980), in *Serapis* 6, p. 118), see the ed. pr. (p. 37) and BL dem., p. 198.

syẖ n t3 iḥ.t, pair of cattle: see comm. on l. 4.

50

The 'Alexandrian Erotic Fragment' or 'Maedchens Klage' (by P. Bing)

Plate XXII

\- H. x W. = 16.5 x 17.8 cm [width incomplete] After October 174 B.C.

British Library, P. inv.no. 605 Verso [purchased from Grenfell on 9 Nov. 1895] = **P. Grenf. I 1** and appendix P. Grenf. II, p. 209-211; I.U. Powell, *Collectanea Alexandrina. Reliquiae minores Poetarum Graecorum Aetatis Ptolemaicae 323-146 A.C.*, Oxford 1970, p. 177-180. See also P. Lond. Lit. 50; R.A. Pack, *The Greek and Latin Literary Texts from Greco-Roman Egypt*, Ann Arbor 1965^2, no. 1743 = Leuven Database of Ancient Books (CD-Rom), Leuven 1998, no. 6867.

Translation. — Rowlandson, *Sourcebook* (1998), no. 84; P. Bing and R. Cohen, *Games of Venus: an Anthology of Greek and Roman Erotic Verse from Sappho to Ovid*, New York 1991, p. 183-184.

Bibliography. — O. Crusius, 'Grenfells Erotic fragment und seine litterarische Stellung', in *Philologus* 55 (1896), p. 353-384; U. von Wilamowitz-Moellendorff, 'Des Mädchens Klage', in *Nachrichten d. K. Ges. in Göttingen* (1896), p. 209-232; G. Manteuffel, *De Opusculis Graecis Aegypti e Papyris, Ostracis Lapidibusque Collectis*, Warsaw 1930, p. 52-55, 153-158; F.O. Copley, *Exclusus Amator. A Study in Latin Love Poetry* (American Philological Association. Monograph Series 17), s.l. 1956, p. 20-22; E. Fraenkel, *Elementi Plautini in Plauto*, Florence 1960, p. 311-320; S.L. Taran, *The Art of Variation in the Hellenistic Epigram* (Columbia Studies in the Classical Tradition 9), Leiden 1979, p. 93; M.L. West, 'Metrical Analyses: Timotheos and Others', in *ZPE* 45 (1982), p. 12-13; idem, *Greek Metre*, Oxford 1982, p. 148-149; I.C. Cunningham, *Herodae Mimiambi cum appendice fragmentorum mimorum papyraceorum*, Leipzig 1987, p. 36-38; R. Hunter, *Theocritus and the Archaeology of Greek Poetry*, Cambridge 1996, p. 7-10; E. Esposito, Il lamento dell' Esclusa (Eikasmos, Quaderni Bolognesi d. Filologia Classica, forthcoming).

Description. — The poem is copied in Dryton's hand (see §64-66) on the back of the loan Text 11 (October 174 B.C.). The poem is written in two columns of which the second is badly damaged. From column I, l. 24 onwards, the text is written in larger characters. For the paragraphoi and the double dots (:), see the introduction.

Transcription (by K. Vandorpe)

Column I

ἐξ ἀμφοτέρων γέγον' αἵρεσις ἐζευγίσμεθα : τῆς φιλίης
Κύπρις ἔστ' ἀνάδοχος : ὀδύνη μ' ἔχει ὅταν ἀναμνησθῶ :
____ὥς με κατεφίλει ἐπιβούλως μέλλων με καταλιμπάν[ει]ν
ἀκαταστασίης εὑρετής : καὶ ὁ τὴν φιλίην ἐκτικώς
____ἔλαβέ μ' Ἔρως : οὐκ ἀπαναίναμαι αὐτὸν ἔχου`σ´' ἐν τῆι διανοίαι
ἄστρα φίλα καὶ : συνερῶσα πότνια νύξ μοι παρά-
πεμψον ἔτι με νῦν πρὸς ὃν ἡ Κύπρις ἔγδοτον ἄγει μ[ε]
καὶ ὁ πολὺς Ἔρως παραλαβὼν συνοδηγὸν ἔχω
τὸ πολὺ πῦρ τὸ ἐν τῆι ψυχῆι μου καιόμενον ταῦτά
____μ' ἀδικεῖ ταῦτά μ' ὀδυνᾶι : ὁ φρεναπάτης ὁ πρὸ τοῦ
μέγα φρονῶν καὶ ὁ τὴν Κύπριν οὐ φάμενος εἶναι τοῦ ἐρᾶν μ̣ε̣τ̣α̣ι̣τ̣ίαν
____οὐκ ἤνεγκε ἐμὴν τὴν τυχοῦσαν ἀδικίην :
μέλλω μαίνεσθαι ζῆλος γάρ μ' ἔχει καὶ κατακάομαι
καταλελειμ̣μένη : αὐτὸ δὲ τοῦτό μοι τοὺς στεφάνους
____βάλε οἷς μεμονωμένη χρωτισθήσομαι :
κύριε μή μ' ἀφῆις ἀποκεκλει{κλει}μένην δέξαι
μ' εὐδοκῶ ζήλωι δουλεύειν : ἐπιμανοῦσ' ὁρᾶν

μέγαν ἔχει πόνον ζηλοτυπεῖν γὰρ δεῖ στέγειν
καρτερεῖν : ἐὰν δ' ἐνὶ προσκαθεῖ μόνον ἄφρων ἔσει
ὁ γὰρ μονιὸς ἔρως μαίνεσθαι ποιεῖ
γινωσχ' ὅτι θυμὸν ἀνίκητον ἔχω ὅταν ἔρις
λάβηι με μαίνομ' ὅταν ἀναμ[νή]σωμ' εἰ μονοκοιτήσω σὺ δὲ χρωτίζεσθ' ἀποτρέχεις
νῦν ἂν ὀργισθῶμεν εὐθὺ δεῖ καὶ δια-
λύεσθαι οὐχὶ διὰ
τοῦτο φίλους ἔχομεν οἳ κρινοῦσι
τίς ἀδικεῖ

1 φιλίας ed., φιλίης ed. (appendix p. 210) et Powell 4 φιλίαν ed., φιλίην Crusius (*Philologus* 55, 1896, p. 354-383) et Powell 5 α in ἀπαναίναμαι corr., Blass (*Jahrbuch f. Klass. Philol.* 1896, p. 347); ἔχουσ' ἐν ed., ἔχου`σ'' ἐν Vandorpe 10 φρ *vacat* εναπατης pap. 11 φαμενος *vacat* ειναι pap.; μ̣ο̣ι̣ α̣ἰ̣τ̣ίαν ed., μ̣ε̣τ̣α̣ι̣τ̣ίαν ed. (p. 4 et appendix p. 210) 12 ἤ̣νεγκε λ̣ι̣αν ed., ἤνεγκ' ἐμήν Blass (*Jahrbuch f. Klass. Philol.* 1896, p. 347) et Powell («incertum»); ἀδικίαν ed., ἀδικίην Crusius (*Philologus* 55, 1896, p. 354-383) 13 εχει *vacat* και pap. 15 χρωτισ *vacat* θησομαι pap. 17 ἐπιμανοῦσ' ὁρᾶν, *l.* ἐπιμανῶς ἐρᾶν 19 προσκαθεῖ, *l.* προσκαθῆι 20 ερως *vacat* μαινεσθαι pap. 22 ἀναμ[νη]σθωμ' cd., ω in ἀναμ[νη]σωμ' corr. ex θ Crusius (*Philologus* 55, 1896, p. 354 383); ει corr. ex αι 24 ἀνοργισθῶμεν ed., ἂν ὀργισθῶμεν Wilamowitz (*Gött. Nachtr.* 1896, p. 212, l. 50); ἄν, *l.* ἐάν; δ *vacat* ει pap. 26 κρι *vacat* νουσι pap.

Column II

ν̣ῦ̣ν̣ [ἂ]ν μὴ ἐπι[- - -]
ἐ̣ρ̣ῶ̣ κ̣ύριε τὸν [- - -]
νῦν μὲν οὐθε[- - -]
πλύτης ο[- - -]
δυνήσομαι · [- - -]
κοίτασον ἧς ἐχ[- - -]
ἱκανῶς σοῦ ἐν̣ . [- - -]
κύριε πῶς μα̣ . . [- - -]
πρῶτός μ' ἐπείρ[ασας - - -]
κύριον ἀτυχῶς οὐ[- - -]
ὀπ[.]α̣σθω με βλέπων [. .]ε̣δε[- - - ἐπι-]
τηδ[εί]ω̣ς αἰσθέσθω μ[. .]ταν[- - -]
ἐγὼ [δὲ] μέλλω ζηλοῦν τω[- - -]
δουλ̣[. . . .] . ταν διαφοροῦ · η[- - -]
ἀνθρ[ώπου]ς ἀκρίτως θαυμά[ζεις - - -]
με . [. . . . . .] . φ[ο]ρη · προσ̣[- - -]
θαυμ̣[α . . . . . .] . χρι̣α̣ν κατ[- - -]
σχω[- - - -]τ̣ω̣ι το[- - -]
κου . [- - -] ἐ̣νόσησα ν̣[- - -]
καὶ . [- - -]μ̣μεν . . [- - -]
λελάλ̣[ηκ - - - πε]ρὶ ἐμὴ̣ν̣ [- - -]

28 ον ed., ἄν Blass 36 πρῶτός με πειρ[- - -] ed., πρῶτός μ' ἐπείρ[ασας - - -] Powell 37 ἀτυχ[.] . ς εδ., ἀτυχῶ̣ς Vandorpe 38 ὀπυασθώμεθα ἐμῶν ed., ὀπ[.]α̣σθω με βλέπων Vandorpe 39 τ̣αν vel γαν 42 ἀνθρ[ώπ . υ]ς ἀκρίτως θαυμά[- - -] ed., ἀνθρ[ώπου]ς ἀκρίτως θαυμά[ζεις - - -] Powell 43 . φ[ο]ρη · [- - -] ed., . φ[ο]ρη · προσ̣[- - -] Vandorpe 45]τ̣ω̣ι vel]τ̣η̣ι 46]νοσησαν[ed., ἐ]νόσησα ν Powell, ἐ̣νόσησα ν̣[Vandorpe

Comment on l. 38: ὀπ[.]α̣σθω με βλέπων (ed. ὀπυασθώμεθα ἐμῶ̣ν): the reading by the editor ὀπυασθώμεθα was interpreted as a passive subjunctive aorist of a verb which appears to be a hapax: ὀπυάζομαι (to marry). The latter verb is listed in LSJ. The structure of my reading ὀπ[.]α̣σθω με βλέπων finds its parallel in the following line: αἰσθέσθω μ[?ε. The addition ὀπ[τ]ά̣σθω may be considered; ὀπτᾶν is a frequently attested verb (to burn); the passive voice may point to the burning by the fire of love. Consequently, the above-mentioned hapax ὀπυάζομαι should be deleted in LSJ.

Introduction (by P. Bing)[1]

The lyric monody, known variously as "The Maiden's Lament", "The Alexandrian Erotic Fragment" and the "Fragmentum Grenfellianum", probably belongs to a genre of popular performance known as *Magodia*, described in detail in Athenaeus (14.621c-d): «The player called *magodos* (μαγῳδός) has tambourines and cymbals and all his clothes are womanish ... Everything he does is indecent, whether playing the role of adulterous women or bawds, or of a drunken man going to his misstress in the *komos*. Aristoxenus says that *hilarodia* is serious and derives from tragedy, but *magodia* from comedy. Often *magodoi* took comic plots (ὑποθέσεις) and acted them in their own style and delivery.»

Our fragment seems well-matched to this description. It is the vividly mimetic song of a woman abandoned by her lover due to some unspecified offense (ἀδικίην vv. 22, 40). Her agitated frame of mind (summed up in the term ἀκαταστασίη, v. 7), causes her to speak in short often asyndetic bursts, her sentiment swinging between anger and abject submission. Following an exposition of her predicament in relatively calm dactyls, iambs and anapaests (vv. 1-10), she sets out for her lover's house, driven through the night by desire, in verses mixing anapaests, cretics, and dochmiacs (vv. 11-22). In the next section (vv. 23-32) she has arrived at his locked door and, addressing her lover directly for the first time (βάλε, v. 25), begs him in the manner of *paraklausithyron* to let her in. Here the key term is "madness" (μέλλω μαίνεσθαι, v. 23; ἐπιμανοῦσ' ὁρᾶν, v. 29; μαίνεσθαι, v. 32), the meter composed entirely of emotionally charged dochmiacs – a typical feature of Tragedy. In the last section before the text becomes fragmentary (vv. 33-40), the woman shifts between threats and a plea for reconciliation, while the rhythm modulates away from the predominately dochmiac.

The poem's meter (which here follows Cunningham's anaylysis) recalls that of the astrophic monodies of late Euripides. In its complex variety, it is unparaleled in Hellenistic poetry. It may, however, have a model in contemporary performance practice. Tragic arias staged as popular entertainment were very fashionable in the Hellenistic era and may, as West suggests, have influenced «the development of a genre of mimetic song» such as ours (p. 148-149).

But if the meter is redolent of late 5th cent. Tragedy, the diction is close to *koine*: for Wilamowitz this was a paradox («Die Versform ist um zwei Jahrhunderte etwa älter als die Sprachform», p. 222). And indeed, the nearest parallels for individual words are repeatedly in Polybius or the Septuagint. But by insistently characterizing the language of the poem as «unmittelbar die Sprache des Lebens» (p. 222), emulating «weder den tragischen noch irgend einen künstlich gesteigerten und geadelten Ton» (p. 220), Wilamowitz underestimated its linguistic artistry.

In fact, the song achieves remarkable effects through repetition and assonance. To this end, it raises almost to an aesthetic principle the exploitation of prepositions in homely compound-verbs, -nouns and -adjectives. See, for instance, the play with *ἀνά* and κατά in vv. 3-10 (*ἀνά*δοχος, ὅ*ταν ἀνα*μνησθῶ, καταλιμπ*άνε*ιν, ἀπ*αναίνα*μαι, δι*ανο*ίαι; *κατε*φίλει, *κατα*λιμπάνειν, ἀ*καταστασί*ης), or most strikingly the *Klangspiel* in vv. 23-35 between *μαίνε*σθαι, με *μονω*μένη, ἐπι*μανοῦσ'*, *μονος*, *μαίνε*σθαι, *μαίνο*μ', *μονο*κοιτήσω,

[1] For the bibliographical references, see the bibliography p. 381.

which suggests a causal link between solitude and madness. (cf. also comm. on v. 18f.). If there is one thing of which we can be sure, it is that no one ever talked like this.

Similarly, Richard Hunter contrasts the "literariness" of Theocritus' *Idyll* 2 in its relationship with Sophron's mimes or its allusions to specific passages from earlier authors, with the straightforward performative aims of our poem. «Idyll 2 is actively engaged with its own literary history; the *Fragmentum* is concerned only with ... its immediate performance» (p. 10). But again, this is to underrate its literary sophistication.

As *paraklausithyron*, our fragment shows considerable historical awareness. We take for granted that Theocritus displays wry literary self-consciousness when he shifts the normal urban setting of the *paraklausithyron* to the entrance of a cave (*Idyll* 3), or that Menander does so when his *exclusus amator* is excluded from his own house, unnerved by a captive concubine (*Misoumenos*). Our poem is no less knowing in its literary play. It sets convention on its head by substituting an *exclusa amatrix* for the stock *amator*; by making the journey to her lover's house transpire in the dark, with only passion's fire to guide her rather than the standard torches (vv. 15-16); by having her beg her paramour, who is at his revels within, to throw her the wreaths that lovers typically bring with them in the *komos* to their lovers' houses (v. 25).

It is tempting, too, to see specific allusions to literary models (to Sappho? comm. on v. 6). One can, for instance, view the whole piece as a response to Asclepiades *AP* 5.164 = G-P 13. There the *exclusus amator* spitefully imagines his female beloved shut out in turn before *his* door: ταὐτὰ παθοῦσα σοὶ [*scil.* Νυκτί] μέμψαιτ' ἐπ' ἐμοὶ στᾶσα παρὰ προθύροις (vv. 3-4). The lover in that epigram, moreover, addresses Night, just as in our poem (v. 11-12), and calls his beloved φιλεξαπάτης, just as the woman in ours calls hers ὁ φρεναπάτης (v. 18). Did the author of our song take this imagined scene as a starting point to spin out an entire scenario? In any case, the considerable artistry of meter and language should prompt us at least to ponder such questions, and indeed to wonder whether the "everyday" register of the diction is meant deliberately to characterize the speaking voice, rather than simply being a generic function of "popular" poetry.

The song was copied in Dryton's own hand on the verso of a loan of wheat taken by him while still a young man in 174 B.C. It seems likely that he copied the poem before moving to the small village of Pathyris in Upper Egypt c. 150 B.C. For Dryton - like his first wife Sarapias - was a citizen of Ptolemais, a bastion of Greek musical culture in the region around Thebes, and the most likely place for him to have encountered poetic performance. We know there was a thriving *koinon* of Dionysiac artists there since we have decrees in which it honored patrons, one signed by its members, including tragic, comic, and epic poets, actors, musicians, and technicians (OGIS I 51 = SB V 8855, mid 3rd cent. B.C., cf. also *BCH* 9 (1885), p. 140; Plaumann, *Ptolemais* (1910), p. 60-65). In such an environment Dryton might have witnessed the performance of a lyric monody, which struck his fancy. The paragraphoi dividing the text into recognizable, if somewhat irregular, sense-units; the double dots (:) marking word-division at grammatical and metrical pauses; the frequent observance in the papyrus of elision, suggest that Dryton may have made his copy directly from an original in which such signs were used as aids in preparation for performance.

Text with Colometry (by P. Bing, after Cunningham)[1]

ἐξ ἀμφοτέρων γέγον' αἵρεσις·	4 da	*Column I*
ἐζευγίσμεθα· τῆς φιλίης Κύπρις	4 da	
ἔστ' ἀνάδοχος· ὀδύνη μ' ἔχει.	2 ia ‖	
ὅταν ἀναμνησθῶ	δ ‖	
ὥς με κατεφίλει 'πιβούλως μέλλων	hδ δ	
με καταλιμπάν[ει]ν	δ	
ἀκαταστασίης εὑρετὴς	an cr	
καὶ ὁ τὴν φιλίην ἐκτικώς.	an cr	
ἔλαβέ μ' Ἔρως	ia	
οὐκ ἀπαναίναμαι αὐτὸν ἔχουσ' ἐν τῆι διανοίαι.	6da ‖	
ἄστρα φίλα καὶ συνερῶσα πότνια νύξ μοι	cr δ ba	
παράπεμψον ἔτι με νῦν πρὸς ὃν ἡ Κύπρις	2 an	
ἔγδοτον ἄγει μ[ε] καὶ ὁ	2 cr	
πολὺς Ἔρως παραλαβών.	2 cr	
συνοδηγὸν ἔχω τὸ πολὺ πῦρ	an cr	
τὸ ἐν τῆι ψυχῆι μου καιόμενον.	2 an	
ταῦτά μ' ἀδικεῖ, ταῦτά μ' ὀδυνᾶι·	2 ia ‖	
ὁ φρεναπάτης,	ia	
ὁ πρὸ τοῦ μέγα φρονῶν, καὶ ὁ τὴν Κύπριν οὐ	δ an	
φάμενος εἶναι τοῦ ἐρᾶν μεταιτίαν.	δ hδ	
οὐκ ἤνεγκ' ἐμὴν	δ	
τὴν τυχοῦσαν ἀδικίην.	lk	
μέλλω μαίνεσθαι· ζῆλος γάρ μ' ἔχει,	2δ	
καὶ κατακα<ί>ομαι καταλελειμμένη.	2δ ‖	
αὐτὸ δὲ τοῦτό μοι τοὺς στεφάνους βάλε.	2δ ‖	
οἷς μεμονωμένη χρωτισθήσομαι.	2δ	
κύριε, μή μ' ἀφῆις ἀποκεκλειμένην·	2δ	
δέξαι μ'· εὐδοκῶ ζήλωι δουλεύειν.	2δ	
ἐπιμανῶς ἐρᾶν μέγαν ἔχει πόνον,	2δ	
ζηλοτυπεῖν γὰρ δεῖ, στέγειν, καρτερεῖν·	2δ	
ἐὰν δ' ἑνὶ προσκαθεῖ μόνον ἄφρων ἔσει,	2δ ‖	
ὁ γὰρ μονιὸς ἔρως μαίνεσθαι ποιεῖ.	2δ	
γινωσχ' ὅτι θυμὸν ἀνίκητον ἔχω,	? 3 chor ‖	
ὅταν ἔρις λάβηι με· μαίνομ' ὅταν ἀναμ[νή]σωμ'	cr 2ia sp	
εἰ μονοκοιτήσω,	δ	
σὺ δὲ χρωτίζεσθ' ἀποτρέχεις.	an cr	
νῦν δ' ἂν ὀργισθῶμεν, εὐθὺ δεῖ	δ ia	
καὶ διαλύεσθαι.	δ ‖	
οὐχὶ διὰ τοῦτο φίλους ἔχομεν	cr δ	
οἳ κρινοῦσι τίς ἀδικεῖ;	lk	
νῦν [ἂ]ν μὴ ἐπι[- - -]		*Column II*
ἐρῶ, κύριε, τὸν [- - -]		
νυν μὲν οὐθε[- - -]		
πλύτης ο[- - -]		
δυνήσομαι. [- - -]		
κοίτασον, ἧς ἐχ[- - -]		
ἱκανῶς σοῦ ἐν. [- - -]		
κύριε, πῶς μ' α. . [- - -]		
πρῶτός μ' ἐπείρ[ασας - - -]		

[1] 48/49 Powell erroneously divided κύριε and πῶς μ' α into separate lines, thus incorrectly adding one to the number of lines.

κύριον ἀτυχῶ̣ς, οὐ[- - -]
ὀπ[̣]α̣σθω με βλέπων [̣ ̣]εδ̣ε[- - - ἐπι-]
τηδ[εί]ω̣ς αἰσθέσθω μ[̣ ̣]τ̣αν[- - -]
ἐγὼ [δὲ] μέλλω ζηλ̣οῦν τω[- - -]
δουλ̣[̣ ̣ ̣ ̣] ̣ταν διαφοροῦ· η[- - -]
ἀνθρ[ώπου]ς ἀκρίτως θαυμά[ζεις - - -]
με ̣[̣ ̣ ̣ ̣ ̣ ̣ ̣] ̣φ[ο]ρη· προσ̣[- - -]
θαυμ̣[α ̣ ̣ ̣ ̣ ̣ ̣ ̣] ̣χρια̣ν κατ[- - -]
σχω[- - - -]τ̣ω̣ι το[- - -]
κου ̣[- - -] ἐ̣νόσησα ν̣[- - -]
καὶ ̣[- - -]μ̣μεν ̣ ̣[- - -]
λελάλ̣[ηκ - - - πε]ρὶ ἐμὴ̣ν̣ [- - -]

Translation (by P. Bing)

Our feelings were mutual,
we bound ourselves together. And Kypris is love's
security. It's torture
to recall
how he kissed me, when he meant
to desert me,
that inventor of confusion,
begetter of my love.
Desire gripped me.
I don't deny that he's on my mind.
O beloved stars and lady Night, companions in my desire,
take me even now to him, whom Kypris
drives me to as a captive, while
potent Eros holds me in his grip.
My guide is the potent torch
that's ablaze in my soul.
But this is what hurts me, this is what aches:
that this cheater of hearts,
so proud before, denied my love had sprung
from Kypris,
and now can't bear
a chance offense.
I'm going to go mad; I'm jealous,
I'm burning up at being deserted.
So throw me the garlands,
which, in my loneliness, I'll press to my skin.
Master, don't lock me out and send me off.
Take me. I'm content to be your eager slave.
Loving to distraction is a heavy task:
you have to be jealous, endure, keep waiting.

And if you devote yourself to just one, you will just go crazy,
for lonely desire makes you go mad.
You should know I have a stubborn temper
when I get in a fight. I go mad when I recall
that I will sleep alone,
while you run off to press your flesh to another's.
If we're angry at each other, we'll have to
make up right now.
Isn't this why we have friends,
to decide who's in the wrong?
....

Notes (by P. Bing)

v.1 In Hellenistic usage, αἵρεσις may denote an emotional "inclination" toward another. See Polybius on his friendship with Scipio: εἰς πατρικὴν καὶ συγγενικὴν ἦλθον αἵρεσιν καὶ φιλοστοργίαν πρὸς ἀλλήλους (31.25.1), cf. 31.23.3, 30.31.17.

2 ζευγίζω is a Hellenistic form for ζεύγνυμι, cf. 1 Macc. 1.15. The idea of being "yoked to a mate" is common in poetry from Sophocles on, cf. *e.g.*, *Trach.* 536.

3 ἀνάδοχος: "a security". The substantive is Hellenistic and prosaic.

ὀδύνη μ' ἔχει: The speaker repeatedly portrays herself as passive victim, cf. the frequency of με as object (με κατεφίλει v. 5, με καταλιμπάν[ει]ν v. 6, ἔλαβέ μ' Ἔρως v. 9, παράπεμψον ... με v. 12, Κύπρις/ ... ἄγει μ[ε] vv. 12-13, μ[ε] ... Ἔρως παραλαβών vv. 13-14, μ' ἀδικεῖ ... μ' ὀδυνᾶι v. 17, ζῆλος ... μ' ἔχει v. 23, μή μ' ἀφῆις v. 27, δέξαι μ' v. 28, ἔρις λάβηι με v. 34), or the accumulation of perfect passive participles in vv. 24-27 (καταλελειμμένη, μεμονωμένη, ἀποκεκλειμένην).

5 'πιβούλως: "treacherously". The adverb only here in poetry.

μέλλων: The first indication of the gender of the object of desire.

6 με καταλιμπάν[ει]ν: cf. Sappho fr.94.2: με ψισδομένα κατελίμπανεν. As here, the female narrator recalls how the object of her desire abandoned her (ἀναμνησθῶ v. 4, ἀναμ[νή]σωμ' v. 34 ~ ὄμναισαι Sappho 94.10, cf. 16.15). λιμπάνω and its compounds (collateral forms of λείπω) are rare in Classical authors (cf. Page *ad* Eur., *Medea* 800), thereafter appearing occasionally in early Hellenistic poetry, cf. Machon fr.9.77, Aratus 128, Posidippus *SH* 705.7. They become a feature, however, of *koine* (cf. *LXX* Gen.39.19, 2 Kings 5.21, etc.). In our poem it may be possible to see the verb as both an allusion to Sappho and a reflection of everyday speech.

Given the paragraphos under vv. 5-6 (= line 3 of the papyrus), we may wish (with Manteuffel) to punctuate after καταλιμπάν[ει]ν, taking vv. 7-9 as a new sentence referring to Eros rather than to the speaker's beloved (the designation "inventor of [*scil.* my] confusion", ἀκαταστασίης εὑρετής v. 7, squares better with the god, though one can imagine it being used hyperbolically of the lover).

7 ἀκαταστασίης εὑρετής: prose idiom, the first word = "confusion", "instability", and is specifically Hellenistic, cf. Polybius 7.4.8; 1 Cor. 14.33, etc.

8 ὁ τὴν φιλίην ἐκτικῶς: ἐκτίκτω, “bring forth, spawn”, a prose word.

9 ἔλαβέ μ' Ἔρως: cf. Posidippus 12.120.2-3: Ἔρως .../ ἤν με λάβῃς.

10 A dactylic hexameter closes the first section (1-10), and ἀπαναίναμαι lends the line a specifically epic coloring, cf. *Il*.7.185, etc. Characteristically, this word is juxtaposed with the prosaic αὐτὸν ἔχουσ' ἐν τῆι διανοίαι.

ἔχουσ': the text’s first indication of the speaker’s gender.

11-2 The speaker’s journey to her lover’s house - a change of scene – is marked by a verbal cue, the imperative παράπεμψον in v. 12. Similarly βάλε, v. 25, indicates that she has arrived before her lover’s door.

ἄστρα φίλα καὶ ... πότνια νύξ: lovers customarily address the night and other heavenly bodies in paraklausithyron, cf. Meleager *AP* 5.190.1 and 5.165.1: σε, φίλη Νύξ,/ ναὶ λίτομαι, κώμων σύμπλανε, πότνια Νύξ, etc. In comedy, cf. Menander, *Misoumenos* A 1: ὦ Νύξ – σὺ γὰρ δὴ πλεῖστον Ἀφροδίτης μέρος / μετέχεις θεῶν, ἐν σοί τε περὶ τούτων λόγοι / πλεῖστοι λέγονται φροντίδες τ' ἐρωτικαί, or Plautus, *Mercator* 3: non ego item facio ut alios in comoediis / vidi amoris facere, qui aut Nocti aut Dii aut Soli aut Lunae miserias narrant suas.

συνερῶσα: as in the epigram of Meleager cited above, where Νύξ appears as “fellow-roamer in the revel” (κώμων σύμπλανε), the temporal coincidence of Night and the *komos* is understood as Night’s *participation* in the amatory situation.

12-3 ἡ Κύπρις / ἔγδοτον ἄγει μ[ε]: ἔκδοτον ἄγειν = “Kypris leads me off as a captive”. For the martial terminology, cf. Herodotus 6.85.10: Τί βουλεύεσθε ποιέειν, ἄνδρες Αἰγινῆται; τὸν βασιλέα τῶν Σπαρτιητέων ἔκδοτον γενόμενον ὑπὸ τῶν πολιητέων ἄγειν;. In an amatory context cf. Posidippus *AP* 12.120.2-3 = 7.2-3 G-P (addressed to Eros) ἤν με λάβῃς ἄπαγ' ἔκδοτον.

15 συνοδηγὸν ἔχω: “I have as my guide”. A hapax, but see the participle in a Christian magical papyrus, Preisendanz 21.26-27. ὁδηγός appears first in Polybius.

τὸ πολὺ πῦρ / τὸ ἐν τῆι ψυχῆι μου καιόμενον: cf. v. 24 κατακα<ί>ομαι. Passion as a fire burning within is ubiquitous in poetry, see, *e.g.*, Pindarus, P.4.219 (of Medea): ἐν φρασὶ καιομέναν, Callimachus, *Ep*.25 Pf. = *AP* 5.6.5: ἀρσενικῷ θέρεται πυρί, Theocritus 2.133-134: Ἔρως ... πολλάκις Ἀφαίστοιο σέλας φλογερώτερον αἴθει, and Gow on Theocritus 3.17. In light of συνοδηγός the fire certainly evokes the torch that lovers bring on the *komos* to the house of their beloved. But, as Wilamowitz observed, «Scham und Angst verwehren ihr das, und so weist ihr nur die Eifersucht den Weg» (p. 223).

Crusius suggests these lines also evoke the torch-lit procession of the bride to the home of the groom (p. 364). παραπέμπειν (v. 12) may = “escort to the bridal chamber”, cf. Plutarchus, *Romulus* 15.5; Lucian, *Dial. mar.* 5.1.

17 ταῦτά μ' ἀδικεῖ, ταῦτά μ' ὀδυνᾶι: this looks ahead to the “chance injury” (τὴν τυχοῦσαν ἀδικίην, v. 22) the woman caused her lover, and which he found intolerable.

18f The accumulation of labial plosives (*φρεναπάτης*, *πρὸ*, *φρονῶν*, *Κύπριν*) suggests the contempt which the speaker here feels for her lover.

ὁ φρεναπάτης: elsewhere only in Paul's letter to Titus (1.10); φρεναπατᾶν in that to the Galatians 6.3 and Philo Judaeus fr.17.

20 μ̣ε̣τ̣α̣ι̣τ̣ίαν: "the joint cause", an elevated word, redolent of Tragedy (cf. Aeschylus, *Ag*. 811, *Eum.* 199, 465). The lover denies that the relationship has divine sanction, thus making it seem less binding. For this gambit cf. Xenopon Ephesius 1.1.5 (ἐφρόνει δὲ τὸ μειράκιον ἐφ' ἑαυτῷ μέγα ... Ἔρωτα γε μὴν οὐδὲ ἐνόμιζεν εἶναι θεόν, ἀλλὰ πάντῃ ἐξέβαλεν οὐδὲν ἡγούμενος, λέγων ὡς οὐκ ἄν ποτέ τις ἐρασθείη οὐδ' ὑποταγείη τῷ θεῷ μὴ θέλων), cited by Crusius (p. 366), who notes that haughty youths denying the power of Kypris are staples of Greek erotic literature from Hippolytus on.

21 ἐμὴν: the papyrus reading cannot be correct. Wilamowitz' conjecture *νῦν* (*i.e.* οὐκ ἤνεγκε *νῦν*) makes for a plausible contrast with ὁ πρὸ τοῦ μέγα φρονῶν (v. 19): "so proud before..., he now was unable to bear a chance offense (ἀδικίην)".

23 ζῆλος: here "jealousy", echoed in ζηλοτυπεῖν v. 30, and probably μέλλω ζη̣λοῦν at v. 54 (though not in v. 28, which introduces the more positive sense of ζῆλος as "passion", ζήλωι δουλεύειν). The speaker is jealous because her lover is at a symposium, presumably in the company of friends and other women (cf. comm. on v. 25 below).

25 αὐτὸ δὲ τοῦτο: "just for this reason", *i.e.* because I am abandoned, cf. Plato, *Symp.* 204a.

στεφάνους βάλε: the first direct address to the lover indicates that the scene has shifted. In a *paraklausithyron* the lover standing before the house of his beloved conventionally hangs wreaths at the door. These are available because he typically comes on a *komos* from a drinking party, where wreaths were standard equipment. The situation here is inverted: the drinking party is within; the speaker is excluded, and must beg her lover to throw wreaths from the house so she can have the requisite prop.

26 μεμονωμένη: the pf. m.-p. pt. is typical of prose, except only Anacreontea 37.13.

27 κύριε: "master". The term expresses servitude in love, cf. also vv. 42, 49, and – with Cunningham – vv. 51 and 60. This is our first instance of κύριος as erotic blandishment. By the time of Martial (cited by Crusius) it seems to have become common. His epigram 10.68.5 chides a Roman patrician matron for using the Greek endearments "κύριέ μου, μέλι μου, ψυχή μου": lectulus has voces, nec lectulus audiat omnis, / sed quem lascivo stravit amica viro, vv. 7-8. Cf. also *AP* 12.28 and Ovid, *Amores* 3.7.11, "et mihi blanditias dixit *dominumque vocavit*". At Xenophon Ephesius 2.4.5, Anthia addresses Habrocomes as τῆς ψυχῆς τῆς ἐμῆς δέσποτα, cf. 5.14.2, Achilles Tatius 5.26.7.

28 εὐδοκῶ: "I am content". The verb is not found before the Hellenistic era.

29 ἐπιμανῶς ἐρᾶν: proposed by H. Diels (*Deutsche Literaturzeit.* 16 May, vol. 20 (1896), p. 614) for the papyrus' corrupt ἐπιμανοῦσ' ὁρᾶν, cf. Lucian, *Verae Historiae* 2.25.4: αὐτὴ δὲ οὐκ ἀφανὴς ἦν ἐπιμανῶς ἀγαπῶσα τὸν νεανίσκον·. Perhaps we should consider ἐπιμανεῖσ' ὁρᾶν, *i.e.* "to look on when you are crazy about (a person)".

30 στέγειν: either "conceal" or, more probably, "endure", a Hellenistic meaning, cf. *e.g.* 1 Cor. 13.7 Ἡ ἀγάπη ... πάντα στέγει; absolute cf. 1 Thess. 3.5 κἀγὼ μηκέτι στέγων ἔπεμψα εἰς τὸ γνῶναι τὴν πίστιν ὑμῶν.

καρτερεῖν: here "to wait", as in Hellenistic prose, cf. 2 Macc. 7.17.

31 ἐὰν δ ἑνὶ προσκαθεῖ: the δέ is adversative, *i.e.* the speaker wavers in her resolve. προσκαθεῖ = προσκαθῇ, 2nd pers. pres. subj. of προσκάθημαι. The verb is in keeping with δουλεύειν v. 28 implying *one-sided* "devotion" and discrepency in status.

32 ὁ γὰρ μονιὸς ἔρως μαίνεσθαι ποιεῖ: μονιὸς ἔρως must mean "lonely desire", not "desire for one person". The principle enunciated in this verse supports and explains (γάρ) the assertion of v. 31: "But if you are devoted to one you will only be frantic. For a μονιὸς ἔρως (and such one-sided devotion is clearly just that) causes madness".

33 γινωσχ' ὅτι θυμὸν ἀνίκητον ἔχω: cf. Plato, ***Republic*** 375 b 1 on the guardian being suitably θυμοειδής: ἢ οὐκ *ἐννενόηκας ὡς* ἄμαχόν τε καὶ *ἀνίκητον θυμός*, οὗ παρόντος ψυχὴ πᾶσα πρὸς πάντα ἄφοβός τέ ἐστι καὶ ἀήττητος; . In pre-Hellenistic literature, ἀνίκητος is mainly a poetic word, but by the time of our papyrus it is also at home in prose (Maccabbees and Diodorus Siculus).

34 ὅταν ἔρις λάβηι με: "when I get angry". The phrase recalls ἔλαβέ μ' Ἔρως (v. 9) and Ἔρως παραλαβών (v. 14). Ἔρως readily lapses into ἔρις.

35 εἰ μονοκοιτήσω: εἰ may = ὅτι following the strongly emotive μαίνομ' ὅταν ἀναμ[νή]σωμ', cf. *KG* II 369,8. In that case the verb is future: "I go mad when I recall that I will sleep alone, while you ...". Alternatively, εἰ may = ἐάν with subjunctive, fairly common in poetry from Homer onwards, rare in prose, cf. *KG* II 474 anm.1: "If I sleep alone, I go mad whenever I remember". μονοκοιτέω previously only at Aristophanes, *Lys*. 592.

36 σὺ δὲ χρωτίζεσθ' ἀποτρέχεις: "you run off to touch your skin to another's". Theocritus has the equivalent χροΐζομαι at *Id.* 10.18 (with Gow's n. *ad loc.*), cf. *Id.* 2.140, χρὼς ἐπὶ χρωτὶ πεπαίνετο. In light of its use here, χρωτισθήσομαι at v. 26 is all the more poignant: the wreaths there substitute for what she truly desires. For ἀποτρέχω of erotic abandonment, cf. Plato, *Symp*. 181d ἐπ' ἄλλον ἀποτρέχοντες.

37 εὐθὺ: temporal, cf. LSJ *s.v.* B I 3.

40 τίς: = ὁπότερος in *koine*, cf. A. Debrunner, *Geschichte der griechischen Sprache*. II (Sammlung Goschen 114), Berlin 1954, p. 71.

42 ἐρῶ: either "I will say" (εἴρω) or "I love" (ἐράω).

46 κοίτασον: "go to bed". The verb is Hellenistic, cf. *LXX* Psalm 103.22, Dan. 4.15.

50 πρῶτός μ' ἐπεί[ρ[ασας: cf. LSJ *s.v.* πειράω A IV. Crusius' supplement suggests one reason why the speaker's attachment to her lover is so intense: he was her first.

51 κύριον ἀτυχῶς: Cunningham reads κύρι' ὂν ἀτυχῶς.

62 λελάλ̣ηκ: the perfect of λαλέω is attested no earlier than Menander.

VII

OSTRAKA

Introduction : §57. Are the ostraka part of the archive of Dryton's family? — §58. Survey of the ostraka of Dryton's family.
Receipt of measurement and harvest tax receipts : §59. Relation between the receipt of measurement and the harvest tax receipts.
Receipts for tax on pigeon house : §60. Tax on pigeon house. — §61. The pigeon house of Dryton's daughters. — §62. The bank in Pathyris and Krokodilopolis.

Introduction

§57. *Are the ostraka part of the archive of Dryton's family?* — The question whether the ostraka belong to the archive of Dryton's family or not is discussed in Vandorpe, *Archives from Pathyris* (2001), §10 and §26. In my view, they were found in the same house as the papyrus archive. There are no ostraka from the time Dryton was still alive (he died in or shortly after 126 B.C.). The ostraka belong to the younger members of the family who inherited part of Dryton's papyrus archive: his son Esthladas took over part of the papyrus archive, but this part is lost, whereas Dryton's oldest daughter and her husband inherited the part which is preserved. Thus, one expects the same scenario for the ostraka: only the ostraka belonging to Dryton's oldest daughter Apollonia alias Senmouthis and her husband Kaies, son of Pates, are expected to be preserved. Indeed, all the ostraka belong to them:

Ostraka 51-53 were issued to Kaies, son of Pates;

Ostraka 54-58 belong to (Apollonia alias) Senmouthis, that is

- either to Senmouthis alone
- or to Senmouthis and others (see survey, §58)
- or to Senmouthis' sisters (Ostrakon 57); in the latter case, Senmouthis undoubtedly kept the ostrakon for her sisters, as she did with some of the papyrus documents.

§58. *Survey of the ostraka of Dryton's family.*

Receipt of measurement				
51	108 B.C.	for Kaies s.of Pates	Pathyris	O. dem. Zürich 36
Harvest tax receipts				
52	108 B.C.	for Kaies s.of Pates	granary, Pathyris	O. dem. *Enchoria* 19/20 no. 2
53	107 B.C.	for Kaies s.of Pates	granary, Pathyris	O. dem. Zürich 12
Pigeon house receipts				
54	108 B.C.	for Senmouthis d.of Dryton and others	[bank, Pathyris]	O. dem. Turin S 12791 ined.
55	101 B.C.	for Senmouthis d.of Dryton	[bank, Pathyris]	O. dem. *Enchoria* 19/20 no. 8
56	100 B.C.	for Senmouthis d.of Dryton	bank, Krokodilopolis	O. Gr. Wilck. II 1617
57	100 B.C.	for sisters of Senmouthis d.of Dryton	bank, Krokodilopolis	O. Gr. Wilck. II 1618
Account				
58	s.d.	Senmouthis d.of Dryton and family member		O. dem. Fs. von Beckerath, p.142

Receipt of measurement and harvest tax receipts (Ostraka **51-53**)

§59. *Relation between the receipt of measurement and the harvest tax receipts.* — Ostrakon 51, issued to Kaies, son of Pates, is a demotic receipt introduced by *r.rḫ=w*. I identify this type of receipt with the receipt of measurement issued after the second survey operation in February-March, when the land under cultivation was measured. In my view, the results of this operation were not only listed in a survey-document kept by an official, but the owner or the lessee also received an excerpt, called a "receipt of measurement"[1]. Thus, Ostrakon 51 records that, within a plot of highland of 16 1/2 1/16 arouras, 7 arouras were cultivated by Kaies and were thus taxable at the normal rate for highland. After the harvest, Kaies went with this receipt to the granary to pay his harvest tax, called *epigraphe* in Greek, *šmw* in demotic; two such harvest tax receipts for Kaies are indeed preserved (Ostraka 52 and 53). Ostrakon 52 dates to October 108 B.C. and may record *part* of the payment of the harvest tax for the 7 arouras of Ostrakon A. As the average tax rate is 4-5 artabas per aroura, one expects a total of 28-35 artabas. Ostrakon 52 records two payments, amounting to 10 1/4 artabas in total:

1. a payment of 5 artabas by Patous, son of Horos, who owes 5 artabas of wheat to Kaies because he took (? leased) two beds of the latter. Instead of returning the 5 artabas to Kaies in person, he hands over the 5 artabas to the granary on the account of Kaies;
2. on the same day, Kaies himself pays another 5 1/4 artabas.

---

1 For my new interpretation of the *r.rḫ=w*-receipts, see Vandorpe, 'The Ptolemaic Epigraphe' (2000), in *AfP* 46, p. 165-228, Part D and E.

Receipts for tax on pigeon house (Ostraka **54-57**)

§60. *Tax on pigeon house*[1]. — The daughters of Dryton pay a tax which in Greek is called πηχισμός, in demotic *p3 tn n s.t-mn.ty* (the tax on (the) pigeon house). The tax is known from demotic receipts of the Ptolemaic and Roman periods[2]. In Pathyris, alongside the common name

p3 tn n s.t-mn.ty (the tax on (the) pigeon house),

a more elaborate name is found in one ostrakon from Pathyris:

p3 tn n grp n s.t-mn.ty (the pigeon-tax on (the) pigeon house)[3].

In Greek the tax is known as

πηχισμὸς Παθύρεως or πηχισμὸς περ(ιστερεώνων) Παθύρεως in Pathyris
πηχισμὸς περιστερεώνων or περιστερεώνων, elsewhere.

The pigeon house tax appears to be a tax on the dimensions (πῆχυς: cubit) of a pigeon house. In some demotic tax receipts of the Roman period the actual cubits of the dovecote are explicitly recorded[4]. It is not clear whether or not this tax is distinct from the τρίτη περιστερεώνων[5].

In SB XX 14372 a tax known as πορθμ(ίδων)? Παθύ(ρεως) (? the ferry-toll of Pathyris) in the Greek receipt and *r p3 iw n t3 s.t-mne* (for the valuation? of the landing place) in the demotic summary. The demotic translation of *t3 s.t-mne* as "landing place" rather than the regular meaning "pigeon house" is undoubtedly inspired by the Greek equivalent πορθμίς (ferry-toll). The reading of πορθμ(ίδων)? Παθύ(ρεως) is, however, doubtful. J.G. Milne already corrected this reading in 1925 into πηχ(ισμοῦ)[6], but his comment, hidden in a footnote, has escaped the attention of most scholars. Consequently, SB XX 14372 forms yet another example of the pigeon house tax, called in Greek πηχ(ισμοῦ) Παθύ(ρεως), as already suggested by P.W. Pestman (personal communication)[7]; the receipt is described in demotic as an *iw n t3 s.t-mne* or "receipt for the tax on pigeon house"[8]. That the pigeon house is involved in SB XX 14372 is confirmed by O. dem. *Enchoria* 19/20 (1992/3) no. 6 and Gallazzi, 'Ricevute' (2000), 2a and 2b, demotic and Greek pigeon house receipts for the same taxpayer and for the same tax amount (1800 dr.) as occurs in SB XX 14372, see the survey below.

---

1 See J.G. Milne, in *JEA* 11 (1925), p. 272; M. Cobianchi, 'Ricerche di ornitologia nei papiri dell' Egitto greco-romano', in *Aegyptus* 16 (1936), p. 119-121; Préaux, *L'économie royale* (1939), p. 238-240; see now also Gallazzi, 'Ricevute' (2000), p. 189-194.
2 See, for instance, O. dem. Mattha, p. 59 (Roman).
3 O. dem. *Enchoria* 19/20 (1992/3), no. 6.
4 See, for instance, O. dem. Mattha 169 and 170.
5 Préaux, *L'économie royale* (1939), p. 238-240: distinct from the τρίτη περιστερεώνων; J.G. Milne, in *JEA* 11 (1925), p. 273: not distinct from the τρίτη περιστερεώνων.
6 J.G. Milne, in *JEA* 11 (1925), p. 273, n. 4.
7 See now also Gallazzi, 'Ricevute' (2000), p. 190.
8 nor is SB XX 14373 a receipt for πορθμίς (ferry-toll), but for the harvest tax, for which see §59; see also BL X: «keine Abgabenquittung für πορθμίς».

The pigeon house tax is paid in cash to the bank in the period March to May (see the survey below). The Greek receipts show that additional taxes amounting to 20% must be paid: these receipts usually record two sums: 1. the tax figure and 2. the total including the tax figure and the additional taxes. The demotic receipts only record one sum: either the total sum, including the extra charge (Ostrakon 55), or the tax sum, exclusive of the extra charge (Ostrakon 54: *irm p3y=w wḏ*).

The purpose of these additional taxes, called προσδιαγραφόμενα in Roman times, is described by Milne[1] as a charge of "an extra percentage to cover the costs of collection [i.e. of the taxes], and in case of taxes assessed in silver a further percentage for the conversion of copper into silver. The percentages were set by the government when the tax was farmed out (which was usually for a year and for a particular nome), and might vary from time to time and from place to place". In Pathyris (2nd half of the 2nd century B.C.), the additional charge was 20%.

1 J.G.Milne, 'Double Entries in Ptolemaic Tax-Receipts', in *JEA* 11 (1925), p. 269-283, esp. p. 282; see also A. Gara, *Prosdiagraphomena e circolazione monetaria* (Testi e documenti per lo studio dell' antichità 56), Milano 1976, App.II, p. 159-171.

Survey: the pigeon house tax in Pathyris.

Ostrakon	*Date B.C.*	*Banker*	*Name of the tax*	*Tax amount*	*Tax payer*
Ostrakon **54**	18 March/ 16 April 108	Patseous s.of Pates (bank Pathyris)	*p3 tn n t3y=w s.t-mn.ty (the tax on their pigeon house)*	6000 dr. for 6 persons + extra charge	Senmouthis d.of Dryton, and others
O. dem. *Enchoria* 19/20 (1992/3) no. 6	In or after 107/6	?	*p3 tn n grp n t3y=f s.t-mn.t (the pigeon tax on his pigeon house)*	1800 dr., extra charge included	Petosiris s.of Harsiesis
Ostrakon **55**	15 March 101	Poregebthis (bank Pathyris)	*[p3 tn s.]t-mn.ty (the tax on the pigeon house)*	1200 dr.	Senmouthis d.of Dryton
O. dem. *Enchoria* 19/20 (1992/3) no. 7	15 March 101	Poregebthis (bank Pathyris)	*p3 tn s.t-mn.ty (the tax on the pigeon house)*	900 dr.	Peteharsemtheus s.of Nechouthes
O. PSI III 258	16 March 100	Paniskos, bank Krokodilopolis	πηχ(ισμὸς) Παθύ(ρεως)[1]	1500 dr. + 20% = 1800 dr.	Patous s.of Pelaias
SB XX 14,372	14 April 100	Paniskos, bank Krokodilopolis	πηχ(ισμὸς) Παθύ(ρεως)[2] = *p3 iw n t3 s.t-mn.ty (the receipt of the pigeon house (tax))*	1500 dr. + 20% = 1800 dr.	Petosiris s.of Harsiesis
Ostrakon **56**	14 May 100	Paniskos, bank Krokodilopolis	πηχ(ισμὸς)[3] Παθύ(ρεως)	1000 dr. + 20% = 1200 dr.	Senmouthis d.of Dryton
Ostrakon **57**	30 May 100	Paniskos, bank Krokodilopolis	πηχ(ισμὸς)[4] Παθύ(ρεως)	3000 dr. + 20% = 3600 dr.	three sisters of Senmouthis d.of Dryton
Gallazzi, 'Ricevute' (2000), 2a and 2b	c. 98	Pankrates, bank Krokodilopolis	2a: πηχι(σμὸς) περ(ιστερεώνων) Παθύρεως 2b: πηχι(σμὸς) περ(ιστερεώνων) Παθύ(ρεως)	1500 dr. + 20% = 1800 dr.	Petosiris s.of Harsiesis

Note: In the Greek receipts of Pathyris πηχισμός is followed by Παθυ( ); ostrakon Gallazzi, 'Ricevute' (2000), 2a, solves the abbreviation into πηχ(ισμὸς) Παθύρεως.

[1] Μενχ̄ παθ̄ ed., Μενχ(είους) Παθύ(ρεως) BL 2; for the reading πηχ(), compare J.G. Milne in *JEA* 11 (1925), p. 273, n. 3 (not in BL)

[2] Ed.: πορθμ(ίδων)? Παθύ(ρεως). [3] Ed. Pr.: πη(ιχ). [4] Ed. Pr.: πηιχ( ).

§61. *The pigeon house of Dryton's daughters.* — Dryton's will of **126** B.C. has shown that he left a dovecote and another, half-finished dovecote to his son Esthladas. His five daughters inherited a lot intended for a dovecote and they were obliged to pay in common the expenses of building this dovecote; strangely, Dryton also asked Esthladas to help to finance this dovecote for the five sisters (Text 4, l. 16-17).

Ostraka 54-57 record the tax payments for the pigeon house of the five sisters for the period **108-100** B.C. Ostrakon 54 of 108 informs us that by that date six people owned an equal part of the dovecote: the five sisters and a woman who was not a family-member: Senminis, daughter of Stotoetis; had the latter bought that part which used to belong to Esthladas? This Senminis may be a daughter of Stotoetis, himself son of Ptaroeris and Senminis[1]; thus, Senminis may have been named after her grandmother.

The tax amounts remain unchanged in the period 108-100 B.C.: 1000 drachmas per person + an extra charge of 20% (see §60), making 1200 drachmas in total per person.

54	108 B.C.	Senmouthis d.of Dryton and her (four) sisters and Senminis d.of Stotoetis = 6 persons = 6000 drachmas, exclusive of extra charge
55	101 B.C.	Senmouthis d.of Dryton = 1 person = 1000 + 200 drachmas = 1200 drachmas
56	100 B.C.	Senmouthis d.of Dryton = 1 person = 1000 + 200 drachmas = 1200 drachmas
57	100 B.C.	three sisters of Senmouthis d.of Dryton = 3 persons = 3000 + 600 drachmas = 3600 drachmas

§62. *The bank in Pathyris and Krokodilopolis.* — It seems odd that inhabitants of Pathyris paid the pigeon house tax either to the bank of Krokodilopolis or to that of Pathyris and that in some cases the banker wrote a demotic receipt instead of a Greek one. How can all this be explained? This is not the place to study the bank system in the Pathyrite nome, but a brief survey will suffice.

Until c. 137 B.C. people from Pathyris had to pay their taxes in cash at the bank of Hermonthis[2], in the northern toparchy of the Pathyrite nome. By 137 B.C. at the latest, Krokodilopolis, located in the southern toparchy not far from Pathyris, had its own bank, and the inhabitants of Pathyris went there to pay their taxes in cash[3]. But when in 116 a bank was installed in Pathyris[4], the people of this town no longer had to travel to go to the bank. But the bank in Pathyris did not function at all times, nor was there always a banker available who could write receipts in Greek. Further, in the period 97-91 B.C., there are no receipts at all found in Pathyris or Krokodilopolis, whereas c. 90 B.C. there seems to have been a short governmental stimulus in Pathyris, when a Greek banker and a Greek granary official were installed shortly before the uprising of 88 B.C. A similar evolution is found in the granary

1 For this Stotoetis, see Vandorpe, 'Paying Taxes to the Thesauroi of the Pathyrites' (2000), Part VII.
2 *E.g.*, SB I 5115 (145 B.C.); see Bogaert, 'Banques et banquiers' (1998), p. 192-193.
3 SB I 4010 (137 B.C.): first payment to the bank of Krokodilopolis; see also Bogaert, 'Banques et banquiers' (1998), p. 193-194.
4 Bogaert, 'Banques et banquiers' (1998), p. 194-195.

receipts of provincial Pathyris[1]. Thus, at certain times the inhabitants of Pathyris were obliged to travel again to nearby Krokodilopolis when they wanted a tax receipt in Greek. The following survey shows in which town people from Pathyris received a Greek or demotic bank receipt from 116 B.C. onwards.

Date B.C.	*Greek receipts*	*Demotic receipts*
116-114	Pathyris[2]	
113-111	Krokodilopolis[3]	
110-109	Pathyris[4]	
109-106	Krokodilopolis[5]	Pathyris[6]
106	Pathyris[7]	
104-98	Krokodilopolis[8]	Pathyris[9]
97-91	*no receipts found*	*no receipts found*
90	Pathyris[10]	

Three bankers are found in the pigeon house receipts from Pathyris (see survey §60). Patseous, son of Pates, wrote two or three demotic bank receipts in 108 B.C., for which see Ostrakon 51, Introduction. Poregebthis wrote demotic bank receipts for the pigeon house tax, the ktamion-tax and the apomoira in Pathyris in the period 109[11] and 103-100 B.C.[12]. Paniskos and Pankrates, bankers of Krokodilopolis, wrote Greek receipts (Paniskos in the period 107 and 104-98 B.C.; Pankrates in 98 B.C.)[13].

---

1 See Vandorpe, 'Paying Taxes to the Thesauroi of the Pathyrites' (2000), esp. the conclusion.

2 P. Lond. VII 2191 (116 B.C.); P. Stras. II 84 (114 B.C.).

3 BGU III 994 (113 B.C.); SB I 5107 (113 B.C.); O. PSI VIII 986; P. Lond. III 1204 (112 B.C.); P. Stras. II 86 (111 B.C.); SB I 5116 (111 B.C.).

4 BGU III 995 (110 B.C.); P. Grenf. I 27 (109 B.C.).

5 P. Stras. II 87 (107 B.C.; banker Paniskos); P. Grenf. I 36 (106 B.C.).

6 O. dem. *MDAIK* 21 (1966) no. 5 (109 B.C.); O. dem. *MDAIK* 21 (1966) no. 7 (109/8 B.C.); O. dem. *MDAIK* 21 (1966) no. 10; O. dem. *MDAIK* 21 (1966) no. 11 (107 B.C.); O. dem. *Enchoria* 19/20 (1992/93) no.6 (107/6 B.C.?); O. dem. *MDAIK* 21 (1966) no. 12 (106 B.C.).

7 O. Cair. 5 (106 B.C.).

8 Banker Paniskos: O. Cair. 22 (104 B.C.); P. Grenf. II 32 (101 B.C.); Ostraka **56** and **57**; O. PSI III 258; SB XX 14372 (100 B.C.); BGU VI 1259 (99 B.C.; ? banker Paniskos); BGU III 999.
Banker Pankrates: BGU III 1000; P. Grenf. II 35 (98 B.C.); Gallazzi, 'Ricevute' (2000), 2a and 2b (98 B.C.).

9 O. dem. *MDAIK* 21 (1966) no. 13; O. dem. *MDAIK* 21 (1966) no. 14 (103 B.C.); Ostrakon **55**; O. dem. *MDAIK* 21 (1966) no. 17 (101 B.C.); O. dem. *MDAIK* 21 (1966) no. 15; O. dem. *MDAIK* 21 (1966) no. 16 (100 B.C.).

10 O. Cair. 21 (90 B.C.).

11 O. dem. *MDAIK* 21 (1966) no. 5.

12 Ostrakon **55**; O. dem. *Enchoria* 19/20 (1992/93) no.7; O. dem. Mattha 231; O. dem. *MDAIK* 21 (1966) no. 13, no. 14, no. 17.

13 Paniskos: Pros. Ptol. I and VIII 1254; for additions, see notes 5 and 8; Pankrates: Pros. Ptol. I 1250; for additions, see note 8; see also Bogaert, 'Banques et banquiers' (1998), p. 194.

51

DEMOTIC RECEIPT OF MEASUREMENT
for Kaies

Pathyris - 108 B.C.

Zürich, O. dem. inv.no. 1875 = **O. dem. Zürich 36**.
Photograph. — Editio princeps, plate VI.

Introduction

Contents. — See Introduction to this chapter, §59.

Date. — Only the year (year 9 = 109/108 B.C.) is recorded; the month and the day, on which the receipt was issued, are lacking. Since receipts of measurement for grain land are always issued after the second survey operation of February-March, the receipt may be dated to 108 B.C., see Vandorpe, 'The Ptolemaic Epigraphe' (2000), in *AfP* 46, p. 165-228, Part E.

Scribe. — The receipt is written by Patseous in 108 B.C. (his father's name is lacking). A Patseous, son of Pates, is attested in the same year as scribe of a pigeon house receipt (Ostrakon 54) and an apomoira-receipt[1]. Is the Patseous of 108 B.C. to be identified with the Patseous who wrote two receipts of measurement and fourteen harvest tax receipts in Pathyris and who was komogrammateus in the period 93-91 B.C.? For the Patseous of 93-91 B.C., see Vandorpe, 'The Ptolemaic Epigraphe' (2000), in *AfP* 46, p. 165-228, Appendix D (IV) and see Vleeming, 'Village Scribes' (1984), especially p. 1055-1056.

Text

1 *R.rḫ=w r Gᶜy s3 Pa-tw qy*
n Pr-Ḥ.t-Ḥr ẖn st3 16 1/2 1/16 st3 7
r st3 3 1/2 r st3 7 ᶜn. Sẖ Pa-t3-s.t-ᶜ3.t n ḥ3.t-sp 9.t (?).

Translation

That which was measured for Kaies, son of Pates: highland in Pathyris: within 16 1/2 1/16 arouras, 7 arouras (are productive), (their half is) 3 1/2 arouras, being 7 arouras again.
Has written Patseous, in year 9 (?).

---

1 O. dem. *MDAIK* 21 (1966) no. 7.

52

DEMOTIC HARVEST TAX RECEIPT
for Kaies

Granary of Pathyris H. x W. = 9.5 x 11.5 cm 10 October 108 B.C.

Cairo, O. dem. inv.no. JE 51235 = **U. Kaplony-Heckel**, in *Enchoria* 19/20 (1992/93), p. 54-55, no. 2 (see also U. Kaplony-Heckel, in *ZPE* 61 (1985), p. 52, n. 26 and p. 54).
Photograph and facsimile. — Editio princeps, plate V and facsimile plate IV.

Introduction

Contents. — See Introduction to this chapter, §59.

Date and scribe or banker. —The editio princeps gives «10. Oktober 108 v. Chr. (oder 9. Oktober 105 v. Chr.)». All ostraka written by Thotortaios son of Kales (see also Ostrakon 54) are written in year 10 which is to be equated with 108-107 B.C. and less probably with 105-104 B.C., since at the late date one expects the double date year 13 = 10 to be used; see Vleeming, 'Village Scribes' (1984), p. 1056 and Vandorpe, 'The Ptolemaic Epigraphe' (2000), in *AfP* 46, p. 165-228, Part E.
For Thotortaios son of Kales, see also pros. 410.

Text

R-in Pa-t3.wy s3 ⸢Ḥr⸣ ẖr p3 ip n Gᶜy s3 Pa-tw
r p3 r3 (n) Pr-Ḥ.t-Ḥr ẖr p3 glg 2
r.ṯ3y=w mtw=f sw 5 r sw 2 1/2 r sw 5 ᶜn ẖr ḥ3.t-sp 9.t.
Sẖ Ḏḥwṱ-i.ir.dy-s s3 Gl3 n ḥ3.t-sp 10 ibd-1 3ḫ.t sw 22.
In ⸢--⸣ R-ẖy Gᶜy n p3y hrw
- - - - - - sw 5 1/4 r sw 2 1/2 1/8 r sw 5 1/4 ᶜn.
Sẖ Ḏḥwṱ-i.ir.dy-s s3 Gl3 n ḥ3.t-sp 10 ibd-1 3ḫ.t sw 22.

Translation

What Patous, son of Horos, has paid for the account of Kaies, son of Pates, to the granary of Pathyris for two beds which were taken from him (i.e. Kaies): 5 artabas of wheat, (their half is) 2 1/2 artabas of wheat, being 5 artabas of wheat again, for year 9.
Has written Thotortaios, son of Kales, in year 10, 22 Thot.

Has paid - - - Has measured Kaies on this day - - - 5 1/4 artabas of wheat, (their half is) 2 1/2 1/8 artabas of wheat, being 5 1/4 artabas of wheat again.
Has written Thotortaios, son of Kales, in year 10, 22 Thot.

Notes

5 *In --- R-ẖy, Has paid - - Has measured*: in her edition, U. Kaplony-Heckel rightly remarked that «*In* ist Anakolouth vor der zweiten Quittung stehen geblieben». The scribe first wrote *In* (*has paid*) after the example of the first receipt, a payment on the account of Kaies (l. 1), but replaced it by *R-ẖy* (*has measured*), an alternative term to denote the payment of the harvest tax in kind.

53

DEMOTIC HARVEST TAX RECEIPT
for Kaies

Granary of Pathyris - 21 June 107 B.C.

Zürich, O. dem. inv.no. 1851 = **O. dem. Zürich 12**.
Photograph. — Editio princeps, plate II.

Introduction

Contents. — See Introduction to this chapter, §59.

Date and Scribe. — For the date and scribe, see Ostrakon 52, Introduction.

Text

In G^{c}y s3 Pa-tw
r p3 r3 n Pr-Ḥ.t-Ḥr
ẖr ḥ3.t-sp 10.t sw 4 2/3 r sw 2 1/3 r sw 4 2/3 ^{c}n.
Sẖ Ḏḥwṱ-i.ir.dy-s s3 ⌜G⌝l3 n ḥ3.t-sp 10.t
ibd-2 šmw sw 6.

Translation

Has paid Kaies, son of Pates, to the granary of Pathyris for (the harvest tax of) year 10: 4 2/3 (artabas) of wheat, (their half is) 2 1/3 (artabas) of wheat, being 4 2/3 (artabas) of wheat again.
Has written Thotortaios, son of Kales, in year 10, 6 Payni.

54

DEMOTIC TAX RECEIPT FOR PIGEON HOUSE

for Senmouthis, daughter of Dryton, her sisters and
Senminis, daughter of Stotoetis

DESCRIPTION

[Bank of Pathyris] - 18 March/ 16 April 108 B.C.

Turin, O. dem. inv.no. S 12791 = **unpublished**, see U. Kaplony-Heckel, in *Enchoria* 19/20 (1992/1993), p. 46, n. 11. My translation below is based on the study of the original ostrakon during my visit to the Egyptological Museum of Turin in May 1998, with the permission of A.M. Donadoni and V. Massa. A full edition will be published by a staff member of the Turin museum in the series of the *Catalogo del Museo Egizio di Torino. Serie Prima - Monumenti e Testi.*

Photograph. — Not available.

Introduction

Contents. —Senmouthis, daughter of Dryton, her sisters and Senminis, daughter of Stotoetis, have paid for the tax of their pigeon's house of year 9: 1 talent with their extra charge[1]. See Introduction to his chapter, §60-62.

Scribe or banker. — See Ostrakon 51, Introduction.

[1] According to this expression, the extra charge of 20% (see §60) is not included. For similar expressions of tax which is not included, see Vandorpe, 'Interest in Ptolemaic Loans' (1998), p. 1467 (*irm p3y=w šmw*; *irm t3y=w ms.t*).

55

DEMOTIC TAX RECEIPT FOR PIGEON HOUSE

for Senmouthis, daughter of Dryton

[Bank of Pathyris]	H. x W. = 6 x 7.5 cm (Width incomplete)	15 March 101 B.C.

Cairo, O. dem. inv.no. JE 51448 = **U. Kaplony-Heckel**, in *Enchoria* 19/20 (1992/93), p. 58, no. 8.
Photograph and facsimile. — Editio princeps, plate IX and facsimile plate VIII.

Introduction

Contents. — See Introduction to this chapter, §60-62.

Scribe or banker. — See Introduction to this chapter, §62.

Text

[In T3-šṛ.t-]Mw.t ta Trwtn ẖn
[p3 tn s.]t-mn.ṱ ḥḏ 60
[r ḥḏ 30 r ḥḏ] 60 ᶜn. St šp (n) ip.
[Sẖ P3-w]r-i3bṱ n ḥ3.t-sp 16 nty ir ḥ3.t-sp 13
[ibd-2 p]r.t ᶜrq.

Translation

Has paid Senmouthis, daughter of Dryton, for the tax of the pigeon house: 60 (deben of) money, (their half is) 30 (deben of) money, being 60 (deben of) money again. They are credited in accounting.
Has written Poregebthis in year 16 which is also year 13, 30 Mecheir.

56

GREEK TAX RECEIPT FOR PIGEON HOUSE
for Senmouthis, daughter of Dryton

Plate XXIII

Bank in Krokodilopolis - 14 May 100 B.C.

Zürich, O. Gr. inv.no. 1904 = **O. Wilck. II 1617**.
Photograph. — Plate XXIII.

Introduction

Contents. — See Introduction to this chapter, §60-62.

Banker. — See Introduction to this chapter, §62.

Text

Ἔτους ιδ Φαρμ(οῦθι) λ̅, τ(έτακται) ἐπὶ τὴν
ἐν Κρο(κοδίλων) πό(λει) τρά(πεζαν) ἐφ' ἧς Πανίσκος
πηχ(ισμοῦ) Παθύ(ρεως) Σεμμοῦθις Δρύ(τωνος)
χιλίας (γίνονται) ʼΑ,
ʼΑσ.
Πανίσκος τρα(πεζίτης).

---

3 πη(ιχ...) ed., πη(χισμοῦ) supplevimus; Παθυ(ρίτου) ed., Παθύ(ρεως) supplevimus (see §60)

Translation

Year 14, 30 Pharmouthi. Has paid to the bank in Krokodilopolis, over which Paniskos (officiates), the pigeon house tax of Pathyris,
Semmouthis, daughter of Dryton, thousand (drachmas), equal to 1000 (drachmas).
1200 (drachmas).
Paniskos, banker.

57

GREEK TAX RECEIPT FOR PIGEON HOUSE

for three daughters of Dryton

Plate XXIII

Bank in Krokodilopolis - 30 May 100 B.C.

Zürich, O. Gr. inv.no. 1905 = **O. Wilck. II 1618**.
Photograph. — Plate XXIII.

Introduction

Contents. — See Introduction to this chapter, §60-62.

Banker. — See Introduction to this chapter, §62.

Text

Ἔτους ιδ Παχὼν ις̅, τ(έτακται) ἐπὶ
τὴν ἐν Κρο(κοδίλων) πό(λει) τρά(πεζαν) ἐφ' ἧς Πανίσκος
πηχ(ισμοῦ) Παθύ(ρεως) Θερμοῦθις χιλίας (γίνονται) ͵Α,
Σενμμῶνθις (*sic*) χιλίας (γίνονται) ͵Α,
Σενπελαίας χιλίας (γίνονται) ͵Α,
(γίνονται) ͵Γ, ͵Γχ.
Πανίσκος τρα(πεζίτης).

---

3 Πηιχ(...) ed., Πηχ(ισμοῦ) legimus et supplevimus; Παθυ(ρίτου) ed., Παθύ(ρεως) supplevimus (see §60)

Translation

Year 14, 16 Pachon. Has paid to the bank in Krokodilopolis, over which Paniskos (officiates), the pigeon house tax of Pathyris,
Thermouthis, thousand (drachmas), equal to 1000 (drachmas),
Senmonthis, thousand (drachmas), equal to 1000 (drachmas),
Senpelaias, thousand (drachmas), equal to 1000 (drachmas),
equal to 3000 (drachmas). 3600 (drachmas).
Paniskos, banker.

58

DEMOTIC ACCOUNT

recording Senmouthis, daughter of Dryton, and her cousin

-	-	s.d.

Cairo, O. dem. inv.no. JE 51234 = **U. Kaplony-Heckel**, *Pathyris* (*Die demotischen Rechts- und Wirtschaftstexte geschrieben auf Kalkstein, Ton und Holz aus der spätptolemäischen Militärkolonie in Oberägypten. Catalogue Général des Antiquités Egyptiennes du Caire*): in print. A provisional transcription and translation are found in U. Kaplony-Heckel, in *Festschrift J. von Beckerath* (HÄB 30), 1990, p. 142, note 2 (DO CG 50.257).

Photograph: not available.

Introduction

Contents. — The account lists names and sums of money. Senmouthis, Dryton's oldest daughter (pros. 506), and a daughter of Dryton's sister-in-law Tiesris (pros. 407) are recorded.

Text

1+x		*ḥḏ 10;*
	T3-šr.t-Mw.t ta Trwtn	*ḥḏ 85;*
	t3 šr.t n T3y-Isr	*ḥḏ 50.*

Translation

1+x		*10 (deben of) money;*
	Senmouthis, daughter of Dryton	*85 (deben of) money;*
	the daughter of Tiesris	*50 (deben of) money.*

VIII

Appendices

§63. *Survey.* — The appendices contain texts which did not belong to the family archive of Dryton, but which are closely related to the family. For the Erbstreit-dossier, connected to the family of Dryton's wife Apollonia, see Vandorpe, *Archives from Pathyris* (2001), §25.1 and 37.

A Gr. descr.	Greek agreement written by Dryton	1 Febr. 136
B Gr.	Greek graffiti by Dryton	s.d.
C Dem. descr.	Demotic temple oath for Esthladas	29 August 124

Appendix A

GREEK CHEIROGRAPHON OF THE PETEHARSEMTHEUS ARCHIVE
written by Dryton

Plate XXIV

[Pathyris] 1 Febr. 136 B.C.

P. Grenf. II 17 = Chrest. Mitt. 138.
Photograph. — See plate XXIV.

Introduction

Contents. — P. Grenf. II 17 is part of the family archive of Peteharsemtheus, son of Panebchounis: it is a private agreement between Patous, son of Patous, and Takmeis, daughter of Patous[1]. Apparently, neither party can write Greek and they apply to Dryton to write down this cheirographon (compare § 34).

Text

The cheirographon consists of 11 lines. In l. 8-10 it is stated that the arrangement has been written by Dryton for the above-mentioned Patous and Takmeis.

ἔγραψεν Δρύτων Παμφίλου ὑπὲρ αὐτῶν διὰ τὸ φάσκειν αὐτοὺς μὴ εἰδέναι γράμματα

Has written Dryton, son of Pamphilos, for them, because they cannot write.

[1] For the contents, see Pestman, 'Pétéharsemtheus' (1965), p. 60, document no. 3.

Appendix B

GREEK GRAFFITI
by Dryton

See facsimiles below

Valley of the Kings H. x W. = see below 2nd cent. B.C.

Tomb of Ramesses IV:
α = Baillet, *Syringes* (1926) no. 306 (facsimile: plate XII): «3e porte, jambage gauche»
β = Baillet, *Syringes* (1926) no. 313 (facsimile: plate XII): «3e porte, jambage gauche»
γ = Baillet, *Syringes* (1926) no. 413 + 414 + 414bis (facsimile: plate XVI): «4e porte, jambage gauche»

Tomb of Ramesses VI:
δ = Baillet, *Syringes* (1926) no. 1780, l. 3 (facsimile: plate LXIX; photograph plate 27a): «mur droit: 1er corridor»
ϵ = Baillet, *Syringes* (1926) no. 1785 (facsimile: plate LXIX; photograph plate 27a): «mur droit: 1er corridor»

Earlier editions: some of the graffiti were edited by Deville, *Archives des missions scientifiques et littéraires*, IIe série, vol. II, Paris 1865:
α = Deville no. 118 = SB I 1836
γ = Deville no. 84 + 85 = SB I 1806 + 1807

For the identification of Dryton and for the date, see Winnicki, 'Besuch Drytons' (1995).

Facsimile: See the facsimiles and photograph in Baillet's edition and the facsimiles below. In addition, a full-scale facsimile of one of the graffiti of Dryton in the tomb of Ramesses IV (=α) was made by J.K. Winnicki, who kindly agreed to my publishing it in this volume.

Introduction

The royal *syringes*-tombs in the Valley of the Kings were a tourist attraction already in Antiquity. Since early Ptolemaic times, several tombs are inscribed or painted with Greek, Latin and demotic graffiti[1]. Five inscribed graffiti show the name of a Dryton (without a father's name): three on the doorjambs of the tomb of Ramesses IV and two in the tomb of Ramesses VI. As Winnicki observed, they are all written in the same way: «in fast gleicher Grösse in Unzialschrift mit einem kleinen, über die Zeile geschriebenen, Omega eingekratzt»[2] (compare the facsimiles below). Baillet already suggested that they were written by the same person[3]. He, however, dated the graffiti to the Roman period, apparently because one of them (no. δ) is written after the name of Ibois, son of Gemellus, a Latin father's name. As Winnicki rightly

1 See Vandorpe, 'Outline of Greco-Roman Thebes' (1995), p. 238.
2 Winnicki, 'Besuch Drytons' (1995), p. 90.
3 Baillet, *Syringes* (1926), p. 456.

pointed out, there is no obvious reason why Dryton's name is to be connected with that of Ibois, son of Gemellus. On the other hand, Winniki points to one of the graffiti (no. γ) where Dryton's name is followed by that of Pelops, son of Alexon, desmophylax; a Pelops who is desmophylax also wrote a graffito (no. 418 in Baillet's edition) some 30 cm to the right of no. γ. A Pelops is often found in the family archive of Dryton: he is apparently closely connected to this family (see pros. 10) and is probably to be identified with the Pelops of the graffiti. One other name follows: ..eonas (?Leonas or ?Kleonas), who is Κρής, a Cretan. As Dryton is also of Cretan origin, the three men (Dryton, Pelops and ..eonas) may have visited the tomb together, since these visits were often made in a group[1].

Text and facsimiles[2]

Tomb of Ramesses IV

α : H. x W. = 8 x 30 cm	Δρύτων	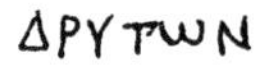
β : H. x W. = 5 x 30 cm	[Δ]ρύτω[ν]	

Tomb of Ramesses VI

γ : H. x W. (of name of Dryton) = 5 x 27 cm	Δρύτων Πέλοψ Ἀλέξων- ο[ς] δεσμο- [φ]ύλαξ ..εονας Κρής	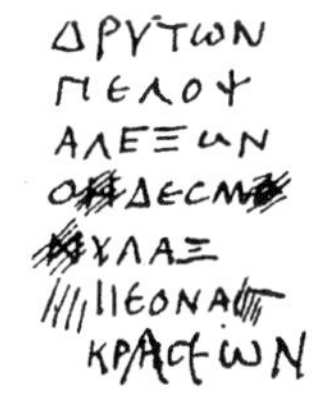
δ : H. x W. = not available	[Δ]ρύτων	
ϵ : H. x W. = 8 x 39 cm	Δρύτων	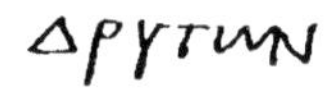

1 Winnicki, 'Besuch Drytons' (1995), p. 91-92.
2 These facsimiles were made on the basis of the plates in Baillet, *Syringes* (1926).

Full-scale facsimile by J.K. Winnicki
of Dryton's graffito α in the tomb of Ramesses IV

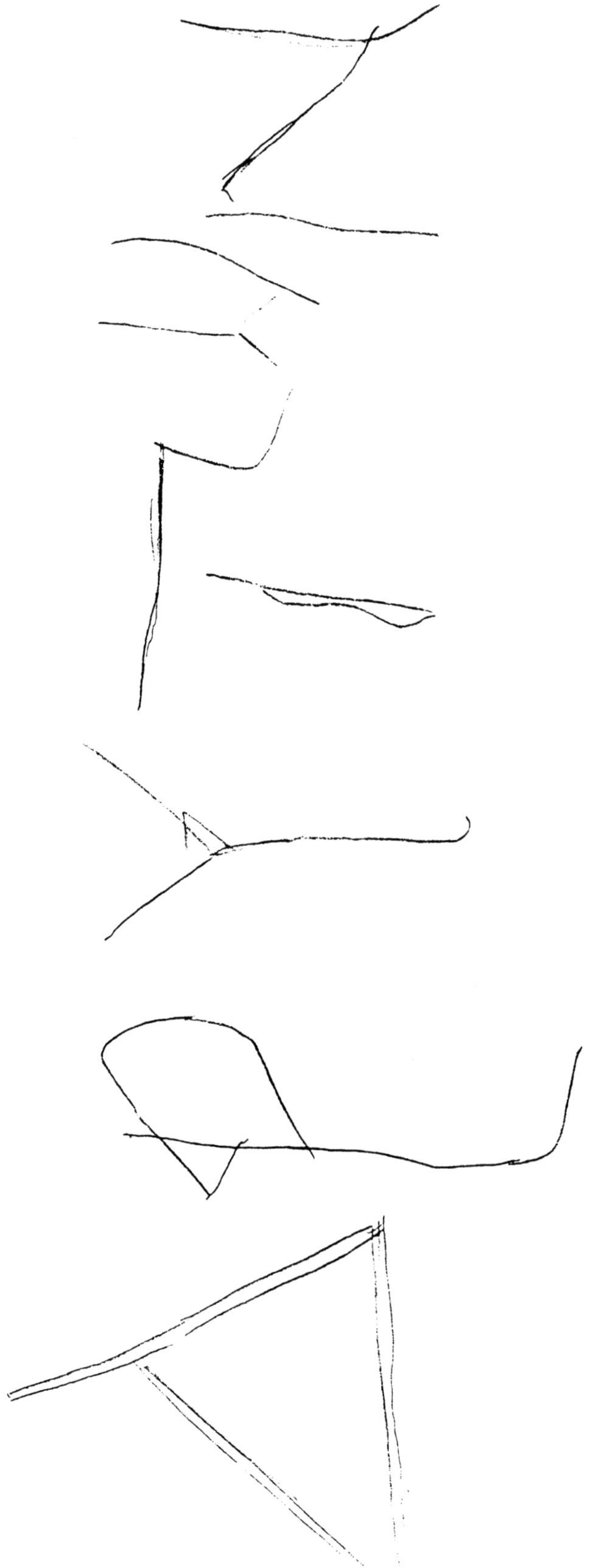

Appendix C

DEMOTIC TEMPLE OATH

for Esthladas

DESCRIPTION

Temple of Souchos [? Krokodilopolis, Pathyris or *Smn*]	H. x W. = 13 x 8.5 cm [incomplete]	29 August 124 B.C.

Turin, O. dem. inv.no. G 5 = **unpublished**, see U. Kaplony-Heckel, in *ZÄS* 118 (1991), p. 132 and n. 49. The edition is being prepared by V. Massa (Massa, *Egyptian Temple Oaths* (2002)).

Photograph. — Not available.

Introduction

Contents. — Dryton's son Esthladas is divorced from his wife Tagombes. According to the Egyptian marriage contract (a *sẖ ḥm.t*, see l. 6 and see §31), Esthladas has to return the goods his wife brought into the house which are listed in the marriage contract, among these two *in-šn*-veils[1] (together worth three talents), a sum of copper money and probably other goods, which are lost in the lacuna of l. 5. Tagombes claims that Esthladas has returned only part of her possessions, among them only one of the two *in-šn*-veils. She has to swear an oath on the subject.

The oath has to be sworn by Tagombes before Souchos. If she swears the oath, Esthladas has to hand over the other veil or he has to pay the countervalue. If she refuses to swear the oath, her claim is dismissed. It is not clear how the dispute ended.

Archive of temple oaths. — Ostrakon Appendix C is a temple oath to be sworn by Tagombes for her former husband Esthladas, son of Dryton. The oath dates from 124 B.C., that is from the period after Dryton's death. As the archive was split up after Dryton's death and as only the part which went to Dryton's oldest daughter is preserved, one does not expect an ostrakon of Esthladas from that period in the archive of Dryton's family.

Where, then, was this ostrakon kept? It is the view of V. Massa, who is preparing a study of temple oaths, and also my view that the temple oaths from Pathyris, written on an ostrakon and sworn in the temple of Hathor, Mistress of Pathyris, or Souchos Lord of Krokodilopolis, were not kept in the family archive of one of the two parties, but were all kept together and were found together. The museum archaeology, the research into the acquisition of the ostraka[2],

---

1 See §31.

2 See Vandorpe, *Archives from Pathyris* (2001), §10.

may prove this. A simple example may suffice: four temple oaths of the Zürich collection have successive inventory numbers: O. dem. Zürich inv. no.

1836[1] : oath sworn before Souchos
1837[2] : oath sworn before Souchos
1838[3] : oath sworn before Hathor
1839[4] : oath sworn before Souchos

As different people are involved in each of these four temple oaths, they were apparently not kept in a family archive, but rather in a common archive, which has been discovered in Pathyris[5].

One of the parties involved could take a copy of the temple oath home, but these copies were written on papyrus, not on ostraka, and were kept in the family archive[6].

The find spot of the temple oaths is problematic (in any case, they were discovered in Pathyris). If they were kept in the temple where they were sworn, how could the temple oaths sworn before Hathor and before Souchos be kept together. Where was the chapel of Souchos, where the major part of the oaths was sworn, located? Souchos is Lord of Krokodilopolis, but it seems odd that inhabitants of Pathyris should travel to Krokodilopolis (or to his temple in *Smn*, a town which cannot be located), while they could swear the same oath before Hathor in their own town. Maybe they went to a chapel of Souchos in Pathyris.

There is another possibility: the oaths were sworn in Pathyris (before Hathor) or in Krokodilopolis or *Smn* (before Souchos), but the ostrakon containing the oath was taken back and kept by a third party (called ὁρκωμότης in Greek texts), who, by order of the judge, accompanied the two parties. The ostrakon was then kept in Pathyris in a public archive.

Temple oaths from Pathyris and from other towns have been published and studied by U. Kaplony-Heckel, *Tempeleide* (1963). A new study is being prepared by V. Massa incorporating several new temple oaths from the Egyptological Museum of Turin (*Egyptian Temple Oaths* (2002)). See also Depauw, *Companion* (1997), p. 138-139.

---

1 = O. dem. Tempeleide, p. 403.
2 = O. dem. *OrSu* 8 (1959), p. 43 = O. dem. Tempeleide 96.
3 = O. dem. *OrSu* 8 (1959), p. 49 = O. dem. Tempeleide 125.
4 = O. dem. *OrSu* 8 (1959), p. 53 = O. dem. Tempeleide 206.
5 And not in Krokodilopolis, since this town cannot be located with certainty and since, as a consequence, no papyri or ostraka have been excavated there.
6 *E.g.*, P. dem. Adler 17, 19 and 28.

EXCURSUS. THE HANDWRITING OF DRYTON AND HIS SON ESTHLADAS

§64. *How to compare handwritings?* — Papyrologists usually identify handwriting on the basis of the ductus and some striking similarities. A real scientific basis for identification cannot be found. On the advice of W. Clarysse, I have examined the way in which the forensic police analyses handwriting nowadays in case, for instance, of forged documents. A basic study is E. Locard, *Les faux en écriture et leur expertise*, Paris 1959 (p. 282-344: Technique de l'expertise; la graphoscopie; la graphométrie). Each letter is split up into different "grammata": the *mu*, for instance, has three "grammata" or downstrokes. The proportion between the different "grammata" is crucial. If someone imitates another handwriting, he may, for instance, make the *g* longer, but he usually betrays himself because the internal proportions (the length and angle) are not correct. These proportions must be examined one by one measuring them under a magnifier with indications up to 100 micrometer presenting a detailed graduation — real drudgery.

I tried this system out with contracts in the hand of the agoranomoi or their representatives of Pathyris and Krokodilopolis: I compared three contracts of each of the following scribes: Areios, Paniskos, Hermias and Ammonios. The drudgery produced few results. The differences which came up may also be observed with the naked eye. On the basis of the other measured values a papyrus could not be attributed with certainty to anyone of the scribes. Consequently, I have not employed the system of the forensic police to examine the handwriting of Dryton and Esthladas.

§65. *General characteristics of the handwriting of Dryton and Esthladas.* — Esthladas is a son of Dryton and this appears to be reflected in his way of writing. Both their handwriting shows a peculiar, otherwise rarely attested characteristic. It is customary to abbreviate words by writing the last letter(s) above or beneath the preceding letter at the *end of a word*. It is, however, exceptional to write letter(s) above or beneath the preceding character *within a word*.

I have found this practice (at least on a regular basis) only in the handwriting of Dryton and Esthladas, especially in their private documents such as accounts or lists and in copies of, for instance, petitions. I can provide only one parallel for this practice, kindly provided by W. Clarysse: in a draft of a letter to Dexilaos, the strategos of Memphis, the first *epsilon* in Σεβε̣ννύ(του) (l. 13) is placed above the initial *sigma*. The latter text is to be dated to the reign of Ptolemy V[1].

[1] See W. Clarysse, 'An Escape from Prison in Ptolemaic Egypt?', to be published in *ZPE*; for the first edition of the text, see M. Müller, in *ZPE* 105 (1995), p. 237-243.

The practice of writing letter(s) above or beneath the preceding letter *within a word* can be analyzed in the following way.

Vowels. — Vowels in open syllables are frequently written above the preceding character. The *iota* is usually put through the preceding or following consonant, or, in case of a *delta*, beneath the *delta*.

Text 41: καρδα-

Text 30: καθηκου-

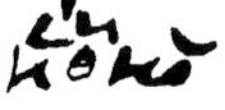

Text 41: Σεμμινι-

Text 41: ιδιος

Text 38: ἐγγυθήκη

Diphthongs. — The *upsilon* (αυ - ου - ευ) in diphthongs is written above the preceding vowel. Diphthongs with *iota* are kept together and are placed above the preceding consonant.

Text 30: τοιούτου

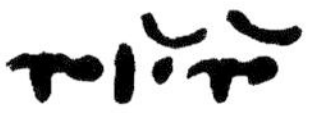

Text 30: αὐτῶι

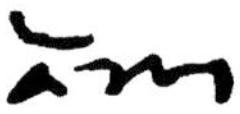

Text 38: σκευ-

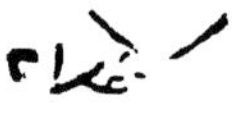

Text 42: παλαι-

Text 42: μωι-

Vowel and consonant. — A vowel with following consonant is rarely put above the preceding character *within a word*. This phenomenon is, however, found when a closed syllable is involved.

Text 42: ἄσφαλτος

On the other hand, a vowel with following consonant is often put above the preceding character *at the end of a word*, a common practice implying an abbreviation. Usually a vowel followed by a liquid or nasal is involved: υρ - ηρ - εγ - υγ - ων - ην.

Text 41: κυρ- 

Text 42: σιδηρ- 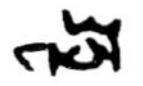

Text 44: μεγ- 

Compare:

Text 38: ποκ- 

Text 40: προς 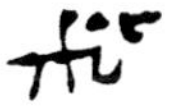

§66. *Dissimilarities in the handwriting of Dryton and Esthladas.* —

Survey

	Text	*Date B.C.*	*Plate*
Texts written by *Dryton* according to information in the text			
Calligraphy	32	137-130	—
Fair copy	App.A	136	XXIV
Scrawl	40	135	XVII
Texts written in a similar hand			
Calligraphy	33-33bis	136-135	XII-XIII; XVII
Fair copy	? 50	after 174	XXII
Scrawl	31	140-131/130	XI
	39	c. 137/136	XVI
	41	135	XVIII
	43	after 154/153 or 143/142	XIX
	44	after 154/3 or 143/142	XX
Texts written by *Esthladas* according to information in the text	22	after 140	see p. 418
	36	130	XIV
Texts written in a similar hand	37	139	—
	42	134	XXI
	4	126	IV
	38	after 153/152 or 142/141	XV

Dryton's hand may be fairly well distinguished from that of Esthladas. Dryton has a broad and, especially in private documents, a rather inconsistent handwriting. Esthladas' hand, on the other hand, is elongated and usually consistent.

For Dryton's hand in App. A, see plate XXIV.

Esthladas' hand in Text 22:

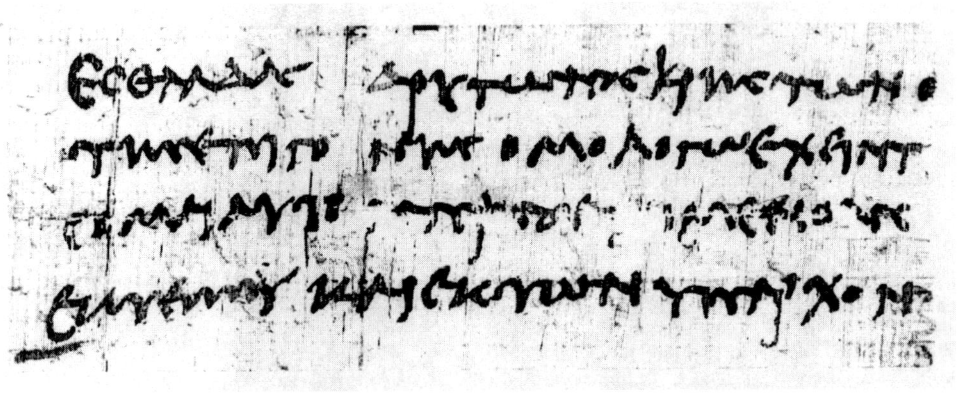

Dryton. — The identification of the handwriting of Dryton is complicated because he uses different types of writing, which may be characterized as calligraphy, fair copy and scrawl.

Calligraphy is found in petitions to the epistrategos: Texts 32 and 33, petitions from himself and his wife, respectively, as well as Text 33bis, a draft of the final petition Text 33, are clearly written by the same hand. The hand may be attributed to Dryton.

A fair copy is, for instance, the private arrangement App. A, which Dryton wrote for members of the family of Peteharsemtheus. Dryton signed the arrangement as scribe at the end. This fair copy is already written in a more careless hand than the above-mentioned petitions, but is still legible and no abbreviations are found in it.

More difficult to read is Dryton's scrawl. Text 40 is an account of Dryton. The hand is very irregular: some parts are written in a clear way, other parts are very cursive. The account contains several abbreviations (see §65).

Texts 41, 43 and 44 and probably Text 39 do not mention the writer, but they may be attributed to Dryton since they show the same particularities as does Text 40. The handwriting of Text 31, a copy of a petition, is more difficult to identify. The copy is probably from the hand of Dryton; compare the way of writing of his name in App. A:

Text 31 

App. A 

Esthladas. — Esthladas' hand is found in Text 36 of 130 B.C., a letter to his parents, and in Text 22, an acknowledgement of debt written by him (not dated). These may be labeled fair copies; they had to be legible for other persons and, thus, neither abbreviations are found nor letters which are written above the preceding character within a word (see §65).

Text 4 of 126 B.C., a copy of Dryton's will, is clearly written in the same hand as the above-mentioned papyri, but since a copy for private use was involved, abbreviations are found as well as letters written above the preceding character within a word. The following accounts are probably also to be attributed to Esthladas: the list Text 37 of c. 139 B.C., written when Esthladas had only just become an adult, Text 38, written in a similar hand (not dated) and the account Text 42 of 134 B.C. written in an already more mature hand. The "scrawl" that Esthladas uses in his private documents is less careless than that of Dryton.

Esthladas' hand in:

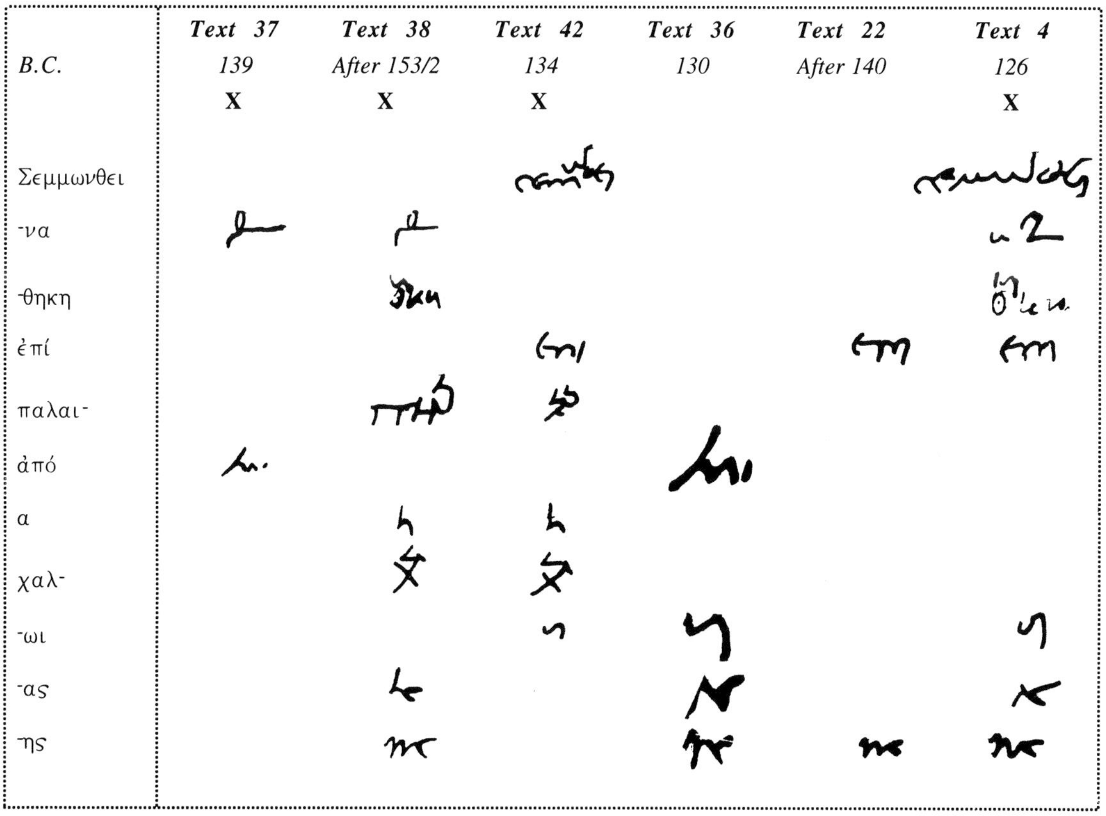
Text 37
Text 38
Text 42
Text 36
Text 22
Text 4
B.C.
139
After 153/2
134
130
After 140
126
X
X
X
X
Σεμμωνθει
-να
-θηκη
ἐπί
παλαι-
ἀπό
α
χαλ-
-ωι
-ας
-ης

X = *Text with characters written above preceding character within the word.*

BIBLIOGRAPHICAL ABBREVIATIONS

Greek and demotic papyri and ostraka

For the abbreviations of Greek papyrus (**P.**, **Pap.**) and ostraka (**O.**) editions, see J.F. Oates, R.S. Bagnall e.a., *Checklist of Editions of Greek, Latin, Demotic and Coptic Papyri, Ostraca and Tablets. Fifth edition* (BASP, Suppl. 9), Oakville (CT)-Oxford 2001; for more recent publications, see:
<http://scriptorium.lib.duke.edu/papyrus/texts/clist.html>

For the abbreviations of demotic papyri (**P. dem.**) and ostraka (**O. dem.**), see S.P. Vleeming and A.A. Den Brinker, *Check-list of Demotic Text Editions and Re-editions, presented on the occasion of the Fifth International Conference for Demotic Studies in Pisa (4th-8th Sept. 1993)* (Uitgaven vanwege de stichting "Het Leids Papyrologisch Instituut" 14), Leiden 1993. See also the above-mentioned *Checklist of Editions of Greek, Latin, Demotic and Coptic Papyri, Ostraca and Tablets. Fifth edition.*

In this volume

Demotic editions in monographs are cited as:	O. dem. Mattha 61
Demotic editions in periodicals are cited as:	O. dem. *Enchoria* 19/20 (1992/3), no. 6

The following abbreviations of text editions are not found in the above-mentioned check-lists:

P. dem. Ackerpachtverträge	: see below, Felber, *Demotische Ackerpachtverträge* (1997)
P. New Pap. Primer^2	= Pestman, Prim^2 in the *Checklist of Editions of Greek and Latin Papyri, Ostraca and Tablets*
P. War of Sceptres	= P. Petr.^{2} in the *Checklist of Editions of Greek and Latin Papyri, Ostraca and Tablets.*

Periodicals and series

AC	Acta Classica. Proceedings of the Classical Association of South Africa (Kaapstad, Pretoria)
AcOr	Acta Orientalia (Leiden, Copenhagen)
Aegyptus	Aegyptus. Rivista italiana di egittologia e papirologia (Milano)
AfP	Archiv für Papyrusforschung und verwandte Gebiete (Leipzig, Stuttgart-Leipzig, München-Leipzig)
AncSoc	Ancient Society (Leuven)
Antiquity	Antiquity (Cambridge)
BASP	The Bulletin of the American Society of Papyrologists (New Haven, Toronto, New York, Chico)
BCH	Bulletin de correspondance hellénique (Paris)
Bd'É	Bibliothèque d'étude de l'Institut Français d'Archéologie Orientale (Le Caire)
BIFAO	Bulletin de l'Institut Français d'Archéologie Orientale (Le Caire)
Chron. d'Ég.	Chronique d'Égypte. Bulletin périodique de la Fondation Égyptologique Reine Élisabeth (Bruxelles)
Enchoria	Enchoria. Zeitschrift für Demotistik und Koptologie (Wiesbaden)
Ét. de Pap.	Études de Papyrologie (Le Caire)
EVO	Egitto e Vicino Oriente (Pisa)
FuB	Forschungen und Berichte (Berlin)

HÄB	Hildesheimer Ägyptologische Beiträge (Hildesheim)
JAOS	Journal of the American Oriental Society (New Haven)
JDAI	Jahrbuch des Deutschen Archäologischen Instituts (Berlin)
JEA	Journal of Egyptian Archaeology (London)
JJP	Journal of Juristic Papyrology (New York, Warsaw)
JRS	Journal of Roman Studies (London)
MDAIK	Mitteilungen des Deutschen Archäologischen Instituts, Abt. Kairo (Augsburg, Wiesbaden, Mainz)
MIFAO	Mémoires publiés par les membres de l'Institut Français d'Archéologie Orientale du Caire
MIO	Mitteilungen des Instituts für Orientforschung (Berlin)
OLA	Orientalia Lovaniensia Analecta (Leuven)
OLP	Orientalia Lovaniensia Periodica (Leuven)
OLZ	Orientalistische Literaturzeitung (Berlin, Leipzig)
Or	Orientalia. Nova Series (Roma)
OrSu	Orientalia Suecana (Uppsala)
Pap. Lup	Papyrologica Lupiensia (Lecce)
Rd'É	Revue d'Égyptologie (Paris)
REA	Revue des études anciennes (Talence)
RecTrav	Recueil de Travaux relatifs à la Philologie et à l'Archéologie Égyptiennes et Assyriennes (Paris)
Serapis	Serapis. The American Journal of Egyptology (Chicago)
Tapha	Transactions of the American Philological Association (Atlanta, Georgia)
ZÄS	Zeitschrift für Ägyptische Sprache und Altertumskunde (Leipzig, Berlin)
ZDMG	Zeitschrift der Deutschen Morgenländischen Gesellschaft (Stuttgart, Mainz)
ZPE	Zeitschrift für Papyrologie und Epigraphik (Bonn)

Monographs and articles

*Studies related entirely or partly to the family archive of Dryton, Apollonia and their oldest daughter, are marked by an asterisk**

Äg.Wb.	A. Erman and H. Grapow (edd.), *Wörterbuch der ägyptischen Sprache*, 7 vol., Berlin 1971
Baillet, *Syringes* (1926)	J. Baillet, *Inscriptions grecques et latines de tombeaux des rois ou syringes* (MIFAO 42), Le Caire 1926
Berger, *Die Strafklauseln* (1911)	A. Berger, *Die Strafklauseln in den Papyrusurkunden. Ein Beitrag zum gräko-ägyptischen Obligationenrecht,* Leipzig-Berlin 1911
Biezuńska - Malowist, *L'esclavage dans l'Égypte gréco-romaine* (1977)	I. Biezuńska - Malowist, *L'esclavage dans l'Égypte gréco-romaine* (Archiwum filologiczne 30/ 35), vol. I. Période ptolémaïque, Wroclaw 1974, vol. II. Période romaine, Wroclaw 1977
BL	*Berichtigungsliste der griechischen Papyrusurkunden aus Ägypten* I (1922) - X (1998)
BL dem.	S.P. Vleeming and A.A. Den Brinker, *A Demotic Berichtigungsliste. Corrigenda and addenda on demotic texts collected and critically presented* (Papyrological Institute Leiden. Special Publications V), Leiden 1996

BL Konkordanz — W. Clarysse, R.W. Daniel, F.A.J. Hoogendijk, P. Van Minnen (edd.), *Berichtigungsliste der griechischen Papyrusurkunden aus Ägypten. Konkordanz und Supplement zu Band I-VII*, Leuven 1989

Bogaert, 'Banques et banquiers' (1998) — R. Bogaert, 'Liste géographique des banques et des banquiers de l' Égypte ptolémaïque', in *ZPE* 120 (1998), p. 165-202

Bonneau, *Le fisc et le Nil* (1971) — D. Bonneau, *Le fisc et le Nil. Incidences des irrégularités de la crue du Nil sur la fiscalité foncière dans l'Égypte grecque et romaine*, Paris 1971

Bouché-Leclercq, *Histoire des Lagides* (1903-1907) — A. Bouché-Leclercq, *Histoire des Lagides*, 4 vol., Parijs 1903-1907 (= Aalen 1978)

Brümmer, 'Griechische Truhenbehälter' (1985) — E. Brümmer, 'Griechische Truhenbehälter', in *JDAI* 100 (1985), p. 1-168

Calderini, *Dizionario* — A. Calderini *e.a.*, *Dizionario dei nomi geografici e topografici dell'Egitto greco-romano*, I, Cairo 1935; I.2, Madrid 1965; II, Milano 1973; III, Milano 1978; IV, Milano 1983-1986; V, Milano 1987; suppl. I, Milano 1998; suppl. II, Bonn 1996

*Chauveau, *L'Égypte* (1997) — M. Chauveau, *L'Égypte au temps de Cléopâtre. 180-30 av. J.-C.*, Paris 1997 [p. 214-219: Un Crétois en Égypte: le cavalier Dryton]

*Clarysse, ' Ἐπάρδιον and ἐγγαίδιον' (1981) — W. Clarysse, ' Ἐπάρδιον and ἐγγαίδιον, delendum and addendum lexicis', in *ZPE* 41 (1981), p. 256

*Clarysse, 'Le mariage et le testament' (1986) — W. Clarysse, 'Le mariage et le testament de Dryton en 150 avant J.-C.', in *Chron. d' Ég.* 61 (1986), p. 99-103

Clarysse, 'Greek Loan-Words' (1987) — W. Clarysse, 'Greek Loan-Words in Demotic', in S.P. Vleeming (ed.), *Aspects of Demotic Lexicography. Acts of the second international conference for demotic studies Leiden, 19-21 September 1984*, Leuven 1987, p. 9-33 [For additions to the list, see Pap. Lugd. Bat. XXX, p. 139]

Clarysse, 'Greeks in Ptolemaic Thebes' (1995) — W. Clarysse, 'Greeks in Ptolemaic Thebes', in S.P.Vleeming (ed.), *Hundred-Gated Thebes. Acts of a colloquium on Thebes and the Theban area in the Graeco-Roman period* (Pap. Lugd. Bat. XXVII), Leiden 1995

Clarysse, 'Ptolemaic Wills' (1995) — W. Clarysse, 'Ptolemaic Wills', in M.J. Geller *e.a.* (edd.), *Legal Documents of the Hellenistic World. Papers from a seminar*, London 1995, p. 88-105

Crum, *Coptic Dictionary* — W.E. Crum, *A Coptic Dictionary*, Oxford 1939

de Ricci, 'Papyrus de Pathyris' (1903) — S. de Ricci, 'Papyrus de Pathyris au musée du Louvre', in *AfP* 2 (1903), p. 515-520

Delebecque, *Xénophon. De l'art équestre* (1978) — E. Delebecque, *Xénophon. De l'art équestre. Texte établi et traduit par E. Delebecque* (Collection des universités de France), Paris 1978

Depauw, *Companion* (1997) — M. Depauw, *A Companion to Demotic Studies* (Pap. Brux. 28), Bruxelles 1997

di Bitonto, 'Le petizioni ai funzionari' (1968) — A. di Bitonto, 'Le petizioni ai funzionari nel periodo tolemaico', in *Aegyptus* 48 (1968), p. 53-107

Erichsen, *Glossar* — W. Erichsen, *Demotisches Glossar*, Kopenhagen 1954

Felber, *Demotische Ackerpachtverträge* (1997) — H. Felber, *Demotische Ackerpachtverträge der Ptolemäerzeit: Untersuchungen zu Aufbau, Entwicklung und inhaltlichen Aspekten einer Gruppe von demotischen Urkunden* (Ägyptologische Abhandlungen 58), Wiesbaden 1997

Foraboschi, *Onomasticon* — D. Foraboschi, *Onomasticon alterum papyrologicum. Supplemento al Namenbuch di F. Preisigke*, (Testi e documenti per lo studio dell' antichità, serie papirologica 2, 16), Milano 1971

Fraser, *Ptolemaic Alexandria* (1972) — P.M. Fraser, *Ptolemaic Alexandria*, 3 vol., Oxford 1972

Gallazzi, 'Ricevute' (2000) — C. Gallazzi, 'Ricevute scritte su etichette di legno', in Pap. Lup. 9 (2000), p. 181-194

*Gerhard, *Ein gräko-ägyptischer Erbstreit* (1911) — G.A. Gerhard, *Ein gräko-ägyptischer Erbstreit aus dem zweiten Jahrhundert vor Chr.* (Sitzungsberichte der Heidelberger Akademie der Wissenschaften, 8. Abhandlung), Heidelberg 1911

Husson, *Oikia* (1983) — G. Husson, *OIKIA, Le vocabulaire de la maison privée en Égypte d'après les papyrus grecs* (Université de Paris IV, Série Papyrologie 2), Paris 1983

Inscr. Fay. II — E. Bernand, *Recueil des inscriptions grecques du Fayoum. II. La «méris» de Thémistos* (Bd'É 79), Le Caire 1981

Kaplony-Heckel, 'Gebelên-Papyri' (1967) — U. Kaplony-Heckel, 'Die demotischen Gebelên-Papyri der Berliner Papyrussammlung', in *FuB* 8 (1967), p. 70-87

*Kaplony-Heckel, 'Soll und Haben' (1990) — U. Kaplony-Heckel, 'Soll und Haben in Pathyris', in *Festschrift J. von Beckerath* (HÄB 30), Hildesheim 1990, p. 139-146

Kaplony-Heckel, 'Zeugen' (1992) — U. Kaplony-Heckel, 'Woher kommen die Zeugen? Zu demotischen Aktenkopien von Urkunden aus Gebelein in Cairo, Heidelberg und London', in U. Luft *e.a.* (edd.), *Intellectual Heritage of Egypt. Studies presented to L. Kákosy by friends and colleagues on the occasion of his 60th birthday* (Studia Aegyptiaca 14), Budapest 1992, p. 323-334

Kaplony-Heckel, 'Pathyris I' (1992/93); 'Pathyris II' (1994); 'Pathyris III' (1995) — U. Kaplony-Heckel, 'Pathyris. Demotische Kurz-Texte in Cairo. I', in *Enchoria* 19/20 (1992/93), p. 45-86; 'Pathyris. Demotische Kurz-Texte in Cairo. II', in *Enchoria* 21 (1994), p. 23-62; 'Pathyris. Demotische Kurz-Texte in Cairo. III', in *Enchoria* 22 (1995), p. 40-122

Kaplony-Heckel, 'Gebelein-Briefe und -Verwaltungsschreiben' (2000) — U. Kaplony-Heckel, 'Der demotische Papyrus *Loeb 80* und ein Überblick über die demotischen Gebelein-Briefe und -Verwaltungsschreiben', in H. Melaerts (ed.), *Papyri in honorem J. Bingen octogenarii* (Studia Varia Bruxellensia 5), Leuven 2000, p. 185-194

Kiessling, *Wörterbuch* — E. Kiessling, *Wörterbuch der griechischen Papyrusurkunden*, IV, 1-4: α - ἐπικόπτω, Berlin - Marburg 1944-71 and Supplement 1 (1940-66), Amsterdam 1971

Kramer and Heinen, 'Der κτίστης Boethos' (1997) — B. Kramer and H. Heinen, 'Der κτίστης Boethos und die Einrichtung einer neuen Stadt', Teil I, in *AfP* 43 (1997), p. 315-339, Teil II, p. 340-363

Kramer, 'κάς, κασῆς und κάσ(σ)ος' (1999) — J. Kramer, 'Warm und wollig, dick und rauh: κάς, κασῆς und κάσ(σ)ος in den Papyri', in *AfP* 45 (1999), p. 192-204

Kreller, *Erbrechtliche Untersuchungen* (1919) — H. Kreller, *Erbrechtliche Untersuchungen auf Grund der graeco-aegyptischen Papyrusurkunden*, Leipzig-Berlin 1919

LÄ — W. Helck *e.a.* (edd.), *Lexikon der Ägyptologie*, 6 vol., Wiesbaden 1975-1986

Lanciers, 'Priester des ptolemäischen Königskulte' (1991) — E. Lanciers, 'Die Priester des ptolemäischen Königskultes', in *Rd'É* 42 (1991), p. 117-143

Launey, *Les armées hellénistiques* (1949-50) — M. Launey, *Recherches sur les armées hellénistiques* (Bibliothèque des Écoles franç. d'Athènes et de Rome 169), 2 vol., Paris 1949-50

Lesquier, *Institutions militaires* (1911) — J. Lesquier, *Les institutions militaires de l'Égypte sous les Lagides*, Paris 1911

*Lewis, 'Dryton's Wives' (1982) — N. Lewis, 'Dryton's Wives: Two or Three?', in *Chron. d'Ég.* 57 (1982), p. 317-321

*Lewis, *Greeks in Ptolemaic Egypt* (1986) — N. Lewis, *Greeks in Ptolemaic Egypt. Case Studies in the Social History of the Hellenistic World*, Oxford 1986 [p. 88-103: 'A Greek stationed among Egyptians: cavalry officer Dryton and his family']

*Lewis, 'Drytoniana' (1993) — N. Lewis, 'Drytoniana', in *Scripta Classica Israelica* 12 (1993), p. 111-112

LSJ — H.G. Liddell, R. Scott, H.S. Jones, *A Greek-English Lexicon*, Oxford, 1940^9. With a Supplement edited by E.A. Barber, 1968

Lüddeckens, *Dem. Namenbuch*	E. Lüddeckens *e.a.*, *Demotisches Namenbuch*, vol. I. 1-17, Wiesbaden, 1980-2000
Mandilaras, *The Verb* (1973)	B.G. Mandilaras, *The Verb in the Greek Non-Literary Papyri*, Athens 1973
Massa, *Egyptian Temple Oaths* (2002)	V. Massa, *Egyptian Temple Oaths in Ptolemaic Egypt. A Comparative Approach at the Cross-Roads of Law, Ethics and Religion* (Catalogo del Museo Egizio di Torino. Serie Prima - Monumenti e Testi), Torino 2002 (in preparation)
Mayser, *Grammatik*	E. Mayser, *Grammatik der griechischen Papyri aus der Ptolemäerzeit mit Einschluss der gleichzeitigen Ostraka und der in Ägypten verfassten Inschriften*, 6 vol., Leipzig 1920-1934
McGing, 'Revolt Egyptian Style' (1997)	B.C. McGing, 'Revolt Egyptian Style. Internal Opposition to Ptolemaic Rule', in *AfP* 43 (1997), p. 273-314
*Mélèze-Modrzejewski, 'Dryton le crétois' (1984)	J. Mélèze-Modrzejewski, 'Dryton le crétois et sa famille ou les mariages mixtes dans l'Égypte hellénistique', in *Aux Origines de l'Hellénisme. La Crète et la Grèce. Hommage à Henri van Effenterre*, présenté par le Centre G.Glotz, Paris 1984, p. 353-377
Messeri Savorelli, 'Lista degli agoranomi' (1980)	G. Messeri Savorelli, 'Lista degli agoranomi di età tolemaico', in Pap. Flor. VII, Florence 1980, p. 185-271
*Messeri, 'P. Grenf. I 19' (1982)	G. Messeri, 'P. Grenf. I 19 + P. Amh. II 166', in *ZPE* 47 (1982), p. 275-280
*Messeri Savorelli, 'Due Atti agoranomici' (1984)	G. Messeri Savorelli, 'Due Atti agoranomici di età tolemaica: SB III 7204, P. Cairo 10357', in G. Crifo *e.a.* (edd.), *Studi in onore di A. Biscardi* V, Milano 1984, p. 515-525
*Messeri Savorelli, 'Frammenti del primo testamento' (1990)	G. Messeri Savorelli, 'Frammenti del primo testamento di Dryton?', in *Miscellanea Papyrologica in occasione del bicentenario dell' edizione della charta borgiana* (Pap. Flor. XIX), Florence 1990, p. 429-436
Mooren, *Prosopography* (1975)	L. Mooren, *The Aulic Titulature in Ptolemaic Egypt. Introduction and Prosopography* (Verhandelingen van de Koninklijke Academie voor Wetenschappen, Letteren en Schone Kunsten van België, Klasse der Letteren, jaargang 37, no. 78), Brussel 1975
Mooren, *La hiérarchie de cour* (1977)	L. Mooren, *La hiérarchie de cour ptolémaïque. Contribution à l'étude des institutions et des classes dirigeantes à l'époque hellénistique* (Studia Hellenistica 23), Leuven 1977
Otto, *Priester und Tempel* (1905-08)	W. Otto, *Priester und Tempel im hellenistischen Ägypten. Ein Beitrag zur Kulturgeschichte des Hellenismus*, 2 vol., Leipzig - Berlin 1905-08

Otto and Bengtson, *Geschichte* (1938) — W. Otto and H. Bengtson, *Zur Geschichte des Niederganges des Ptolemäerreiches. Ein Beitrag zur Regierungszeit des 8. und 9. Ptolemäers* (Abhandlungen der Bayerischen Akademie der Wissenschaften, Philos.-hist. Abteilung, Neue Folge 17), München 1938

*Peremans, 'Wilck. Chrest. 10' (1953) — W. Peremans, 'Notice concernant Wilck. Chrest. 10', in W. Peremans and E. Van 't Dack, *Prosopographica* (Studia Hellenistica 9), Louvain 1953, p. 83

*Peremans, 'Les mariages mixtes' (1981) — W. Peremans, 'Les mariages mixtes dans l'Égypte des Lagides', in E. Bresciani *e.a.* (edd.), *Scritti in onore di O. Montevecchi*, Bologna 1981, p. 273-281

Pestman, *Marriage* (1961) — P.W. Pestman, *Marriage and Matrimonial Property in Ancient Egypt* (Pap. Lugd. Bat. IX), Leiden 1961

Pestman, 'Pathyris II' (1963) — P.W. Pestman, 'A proposito dei documenti di Pathryis II : Πέρσαι τῆς ἐπιγονῆς', in *Aegyptus* 43 (1963), p. 15-53

Pestman, 'Pétéharsemtheus' (1965) — P.W. Pestman, 'Les archives privées de Pathyris à l'époque ptolémaïque. La famille de Pétéharsemtheus, fils de Panebkhounis', in Pap. Lugd. Bat. XIV, Leiden 1965, p. 47-105

Pestman, 'Loans Bearing no Interest?' (1971) — P.W. Pestman, 'Loans Bearing no Interest?', in *JJP* 16-17 (1971), p. 7-29

Pestman, 'L' agoranomie' (1978) — P.W. Pestman, 'L'agoranomie : un avant-poste de l'administration grecque enlevé par les égyptiens', in H. Maehler and V. Strocka (edd.), *Das Ptolemäische Aegypten*, Mainz am Rhein 1978, p. 203-210

Pestman, 'L'impôt-ἐγκύκλιον' (1978) — P.W. Pestman, 'L'impôt-ἐγκύκλιον à Pathyris et à Krokodilopolis', in Pap. Lugd. Bat. XIX, Leiden 1978, p. 214-222

Pestman, 'Nahomsesis' (1981) — P.W. Pestman, 'Nahomsesis, una donna d'affari di Pathyris. L'archivio bilingue di Pelaias, figlio di Eunus, in E. Bresciani *e.a.* (edd.), *Scritti in onore di O. Montevecchi*, Bologna 1981, p. 295-315

Pestman, 'Agoranomoi' (1985) — P.W. Pestman, 'Agoranomoi et actes agoranomiques', in Pap. Lugd. Bat. XXIII, Leiden 1985, p. 9-27

Pestman, ' "Inheriting" in the Archive of the Theban Choachytes' (1987) — P.W. Pestman, ' "Inheriting" in the Archive of the Theban Choachytes (2nd cent. B.C.)', in Vleeming, *Aspects of Demotic Lexicography* (1987), p. 57-73

Plaumann, *Ptolemais* (1910) — G. Plaumann, *Ptolemais in Oberägypten. Ein Beitrag zur Geschichte des Hellenismus in Ägypten* (Leipziger Historische Abhandlungen 18), Leipzig 1910

*Pomeroy, *Women in Hellenistic Egypt* (1990) — S.B. Pomeroy, *Women in Hellenistic Egypt. From Alexander to Cleopatra*, Detroit 1990 [p. 103-124: 'Apollonia (also called Senmonthis), wife of Dryton: woman of two cultures']

Powell, *Collectanea Alexandrina* (1970) — I.U Powell, *Collectanea Alexandrina. Reliquiae minores Poetarum Graecorum Aetatis Ptolemaicae 323-146 A.C.*, Oxford 1970

Préaux, *L'économie royale* (1939) — Cl. Préaux, *L'économie royale des Lagides*, Brussel 1939

Preisigke, *Namenbuch* — F. Preisigke, *Namenbuch enthaltend alle griechischen, lateinischen, ägyptischen, hebraeischen, arabischen und sonstigen Menschennamen, soweit sie in griechischen Urkunden Ägyptens sich vorfinden*, Heidelberg 1922

Preisigke, *WB* — F. Preisigke, *Wörterbuch der griechischen Papyrusurkunden*, 3 vol., Berlin 1925-31.

Pros. — See p. 16-17. A prosopographical study of the family members of Dryton and his wives Sarapias and Apollonia is to be found in Vandorpe, *Archives from Pathyris* (2001), chapter V

Pros. Ptol. — W. Peremans, E. Van 't Dack *e.a.*, *Prosopographia Ptolemaica* (Studia Hellenistica), Louvain 1 (1950)-

RE — A. Pauly, G. Wissowa, W. Kroll *e.a.*, *Realencyclopädie der classischen Altertumswissenschaft*, Stuttgart (from 1972 onwards: München) 1893-

Reekmans, 'Ptolemaic Copper Inflation' (1951) — T. Reekmans, 'The Ptolemaic Copper Inflation', in E. Van 't Dack and T. Reekmans (edd.), *Ptolemaica* (Studia Hellenistica 7), Leuven 1951, p. 61-118

Reil, *Kenntnis des Gewerbes* (1913) — Th. Reil, *Beiträge zur Kenntnis des Gewerbes im hellenistischen Ägypten,* Leipzig 1913

*Ritner, 'Property Transfer' (1984) — R. K. Ritner, 'A Property Transfer from the Erbstreit Archives', in H.-J. Thissen and K.-Th. Zauzich (edd.), *Grammata Demotika. Festschrift für E. Lüddeckens zum 15. Juni 1983*, Würzburg 1984, p. 171-187

Rowlandson, *Sourcebook* (1998) — J. Rowlandson *e.a.* (edd.), *Women and Society in Greek and Roman Egypt. A Sourcebook*, Cambridge 1998

Sandy, *Vegetable Oils* (1989) — D.B. Sandy, *The Production and Use of Vegetable Oils in Ptolemaic Egypt* (BASP, Suppl. 6), Atlanta (Georgia) 1989

Schnebel, *Die Landwirtschaft* (1925) — M. Schnebel, *Die Landwirtschaft im hellenistischen Ägypten* (Münchener Beiträge zur Papyrusforschung und antiken Rechtsgeschichte 7), München 1925

*Scholl, 'Drytons Tod' (1988) — R. Scholl, 'Drytons Tod', in *Chron. d'Ég.* 63 (1988), p. 141-144

Seidl, *Der Eid* (1929) — E. Seidl, *Der Eid im ptolemäischen Recht*, München 1929

Seidl, *Ptolemäische Rechtsgeschichte* (1962²) — E. Seidl, *Ptolemäische Rechtsgeschichte* (Ägyptologische Forschungen 22), Glückstadt 1962²

Seidl, 'Bilaterale Urkunde' (1980) — E. Seidl, 'Eine bilaterale demotische Urkunde (?)', in *Serapis* 6 (1980), p. 117-120

Semeka, *Ptolemäisches Prozessrecht* (1913) — G. Semeka, *Ptolemäisches Prozessrecht. Studien zur ptolemäischen Gerichtsverfassung und zum Gerichtsverfahren*, München 1913

Spence, *Cavalry* (1993) — I.G. Spence, *The Cavalry of Classical Greece*, Oxford 1993

*Spiegelberg, 'Papyrus Erbach' (1905) — W. Spiegelberg, 'Papyrus Erbach. Ein demotisches Brieffragment', in *ZÄS* 42 (1905), p. 51

Spiegelberg, *Demotische Grammatik* (1925) — Spiegelberg, *Demotische Grammatik*, Heidelberg 1925

Swarney, *Idios Logos* (1970) — P.R. Swarney, *The Ptolemaic and Roman Idios Logos* (American Studies in Papyrology 8), Toronto 1970

Taubenschlag, *Law* (1955²) — R. Taubenschlag, *The Law of Greco-Roman Egypt in the Light of the Papyri (332 B.C. - 640 A.D.)*, Warszawa 1955²

Thomas, *The Epistrategos* I (1975) — J.D. Thomas, *The Epistrategos in Ptolemaic and Roman Egypt*, vol. I. *The Ptolemaic Epistrategos* (Pap. Colon. 6), Opladen 1975

Vandier, *Manuel* IV — J. Vandier, *Manuel d'archéologie égyptienne*. IV. *Bas-reliefs et peintures: scènes de la vie quotidienne*, Paris 1964

Van 't Dack, *Ptolemaica Selecta* (1988) — E. Van 't Dack, *Ptolemaica Selecta* (Studia Hellenistica 29), Leuven 1988

Vandorpe, 'Strategen der Thebais' (1988) — Vandorpe, 'Der früheste Beleg eines Strategen der Thebais als Epistrategen', in *ZPE* 73 (1988), p. 47-50

*Vandorpe, 'Zwei Hypepistatai' (1988) — K. Vandorpe, 'Zwei Hypepistatai in Pathyris', in *ZPE* 73 (1988), p. 51-52

*Vandorpe, 'Museum Archaeology' (1994) — K. Vandorpe, 'Museum Archaeology or How to Reconstruct Pathyris Archives', in *Acta demotica. Acts of the Fifth International Conference for Demotists (Pisa, 4th-8th Sept. 1993)* (= *EVO* 17 (1994)), Pisa 1994, p. 289-300

Vandorpe, 'Outline of Greco-Roman Thebes' (1995) — K. Vandorpe, 'City of Many a Gate, Harbour for Many a Rebel. Historical and Topographical Outline of Greco-Roman Thebes', in S.P.Vleeming (ed.), *Hundred-Gated Thebes. Acts of a colloquium on Thebes and the Theban area in the Graeco-Roman period* (Pap. Lugd. Bat. XXVII), Leiden 1995, p. 203-239

*Vandorpe, 'Greek Horsemanship' (1997) K. Vandorpe, ' "When a Man has found a horse to his mind" (Xen., *De equitandi ratione*, IV.1)". On Greek Horsemanship in Ptolemaic Egypt', in B. Kramer *e.a.* (edd.), *Akten des 21. internationalen Papyrologenkongresses Berlin 13-19.8.1995* (*AfP*, Beiheft 3), Stuttgart-Leipzig 1997, p. 984-990

Vandorpe, 'Horos son of Amenothes' (1997) K. Vandorpe, 'Horos son of Amenothes, Scribe at the 'Thesauroi of the Pathyrites' ', in *JJP* 27 (1997), p. 75-81

Vandorpe, 'Seals in and on the Papyri' (1997) K. Vandorpe, 'Seals in and on the Papyri of Greco-Roman and Byzantine Egypt', in M.-Fr. Boussac and A. Invernizzi (edd.), *Archives et Sceaux du monde hellénistique* (Bulletin de correspondance hellénique, Suppl. 29), Paris 1997, p. 231-291

Vandorpe, 'Interest in Ptolemaic Loans' (1998) K. Vandorpe, 'Interest in Ptolemaic Loans of Seed-Corn from the 'House of Hathor' (Pathyris)', in W. Clarysse *e.a.* (edd.), *Egyptian Religion. The Last Thousand Years. Studies Dedicated to the Memory of J. Quaegebeur* (OLA 84-85), Leuven 1998, II, p. 1459-1468

Vandorpe, 'Agoranomic Loans with Demotic Summary' (2000) K. Vandorpe, 'Two Agoranomic Loans with Demotic Summary (Pathyris)', in H. Melaerts (ed.), *Papyri in honorem J. Bingen octogenarii* (Studia Varia Bruxellensia 5), Leuven 2000, p. 195-204

*Vandorpe, 'Feminisme avant la lettre?' (2000) K. Vandorpe, 'Feminisme avant la lettre? Het leven van een zakenvrouw in hellenistisch Egypte', in *De uitstraling van Hellas* (Nieuw Tijdschrift van de Vrije Universiteit Brussel 13.1), Brussel 2000, p. 107-133

Vandorpe, 'Paying Taxes to the Thesauroi of the Pathyrites' (2000) K. Vandorpe, 'Paying Taxes to the Thesauroi of the Pathyrites in a Century of Rebellion (186-88 BC)', in L. Mooren (ed.), *Politics, Administration and Society in the Hellenistic and Roman World. Proceedings of the international colloquium, Bertinoro 19-24 July 1997* (Studia Hellenistica 36), Leuven 2000, p. 405-436

Vandorpe, 'The Ptolemaic Epigraphe' (2000) K. Vandorpe, 'The Ptolemaic Epigraphe or Harvest Tax (shemu)', in *AfP* 46 (2000), p. 165-228

*Vandorpe, 'Apollonia, a Businesswoman' (2001) K. Vandorpe, 'Apollonia, a Businesswoman in a Multicultural Society (Pathyris, 2nd-1st centuries B.C.)', in H. Melaerts and L. Mooren (edd.), *Le rôle et le statut de la femme en Égypte hellénistique, romaine et byzantine (Bruxelles et Louvain, 27-29/ 11/ 1997)* (Studia Hellenistica) (in print)

*Vandorpe, *Archives from Pathyris* (2001) K. Vandorpe, *The Archives from Pathyris Reconstructed. With an Introduction to the Bilingual Family Archive of Dryton, his Wife Apollonia and their Daughter Senmouthis* (Collectanea Hellenistica 3), Brussels 2001

Vandorpe, 'Greek and Demotic Loan Contracts from Pathyris' (2001) K. Vandorpe, 'Greek and Demotic Loan Contracts from Pathyris', in preparation

Vandorpe and Clarysse, 'The Ptolemaic Apomoira' (1998)	K. Vandorpe and W. Clarysse, 'The Ptolemaic Apomoira', in H. Melaerts (ed.), *Le culte du souverain dans l'Égypte ptolémaïque au IIIe siècle avant notre ère* (Studia Hellenistica 34), Leuven 1998, p. 5-42
Veïsse, *Les «révolutions égyptiennes»* (2000)	A.-E. Veïsse, *Les «révolutions égyptiennes». Recherches sur les troubles intérieurs en Égypte du règne de Ptolémée IV Philopator aux premiers temps de la domination romaine (221-29 av. n.è.)*, thèse de doctorat, Univ. de Versailles-Saint-Quentin-en-Yvelines 2000 (to be published in Studia Hellenistica)
Vigneron, *Le cheval dans l'Antiquité* (1968)	P. Vigneron, *Le cheval dans l'Antiquité gréco-romaine (des guerres médiques aux grandes invasions). Contribution à l'histoire des techniques* (Annales de l'Est 35), Nancy 1968
Vleeming, 'The Artabe in Pathyris' (1979)	S.P. Vleeming, 'Some Notes on the Artabe in Pathyris', in *Enchoria* 9 (1979), p. 93-100
Vleeming, 'Village Scribes' (1984)	S.P. Vleeming, 'The Village Scribes of Pathyris', in *Atti del 17 congresso internazionale di papirologia*, Napoli 1984, vol. III, p. 1053-1056
Vleeming, 'The Title 'Man Receiving Pay'' (1985)	S.P. Vleeming, 'The reading of the Title 'Man Receiving Pay' ', in Pap. Lugd. Bat. XXIII, Leiden 1985, p. 204-207
Vleeming, *Aspects of Demotic Lexicography* (1987)	S.P. Vleeming *e.a.* (edd.), *Aspects of Demotic Lexicography. Acts of the Second International Conference for Demotic Studies, Leiden, 19-21 September 1984* (Studia Demotica 1), Leuven 1987
Vycichl, *DELC*	W. Vycichl, *Dictionnaire étymologique de la langue copte*, Leuven 1983
*Winnicki, 'Ein ptolemäischer Offizier' (1972)	J.K. Winnicki, 'Ein ptolemäischer Offizier in Thebais', in *Eos* 60 (1972), p. 343-353
Winnicki, *Ptolemäerarmee* (1978)	J.K. Winnicki, *Ptolemäerarmee in Thebais* (Archiwum Filologiczne 38), Warszawa 1978
*Winnicki, 'Soldaten aus Pathyris' (1994)	J.K. Winnicki, 'Verlegungen von drei Soldaten aus Pathyris', in A. Bülow-Jacobsen (ed.), *Proceedings of the 20th International Congress of Papyrologists Copenhagen, 23-29 August, 1992*, Copenhagen 1994, p. 600-603
*Winnicki, 'Besuch Drytons' (1995)	J.K. Winnicki, 'Der Besuch Drytons in den Königsgräbern von Theben', in M. Capasso, *Papiri documentari greci* (Pap. Lup. 2), Lecce 1995, p. 89-94
Wipszycka, *L' industrie textile* (1965)	E. Wipszycka, *L'industrie textile dans l'Égypte romaine*, (Archivum filologiczne 9), Wroclaw-Warszawa-Krakow 1965

Wolff, *Justizwesen* (1970^2) — H.J. Wolff, *Das Justizwesen der Ptolemäer* (Münchener Beiträge zur Papyrusforschung und antiken Rechtsgeschichte 44), München 1970^2

Wolff, *Recht der griechischen Papyri* (1978) — H.J. Wolff, *Das Recht der griechischen Papyri Ägyptens in der Zeit der Ptolemäer und des Prinzipats. 2. Organisation und Kontrolle des privaten Rechtsverkehrs* (Handbuch der Altertumswissenschaft 10.5.2/ Rechtsgeschichte des Altertum 5.2), München 1978

Concordances

Previous editions — Inventory numbers — Plates

Previous editions (of Greek and demotic texts)	*P. Dryton*
Baillet, *Syringes* (1926), no. 306, 313, 413, 1780 and 1785	**App. B** Gr.
Clarysse, 'Le mariage et le testament' (1986), in *Chron. d'Ég.* 61, p. 99-103	**2** Gr.
Gerhard, *Ein gräko-ägyptischer Erbstreit* (1911)	**33** Gr. and **33bis** Gr.
Gerhard, *Ein gräko-ägyptischer Erbstreit* (1911), p. 8-9	**2** Gr.
Kaplony-Heckel, 'Pathyris I' (1992/93), in *Enchoria* 19/20, no. 2	**52** Dem.
Kaplony-Heckel, 'Pathyris I' (1992/93), in *Enchoria* 19/20, no. 8	**55** Dem.
Kaplony-Heckel, 'Soll und Haben' (1990), p. 142, note 2	**58** Dem.
Kaplony-Heckel, 'Gebelên-Papyri' (1967), p. 76-77, no. 2	**24** Dem.
Kaplony-Heckel, 'Gebelên-Papyri' (1967), p. 77, no. 3	**28** Dem.
Kaplony-Heckel, 'Soll und Haben' (1990), p. 139-146	**45** Dem.
Messeri Savorelli, 'Due Atti agoranomici' (1984), p. 522-525	**30** Gr.
Messeri Savorelli, 'Frammenti del primo testamento' (1990); the verso is unpublished	**1** Gr.-Dem.
Messeri, 'P. Grenf. I 19' (1982), in *ZPE* 47, p. 275-280	**17** Gr.
Powell, *Collectanea Alexandrina* (1970), p. 177-180	**50** Gr.
de Ricci, 'Papyrus de Pathyris' (1903), in *AfP* 2, p. 517-518	**36** Gr.
Spiegelberg, 'Papyrus Erbach' (1905), in *ZÄS* 42, p. 51	**35** Dem.
White, J.L., *Light from Ancient Letters*, Philadelphia 1986, no. 43	**36** Gr.

C. Ptol. Sklav. 56	**46** Gr.
C. Ptol. Sklav. 57	**4** Gr.
Chrest. Mitt. 18	**34** Gr.
Chrest. Mitt. 138	**App. A** Gr. descr.
Chrest. Mitt. 302	**4** Gr.
Chrest. Wilcken 10	**36** Gr.
O. dem. Zürich 12	**53** Dem.
O. dem. Zürich 36	**51** Dem.
O. Wilck. II 1617	**56** Gr.
O. Wilck. II 1618	**57** Gr.

P. Amh. II 36	**32** Gr.
P. Amh. II 166	**17** Gr.
P. Baden II 5	**46** Gr.
P. Baden II 6	**22** Gr.
P. Bour. 9	**3** Gr.
P. dem. Baden I 6	**8** Dem.
P. dem. Baden I 7	**5** Dem.
P. dem. Baden I 8	**6** Dem.
P. dem. Cairo II 30674	**45** Dem.
P. dem. Cairo II, p. 337, demotic note	**48** Gr.-Dem.
P. dem. Gebelein Heid. 11	**49** Dem.
P. dem. Gebelein Heid. 16	**27** Dem.
P. dem. Gebelein Heid. 18	**18** Dem.
P. dem. Gebelein Heid. 22	**13** Dem.
P. dem. Gebelein Heid. 25	**14** Dem.
P. dem. Gebelein Heid. 30	**23** Dem.
P. Grenf. I 1	**50** Gr.
P. Grenf. I 10	**11** Gr.
P. Grenf. I 12	**2** Gr.
P. Grenf. I 14	**37** Gr.
P. Grenf. I 15	**33bis** Gr.
P. Grenf. I 16	**40** Gr.
P. Grenf. I 17	**33** Gr.
P. Grenf. I 18	**16** Gr.
P. Grenf. I 19	**17** Gr.
P. Grenf. I 20	**19** Gr.
P. Grenf. I 21	**4** Gr.
P. Grenf. I 23	**25** Gr.
P. Grenf. I 29; the demotic receipt is unpublished	**29** Gr.-Dem.
P. Grenf. I 44	**3** Gr.
P. Grenf. II 17	**App. A** Gr. descr.
P. Lond. II 401 (p. 12-14)	**34** Gr.
P. Lond. II 402 Verso (p. 11-12)	**38** Gr.
P. Lond. III 889a (p. 22); the verso is unpublished	**21** Gr.-Dem.
P. Ryl. II 67	**31** Gr.
Pap. Lugd. Bat XIX 4	**3** Gr.
SB I 1806 + 1807 and 1836	**App. B**
SB I 4637	**2** Gr.
SB I 4638	**33** Gr. and **33bis** Gr.

SB XVI 12716	**17** Gr.
SB XVI 12986	**30** Gr.
SB XVIII 13330	**2** Gr.
SB XX 14579	**1** Gr.-Dem.
Sel. Pap. I 83	**4** Gr.
Sel. Pap. I 101	**36** Gr.

Inventory numbers	*P. Dryton*
Berlin, P. dem. inv.no. 13385	**28** Dem.
Berlin, P. dem. inv.no. 13388	**24** Dem.
Bibliotheca Medicea Laurenziana, P.L. III/155 recto	**1** Gr.-Dem.
Bibliotheca Medicea Laurenziana, P.L. III/155 verso	**1** Gr.-Dem. = *editio princeps*
British Library, P. inv.no. 401	**34** Gr.
British Library, P. inv.no. 402 verso	**38** Gr.
British Library, P. inv.no. 605 recto	**11** Gr.
British Library, P. inv.no. 605 verso	**50** Gr.
British Library, P. inv.no. 607	**2** Gr.
British Library, P. inv.no. 609 verso	**37** Gr.
British Library, P. inv.no. 611 recto a	**33bis** Gr.
British Library, P. inv.no. 611 recto b	**40** Gr.
British Library, P. inv.no. 611 verso	**41** Gr. = *editio princeps*
British Library, P. inv.no. 612	**33** Gr.
British Library, P. inv.no. 613	**16** Gr.
British Library, P. inv.no. 614	**17** Gr.
British Library, P. inv.no. 614 addendum	**17** Gr.
British Library, P. inv.no. 616	**19** Gr.
British Library, P. inv.no. 617	**4** Gr.
British Library, P. inv.no. 619	**25** Gr.
British Library, P. inv.no. 625	**29** Gr.-Dem.
British Library, P. inv.no. 625, demotic receipt below the Greek text	**29** Gr.-Dem. = *editio princeps*
British Library, P. inv.no. 640	**3** Gr.
British Library, P. inv.no. 641	**39** Gr. = *editio princeps*
British Library, P. inv.no. 686e	**39** Gr. = *editio princeps*
British Library, P. inv.no. 686f	**31** Gr. = *editio princeps*
British Library, P. inv.no. 687a	**3** Gr. = *editio princeps*
British Library, P. inv.no. 687b	**31** Gr. = *editio princeps*
British Library, P. inv.no. 687e	**3** Gr. = *editio princeps*
British Library, P. inv.no. 889a recto	**21** Gr.-Dem.

British Library, P. inv.no. 889a verso	**21** Gr.-Dem. = *editio princeps*
British Museum, old inv.no. P. dem. 03 (new no.: 74901)	**15** Dem. = *editio princeps*
British Museum, P. dem. inv.no. 10484	**26** Dem. descr.
British Museum, P. dem. inv.no. 10514	**9** Dem. descr.
British Museum, P. dem. inv.no. 10515	**10** Dem. descr.
British Museum, P. dem. inv.no. 74901	**15** Dem. = *editio princeps*
Cairo, O. dem. inv.no. JE 51234	**58** Dem.
Cairo, O. dem. inv.no. JE 51235	**52** Dem.
Cairo, O. dem. inv.no. JE 51448	**55** Dem.
Cairo, P. dem. inv.no. 30674	**45** Dem.
Cairo, P. Gr. inv.no. 10343	**48** Gr.-Dem. = *editio princeps*
Cairo, P. Gr. inv.no. 10349	**2** Gr.
Cairo, P. Gr. inv.no. 10354	**17** Gr. = *editio princeps*
Cairo, P. Gr. inv.no. 10355	**47** Gr. = *editio princeps*
Cairo, P. Gr. inv.no. 10357	**30** Gr.
Heidelberg, P. dem. inv.no. 712	**18** Dem.
Heidelberg, P. dem. inv.no. 724	**27** Dem.
Heidelberg, P. dem. inv.no. 725	**49** Dem.
Heidelberg, P. dem. inv.no. 739a	**14** Dem.
Heidelberg, P. dem. inv.no. 742a	**35** Dem.
Heidelberg, P. dem. inv.no. 749d	**13** Dem.
Heidelberg, P. dem. inv.no. 754c	**6** Dem.
Heidelberg, P. dem. inv.no. 762	**8** Dem.
Heidelberg, P. dem. inv.no. 770a	**8** Dem.
Heidelberg, P. dem. inv.no. 770b	**23** Dem.
Heidelberg, P. dem. inv.no. 773	**8** Dem. = *editio princeps*
Heidelberg, P. dem. inv.no. 774	**8** Dem.
Heidelberg, P. dem. inv.no. 779a	**5** Dem.
Heidelberg, P. Gr. inv.no. 313	**20** Dem.-Gr. = *editio princeps*
Heidelberg, P. Gr. inv.no. 314	**43** Gr. = *editio princeps*
Heidelberg, P. Gr. inv.no. 315	**44** Gr. = *editio princeps*
Heidelberg, P. Gr. inv.no. 1280	**33** Gr.
Heidelberg, P. Gr. inv.no. 1285	**2** Gr.
Heidelberg, P. Gr. inv.no. 1291	**22** Gr.
Heidelberg, P. Gr. inv.no. 1301	**31** Gr. = *editio princeps*
Heidelberg, P. Gr. inv.no. 1316	**46** Gr.
Heidelberg, P. Gr. inv.no. 1320	**42** Gr. = *editio princeps*
John Rylands Library, P. inv.no. 67	**31** Gr.
Louvre, P. inv.no. E 10440	**12** Dem. = *editio princeps*
Louvre, P. inv.no. E 10594	**36** Gr.
Louvre, P. inv.no. E 10595	**23** Dem. = *editio princeps*
Moskow, P. dem. inv.no. 431	**7** Dem. descr.
New York Pierpont Morgan Library, P. Gr. inv.no. 36	**32** Gr.

New York Pierpont Morgan Library, P. Gr. inv.no. 166	**17** Gr.
Sorbonne Bouriant, P. inv.no. 46	**3** Gr.
Turin, O. dem. inv.no. G 5	**App. C** Dem. descr.
Turin, O. dem. inv.no. S 12791	**54** Dem. descr.
Zürich, O. dem. inv.no. 1851	**53** Dem.
Zürich, O. dem. inv.no. 1875	**51** Dem.
Zürich, O. Gr. inv.no. 1904	**56** Gr.
Zürich, O. Gr. inv.no. 1905	**57** Gr.

P. Dryton	*Previous editions*
1 Gr.-Dem.	Messeri Savorelli, 'Frammenti del primo testamento' (1990) (= SB XX 14579); the verso is not published
2 Gr.	P. Grenf. I 12; Gerhard, *Ein gräko-ägyptischer Erbstreit* (1911), p. 8-9 (l. 1-17 = SB I 4637) + Clarysse, 'Le mariage et le testament' (1986), in *Chron. d' Ég.* 61, p. 99-103 (= SB XVIII 13330)
3 Gr.	P. Grenf. I 44 + P. Bour. 9 = Pap. Lugd. Bat. XIX 4 + **ined.** [British Library, P. inv.no. 687a and 687e]
4 Gr.	P. Grenf. I 21 = Chrest. Mitt. 302 = Sel. Pap. I 83 = C. Ptol. Sklav. 57
5 Dem.	P. dem. Baden I 7
6 Dem.	P. dem. Baden I 8
7 Dem. descr.	**Ined.** [Moskow, P. dem. inv.no. 431]
8 Dem.	P. dem. Baden I 6 + **ined.** [Heidelberg, P. dem. inv.no. 773]
9 Dem. descr.	**Ined.** [British Museum, P. dem. inv.no. 10514]
10 Dem. descr.	**Ined.** [British Museum, P. dem. inv.no. 10515]
11 Gr.	P. Grenf. I 10
12 Dem.	**Ined.** [Louvre, P. dem. inv.no. E 10440]
13 Dem.	P. dem. Gebelein Heid. 22
14 Dem.	P. dem. Gebelein Heid. 25
15 Dem.	**Ined.** [British Museum, old inv.no. P. dem. 03 / on 11-6-1980 put under the same glass as inv.no. 69008 / registered on 12-7-1995 as inv.no. 74901]
16 Gr.	P. Grenf. I 18
17 Gr.	P. Grenf. I 19 + P. Amh. II 166 = Messeri, 'P. Grenf. I 19' (1982), in *ZPE* 47, p. 275-280 (= SB XVI 12716) + **ined.** [Cairo, P. inv.no. 10354]
18 Dem.	P. dem. Gebelein Heid. 18
19 Gr.	P. Grenf. I 20
20 Dem.-Gr.	**Ined.** [Heidelberg, P. Gr. inv.no. 313]
21 Gr.-Dem.	P. Lond. III 889a (p. 22): the verso is unpublished
22 Gr.	P. Baden II 6
23 Dem.	P. dem. Gebelein Heid. 30 + **ined.** [Louvre, P. dem. inv.no. 10595]
24 Dem.	Kaplony-Heckel, 'Gebelên-Papyri' (1967), p. 76-77, no. 2
25 Gr.	P. Grenf. I 23
26 Dem. descr.	**Ined.** [British Museum, P. dem. inv.no. 10484]
27 Dem.	P. dem. Gebelein Heid. 16
28 Dem.	Kaplony-Heckel, 'Gebelên-Papyri' (1967), p. 77, no. 3
29 Gr.-Dem.	P. Grenf. I 29: the demotic receipt is unpublished
30 Gr.	Messeri Savorelli, 'Due Atti agoranomici' (1984), p. 522-525 (= SB XVI 12986)

31 Gr.	P. Ryl. II 67 + **ined.** [British Library, P. inv.no. 686f + 687b + Heidelberg, P. Gr. inv.no. 1301]
32 Gr.	P. Amh. II 36
33 Gr.	P. Grenf. I 17; Gerhard, *Ein gräko-ägyptischer Erbstreit* (1911), l. 1-27 and 39-41 (= SB I 4638, l. 1-27 and 39-41)
33bis Gr.	P. Grenf. I 15; Gerhard, *Ein gräko-ägyptischer Erbstreit* (1911), l. 28-38 (= SB I 4638, l. 28-38)
34 Gr.	P. Lond. II 401 (p. 12-14) = Chrest. Mitt. 18
35 Dem.	Spiegelberg, 'Papyrus Erbach' (1905), in *ZÄS* 42, p. 51
36 Gr.	de Ricci, 'Papyrus de Pathyris' (1903), in *AfP* 2, p. 517-518 = Chrest. Wilcken 10 = Sel. Pap. I 101 = J.L. White, *Light from Ancient Letters*, Philadelphia 1986, no. 43
37 Gr.	P. Grenf. I 14
38 Gr.	P. Lond. II 402 Verso
39 Gr.	**Ined.** [British Library, P. inv.no. 641 + 686e]
40 Gr.	P. Grenf. I 16
41 Gr.	**Ined.** [British Library, P. inv.no. 611 Verso]
42 Gr.	**Ined.** [Heidelberg, P. Gr. inv.no. 1320]
43 Gr.	**Ined.** [Heidelberg, P. Gr. inv.no. 314]
44 Gr.	**Ined.** [Heidelberg, P. Gr. inv.no. 315]
45 Dem.	P. dem. Cairo II 30674 = Kaplony-Heckel, 'Soll und Haben' (1990), p. 139-146
46 Gr.	P. Baden II 5 = C. Ptol. Sklav. 56
47 Gr.	**Ined.** [Cairo, P. inv.no. 10355]
48 Gr.-Dem.	**Ined.** [Cairo, P. inv.no. 10343]; the demotic note is published in P. dem. Cairo II, p. 337
49 Dem.	P. dem. Gebelein Heid. 11
50 Gr.	P. Grenf. I 1 = Powell, *Collectanea Alexandrina* (1970), p. 177-180
51 Dem.	O. dem. Zürich 36
52 Dem.	Kaplony-Heckel, 'Pathyris I' (1992/93), in *Enchoria* 19/20, no. 2
53 Dem.	O. dem. Zürich 12
54 Dem. descr.	**Ined.** [Turin, O. dem. inv.no. S 12791]
55 Dem.	Kaplony-Heckel, 'Pathyris I' (1992/93), in *Enchoria* 19/20, no. 8
56 Gr.	O. Wilck. II 1617
57 Gr.	O. Wilck. II 1618
58 Dem.	Kaplony-Heckel, 'Soll und Haben' (1990), p. 142, note 2
App. A Gr. descr.	P. Grenf. II 17 = Chrest. Mitt. 138
App. B Gr.	SB I 1806 + 1807, 1836; Baillet, *Syringes* (1926), no. 306, 313, 413, 1780 and 17
App. C Dem.descr.	**Ined.** [Turin, O. dem. inv.no. G 5]

You may consult several photographs of Dryton-papyri on
http://millennium.arts.kuleuven.ac.be/LHPC

Plates in this volume	*P. Dryton (facs. = facsimile)*	*Plates in previous editions and on World Wide Web*
I (New collage)	**1** Gr.-Dem. (recto) [facs. of verso p. 55]	Messeri Savorelli, 'Frammenti del primo testamento' (1990), pl. 41 (recto and verso)
II (Collage by W. Clarysse)	**2** Gr. (recto)	Plates of the fragments kept in Heidelberg are to be found on http://www.rzuser.uni-heidelberg.de/~gv0/Papyri/P.Heid._Uebersicht.html (see SB I 4637); Plate of the verso in Clarysse, 'Le mariage et le testament' (1986), in *Chron. d' Ég.* 61, p. 100
III (New collage)	**3** Gr.	Pap. Lugd. Bat. XIX, pl. 6 and P. New Pap. Primer^2, p. 57 (col. II) (no photographs of the fragments British Library, P. inv.no. 687a and 687e)
IV	**4** Gr.	—
—	**5** Dem. [facs. p. 90]	—
—	**6** Dem. [facs. p. 94]	—
—	**7** Dem. descr.	—
—	**8** Dem. [facs. p. 100]	—
—	**9** Dem. descr.	—
—	**10** Dem. descr.	—
—	**11** Gr. (recto) [verso = Text 50]	—
V-VI	**12** Dem. (recto-verso) [facs. of verso p. 131 and 134]	—
—	**13** Dem. [facs. p. 139]	Facsimile in P. dem. Gebelein Heid., p. 101, no. 22
—	**14** Dem. [facs. p. 143]	Facsimile in P. dem. Gebelein Heid., p. 102, no. 25
VIII	**15** Dem. [scanned photograph. p. 148]	—
—	**16** Gr. (recto-verso)	—
VII (Collage by P.W. Pestman)	**17** Gr. (recto)	Messeri, 'P. Grenf. I 19' (1982), in *ZPE* 47, pl. 16, recto-verso (no photograph of Cairo, P. inv.no. 10354)
—	**18** Dem. [facs. of recto-verso p. 164]	Facsimile in P. dem. Gebelein Heid., p. 100, no. 18
—	**19** Gr. (recto-verso)	—
VIII	**20** Dem.-Gr. (recto-verso) [facs. p. 174]	—
—	**21** Gr.-Dem. (recto-verso) [facs. of verso p. 179]	—

—	**22** Gr. [scanned photograph p. 418]	http://www.rzuser.uni-heidelberg.de/~gv0/Papyri/P.Heid._Uebersicht.html (see VBPII 6)
IX (New collage)	**23** Dem. [facs. p. 186]	Facsimile in P. dem. Gebelein Heid., p. 104, no. 30 (no facsimile of Louvre, P. dem. inv.no. 10595)
—	**24** Dem. [scanned photograph p. 192]	Facsimile in Kaplony-Heckel, 'Gebelên-Papyri' (1967), p. 76-77
—	**25** Gr. (recto-verso)	—
—	**26** Dem. descr.	—
—	**27** Dem. [facs. p. 203]	Facsimile in P. dem. Gebelein Heid., p. 98, no. 16
—	**28** Dem. [scanned photograph p. 208]	Facsimile in Kaplony-Heckel, 'Gebelên-Papyri' (1967), p. 77
X	**29** Gr.-Dem. (recto-verso) [facs. of demotic part p. 214]	—
—	**30** Gr.	Messeri Savorelli, 'Due Atti agoranomici' (1984), p. 523
XI (New collage)	**31** Gr.	—
—	**32** Gr.	—
XII-XIII (Collage)	**33** Gr. (recto-verso)	Photograph of fragment Heidelberg, P. Gr. 1280, and of the verso in R. Seider, *Paläographie der griechischen Papyri* III.1, Stuttgart 1990, p. 394-395; http://www.rzuser.uni-heidelberg.de/~gv0/Papyri/P.Heid._Uebersicht.html (see SB I 4638)
XVII	**33bis** Gr.	—
—	**34** Gr.	—
XIII	**35** Dem. (recto-verso) [facs. of recto-verso p. 268]	Facsimile in Spiegelberg, 'Papyrus Erbach' (1905), in *ZÄS* 42, p. 51
XIV	**36** Gr. (recto)	—
—	**37** Gr.	—
XV	**38** Gr. (verso)	—
XVI (Collage)	**39** Gr. (verso-recto) [facs. p. 319]	—
XVII	**40** Gr. (recto) [facs. p. 324]	—
XVIII	**41** Gr. (verso) [facs. p. 329]	—
XXI	**42** Gr. (verso- recto) [facs. p. 332]	—
XIX	**43** Gr. (recto-verso) [facs. p. 338; 340] and part of **43 App.** Dem. [facs. p. 344]	—
XX	**44** Gr. (verso-recto) [facs. p. 349] and part of **43 App.** Dem. [facs. p. 344]	—

—	**45** Dem. [facs. p. 354]	P. dem. Cairo II, pl. 50; Kaplony-Heckel, 'Soll und Haben' (1990), pl. 8b.
—	**46** Gr.	http://www.rzuser.uni-heidelberg.de/~gv0/Papyri/P.Heid._Uebersicht.html (see VBPII 5)
XXI	**47** Gr.	—
—	**48** Gr.-Dem. [scanned photograph of demotic part p. 370]	P. dem. Cairo II, pl. 146
—	**49** Dem.	Facsimile in P. dem. Gebelein Heid., p. 92-93, no. 11
XXII	**50** Gr. (verso) [recto = Text 11]	—
—	**51** Dem.	O. dem. Zürich 36, pl. VI
—	**52** Dem.	Kaplony-Heckel, 'Pathyris I' (1992/93), in *Enchoria* 19/20, no. 2, pl. 5 and facs. pl. 4
—	**53** Dem.	O. dem. Zürich 12, pl. II
—	**54** Dem. descr.	—
—	**55** Dem.	Kaplony-Heckel, 'Pathyris I' (1992/93), in *Enchoria* 19/20, no. 8, pl. 9 and facs. pl. 8
XXIII	**56** Gr.	—
XXIII	**57** Gr.	—
—	**58** Dem.	—
XXIV	**App. A** Gr. descr.	—
—	**App. B** Gr. [facs. p. 411-412]	Baillet, *Syringes* (1926), facsimiles: pl. XII, XVI and LXIX; photograph: pl. 27a
—	**App. C** Dem. descr.	—

INDICES

Dating

Rulers and years

Ptolemy VI

Πτολεμαῖος τοῦ Πτολεμαίου καὶ Κλεοπάτρας θεῶν Ἐπιφανῶν **11** 1
Ptlwmysʿws s3 Ptlwmysʿws irm Glwptrʿws n3 ntr.w nty pr **12** 1

Year 8	174 B.C.	**11**
Year 10	171	**12**

Ptolemy VI, Ptolemy VIII and Kleopatra II

Πτολεμαῖος καὶ Πτολεμαῖος ὁ ἀδελφὸς καὶ Κλεοπάτρα ἡ ἀδελφὴ τῶν Πτολεμαίου καὶ Κλεοπάτρας θεῶν Ἐπιφανῶν **1** [1-2]
Φιλομήτωρ **3** [7-9]; **4** 5

Year 6	164 B.C.	**1**

Ptolemy VI and Kleopatra II

Πτολεμαῖος καὶ Κλεοπάτρα ἡ ἀδελφὴ τῶν Πτολεμαίου καὶ Κλεοπάτρας θεῶν Ἐπιφανῶν **2** 1-2

Year 31	150 B.C.	**2**

Ptolemy VIII (and Kleopatra II and/ or III)

Πτολεμαῖος **48** [7], 8
Ptlwmysʿws irm Glwptr3ʿws - - Ptlwmysʿws irm Glwptr3ʿws n3 ntr.w nty pr **13** 1-2
Ptlwmysʿws p3 mnḫ s3 Ptlwmysʿws irm Glwptr3ʿws n3 ntr.w nty pr.w irm t3 Pr-ʿ3ʿws.t Glwptr3ʿws t3y=f sn.t t3y=f ḥm.t t3 ntr.t mnḫ.t **14** 1-3
Ptlwmysʿws **15** 1
Ptlwmysʿws p3 mnḫ s3 Ptlwmysʿws irm Glwp[t]r3ʿws **18** 2-3
Ptlwmysʿws p3 mnḫ s3 Ptlwmysʿws irm Glwptr3ʿws n3 ntr.w nty pr.w **5** 1-3
Ptlwmysʿws p3 ntr mnḫ s3 Ptlwmysʿws irm Glwptr3ʿws n3 ntr.w nty pr.w irm ?n3 ?Pr-ʿ3ʿws.wt n3 ntr.w mnḫ.w **23** 1-4 (Ptolemy VIII and Kleopatra II and/or Kleopatra III)

Year ?	145-143/2 B.C.	**13**
Year ?	143/2-138/7	**14**
Year 30	141/40	see **33**
Year 32	139/38	see **33**
Year 32	139	**15**, **37**
Year 34	137/36	see **33**
Year 35	135	**40**, **41**
Year 36	134	**42**
Year 39	131	**16**
Year 40	130	**36**
Year 41	129	**17**
Year 42	128	**18**
Year 44	127	**19**
Year 44	126	**3**, **4**
Year 47	123	**5**
Year 52	118	**24**
Year 53	117	**25**
Year ?	124-116	**23**

Kleopatra III and Ptolemy IX Soter II
Glwptr3 ʿws *n3 ntr.w nty pr irm Ptlwmys* ʿws *p3 nty mr mw.t p3 Swtr* **27** 1-3

Year 5	112 B.C.	**27**
Year 9	108	**51**, **54**
Year 10	108	**52**
Year 10	107	**53**

Kleopatra III and Ptolemy X Alexander I

Year 12=9	105 B.C.	**29**
Year 16=13	101	**55**

Ptolemy X Alexander I and Kleopatra Berenike
Ptlwmys ʿws *nty iw=w ḏd n=f 3lgsntrws* ʿws *irm t3 Pr-ʿ3* ʿws*.t Brnyg3* ʿws *t3y=f sn.t t3y=f ḥm.t* **8** 1-2

Year 14	100 B.C.	**56**, **57**
Year 15	100	**8**
Year 21	94	**49**

ἔτος **1** [13], 30; **2** 2, [15], 29, 30, verso 4; **3** [1], [7-9], [29], [30], [31-32], 45, 49, 54, 58, 65; **4** [1], 18, 19, [22]; **11** 1, 8, [11], 12; **12** verso II 1, [3]; **16** 1, 15, verso 2a, 1b; **17** 1, verso 2a; **19** [1], 9; **25** 1, 10; **29** 1, 9; **33** 13, 18, 27, verso 1; **36** 15; **37** 1, 19, 20; **39** 24, 29; **40** 1; **41** 1; **42** 1; **48** 5; **56** 1; **57** 1
ḥ3.t-sp, year **5** 1; **8** 1; **12** 1, [12], [13]; **13** [1], [10]; **14** [1], [7]; **15** 1; **18** 1; **20** 5; **23** [1]; **24** 7, [10]; **27** 1, 9; **49** 19; **51** 3, 4, 7; **52** 3, 4, 7; **53** 3, 4; **55** 4

Months and days

3ḫ.t-season, inundation season

Θωύθ	**11** 5-6
ibd-1 3ḫ.t	**8** 1; **15** 1; **49** 19; **51** 4, 7
Φαῶφι	**19** 1, 9; **37** 1, 20
Ἀθύρ	**43** 1
Χοίαχ/ Χοίακ	**16** 1; **25** 1; **29** 8; **43** 2, 3
ibd - - 3ḫ.t	**14** 1

pr.t-season, germination season

Τῦβι	**36** 9
ibd-1 pr.t	**27** 1
Μεχείρ	**2** 13, verso 4; **19** 9, 11
ibd-2 pr.t	**18** 1; **55** 5
Φαμενώθ	**12** verso II 3; **29** 11
ibd-3 pr.t	**5** 1; **12** [12]; **23** 13
Φαρμοῦθι	**17** 1; **37** 19; **56** 1
ibd-4 pr.t	**12** [13]

šmw-season, harvest season

Παχών	**1** 11, 30; **16** 15; **25** 9; **33** verso 1; **43** 6, 7; **57** 1
ibd-1 šmw	**13** [10]; **14** [7]; **24** 7; **27** 9
Παῦνι	**3** [1]; **4** [1], 22; **11** [14]
ibd-2 šmw	**53** 5
Ἐπείφ	**42** 1
Μεσορή	**12** verso II 1; **29** 1; **39** 1; **41** 1
ibd-4 šmw	**12** 1; **24** 10

sw 2	**12** 1
sw 4	**5** 1
sw 5	**8** 1
sw 6	**49** 19; **53** 5
sw 10	**15** 1
sw 18	**14** 1
sw 22	**51** 4, 7
sw 25	**18** 1
sw 26	**24** 10; **27** 1
(sw) ʿrq(y) (30)	**12** [12]; **13** [10]; **14** [7]; **23** 13; **24** 7; **27** 9; **55** 5

Gods

Greek

Ἀφροδίτη **3** 43
Σουχος **3** 43

Demotic

Imn, Amon **12** 9
Imn-Rᶜ-nsw-ntr.w, Amonrasonther **12** 17
Ḥ.t-Ḥr nb In.ty, Hathor, Mistress of Inty **8** 11; **27** 22
Sbk nb 3mwr, Souchos, Lord of Krokodilopolis **23** 26
Sbk p3 ntr ᶜ3, Souchos, the great god **35** 3

Personal names

(A: army; E: eponymous priest(ess); N: notary or subordinate of the notary; P: priest(ess); Pros.: see Prosopography p. 17; W: witness; s.: son of; d.: daughter of; f.: father of; m.: mother of)

Greek personal names

Ἀγαθόκλεια d. Noumenios (E) **1** [9]
Ἀθηνόδοτος f. Ariston **34** 17
Ἀλῦκις **40** 4
Ἀμμωνία ἢ καὶ Σενμῖνις d. Ptolemaios (pros. 405) **33** 1, verso 3
Ἀμμώνιος (?N) **11** 20
Ἀμμώνιος s. Areios (A) **3** 64
Ἀμπέλιον (pros. 08) **3** [10]; **4** 7
Ἀνδρείας **40** ?5
Ἀνίκητος (N) **17** 2, 27
Ἀνίκητος ὃς καὶ Νεχούτης s. Ptolemaios~Panobchounis **17** 10-11, 16, verso 2b, upper margin
? Ἀντιοχ[**1** Fr.10
Ἀντίπατρος f. Antipatros **2** 7
Ἀντίπατρος s. Antipatros (E) **2** 7
Ἀπολλόδοτος ὃς καὶ Ἁρσιῆσις f. Apollonios~Psennesis (pros. 310) **16** 8
Ἀπολλωνία d. Dryton (pros. 506) **3** [17-18], [25], [26-27]; **4** 7, 12, 15, 16; see Ἀπολλωνία ἢ καὶ Σενμοῦθις
Ἀπολλωνία ἢ καὶ Σενμοῦθις d. Dryton (pros. 506) **34** 3
Ἀπολλωνία d. Ptolemaios~Pamenos (pros. 404) **2** 21, verso 1; **3** [10]; **16** 3, 15, 25, verso 1b; **17** 3, 21, verso 1b-2b; **19** 2, 10, 17, verso 1; see Ἀπολλωνία ἢ καὶ Σενμῶνθις
Ἀπολλωνία ἢ καὶ Σενμῶνθις d. Ptolemaios~Pamenos (pros. 404) **3** [17-18], [29]; **4** 12, 17; **33** 1, verso 2; **46** 5-6
Ἀπολλωνία the younger, d. Dryton (pros. 509) **3** 14-15, [17-18]; **4** 9, 12; see Ἀπολλωνία the younger ἢ καὶ Σενπελαία
Ἀπολλωνία the younger ἢ καὶ Σενπελαία d. Dryton (pros. 509) **34** 7
Ἀπολλώνιος s. Asklepiades (W) **2** 27
Ἀπολλώνιος ὃς καὶ Ψενμῶθης f. Kallimedes~Patous (pros. 207) **33** 2-3
Ἀπολλώνιος ὃς καὶ Ψεννῆσις s. Apollodotos~Harsiesis (pros. 408) **16** 7-8, 11-12
Αρ. . . . s. [ ]is **39** 27
Ἄρειος (N) **16** 30; **17** 27; **19** 21; **25** [24]; **30** 15
Ἄρειος f. Ammonios **3** 64
Ἁρεκῦσις **37** 21
Ἀριστόδημος f. Polykritos **1** [1-2]
Ἀριστονίκη d. *Nwl3ts* (E) **1** 4
Ἀριστώ d. Dryton (pros. 507) **3** [17-18]; **4** 12; see Ἀριστὼ ἢ καὶ Σενμῶνθις
Ἀριστὼ ἢ καὶ Σενμῶνθις d. Dryton (pros. 507) **34** 6
Ἀρίστων s. Athenodotos **34** 17
Ἀρίστων s. Kallikles (E) **1** [8]
Ἁρμάις s. Horos **19** 5
Ἁρπαῆσις s. Portis **25** 5, 20, verso 2
Ἀρσάκης f. Herodos **2** 31
Ἀσκληπιάδης (N) **3** [1]; **4** 1; **19** 1, 21
Ἀσκληπιάδης f. Apollonios **2** 27
Ἀφροδισία d. Dryton (pros. 510) **3** [17-18]; **4** 12
Ἀφροδισία ἢ καὶ Ταχράτις d. Dryton (pros. 510) **34** 3-4

Βόηθος **32** 1; **33** 1*

Δημαρίον d. Metrophanes (E) **1** [5]
Δημήτριος f. Nikias **2** 10
Δι[- - - f. Diodoros **2** 9
Διδυ(μ) **39** 18
Διόγνητος f. - - -te **2** 12
Διόδοτος (A) **2** 15; **33** 5
Διόδωρος s. Di- - - (E) **2** 9
Διονύσιος (N) **1** [11]; **3** [7-9]; **4** 5
Διοσκουρίδης (N) **30** 3
Δρύτων s. Pamphilos, f. Esthladas (pros. 403) **1** [12], 17; **2** 15, 22, verso 2; **3** [1], 33, [35]; **4** 1, 20; **11** [11], 15, 17; **16** 5; **17** 6; **19** 3; **21** 6; **22** 1; **30** 1; **31** 2, 7; **32** 3; **34** 4; **40** 1; **46** 8; **47** 3, 5; **56** 3

Εἰρήνη (pros. 07) **3** [10]; **4** 7
Ἑριεύς **41** 5
Ἑριεύς f. Patous **3** 52
Ἑρμ.φιλος s. Pamphilos (pros. 01) **1** [17]; **2**

22; **3** [7-9]; **4** 6
Ἑρμίας **31** 2
Ἑρμίας (N) **29** 2, 16
Ἑρμοκρατεία d. Hermokrates (E) **1** [5]
Ἑρμοκράτης **43** 5
Ἑρμοκράτης f. Hermokrateia **1** 5
Ἑρμοκράτης f. Ptolemaios (pros. 205) **16** 3; **33** 4
Ἐσθλάδας s. Dryton (pros. 504) **2** 18, 19; **3** 5, [14], [15], [17-18], [19-24], [25], [26-27]; **4** [4], 9, 10, 11, 14, 15, 16; **21** 6; **22** 1; **31** 7; **36** 1; **39** 3, 29; **46** 7; **48** 3
Ἐσθλάδας s. Esthladas (pros. 03) **2** 23
Ἐσθλάδας f. Esthladas **2** 23
Ἐσθλάδας f. Petras- - - (?pros. 504) **3** [15]; **4** 10
Ἐσθλάδας f. Sarapias, s. Theon (pros. 301) **1** [15]; **2** 19; **3** [6]; **4** 4
Εὐρύμαχος **1** [7]
Εὐχαρίστη d. Ptolemaios (E) **1** 10

Ζήνων (E) **2** 10
Ζωὶς ἣ καὶ Ὀγχᾶσις d. Isidoros **21** 1

Ἡλιόδωρος (N) **25** 2, [24]
Ἡραὶς ἣ καὶ Τίσρις d. Ptolemaios~Paous (pros. 407) **16** 9-10; **33** 2 (Τάσρις)
Ἡρακλεία ἣ καὶ Σεναπᾶθις d. Ptolemaios (pros. 406) **33** 1
Ἡρακλείδης **33** 14
Ἡρακλείδης (W) **2** 28
Ἡρακλεόδωρος f. Noumenios **1** [7]
Ἥροδος s. Arsakes (W) **2** 31

Θαῖβις **39** 27
Θαίς d. *3pr*.. (E) **1** [10]
Θεοδώρα d. - - -agros (E) **2** 11
Θερμοῦθις (pros. 508) **57** 3; see Νικάριον ἣ καὶ Θερμοῦθις
Θέων f. Esthladas (pros. 201) **1** [15]; **3** [6]; **4** 4
Θορτ[ ] **39** 28
Θορταῖος (N) **33** 26
Θοτορταῖος f. Nechoutes **3** 48
Θοτορταῖος s. Nechthminis **44** verso 9
Θράσων f. Senenouphis (pros. 305) **41** 4

Ἰσίδωρος f. Zois~Onchasis **21** 1

Καίης s. Pates (pros. 505) **25** 2, 9, 20, verso 1
Καλῖβις (pros. 307) **33** 3
Καλλικλῆς f. Ariston **1** [8]
Καλλιμήδης ὃς καὶ Πατοῦς s. Apollonios~Psenmonthes (pros. 308) (A) **33** 2-3, 24, 25
Κεφάλων s. Panobchounis **17** verso 3b, upper margin

Λαμένθις **40** 2
Λεοννα.( ) **39** 6
Λυκόφρων f. - - -ios **2** 6

Μητροφάνης f. Demarion **1** [5]
Μυρσίνη (pros. 05) **3** [7-9]; **4** 6; **43** 2, 5; **44** verso 3, 5

Νεχθμῖνις f. Thotortaios **44** verso 9
Νεχούτης s. Thotortaios (P) **3** 48
Νεχούτης see Ἀνίκητος ὃς καὶ Νεχούτης
Νεχοῦτις see Νικαία ἣ καὶ Νεχοῦτις
Νικαία ἣ καὶ Νεχοῦτις d. ?~P[ ]ais **17** 13-14
Νικάριον d. Dryton (pros. 508) **3** [17-18]; **4** 12; see Νικάριον ἣ καὶ Θερμοῦθις
Νικάριον ἣ καὶ Θερμοῦθις d. Dryton (pros. 508) **34** 6-7
Νικίας s. Demetrios (E) **2** 10
Νουμήνιος f. Agathokleia **1** 9
Νουμήνιος s. Herakleodoros (E) **1** [7]

Ὀνῆς **33** 19, 20
Ὀνθονμοῦθις **43** verso 8
Ὀρσῆς s. Kallimedes~Patous (pros. 415) **33** 4

Π. τα[ ] **41** 8
Π[ ].αις f. Nikaia~Nechoutis **17** 14
Πάμφιλος f. ? **11** 12
Πάμφιλος f. Dryton (pros. 302) **1** 18; **2** 15, 22; **3** [1], [35]; **4** 1; **11** [12]; **16** 5; **17** 6-7; **19** 3; **31** [2]; **32** 3
Πάμφιλος f. Herm.philos **1** [17]; **2** 22
Πανίσκος **56** 2, 6; **57** 2, 7
Πανίσκος (N) **29** 2, 16
Πανοβχοῦνις s. Kallimedes~Patous (pros. 414) **33** 4
Πανοβχοῦνις f. Phagonis (pros. 502) **29** 5
Πανοβχοῦνις see Πτολεμαῖος ὃς καὶ Πανοβχοῦνις
Πατής f. Kaies (pros. 401) **25** 2
Πατοῦς (P) (pros. 04) **21** 2; **37** 2
Πατοῦς see Καλλιμήδης ὃς καὶ Πατοῦς
Πατοῦς s. Herieus (P) (?pros. 04) **3** 52
Πατοῦς s. Horos (A) **3** 56
Πατοῦς f. Peteharsemtheus **20** verso 2
Πατσεοῦς **31** 3
Πατσεοῦς f. Phibis **39** 23
Πατσεοῦς f. Sennesis **29** 4
Παχνοῦβις s. . e[**12** verso II 2
Παῶς **36** 8
Πέλοψ (pros. 10) **36** 13; **39** 18; **40** 8, 8-9, 26
Πετεαρσεμθεῦς s. Patous **20** verso 1
Πετρασ- - - s. Esthladas (pros. 610) **3** [15]; **4** 10
Πολύκριτος s. Aristodemos (E) **1** [1-2]
Πόρτις f. Harpaesis **25** 5
Πρώταρχος f. Ptolemaios **2** 8
Πτολεμαῖος **33** 22
Πτολεμαῖος (N) **2** 14, 33, verso 3
Πτολεμαῖος f. Apollonia~Senmonthis, f. Ammonia~Senminis, f. Herakleia~Senapathis, f. Herais~Tisris (pros. 304) **33** 2
Πτολεμαῖος f. and grandf. Euchariste **1** [10]
Πτολεμαῖος s. Hermokrates, f. Apollonia (pros. 304) **16** 3; **17** 4; **19** 2; **33** 4
Πτολεμαῖος s. Protarchos (E) **2** 8
Πτολεμαῖος s. Ptolemaios (A) **2** 30
Πτολεμαῖος f. Ptolemaios **2** 30

Demotic personal names

T3-šr.t-Ḏḥwty, Senthotis m. Pamenos (pros. 516) **8** 4
T3y-Išr, Tiesris (pros. 407) **45** 5, 11; **58** 3
T3mgls, Demokles f. Demetrios **12** 2
Ta-ḫrd.ṯ, Tachratis d. Dryton and Senmonthis (pros. 510) **5** 7
Ty3twtws, Diodotos (A) **14** 4
Twtw, Totoes f. Psenthotes **12** verso 8
Twtw, Totoes f. Semtheus **12** verso 9
Tmtrys, Demetrios s. Demokles (E) **12** 2
Trwtn, Dryton f. Peteharsemtheus **27** 24
Trwtwn, Dryton s. Pamphilos (pros. 403) **1** [verso]; **5** 7; **6** 4; **12** 10 (*Trwtn*); **35** 2 (*Trwtn*), verso (*Trwtn*); **55** 1 (*Trwtn*); **58** 2 (*Trw͑tn*)
Th3mnsts ͑*ws*, Theomnestos s. Hippalos (E) **12** 6
Tsythws, Dositheos f. Kineas **12** 7

Ḏḥwṯ-i.ir.dy-s , Thotortaios s. Kales (pros. 410) **52** 4, 7; **53** 4
Ḏḥwṯ-i.ir.dy-s, Thotortaios f. Phibis **15** 2
Ḏḥwṯ-sḏm, Thotsytmis s. Amphiomis (W) **12** verso 3
Ḏd-ḥr, Teos f. Espnouthis **23** 25
Ḏd-ḥr, Teos f. Spemminis **23** 28

- -*[- - -]*, - - f. Nechthminis **8** 13
[- - -]~Pa-n3, [- - -]~Panas f. Hr- - - ~ Harmais **14** 4-5
[- - -] ͑*nḫ*, - - - ͑nḫ f. ? **23** 30
]-Is.t, -esis s. Harsiesis **13** 4
⌜- ⌝*[- - -]*⌜*Is.t*⌝, --?esis f. Pachnoubis **12** 10

For the Greek name

Alexander, see *3lgsntrs*
Ammonios, see *3mwnys*
Apollonia, see *3pwlny3*
Arsinoe, *3rsyn3*
Demetrios, see *Tmtrys*
Demokles, see *T3mgls*
Diodotos, see *Ty3twtws*
Dositheos, see *Tsythws*
Dryton, see *Trwtn* and *Trwtwn*
Eirene, *see Hyrn3*
Esthladas, see *3stlts*
Euboulos, see *3wbwls*
Hippalos, see *Hyplws*
Hr- - -, see *Hr[- - -]*
Kineas, see *Gyn3s*
Kleainete, see *Gl3ynt*
Komanos, see *Qmnw*
Lochos, see *L3qhws*
Pamphilos, see *Pnphylws*
Philotera, see *Phyltr*
Ptolemaios, see *Ptlwmys*
Ptolemais, see *Ptwlm3*
Sarapias, see *Srpy3s*
?Sogenes, see *Sgn*
Sosos, see *S3s*
Theomnestos, see *Th3mnsts*

Double names

Ἀμμωνία~Σενμῖνις
Ἀνίκητος~Νεχούτης
Ἀπολλόδοτος~Ἁρσιῆσις
Ἀπολλωνία~Σενμοῦθις
Ἀπολλωνία~Σενμῶνθις
Ἀπολλωνία the younger~Σενπελαία
Ἀπολλώνιος~Ψενμῶθης
Ἀπολλώνιος~Ψεννῆσις
Ἀριστώ~Σενμῶνθις
Ἀφροδισία~Ταχράτις
Ἡραίς~Τίσρις
Ἡρακλεία~Σεναπᾶθις
Καλλιμήδης~Πατοῦς
Νικαία~Νεχοῦτις
Νικάριον~Θερμοῦθις
Πτολεμαῖος~Πανοβχοῦνις
Πτολεμαῖος~Παοῦς
Σόλων~Σλῆις

3pwlny3~T3-šr.t-Mnṯ, Apollonia~Senmonthis
Ptlwmys~Pa-mnḥ, Ptolemaios~Pamenos
Hr[- - -]~ Ḥr-m-ḥb, Hr- - - ~ Harmais s. [- - -]~Panas
[- - -]~Pa-n3, [- - -]~Panas

Titles and occupations

Greek titles and occupations

ἀγορανόμος **1** 12; **2** 14, verso 3; **3** 1, [7-9]; **4** 1, 5; **16** 2; **17** 2; **25** 2; **29** 3; **30** [3]
ἀθλοφόρος Βερενίκης Εὐεργετίδος **1** 4; **2** 4-5; **11** 3
ἀρχεῖον see General word index
ἀρχιφυλακίτης **33** 14
ἀστή see General word index
γραμματεύς **40** ?5
διάδοχος **3** [2], 35; **4** 1; **16** 7; **17** 7; **19** 4; **22** 1; **31** 2; **32** 5; **46** [3]
ἐπιμελητής **31** 2
ἐπιστράτηγος **32** 1; **33** 1*; **34** 1
ἐπίταγμα see General word index
ἱερεία Ἀρσινόης Φιλοπάτορος **1** [5]; **2** 5; **11** 3-4
ἱερεία βασιλίσσης Κλεοπάτρας **1** [8]; **2** 11
ἱερεία Κλεοπάτρας τῆς μητρός **2** 11-12
ἱερεία Κλεοπάτρας τῆς μητρὸς Πτολεμαίου Θεοῦ Ἐπιφανοῦς Εὐχαρίστου **1** 9
ἱερεύς **3** <48>, 52; **20** verso 2; **21** 2, 3; **37** 2
ἱερεὺς Ἀλεξάνδρου καὶ θεῶν Σωτήρων καὶ θεῶν Ἀδελφῶν καὶ θεῶν Εὐεργετῶν καὶ θεῶν Φιλοπατόρων καὶ θεῶν Ἐπιφανῶν καὶ θεῶν Φιλομητόρων **1** 1-3; **11** 1-3

Demotic titles and occupations

Geography

Greek

Demotic

Place of redaction of the texts

Money, measures, weights, taxes

Greek

Demotic

Varia

it 1 1/3 r it 2/3 r it 1 1/3 ʿn, 1 1/3 (artaba) of barley — (their half is) 2/3, being 1 1/3 (artaba) of barley again **20** 4
it 3 1/2 r 1 1/2 1/4 r̥ 3 1/2 ʿn, 3 1/2 (artabas) of barley — (their half is) 1 1/2 1/4, being 3 1/2 again **28** 3
rdb sw 4 t3y=w ps(.t) 2 r rdb sw 4 ʿn, 4 artabas of wheat — their half is 2, being 4 artabas of wheat again **15** 2-3
rdb n sw 15 t3y=w pš 7 1/2 (r) rdb n sw 15 ʿn, 15 artabas of wheat — their half is 7 1/2, being 15 artabas of wheat again **27** 6-7
ḥḏ 60 r ḥḏ 30 r ḥḏ 60 ʿn, 60 (deben of) money — (their half is) 30 (deben of) money, being 60 (deben of) money again **55** 2-3
ḥḏ 261 qd 5 r sttr 1305 1/2 r ḥḏ 261 ḳd 5 ʿn, 261 (deben of) money and 5 kite — that is 1305 1/2 staters, being 261 deben and 5 kite again **12** 11
sw 4 2/3 r sw 2 1/3 r sw 4 2/3 ʿn, 4 2/3 (artabas) of wheat — (their half is) 2 1/3 (artabas) of wheat, being 4 2/3 (artabas) of wheat again **53** 3
sw 5 r sw 2 1/2 r sw 5 ʿn, 5 artabas of wheat — (their half is) 2 1/2 artabas of wheat, being 5 artabas of wheat again **52** 2
sw 5 1/4 r sw 2 1/2 1/8 r sw 5 1/4 ʿn, 5 1/4 artabas of wheat — (their half is) 2 1/2 1/8 artabas of wheat, being 5 1/4 artabas of wheat again **52** 6
st3 7 r st3 3 1/2 r st3 7 ʿn, 7 arouras — (their half is) 3 1/2 arouras, being 7 arouras again **51** 2-3

Interest clauses (see §35)

ἄτοκα **16** 13; **17** [19]; **19** 8; **29** 6
τόκος **19** 13 (καὶ τοῦ ὑπερπεσόντος χρόνου τόκους [διδράχμο]υς τῆς μνᾶς τὸν μῆνα ἕκαστον); **39** 8, 9 (σὺν τόκωι)
iw p3y=w ḥw ẖn=w, interest included **12** [11]; **13** [9-10]; **14** 7; **15** [3]; **23** 11; **27** 8
irm p3y=w 1 r 1 1/2, increased by 50% **14** 10; **23** 14; **27** 13
irm t3y=w ms.t r-ẖ t3 ms.t nty iw=s r smn (n) wʿ irm 2 Pr-Ḥ.t-Ḥr, together with their interest according to the interest to be established for each and everyone of Pathyris **24** 5-7 and notes

General word index of documentary texts

Greek general word index[1]

ἄβαξ see §52 (p. 293); **38** 29
ἀγνοεῖν **31** 1
ἀγορά **11** [18]; **16** 22; **25** 18; **30** [8]
ἀγωγεύς see §52 (p. 286); **38** 28
ἀδελφή **3** [10], [26-27]; **4** 7, 15; **34** 6; **36** 13
ἀδιάθετος **33** 5
ἀδικεῖν **33** 2
ἀδίκως **34** 21
ἄδολος **16** 16
ἀδυνατεῖν **31** 6
ἀεί **33** 10
αἱρεῖν **2** 17; **16** 27; **17** 24; **19** 19; **30** 13
αἰτία **32** 12
ἀκίνδυνος **11** [14]
ἄκρος **1** [13]; **2** 16; **11** [12]; **46** 4
ἄκυρος **47** 6
ἀλαβάστρινος **39** 1
ἀλαβαστροθήκη see §52 (p. 293); **38** 28
ἀλήθεια **48** 10
ἀλλά **47** 3
ἀλλήλων **16** 22; **17** 19+x; **19** 15; **30** 9
ἄλλος **1** [16]; **2** [24]; **3** [7-9], [12], [13], [26-27]; **4** 5, 8, 9, [16]; **19** verso 2; **33** 7; **34** 14; **37** 3; **38** 5, 11, 19, 26, 30, 32, 33; **42** 3, 7, 8, 10, 15, 19, 20; **43** 2, 7; **44** verso 5, 9, recto 2; **48** 6
ἀλλότριος **33** 17
ἅλς **29** 6, verso 2
ἅμαξα see §55; **3** [12]; **4** 8; **40** 7; **43** verso 2; **44** verso 2
ἀμειξία **34** 20
ἄμπελος **34** 22
ἀμπελών **3** [11]; **4** 8; **34** 11, 19, 27-28
ἀμφότερος **2** 31; **16** 25; **34** 4
ἄν passim
ἀναγκαῖος **33** 12
ἀναγνωστικά see §52 (p. 299); **37** 12
ἀναγράφειν **31** 3
ἀναπλεῖν **36** 8-9
ἀνάσιλλος **2** [16]; **11** 11
ἀναφάλαντος **2** 28
ἀνδρεῖος **47** ?4
ἀνέγκλητος **3** 29; **4** 18
ἄνευ **47** [3]
ἀνήλωμα **3** [28]; **4** 17; **11** 15; **16** 18; **25** 12-13
ἀνήρ **3** 2, 35; **4** 2; **16** 5, 7, 11; **17** 6, 9, 16; **19** 3, 4; **31** 6, 7; **32** 6; **46** [4]
ἀνθεινός **42** 3
ἀνθρώπινος **1** 14; **2** 17; **3** [3]; **4** 2
ἀνοιγνύναι **3** 15; **4** 10
ἀνομολογεῖσθαι **33** 14
ἀντί **40** 8
ἀντιλαμβάνειν **33bis** 37; **34** 30
ἀντίληψις **33bis** 28
ἀντιποιεῖν **33** 11, 20; **34** 21
ἀνχιστεία **33** 7
ἀξιοῦν **31** 8; **32** 14; **33** 21; **33bis** [30]; **34** 25
ἀπαίτησις **31** 4
ἀπέναντι **3** [19-24]; **4** 14
ἀπηλιώτης **3** [15]; **4** 10, 12
ἀπό **2** [18]; **3** [7-9], [17-18], [19-24]; **4** 6, 11, 14; **11** [10], 14; **19** [9]; **31** 5; **32** 7; **33** 10; **34** 11, 12, 18; **37** 13, 14, 19; **43** 1; **48** 5
ἀπογράφειν **33** 7
ἀποδεικνύναι **3** [17-18], [28]; **4** 11, 17
ἀποδημεῖν **43** 4
ἀποδιδόναι **11** 13; **16** 14, 19; **19** 10, 11; **25** 7-8, 15; **29** 7, 9; **30** 6; **33** 13, 14, 16; **36** verso 1
ἀπόδοσις **16** verso 1a; **17** verso 1a
ἀποκαθιστάναι **11** 14-15, 15-16; **16** 16-17; **25** 11; **36** 5
ἀποκλύζειν **33** 16
ἀπολείπειν **33** 5, 6, 7-8, 9
ἀποστάτης **36** 12
ἀποτίνειν **11** 17; **16** 20; **19** 12; **25** 16; **29** 11; **30** 7
ἀποφέρειν **33** 10, 19; **34** 29
ἄπρακτος **33** 18
ἀργυρικός **3** [26-27]; **4** 16
ἀριστερός **1** [13]; **2** 16; **3** 55; **11** [12]; **46** [4]
ἀριστοφόρον see §52 (p. 294); **37** 7
ἀρχεῖον see §34; **3** [7-9]; **4** 5
ἀσκός **38** 10
ἀστή **1** [15]; **2** 19; **3** [6]; **4** 4
ἀσφαλιών see §52 (p. 283); **37** 8
ἄσφαλτος see §52 (p. 300); **42** 15
ἄτοκα, see Money, measures, weights, taxes
αὐλή **3** 13; **4** 9
αὐτός **3** [14], [31-32], 53; **4** 9, 19
ἀφιστάναι **11** 9

βασιλεύς **48** 4, [7], 8
βασιλεύω **1** [1]; **2** 1; **11** [1]
βάσις **37** 15
βία **33** 9, 19; **34** 30
βίαιος **34** 18
βῖκος see §52 (p. 283); **37** 4
βίος **33** 5
βλάπτειν **33** 15
βορρᾶς **3** [14]; **4** 9
βοῦς **3** [19-24]; **4** 13
βυβλιοθήκη see §34; §52 (p. 299); **38** 8
βυβλίον see §52 (p. 299); **38** 9; **42** 12, 14, 20

γάμος **2** verso 1
γάρ **32** 10; **36** 8
γείτων **3** [14]; **4** 9
γένημα **34** 29
γῆ **34** 14
γίγνεσθαι **2** verso 1; **11** 16-17; **31** 8; **33** 12, 14; **33bis** 30, 36; **38** 33; **39** 14; **41** 11; **42** 4; **43** 2, 3, 6, 7; **44** verso 2, 4, 5,

[1] Exclusive of the poem Text 50. Exclusive of numerals and pronouns.

ἐπίγρυπος **2** [16]; **11** 9, 11-12
ἐπιδιδόναι **33** 13
ἐπικρεμαστός see §52 (p. 297); **42** 5
ἐπίκτητος **3** [33]; **4** 20
ἐπιμέλεσθαι **36** 4
ἔπιπλα **2** 18; **3** 4, [26-27]; **4** 3, 16; **33** 9, 16
ἐπισκευή **3** 12; **4** [9]
ἐπισκοπεῖν **34** 26; **36** 12
ἐπίστατον **37** 6
ἐπίταγμα **3** [2], 35; **4** [2]; **16** 6; **17** 8; **19** 3-4; **32** 5-6; **46** 3
ἐπιτελεῖν **3** 28; **4** 17
ἐπίτροπος see §6; **1** [17]; **2** 21; **3** [7-9]; **4** [6]; **33** 8
ἐπιφέρειν **11** 19
ἐποίκιον **34** 13
ἐποικονομ[**31** 7
ἐρεοῦς see ἐριοῦς
ἐριοῦς **38** 15
ἕτερος **33** 15; **34** 23
ἔτι **36** 6
ἔτος, see Dating

εὖ **48** [11]
εὐαισθητεῖν **1** 12
εὐθύριν **3** 46, 50, 55, 59, 66
εὐμεγέθης **2** 29; **3** 45; **11** 12
εὐορκεῖν **48** 11
εὑρίσκειν **39** 25
εὐτυχεῖν **31** 9; **33bis** 37; **34** 31
εὐχερῶς **34** 24
ἐφάπτειν **33** 17
ἔφεσις **33** 26
ἐφιορκεῖν **48** [11]
ἐφίππιος/ἐφίππιον see §52 (p. 286); **38** 5; **42** 6
ἔχειν **3** [25], [33]; **4** 15, 20; **21** 5; **22** 2; **39** 29; **41** 2; **43** verso 7
ἕως **3** [15], [28], [31-32]; **4** 10, 17, 19; **12** verso II 3; **19** 9; **37** 20; **43** 3

ζμύρνα **37** 9
ζωστήρ see §52 (p. 287); **38** 8; **39** 5

ἤ passim
ἡμιόλιος **11** [18]; **16** 21; **19** [13]; **25** 17; **30** 8
ἥμισυς **2** 20; **3** [25], [26-27], [30]; **4** 15, 16, 18; **34** 8, 11, 12, 21, 27
ἡμιτέλεστος **3** 13; **4** 9
ἥσσων/ ἥττων **11** 19; **47** 7

θηλυκός **3** [7-9], [19-24]; **4** 7, 13
θῖβις see §52 (p. 284); **37** 10
θυγάτηρ **3** [30]; **4** 18; **34** 4; **39** 25; **41** 5
θύρα **3** [16], [17-18], [19-24]; **4** 10, 11, 14
θώραξ see §52 (p. 287); **38** 6

ἴδιος **11** [16]; **16** 17; **25** 12; **31** 3 (ἴδιος); **40** 1; **41** 1
ἰδιόχρεος **33** 15
ἱδρωιον see §52 (p. 287); **38** 18
ἱερόν **3** 49, 53; **21** 4; **37** 2
ἱκανός **36** 10
ἱμάς see §52 (p. 287); **42** 17
ἱμάτιον **38** 16
ἵνα **31** [1]; **34** 30
ἵνιον see §52 (p. 294); **38** 14
ἱππικός **38** 8, 22; **42** 17, 18
ἵππος **2** 20; **3** [4]; **4** 3
ἴσος **3** [19-24], 62; **4** 13

καθάπερ **16** 28-29; **17** 25; **19** 20; **22** [4]; **25** 22; **29** 15; **30** [14]
καθαρός **16** 16; **25** 10
καθήκειν **31** 3, 8; **33** 12; **33bis** [33], 34
καθιστάναι **3** [7-9]; **4** 6; **33** 18
καθότι **11** [16]; **29** 10
καί passim
καινός **38** 12, 18
καιρός **34** 20
καλῶς **36** 6
καμάρα **3** [17-18]; **4** 11
καμαροῦν **3** 14; **4** 9
κάρδαμον **41** 7, 8
καρπός **11** 9
κασῆς see §52 (p. 287); **38** 4, 5
κατά **1** [15]; **3** [6], [19-24], [25], [26-27]; **4** 4, 13, 15, 16; **30** [1]; **31** 3; **33** 6, 7, 8, 12; **33bis** 35; **40** 5; **48** 10
καταβλάπτειν **33** 11
καταγιγνώσκειν **34** 22
καταλείπειν **1** [14], 17; **2** 17-18, 22, 24; **3** [3]; **4** 2
καταπεριϊστάναι **33** 18-19
καταστέλλειν **36** 10
καταφεύγειν **34** 25
καταφρονεῖν **33** 6
καταφυγή **33bis** 29
καταφυτεύειν **34** 22
κάτεργον see §55; **44** verso 1-2
κατοικεῖν **34** 5, 23
κατωμηλ( ) **38** 9
κεῖσθαι **38** 29; **44** verso 7
κελλίβας see §52 (p. 294); **38** 30
κενός **38** 26
κεράμιον **41** 11
κινδυνεύειν **32** 13-14
κίνδυνος **11** 14
κίστη see §52 (p. 284); **37** 3, 9; **39** 12
κληρ( ) see §52 (p. 299); **37** 11
κληρονομεῖν **33** 12
κληρονομία **33** 23
κλίβανος **3** [19-24]; **4** 14
κλῖμαξ see §55; **39** 17; **43** verso 4
κλίνη see §52 (p. 297); **37** 7; **38** 27, 31; **39** 3
κοιλογένειος **11** 13
κοινός **3** [26-27], [31-32], 31-32; **4** 16, 19, 20
κόνδυ see §52 (p. 294); **38** 13, 33
κρατεῖν **34** 15, [17]
κριθή **20** verso 2; **33** 20; **40** 3, 5, 7; **41** 6
κριτήριον **33bis** 34
κρόταφος **3** 47
κροτών **3** [30]; **4** 18; **44** verso 3, 4
κτῆνη **3** 4; **4** 3; **43** 1, verso [1]
κτῆσις **34** 25
κύαθος **39** 3
κυρ[ευ **47** 3
κυριεύειν **3** [19-24], 33; **4** 13, 20; **33** 12-

10, 11, 14, 15; **31** 4, 5; **34** 23, 28
τορνευτός **38** 31
τράπεζα **56** 2; **57** 2
τρόπος **2** 17
τροφή **3** [30]; **4** 18

ὑγιαίνειν **1** [13]; **2** 14, 16; **3** [1], [2]; **4** 1, 2
υἱός **2** 19, 20; **19** 7; **33** 4; **39** 13; **43** verso 6
ὕπαιθρον **32** 8
ὑπάρχειν **2** 18; **3** [4], 10, [26-27]; **4** [3], 7, 16; **11** [19]; **16** 28; **17** 24-25; **19** 19; **22** 4; **25** 21; **29** 14; **30** [13]; **32** 9-10; **33** 5, 8; **34** 5
ὑπεπιστατεῖν **33** 19
ὑπέρ **21** 6; **33** 17; **47** 5
ὑπερβολή **32** 13
ὑπερέχειν **33** 18
ὑπερισχύειν **33** 6
ὑπερπίπτειν **19** 13
ὑπό **31** 4; **33** 2, 9; **33bis** 30
ὑπογράφειν **31** 7; **33** 24
ὑπογραφή **33** 25
ὑπόδημα **38** 10
ὑποθήκη **1** 21
ὑποκάτω **3** 66
ὑπόκλαστος **3** [17-18]; **4** 11

φαίνειν **3** [31-32]; **4** 20; **31** 8; **33bis** 31; **34** 25
φέρειν **44** verso 2
φερνή **3** [31-32]; **4** 19
φιλανθρωπεῖν **31** 8
φιλάνθρωπον **33bis** 32
φοινικοῦς **38** 5
φορολογία **34** 14
φρέαρ **3** [12]; **4** 8; **34** 13
φρονεῖν **1** [12]; **2** 14; **3** [1]; **4** 1
φυλακή **31** 5
φυτεύειν **34** 28
φωρά **33** 17

χαίρειν **21** 5; **36** 1
χαλινός/ χαλινόν see §52 (p. 292); **38** 7, 33
χαλκοῦς **38** 13; **39** 24; **42** 16
χάλκωμα **42** 19
χειρόγραφον see §34; **39** 27
χέρσος **34** 14
χιλωτήρ see §52 (p. 285); **38** 9, 24
χιτών **38** 14; **42** 7
χλαμύς **38** 16
χρῆσθαι **36** 11
χρηματίζειν **2** 3; **3** [6]; **4** [5]; **16** 30; **17** 27; **19** 21; **25** [24]; **29** 16; **30** [15]
χρηστήρ (for χρηστήριον?) **3** [16]; **4** 10
χρόνος **11** 10, [16]; **16** 20; **19** 12, 13; **25** 16; **29** 10; **30** 7; **34** 16

ψιλός **3** [14], [15], 16, [19-24]; **4** 9, 10, 11, 14, 15

ὠνητής **31** 7
ὡς **1** [13]; **2** [15], 29, 30; **3** 45, 49, 54, 58, 65; **11** 8, [11], 12; **33** 6, 21; **36** 12; **40** 4
ὧς **2** 29; **11** 9
ὡσαύτως **33** 22
ὥστε **43** 5

Demotic general word index

3rghn, archeion **21** verso
3ḥ, land **49** 2, 8, 9
3ẖ.t, see Dating

i-ir-n=, against, owing from **12** 11; **13** [9]; **14** 7; **15** 3; **23** 12; **24** [3]; **27** 7; **28** 4
iw (circumstantial, future, relative clause) passim
iw, receipt **12** 14; **14** [11]; **23** 19; **27** 16
iwy(.t), security **12** 15; **23** 20 (*iwi*); **27** 20
iwṱ, without **12** [13], 14, 16; **13** 11; **14** 8, [10], [11]; **23** 19, 24; **24** 8; **27** 10, 14, 16, 21
ibd, month **12** [13]; **14** 10; **23** 14, 15; **27** 13, 14; see Dating
ip, account **45** 1; **51** 1; **55** 3
in, to pay **51** 1, 5; **53** 1; **55** [1]
ir, to do, make **1** [verso]; **5** 12; **6** [8], [10]; **8** [7], 8; **12** 16; **14** 12; **18** verso 1; **21** verso; **23** 17, 21, 23; **27** 17, 20; **29** dem. receipt 2; **35** 2; **49** 12, 14, verso 1; **55** 4; in *i.ir ir n3 nfr.w*, see Titles (*wʿb*)
iry, companion **49** 16
irm, with, and passim
iḥ.t, cow **49** 4, 6, 12, verso 3
it, barley **20** 4 = κριθή **20** verso 2; **24** 2, 3, 4; **28** 3
it, in *n3 ntr.w mr it.ṱ=w*, see Titles (*wʿb*); in *wʿb 3rsyn ʿws t3 mr it.ṱ=s*, see Titles

ʿ.wy, house, place **6** [9]; **8** 8; **13** 12; **14** 9; **27** 11
ʿ3, great **35** 3
ʿn, again **12** [11]; **13** [8]; **14** [7]; **15** 3; **20** 4; **27** 7; **28** 3; **51** 3, 6; **52** 3, 6; **53** 3; **55** 3
ʿnḫ, life **35** 4; in *ʿnḫ ḏ.t*, may he live forever **15** 1
ʿḥʿ, to stand **6** 8; **8** 7; in *iw iw=f ʿḥʿ rd.ṱ*, a valid receipt **12** 14; **14** [11-12]; **23** 19; **27** 16
ʿš, (bronze) stove **45** 9, 11

wy, to be far, to recede **5** 9; **6** 5; **8** 5; **29** dem. receipt 3
wyʿ, farmer **49** 6, 9
wʿb(.t), priest(ess) **8** 11; **12** 2, 5, 7, 8; see Titles
wʿb, pure **13** [11]; **14** 8; **27** 9
wp.t, work **49** 9, 12
wn, in *wn-mtw=*, to possess **12** 10; **13** [8]; **14** 6; **15** 2; **23** 10; **24** 2; **27** 6; **28** 3
wṱ, in *irm p3y=w wṱ*, with their extra charge **54** notes

b3ḥ, in *m-b3ḥ*, before **35** 3; in *f3y tn nb m-b3ḥ 3rsyn ʿws t3 mr sn*, see Titles
bn iw, negative future III **6** 8, [11]; **8** 7, 9; **12** 12, 13; **14** [10], 11, 12; **23** 15, 16, 18; **27** 14, 15, 17
bk, document see §34; **49** verso 1

For the Greek word

Addenda and corrigenda to LSJ

ἀσφαλιών to be added , see Text **37**, l. 8 comm. and p. 283

ἀσφαλών to be deleted (hapax legomenon in LSJ), see Text **37**, l. 8 comm. and p. 283

ἐντύλη for the meaning (LSJ has: «rug or cushion»), see p. 296-297

ἐπικρεμαστός to be added, see Text **42**, l. 5 and p. 297

κήθιν to be deleted (hapax legomenon in LSJ), see Text **38**, l. 23 comm.

μώστιον for the etymology (LSJ has «= μώϊον»), see p. 285

ὀπυάζομαι to be deleted (hapax legomenon in LSJ: «dub. l.»)), see Text **50** col. II, l. 38 and comm. (p. 382)

σφαιρωτήρ P.Lond.2.402v22 (= Text **38**) is to be deleted from the examples listed in LSJ, see p. 290

χρητήρ to be deleted (hapax legomenon in LSJ), see Text **4**, l. 10 comm.

PLATES

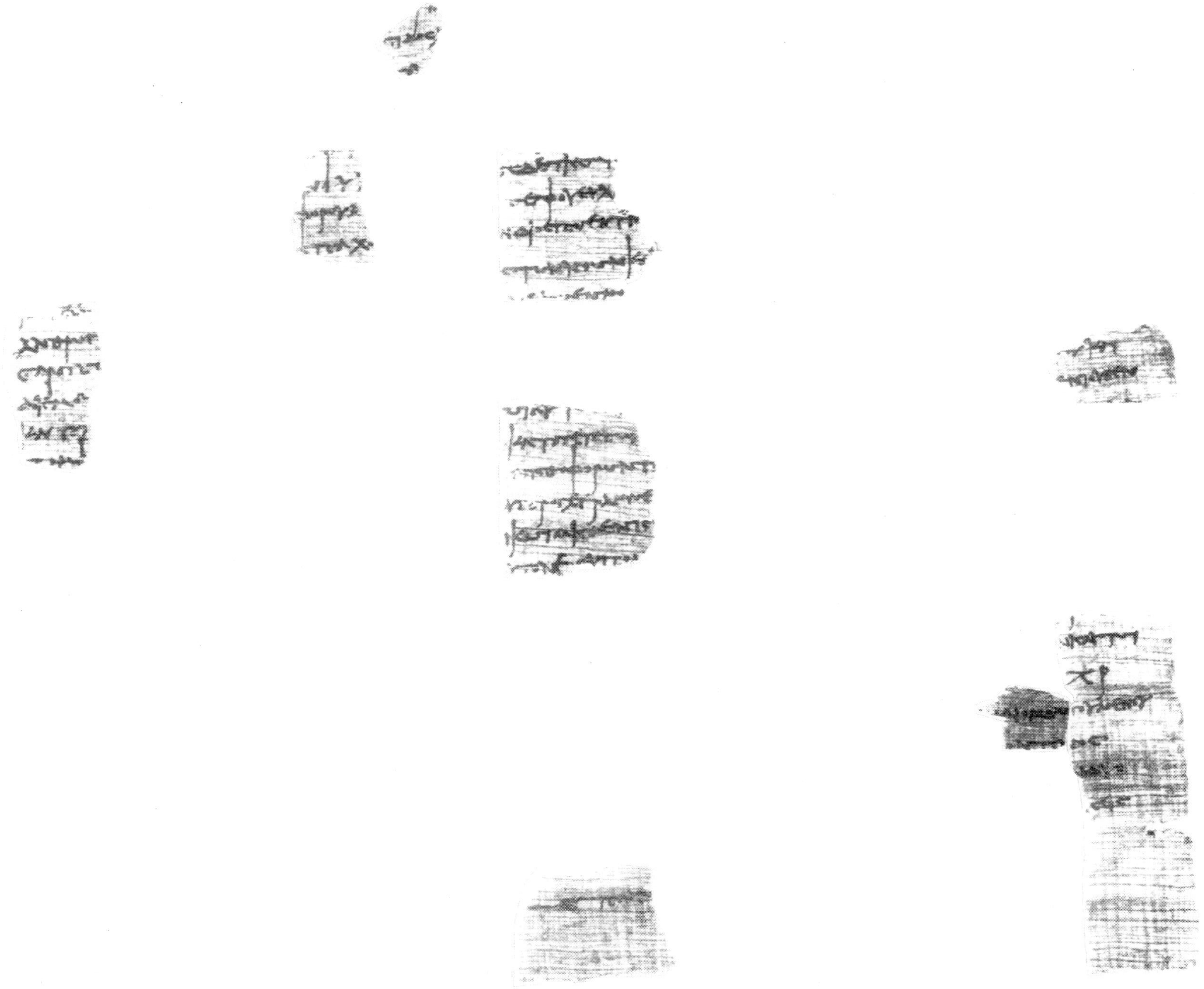

I — No. 1 recto [new collage] — Bibliotheca Medicea Laurenziana P. L. III/155.

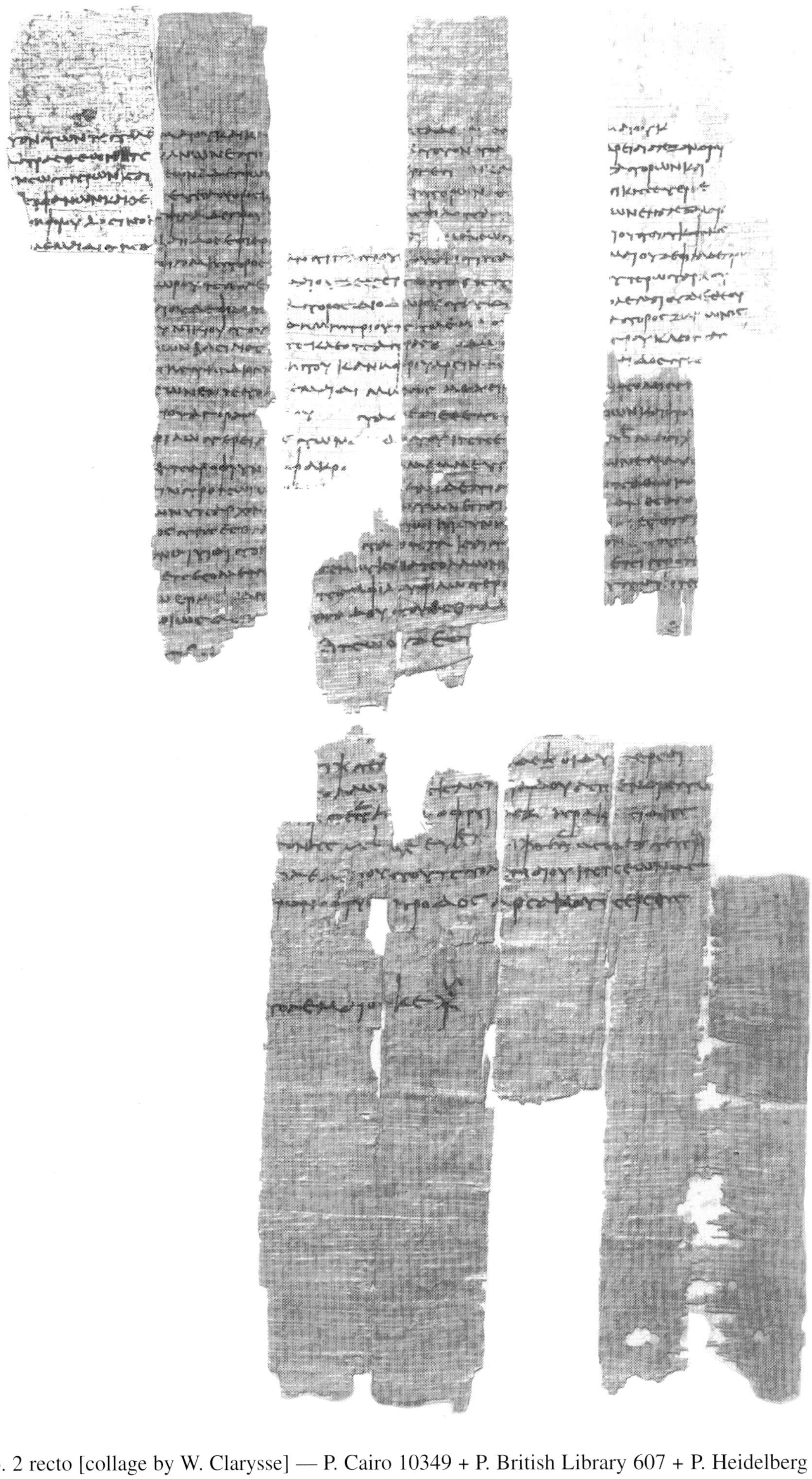

II — No. 2 recto [collage by W. Clarysse] — P. Cairo 10349 + P. British Library 607 + P. Heidelberg Gr. 1285.

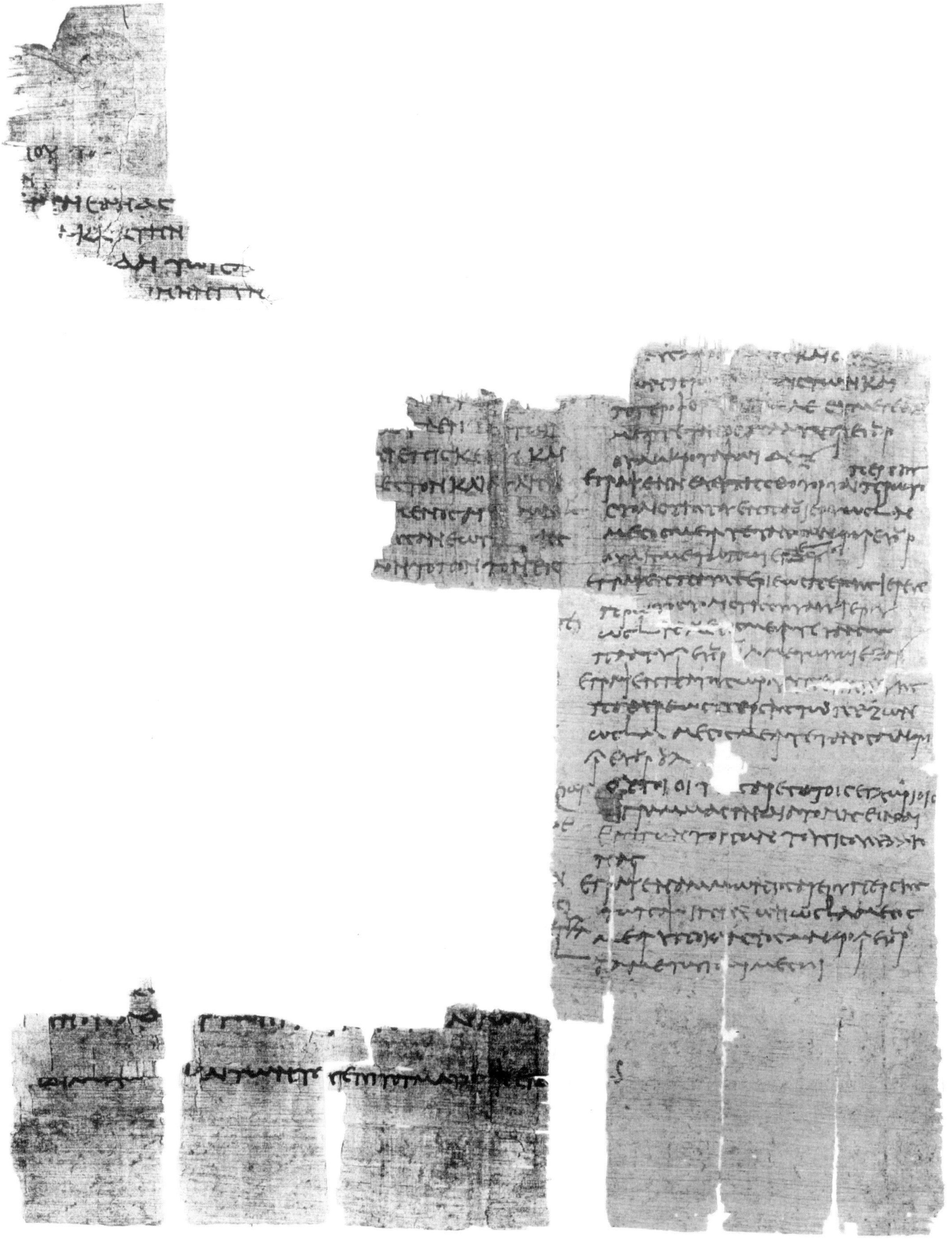

III — No. 3 [new collage] — P. British Library 687a + 640 + 687e + P. Sorbonne Bouriant 46.

IV — No. 4 — P. British Library 617.

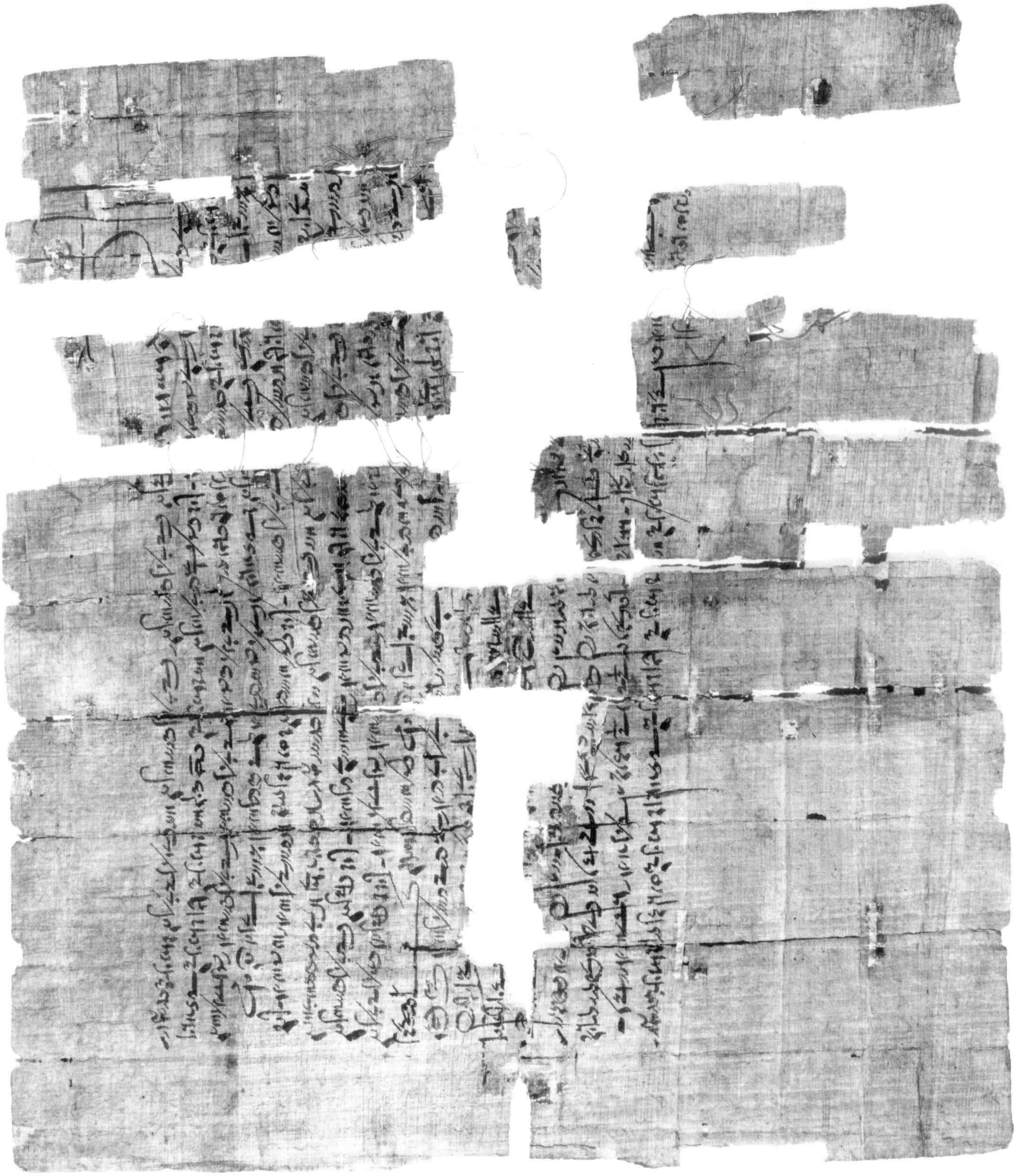

V — No. 12 recto — P. Louvre E 10440 (© Photo R.M.N.).

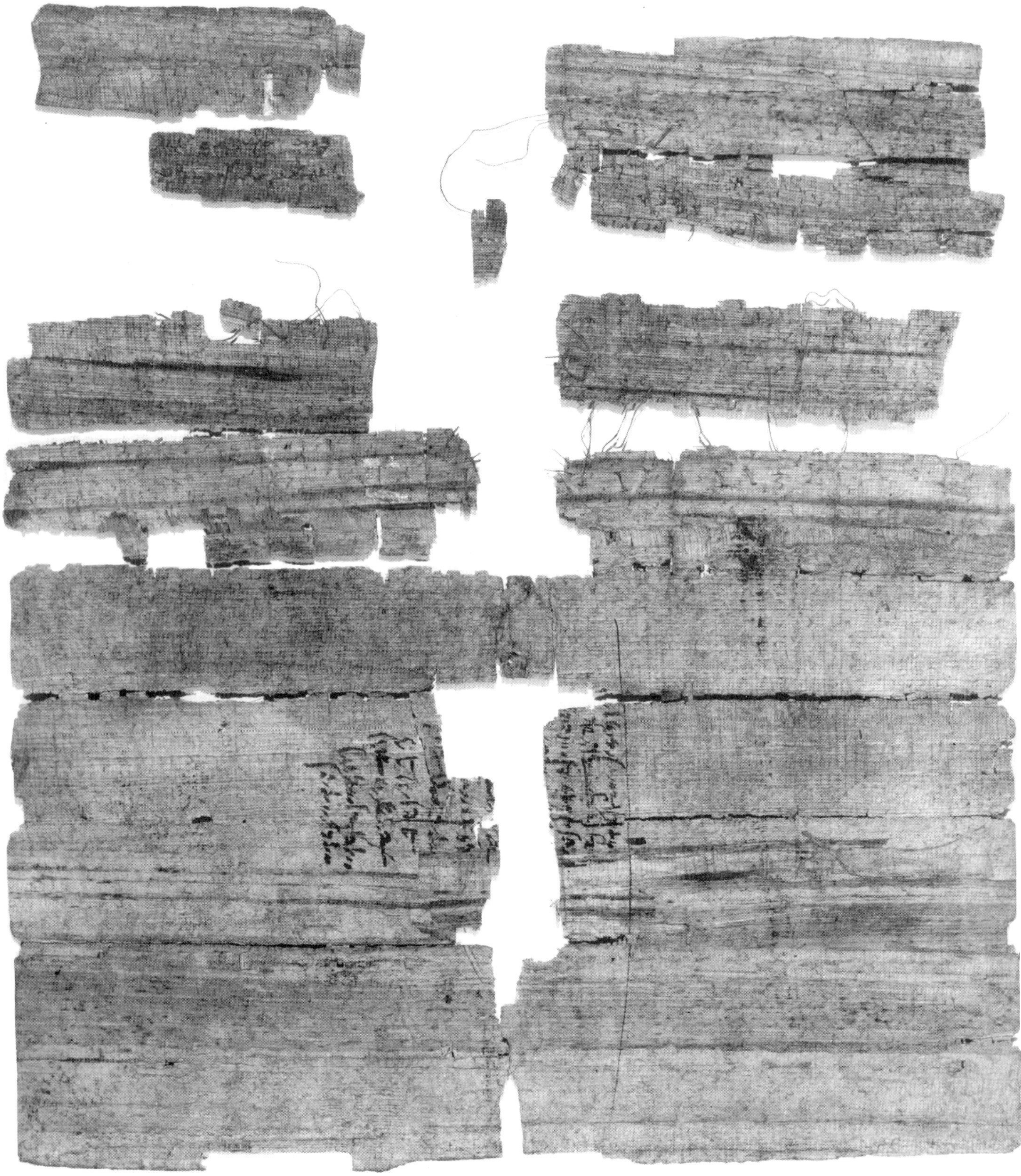

VI — No. 12 verso — P. Louvre E 10440 (© Photo R.M.N.).

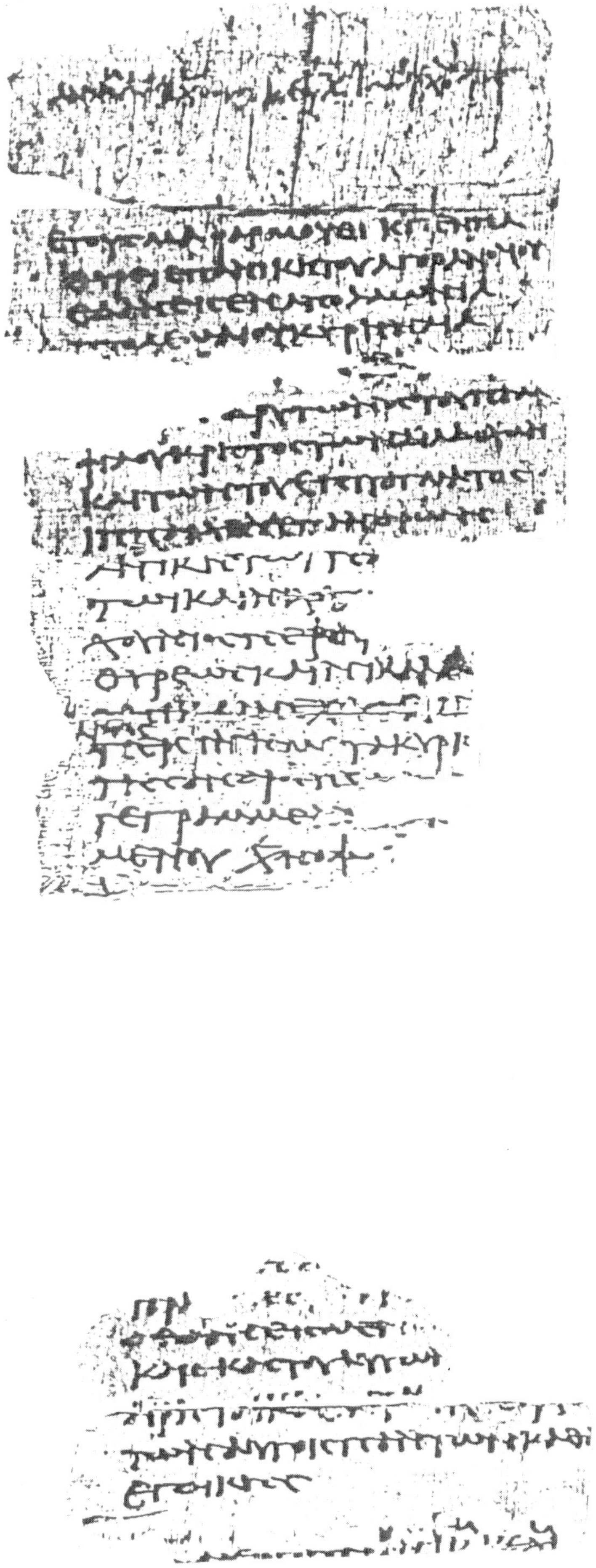

VII — No. 17 recto [collage by P. W. Pestman] — P. British Library 614 + 614 add. + P. Cairo 10354 + P. Pierpont Morgan Library Gr. 166.

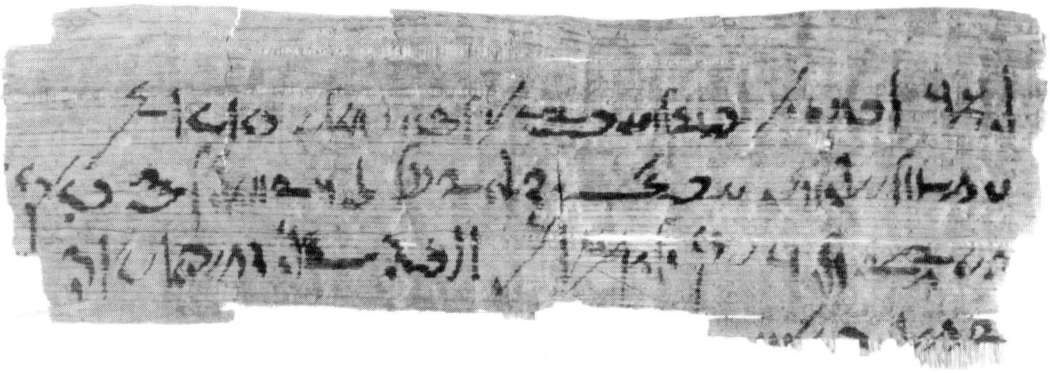

VIIIa — No. 15 — P. British Museum 74901 (© British Museum).

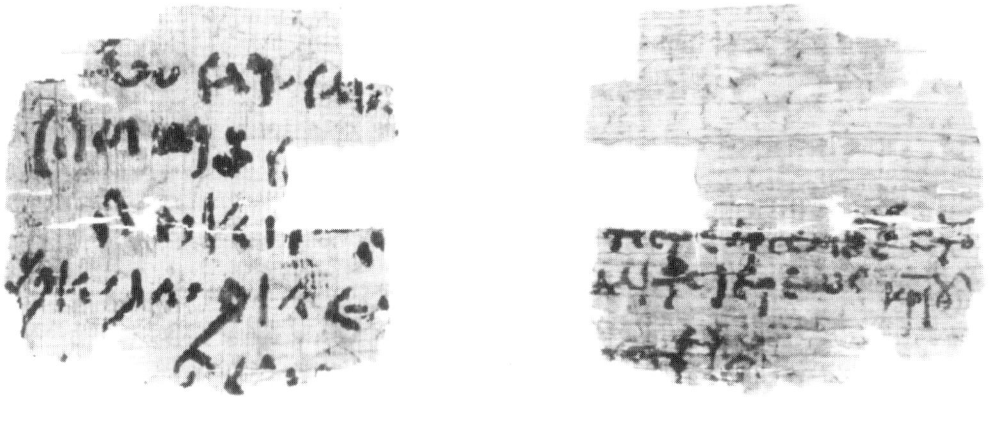

VIIIb — No. 20 recto and verso — P. Heidelberg Gr. 313.

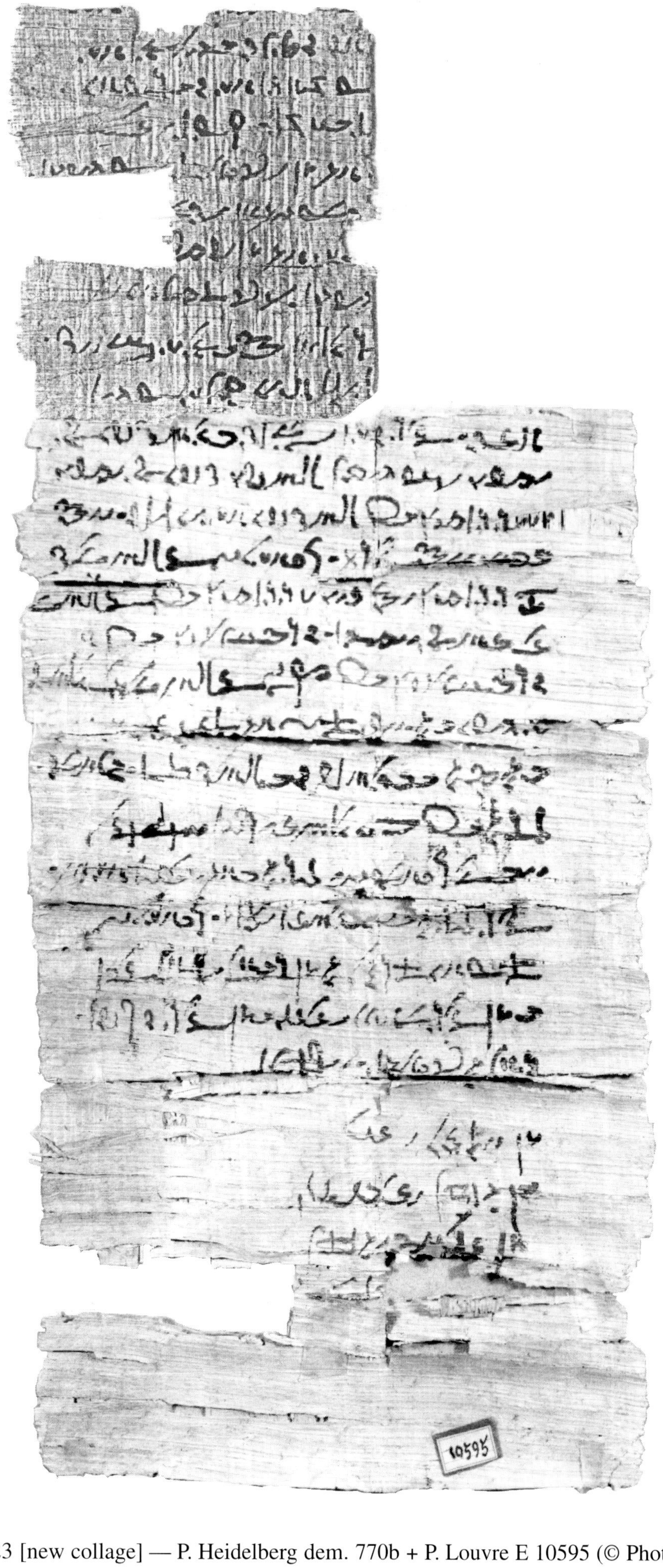

IX — No. 23 [new collage] — P. Heidelberg dem. 770b + P. Louvre E 10595 (© Photo R.M.N.).

Recto

Verso

X — No. 29 recto and verso — P. British Library 625.

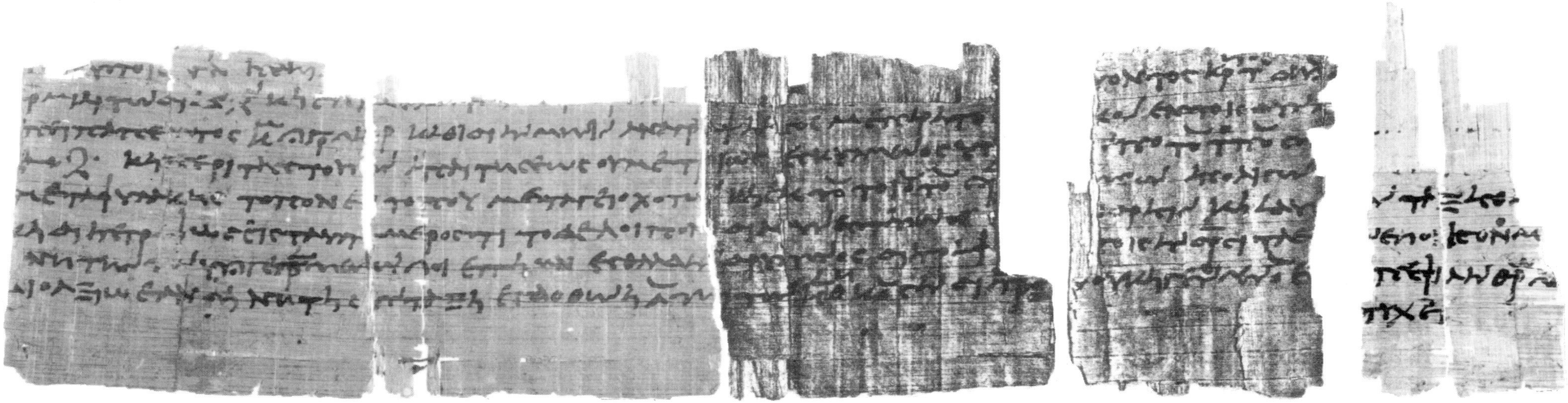

XI — No. 31 [new collage] — P. John Rylands Library 67 + P. British Library 686f + 687b + P. Heidelberg Gr. 1301.

XII — No. 33 recto [collage] — P. Heidelberg Gr. 1280 + P. British Library 612.

XIIIa — No. 33 verso — P. Heidelberg Gr. 1280.

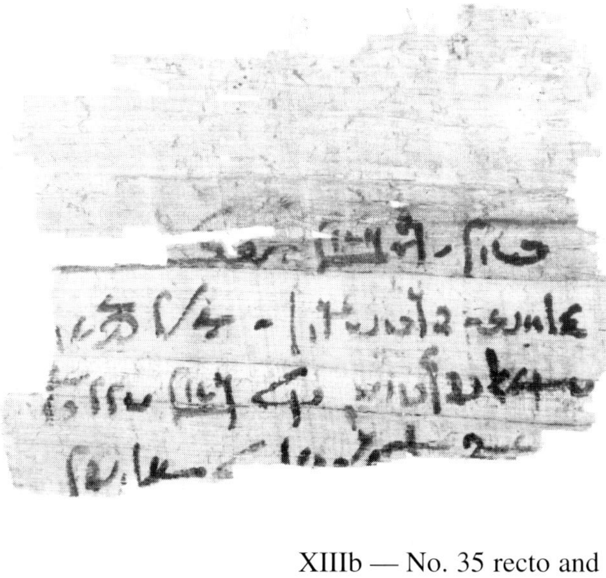

XIIIb — No. 35 recto and verso — P. Heidelberg dem . 742a.

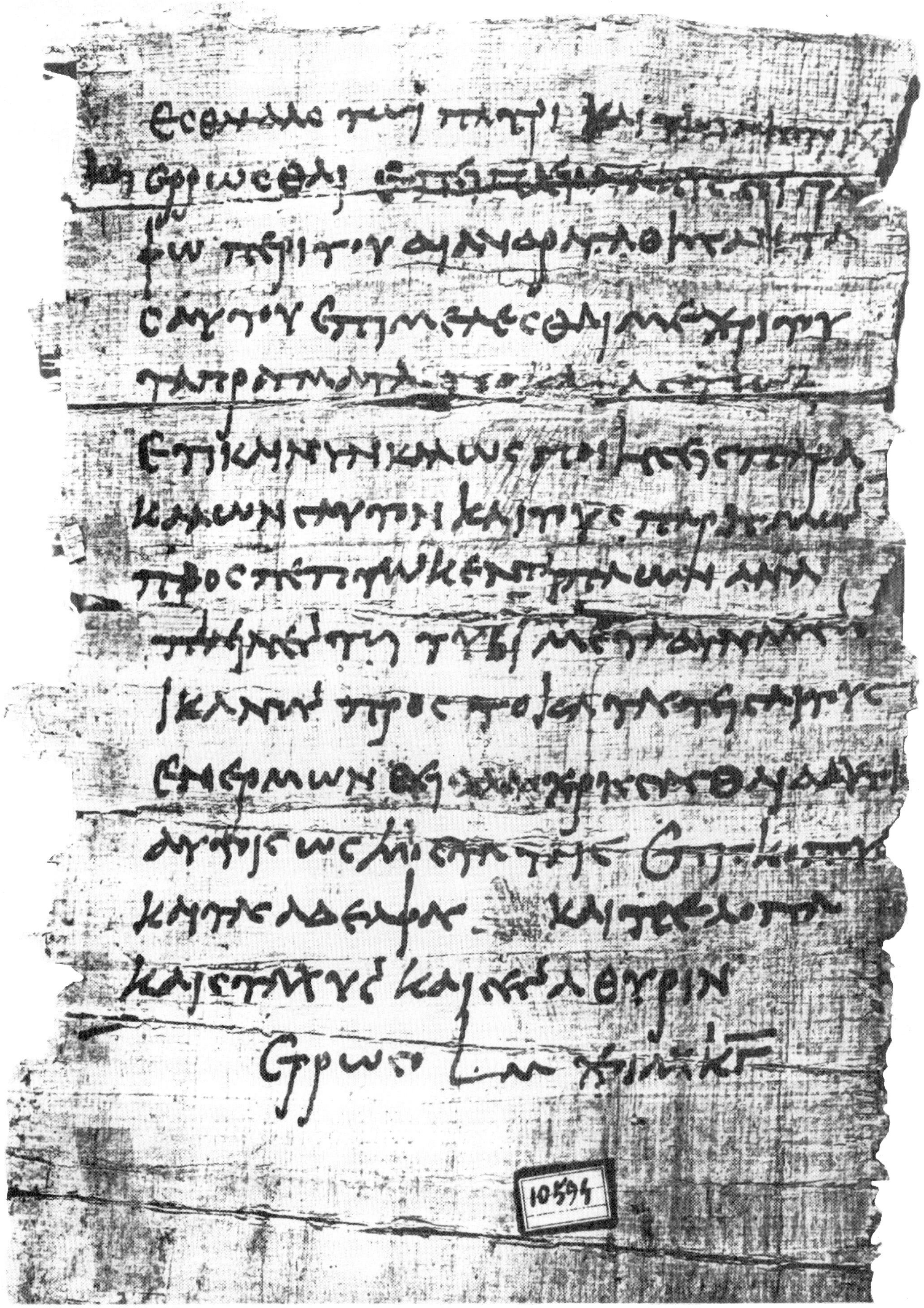

XIV — No. 36 recto — P. Louvre E 10594.

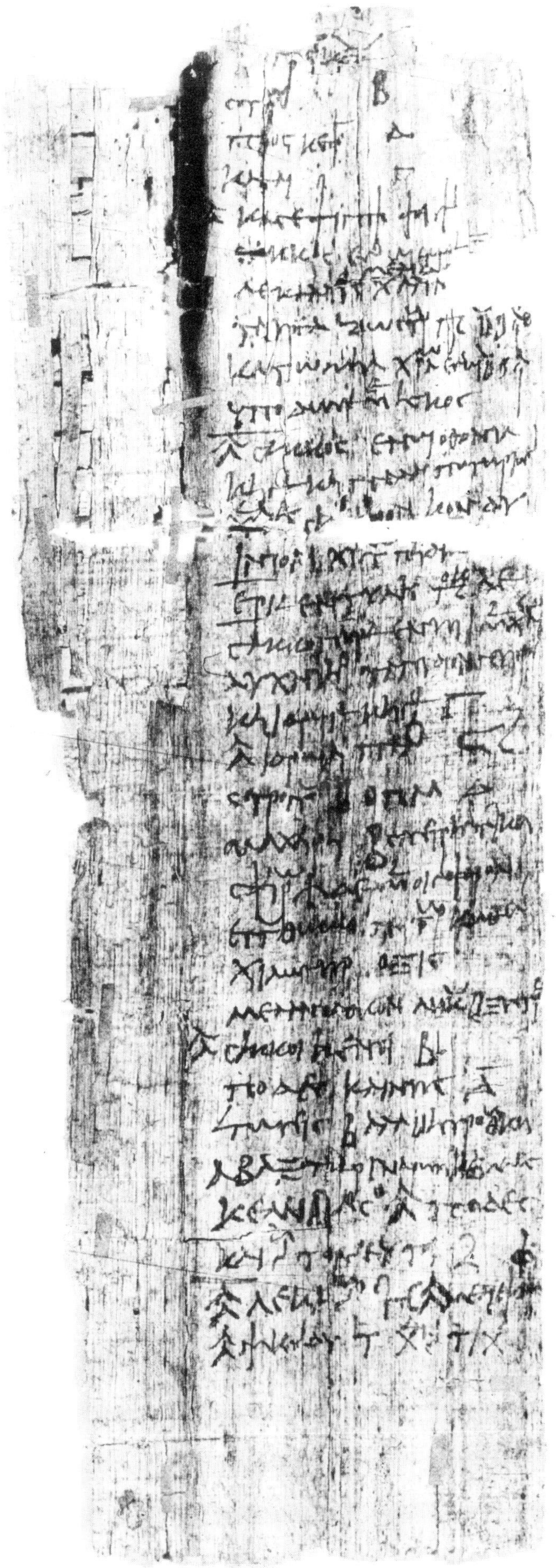

XV — No. 38 verso — P. British Library 402.

XVI — No. 39 verso [collage] and recto — P. British Library 641 + 686e.

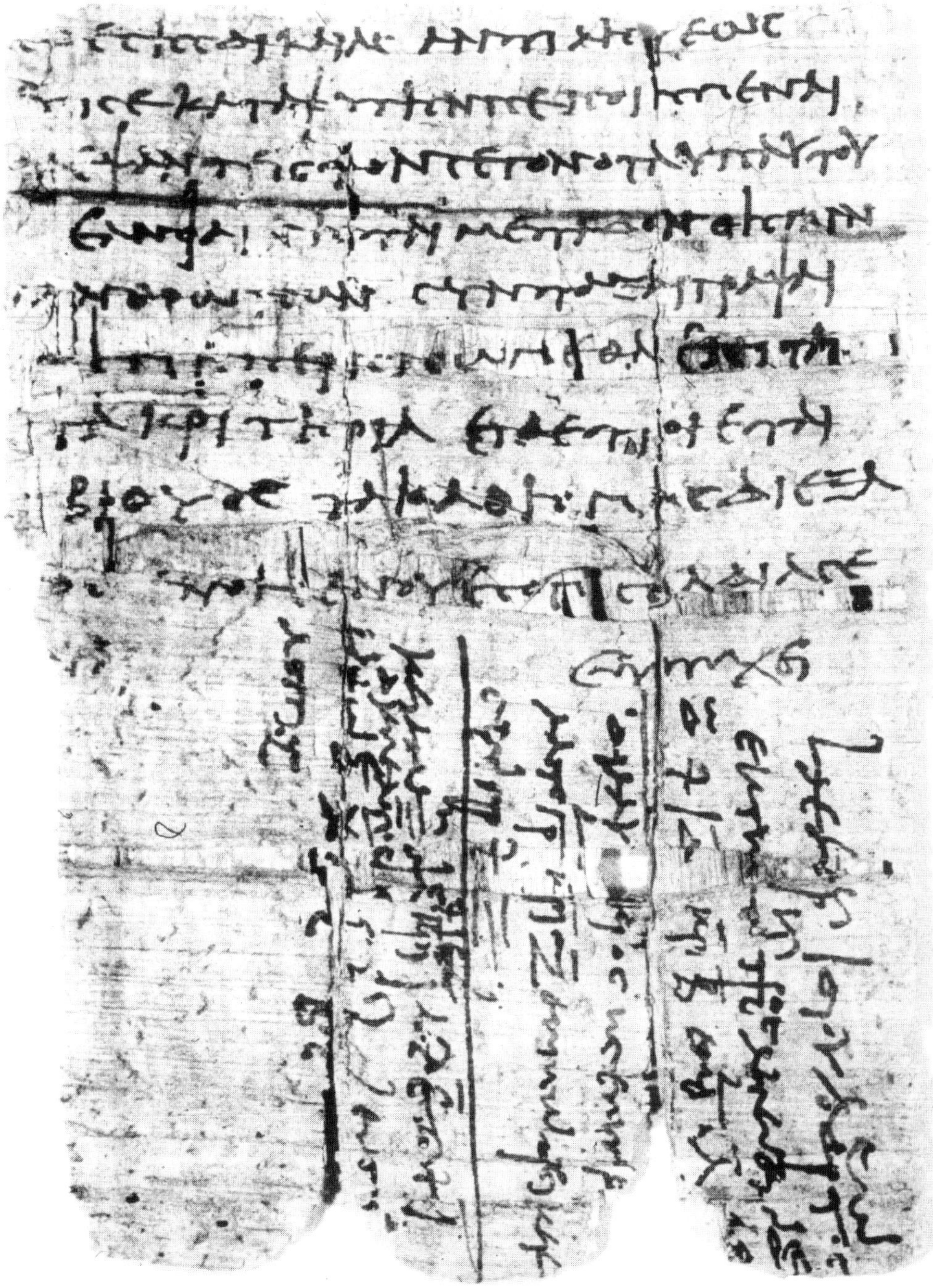

XVII — No. 40 recto — P. British Library 611 recto.

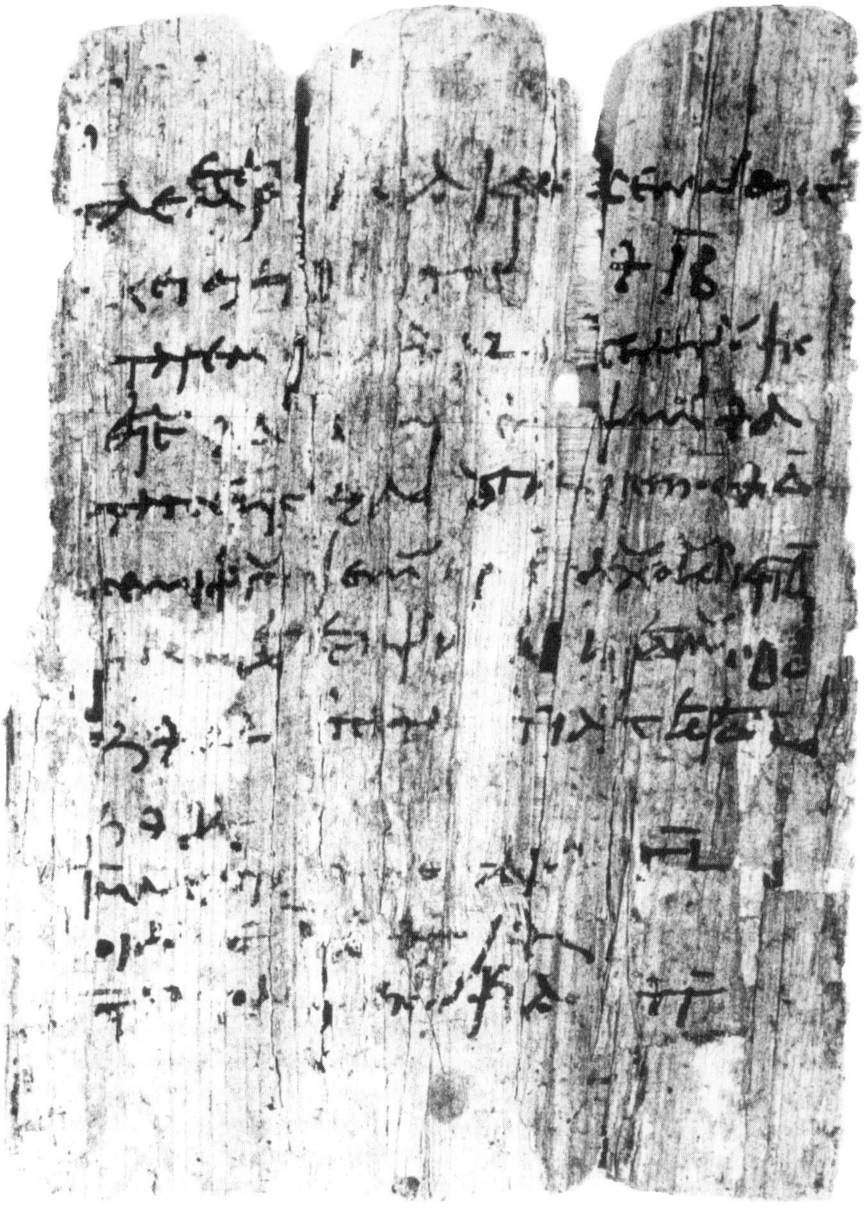

XVIII — No. 41 verso — P. British Library 611 verso.

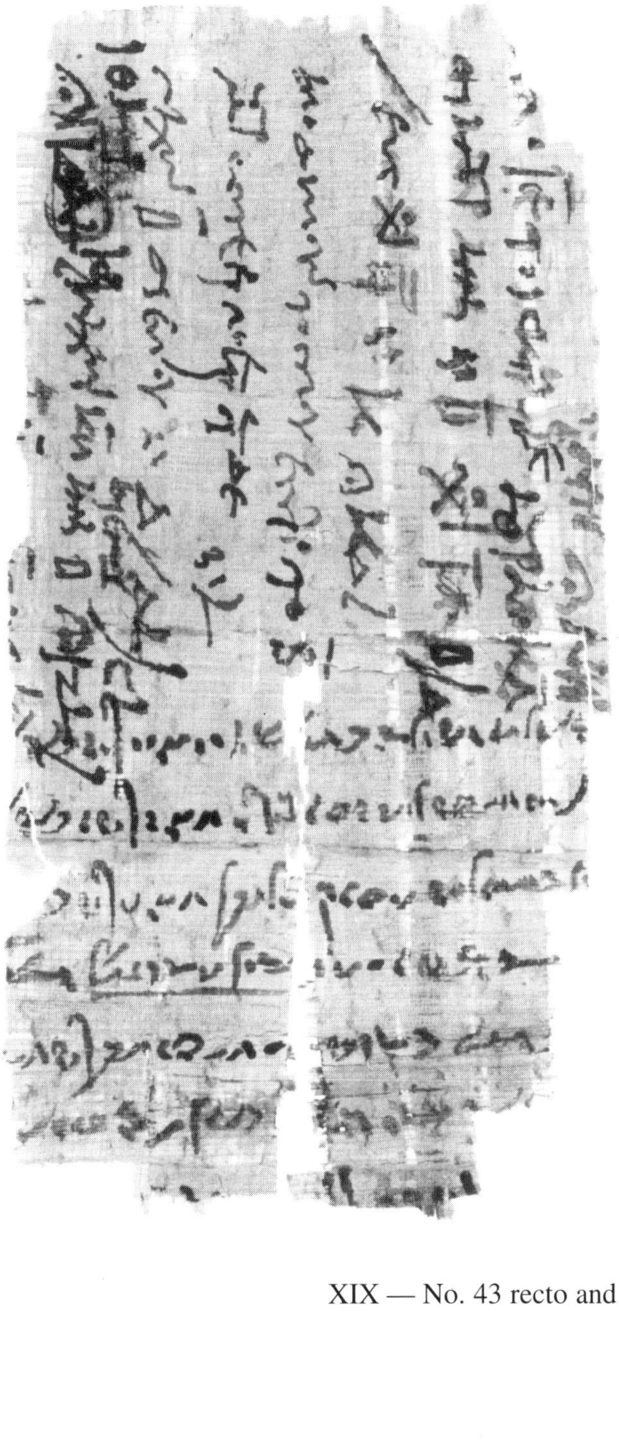

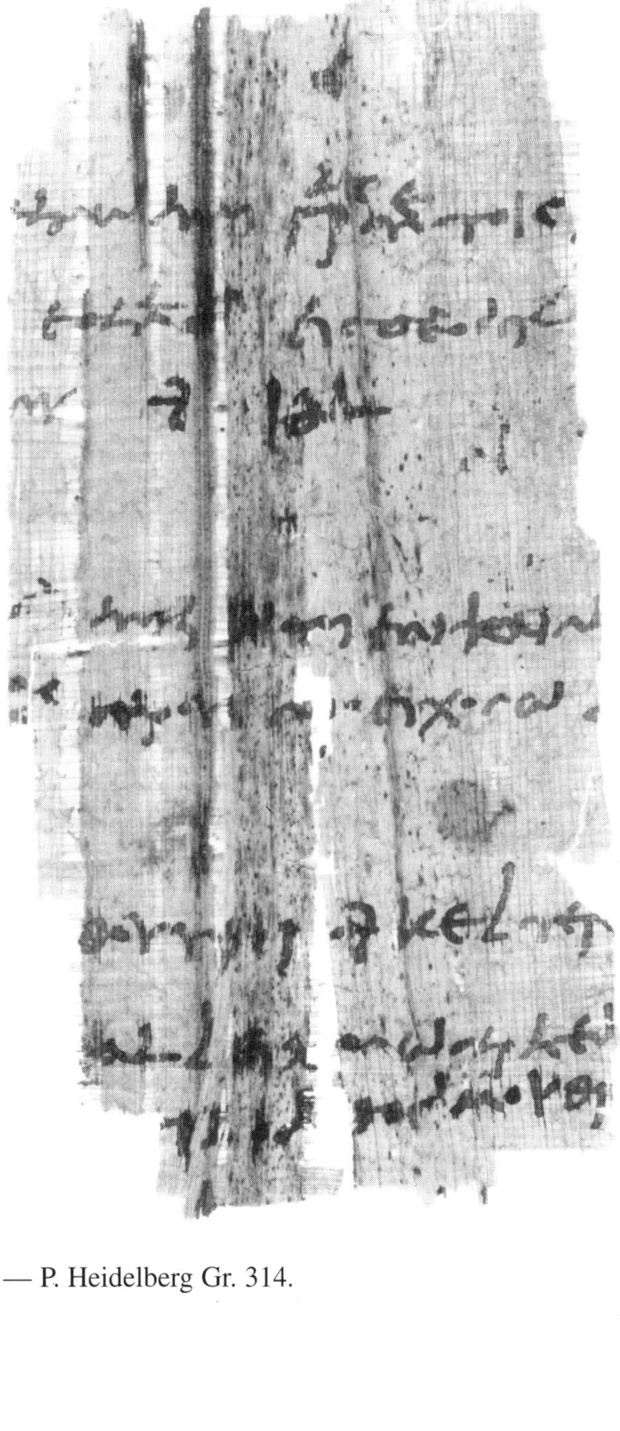

XIX — No. 43 recto and verso — P. Heidelberg Gr. 314.

Verso

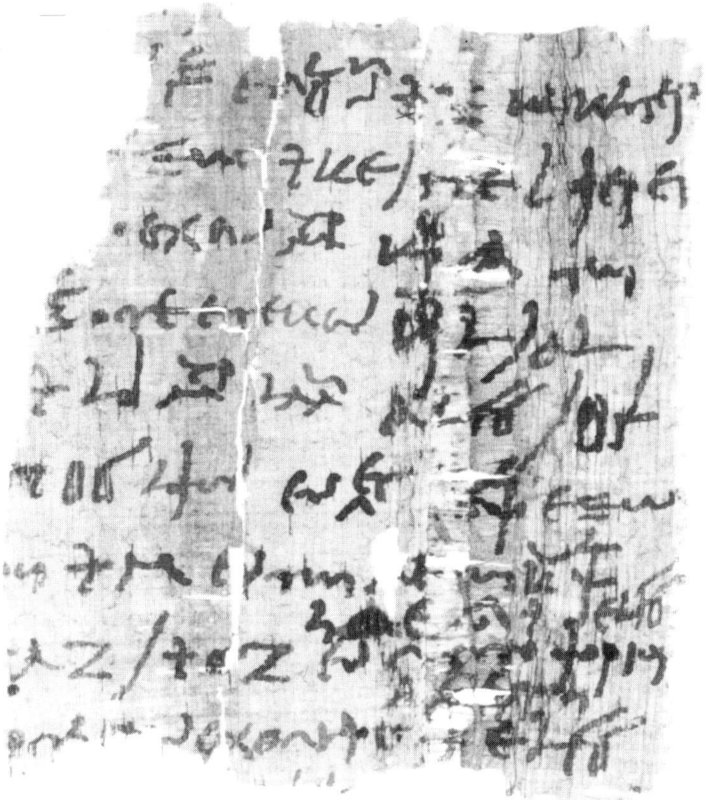

Recto

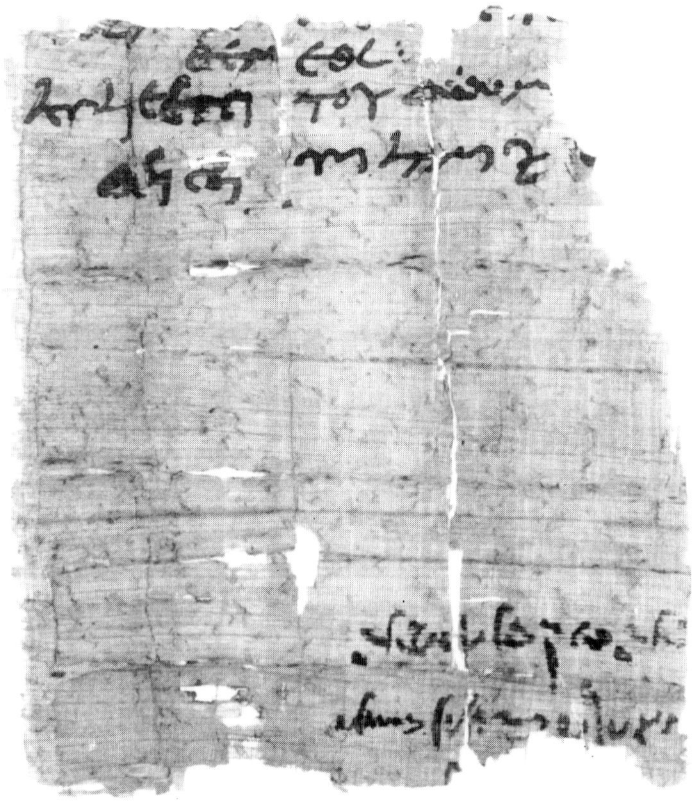

XX — No. 44 verso and recto (see also No. 43 Appendix) — P. Heidelberg Gr. 315.

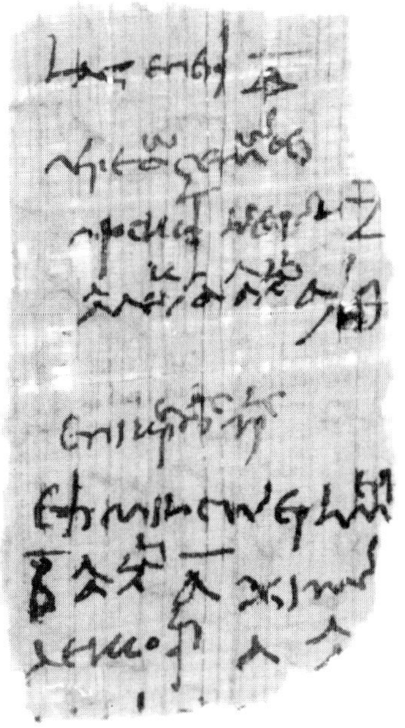 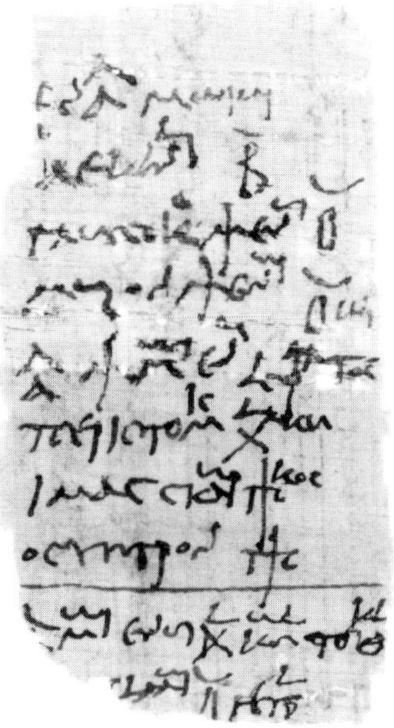

XXIa — No. 42 verso and recto — P. Heidelberg Gr. 1320.

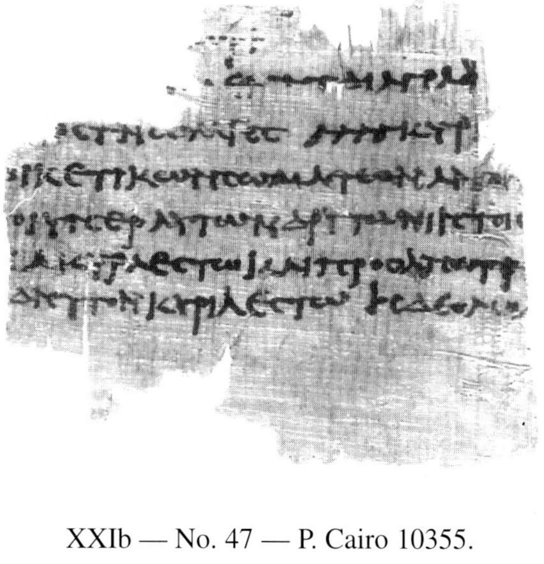

XXIb — No. 47 — P. Cairo 10355.

XXII — No. 50 — P. British Library 605 verso.

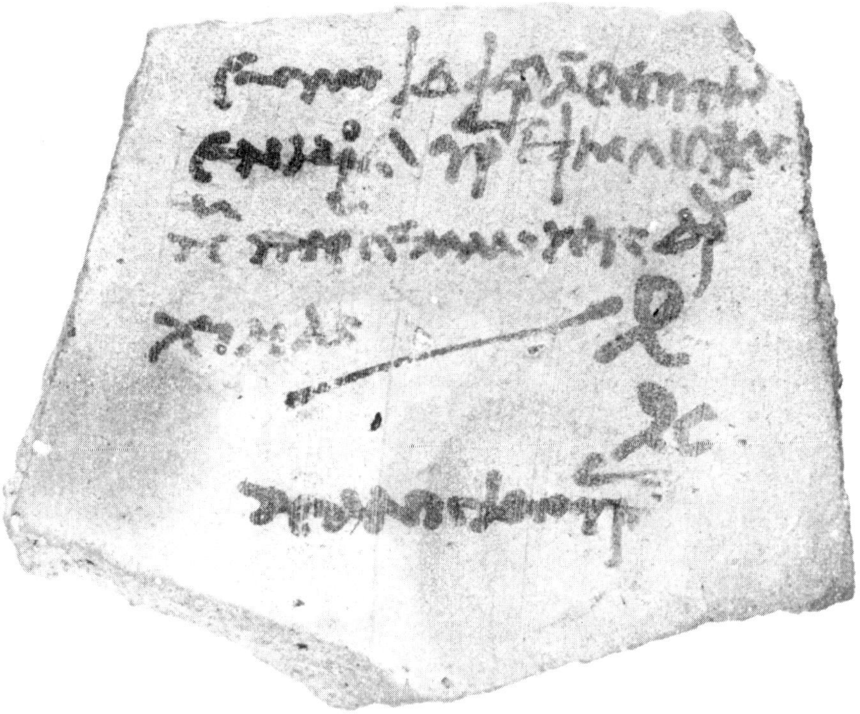

XXIIIa — No. 56 — O. Zürich Gr. 1904.
(Photo, Silvia Hertig, Archäologisches Institut der Universität Zürich)

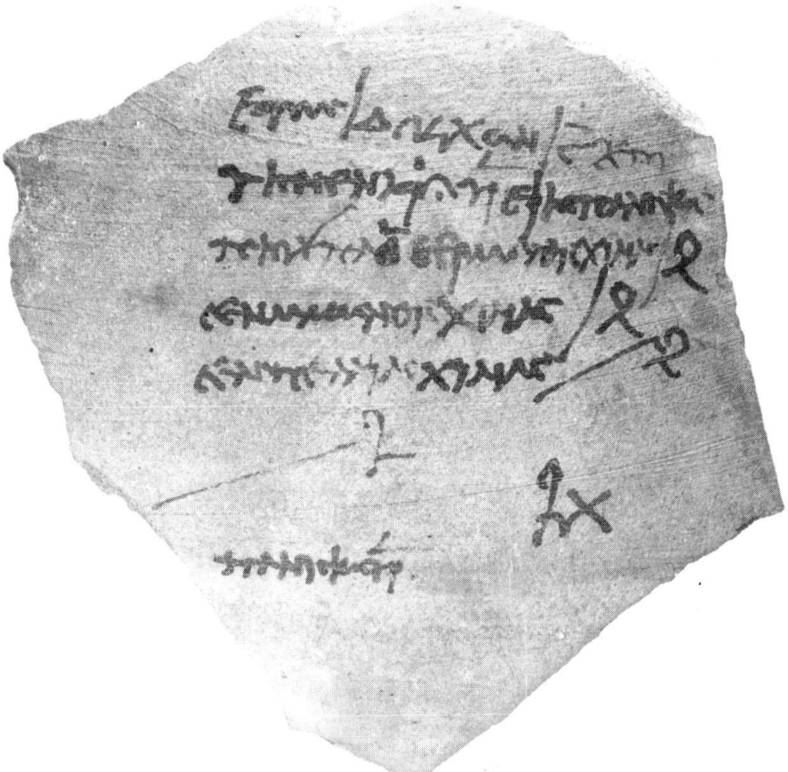

XXIIIb — No. 57 — O. Zürich Gr. 1905.
(Photo, Silvia Hertig, Archäologisches Institut der Universität Zürich)

XXIV — No. App. A — P. British Library 668.